MINUTES OF THE JONES COUNTY NORTH CAROLINA

COURT OF COMMON PLEAS AND QUARTER SESSIONS

1826-1841

ABSTRACTED AND ANNOTATED BY

Nancy Bryan Aiken

HERITAGE BOOKS
2008

HERITAGE BOOKS
AN IMPRINT OF HERITAGE BOOKS, INC.

Books, CDs, and more—Worldwide

For our listing of thousands of titles see our website
at
www.HeritageBooks.com

Published 2008 by
HERITAGE BOOKS, INC.
Publishing Division
100 Railroad Ave. #104
Westminster, Maryland 21157

Copyright © 2002 Nancy Bryan Aiken

All rights reserved. No part of this book may be reproduced or transmitted in any form or by any means, electronic or mechanical, including photocopying, recording or by any information storage and retrieval system without written permission from the author, except for the inclusion of brief quotations in a review.

International Standard Book Numbers
Paperbound: 978-0-7884-2044-3
Clothbound: 978-0-7884-7063-9

CONTENTS

Acknowledgements	iv
Preface	v
Introduction	1
Minutes of the Court	10
References	235
Index	237

ACKNOWLEDGEMENTS

    I wish to thank my cousin, James E. White III, for loaning me the microfilm copy of the Jones County North Carolina Court of Common Pleas and Quarter Sessions which he purchased from the North Carolina State Department of Archives and History.

    I also wish to thank Gerry Weir of West Monroe, LA, a descendant of Joseph and Sarah Green, for information on the Green family of Jones County.

    Also, my thanks go to my friend, Mary L. Bowman, for loaning me a microfilm reader; it saved many trips to the library. However, I was supposed to be transcribing census records for her massive 1880 Ohio Census Index project, but I worked on these court records instead. My guilt remains even though she forgave me years ago.

PREFACE

I began this project many years ago. It has been a slow and arduous process with many starts and stops. Other projects forced these court records back on the shelf several times. I discovered that abstracting records is not what I call fun. To keep up my interest I did some research on the Nat Turner rebellion, slave ownership, law terms, and North Carolina geography besides some research on the people who were active in this court. I include all of that in notes within the text of the court minute abstracts. I hope it adds interest for you as it did for me.

These are abstracts of the Minutes of the Jones County North Carolina Court of Common Pleas and Quarter Sessions for the years 1826 through part of 1841. Quotations in the text are transcribed exactly from the original (as much as that is humanly possible). Unfortunately, court minutes generally offer researchers very little detail, and that is the case here. However, so few records are extant from this place and time that even court minutes become important.

My old cousin, Hardy Bryan was the clerk for most of the years of these court minutes. I believe Hardy and I may share a gene for bad spelling. I hope that we have not collaborated to mutilate too many names. I tried to follow his spelling as much as I could which lead to several spellings for what, no doubt, is one name. I think that sometimes names were spelled the way the writer pronounced the name. For example, my guess is that Hardy Bryan pronounced Henry with an extra vowel before the r so that the spelling became Henery. Hardy was not consistent in his spelling either. Saml Dillahunt was very likely the same person as Samuel Dillahunty. I had considerable difficulty differentiating among o, a, and e. I, L, and S also presented problems. Wilson and Wilcox were most difficult to distinguish. Maids could be Mades; Hiles might be Hill; and Small might be Smaw. I attempted to check difficult to read names with the censuses. This afforded some help as is noted in the text.

My cousin, James E. White, III loaned me the microfilm copy of these records urging me to hunt for all the Bryan references. There turned out to be a Bryan on nearly every page, so I thought I might as well abstract every entry. Since the original had no index and no page numbering, finding specific items was very difficult. To find the entry on the microfilm of the original, find the term and year. I hope that my effort makes researching these court records a much easier task.

INTRODUCTION

County Formation

Jones County was formed in 1779 from CRAVEN COUNTY. Named in honor of WILLIE JONES of HALIFAX, who was a leader during the Revolution. It is in eastern North Carolina and is bounded by CRAVEN, CARTERET, ONSLOW, DUPLIN, and LENOIR COUNTIES. The first court was held at the home of THOMAS WEBBER at TRENT BRIDGE. In 1784 an act authorized the town of TRENTON to be laid out as the county seat (Corbitt, pp. 134, 135).

The County Court

I studied the 1830 and 1840 censuses for information on the people who were active in court and how they fit into the general population. Most of those notes are in the text, but some general items might be mentioned here. Also, I found some background material on the court system in North Carolina before the Civil War. This, too, I thought would be of interest, and the information comes from Johnson (1937) unless otherwise noted.

Jones was a rather atypical county during the antibellum period in North Carolina. On the eve of the Civil War only sixteen North Carolina counties had more slaves than whites. Jones County was one of those sixteen. All sixteen counties were heavy producers of cotton or tobacco, both of which were labor intensive commodities. Of Jones County's neighbors, only LENOIR COUNTY was similar to Jones in its heavy reliance upon cotton production and slave labor. The number of families owning slaves in North Carolina hovered around 30% between 1790 and 1860. In 1830 55% of Jones County families owned slaves.

Those men who participated in the County Court were predominately slave owners. Of the 138 people whose names appear in the Court Minutes for December Term, 1830, only seventeen did not own slaves. December Term, 1830 was not an a typical term for the Jones County Court of Common Pleas and Quarter Sessions; it can safely be assumed that slave owners dominated the proceedings of the court.

This finding is not surprising since the North Carolina Constitution of 1776 practically gave all political power to slave owners. Political office depended on land ownership, and ownership of land in quantity meant slave ownership. In order to qualify for a seat in the Senate of the State General Assembly a man had to own 300 acres of land. Just to vote in a senatorial election a white man had to own 50 acres of land. To qualify for a seat in the House of Commons of the State Assembly, a man had to own 100 acres. However, one needed only to be a white, male taxpayer to vote in a house election. The governor, elected by the General Assembly and not by popular vote, had to have a "freehold" evaluated at over 1000 pounds sterling. Thus, "freeholders" ran the government and of those "freeholders" the government was run in effect by the two upper classes in North Carolina: the gentry and the middle class.

The gentry probably comprised only about 2% of the total free families in North Carolina on the eve of the Civil War. Wealth contributed to one's entry into the gentry class but more emphasis was placed on family prestige. Several generations of "respectability" were necessary for a North Carolinian to move in "gentry society." Once wealth was obtained and the family had the leisure to acquire education, refined manners, and sophistication, it could be accepted as gentry. Once accepted, a family generally would retain its status for several more generations despite financial reverses. Planters were not the only contributors to the gentry. Doctors, lawyers, educators, and educated clergymen often moved in "polite society."

The middle class, next below the gentry, was made up of small planters, merchants, manufacturers, successful artisans, small office holders, country school teachers, lawyers, doctors, and parsons. The small planter generally owned two or three hundred acres and as many as ten or fifteen slaves. He sometimes worked beside his slaves in the fields and seldom hired an overseer to manage his farm. These were the men who sought county offices and enjoyed the title of Esquire given Justices of the Peace.

A study of the persons who appeared in court December Term, 1830 offers support for Johnson's conclusion that the middle class and the gentry were the major participants in local North Carolina government. The largest group of court participants (26%) owned ten to nineteen slaves. These would, by Johnson's standards, have been the middle class. In this group were the justices: JOHN H. HAMMOND (10 slaves), NATHAN B. BUSH (11 slaves), OWEN B. COX (11 slaves), WILLIAM HUGGINS (11 slaves), ABNER GREEN (13 slaves), and ALFRED HARGET (14 slaves). HARDY BRYAN, clerk of courts, owned 19 slaves in 1830; he may have been considered gentry.

Twenty percent of those who appeared in court owned five to nine slaves. These men included such recurring names in the court minutes as: BENJAMIN HUGGINS (5 slaves), DANIEL MALLARD (5 slaves), MILLINGTON MEADOWS (5 slaves), LEWIS SMALL (5 slaves), LOTT EUBANKS (6 slaves)1, URBAN OLDFIELD (6 slaves), WILLIAM GILES (7 slaves), COUNCIL GOODING (7 slaves), LEWIS KINSEY (7 slaves), RISDON McDANIEL (7 slaves), NATHAN FOSCUE (8 slaves), JOHN HEATH (8 slaves), JONAS JONES JR. (8 slaves), WILLIAM LAROQUE (8 slaves), JOHN FORDHAM (9 slaves), FREDERICK FOSCUE (9 slaves), and HENRY RHODES SR. (9 slaves).

Eighteen percent of court participants during the December Term of 1830 were owners of twenty to forty-two slaves. These men were either newly wealthy or gentry. They included men who often took part in the county court such as FREDERICK BECTON and MARTIN F. BROCK (each with 20 slaves), EMANUEL JARMAN (22 slaves), CHRISTOPHER GREEN (23 slaves), DANIEL Y. SHINE and JOSEPH WHITTY (each with 24 slaves), SIMMONS HARRISON (28 slaves), JAMES B. SHINE (30 slaves), JOSEPH KINSEY, HARDY PERRY, and ELIJAH SIMMONS (each with 32 slaves), EDMOND B. HATCH and JAMES W. HOWARD (each with 34 slaves), WILLIAM ISLER (39 slaves), and JAMES ROBERTS (42 slaves). Only four court participants during December Term, 1830 owned more than 42 slaves. LEMUEL SIMMONS was the most active in the court system of this group. He owned 52 slaves. Others were ENOCH FOY (53 slaves), DURANT HATCH (71 slaves), and JOBE SMITH, who owned 198 slaves placing him among the less than 1% of North Carolina slave owners who owned 100-199 slaves. Of the four, the first three men were regular participants in local government.

County officers were elected by the County Court and Court Officers were appointed by the governor on recommendation of the legislators of their respective counties. Although movements began early in the nineteenth century to rid the government of property qualifications and require popular elections, it was not until the new constitution was adopted after the Civil War that the changes were made.

Court Week

Court week was a bustle of activity. Besides judges, litigants, witnesses, prospective jurors, and lawyers making their regular rounds of the courts, there were vendors, entertainers, and spectators in town for the court. Political meetings, agricultural fairs, and temperance and Bible societies were held at the same time as the county court.

Court proceedings could be described as a state of confusion with constant talking and justices going on and off the bench. Court rooms reeked of sweating bodies, tobacco, and alcohol - especially on a winter day when the room would be closed and the stove would be belching smoke.

North Carolina Court System

The lowest court in the North Carolina system was the oldest, the Magistrate's Court. Its jurisdiction extended over petty offenses up to $100 judgments. It was presided over by one or, perhaps, two justices of the peace. The Magistrate Court met when and wherever it was convenient.

The County Court or Court of Common Pleas and Quarter Sessions was the next higher court in North Carolina. A court of three justices of the peace held terms quarterly for periods of from one to six days. This court summoned grand and petit juries and could dispense with a jury at two of the four terms if court business did not require a jury. Its jurisdiction extended to suits of $100 or more for violation of the penal code, and to suits for dower, partition, and legacies. It served as an orphans' court and had criminal jurisdiction in all cases in which judgment did not extend to death or *dismemberment*. The state legislature delegated an assortment of duties to the county court which gave it a pervasive sphere of influence. It appointed county officers, approved licenses to peddlers and retailers of spirituous liquor, bound out apprentices, heard petitions, emancipated slaves, and levied county taxes among other duties.

The Superior Court and Supreme Court were North Carolina's highest courts. The Superior Court had jurisdiction over felonies. The Supreme Court was the court of final appeal.

An 1845 review of the North Carolina court system found the greatest need for reform in the County Court. A major complaint was that justices continually went on and off the bench. This situation occurred because J.P.s would come into court when other business allowed and leave when their business demanded.

Problems inherent in the county court system were: justices need not have knowledge of the law, justices were paid only a token amount (about $1.00 to $3.00 a day) which would not inspire devotion to duty, the constant changes in persons on the bench which made consistency difficult, and there were solicitations of certain justices to try particular cases. (Jones County attempted to deal with some of these problems by assigning justices to particular terms.) Often the jury was left to determine the law and the facts in cases for themselves. To counterbalance this, every case heard in county court could be appealed to Superior Court. Unfortunately, a poor person, having to give bond in a appeal, probably could not afford an appeal.

Some county courts were shameful in their proceedings. They were so noisy the jury could not hear testimony and the judges would be drunk. Some judges were no doubt bribed to make certain decisions. (However, the Minutes of the Jones County Court give no indication of such occurrences although they may have been happening. The appearance given by the Minutes is one of decorum. Business like proceedings appear in the clerk's carefully worded minutes which are liberally spiced with Latin legal terms giving the overall appearance of a court which knew what it was doing and performed its duties with dispatch.)

Pleas for reform of the North Carolina County Courts finally resulted in its abolishment by the Constitution of 1868. Its powers were divided between the Magistrate's Court and the Superior Court until 1923 when it was reestablished as a subordinate to the Superior Court.

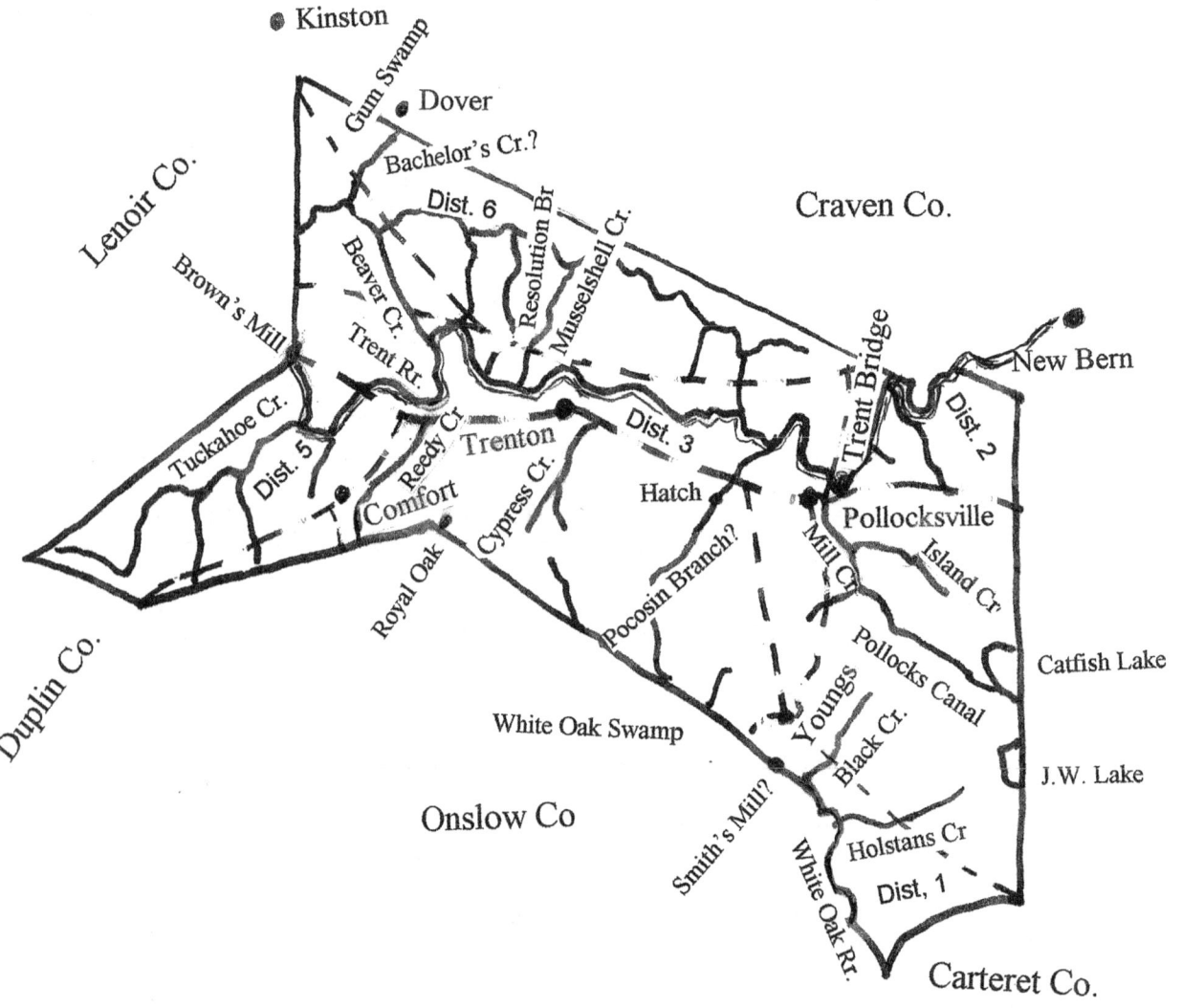

Map of Jones County, North Carolina

Introduction

This map is based on a U.S. Coast Survey map of 1865 (Cummings, Plate XIII). The positions of CYPRESS and REEDY CREEKS come from the COLLETT MAP of 1770 (Cummings, Plate VII). The hatched lines indicate roads on the 1865 map, and the MAC RAE-BRAZIER MAP of 1833 (Cummings, Plate X) shows essentially the same roadways.

A few notes from the Minutes add detail. During the September 1831 Term, it was mentioned that the road running from TRENTON to KINSTON ran across MUSSELSHELL BRANCH after the fork at RISDEN M. McDANIEL's place. (There was a bridge at TRENTON which must have connected the road south of the TRENT RIVER with the road north of the river.) A note in the December 1831 Minutes indicates the fork in this road was at B. HUGGINS' place. During that same term RATTLESNAKE BRIDGE was mentioned in the vicinity of the crossroads which would appear to be near COMFORT. During the March 1832 term it was mentioned that JAMES B. SHINE planned to rebuild a mill on REEDY BRANCH which had formerly been owned by FRED. I. BECTON. In 1835 the road from BLACK SWAMP, which is in the area of BLACK CREEK, ran to TRENTON past JOHN YOUNG's. In 1836 the DOVER ROAD went through GUM SWAMP to the County Line near JOHN COBB and JOHN WISE. (This must have been an extension of the road that appears to go to KINSTON.)

I attempted to map the various districts which are mentioned in the Minutes. Although I feel comfortable locating Districts 1, 2, 3, 5, and 6 where they are placed on the map, I do not feel as confident about the locations of Districts 4 and 7. Given the names of District 4 (Cypress Creek) and District 7 (Beverdam), one would guess District 4 was in the vicinity of Cypress Creek and District 7 was in the general area near BROWN's MILL because a BEAVERDAM CREEK flows into the TRENT RIVER just west in LENOIR COUNTY according to the 1865 map.

In addition, I made lists of men who were patrols or held elections in the various districts on the assumption they lived in the designated district. Following are the lists of Districts and men who served as patrols or who held elections in those Districts and the year or years they served. You will see that some names are repeated and sometimes are repeated in different districts. Perhaps they moved or were patrols or held elections in districts other than their home district, or perhaps, two men shared the same name.

District 1 (White Oak)
THOMAS GILLET (1831, 1833-1834, 1836-1841)
DANIEL YATES (1831, 1833-34)
LEVI EUBANKS (1831, 1834-1837, 1839)
DANIEL DICKSON (1831, 1836-1841)
JOHN BINDER (1831)
RIGDON HEWIT (1831)
DANIEL SMITH (1831)
LOT EUBANKS (1831)
HARDY MUNDINE (1831)
JAMES ROBERTS (1833-34)
FRANCIS MATTOCKS (1833)
LEVI EUBANKS (1834)

District 2 (Trent Bridge)
ROSCO BARRUS (1831, 1833-1840)
JNO OLIVER (1831 & 1838)
OWEN ADAMS (1838)
ENOCH FOY (1837-1839)
EDMOND HATCH (1838)
DANIEL WILLIAMSON (1831, 1833-34, 1839-40)
JAMES W. HOWARD (1833, 1836-37, 1840)
JAMES FOY (1833-36, 1838-39)
WALTER P. ALLEN (1834, 1838)
JOSEPH S. FOY (1834-36)
JOHN YOUNG (1834-35)
JONATHAN WOOD (1836)

JOHN YOUNG (1835, 1837, 1841)
THOS. GILBERT (1835)
NATHAN F. PARSONS (1836-38)
MICAJAH F. MATTOCKS (1837-40)
JOHN BINAM (1837)
FERDINAN DICKSON (1836 & constable in 1837)
JOHN HUGGINS (1838-39)
JOHN L. PARSONS (1838-39)
BARTHALOMEW MEADOWS (1838-39)
GEORGE SIMMONS (1840)
STEWART SCOTT (1840)
READING SCOTT (1840/41?)
F. PARSONS (1841)
RICHARD OLDFIELD (1841)
THOMAS PARSONS (1841)
ELIJAH LOVETTE (1841)

JOSEPH I. FOY (1836)
JOSEPH WHITTY (1837, 1840)
STEPHEN SMITH (1835)
ISRAEL HOWARD (1835)
ALFRED WHITTY (1835, 1838)
JAMES MORTON (1835, 1837)
GEORGE S. BENDER (1835, 1840-41)
GEORGE W. SIMMONS (1837-38)
FREDERICK MARKET (1837)
HENRY FOY (1837, 1841)
JAMES PRIGET? (1837)
JOHN HANCOCK (1838)
JOHN HALL (1840)
ELIJAH SIMMONS JR (1840)
RICHARD PARSONS (1840)
WM W. FRANK (1841)
JOHN R. BENDER (1841)
BRYAN BENDER (1841)
THOMAS HALL (1841)

District 3 (Trenton)
CHRIS. A. HATCH (1831)
WILLIAM HUGGINS (1831, 1833-34, 1836-39)
HARDY BRYAN (1831, 1834, 1836)
WILLIAMS BROWN (1831)
JACOB HUGGINS (1831)
HARDY O. CONNER (1831, 1840)
RESDON M. McDANIEL (1833, 1837 1841)
SAMUEL HILL (1833, 1837, 1839-1840)
JAMES B. LARAQUE (1833)
JAMES McDANIEL (1834, 1837)
JOHN HOUSTON (1834-35)
ABNER GREEN (1835)
LEML BUSACK (1835, 1837-38, 1841)
NATHAN FOSCUE (1836)
CALVIN J. MORRIS (1836)
JOHN WILLIAM (1837)
BRYAN THOMAS SR (1837)
FARNIFOLD McDANIEL (1837-38, 1840)
BAZEL McDANIEL (1837, 1840)
JOHN HARRISON (1837)
CHARLES GEROCK (1837-38, 1841)
BENJAMIN HUGGINS (1838)
ADONIJAH McDANIEL (1838, 1841)
JAMES C. BRYAN (1838, 1840)

District 4 (Cypress Creek)
JOHN H. HAMMOND (1831, 1834-35, 1837-38)
DANIEL Y. SHINE (1831)
ROBERT GILBERT (1831)
FRED. I. BECTON (1831)
JAMES HARRISON (1831, 1837)
ISAAC BROWN (1831, 1833)
SIMMONS HARRISON (1831, 1833)
CALVIN KOONCE (1833-1841)
JOSEPH BROCK (1833)
JAMES B. SHINE (1834, 1836-41)
FURNIFOLD G. HERRITAGE (1834)
JOHN L. PARSONS (1834)
JNO JONES (1835-36, 1838-41)
FURNIFOLD H. JARMAN (1836-38)
ZACHEUS BROWN (1836, 1838)
JOHN HANCOCK (1836-38)
WILLIAM HARRISON (1837)
RICHARD PARSONS (1837)
BENJAMIN BROCK (1838, 1840)
SIMON KOONCE (1840)

JOHN McDANIEL (1838)
JOHN H. DILLAHUNT (1839)
LEMUEL H. SIMMONS (1840)
BENJAMIN ASKEW (1841)

District 5 (Tuckahoe)
EMANUEL JARMAN (1831, 1834, 1837-38)
ISAAC BROWN (1831, 1833, 1839)
JOSEPH KINSEY (1831, 1833-34, 1836)
HENRY RHODES SR (1831, 1833-34)
OWEN B. COX (1831, 1833-39, 1841)
FURNIFOLD H. JARMON (1834-35)
ROSCO BRYAN (1835)
LEWIS WILLIAMS (1836-37, 1840-41)
CALVIN KOONCE (1838)
HENRY RHODES (1837-40)
EML F. JONES (constable 1836)
JAMES KINCEY (1837-38)
JOHN KINCEY (1837)
JOHN JARMON JR (1837-39, 1841)
JOSEPH KINCEY JR (1838-39, 1841)
EMORY METTS (1839)
SAMUEL HILL (1840)
JOHN H. DILLAHUNT (1840)
JONAS WILLIAMS (1840)
LEWIS JONES (1840)
JOHN A. COX (1840)
JONAS JONES JR (1841)

District 7 (Beverdam)
ALFRED HARGET (1831)
JOHN L. PARSONS (1831)
RISDON M. McDANIEL (1831)
FREDERICK FOSCUE (1831)
NATHAN B. BUSH (1831)
BENJ. HUGGINS (1831)
WILLIAM STANLY (1831)
NATHAN FOSCUE (1833-37, 1840)
AMOS SIMMONS (1835, 1837)
HARDY O. NEWTON (1835-37)
JAMES MARRET (1836-37, 1840)
LEML H. SIMMONS (1838)
WILLIAM C. MURPHY (1838-39)
DANIEL HARRISON (1838-40)
FRANCIS MERRITT (1838-39)
JOHN MERRITT (1839)
THOMAS HARRISON (1840)
NATHANIEL WAPLES (1841)

District 6 (Bever Creek)
CALVIN KOONCE (1831)
ABNER GREEN (1831, 1837, 1839-40)
WMS ISLER (1831, 1833)
PETER HARGET (1831, 1833, 1837, 1839-40)
HARDY SHELFER (1831)
MARTIN F. BROCK (1831, 1834)
JOHN STANLY (1831)
RISDEN M. McDANIEL (1831)
DANIEL HARRISON (1831)
JOHN S. KOONCE (1833-34)
FREDERICK I. BECTON (1833-35, 1837-41)
SIMMONS ISLER (1834, 1836, 1838)
BENJAMIN HUGGINS (1834, constable 1836)
JAS S. KOONCE (1835)
SIMON I. BECTON (1835, 1841)
AMOS HEATH (1835, 1840)
WILLIAM STANLY (1835, 1837, 1840)
FREEMAN SMITH (1835, 1837, 1840)
AUTUS GILBERT (1835, 1837)
JOHN B. REYNOLDS (1835, 1838, 1840)
MICHAEL SHELFER (1835, 1839)
BENJN F. STANLY (1835, 1837)
ALFRED H. REYNOLDS (1836-37)
MICHAEL KOONCE (1836)
DAVID GREEN (1837)
H. PARRY (1837, 1839)
WILLIAM POLLOCK (1838)
BENJAMIN KOONCE (1838-39, 1841)
HARRISON HEATH (1839)
AMOS I. KOONCE (1839)
NEEDHAM BEASLEY (1841)
NATHAN STANLEY (1841)
JAMES G. HERRITAGE (1841)
AMOS RHEM (1841)

Introduction

A number of Latin law terms are used in the Minutes. I attempted to find definitions for them; they are defined in the text. I also tried to define other terms with which the researcher may not be familiar. The patrols, many of whom are listed above, had the duty of keeping slaves under control by enforcing the rules and giving them 15 lashes for infractions. Patrols were fined $20.00 for failing to enforce the rules. (in 1829 BENJAMIN COLLINS was given a three month jail sentence for harboring a runaway Negro. This may have been the only jail sentence handed out by the court between 1826 and 1841.) A freeholder was a person (white male) who owned in his right or the right of another 50 acres or a lot in a town.

I abbreviated a few well-used terms:
shff = sheriff
admr or admx = male or female administrator
decd = deceased
guard = guardian
admin = administration
Esq. = esquire
pltfs = plantiffs
exr = executor

Places and legal terms identified in text for Jones County Court Records

PLACES

Beaver Dam/Bever Dam
Beaverdam Branch/Beverdam Branch
Big Chinquipen
Black Swamp

Cypress Creek

Deep Gully
Dover (Craven Co.)

Ginger Branch
Grape Branch
Gum Swamp

Indian Grove

Little Chinquipen

Jack Cabin Branch
Joshways Resolution

Mill Creek
Mill Run
Musselshell

New River

Pocosin Branch

Rattlesnake Branch
Read Hill
Ready Branch
Red Hill
Red Oak
Resolution Branch
Ruby Branch

Sand Ridge (Lenor Co.)
Sandy Bottom
Sandy Ridge
Smith's Mill

Ten Mile Fork
Ten Mile House
Tom's Swamp
Trent Bridge Road
Trent River

Tuckehoe

Wards/Words Hill
White Oak River

LEGAL TERMS:

affray
capeas ad satisfaciendum or ca.sa.
de bonis non
fi fa/fieri facias
non pros.
nut aut void
scire facias
sie fa/sei fa
to the use of
vendition (veneres)
vinera

    The County Clerk abbreviated names; I tried to copy what he wrote. The difference is that in the original the final letter is elevated.
    I read these minutes from the microfilm copy available from the North Carolina State Library and Archives. The pages were not numbered. Items entered in this abstraction are in the order in which they appear in the microfilm copy with one exception which is noted in the text. Since the number of pages for each term is relatively small, the way to find items in the microfilm copy from this abstraction is to find the term and then locate the item within the court term. Lists of names which appear in columns may not always be in the exact order in which they appeared on the microfilm. Sometimes I moved them around so that they would better fit the columns, but, of course, they are on the same list in which they appeared on the microfilm.

Jones County Court of Common Pleas Minutes 1826

The first two pages appear to be notes inserted (possibly from 1828) before the minutes for the March term, 1826. The notes are as follows:

DOCT LAROQUE probate of bill of sale from WHITE	6/"
JAS GREEN for probate of deed	6/"

LEML SIMMONS
 Order & return of settlement of estate A.W.S.   1.00
 Order & return of settlement of estate ELIZAH SIMMONS
    1.00
 Probate of power of attorney from F. FOY   .60
 Order to sell Negroes of T. FOY

SIMON FOSCUE
 Order of settlement of accounts of admr. & accounts returned
    .60
 Order for D. FOSCUE (The rest is smudged.)   .60
 Motion for settlement...by shff   .60
    1.80

C. BRYAN admr of HATHAWAY
R.M. McDANIEL admr of M. McDANIEL
 Administration bond & letters   1.60
 Guardian to WM POLLOCK
 Order bond   .80

DURANT HATCH admr of ROBT KORNEGAY
 Administration bond, etc. $2.40

Executor of THOS MURPHEY
 Same as above and recording of deed J.W. LEE to
 JNO G. KINSEY and mortage from T. BROWN TO R.
 KORNEGAY $6.00

D. HATCH JR. admr of R. KORNEGAY for probate and
 registration of shff bond   .90
DU HATCH received of decd J.G. KINSEY Mar Term, 1828   .60
DU. HATCH received of decd ELIJAH SIMMONS Mar term, 1828   .60
    2.70

Note: I copied the above as close as I could to the original. It was obviously added later and possibly by someone other than the regular clerk since it was not composed in the same format as was used by Hardy Bryan, clerk.

MARCH TERM, 1826
TRENTON, Monday the 13th

Justices: BENJAMIN HARRISON, OWEN B. COX, RESDEN M. McDANIEL, JAMES REYNOLDS, JAMES ROBERTS, ESQ.
Shff: WILLIAM HUGGENS
Clerk: HARDY BRYAN

Jurers:
JAMES B. SHINE	COUNCIL GOODING	LEWIS WILLIAMS
THOMAS McDANIEL	JOHN McDANIEL	LEML BUSICK
JAMES HUGGINS SR	LUKE SHELFER	HARDY MUNDINE
PETER HARGET	THOS B. HARRISON	JOHN HEATH
JOHN POLLACK		

CHRISTOPHER BRYAN, RESDEN M. McDANIEL, and HARDY BRYAN ordered to settle accounts of JAMES REYNOLDS, admr of JAMES GREEN, decd.

RESDEN M DANIEL, JAMES REYNOLDS, and ISAAC HATHAWAY ordered to settle accounts of CHRIST BRYAN, admr of WILLIAM H. CONNER, decd.
[Note: CHISTOPHER BRYAN, Esq., Clerk of Superior Court of Jones County married REBECCA CONNER, daughter of the late WILLIAM H. CONNER, Esq., 13 Jul 1826 (Kammerer, Vol. I, p. 65 as reported in the North Carolina *Star*). He died in TRENTON 13 Sep 1827 (Kammerer, Vol. 2, p. 6 and, again, from the *Star*).]

CHRIST BRYAN, JAMES REYNOLDS, and RISDEN M. McDANIEL ordered to settle accounts of ISAAC HATHAWAY, admr of JOSEPH BRYAN, decd.

JAMES ROBERTS, ASA SMITH, and THOS GILLET to settle accounts of estate of THOS MEADOWS with his admr.

RISDON M. McDANIEL ordered to be a commissioner in place of ENOCK FAY (resigned) to superintend the buildings of the court house in Trenton.

JAMES ROBERTS, THOMAS GILLET, JOSEPH WHITTY, DANIEL YATES, and GEORGE OLDFIELD ordered to divide lands of THOMAS L. MEADOWS and allot off to BARTHALOMEW MEADOWS his distributive share of said lands.

JAMES ROBERTS ordered to be overseer of road from THOMAS M. (remainder of name lost in book binding) to BLACK SWAMP. (**Note:** Black Swamp Creek, according to Powell, is in south east Jones County and flows south into White Oak River. The White Oak River rises in northern Onslow and southern Jones Counties and flows southeasterly on the Jones-Onslow County line to the Carteret-Onslow Couny line and into the Atlantic Ocean through Bogue Inlet.)

JAMES ROBERTS to "turn" road leading across GINGER BRANCH between lines of JOSIAH HOWARD and JAS ROBERTS. (Note: Powell does not have a Ginger Branch.)

DANIEL STANLEY to be full admr of estate of JOHN H. STANLEY, decd., $2,500 bond with JAMES REYNOLDS and RESDON M. McDANIEL, securities.

NATHAN B. BUSH to turn that part of the public road leading from MUSSELSHELL up to his house. (Note: According to Powell, Musselshell Creek rises in northeastern Jones County and flows into the Trent River.)

THOS MURPHEY, JAMES N. SMITH, and SOLOMON E. GRANT ordered to allot off to the widow of JOHN H. STANLY, decd., one year's provisions.

LEWIS SMALL ordered to oversee road in place of JOHN STRECKLIN.

JOSEPH KINSEY to turn that part of public road opposite the WM KING plantation. [Note: A biography of JOSEPH KINSEY SR. was published in the NEW BERN *Daily Journal* 30 Jan 1886. It indicated that his ancestor, MAURICE or MORRIS KINSEY, a native of HOLLAND, was one of the first settlers of NEW BERN. His son, JOSEPH KINSEY, moved to Jones County to the headwaters of the TRENT RIVER. A blacksmith and bell maker, JOSEPH KINSEY, son of the immigrant, had seven children, and JOSEPH KINSEY, born 27 Oct 1777, was the youngest. He inherited his father's estate and was a blacksmith, carpenter, wheelright, and shoemaker. The name of his first wife is unknown, but the second was a Miss BROCK who gave him four boys and two girls. The third wife was Miss SUSAN RHEM who gave him nine boys and three girls. All of the children's names began with a "J." The youngest son was JAY ROBERT KINSEY (Kammerer, Vol. 2, pp. 22-23).]

ALFRED HARGET given leave to sell spirits by small measure in Trenton for one year.

JOHN H. BRYAN given leave to sell spirits by small measure in Trenton for one year.

JOHN MORRIS, HASKEL F. HATCH, EDWD S. FRANK, and RESDON M. McDANIEL ordered to allot off to PENNY SIMMONS, widow of F.G. SIMMONS, decd., one year's provisions for self and family.

DURANT HATCH JR., WILLIAM HARGET, and AMOS AMYET ordered to settle accounts of JOHN MORRIS, guard. to LEWIS MORRIS (minor).

FANNY KNIGHTS, dau of KADER KNIGHTS, decd., ordered to be bound to NANCY (WATSON).

IVY CONAWAY ordered to have letters of admin of the estate of JAMES CONAWAY, decd., $500 bond with JAMES SIMMONS and JONATHAN LEE, securities.

THOMAS GILLET, THOMAS HILL, and ASA SMITH ordered to settle estate of WM. BRAY, decd.

At the request of MORRIS WARD, THOS GILLET and JAMES ROBERTS are ordered to take the depositions of DANIEL SMITH and EDWD. S. FRANK in the case between said WARD and WILLIAM ORME.

ELIJAH SIMMONS, JAMES ROBERTS, and ASA SMITH ordered to settle accounts of ANN WATSON, admr of IVEY WATSON, decd.

CHARLES WHITTY ordered to oversee road from the corner of ROBT. DICKSON'S fence to the upper bridge on MILL CREEK. (Note: According to Powell, MILL CREEK rises in southern JONES COUNTY and flows north into the TRENT RIVER. It appears on the MOSELEY map of 1733 which also has FRANKS FERRY across the TRENT near the mouth of MILL CREEK.)

JOHN YOUNG ordered to oversee road from the fork to MILL CREEK bridge.

GEORGE C. HATCH ordered to oversee road in room of LEWIS FOSCUE.

IVEY ANDREWS ordered to oversee road in room of JOHN B. HARGET (moved) from the bridge at TRENTON to DEEP GULLY. (Note: According to Powell, DEEP GULLY rises on the JONES-CRAVEN COUNTY line and flows south east into the TRENT RIVER. Part or all of this waterway was a canal.)

RHODES WEEKS vs CHRIST. BRYAN, admr of WM. H. CONNER, decd.
Jurers for this case:

JOHN C. WOOD	THOS. HARRISON	FRED. I. BECTON
JAS. MARRET	JONATHAN LEE	RISDEN McDANIEL
WILLIAM COMBS	BENJ. KOONES	GEORGE KING
WRIGHT SIMMONS	RICHARD B. HATCH	RICHARD RENOLDS

find for the defendant (He has fully administered).

State vs BENJ. COLLINS
Jurers for this case:

THOS. HARRISON	J.L.C. WOOD	FREDK. I. BECTON

Jones County Court of Common Pleas Minutes 1826

I.L. MARRET	JONATHAN LEE	RISDON McDANIELS
WILL COMBS	WRIGHT SIMMONS	BENJ. M. KOONCE JR.
RICH. B. HATCH	RICHARD REYNOLDS	
find defendent guilty.	Fined $2.00.	

THOS. SPIGHT ordered to enter a guardianship bond of $3000 with RICH. REYNOLDS and JAS. B. SHINE, sureties, for the orphan children of MICHAEL KOONCE, decd.

Tuesday, March 14, 1826

Justices: RISDON M. McDANIEL, SOLM. E. GRANT, and NATHAN FOSCUE
Shff: WM HUGGINS
Clerk: H. BRYAN

    By petition of ABNER GREEN, admr. of estate of THOS BROWN, decd, the court orders GREEN to sell jointly with the admr. of ROBERT KORNEGAY, decd., a female slave, DELIAH, of the estate of BROWN but under mortage to KORNEGAY, to pay debts of the estate.
    Court orders sale of lands of AMOS W. SIMMONS in the hands of his heirs. Also the same order as to judgments against the heirs of WILLIAM H. CONNER, decd.
    JOSEPH LOFTIN given full administration of estate of FURNIFOLD G. SIMMONS, decd., he entering into $5000 bond with LEML. SIMMONS, FRED. I. BECTON and JOSEPH PEIRCE, securities. JOSEPH LOFTIN also given guardianship of the children of F.G. SIMMONS, ELIZABETH and FURNIFOLD, he entering $5000 bond for them with the same securities.
    DANIEL YATES appointed guardian to ELIZABETH, JAMES, and SUSAN STAFFORD, heirs of ELISHA STAFFORD, decd. $3000 bond with JAMES ROBERTS and LEVI EUBANKS, securities.
    WILLIAM B. HATCH, ISAAC HATHAWAY, and ALFORD HARGET ordered to audit and settle accounts of TOBIAS KOONCE, admr of estate of MARY WRIGHT, decd.
    JAMES ROBERTS, ASA SMITH, and LEVI EUBANKS ordered to settle accounts of the executor of ELISHA STAFFORD, decd.
    Letters of admin. granted to SIMMONS HARRISON on the estate of MICHAEL KOONCE, decd. $8000 bond with JAMES REYNOLDS and RISDON McDANIEL, securities. [Note: RISDON McDANIEL served in the House of Commons 1818-1823 and the state Senate 1824-1831 (Wheeler), but this Risdon may or may not have been the politician since more than one Risden/Risdon McDaniel lived in Jones County during this era.]
    By petition of PENNY KOONCE, widow of MICHAEL KOONCE, decd., court orders JAMES REYNOLDS, ELIJAH PARRY, SAML. DILLAHUNT, and JOHN WOOD to allot off a year's provisions to said widow.
    Admr. of MICHAEL KOONCE, decd, given leave to sell enough slaves to pay debts of the estate.
    Letters of admin. given to WILLIAM DUNKEN on the estate of ISAAC KORNEGAY, decd. $8000 bond with ERASMUS HILL and SUSAN KORNEGAY, securities.
    Executors of BENJ. SMALL, decd, ordered to sell enough of his real estate that will satisfy claims of the admr., EML. JARMEN.

Jones County Court of Common Pleas Minutes 1826

The following deeds and bills of sale were proved with JAS. REYNOLDS, registrar:

    Shff HUGGINS to RICH. REYNOLDS
    Shff HUGGINS to RACHEL CONNER
    Shff HATCH to HARDY BROWN
    MILTON ARNOLD to WM WATSON
    ISAAC C. HUGGINS to WM. STANLY JR.
    Shff HATCH to FRANCIS DuVAL
    ISAAC HATHAWAY to WM HUGGINS
    JACOB HUGGINS to WM HUGGINS
    GEO. and JAS. FRANER to RICH. REYNOLDS
    COUNCIL YATES to JNO. MALLARD
    LEVIN B. LANE to JNO. STANLY
    GEORGE OLDFIELD to RICH. B. HATCH
    IVY SPIGHT to SIMMONS HARRISON
    JOHN KOONCE to RICH. KOONCE
    JAS. N. SMITH to JNO. PARKER
    JAS. N. SMITH to JNO. PARKER [Note: JAMES N. SMITH served in the North Carolina House of Commons in 1825 (Wheeler).]
    JOHN B. HARGET to RICH. KOONCE
    DANL. and (N.) MILLER to WM P. GILBERT
    Marriage contract between LEML HATCH, MARY A. SIMMONS and CHRIST. BRYAN

EDWD DEBRULE appointed guardian to ASA and DANIEL KNIGHT, minors.

SIMON FOSCUE, guardian to DARCUS FOSCUE, ordered to bring his accounts to court next term.

Jurers drawn for June term, 1826:

WILLIAM JARMON	WILLIAM RHEM	WILLIAM GILBERT
SIMMONS ISLER	ISAAC KORNEGAY	CULLEN POLLACK
JOHN WISE	SILAS McDANIEL	EDWD.S. FRANK
ASA EUBANKS	JOHN H. BECTON	JOHN FORDHAM
JAMES READ	LOT EUBANKS	MORRIS McDANIEL
THOMAS H. HILL	STEPHEN WALLACE	LEROY BROWN
JOHN D. COLVET	JOHN MALLARD	FARNIFOLD G. HERRITAGE
RUBIN G. CORMON	WILLIAM ORME	WALTER HELLEN
BENJ. KOONCE	WILLIAM JONES	ELIJAH KOONCE
ELIJAH MARKET	HARDY JARMON	LEVI EUBANKS

JUNE TERM, 1826 TRENTON, June 12th

Justices: BENJ. HARRISON, RISDON M. McDANIEL, and HARDY PARRY, Esquires

Shff: WILLIAM HUGGINS
Clerk: HARDY BRYAN

Inventory and account of sales of estate of FURNIFOLD GEORGE, decd., returned by admr., RICHD. REYNOLDS.

Grand jurors drawn for this term:
EDWARD S. FRANK, foreman
ELIJAH MARKET   JOHN MALLARD   WILLIAM READ
JOHN FORDHAM   JOHN D. COLVERT   WILLIAM ORME
LOTT EUBANKS   RUBIN G. CORMAN   MORRIS McDANIEL
LEROY BROWN   THOMAS H. HILL   SILAS McDANIEL

ADONIJAH PARRY sworn in as constable.

JOHN SHELFER appointed admr. of estate of JESSE SHELFER, decd. $1000 bond with JAMES REYNOLDS and LUKE SHELFER, securities.

LEWIS OLIVER to be bound to JAMES ROBERTS until he arrives at lawful age. ROBERTS to teach LEWIS reading and writing.

PENELOPE PENUEL to be bound to JOSEPH SMALL. He to teach her reading and writing.

THOMAS WILCOX entered bond with DANIEL STANLY and BENJ. W. HARGET, sureties, to clear wardens and county from charge or expense of bastard child which WILCOX is charged with begetting on body of SUSANNA PENUEL, a single woman.

JAMES ROBERTS, JOSEPH WHETTY, and THOMAS H. HALL to settle estate of JAMES SCOTT, decd., with the executor.

JAMES REYNOLDS, HARDY BRYAN, and WM RHEM to lay off one year's provisions to SALLY SHELFER, widow of JESSE SHELFER.

Shff to summon a jury to allot off to SALLY SHELFER, widow of JESSE SHELFER, decd., her dower in lands of said decd.

Same as immediately above for PENELOPE KOONCE except her husband was not named.

Letter of admin. issued to OWIN B. COX on estate of FELIN COX, decd. $200.00 bond with J.S. REYNOLDS and RISDON M. McDANIEL, sureties. [Note: OWEN B. COX served in the North Carolina House of Representatives 1826-1829 and again in 1831 (Wheeler).]

NATHAN FOSCUE resigned as county surveyor. JNO H. HAMMONS to succeed him.

BRYAN BECTON, JAS G. OLIVER, and WILLIAM ISLER to settle estate of HARDY JONES, decd.

MODICA WHITE, guard. to WINIFORD ISLER. $2000.00 bond with JAMES REYNOLDS and JAS G. OLIVER, sureties.

FREDK FOSCUE, JAMES MARRIT, and NATHAN FOSCUE to settle estate of THOS FOY, decd., with LEML SIMMONS, admir.

SIMMONS ISLER, GEO H. HOWARD, and LEML HATCH, esquires, qualified as justices of the peace.

FREDK FOSCUE, JAMES MARRIT, and NATHAN FOSCUE to settle estate of AMOS W. SIMMONS, decd, with LEML. H. SIMMONS, admr.
Also the estate of ELIZABETH SIMMONS, decd., widow of the late AMOS W. SIMMONS. Also the same men to settle accounts of LEML H. SIMMONS, guard. to AMOS and SOPHIA SIMMONS, minors. [Note: LEMUEL H. SIMMONS served in the North Carolina House of Commons 1824-1825 (Wheeler). According to a biography

published in the NEW BERN *Daily Journal* 13 Dec 1885, he also had served as county treasurer and trustee besides a county magistrate. His wife was MARIA FOY. Their oldest daughter, ELIZABETH LANE SIMMONS, married WILLIAM P. WARD of ONSLOW COUNTY. She died young leaving two children, a daughter who died without issue and a son, W.E. WARD of TRENTON. Their next oldest daughter, MARY ANN SIMMONS married RICHARD OLDFIELD, but she died soon afterwards. Another daughter, EMILY SIMMONS, married F.B. HARRISON and was still living in TEXAS when the article was published. They had two sons, NEEDHAM and FRANK SIMMONS, but FRANK died young (Kammerer, Vol. 2, pp. 25-26.) LEMUEL H. SIMMONS' will is abstracted by Gwynn, p. 445. Written 14 Jun 1844 and probated March term, 1846, it names his wife, MARIA, son-in-law, WILLIAM P. WARD, daughters EMILY and MARY ANN SIMMONS, son, BENJAMIN FRANKLIN SIMMONS, sister, MARY, wife of GEORGE C. HATCH and their son, LEMUEL L. HATCH. JACOB GOODING, AMOS D. SIMMONS, and WILLIAM P. WARD were named exrs., and the witnesses were NATHAN FOSCOE and JOHN STANLY.

ELIZABETH SIMMONS left a will which was written 30 Oct 1820. Named were NATHAN FOSCUE, POLLY and BENETER SIMMONS, JANE SHEPHERD and REZON GUNTER (no relationships were mentioned). NATHAN FOSCUE was named exr. and the witnesses were RISDON McDANIEL and DANIEL MALLARD (Gwynn, p. 445).]

JAMES REYNOLDS, MARTIN F. BROCK, and DURANT H. WHITE to settle estate of BENJAMIN GRIFFEN, decd.

Will of THOMAS MURPHY, decd, proved in court by oath of JAMES MARRET, a witness. DURANT HATCH, JR., executor. [Note: Gwynn abstracted this will (pp. 438-439) which was written 6 Dec 1823. It names his wife, MARY, and infant son, THOMAS. Also, it names son, WILLIAM CLARK MURPHY, and four daughters: FRANCES (FANNY), ELIZA, CAROLINE and MIRANDA. Exr was DURANT HATCH, JR., of Jones County, and the witnesses were STEPHEN B. FORBIS and JAMES MARRET.]

Account of sale and inventory of estate of F.G. SIMMONS, decd., returned by admir., JOSEPH LOFTON.

Settlement of estate of THOS MEADOWS, decd, returned.

Same for IVY WATSON, decd.

Year's provisions allotted to widow of MICHAEL KOONCE, decd.

Inventory and account of sale of estate of JOHN H. STANLY, decd., returned by DANIEL STANLY, admir.

Settlement of estate of MARY WRIGHT, decd, returned.

Same of WM H. CONNER, decd.

Account of sale of estate of DAVID FONVILLE, decd, returned.

Inventory of property, left in hands of E. FIELDS and wife and supposed to belong to her children at her death, returned.

Inventory and account of sale of estate of JAMES CONWAY, decd, returned by IVEY CONWAY.

Settlement filed of O.W.B. COX, guard. to JESSE B. GREGORY, minor.

Settlement of estate of JAMES GREEN, decd, filed by JAMES REYNOLDS, admr.

Settlement of estate of ELISHA STAFFERD, decd, filed by C. FIELDS, executor.

Jones County Court of Common Pleas Minutes 1826

Account of sales of property of heirs of ELISHA STAFFERD, decd, returned by DANIEL YATES.

Inventory and account of sale of estate of F.G. GEORGE, decd, filed by RICHD REYNOLDS, admr.

ELIZABETH PICKERIND (Note: Potter, 1970, read this name as PICKRON.) vs RACHEL JARMON:

Jurers: CULLEN POLLACK   JAS READ   ASA EUBANKS
         HARDY MUNDINE   JOHN STANLY   WALTER HELLIN
         JOHN M. FRANKS   LEVI EUBANKS   ABIJAH HEATH
         LUKE SHELFER   ELIJAH KOONCE   RISDON McDANIEL JR

Jury found for defendant; "no cause of action."

Thursday, June 13, 1826

CHARLES WATSON, an orphan, to be bound to THOS HILL until WATSON is 21 years old.

Issued letters of admin. to EML JARMON on estate of ROBT WALLACE, decd. $1000 bond with WMS BROWN and HARDY PARRY, sureties.

GEORGE OLDFIELD appointed special guard. to AMOS FOSCUE. $1000 bond with JAMES ROBERTS and ASA SMITH, sureties.

CHRISTOPHER BRYAN, LEML HATCH, and WILLIAM HUGGINS to allot to widow of ROBERT WALLACE, decd, one year's support for self and family.

JAMES HARRISON, FREDK I. BECTON, and JACOB GILES to settle estate of NANCY BROWN, decd.

CHRISTOPHER BRYAN, HARDY BRYAN, and HARDY PARRY to divide Negroes belonging to heirs of EML KOONCE, decd, and allot to BRADERIK NOBLE his distributive share.

CHRISTOPHER BRYAN, HARDY BRYAN, and WMS BROWN to settle accounts of JAMES HARRISON, guard. to heirs of BRYAN MUMFORD, decd.

HARDY MUNDINE permitted to amend an inventory of property of WM W. BRAY, decd, returned by him as admr. to strike out unnamed Negro.

JOHN H. BRYAN resigned as county attorney and JAMES W. BRYAN appointed to the vacancy.

$600 added to the appropriation made to build a new courthouse in TRENTON.

$200 approved for repairs to TRENT BRIDGE.

ROBERT KORNEGAY, former clerk, allowed $25 for extra services "up to his death."

HARDY BRYAN, clerk, allowed $27 for extra services up to this term.

WILLIAM HUGGINS, shff, allowed $75 for his entire services for the past year.

Elections were held for county officers. Present and voted were "the worshipfuls" RISDEN M. McDANIEL, LEML HATCH, LEML HARRISON, LEML ISLER, DURANT HATCH, BRYAN BECTON, HARDY PARRY, ELIJAH SIMMONS, JAS ROBERTS, DANIEL SMITH, JAMES HARRISON, O.B. COX, THOMAS GELLIT, NATHAN FOSCUE, JAMES REYNOLDS, and ASA SMITH, Esquires. Chairman, BENJ HARRISON counted the votes. NATHAN B. BUSH was elected county trustee; JOHN H HAMMONS, county surveyor; and WILLIAM HUGGINS, shff. The constables elected for each district:

Jones County Court of Common Pleas Minutes 1826

1) DANIEL DICKESON
2) ALFRED HARGET
3) ADONIJAH PARRY
4) EML JARMON
5) JAMES HUGGINS
6) SAML WIGGINS

WRIGHT STANLY, JOHN STANLY JR, JAMES and SIMMONS ISLER to be patrols in District 5.

JOHN H. HAMMONS, F.G. HERETAGE, SAML DILLAHUNTY, DURANT McDANIEL, and SAML HILL to be patroles in District 3.

DANIEL WILLIAMSON, THOS HALL, G.W. HOWARD, and JOHN RAMSEY to be patroles in District 2.

Ordered tax of 35 cents on the pole and 12 1/2 cents on the $100 value of land and town lots for present year.

The following justices are to hold the elections for the present year:
District 1: DANIEL SMITH, Esq.; JNO BINDER, and DANIEL YATES
District 2: ELIJAH SIMMONS, Esq.; WALTER HELLEN, and EDMD HATCH
District 3 or 4 (number obscured): JAS HARRISON, Esq.; F.I. BECTON, and JACOB GILES.
"at Jones:" ISAAC BROWN, Esq.; ELIJAH KOONCE, and EML JARMON
District 5: BENJ HARRISON, Esq.; JAMES REYNOLDS, and B. BECTON
District 6: NATHAN FOSCUE, Esq.; JAMES MARRIT, and IVY ANDREWS

The following justices shall take the tax list this year:
JAMES ROBERTS, Esq. in District 1
GEO W. HOWARD in District 2
LEML HATCH in District 3
JAMES HARRISON in District 4
SIMMONS ISLER in District 5
RESDON M. McDANIEL in District 6

The following freeholders were drawn as jurers for the September term:

FRANCIS ANDREWS	TOBIAS KOONCE	JAMES MADES
JOHN BINDER	JAMES WISE	COUNCIL FIELDS
ARCHIBALD B. COX	WM H. MEADOWS	EDWD DEBRUELE
ELIJAH PARRY	JOHN COLLINS	JOHN H. BRYAN
THOS STILLY	AARON EUBANKS	CHARLES WHITTY
RICHARD KOONCE	JEREMIAH CONNOR	JOHN ANDREWS JR
HENRY ROADS	JOSEPH BROCK	EDWIN BECTON
HARDY HILL	OWEN ADAMS	DANIEL WILLIAMSON
BARTHOLOMEW WILLIAMS	JACOB GILES	WILLIAMS ISLER

Inventory and sale of estate of ROBERT KORNEGAY, decd, filed by DURANT HATCH, admr.

Settlement of JNO MORRIS, guard. to LEWIS MORRIS, filed.

Division of property of SAML WESTBROOK, decd, filed.

Inventory and sale of estate of ISAAC KORNEGAY, decd, filed by EDWD GRAHAM for WM DUNKIN, admr.

Deeds and bills of sale proved this term by JAS REYNOLDS, registrar, and received from HARDY BRYAN, clerk:
1) deed: THOS SMART to MICHAEL KOONCE
2) bill of sale: F. GREEN to SIMMONS ISLER
3) deed: N.B. BUSH to HANNAH WOOD

4) bill of sale: BENJAMIN KOONCE to LEVIN B. LANE
5) deed: Shff. of Jones to THOS BROWN
6) deed: ISAAC HATHAWAY to (N. GUNTER) and E. WRIGHT
7) deed: DANIEL ALPHEN to WILLIAM HUGGINS
8) bill: LEML HARRISON to LEML H. HARRISON
9) deed: LEML HATCH, shff to JAMES ROBERTS
10) shff of Jones to RISDEN M. McDANIEL
11) bill: H. HUMPHREY to THOS WILSON
12) deed: THOS POLLOCK to JOHN POLLOCK
13) bill: LEVIN B. LANE to DANIEL WILLIAMSON
14) bill: LEVIN B. LANE to BENJM KOONCE
15) deed: LEVIN B. LANE to JOHN B. HARGET
16) bill: GEO OLDFIELD to BENJM KOONCE
17) deed: shff of Jones to ISAAC BROWN
18) deed: shff of Jones to WM ORME
19) deed: JAMES and WIGHT SIMMONS to EDWD S. FRANKS
20) deed: ISAAC HATHAWAY to DANIEL WILLIAMSON
21) deed: SOL E. GRANT to RISDON JARMON
22) deed: LEML HATCH, shff to JNO STANLY
23) deed: JNO C. BRYAN to JOHN B. HARGET
24) bill: ISAAC HATHAWAY to DANIEL HARRISON
25) bill: JESSE W. LEE to JOHN G. KINSEY
26) power of attorney: WM R. JONES to WM B. PENUEL
27) power of attorney: CALVIN JONES to WM B. PENUEL

Freeholders drawn as jurors for Superior Court, Sept. term, 1826:

JOHN MORRIS	JESSE LEE	BENJM HARRISON
FREDK FOSCUE	LEML HILL	ASA SMITH
SAML DELAHUNT	WILLIAM GILES	ALEXANDER HICKS
WILLIAM RICHARDS	SIMMONS HARRISON	ELIJAH SIMMONS
DANIEL SIMMONS	ADONIJAH PARRY	HARDY PARRY
MARTIN F. BROCK	JAMES REYNOLDS	JAMES ROBERTS
LEML HATCH	RIGDON HEWIT	RISDEN M. McDANIEL
JOHN ADAMS	WILLIAMS BROWN	WILLIAM ADAMS
ISAAC BROWN	JOSEPH KINSEY	WILLIAM COMBS
PETER HARGET	WALTER HELLEN	LEML H. SIMMONS
JOHN JARMON	ELIJAH KOONCE	EDMD HATCH
BRYAN BECTON	EDWD GILBERT	COUNCIL GOODIN

SEPTEMBER TERM, 1826 TRENTON, Sept 11

Justices: "the worshipfull" BRYAN BECTON, RISDON M. McDANIEL, and ELIJAH SIMMONS, esquires

Shff: WILLIAM HUGGIN
Clerk: HARDY BRYAN

Jones County Court of Common Pleas Minutes 1826

Grand jurers for this term:
WILLIAMS ISLER, foreman

JOSEPH BROCK	RICHARD KOONCE	CHARLES WHITTY
JOHN H. BRYAN	DANIEL WILLIAMSON	JOHN BENDER
ARCHIBALD B. OWINS	TOBIAS KOONCE	WILLIAM H. MEADOWS
EDWARD DEBRULE	HARDY HILL	JOHN ANDREWS JR

BENJAMIN HARRISON, BRYAN BECTON, and EDWIN BECTON to settle estate of JOHN ISLER, decd, with executor.

CHRISTOPHER BRYAN, RISDEN M. McDANIEL, and WILLIAM B. HATCH to settle accounts of AMOS AMYET/AMGET, guardian to heirs of ADONIJAH ANDREWS, decd.

BRYAN LAVENDER granted license to sell spirits by the small measure at his store near TRENT BRIDGE.

Tax list for District 4 returned and filed.

ISAAC BROWN, EML JARMON and JAMES HUGGINS SEN to take private exam of LEAH SMALL, wife of (a blank space was left here), and MARIAH SMALL, wife of (another unfortunate blank space), for their voluntary consent in a deed for lands heired to them by the death of their father, SAML WESTBROOK, decd, and sold to DURANT WESTBROOK.

JAMES HARRISON, WILLIAM ORME and ASA SMITH to settle accounts of SIMON FOSCUE, guard. to AMOS FOSCUE (minor).

EDMOND HATCH, WILLIAM B. HATCH, RISDEN M. McDANIEL, and NATHAN FOSCUE to allot off to PENELOPE SIMMONS, widow of FURNIFOLD SIMMONS, decd, one year's provisions.

HARDY PARRY, EML JARMON, and ELIJAH SIMMONS to act as board of appeals to hear grievances of people on adjustment of their lands.

Letters of admin. to JAMES SIMMONS on estate of WRIGHT SIMMONS, decd. $12,000 bond with JAMES N. SMITH, ELIJAH SIMMONS, and JAMES MARRITT, sureties.

Account of sale and inventory of estate of FELON COX, decd, filed.

Account of sale and inventory of estate of JESSE SHELFER, decd, filed.

Tax list returned for District 1.

Will of ELANY COX, decd, proved in court; OWIN B. COX, executor. [Note: Gwynn abstracted this will (p. 408) which was written 15 May 1826. It names her sons, LEWIS KINSEY and OWEN B. COX, and daughters, SARAH M. HUMPHREY and DELILA MIDDLETON. Her late husband was ANDREW COX. The names of the witnesses could not be read.]

Settlements of estates of JOSEPH BRYAN, THOS FOY, BENJM GRIFFEN, HARDY JONES, and WM W. BRAY, all decd, returned.

Settlement of accounts of LEML H. SIMMONS, guard to AMOS and SOPHIA (minors) filed. (No last name was given the children.)

Tax lists for Districts 3 and 5 filed.

Account of sale and inventory of the estate of ROBT WALLACE, decd, filed.

Division of Negroes of estate of EML KOONCE, decd, filed.

Thursday: 12 Sept 1826

Justices: BENJM HARRISON, THOMAS GILLET, and HARDY PARRY
Shff: WILLIAM HUGGINS
Clerk: HARDY BRYAN

Jones County Court of Common Pleas Minutes 1826

RICHARD REYNOLDS, BENJM HARRISON, JAMES HARRISON, and CHRISTOPHER BRYAN to allot off to MARY ANN HATCH, widow of LEML HATCH, decd, a year's provisions.

RICHARD REYNOLDS, admr of FURNIFOLD G. GEORGE, petitioned the court for distribution of two Negroes, EPOCKS, a blacksmith, and DENNIS, belonging to said estate, among BRICE GEORGE, CHRISTIAN and FURNIFOLD who are minors and represent their father DAVID GEORGE, all of the state of GEORGIA, and BETSY, wife of JOHN LEVANDER, also of GEORGIA, and CLARRISA and LEWIS GEORGE, both of ONSLOW CTY. Court allowed Negroes to be sold at the courthouse of Jones Co. after advertising the sale.

EDMD HATCH appointed guard. to EDMOND HATCH and RICHD W. HATCH, heirs of BUCKNER HATCH, decd. $20,000 bond with JOHN MORRIS, ELIJAH SIMMONS, and SIMON FOSCUE, sureties.

Renew order to lay off dower in the lands of BUCKNER HATCH, decd, to his widow, ALICE HATCH.

ENOCK FOY, EDMD HATCH, ELIJAH SIMMONS, and SIMON FOSCUE to be patrols this year.

Letters of admin. to WILLIAM I. BLACKLEDGE on estate of LEMUEL HATCH, decd. $50,000 bond with BENJM HARRISON, RICHD REYNOLDS, EDMD HATCH, and S. FOSCUE, sureties.

ASA SMITH, DANIEL YATES, and LEVI EUBANKS to settle estate of RACHEL STEPHENS.

FREDK I. BECTON appointed guard. to READING JONES. $300 bond with EML JARMON and RISDEN M. McDANIEL, sureties.

OWEN B. COX appointed county surveyor.

Ordered that no Negro, slave or free, shall preach in this county except at funerals for three months.

The following justices are to take the tax list for this year:
District 1: ASA SMITH   District 4: ISAAC BROWN
District 2: WALTER HELLEN   District 5: BRYAN BECTON
District 3: HARDY PARRY   District 6: ROSCO BARRIS
(Note: Those listed for Districts 1,2 and 3 were marked "error."

Deeds and bills of sale delivered to registrar, JAS REYNOLDS, this term:
1) MILES SPIGHT to THOS HARRISON
2) WM ORME to BRYAN LAVENDER
3) JAS N. SMITH to ROSCO BARRIS
4) JAMES WISE to LEWIS O. BRYAN
5) ELIZABETH PICKERING to ADONIJAH PARRY
6) RISDEN McDANIEL to LEVI HARRISON
7) JOHN KOONCE to JOSEPH RHEM
8) JOSHUA DAVIS to BENJM HARRISON (mortgage)
9) JNO MILLER to BENJM HARRISON (mortgage)
10) J.W. LEE to WM ORME (mortgage)

Jurors drawn for December Term:
JOSEPH KINSEY   WILLIAMS BROWN   HARDY JARMON
STEPHEN WALLACE   BENJM HARGET   ISAAC KORNEGAY
LEWIS WILLIAMS   WALTER HELLIN   THOS H. HILL

THOS STILLY	DURANT WESTBROOK	LUKE SHELFER
ELIJAH MARKET	CULLEN POLLOCK	JAMES READ
MICAJAH PITAWAY	THOS B. HARRISON	JOHN S. COLLINS
ROBERT GILBERT	SAML HILL	OWEN ADAMS
JNO M. FRANK	COUNCEL FIELDS	JNO C. WOOD
JACOB GILES	LEVI EUBANKS	JONATHAN LEE
SAML DILLAHUNT	FREDK I. BECTON	HARDY MUNDINE

DECEMBER TERM, 1826 TRENTON, Monday 11 Dec 1826

Justices: RISDEN M. McDANIEL, HARDY PARRY, and OWEN B. COX, Esqs.

Shff: WILLIAM HUGGINS
Clerk: HARDY BRYAN

Jurors summoned for this court:
ISAAC KORNEGAY, foreman

THOMAS B. HARRISON	SAMUEL HILL	ELIJAH MARKET
CULLEN POLLACK	JAMES READ	JOHN M. FRANKS
DURANT WESTBROOK	LUKE SHELFER	JOHN C. WOOD
STEPHEN WALLACE	BENJM HARGET	LEWIS WILLIAMSON

ALFRED HARGET, "Con...e" (Note: I presume this abbreviation is for constable.) was sworn and sent to attend the jury.

JEREMIAH WATSON named admr. of estate of WILLIAM WATSON, decd. $200 bond with ISAAC H. MEADOWS and MICAJAH F. MATTOCKS, sureties.

JOHN MORRIS named admr. of estate of LEWIS MORRIS, decd. $2000 bond with DURANT HATCH JR and FRANCIS DuVAL, sureties.

Petit jurors for this day:

ROBERT GILBERT	LEVI EUBANKS	WALTER HELLEN
JAMES B. SHINE	ISAAC MEADOWS	BENJM HUGGINS
LEML H. SIMMONS	JAMES MARRET	JOHN MALLARD
ELIJAH PARRY	BRODRICK NOBLE	DANIEL YATES

DANIEL YATES, ASA SMITH, and GEORGE OLDFIELD to settle accounts of JOHN BENDER JR., executor of RACHEL STEPHENS, decd.

JAMES SIMMONS ordered to appear next court to renew his bond as guard. to heirs of JOHN SIMMONS, decd, and find surety in room of NATHAN FOSCUE.

HEPHZIBAH BRAY appointed guard. to "her children, HARDY, ELIZA, MARGARET, NICHOLAS, and WILLIAM BRAY." $2000 bond with ASA SMITH and JAMES READ, sureties.

RISDEN M. McDANIEL named guard. to WILLIAM POLLACK. $2400 bond with JOHN MORRIS and "RISDEN McDANIEL (son of JAMES)," sureties.

JAMES HARRISON, FREDERICK I. BECTON, and EML JARMON shall set off to LAVINIA COX, widow of JNO B. COX, decd, her distributive share of Negroes out of estate of her said husband.

JOHN YOUNG to "turn" the public road.

ENOCH FOY, ROSCO BARRIS, and JESSE W. LEE shall set off to WILLIAM HELLEN his distributive share of Negroes from the estate of "WM HELLEN, decd, (his father)."

BENJN HARRISON Esq., JAMES B. SHINE, and SAMUEL DILLAHUNT shall allot off to "MARY HELLEN, wife of WILLIAM HELLEN formerly MARY BRYAN heir at law of JOSEPH BRYAN decd" her distributive share of Negroes of BRYAN'S estate.

JAMES HARRISON, EMANUEL JARMON, and FREDERICK I. BECTON shall settle accounts of heirs of FOUNTIN WILLIAMS, decd, with their guard.

JAMES HARRISON, Esq., JAMES B. SHINE, and JOHN B. HARGET shall allot off to JOHN PARSONS his distributive share of Negroes out of estate of "his father, JEREMIAH PARSONS, decd."

ROSCO BARRIS, JAMES B. SHINE, and JESSE W. LEE shall settle accounts of SIMON FOSCUE, guard. to DARCUS FOSCUE.

WILLIAM B. HATCH, GEO C. HATCH, and JOSEPH GREEN shall settle accounts of LEML H. SIMMONS, admr of estate of AMOS W. SIMMONS and ELIZABETH SIMMONS, decd.

HARDY BRYAN, WILLIAMS BROWN, and NATHAN B. BUSH shall settle accounts of heirs of ZEADOCK ASKEY, decd, with admr of ISAAC HATHAWAY, decd, their guard.

JAMES HARRISON, JAMES B. SHINE, and JNO B. HARGET shall settle accounts of guard. of heirs of JEREMIAH PARSONS, decd.

THOMAS GILLET, JAMES ROBERTS, and THOMAS DUDLEY shall settle accounts of estate of JAMES MADES, decd.

LEML H. SIMMONS, admr of THOS FOY, decd, may sell two Negroes of the estate of FOY to pay FOY's debts.

ELIJAH SIMMONS, ENOCH FOY, and JAMES N. SMITH to take private exam of HANNAH CORMAN and SUSAN RICHERSON.

ROSCO BARRIS, WALTER HELLEN, and DANIEL SMITH, Esq. shall settle account of guard. of heirs of RICHD OLDFIELD.

JAMES HARRISON to oversee road in place of JAS B. SHINE.

WINDAL DAVIS to be guard. (in place of LEWIS KINSEY) to heirs of CHRISTOPHER KINSEY, decd. $5,000 bond with EML JARMON and OWEN B. COX, sureties.

EMANUEL JARMON, HENERY RHODES SR., and JOHN JONES shall settle account of LEWIS KINSEY, former guard. to heirs of CHRISTOPHER KINSEY, decd, with WINDAL DAVIS, their present guard.

(Note: My old cousin, Hardy Bryan as clerk of the court, resorted on occasion to creative spelling, but I wonder if he spelled Henry this way because he pronounced it Henery?)

BENJN HARRISON, EDWIN BECTON, and JAMES REYNOLDS to settle estate of JOHN ISLER, decd, with WMS ISLER, executor and guard. to heirs.

CHRISTOPHER BRYAN, HARDY BRYAN, and SAML C. FORBES (Note: This name could be FOSTER; it was very difficult to read.) to settle accounts of guard. of heirs of EML KOONCE, decd.

HARDY COLLINS appointed admr of estate of MARTHA COLLINS, decd. $1000 bond with ASA SMITH and M.F. MATTUKS, sureties.

Shff to summon a jury to allot off to widow of MICHAEL KOONCE, decd, her dower in lands of her decd husband.

BENJN HARRISON, RICHARD KOONCE, PETER HARGET, and HARDY BRYAN shall allot to MAHALA McDANIEL, widow of MORRIS McDANIEL, decd, one year's provisions for self and family.

Tuesday, 12 Dec 1826

Justices: ELIJAH SIMMONS, OWEN B. COX, and SIMMONS ISLER, Esqs.
Shff: WILLIAM HUGGINS
Clerk: HARDY BRYAN

Jurers for this day:
ROBERT GILBERT
JAMES MARRET
PETER HARGET
JOHN MALLARD
RISDEN McDANIEL (son of JAS)
LEVI EUBANKS
ELIJAH KOONCE
JOHN H. HAMMONS
JAMES SIMMONS
WALTER HELLEN
DURANT RICHARDS
LEWIS SMALL

ISAAC BROWN, HENERY RHODES SENR, and JOHN JONES to settle accounts of guard. of heirs of SAML WESTBROOK, decd, and to settle accounts of guard. to heirs (or heir) of JOHN SHELFER, decd, and to settle account of guard. to heirs of ZENOS KOONCE, decd. (Note: Potter has this name as GENAS KOONCE.)

JAMES HARRISON, ISAAC BROWN, and FREDK I. BECTON to settle accounts of guard. to WM A. COX (minor).

WALTER HELLEN, guard. to heirs of WILLIAM HELLEN, decd, allowed to sell two Negro girls, LEDIA and TAMIRS, in order to make an equal division between the heirs.

ENOCH FOY, ROSCO BARRES, and JESSE W. LEE to allot to each heir of WRIGHT SIMMONS, decd, his distributive share of Negroes of SIMMONS' estate.

WALTER HELLEN, JOHN MORRIS, and ENOCH FOY to set off to ALICE HATCH, wife of EDMD HATCH, her distributive share of Negroes of "her decd son, LEMUEL HATCH."

THOMAS HALL to oversee road in place of "E.S. FRANKS (dead)."

WM B. HATCH may sell liquor for one year.

ROBERT V. ORME to admr estate of WILLIAM ORME, decd. $20,000 bond with JAMES N. SMITH and ASA SMITH, sureties.

DURANT HATCH, CULLEN POLLACK, and AMOS AMGET to settle accounts of guard. to heirs of WM MORRIS, decd.

DANIEL DEEKSON appointed guard. to MARY C. HUNTINGTON in place of THOS SPIGHT. $2000 bond with JAS SIMMONS, ASA SMITH, and GEO OLDFIELD, sureties.

JAMES ROBERTS, THOS GELLIT, and JOSEPH WHITTY to settle accounts of THOS SPIGHT, former guard. to MARY C. HUNTINGTON, with DANIEL DEEKSON, present guard.

PETER HARGET appointed guard. to JOSEPH and WILLIAM BRYAN, heirs of JOSEPH BRYAN, decd. $8,000 bond with RISDEN McDANIEL and JNO HARGET, sureties.

HARDY BRYAN, WILLIAMS BROWN, and NATHAN B. BUSH shall settle accounts between PETER HARGET, present guard. to JOSEPH and WILLIAM BRYAN (heirs of JOSEPH BRYAN, decd) and CHRISTOPHER BRYAN, admr of ISAAC HATHAWAY, decd, former guard. to JOSEPH and WILLIAM.

Jones County Court of Common Pleas Minutes 1826

ALFRED HARGET to admr estate of HARDY BRYAN, son of JOSEPH BRYAN, decd. $2,000 bond with OWEN B. COX and RISDEN M. McDANIEL, sureties.

Shff to summon a jury of 12 freeholders to ____ & ____ MARTH COLLINS, an "insane" or "limited" young woman.

RISDEN M. McDANIEL, Esq., ALFRED HARGET, SAML C. FISHER, and NATHAN B. BUSH shall allot to NANCY HATHAWAY, widow of ISAAC HATHAWAY, decd, one year's provisions.

Next day:

Justices: BENJN HARRISON, OWEN B. COX and ASA SMITH, Esqs.
Sheriff: WILLIAM HUGGINS
Clerk: HARDY BRYAN

Jurors for the day:
ROBERT GILBERT	WALTER HELLEN	WILLIAMS BROWN
JAMES MARRET	DURANT McDANIEL	WILLIAM STANLY
HARDY HILL	WILLIAM B. HATCH	DURANT RICHARDS
NATHAN B. BUSH	JOHN MALLARD	WILLIAM WATERS

CHRISTOPHER BRYAN to admin. estate of ISAAC HATHAWAY, decd. $4000 bond with RISDON M. McDANIEL and WM HUGGINS, secureties.

RISDON McDANIEL to admin. estate of MORRIS McDANIEL, decd. $4000 bond with CHRISTOPHER BRYAN and EMANUEL JARMON, sureties.

By petition of DURANT HATCH JR, admr of ROBERT KORNEGAY, decd, he may sell slaves of the KORNEGAY estate to pay debts of said estate.

Report of commission to lay off year's provision for MARY A. HATCH (widow of LEML HATCH, decd) and family returned for amount of $583.25 and filed.

Case: JAMES FRAZER SENR vs JAMES N. SMITH, admr of BAZEL R. SMITH, decd. ASA SMITH, Esq. appointed special guardian to CHRISTEEN SMITH, EDWD WARD SMITH and SALLY ANN SMITH (minors) heirs at law of BAZEL R. SMITH.

CHRISTOPHER BRYAN, admr of ISAAC HATHAWAY, decd, may sell "all" the property of "his intestate in his hands and particularly Negro girl VIOLET" to pay debts of the estate.

MARY FRANKS, widow of EDWD S. FRANKS, decd, appeared in court to protest the will of her husband and file her petition for dower and portion of personal estate "and services of the same being made on the executors and WILLIAM W. FRANKS (minor) heir at law by the said executors last testamentary guardian." Ordered "Writ of Veneres" (Note: This would be _Venditioni exponas_ which is a writ commanding the sheriff to sell property already seized according to Swaim, 1987 and Black, 1979.) issued to shff of ONSLOW to lay off her dower and to shff of JONES to allot to her her portion of the slaves of the estate.

Case: President and Board of Directors of State Bank of N.C. vs CHRISTOPHER BRYAN, admr of ISAAC HATHAWAY, CHRIST. BRYAN, RESDEN McDANIEL and NATHAN FOSCUE. The defendants, C. BRYAN, NATHAN FOSCUE, and R.M. McDANIEL confess judgment for sum of $644.56. CHRIST BRYAN, admr of ISAAC HATHAWAY, admits the debt to be $644.56. Judgment for same and costs, but the admr pleads no assets. Pltf prays process the real estate in the hands of

the heirs at law. Court ordered *Sie fa* (Note: This is probably *Scire facias* which is a writ ordered for the purpose of giving the defendant an opportunity to show cause why a judgment, or other matter equal to a judgment, should not be enforced according to Swaim, 1987.) issued to SUSAN, the infant, heir of ISAAC HATHAWAY. NATHAN B. BUSH appointed special guardian to defend the suit for the infant heir.

Case: State Bank vs SUSAN HATHAWAY, heir at law of ISSAC HATHAWAY. *Sie fa*. Defendant by her guardian, NATHAN B. BUSH, pleads *nut tut vioid*. Judges determined that there is such *void* and award judgment according to *Sie fa*. Principal: $642.00 with $2.56 interest = $644.56. (Note: Neither Black nor Swaim could help much with *nut tut vioid*.)

Case: President and directors of State Bank of N.C. vs CHRISTOPHER BRYAN, admr of ISAAC HATHAWAY, decd, and RESDEN M. McDANIEL. Same situation as the two preceding cases. This time the amount was $140.30 and the outcome was the same.

    Inventory of ELANY COX returned and filed.
    Inventory of WRIGHT SIMMONS, decd, returned and filed.
    Inventory of ANDREW COX, decd, returned and filed.
    Settlement of estate of A.W. SIMMONS, decd, with LEML H. SIMMONS, admr, returned and filed.
    Settlement of estate of ELIZA SIMMONS, decd, with LEML H. SIMMONS, admr, returned and filed.
    Accounts of SIMON FOSCUE, guard. to DARIUS FOSCUE, filed.
    Accounts of AMOS AMYET, guard. to heirs of AD ANDREWS, filed.
    Settlement of estate of JEHU SEAT (Note: Although no SEATS were in the index to the 1820 federal census for JONES COUNTY, there were SEATS in ASHE, HALIFAX, and NORTHAMPTON COUNTIES.) with THOS GILLET, esq., filed.
    Account of JONAS JONES, guard. to heirs of FOUNTEN WILLIAMS, decd, filed.
    Will of EDWD S. FRANKS proved by oath of SOLE E. GRANT. ROSCO BARRIS and ABRAHAM MITCHEL, executors.
    Will of BENJN WILCOX or WILSON, decd, proved by oath of BENJN HARRISON. THOMAS WILSON or WILCOX, executor. (Note: Potter has both BENJ and THOMAS WILCOX in JONES COUNTY in 1820.)
    Will of JOHN HARRISON, decd, proved by oath of the witnesses (unnamed). LEVI HARRISON, executor. (Note: An abstract of this will is found in Gwynn, p. 416. It names sons, LEVY and AMOS HARRISON, minor, and other unnamed children. His wife, ELIZABETH, was named exr. in the will which was written 30 Mar 1822. Witnesses: RICHARD MORRIS and WILSON MORRIS.)

Deeds and bills of sale received for registration with JAS REYNOLDS, registrar.
1) RIGDON WHITE to JAMES LARAQUE
2) MARTH.. COLLINS to BENJN COLLINS
3) MARTH.. COLLINS to her children
4) JOB MEADOWS to ISAAC H. MEADOWS (mortgage)

5) JOHN B. HARGET to JOHN C. BRYAN
6) C. BRYAN and WM HUGGINS, shff to LEML HATCH
7) C. BRYAN and WM HUGGINS, shff to LEML HATCH
8) FREDK FOY to LEML H. SIMMONS

Freeholders drawn as jurors for next court:

WILLIAM ADAMS	JAMES WISE	JOHN H. BECTON
PETER ANDREWS	DANIEL SMITH	EDWD DEBRULE
DANIEL SIMMONS	TOBIAS KOONCE	WILLIAM H. MEADOWS
JOHN FORDHAM	BENJN HARRISON	BENJN KOONCE JR
EDMD HATCH	MILLETON MEADOWS	ASA SMITH
JOHN HEATH	ISAAC BROWN	DURANT RICHARDS
DANIEL WILLIAMSON	JOHN BALL	JAMES McDANIEL
JOHN MALLARD	WILLIAM GOODING	ADONIJAH PARRY
BENJN HUGGINS	LEWIS O. BRYAN	SILAS McDANIEL
FREDK FOSCUE	IVY ANDREWS	LEML BUSICK
JAMES MARRET	CHARLES WHITTY	JAMES REYNOLDS
COUNCEL GOODING	JOSEPH BROCK	HENERY RHODES JR

Jurors drawn for next county court:

EDWIN BECTON	DANIEL YATES	FRANCIS ANDREWS
MARTIN F. BROCK	THOS HARRISON	WM RICHARDS
JOHN ROUSE	WILLIAM COOMBS	JEREMIAH CONNER
JOHN MORRIS	ASA EUBANKS	FURNEY G. HERITAGE
STEPHEN KINSEY	JOHN D. COLVET	HARDY HILL
JAMES MADIS	JOHN STANLY SENR	LOT EUBANKS
THOS McDANIEL	EDWD GILBERT	JESSE W. LEE
ELIJAH KOONCE	JOHN BENDER	ARCHIBALD B. OWINS
JOHN McDANIEL	RIGDON HEWIT	LEWIS KINSEY
WILLIAM GILBERT	WILLIAMS ISLER	PETER HARGET

(Note: Potter has JEREMIAH CANNON and JAMES MADES in the 1820 census for JONES COUNTY.)

More deeds and bills of sale:
9) JOHN H. BRYAN to WILLIAM HELLEN [Note: WILLIAM HELLEN married 16 Nov 1826 in Jones County to Miss MARY BRYAN (North Carolina Star/Kammerer, Vol. 1, p. 65)]
10) ISAAC HATHAWAY to JOSEPH GREEN
11) GEO POLLACK to ENOCK FOY
12) CATHARINE to E. SIMMONS
13) CHRIST BRYAN to JNO MALLARD
14) Shff LEML HATCH to JNO PARKER
15) Shff WM HUGGINS to LEML HATCH
16) Shff WM HUGGINS to ROBT KORNEGAY
17) LEML HATCH to BENJN SMALL JR

MARCH TERM 1827
TRENTON, Second Monday of March, the 12th

Justices: OWEN B. COX, SIMMONS ISLER, and BRYAN BECTON, Esquires

Shff: WILLIAM HUGGINS
Clerk: HARDY BRYAN

Grand jurors for this term:
MARTIN F. BROCK, foreman

JAMES MADIS	JOHN MORRIS	JESSE W. LEE
JOHN STANLY SENR	RIGDON HEWET	DANIEL YATES
EDWIN BECTON	FRANCIS ANDREWS	JOHN ROUSE
STEPHEN KINSEY	PETER HARGET	WILLIAM RICHARDS
LEWIS KINSEY	ARCHIBALD B. OWINS	

    STEPHEN B. FORBES, admr of THOMAS O. BRYAN, decd, motioned court to sell so many of Negroes of said decd at a credit of six months as will be sufficient to attain a sum of $2,500 to enable FORBES to pay the debts of the said THOS O. BRYAN, decd. [Note: THOMAS O. BRYAN died 16 Jan 1827 in Jones County according to the NEW BERN *Sentinel* (Kammerer, Vol. 2, p. 70).]

    BRYAN BECTON, JAMES REYNOLDS, and WILLIAMS ISLER shall audit and settle accounts of estate of JACOB KOONCE, decd, and LIDEA KOONCE at request of SIMMONS ISLER.

    STEPHEN B. FORBES to take full admin. on estate of THOS O. BRYAN, decd. $6000 bond with WM S. BLACKLEDGE and JACOB GOODING, sureties. (Note: THOMAS O. BRYAN was censused in NEW BERN in 1820 and the records of his estate are in the estate records of CRAVEN COUNTY in the N.C Archives, RALEIGH.)

    FURNIFOLD G. HERETAGE to admr estate of THOMAS STILLEY, decd. $2000 bond with N.B. BUSH and ALFRED HARGET, sureties.

    EML JARMON, ISAAC BROWN, and OWEN B. COX to settle accounts of estate of MICAJAH ADAMS, decd.

    WILLIAM WATERS appointed guard. to SIMMONS COLLINS (minor). $1000 bond with ISAAC H. MEADOWS, ARCHIBALD B. OWINS, and MICAJAH MATTECKS, sureties.

    CHRISTOPHER BRYAN to admr estate of MARY A. HATCH, decd. $3000 bond with RISDON M. McDANIEL and WILLIAM HUGGINS, sureties.

    JAMES MARRIT to oversee road from SOLO E. GRANT's to the BEAVERDAM BRANCH near said MARRIT's heading from NEWBERN to TRENTON in place of L. FOSCUE. (Note: According to Powell, BEAVERDAM BRANCH rises in southern JONES COUNTY and flows north into MILL RUN which rises in central JONES COUNTY and flows north east into TRENT RIVER.)

    THOMAS HARRISON to oversee road in place of IVEY ANDREWS from bridge at TRENTON down to BEAVERDAM also from fork at R.M. McDANIEL's up to MESSELSHELL.

    COUNCIL FIELDS to oversee roads in room of ISAAC H. MEADOWS from BLACK SWAMP BRIDGE to SMITHS MILL and from cross roads to TOM'S SWAMP. (Note: According to Powell, BLACK SWAMP CREEK rises in south east JONES COUNTY and flows south into WHITE OAK RIVER, but Powell is unable to help with SMITHS MILL and TOM'S SWAMP.)

    JAMES W. HOWARD to oversee road in room of GEO HOWARD from POCOSIN to

BUCKNER HATCH's mill and to bridge near RICHD B. HATCH's roads leading from HATCH's MILL to WHITE OAK and to TRENT BRIDGE. (Powell tells us that POCOSIN BRANCH rises in southern JONES COUNTY and flows north into the TRENT RIVER.

SIMMONS HARRISON JR. to oversee road in place of STEPHEN BROWN from the READ HILL to RATTLESNAKE. (Note: The best Powell can do is READY BRANCH which rises in southern JONES COUNTY and flows north into TRENT RIVER, and RATTLESNAKE BRANCH which rises in northern JONES COUNTY and flows southeast into BEAVER CREEK.)

ELIJAH S. BELL may retail spirits for one year.

Will of BENJN KOONCE, decd, proved in open court by oath of WILLIAM HUGGINS, a witness; SIMMONS ISLER, executor. [Gwynn abstracted this will (p. 430) which was undated. It names the deceased's wife, ZILPAH; daughters, WINIFRED and MARTHA; son, BENJAMIN; and grandson, EMANUEL KOONCE HARGET. Exrs: SIMMONS ISLER and PETER HARGET; witnesses: WM. HUGGINS and L.G. HAYWOOD.]

Will of PENELOPE ANDREWS, decd, proved by oath of HARDY BRYAN, a witness; LEML BUSICK, executor. [Note: Gwynn abstracted this will (p. 400) which was written 11 Jul 1825. In it she named her cousin, PETER ANDREWS, and his children: SUSAN, MELITO (a daughter), JOHN, PETER, MARYANN, and ADAM ANDREWS. She also named LEMUEL BUSICK but mentioned no relationship. Also named were LEMUEL BUSICK's daughter, SALLY, and MORRIS McDANIEL and his sons, MITCHEL BUSICK McDANIEL and JOHN McDANIEL. Exrs. were LEMUEL BUSICK and PETER ANDREWS. Witnesses were HARDY BRYAN and TOBIAS KOONCE.]

Commissioners returned division of Negroes of I. PARSONS, decd, to allot off to JNO PARSONS his share.

Inventory and sale of estate of WM WATSON returned and filed by I. WATSON.

Inventory of estate of JOHN HARRISON, decd, returned and filed by LEVI HARRISON, executor.

Account of sale of Negroes of F.G. GEORGE filed by RICHD REYNOLDS, admr.

Inventory and account of sale of estate of THOS O. BRYAN, decd, filed by S.B. FORBES, admr. (Note: The inventory is to be found in the courthouse at TRENTON.)

Inventory and account of sale of estate of ISAAC HATHAWAY, decd, filed by C. BRYAN, admr.

Settlement of estate of JNO MADES, decd, in account with JAMES MADES, admr, filed by commissioners.

Current accounts of JOHN H. HAMMONS, guard. to N. PARSONS (minor), filed by commissioners.

Tuesday, MARCH 13, 1827

Justices: RESDEN M. McDANIEL, OWEN B. COX, and BRYAN BECTON
Shff: WILLIAM HUGGINS
Clerk: H. BRYAN

JAMES N. SMITH may sell liquor at T. BRIDGE for one year.

WILLIAMS ISLER motioned that BRYAN BECTON, EDWIN BECTON and JAMES REYNOLDS settle estate of JOHN ISLER, decd, with WM ISLER, executor.

SIMMONS ISLER to be guard. to RICHD KOONCE (minor); $1000 bond with BRYAN BECTON and WILLIAMS ISLER securities.

Jones Cty Court of Common Pleas Minutes 1827

SIMMONS ISLER to be guard. to PATSEY WENNEY and EML KOONCE (minors); $3000 bond with BRYAN BECTON and WILLIAMS ISLER securities.

RESDON M. McDANIEL, admr of MORRIS McDANIEL, decd, may sell a Negro boy, PETER, of the estate of said MORRIS at a credit of six months to pay debts.

JAMES SIMMONS renewed his bond as guard. to JNO SIMMONS (minor); $4000 bond with JAMES MARRIT and JESSE W. LEE, securities.

B. NOBLE motioned to renew order for CHRISR BRYAN, HARDY BRYAN, and S.C. FISHER to settle accounts of B. NOBLE, guard. to heirs of EML KOONCE.

WILLIAMS BROWN motioned that CHRISR BRYAN, WILLIAM HUGGINS, and SAML C. FISHER settle estate of NANCY BROWN, decd, with admr.
(Note: SAML C. FISHER could be SAML C. FORBES or FOSTER.)

EDWD DEBRULE motioned that NATHAN FOSCUE, RESDON M. McDANIEL, and JOHN D. COLVET settle accounts of E. DEBRULE, guard. to heirs of KADER KNIGHT JR., decd.

HEPSEY BRAY to be guard. to her five children: THOMAS, ELIZA, MARGARET, and NICHOL__ (the rest was lost in binding of book) BRAY (minors); $1500 bond with ASA SMITH and JAMES READ, securities.

Letters of admin. on estate of SAMUEL S. WIGGENS, decd, granted to HARDY PARRY; $5000 bond with ELIJAH PARRY and EML JARMON, sureties.

JOHN TURNER motioned court to order county surveyor to run lands in dispute between JOHN TURNER, GEORGE KING, and RIGDON WHALEY.

ROSCO BARRES and WALTER HELLEN qualified as Justices of the Peace.

OWEN B. COX motioned court that ISAAC BROWN, F.I. BECTON, and JAMES HARRISON to settle accounts of guard. of WILLIAM A. COX (minor).

Renew order to allot off to SARAH SHELFER, widow of JESSE SHELFER, decd, her dower in lands of her decd husband.

WILLIAMS BROWN to be constable in DIST. 6 in place of S.S. WIGGINS, decd. He should enter into a bond with ALFRED HARGET and EML JARMON, sureties.

EML JARMON shall be guard. to heirs of ZEADUK ASKEY, decd; $1000 bond with THOMAS WILCOX and LEWIS SMALL, securities.

ASA SMITH, JAMES ROBERTS, and THOMAS GILLET to settle accounts of estate of WILLIAM BRAY, decd, with admir.

EML JARMON motioned court that RISDON M. McDANIEL, HARDY PARRY, and WILLIAM B. HATCH should settle accounts between EML JARMON, present guard. to heirs of ZEA ASKEY, decd, and ISAAC HATHAWAY, former guard.

JACOB GILES motioned court that ABNER KILLEBREW, (minor) aged 14 or 15, be bound to said GILES until he is 21 years old and GILES should give him 12 months schooling.

AMOS HEATH, JAMES G. OLIVER, DURANT H. WHITE, and BRYAN BECTON to be patrols for DIST. 5.

LEWIS WILLIAMS, JOHN M. FRANK, EML JARMAN, and HENERY RHODES to be patrols for DIST. 4.

JOHN HOUSTON, THOMAS DAVIS, REUBIN G. CORMAN, and THOMAS HAZARD to be patrols for DIST. 2. (Note: CORMAN could be CARMAN, CONNON, CANNON, or CONNER.)

SIMON FOSCUE, GEORGE C. HATCH, LEML H. SIMMONS, and NATHAN FOSCUE to be patrols in DIST. 6.

JOHN TURNER motioned court that deposition of ANN TURNER be taken in suit brought by JNO TURNER against RIGDON WHALEY.

LEAH STILLEY, widow of THOS STILLEY, decd, petitioned court to allot off one year's provisions for self and family. JAMES HARISON, Esq., FREDK I.

BECTON, SAMUEL DILLAHUNT, and EML JARMON were to do so.

Admin., "pending the contest about JOHN ANDREWS, will be granted to PETER ANDREWS;" $10,000 bond with NATHAN FOSCUE and THOS HARRISON, sureties. Admr may sell all perishable property of the estate. (There was no indication of whose estate.)

HARDY PARRY, admr of SAMUEL S. WIGGINS, may sell slaves of the estate to pay debts.

Case: WM ORME "to the use of" THOS McBINE vs GEO. OLDFIELD. Since executor went into bond with WILLIAM HUGGINS, shff, 20 days before sitting of court and has not returned the execution, he is fined $100. (Note: "to the use of" refers to one for whose use or benefit an action is brought in the name of another. That is, where the assignee of a case in action is not allowed to sue in his own name, in this instance THOS McBINE is not allowed to or cannot sue in his name so WM ORME is the assignor for McBINE.)

Case: GEORGE A. HALL vs SIMMONS HARRISON: same kind of suit and order as above. (Note: HALL could be HALE.)

Jurors drawn for June term, 1827:

WILLIAM GOODING	PETER ANDREWS	RUBIN G. CONNON
JOHN ANDREWS JNR	RICHARD FOSCUE	WM M. GILES
JAMES HUGGINS SNR	JOHN ADAMS	BARTHOLOMEW MEADOWS
GEORGE KING	JAMES B. SHINE	JOHN JONES
ENOCH FOY	ALEXANDER HICKS	LEMUEL H. SIMMONS
JOHN JARMON	JAMES N. SMITH	JOHN D. COLVET
JOHN WISE	ASA EUBANKS	WILLIAM RHEM
JOHN POLLACK	DURANT McDANIEL	ELIJAH PARRY
WILLIAMS JONES	ISAAC H. MEADOWS	FREDERICK COLVET
DANIEL ANDREWS	JOHN PARSONS	

Letters of admin. granted JOHN H. HAMMON on estate of JOSEPH BRYAN, decd; $100 bond with DURANT H. WHITE and JAMES G. OLIVER, sureties.

Shff returned proceedings of the jury summonded to lay off to PENELOPE KOONCE, widow of MICHAEL KOONCE, dower in the lands of her decd husband. Due to dissatisfaction with the dower by WILLIAM McDANIEL, present husband of said widow, court orders Sei fa issued to THOS SPEIGHT, guard. to heirs of MICHAEL KOONCE, to appear next term and show, if he can, why another jury should not lay off new dower.

Admin. D. bonis non on estate of BUCKNER HATCH, decd, granted to WILLIAM HATCH. No dollar amount given for bond, but N.B. BUSH and DURANT HATCH, JR., sureties. (Note: An administrator De bonis non is appointed to fill the vacancy left by a deceased or removed executor of an estate so that the unsettled portion of the estate can be settled, according to Black.)

ALFRED HARGET, JAMES MARRIT, SIMMONS HARRISON, RESDEN M. McDANIEL, and LEMUEL H. SIMMONS to divide the lands of ADAM ANDREWS, decd, among his heirs.

Settlement of estate of RACHEL STEPHENS returned; JNO BENDER, executor.

Will of DANL SIMMONS, decd, proved by oath of JOHN JACKSON, a witness; PETER HARGET, executor.

Division of Negroes of LEML HATCH JR. filed.

Division of Negroes of WRITE SIMMONS and of WM HELLEN, decd, filed.

ISAAC HATHAWAY, former guard. to JOSEPH and WILLIAM BRYAN (minors), accounts filed.

EML JARMON, guard. to heirs of S. WESTBROOK, accounts filed.

Jones Cty Court of Common Pleas Minutes 1827

E. JARMON, guard. to JNO KOONCE (minor), accounts filed.
EML JARMON, guard. to heirs of JOHN SHELFER, decd, accounts filed.
TOBIAS KOONCE, guard. to E.M. WRIGHT (minor), accounts filed.
WILLIAMS BROWN, guard. to heirs of SMALL, decd, accounts filed.
Inventory and account of sale of estate of LEML HATCH, decd, filed.
Account of sale of estate of WRIGHT SIMMONS, decd, filed.
Inventories and accounts of sales of estates of T. MURPHEY, decd, E.S. FRANKS, decd, and BENJN KOONCE, decd, filed.
Account of sale of two Negroes of estate of WILLIAM HELLEN, decd, filed.
Inventories and accounts of sales of estates of MARTHY COLLINS, decd, and B. KOONCE, decd, filed.
Inventory and account of sale of estate of BUCKNER HATCH, decd, by LEML HATCH, admr, Jny 13, 1825; filed by W.S. BLACKLEDGE.
Inventory of property of WM ORME, decd, filed.
ISAAC HATHAWAY, guard. to H. BRYAN (minor), accounts approved and filed.
ISAAC HATHAWAY, guard. to heirs of Z. ASKEY, accounts approved and filed.
Division of Negroes of JNO B. COX, decd, filed.
LEWIS KINSEY, guard. to heirs of CHRISR KINSEY, decd, accounts filed.
Deeds, bills of sale, and mortgages proved and recorded by registrar, JAS REYONLDS:
1. DURANT RICHARDS to FRANCIS ANDREWS
2. ISAAC BROWN to WILLIAM BROWN
3. DURANT RICHARDS to PETER ANDREWS
4. Shff to F.G. SIMMONS
5. GEORGE C. HATCH to F.G. SIMMONS
6. F.G. SIMMONS to GEORGE C. HATCH
7. ISAAC BROWN to WILLIAM BROWN
8. ALLEN JONES to JOHN TURNER
9. ISAAC BROWN to P. GILES
10. J.B. HARGET to WM M. GILES
11. GEORGE C. HATCH to F.G. SIMMONS
12. GEORGE C. HATCH to F.G. SIMMONS
13. F.G. SIMMONS to GEORGE C. HATCH
14. S. SMALL and wife and I. SMALL and wife to DURANT WESTBROOK
15. W.A. SIMMONS to JAMES SIMMONS
16. LEMUEL H. SIMMONS to JAMES G. OLIVER
17. Shff to HUBAND STANLY
18. JAMES SIMMONS to M.A.F. SIMMONS
19. ISAAC MEADOWS to WM ORME
20. ISAAC KOONCE to JOHN KOONCE
21. SARAH BRYAN to ISAAC HATHAWAY
22. JESSE W. LEE to BRYAN LAVINDER
23. ABIJAH HEATH to H. PARRY and B. HARRISON

JUNE TERM, 1827   2nd Monday, 11 June 1827

Justices: ISAAC BROWN, ROSCO BARRES, and _____ B. COX (Note: the first name was blotted out.)

Jones Cty Court of Common Pleas Minutes 1827

Shff: WM HUGGINS
Clerk: HARDY BRYAN

Grand Jurors:
ENOCK FAY, foreman
JOHN PARSONS
ISAAC H. MEADOWS
JOHN POLLACK
WILLIAM M. GILES
ASA EUBANKS
GEORGE KING
ELIJAH PARRY
PETER ANDREWS
WILLIAM GOODING
JAS B. SHINE
WILLIAMS JONES
JNO ANDREWS

JAMES N. SMITH to admr estate of VINCENT M. JENTRIES; $300 bond with I.S. ROBERTS and WM HUGGINS, sureties.

WILLIAM McDANIEL to oversee road from HARRISON'S BRIDGE to WILLIAM RIMS road in place of RICHD KOONCE.

HARDY BRYAN, CHRISTOPHER BRYAN, and HARDY PARRY to settle accounts of admr of JOHN H. STANLY, decd.

ROSCO BARRIS to oversee road in room of JNO DAVIS.

MORDICA WHITE to oversee road in room of RIGHT STANLY.

WILLIAM ADAMS to oversee road from BLACK SWAN to fork at WILLIAM McDANIEL's. (Note: BLACK SWAN is probably BLACK SWAMP CREEK.)

JOHN MORRIS and DANL FRANCIS DuVAL may retail liquor at the grocery in TRENTON for one year.

DANIEL Y. SHINE to oversee road from JACK CABIN BRANCH to RED OAK. (Note: According to Powell, JACK CABIN BRANCH rises in southern JONES COUNTY and flows north west into the TRENT RIVER, but he is unable to help with RED OAK. Could RED OAK be ROYAL OAK? ROYAL OAK, as described by Powell, appears on the Price map of 1808 and the MacRae map of 1833 on the JONES-ONSLOW COUNTY line. It was a tree where legend has it a British soldier was hung after he was found spying from its branches. The stump was removed about 1916 when the road from RICHLANDS to COMFORT was widened.)

SIMMONS ISLER to be guard to JOSEPH and WILLIAM BRYAN (minors). $2000 bond with PETER HARGET and JAS REYNOLDS, sureties.

(MAPS?) M. SANDERS (minor), about 13 years, to be bound to JOHN M. FRANK until he is 21 years and FRANK to give him 15 months schooling.

By consent of J. SMALL, PENELOPE PENEUL (minor) to be bound to WILLIAM STANLY until she is 21; she should learn to read and write.

SIMMONS HARRISON to oversee road from JACK CABBIN to INDIAN GROVE in place of WM JARMEN.

JAMES REYNOLDS to be guard of NANCY MCQUILIN. $200 bond with SIMMONS ISLER and EDWD DEBRULE, sureties.

Settlement of EDWD DEBRULE, guard to heirs of KNIGHT, filed. (Note: Only the one name was given.)

Settlement of estate of (JNOS IHS?), decd, filed.

Settlement of JNO MORRIS, guard to L. MORRIS, filed.

Inventory and account of sale of estate of THOS STILLEY, filed.

Inventory of property of LEWIS MORRIS, decd, filed.

Inventory and account of sale of the estate of SAML S. WIGGINS, decd, filed.

Inventory of estate of PENELOPE ANDREWS, decd, filed.

Inventory and account of sale of estate of DANIEL SIMMONS, decd, filed.

Inventory and account of sale of estate of MRS. M.A. HATCH, decd, filed.

Jones Cty Court of Common Pleas Minutes 1827 35

Year's provision to widow of T. STILLEY, decd, filed.
Settlement of WILLIAM ADAMS, admr of M. ADAMS, filed.

Next day:

Justices: DURANT HATCH, ISAAC BROWN, and OWEN B. COX, esquires
Shff: WILLIAM HUGGINS
Clerk: HARDY BRYAN

JOHN JONES, HENERY RHODES SENR, EML JARMEN, JACOB GILES, and ISAAC BROWN to divide real estate which descended to them from their father, WILLIAM KILLEBREW, between JOHN KINSEY and wife and ABNER KILLEBREW.

ROSCO BARRIS to oversee road from DEEP GULLY BRIDGE up to TRENT BRIDGE ROAD leading from TRENT BRIDGE to NEWBERN.

Ordered that ALFRED HARGET be paid #11.20 for his duties as constable June term 1826 through March term 1827.

Ordered that ADONIJAH PARRY be paid $16.00 for services rendered the court from Sept term 1825 through June term 1827.

WILLIAM HUGGINS, shff, allowed $50.00 for extra services the past year.

HARDY BRYAN, clerk, allowed $40.00 for extra services and stationary the past year.

EML JARMON, constable, allowed $13.60 for his attention to the court up to this term.

WILLIAM BROWN, constable, to be paid $1.60 for 2 days court attendance March, 1827.

ALFRED HARGET, admr of HARDY BRYAN (minor), decd, may sell Negroes of the estate of said decedent to affect a division among the heirs.

CHRISR BRYAN, FREDK BECTON, and HARDY BRYAN to settle accounts of JAS HARRISON, guard to heirs of B. MUMFORD.

GEO S. ATTMORE, attor., motioned that HARDY BRYAN and NANCY HARRISON be appointed admrs to BENJAMIN HARRISON. $20,000 bond with CHRISTOPHER BRYAN and WILLIAMS BROWN, sureties. The admrs may sell 16 Negroes of the estate to pay its debts should it
become necessary.

HARDY BRYAN appointed guardian to FRANKLIN B. HARRISON. $10,000 bond with ADONIJAH PARRY and RISEN M. McDANIEL, sureties.

JOHN ANDREWS appointed admr of JAMES ANDREWS, decd. $200 bond with JAMES MARRIT and RISDON M. McDANIEL, sureties.

SIDNEY JARMEN (widow) appointed admx of HARDY JARMON, decd. $200 bond with THOS McDANIEL and SILAS McDANIEL, sureties.

N.B. BUSH to enter $3000 bond as county trustee with RISDON M. McDANIEL and WILLIAM HUGGINS, securities.

ROSCO BARRIS, esq., to estimate value of the work done on TRENT BRIDGE at POLLOCK PLANTATION by MR. BRAWER.

ABNER GREEN appointed admr of MARY GREEN, decd. $2,000 bond with JAS N. SMITH and N.B. BUSH, sureties.

Sie fa issued to SARAH OLDFIELD to show cause why ELIJAH SIMMONS should not be released from the guard bond of heirs of RICHD OLDFIELD.

Will of PENELOPE KOONCE proved by BRADICK NOBLE, a witness. [Note: Gwynn abstracted this will (p. 430) which was written 10 Oct 1826. In it PENELOPE (or PHILPINY or PHILPENIA) named her daughter, ANNY PENEWILL; grandsons, JERRY and DANIEL NOBLES; and DICY GRIFFIN's two heirs; ELEY

MILLER's two children; and MARY FORDHAM. No executors were named. The witnesses were B. HARRISON and BRADDOCK NOBLE.]

    Accounts of OWEN B. COX, guard to WILLIAM COX (minor), filed.
    Accounts of BRADICK NOBLE, guard to heirs of EML KOONCE, filed.
    Since a majority of the justices were present, officers for the county were elected:
WILLIAM HUGGINS, shff. He entered into a bond with JAMES B. SHINE and CHRISTOPHER BRYAN.
Constables and their bondsmen:
    District 1: DANIEL DECKSON with ASA SMITH, T.B. [JONES and __ OLDFIELD] (Note: The bracketed names were written so close to the binding that I can offer only fair guesses as to what they were.)
    District 2: FREDK DEEKSON with JAS N. SMITH and ROBT V. ORME
    District 3: ALFRED HARGET with WMS BROWN, JAS REYNOLDS, and B. NOBLE
    District 4: DANIEL Y. SHINE with JAS B. SHINE and JAS HARRISON
    District 5: BRADECK NOBLE with JAS REYNOLDS, JAS B. SHINE and ALFRED HARGET
    District 6: WMS BROWN with ALFRED HARGET and WM M. GILES

    N.B. BUSH's accounts as county trustee filed.
    Accounts of WILLIAMS BROWN, admr of NANCY BROWN, filed.
    Settlement of accounts of ISAAC HATHAWAY, former guard to heirs of ZEADOCK ASKEY, decd, with EML JARMON, present guard, filed.
    County trustees to pay ABNER GREEN, admr of THOS BROWN, decd, "former jaylor" $11.60 for maintaining ESEREAL WILLS, a prisoner, from 12 Aug to 15 Sept 1825.
    WILLIAM S. BLACKLEDGE, admr of LEMUEL HATCH, decd, may return an amended and corrected supplemental inventory of estate
of BUCKNER HATCH, decd, to whom said LEML HATCH was admr.

    The following justices should take the tax list for the present year:
District 1: ASA SMITH   District 4: ISAAC BROWN
District 2: WALTER HELLEN   District 5: BRYAN BECTON
District 3: HARDY PARRY   District 6: ROSCO BARRIS

    Jurors for next superior and county court:

DURANT RICHARDS	WILLIAM COOMBS	JOHN STANLY (TRENTON)
JOSEPH GREEN	SIMON FOSCUE	THOMAS B. HARRISON
JOHN BALL	CULLEN POLLACK	SIMMONS HARRISON
RISDON McDANIEL (son of JAS)		WILLIAM McDANIEL SENR
WILLIAM B. HATCH	THOMAS HARRISON	NATHAN FOSCUE
WALTER HELLEN	THOMAS DUDLEY	JAMES MARRIT
BENJN HUGGINS	EDMD HATCH	FREDRICK I. BECTON
HENERY RHODES SR	BRYAN LAVENDER	JOHN H. HAMMONS
HARDY HILL	NATHAN B. BUSH	JAMES HARRISON
RISDON McDANIEL (son of RIS)		FREDERICK FOSCUE
WILLIAMS BROWN	JOHN FORDHAM	RISDEN M. McDANIEL
DANIEL SMITH	GEO C. HATCH	ISAAC KORNEGAY
JOHN H. BECTON	SAMUEL HILL	

Jones Cty Court of Common Pleas Minutes 1827

County Court Jurors:

WILLIAM STANLY	JAMES READ	EDWD DEBRULE
EML JARMON	DANIEL Y. SHINE	WILLIAMS ISLER
WILLIAM HELLEN	JESSE W. LEE	THOS H. HILL
JOHN McDANIEL	JAMES TURNAGE	JOSEPH KINSEY
JOHN TURNER	GEORGE WILLCOX	CHARLES WHITTY
JOSEPH HAY	JAMES MADES	MICAJIAH PETTEWAY
LOTT EUBANKS	JOSEPH WOOD	BENJAMIN COLLINS
LEWIS O. BRYAN	SILAS McDANIEL	RIGDON HEWIT
WILLIAM WATERS	ALFRED HARGET	JOHN C. WOOD
HUBARD STANLY	SHADERACK MALLARD	COUNSEL GOODING

Next day:

Justices: ISAAC BROWN, RISDEN M. McDANIEL, and SIMMONS ISLER, esquires
Sheriff: WILLIAM HUGGINS
Clerk: HARDY BRYAN

ELIJAH PARRY, DURANT McDANIEL, SAMUEL HILL, BRADICK NOBLE, WILLIAM McDANIEL, WILLIAMS BROWN, GEORGE WILCOX, WILLIAM JARMON, NATHAN B. BUSH, WRIGHT STANLY, CALVIN KOONCE, DURANT WHITE, BENJN. KOONCE and JAMES OLIVER to be patrols for one yr.

The following should "hold the poles at the next election:"
Dist. 1: THOS. GILLET   Dist. 4: BEVIN (___)
Dist. 2: WALTER HELLEN   Dist. (_): SIMMONS ISLER,
Dist. 3: WM. HUGGINS, Shff   EDWD BECTON, and
                                        M.F. BROCK

TUCKAHOE: ISAAC BROWN

The following should hold the election:
WHITE OAK: THOMAS GILLET, JAMES ROBERTS, and ISAAC N. MEADOWS
TRENT BRIDGE: WALTER HILLEN, EDMD HATCH and JESSE W. LEE
TRENTON: WILLIAM HUGGINS, shff; RESDON McDANIEL ("son of JAS."),
    and CHRISR. BRYAN
CYPRESS CREEK: SIMMONS HARRISON, FREDK. I. BECTON, and DANIEL Y.
    SHINE
TUCKEHOE: ISAAC BROWN, EML JARMEN, and HENERY RHODES SENR.
BEVER CREEK: SIMMONS ISLER, EDWIN BECTON, and MARTIN F. BROCK

ABNER GREEN, admr of MARY GREEN, decd, may sell Negro man, LEMON, to make a division among heirs

RISDON M. McDANIEL granted admin. on estate of JOHN T. McDANIEL; $1500.00 bond; NATHAN B. BUSH and DURANT McDANIEL, sureties

HARDY BRYAN, NATHAN B. BUSH, and CHRISTOPHER BRYAN to settle accounts of RISDON M. McDANIEL, admr of MORRIS McDANIEL, decd, who was guard. to FANNY POLLACK (minor)

LEWIS GREGORY appointed admr of JOSEPH GILBERT "whose will was admitted to probate at June term 1784 of this county the executor therein named renouncing;" $6,000.00 bond; JOHN VANN, EDWD GILBERT, and JAMES REYNOLDS, sureties

Jones Cty Court of Common Pleas Minutes 1827

Deeds and bills of sale proved and recorded with the registrar, JAS REYNOLDS:
1. WILLIAM HUGGINS, shff to NATHAN FOSCUE
2. ISAAC HATHAWAY to ELIJAH PARRY
3. COUNCEL S. YATES to NATHAN FOSCUE
4. ALLEN DAVIS to JOSEPH KAY
5. WM. HUGGINS, shff to CHRISTOPHER BRYAN
6. BENJN W. HARGET to PETER HARGET
7. JOHN B. HARGET to JAMES B. SHINE
8. JOHN B. HARGET to A. HARGET and LEML. HARRISON
9. WM. HUGGINS, shff to ALFRED HARGET
10. ARIAL JONES to SILAS TURNER
11. SILVESTER BROWN to DANIEL WILLIAMSON
12. WM. HUGGINS, shff to H. CARTER
13. ELIJAH JONES to BAZEL JONES and WM. JONES
14. COUNCEL S. YATES to ISAAC HATHAWAY
15. DURANT RICHARDS to PETER ANDREWS
16. WM. HUGGINS, shff to JAMES BEASLEY
17. L. SANDERSON to NATHAN FOSCUE
18. ELIZABETH and JOHN HOLDEN to ISAAC BROWN
19. VARTIER KING to ELIZABETH HOLDEN
20. REUBIN G. CORMON to WILLIAM B. HATCH
21. EML JARMON to ELIZABETH HOLDEN
22. WM HUGGINS, shff to DANIEL STANLY
23. SAML C. FISHER to M. STEPHENSON
24. ISAAC HATHAWAY to WILLIAM B. HATCH
25. WM HUGGINS, shff to NANCY HATHAWAY
26. COMS. (?) to WM B. HATCH

SEPTEMBER TERM, 1827 TRENTON, 2nd Monday, 10 Sept 1827

Justices: ISAAC BROWN, RESDON M. McDANIEL and OWEN B. COX, esqs.
Sheriff: WILLIAM HUGGINS
Clerk: HARDY BRYAN

Grand Jurors:
1. EMANUEL JARMON, forman
2. JAMES MADES
3. HUBARD STANLY
4. JAMES READ
5. GEORGE WILCOX
6. EDWARD DEBRULE
7. SILAS McDANIEL
8. RIGDON HEWIT
9. LEWIS O. BRYAN
10. WILLIAM HELLEN
11. WILLIAM WATERS
12. DANIEL Y. SHINE
13. SHADERACK MALLARD

JAMES G. HERITAGE appeared in court and qualified as acting justice of the peace
JOSEPH WALLACE to be admr of estate of STEPHEN WALLACE, decd; $1000.00 bond; ENOCK FAY and BRYAN LAVINDER, sureties
JAMES HARRISON, SIMMONS HARRISON, SENR and DANIEL Y. SHINE should divide estate of HARDY BRYAN (minor), decd, among the lawful heirs
JAMES REYNOLDS appointed guard to WINIFRED ISLER in place of MORDICA

Jones Cty Court of Common Pleas Minutes 1827

WHITE; $2000.00 bond; ELIJAH KOONCE, GEO. KING, and BRADICK NOBLE, sureties

JAMES HERITAGE, DURANT WHITE, LEWIS O. BRYAN, JOHN ROUSE, JOHN H. BECTON, and JAMES WISE to be patrols for one year in DIST. 5

DANIEL WILLIAMSON to oversee rd from MILLCREEK to RIDY BRANCH at the CRAVEN COUNTY line (Note: RIDY BRANCH is not in Powell, but perhaps it is REEDY BRANCH.)

DURANT HATCH JR. to admr estate of JNO. MORRIS, decd; $8,000.00 bond; WILLIAM B. HATCH and EDMD HATCH, sureties

RISDON M. McDANIEL, esq., C. POLLACK, JNO. McDANIEL, and THOS. DAVIS shall set off a year's provisions for herself and family from the estate to the widow of JOHN MORRIS, decd

JOHN ANDREWS to admr estate of LEWIS HARRISON, decd; $400.00 bond; FRANCIS ANDREWS and IVY ANDREWS, sureties

WALTER HELLEN, esq., AMOS AMYET, CULLEN POLLACK, and JOHN McDANIEL to set off to widow of LEWIS HARRISON, decd, one yr's provisions out of the estate for herself and family

WILLIAM GRIFFEN "(supposed to be about eleven years old)" to be bound to BENJN HUGGINS as an apprentice servant until he is 21; 18 mos schooling

WALTER HELLEN, esq., ENOCK FAY, BRYAN LAVENDER, and JAS. N. SMITH shall set off to widow of STEPHEN WALLACE, decd, one yr's provisions out of the estate for herself and family

ALFRED HARGET to admr estate of JOHN B. HARGET, decd; $1000.00 bond; JAMES REYNOLDS and THOS. SPAIGHT, sureties

JAMES HARRISON, esq., N.B. BUSH, JAMES B. SHINE, and JAS. MILLER shall set off to ZETPHEY HARGET, widow of JNO. B. HARGET, one yr's provisions out of the estate for herself and family

WILLIAMS ISLER to oversee rd from fork at JAMES REYNOLD's to fork at JOHN WISE's in room of BRYAN BECTON

JOHN H. BECTON to oversee rd from GUM SWAMP on DOVER RD to county line near JOHN COBBS's and from JOHN WISE's to southwest bridge in place of JOHN ROUSE (Note: According to Powell, GUM SWAMP rises in NW JONES COUNTY, west of the town of DOVER which is in CRAVEN COUNTY, and flows NW into CRAVEN COUNTY where it merges with what is now TRACEY SWAMP but formerly also called GUM SWAMP. Site of two Civil War engagements)

DURANT WESTBROOK to oversee rd from BLACK SWAMP to LENOIR COUNTY line rd from TRENTON to LENOIR in place of ELIJAH KOONCE   On behalf of WILLIAM G. TAYLOR, jailor of CRAVEN COUNTY, court orders execution against admr of JACOB DUDLEY and SOLOMAN E. GRANT, the state bank may collect $9.00

RISDON M. McDANIEL, esq., C. BRYAN, HARDY BRYAN and ALFRED HARGET shall set off to NANCY HATCH, widow of HASKEL F. HATCH, one yr's provision out of the estate for herself and family

DAVID BALL to oversee rd from SAND RIDGE to fork of rd at JAMES FRAZAR's place and from fork below FRAZAR's to state rd. toward TRENT BRIDGE in place of JOHN BENDER (Note: SAND RIDGE probably is SANDY BOTTOM in western LENOIR COUNTY since Powell indicates this community was known as SANDY RIDGE during the Civil War.)

Inventory of estate of HARDY BRYAN (minor) returned by A. HARGET, admr

Settlement of estate of LIDIA KOONCE, decd, filed

ROSCO BARRIS, esq., reported on work done on TRENT BRIDGE by M. BROWDER

Jones Cty Court of Common Pleas Minutes 1827

Next day:

Justices: ISAAC BROWN, NATHAN FOSCUE, and HARDY PARRY, esqs

EML JARMON, JACOB GILES, and JOHN JONES should settle accounts of HINCHEY KILLIBREW, guard. to heirs of WILLIAM KILLEBREW, decd

JAMES McDANIEL to oversee rd in place of JOHN MORRIS

PETER ANDREWS to be guard. to NANCY ANDREWS (minor); $5,000.00 bond; LAWSON MALLARD and DANIEL MALLARD, sureties

ASA KNIGHT bound to THOS. GILLET

OWEN ADAMS appointed guard. to FANNEY, DANIEL, and MATILDA KNIGHT; $1,000.00 bond; BRYAN LAVENDER and URBAN OLDFIELD, sureties

ENOCK FAY, HARDY PARRY, and EML. JARMON to hold the board of appeals for JONES CO.

HARDY BRYAN to admr estate of JOSHUA DAVIS; $500.00 bond; PETER ANDREWS and RESDON M. McDANIEL, sureties

The "eisee" of JOHN ANDREWS proved in court on trial ("See trial docket this term") and PETER ONE (Note: Could this be ORME?), executor therein named, qualified as such

Settlement of estate of JOHN H. STANLY, decd, filed

Inventory and account of sale of estate of BUCKNER HATCH, decd, returned by admr of L. HATCH, March term 1827, revised by L. HATCH and returned and filed this term

Inventory of estate of MARY GREEN, decd, returned by ABNER GREEN, admr, filed

Account of sale and inventory of estate of JOHN ANDREWS SR. returned and filed by P. ANDREWS, admr and executor

Inventory of estate of HARDY JARMON, decd, returned & filed

Deeds, bills of sale, and mortgages proved this term for registration with JAS. REYNOLDS, registrar:
1. JOHN FORDHAM to ELIAS FORDHAM
2. JOHN FORDHAM to ELIAS FORDHAM
3. GEO. POLLACK to STEPHEN WALLACE
4. ALFRED HARGET, adm. to JOHN FORDHAM
5. MORDICAI WHITE to EDWIN BECTON
6. LEROY BROWN to SIMS. HARRISON JR.
7. B. LAVINDER to WM. H. MEADOWS
8. STEPHAN WALLACE to JOSEPH WALLACE
9. MOLSEY CONNER to JNO. STANLY SR.
10. Sheriff to JNO. JONES
11. JOHN COLLINS to SIMEON MEADOWS
12. DANIEL STANLY to JOHN (V. ?) STANLY
13.& 14. HOLLON KOONCE to N. GUNTER & E. WRIGHT
15. JAMES READ to JOSEPH WHILLY
16. ARIAL JONES to SILAS TURNER
17. Admr of B. HARRISON to JAMES BEASLEY
18. WILLIAM HUGGINS to SARAH SHELFER
19. DURANT HATCH JR to JOHN P. DAVIS

Jurors for next term:
1. EDWIN BECTON   11. LEWIS KINSEY   21. JOHN DAVIS

2. TOBIAS KOONCE
3. MARTIN F. BROCK
4. PETER HARGET
5. WILLIAMS BROWN
6. JOHN STANLY SR
7. THOMAS SMITH
8. ELIJAH MARKET/ MASKET
9. JOSEPH BROCK
10. JAMES WALLACE
12. HARDY COLLINS
13. JAMES SIMMONS
14. HENERY RHODES JR.
15. IVY ANDREWS
16. LUKE SHELFER
17. AMOS TAYLOR
18. WILLIAM JARMON
19. ROBERT GILBERT
20. DURANT WESTBROOK
22. JOSIAH ASKEY
23. JOHN WOOD
24. ISAIAH WOOD
25. LEVI HARRISON
26. JAMES McDANIEL
27. THOMAS WILCOX
28. FURNIFOLD HERITAGE
29. DANIEL WILLIAMSON
30. JAMES W. HOWARD

DECEMBER TERM, 1827
TRENTON, 2nd Monday in December, 1827

Justices: SIMMONS ISLER, SIMON FOSCUE and ROSCO BARRUS, Esquires
Sheriff: WILLIAM HUGGINS
Clerk: HARDY BRYAN
Jurors: EDWIN BECTON, foreman

IVY ANDREWS	DANIEL WILLIAMSON	ISAIAH WOOD
JOHN WOOD	MARTIN F. BROCK	TOBIAS KOONCE
THOMAS WILCOX	ROBERT GILBERT	JAMES McDANIEL
LEVI HARRISON	PETER HARGET	THOMAS SMITH

Petit-Jurors:

ELIJAH MARKET	JAMES SIMMONS	JOHN STANLY SR
LUKE SHELFER	JAMES W. HOWARD	JOSEPH BROCK
HARDY COLLING	JOSIAH ASKEY	JOHN STANLY "(of TRENTON)"
JOHN FORDHAM	DURANT WESTBROOK	RISDEN McDANIEL

HARDY BRYAN appointed admr of estate of CHRISTOPHER BRYAN, decd; $10,000 bond; EDWIN BECTON and TOBIAS KOONCE, securities

HARDY BRYAN, MASTEN T. BROCK and JAMES REYNOLDS to settle accounts of J. LOFTEN, "____" of FURNIFOLD G. SIMMONS, decd

HARDY BRYAN, FRANCIS DUVAL, and RISDON M. McDANIEL to settle account of AMOS AMYET, guardian to heirs of ADONIJAH ANDREWS

ASA SMITH, JAMES CR. SMITH, and ELIJAH SIMMONS to settle account of SARAH OLDFIELD, guardian to heirs of RICH. OLDFIELD, decd

JAMES N. SMITH, BRYAN LAVENDER, JOHN HOUSTON, and WALTER HELLEN, esq. to set off to the widow of STEPHEN WALLACE, decd, one year's provison

GEORGE C. HATCH, LEMUEL H. SIMMONS and ROSCO BARRUS, esq. to allot to THOMAS J. FONVIELLE his share of Negroes of estate of THS. MURPHEY, decd, in right of his wife, FANNEY, as heir of said MURPHY agreeable to the will

ASA SMITH, THOMAS GILLET, THOMAS H. HILL, WALTER HELLEN, and JAMES N. SMITH to settle accounts of JAMES ROBERTS, guardian to AGRIPPA ROBERTS, and to set off to AGRIPPA his share of estate of his father agreeable to the will

JONAS JONES may sell liquor at his house for on yr

JOHN FORDHAM to admr estate of PENELOPE KOONCE, decd; SAMUEL DILLAHUNT and EML JARMON, surities

NATHAN FOSCUE, Esq., NATHAN B. BUSH, TOBIAS KOONCE, and JAMES McDANIEL to set off to REBECKAH BRYAN, widow of C. BRYAN, decd, one yr's provisions

EML JARMAN, HENRY RHODES, SR., and ISAAC BROWN, Esq. ordered to settle estate of CHRIST. KINSEY, decd, and to allot to CHARLES A. HINES his share of

Jones Cty Court of Common Pleas Minutes 1827

said estate in right of his wife, BETSY, heir at law of said C. KINSEY

Ordered that a commisssion issue to THOMAS GILLET and JAMES ROBERTS, Esq., leave to take the private examination of NARCISA DUDLEY, wife of THOMAS DUDLEY, to obtain her free consent in the execution of a deed signed to EDWD JONES

EML JARMAN, JACOB GILES and ISAAC BROWN, Esq. ordered to settle estate of DANIEL NOBLE, decd, and to allot a share to JERIMIAH NOBLE, one of the heirs

Account of sale of estate of JAS ANDREWS, dec
Account of sale and inventory of BENJN HARRISON, decd
Account of sale and inventory of J. DAVIS returned and filed
Account of sale and inventory of STEPHEN WALLACE, decd

Tuesday, 11 December 1827

Court met. Present the worshipful justices: NATHAN FOSCUE, SIMMONS ISLER and ASA SMITH, Esquires

Jurors:

ELIJAH MARKET	JAMES SIMMONS	JOHN STANLY SR
LUKE SHELFER	JAMES W. HOWARD	FREDRICK I. BECTON
JOSIAH ASKAY	DAVID GREEN	DURANT WESTBROOK
RESDON McDANIEL	JOSEPH BROCK	JOHN STANLY-TRENTON

Account of sale and inventory of estate of HASKEL F. HATCH, decd

NATHAN FOSCUE and HARDY PARRY ordered to be com____ for buildings in the courthouse in place of C. BRYAN and LEML HATCH, dead

SAMUEL HILL overseer of road from head of the straight reach above TRENTON to INDIAN GROVE OLDFIELD in room of LEML BUSICK, resigned

HARDY BRYAN ordered to admr estate of JOSEPH GREEN, decd; $2000 bond with EML JARMAN and DURANT McDANIEL sureties

ROSCO BARRUS, JAMES N. SMITH, and RESDON M. McDANIEL, Esq. ordered to settle accounts of SIMON FOSCUE, guardian to DARCUS FOSCUE and AMOS FOSCUE, his wards

JOHN STANLY to oversee rd from TRENTON bridge to head of the "streight reach" in room of JOSEPH GREEN, dead (Note: According to a descendant, JOSEPH GREEN married SARAH ARNOLD in CRAVEN COUNTY and had issue: JOHN, ABNER, HAMELTON (b. 17 Oct 1824, d. 1879), CORNELIA, and SARAH. The family, after Joseph's death was censused in JONES COUNTY in 1830 and in UNION PARISH, LOUISIANA in 1840.)

LEVI JONES overseer of rd from RATTLESNAKE to DUPLIN COUNTY line in room of HENERY RHODES JR., resigned (Note: Perhaps this is the road that went through the community of COMFORT.)

FREDK. I. BECTON, JAMES HARRISON, and JACOB GILES ordered to settle estate of the heirs of DANIEL MASHBURN with JAMES B. SHINE, guardian

RISDEN M. McDANIEL, admr of JOHN McDANIEL, decd, ordered to sell Negroes belonging to the estate in order to make an equal division among the heirs

WILLIAM HUGGINS, SAML C. FISHER and NATHAN B. BUSH ordered to settle estate of THOMAS McQUILLIN, decd

CHRISTOPHER A. HATCH ordered to admr estate of WM. B. HATCH, decd; $10,000 bond; EDMD HATCH and DURANT HATCH, JR., sureties

JAMES B. SHINE, DANIEL Y. SHINE, and ROBERT GILBERT ordered to settle

Jones Cty Court of Common Pleas Minutes 1827

accounts of I. GILBERT, admr of JAMES REYNOLDS, decd

BENJAMIN HUGGINS allowed to alter and turn public rd from WM. COMBS's place to TOBIAS KOONCE's

FRANCIS DuVAL guardian to heirs of THOMAS MURPHEY, decd; $10,000 bond; JAMES MERRET and WILLIAM HUGGINS, sureties

SETH MORRIS bound to FRANCIS DuVAL until he arrives at age 21 and said DuVAL should give him a reasonable education

Wednesday, 12 December 1827

Justices: ISAAC BROWN, NATHAN FOSCUE, and SIMMONS ISLER, Esqs.

HARDY BRYAN, WILLIAMS BROWN, and RISDON M. McDANIEL, Esq. to settle accounts of HARDY PARRY, guardian to heirs of SILAS PARRY, decd

ROSCO BARRUS, JAMES N. SMITH, and WALTER HELLEN, Esq. to settle accounts of THOS. SPEIGHT, former guard. to MARY HUNTINGTON (minor) with DANIEL DICKSON, present guardian

FREDK. I. BECTON to be guardian to JAMES CHRISTOPHER BRYAN; $30,000 bond; JAMES HARRISON and THOMAS BATTLE, sureties (Note: Could this have been James and Christopher Bryan even though there was no "and" in the record?)

ISAAC BROWN, HENERY RHODES, and JAMES HUGGINS SR. to settle accounts of EML JARMAN, guard. to heirs of SAML WESTBROOK, decd, and allot to NATHAN WESTBROOK his share

EML JARMAN, HENERY RHODES, and JOHN M. FRANKS ordered to settle accounts of JONAS JONES, guard. to heirs of FOUNTIN WILLIAMS, decd

JOHN GILBERT ordered to be guardian to heirs of JAMES REYNOLDS, decd; $1000 bond; ROBT GILBERT and WILLIAM GILBERT, sureties

County trustee ordered to pay WILLIAM COOMBS $5.00 for burial of Negro, TEEL "killed under outlaw"

All hands of LEML SIMMONS ordered to work the public rd are to be added to JAMES MERRIT's district or from BEVER DAM down and they are now cleared from working under the overseer above BEVER DAM

The following freeholders were drawn as jurors to the next Superior Court, March Term, 1828:

JOHN SHELFER	JAMES ROBERTS	BRODRICK NOBLE
OWEN ADAMS	OWEN B. COX	LEWIS WILLIAMS
BRYAN BECTON	ISAAC BROWN	DURANT HATCH JR
SIMMONS ISLER	ASA SMITH	THOMAS GILLET
JAMES REYNOLDS	DANIEL YATES	LEVI EUBANKS
HARDY PARRY	SIMMONS HARRISON	ELIJAH SIMMONS
SAMUEL DILLAHUNT	JOHN GODWIN	JOHN HEATH SR
JAMES HERITAGE	SOLOMON CASY	WILLIAM ADAMS
JOHN McDANIEL	BARTHOLOMEW MEADOWS	WILLIAM BROWN
JOHN STANLY SR	JOHN POLLOCK	WILLIAM WATERS
RISDON McDANIEL	WILLIAMS JONES	WILLIAM M. GILES
DURANT RICHARDS	JOHN STANLY (TRENTON)	

The following freeholders were drawn as jurors for the next county court, March Term, 1828:

LAWSON MALLARD	JAMES WISE	ELIJAH KOONCE
THOMAS POLLOCK	HARDY MUNDINE	JOHN STILL
WILLIAM H. MEADOWS	JAMES GODWIN	ARCHIBALD B. OWENS

Jones Cty Court of Common Pleas Minutes 1827

JACOB GILES	WILLIAM MEADOWS	EDWARD GILBERT
THOMAS McDANIEL	JOHN MALLARD	JACOB HUGGINS JR
LEWIS FOSCUE	LEMUEL BUSICK	REEVES R. FOSCUE
JOSEPH RHEM	JOHN BENDER	FRANCIS ANDREWS
ZEADOCK MEADOWS	SHADERACK MALLARD	JOHN M. FRANKS
JOHN ROUSE	JOHN FRIEZD (Note: Potter has this name as JOHN FIZLOW)	
BENJAMIN KOONCE	GEORGE ROBERT	WILLIAM GILBERT

Deeds of sale and marriage contracts approved this term and received by JAS. REYNOLDS, registrar:

Sheriff to SUSAN FAY
Sheriff to ZILPHA HARGET
Sheriff to JOHN LOVICK
JAMES P. STEELE to WILLIAM HUGGINS
JOHN H. BRYAN to WILLIAM HUGGINS
ALFRED HARGET to WILLIAM HUGGINS
HARDY PARRY to WILLIAM HUGGINS
B. KOONCE to H. NICKBIREN
ISAAC H. MEADOWS to THS. DUDLEY
JAMES BEVINS to MARTIN F. BROCK
MARTIN F. BROCK to JNO. FORDHAM
JAMES SIMMONS to JAMES N. SMITH
JAMES SIMMONS to JAMES N. SMITH
RACHEL SANDERS to MOSES SANDERS
D. HATCH, admr of R. KORNEGAY to R. CONNER
JACOB HUGGINS to THOMAS SHELFER
THS. DUDLEY to EDWD S. JONES
LEML and MARY A. HATCH, marriage contract
NANCY HARRISON and ABNER GREEN, marriage contract
RACHEL SANDERS to her children

Case: State Bank vs HARDY PITTS, STEPHEN GRANT, ISAAC GRANT, ROBT. V. ORME, and MOSES JARVIS. On motion of EDWD GRAHAM, plantiff's attorney, BRICE FONVILLE, sheriff of ONSLOW COUNTY, "_____ _____" $100.00 for an unlawful return.

Case: State Bank vs HARDY PITTS, RICHD PITTS, ROB. V. ORME, and MOSES JARVIS. Same order as immediately above.

Case: Admr of WM ORME to use of THOS. McLIN vs (smugged). WILLIAM HUGGINS, shff of JONES COUNTY, fined $100.00 for not making a return to court

HUGGINS again fined $100.00 for not collecting money due in suit JAMES E. BETNER vs GEORGE C. HATCH

NATHAN B. BUSH, JAS. McDANIEL, and HARDY BRYAN to divide Negros of estate of THOS. FAY, decd, and allot to SUSAN FAY, widow, her share

MARCH TERM, 1828
TRENTON, 10 MARCH

Justices: ISAAC BROWN, OWEN B. COX, and DANIEL SMITH, Esquires
Sheriff: WILLIAM HUGGINS
Clerk: HARDY BRYAN

Grandjurors for this term:
JOHN BENDER, foreman

JOHN MALLARD	EDWD GILBERT	JOSEPH RHEM
THOMAS McDANIEL	LEMUEL BUSICK	SHADERACK MALLARD
HARDY MUNDINE	ARCHIBALD B. OWINS	JOHN STELE
FRANCIS ANDREWS	JOHN ROUSE	REAVES R. FOSCUE

(Note: A JOHN STILL was in the WAKE COUNTY tax list for 1820.)

By suggestion of JOS. W. BRYAN, county solicitor, the court orders JOHN FROST to be overseer in place of THOMAS HARRISON, resigned

HARDY BRYAN, JAMES REYNOLDS, and MARTIN F. BROCK ordered to settle accounts of JOSEPH LOFTIN, admr of F.G. SIMMONS, decd

JESSE W. LEE may sell "spirits" at his residence

ENOCK FOY, EDMD HATCH and JOHN YOUNG ordered to divide lands of WILLIAM TAYLOR, decd, among the heirs [Note: ENOCK FOY served in the North Carolina House of Commons 1826-1828 and in the senate in 1838 (Wheeler). Gwynn abstracted his will (p. 413) which was written 25 Jul 1842 and probated December term 1842. He named his wife, RACHEL; daughters: NANCY STANTON, CAROLINE FOY; son: JOSEPH S. FOY, MILES FOY, CHARLES HENRY FOY, THOMAS D. FOY, and FRANLIN FOY. His six youngest children were FRANCIS, ELIZABETH, REBECCA, FRANKLIN, SALLY, and HARRIET FOY. He also left a portion of his estate to two grandchildren, MARIAH and ENOCH, children of his deceased son, JAMES FOY. Sons, MILES and CHARLES H. FOY, and a friend from CRAVEN COUNTY, WILLIAM WASHINGTON, were named exrs. Witnesses were JAMES MESSER, T.D. FOY, and CAROLINE MESSER.]

SIMON FOSCUE, HARDY PARRY, and JAMES MERRET to divide Negroes belonging to estate of JAMES McDANIEL between JOHN F. McDANIEL and LANEY McDANIEL

DANIEL STANLY ordered to oversee road in room of JAMES MARRET, resigned

ENOCK FAY, EDMD HATCH, and ELIJAH SIMMONS ordered to settle accounts of IVEY CONWAY, admr of JAS CONWAY

THOS GILLET to be overseer of road from EDWD S. JONES to CARTERET COUNTY line

SARAH OLDFIELD to renew her bond as guardian to SUSAN, PRUDY, and RICHARD OLDFIELD; JAMES N. SMITH and ANTHONY HATCH, securities; $10,000 bond

HARDY PARRY, RESDON M. McDANIEL, and WILLIAM HUGGINS to settle accounts of estate of PENELOPE KOONCE, decd; BENJM. HARRISON, executor, and JNO. FORDHAM, admr

OWEN B. COX, DANIEL Y. SHINE, JAMES B. SHINE, and JACOB GILES ordered to be patrols for DISTRICT 4

LEML H. SIMMONS ordered to be overseer of road in room of THOS HARRISON, resigned

EML JARMON to admin. estate of HENERY KELLEBREW, decd; $5,000 bond; ISAAC BROWN and RESDON M. McDANIEL, securities

T.L. HAWKS resigned as guardian to OLIVER E. STRONG (minor) and ROSEA BARRIER appointed to replace him; $6,500 bond; JAMES N. SMITH and BRYAN

LAVENDER, securities

JOHN HARRISON to admin. estate of LEVI HARRISON, decd; $2,000 bond; PETER ANDREWS and JAMES McDANIEL, securities

EML JARMON to oversee road in room of SIMMONS HARRISON, resigned

Inventory and accounts of sales of estate of CHRISTOPHER BRYAN, decd, returned and filed

Same for estate of JOSEPH GREEN, decd, JOHN T. McDANIEL, decd, and MARTHY COLLINS, decd

Division of Negroes of THOS MURPHY, decd, filed
Same for THOMAS FOY, decd
Division of lands of ISAAC KORNEGAY, filed
Division of Negroes of JAS McDANIEL, filed
Division of lands of LEML HATCH, decd, filed

Tuesday, 11 March, 1828

Justices: ISAAC BROWN, OWEN B. COX, and NATHAN FOSCUE, Esquires
Sheriff: WILLIAM HUGGINS
Clerk: HARDY BRYAN

JAMES MARRET ordered to be guardian to heirs of JOHN SIMMONS, decd, in room of JAMES SIMMONS; $1000 bond; ELIJAH SIMMONS and LEMUEL H. SIMMONS, securities

ENOCK FOY, ROSCO BARRES, and WALTER HELLEN ordered to settle accounts of JAMES SIMMONS, former guardian, with JAMES MARRET, present guardian to heirs of JNO. SIMMONS, decd

ENOCK FOY, SIMON FOSCUE, and ROSCO BARRES, Esq., to settle accounts of ISAAC KORNEGAY and to divide personal estate and Negroes between heirs

ELIJAH LOVETT to oversee road

Admr of MICHAEL KOONCE, decd, to settle with WM McDANIEL and wife, heirs of said KOONCE

Mistake in orders of last term: JOHN TURNER was ordered to pay but he was plantiff and GEORGE KING was the defendant

JOHN CONWAY ordered to oversee road in room of CHARLES WHITTY (moved)

LEWIS HALE (minor) ordered to be bound to DANIEL YATES and YATES should give him six months of schooling

County trustees ordered to pay EMANUEL JARMON and HARDY PARRY each $4.00 for their services on board of appeals in 1826 & 1827

JACOB GILES ordered to be guardian to ABNER KILLIBREW (minor); $2,000 bond; FREDK. I. BECTON and JAMES B. SHINE, securities

HENERY RHODES, SENR., OWEN B. COX, and ISAAC BROWN ordered to settle accounts of HINCHEY KILLIBREW, former guardian to the heirs of WILLIAM KILLIBREW and EML JARMON, admr of said HINCHY KILLIBREW, decd, to report same to court

JAMES N. SMITH permitted to sell liqueurs at TRENT BRIDGE by small measure

JOHN D. SMAW permitted to sell spirits at his residence (Note: The 1820 census index has BENJAMIN and ELIZABETH SMALL in Jones County and several JOHN SMALLs in other N.C. counties; however, there was a JOHN SMAW in BEAUFORT COUNTY.)

JOHN M. FRANKS, HENERY RHODES, SENR. and EML JARMON ordered to settle accounts of JONAS JONES, guardian to LEVINA and JOHN COX (minors)

Jones Cty Court of Common Pleas Minutes 1828

ENOCH FOY, SIMON FOSCUE, and ROSCO BARRUS ordered to settle accounts of WILLIAM DUNKEN, admr of ISAAC KORNEGAY, decd, and to divide Negroes of said decd among his heirs

JAMES REN bound to DANIEL Y. SHINE to learn art of farmer

BENJAMIN HUGGINS ordered to oversee road in room of N.B. BUSH, resigned

HARDY BRYAN, JAMES B. SHINE, and FREDK I. BECTON ordered to settle accounts of JAMES HARRISON, guardian to JAMES and PENELOPE MUMFORD (minors)

RESDON M. McDANIEL, esq., FRANCIS DUVAL, and HARDY BRYAN ordered to settle accounts of RICH. REYNOLDS, admr of FURNIFOLD GEORGE, decd

CHRISTOPHER BROCK ordered to appear next term and renew his guardian bond

WILLIAM S. BLACKLEDGE ordered to adm. estate of MARY A. HATCH, decd; $10,000 bond; MOSES JARVIS and NATHAN B. BUSH, securities

BENJAMIN KOONCE entered bond for the maintenance of a child begotten on the body of WELTHY HARRISON

Inventory of sale of estate of WM B. HATCH, decd, filed

Division of Negroes of estate of CHRISTOPHER KINSEY, decd, filed

Account of settlement of EML JARMON, guardian to heirs of SAML WESTBROOKE, decd, and divisions among the heirs, filed

Settlement of T.L. HAWKS, guardian to O.E. STRONG (minor), filed

Settlement of RICHD NOBLE, guardian to heirs of D. NOBLE, filed

Settlement of EML JARMON, guardian to heirs of SAML WESTBROOK, decd, filed

Settlement of TOBIAS KOONCE, guardian to ELISA M. WRIGHT (minor), filed

Settlement of estate of T. WILLIAMS filed

Settlement of LEML H. SIMMONS, guardian to AMOS and SOPHIA SIMMONS, filed

Settlement of SIMON FOSCUE, guardian to DARCUS FOSCUE, filed

Settlement of HARDY PARRY, guardian to heirs of SILAS PARRY, decd, filed

Year's provisions to REBEKAH BRYAN, widow of CHRIS BRYAN, decd

Year's provisions to S. or L. GREEN, widow of JOS. GREEN

Year's provisions to widow of STEPHEN WALLACE

Deeds and bills of sale filed with JAS REYNOLDS, registrar:

BRYAN BECTON to FREDK I. BECTON
JOHN G. KINSEY to DURANT HATCH JR.
ELIJAH SIMMONS to DURANT HATCH JR.
ISAAC BROWN to SUSANNA BROCK
THOMAS P. IVES to PENELOPE ELIZABETH IVES
H. TWILLEY to BENJM KOONCE
JAMES REED to JOB SMITH
DANIEL SMITH to JOB SMITH
JOB SMITH to JAMES REED
THOMAS WALTON to JAMES SHINE
DANIEL WALTON to JAMES SHINE
NATHAN I. or S. WESTBROOK to DURANT WESTBROOK
JOHN H. BECTON to JOHN HEATH
ELIJAH S. MILE (?) to ELIJAH SIMMONS
DURANT RICHARDS to IVEY ANDREWS
HINCHY KILLIBREW and others to JOHN JONES
JOHN MORRIS to BENETER, LEML, and ALEXANDER MORRIS
GEORGE POLLOCK to ENOCH FOY
SHFF. HATCH to CHARLES WHITTY

CLERK MARTIN in equity to WILLIAM HUGGINS
WM HUGGINS, Shff. to HARDY CONNER (Note: this line was crossed out.)
GEORGE POLLOCK to ENOCH FOY
ENOCH FOY to GEO. POLLOCK

Jurors drawn for June term:

HENERY RHODES SENR	ISAAC KORNEGAY	LEWIS FOSCUE, JR
DURANT WESTBROOK	MECAJAH PETHAWAY	HARDY HILL
FREDERICK FOSCUE	HARDY COLLINS	LEMUEL BUSICK
GEORGE C. HATCH	JOSEPH BROCK	LEMUEL H. SIMMONS
RIEVES R. FOSCUE	JOHN H. HAMMONS	WILLIAM ADDAMS
LEWIS KINSEY	WILLIAM STANLY	SAMUEL HILL
NATHAN B. BUSH	EDWD C. DEBRULE	EMANUEL JARMEN
WILLIAM McDANIEL SENR	JOHN TURNER	RIGDON HEWET
IVEY ANDREWS	GEORGE WILCOX	JOHN WOOD
THOMAS H. HILL	JOHN H. BECTON	

JUNE TERM 1828
TRENTON, Monday June 2

Justices: ISAAC BROWN, DANIEL SMITH, and HARDY PARRY
Sheriff: WILLIAM HUGGINS
Clerk: HARDY BRYAN

Jurors: JOHN H. HAMMON, forman

LEML BUSICK	GEORGE C. HATCH	IVEY ANDREWS
WILLIAM STANLY	GEORGE WILCOX	SAML HILL
MICAJAH PETTEAWAY	WM. McDANIEL, SENR	ISAAC KORNEGAY
DURANT WESTBROOK	RIGDEN HEWET	JOHN WOOD

FREDK I. BECTON to admin. goods and chattles of BRYAN BECTON, decd; $10,000 bond with JAMES B. SHINE and JACOB GILES
Said BECTON given leave to sell 5 Negroes to pay debts of the deceased's estate
FREDERICK I. BECTON and JACOB GILES ordered to audit and settle accounts of JS. B. SHINE, guardian to the heirs of DANIEL MASHBIRN, decd
SAML DILLAHUNT to admin. estate of SUSANNAH DILLAHUNT, decd; $500 bond with EML JARMON and DAVID GREEN, securities
ARCHIBALD B. OWENS to admin. estate of MERIEM? MEADOWS, decd; $600 bond with ASA SMITH and HARDY COLLINS, securities
ASA SMITH to admin. estate of NANCY LIETZ, decd; $800 bond; JAMES N. SMITH and URBAN OLDFIELD, securities (Note: LIETZ might be FIETZ or FRISZD or, even, FIZLOW.)
SAML DILLAHUNT, admr of SUSANNAH DILLAHUNT, has leave to sell Negro, PATSY, belonging to said estate to effect a division among the heirs
EDMD HATCH, WALTER HELLEN, and ROSCO BARRUS to audit and settle accounts of JAS. SIMMONS, admr of WRIGHT SIMMONS, decd
CHRISTOPHER BROCK, guardian to his children: JOHN, ELIZABETH, and MARTIN BROCK, minors, entered into $2,500 bond with ISAAC BROWN and WILLIAM RHIM, sureties
SAMUEL B. HEATH, guardian to his children: HENRY, SOLEAH?, and WILLIAM

Jones Cty Court of Common Pleas Minutes 1828

HEATH, minors, entered into $800 bond with EMANUEL JARMON, surety

ALFRED HARGET to admin. estate of ISAAC HATHAWAY, decd; $500 bond; JAMES N. SMITH and JNO. H. HAMMON, sureties

EML JARMAN resigned as entry taker for the county

JAMES HARRISON, DANIEL Y. SHINE, and JAMES B. SHINE to audit and settle accounts of the guardian to FREDK BRYAN (minor)

RACHEL McDANIEL, guardian to her child, EDNEY S. McDANIEL (minor), entered into $1,000 bond with JAMES McDANIEL and RESDEN M. McDANIEL, securities

HARDY BRYAN, WILLIAM HUGGINS, and ALFRED HARGET to audit and settle accounts of DURANT HATCH JR., admr of ROB. KORNEGAY, decd, and settle accounts of DURANT HATCH, executor of THOS MURPHY, decd

FREDERICK FOSCUE, JOSEPH BROCK, RIVERS R. FOSCUE, EDWD C. DEBRULE, JOHN TURNER, THOS H. HILES/HILL, and JOHN H. BECTON each fined $4.00 for nonattendance as jurors at this term

More jurors for this term:

HARDY COLLINS	WILLIAM ADAMS	LEWIS KINSEY
HENERY RHODES SENR	GEORGE KING	JNO. M. FRANKS
WILLIAM HELLEN	THOMAS McDANIEL	MARTIN BROCK
JACOB GILES	COUNCIL GOODING	THOS J. FONVIELLE

The following justices should take the tax list for the present year:
District 1: JAMES ROBERTS
District 2: JAMES N. SMITH
District 3: JAMES HARRISON
District 4: OWEN B. COX
District 5: JAMES G. HERITAGE
District 6: SIMON FOSCUE

NATHAN B. BUSH, CHRISTOPHER A. HATCH, JOHN STANLY, and JOSIAH? HUGGINS to be patrols for the town of TRENTON

Freeholders drawn as jurors for the next court:

ELIJAH PARRY	SHADRACK MALLARD	TOBIAS KOONCE
HARDY MUNDINE	HUBARD STANLY	JOHN C. WOOD
JAMES MAIDS	FURNEY G. HERITAGE	THOMAS WILSON
ELIJAH MARKET	JOHN JONES	JAMES SIMMONS
JOSIAH ASKEW	EDWIN BECTON	THOMAS HARRISON
JOSEPH KINSEY	LOT EUBANK	WILLIAM GILBERT
ISAAC H. MEADOWS	JOSEPH HAY	LAWSON MALLARD
ARCHIBALD B. OWENS	BENJM KOONCE	GEORGE ROBERTS
JACOB GILES	JAMES MARRET	JOHN BENDER
JOHN FORDHAM	BENJAMIN HUGGINS	OWENS ADAMS

Thursday, June 10, 1828

Justices: ISAAC BROWN, DAVID HATCH, and HARDY PARRY

Jurors for this day:
HARDY COLLINS   WILLIAM ADAMS   LEWIS SMALL
HENRY RHODES SR (but this name is crossed out with FREDK I. BECTON written above it)   CHRIST. A. HATCH
LEM H. SIMMONS (This name is also crossed out and JAMES B. SHINE is written

Jones Cty Court of Common Pleas Minutes 1828

above it.)
JOHN POLLOCK (This name is crossed out and JOHN FORDHAM is written above)
ELIJAH PARRY
PETER ANDREWS

IGNATIUS BROCK

MARTIN F. BROCK
JACOB GILES

THOS I. FONVIELLE, JOHN OLIVER, DANIEL STANLY and GEORGE HAZARD to be patrols in DISTRICT 6

SIMMONS ISLER, esq., JAMES B. SHINE, and LEMUEL H. SIMMONS to audit and settle accounts of NATHAN B. BUSH, county trustee

The fine of FREDK FOSCUE for no attendance as a juror at this term is remitted; his excuse heard by the court

WILLIAM DUNKEN to oversee road in room of ROSCO BARRUS from DEEP GULLY BRIDGE to TRENT BRIDGE

JOHN OLIVER, GEORGE HAZZARD, THOMAS I. FONVIELLE, and DANIEL STANLY to patrol DISTRICT 6 (This entry is crossed out.)

JAMES N. SMITH, ROSCO BARRUS, and WALTER HELLEN to audit and settle the accounts between THOS SPIGHT, former guardian to MARY HUNTINGTON, and DANIEL DICKSON, present guardian to said MARY

WILLIAM BINAM? to be overseer of road from WHITE OAK to SAND RIDGE in place of JOHN BALL, resigned

HARDY BRYAN, admr of JOSEPH GREEN, decd, has leave to sell all the Negroes of the estate of said GREEN in order to pay debts

Jurors present:
JAMES HARRISON   NATHAN FOSCUE   SIMMONS HARRISON
ASA SMITH   HARDY PARRY   ROSCO BARRUS
OWEN B. COX   JAMES N. SMITH   DURANT HATCH
ISAAC BROWN   RISDON M. McDANIEL   SIMMONS ISLER, Esquire

WILLIAM HUGGINS, sheriff, in bond with RICHD REYNOLDS? and NATHAN B. BUSH, securities

FRANCIS DUVAL, coroner, in bond with N.B. BUSH and WILLIAM HUGGINS, sureties

NATHAN B. BUSH, county trustee, in bond with RISDEN M. McDANIEL and WM HUGGINS, sureties

Constables for District 1: DANIEL DICKSON in bond with ASA SMITH and URBEN OLDFIELD, sureties

District 2: WILEY HEGGINS in bond with RIGDEN HEWIT, URBEN OLDFIELD, and JOHN D. SMALL/SMAW, sureties

District 3: ALFRED HARGET in bond with OWEN B. COX, BRODRICK NOBLE, and SAML DILLAHUNT

District 4: LEWIS JONES; OWEN B. COX, and WM HUGGINS (sureties)

District 5: BRODRICK NOBLE in bond with EML JARMON and ALFRED HARGET

District 6: WILLIAM BROWN in bond with JOSEPH KINSEY and JAMES MARRET

EML JARMON, executor of RESDEN McDANIEL, decd, has leave to sell these Negroes: MARY ELIZA and BYER, to pay debts [Note: Gwynn abstracted the will of RISDON McDANIEL (pp. 436-437) which was written 23 April (year uncertain) and probated June term 1828. He named his wife, RACHEAL, daughters, EDNEY McDANIEL and CHARLOTTE LAVENDER, wife of LEWIS LAVENDER; sons, JOHN, DAVID,

Jones Cty Court of Common Pleas Minutes 1828

ELIJAH, BENJAMIN, BUCKNER and WILLIAM; and grandchildren, SARAH and THOMAS BUSICK. Exrs. were WM. BROWN, EMANUEL JARMAN, and FRANCIS DEVAL. Witnesses were HARDY PERRY and JOSEPH M. PEARSON.]

The following freeholders were drawn as jurors for next term:

EDWD M. GILBERT	DANIEL SMITH	DANIEL Y. SHINE
JOHN SHELFER	JOHN MALLARD	JOHN FRIZE
JAMES HARRISON	SIMON FOSCUE	JAMES GODWIN
JACOB HUGGIN JR	PETER ANDREWS	RISDON M. McDANIEL
SHADRACK MALLARD	BENJAMIN COLLINS	JAMES B. SHINE
JAMES McDANIEL	HENERY RHODES JR	SILAS McDANIEL
WILLIAMS ISLER	WILLIAMS BROWN	SIMMONS ISLER
ALFRED HARGET	ENOCK FOY	SIMMONS HARRISON
AMOS TAYLOR	OWEN B. COX	LEVI HARRISON
FREDK I. BECTON	MILLENTON MEADOWS	ASA EUBANKS
JAMES G. HERITAGE	THOMAS McDANIEL	JOHN L. PARSONS
WILLIAM H. MEADOW	ELIJAH KOONCE	JAMES WISE

Account of RICHD REYNOLDS, admr of F.G. GEORGE, decd, filed

Account of JOSEPH LOFTEN, admr of F.G. SIMMONS, decd, filed

Same for WM DUNKEN/DUNKER, admr of ISAAC KORNEGAY, decd

WILLIAMS BROWN to be paid $11.20 for his services as constable the last year

DANIEL DICKSON to be paid $19.20 for his services as constable the last year

The sheriff is to be paid by the county trustee $70.00 for his extra services for the last year

Sheriff allowed $82.84 from the county treasury for jail expenses

HARDY BRYAN, clerk, to be paid $40.00 for extra services

HENERY H. NICKLESON allowed license to stock liquor in his grocery in TRENTON for one year

URIAH MORSE bound to BRYAN LAVENDER

Account of JAMES HARRISON, guardian to heirs of BRYAN MUMFORD, filed

Accounts of estate settlements of FELPINCA KRUONCE (KOONCE?) and B. HARRISON filed by the admr

Account of settlement between EML JARMAN, admr of HENCHEY KILLEBREW who was guardian to the heirs of WILLIAM KILLEBREW, decd, filed

Settlement of IVEY CONWAY, admr of JOS. CONWAY, decd, filed

Account of JAS SIMMONS, guardian to BENJN and JAS SIMMONS, minors, filed

Inventory and account of estate sale of JOHN MORRIS, decd, filed by admr

Same for LEVI HARRISON, decd

Same for HENCHY KILLEBREW, decd

Will of DURANT McDANIEL, decd, proved in court by EML JARMEN, one of the executors [Note: Gwynn abstracted this will (pp. 434-435). It was written 17 Apr 1828 and names his wife, MARY ANN, and son, CHRISTOPHER. ISAAC BROWN and EMANUEL JARMAN were exrs. and HARDY PERRY and THOMAS BALEY were witnesses.]

Will of RESDEN McDANIEL, decd, proved in court by EML JARMAN, one of the executors

WILLIAM HELLEN to oversee road from JACK CABIN to the RED OAK in room of D.Y. SHINE, resigned

RESDEN M. McDANIEL to admr estate of McCULLEN POLLOCK, decd; $800 bond; EMANUEL JARMAN and THOMAS McDANIEL, securities

LETITIA KORNEGAY appointed guardian to MARGARET, THOMAS, HAMILTON, and

MARY KORNEGAY, infants of ROBERT KORNEGAY, decd; $400 bond; MARY SMITH and JAMES SMITH, sureties

Deeds/bills of sale received for registration by JAS REYNOLDS:
Sheriff to ISAAC BROWN
WM HUGGINS to HARDY BRYAN
Sheriff to HARDY O. CONNER
WM HUGGINS, shff to JOSHUA B. OLIVER
Sheriff to JAMES McDANIEL (There were four entries like this.)
BRADDOCK NOBLE to DAVID GREEN
SIMMONS HARRISON to ALFRED HARGET
JOHN B. HARGET to JOHN OLIVE
THOS DUDLEY and N. DUDLY with Constable to EDWD S. JONES
MARY KINSEY and others to JOHN BENDER
JESSE W. LEE to JOHN BENDER (There were two entries like this.)
BENJN WALLACE to ENOCK FOY
JONAS JONES to WILLIAM JONES
CHARLES WHITTY to ELIJAH SIMMONS (There were two like this.)
D. HATCH JR, admr of R. KORNEGAY to GEO. B. HATCH

SEPTEMBER TERM 1828
TRENTON, Monday, Sept. 8, 1828

Justices: ISAAC BROWN, WALTER HELLEN, and DANIEL SMITH
Sheriff: WILLIAM HUGGINS
Clerk: HARDY BRYAN

Grand jurors this term:
OWEN ADAMS	THOS HARRISON	JAMES SIMMONS
JOHN C. WOOD	BENJN HUGGINS	ELIJAH MARKET
JOHN BENDER	ISAAC H. MEADOWS	THOS WILCOX
HARDY MUNDINE	JAMES MARRET	ELIJAH PARRY

Petit jurors this term:
SHADRACK MALLARD	HUBBARD STANLY	F.G. HERITAGE
JOSIAH ASKEW	JOSEPH KINSEY	WM./W. GILBERT
LAWSON MALLARD	BENJAMIN KOONCE	JOHN FORDHAM
THOS McDANIEL	WILLIAM HELLEN	WILLIAMS ISLER
ISAIAH WOOD		

JAMES HARRISON, Esq., FREDERICK I. BECTON, and JACOB GILES to audit accounts of JAS B. SHINE, guardian to heirs of DANIEL MASHBERN, decd

RISDON M. McDANIEL, Esq., HARDY BRYAN, and FRANCIS DUVAL to audit accounts of I. AMYET, guardian to heirs of ADONIJAH ANDREWS

THOS GILLET and JAMES ROBERTS, Esqs. to take private examination of CHARITY MEADOWS, wife of BARTEY MEADOWS, for her voluntary consent to a deed

JAMES HARRISON, Esq., JAMES B. SHINE, and DANIEL Y. SHINE to audit accounts of JOHN GILBERT, admr of DAVID FONVIELLE, decd, and of JAMES REYNOLDS, decd

On hearing application of WINIFRED HARRITT, the court orders ENOCK FOY, SIMON FOSCUE, ROSCO BARRUS, and JAMES MARRIT to divide the lands of ISAAC

Jones Cty Court of Common Pleas Minutes 1828

KORNEGAY, decd, among the lawful heirs

JAMES N. SMITH and WALTER HELLEN to audit accounts of SARAH OLDFIELD, guardian to heirs of RICHD OLDFIELD, decd

THOMAS GILLET, ROSCO BARRUS, and WALTER HELLEN, Esquires, to audit accounts of JAMES READ, executor of WM READ, decd

THOMAS GILLET, ROSCO BARRUS, and WALTER HELLEN to audit estate of ABIGAIL READ with JAMES READ her admr

JAMES READ allowed to sell Negro, DARBY, from the estate of _____ (This was left blank.)

ALFRED HARGET, admr of JOHN B. HARGET, has leave to sell Negroes, LOTT and NATHAN, for the benefit of the estate

Justices: ISAAC BROWN, ELIJAH SIMMONS, and JAMES HERITAGE, Esqs

MICAJAH F. MATTECKS to oversee road in room of COUNCIL FIELDS

MARTIN F. BROCK to oversee road in room of WINIF____ STANLY (This name was crossed out and MORDICS? WHITE written above) resigned

JOB SMITH to be guardian of HOLLON and SARAH READ; $500 bond with WILLIAM FOSCUE and WALTER HILLEN, sureties

PETER HARGET to oversee road in room of EDWIN BECTON, resigned

WILLIAM L. LARAQUE may sell spirits by small measure for one year in his shop in TRENTON

WILEY N. TENDALE may sell spirits at his house in TRENTON for one year

GEORGE HARRIETT excused from military duty due to a rupture and until said rupture be removed

SAMUEL DILLAHUNT, admr of SUSANNAH DILLAHUNT, permitted to sell Negro woman, SILVEY, the property of the intestate, to afford a division among the heirs

These persons are to count taxpayers:
District 1: DANIEL SMITH, esq., DANIEL YATES and ISAAC H. MEADOWS
District 2: WALTER HILLEN, esq., JAS W. HOWARD and JAS N. SMITH
District 3: Sheriff, NATHAN FOSCUE, and LEML BUSECK
District 4: ISAAC BROWN, HENERY RHODES, and JOSEPH KINSEY
CYPRESS CREEK: JAS HARRISON, esq., F.I. BECTON, and JACOB GILES
District 5: SIMMONS ISLER, esq., EDWIN BECTON, and PETER HARGET

THOS HARRISON living in the fork of MUSSELSHELL (Note: It was not clear whether HARRISON was to count taxpayers in his area or whether he was to oversee road work in his area.)

Jurors for next term:

JAMES WALLACE	BRYAN LAVENDER	JOSEPH WOOD
JOHN M. FRANKS	THOMAS SMITH	THOMAS POLLOCK
JAMES TURNAGE	COUNCIL GOODING	FRANCIS ANDREWS, SEN.
LEWIS O. BRYAN	JOSEPH RHEM	DANIEL STANLY, SEN.
ISAIAH WOOD	LEWIS W. KORNEGAY	DANIEL WILLIAMSON
JOHN ROUSE	MARTIN F. BROCK	ZEADOCK MEADOWS
THOMAS DUDLEY	LEVI EUBANKS	WILLIAM RHEM
JAMES W. HOWARD	JOHN HEATH	JOHN BALL
EDMUND HATCH	WILLIAM GOODING	JOHN GODWIN
WILLIAM GOODING	JOHN ADAMS	DANIEL YATES

(Note that WILLIAM GOODING was listed twice.)

ROSCO BARRUS, JAMES N. SMITH, and WALTER HELLEN to audit accounts of SIMON FOSCUE, guardian to AMOS FOSCUE

JOHN BALL confined in jail for 21 days because of debts, came to court and took the oath of insolvency. His property being assigned to his creditors, he was set free.

NANCY WATSON ordered to appear at court next term to show why FANNY KNIGHT, an orphan and bound to her by a former term of this court, should not be taken from her for ill treatment

RESDON M. McDANIEL, BENJN HUGGINS, and ALFRED HARGET to audit accounts of DURANT RICHARDS, executor of JOHN RICHARDS, decd

The following persons ordered to be patrols for one year:

District 1 (WHITE OAK): JOSEPH WHITTY, MICAJAH F. MATTOCKS, and NATHAN EASTON
District 2 (TRENT BRIDGE): JNO HARRISON, DANL WILLIAMSON, and DURANT HATCH JR
District 3 (TRENTON): JOHN RAMSEY, C.A. HATCH, and LEML BUSICK
District 4 (CYPRESS CREEK): JACOB GILES, JAS B. SHINE, and JNO HAMMON
District 5 (TUCKAHOE): HENERY RHODES SR, JNO M. FRANKS, and JOSEPH KINSEY
District 6 (BEAVER CREEK): SIMMS ISLER, R. STANLY, CALVIN KOONCE, and B. NOBLE
District 7: L.H. SIMMONS, JNO OLIVER, and NATHAN FOSCUE

FREDERICK I. BECTON, admr of BRYAN BECTON, decd, has leave to sell Negroes of intestate to pay debts: two old women, one child about four years old and one child about nine years old

HARDY PARRY, ISAAC BROWN, JOHN H. HAMMONS, WILLIAMS BROWN, and SAMUEL DELLAHUNT, Esquires, to examine the RIVER TRENT from the mouth of TUCKEHOE down to COLVETT'S FORD and make a scale of the expense and labor with which the openings and clearings will be attended should the county be responsible for the expense

JAMES HARRISON, Esq., FREDERICK I. BECTON, and ISAAC BROWN to audit accounts of OWEN B. COX, executor of ANDREW COX, decd; ANDREW'S wife was E. COX

JAMES HARRISON, Esq., ISAAC BROWN, and FREDERICK I. BECTON to audit accounts of OWEN B. COX, admr of FILIA? COX, decd

Same men to audit accounts of ____C.B. COX, executor of ELANY COX, decd. (Could this be Andrew's wife since it was not clear above whether his wife was living or dead?)

DANIEL SMITH to oversee road from head of WHITE OAK down to _____

JAMES HARRISON, ISAAC BROWN, and FREDERICK I. BECTON to audit accounts of OWEN B. COX, guardian of WILLIAM A. COX, minor, and report next court

ASA SMITH, Esq., JAMES ROBERTS, and SIMEON MEADOWS to audit accounts of HARDY COLLINS, admr of MARTHY COLLINS, decd

RESDEN M. McDANIELS, ALFRED HARGET, and BENJAMIN HUGGINS to audit accounts of DURANT RICHARDS, admr of SARAH SMITH, decd

Estate settlements of WRIGHT SIMMONS, ROBT KORNEGAY, and THOS MURPHY, all decd, filed

Guardian settlement of SARAH OLDFIELD to heirs of R. OLDFIELD, filed

Account of sales of estates of SARAH SMITH, JNO? RICHARDS, and BRYAN BECTON, all decd, filed

Bills of sale, etc., registered in court this term by JAS. REYNOLDS:
    FRANCIS DUVAL to DURANT HATCH JR
    SILAS TURNER to SILAS M. TURNER
    SILAS TURNER to LEVI JACKSON TURNER
    HARDY ADAMS to WILLIAM ADAMS

Sheriff HUGGINS to WILLIAM ADAMS
THOMAS B. HAUGHTON to HARDY O. NEWTON
HOUSTON ROBERTS to SARAH OLDFIELD
HOUSTON ROBERTS to SARAH OLDFIELD
DANIEL ANDREWS to PETER ANDREWS
Sheriff HUGGINS to URBIN OLDFIELD
DANIEL ANDREWS to PETER ANDREWS
NERCISON? HARDY to DANIEL WILLIAMSON
JOSEPH WHILLY to BENJN WALLACE
WILLIAM KING to KING G. JONES
COUNCIL FIELDS to MICAJAH F. MATTOCKS
URBEN OLDFIELD to JOHN SMITH
JAMES WISE and NANCY WISE to OLIVE WISE
WILLIAM HUGGINS, sheriff, to SIMMONS HARRISON
DEMPSEY BROWN and others to ISAAC BROWN

DECEMBER TERM, 1828
TRENTON, Monday the 8th

Justices: ISAAC BROWN, SIMMONS ISLER, and WALTER HILLEN
Sheriff: WILLIAM HUGGINS, esquire
Clerk: HARDY BRYAN

Freeholders drawn as jurors:
DANIEL YATES, foreman
WILLIAM RHEM   THOS SMITH (LEVI EUBANK crossed out here)
THOS POLLOCK   ISAIAH WOOD   JAS W. HOWARD
JNO. M. FRANKS   FRANCIS ANDREWS   COUNCIL GOODING
LEWIS W. KORNEGAY   JOHN BALL   JOSEPH RHEM

    RACHEL McDANIEL, widow of RISDON McDANIEL, decd, "signifyed her descent from the will of her late husband"
    RIGDEN WHITE filed with HARDY PARRY a schedule of his property and notes and took the oath of insolvency
    EMANUEL JARMAN, executor of RESDEN McDANIEL, decd, has leave to sell Negroes of the estate to pay debts
    WALTER HILLEN, JAMES SIMMONS, BRYAN LAVENDER, ELIJAH SIMMONS, and JAMES N. SMITH to divide the land left to DEMPSEY LOVITT and DAVID LOVITT by their father agreeable to the will
    JAMES SIMMONS, admr of WRIGHT SIMMONS, decd, said he had made an error in the accounts returned by him last court; WALTER HILLEN, EDMD HATCH and ROSCO BARRUS, esqs. to examine the accounts
    ELIJAH SIMMONS ordered to be guardian to FREDERICK M. FIELDS; $800 bond; JAMES HARRISON and WILLIAM FOSCUE, securities
    THOMAS H. DAVIS, JAMES McDANIELS, and JNO HOUSTON? to divide Negroes of the estate of FURNIFOLD G. SIMMONS, decd; PENELOPE SIMMONS, widow; ELIZABETH and FURNIFOLD SIMMONS, children of said decd
    WALTER HELLEN, THOS H. DAVIS and JAMES N. SMITH, esq., to audit and settle accounts of ROSCO BARRUS, executor of EDWARD S. FRANKS, decd
    Same persons to audit and settle accounts of ROSCO BARRUS, guardian to WM W. FRANKS (minor)

Jones Cty Court of Common Pleas Minutes 1828

WILLIAM HUGGINS, JAMES REYNOLDS and BENJAMIN HUGGINS to audit and settle accounts of SIMMONS ISLER, guardian to EMANUEL HARGET (minor)

LEWIS HARGET ordered to be guardian to EMANUEL HARGET; $2,000 bond with WILLIAM HUGGINS and BENJM HUGGINS, securities

JAMES REYNOLDS allowed $7.00 of county funds to buy a blank book for his office as registrar

DANIEL Y. SHINE, JAMES B. SHINE and JAMES HARRISON, esq., to audit and settle the accounts of JOHN HAMMON, guardian to the heirs of JEREMIAH PARSONS, decd

Same persons to audit and settle accounts of JOHN HAMMON, guardian to FREDK BRYAN (minor)

FRANCIS DUVAL, HARDY BRYAN, and RESDON M. McDANIEL to audit and settle accounts of (blank space) AMYET, guardian to the heirs of ADONIJAH ANDREWS

GEORGE WILCOX to oversee road above TRENTON to the INDIAN GROVE in place of SAMUEL HILL, resigned

JAMES JONES has leave to sell liquor at his residence for one year

ISAAC BROWN, JAMES HARRISON, FREDK I. BECTON, HENERY RHODES SENR, and JOHN M. FRANKS to divide Negroes of estate of FAUNTIN WILLIAMS, decd, among the heirs

JOHN HAMMONS, guardian to heirs of JEREMIAH PARSONS, decd, allowed to sell a Negro boy of the estate named LIMONE (but the name is crossed out) for the purpose of (just lines here) at a credit of six months

Settlement of estate of A. COX, decd, returned and filed by O.B. COX, executor

Settlement of LEML H. SIMMONS, guardian to AMOS and SOPHIA SIMMONS (minors) filed

Settlement of estate of FELIX? COX filed

Settlements of estates of ELENA COX, JOHN RICHARDS, and SARAH SMITH, decd, filed

Account of sale of property of MARCUM MEADOWS filed; $92.40

Tuesday, December 9, 1828

Justices: ISAAC BROWN, JAMES N. SMITH, and SIMON FOSCUE

JAMES READ, executor of WILLIAM READ, decd, may sell Negro man, JERRY, to affect a division among the heirs of WILLIAM READ

JAMES N. SMITH ordered to be guardian to DAVID LOVETT; $3,000 bond with ASA SMITH and ALFRED HARGET, securities

ENOCH FOY, THOMAS H. DAVIS, and JOHN HOUSTON to "divide Negroes of LEMUEL HATCH, decd, among heirs of said decd so as to set off to MARY F. BLACKLEDGE, wife of WILLIAM S. BLACKLEDGE, her distributive share agreeable to law"

JOB SMITH to admin. SUSAN READ; $500 bond with WILLIAM FOSCUE and JAMES N. SMITH, securities

WILEY HUGGINS, constable, allowed $12.00 which is his cost of removing ELIZABETH WAINWRIGHT from the county

GEORGE PENUEL to be paid for his services as constable

EML JARMAN, admr of HENCHEY KILLEBREW, decd, to sell at credit of six mos. two Negroes of the estate of his intestate to make distribution among the

Jones Cty Court of Common Pleas Minutes 1828

heirs of said decd

JOB SMITH, admr of SUSAN READ, to sell at six mos. credit one Negro man, DARBY, of the estate of the intestate so as to affect a division among the heirs of said decd

ISAAC BROWN and HARDY PARRY, esqs., to take private examination of LEAH SMALL and MARIA SMALL in the matter of a deed of land which their husbands conveyed to NATHAN WESTBROOK

WILLIAM ANTWINE to oversee road from INDIAN GROVE to OLDFIELD's? to JACK CABBIN in room of SIMMONS HARRISON, esq., resigned

ASA SMITH, JAMES ROBERTS, and SIMEON MEADOWS to audit and settle accounts of HARDY COLLINS, admr of MARTHEY COLLINS, decd

JAMES REYNOLDS, PETER HARGET, and SIMMONS ISLER, esq., to audit and settle accounts of JOHN SHELFER, admr of JESSE SHELFER, decd

Settlement of estate of EDWD S. FRANKS filed by executor, R. BARRUS

Settlement of R. BARRUS, guardian to WILLIAM W. FRANKS (minor) filed

Settlement of estate of WILLIAM READ filed

Accounts of sales of estates of WILLIAM READ, SUSANNAH READ, and EDWD S. FRANK, all decd, filed

Inventory and sale of estate of MRS. NANCY FIELDS, decd, filed

JACOB HUGGINS vs HARDY BRYAN, admr of JOSEPH GREEN: Find for plaintiff for sum of $462.85 with interest from 19 June 1827 until paid in cash. WILLIAM HUGGINS appointed special guardian to ABNER GREEN, JOHN GREEN, CORNELIUS GREEN, HAMBLETON GREEN, and SARAH ANN GREEN (infants) and heirs at law of JOSEPH GREEN, decd

JACOB HUGGINS and ANN, his wife, vs. HARDY BRYAN, admr of JOSEPH GREEN, decd: Judgment for the plaintiff for $190.69 principal and $10.15 interest and costs. Again the heirs are listed as above

Freeholders drawn for jury duty next court:

WILLIAM GILBERT	DANIEL Y. SHINE	JACOB GILES
A.B. OWENS	JACOB HUGGINS JR.	EDWARD GILBERT
GEORGE C. HATCH	JAMES B. SHINE	PETER ANDREWS
FURNIFOLD HERITAGE	JOHN BENDER	EMANUEL JARMON
JOHN SHELFER	JOHN FORDHAM	THOS WILSON
ASA EUBANKS	WILLIAM BROWN	THOMAS H. HILL
RICHD R. FOSCUE	WILLIAM McDANIEL SR	JAMES SIMMONS
LOTT EUBANKS	BENJAMIN KOONCE	JOHN C. WOOD
MILENTON MEADOWS	SHADRACK MALLARD	COUNCIL GOODING
HENERY RHODES SENR	HUBARD STANLY	SILAS McDANIEL

Settlement of AMOS AMYET, guardian to LEML ANDREWS (minor) filed

Jones Cty Court of Common Pleas Minutes 1829

MARCH TERM, 1829
TRENTON, Monday, the 9th

Justices: SIMMONS ISLER, RESDEN M. McDANIEL, and HARDY PARRY, esqs.
Sheriff: WILLIAM HUGGINS
Clerk: HARDY BRYAN

ABNER GREEN, DANIEL Y. SHINE, EMANUEL JARMAN, and FRANCIS DUVAL, esqs., sworn in as justices of the peace

JAMES RUSSEL took the oath of insolvency and was set at liberty. MOSES W. JARVIS mentioned (Note: He was possibly a creditor.)

FRANCIS B. AMYET, admr of estate of ENOCH AMYET, decd; bond set at $150.00 with JAMES W. HOWARD and CHARLES WHILLY, securities

FURNIFOLD G. HERITAGE, admr of estate of JAMES MILLER, decd; bond set at $2500? with JOHN H. HAMMON and ALFRED HARGET, securities

SIMMONS HARRISON, JNO. H. HAMMON, JNO. PARSONS, and WM HELLEN to allot off to SARAH MILLER, widow of JAS MILLER, one yr's provisions

RESDON M. McDANIEL, esq., HARDY BRYAN, and JAMES MARRET to audit and settle accounts of PETER ANDREWS, executor of JNO. ANDREWS, decd

BENJM KOONCE to oversee road from the bridge at TRENTON to WORDS/WARDS HILL and from fork at COOMBS to MUSSELSHELL BRANCH to R.M. McDANIEL'S in place of BENJM HUGGINS, resigned

ABNER GREEN to oversee road in room of WILLIAM McDANIEL, resigned, from HARRISON'S bridge to WILLIAM RHEM'S road

NATHAN FOSCUE to oversee road in room of LEML H. SIMMONS, resigned, from bridge at TRENTON down to BEAVERDAM BRANCH and from fork of road at R.M. McDANIEL'S up the KINSTON ROAD to MUSSELSHELL BRANCH

JOHN OLIVER to oversee road in room of DANIEL STANLY, resigned, from BEAVERDAM near JAMES MARRET'S down to fork of road at SOLOMON E. GRANT'S

GEORGE WILCOX to admr estate of THOMAS WILCOX, decd; bond of $2500.00; EML JARMAN and SAML HILE/HILL, securities

Inventory and account of sale of estate of MARY GREEN, decd, filed by ABNER GREEN, admr

Amount current of TOBIAS KOONCE, guardian to ELIZA M. WRIGHT, filed and approved

Same for JOHN H. HAMMON, guardian to NATHAN PARSONS

Same for JOHN H. HAMMON, guardian to JEREMIAH PARSONS, RICHD PARSONS, HARRIET PARSONS, and FREDK BRYAN

Same for HARDY PARRY, guardian to heirs of ISLER PARRY, decd

Tuesday, 10 MARCH 1829

Justices: RESDON McDANIEL, EMANUEL JARMAN, and SIMMONS ISLER, esqs.
Sheriff: WILLIAM HUGGINS
Clerk: HARDY BRYAN

Freeholders drawn for jury this term:
WILLIAM GILBERT	JACOB GILES	EDWARD GILBERT
JAMES B. SHINE	JOHN BENDER	JNO. SHELFER
FURNIFOLD G. HERITAGE	JOHN FORDHAM	ASA EUBANKS

Jones Cty Court of Common Pleas Minutes 1829

RICHARD R. FOSCUE		JAMES SIMMONS		WILLLIAM McDANIEL SR

JOHN HEATH, WILLIAMS ISLER, and JAMES REYNOLDS to settle accounts of SIMMONS ISLER, executor of BENJM KOONCE, decd

JACOB GILES to oversee road in room of EMANUEL JARMON, resigned, west side of REEDY BRANCH up to RATTLESNAKE BRIDGE

ALFRED STANLY, JAMES FOY, OWEN ADAMS, and THOMAS HALL to be patrols for one year

DANIEL GILBERT, orphan boy aged about 12 yrs, bound to GARSHAM ANTWINE, farmer; said ANTWINE to give said child 12 mos schooling (Note: This is probably GRAHAM ANTWINE who was in the 1820 federal census for JONES COUNTY according to Potter.)

ELIAS FORDHAM to oversee road in place of DURANT WESTBROOK from BLACK SWAMP to LENOIR COUNTY line

JOHN STELL/STELE/HILL/HILE to oversee road in place of JOHN STANLY, resigned, from bridge at TRENTON and including the streets of TRENTON up to head of the straight road one mile above town

LEWIS KORNEGAY to oversee road from fork at SHINE'S to west side of REEDY BRANCH in place of IGNATIOUS BROCK [Note: From March term, 1929 of CRAVEN COUNTY court records is a release of claim to property which is of interest here. ISAAC KORNEGAY, who was decd by March, 1828, was married to CATHARINE BROCK, widow of BENJ BROCK. CATHARINE was entitled to Negroes from her late husband's (BROCK'S) estate and from the estate of IGNATIOUS WADSWORTH at the death of his widow. ISAAC KORNEGAY released all claims he had to his late wife's (CATHERINE'S) properties to JOSEPH, IGNATIOUS, and BENJAMIN BROCK and MICAJAH PETTEWAY. (CATHERINE was the daughter of IGNATIOUS WADSWORTH SR. She married BENJAMIN BROCK in CRAVEN COUNTY 6 Mar 1795.)]

HARDY PARRY and LEML BUSECK to take private examination of SUSAN BROWN for her voluntary consent of a deed to MOSES JARVIS and JOHN D. DAVIS

RESDON M. McDANIEL, guardian to JAMES HENERY (minor); $400.00 bond with JAMES McDANIEL and HARDY PARRY, securities

Account of JOHN H. HAMMON, guardian to THOS PARSONS, filed
Same for JNO. GILBERT, admr of DAVID FONVILLE; G. GREEN? mentioned
Same for JAS SIMMONS, admr of WRIGHT SIMMONS, decd
Division of Negroes beween JAMES WILLIAMS and JAMES JONES filed
Account of JAMES B. SHINE, guardian to heirs of DANIEL MASHBURN, filed
Freeholders drawn as jurors for next term:

JOHN FRIZE/FIETZ/FRISZD/FIZLOW

LAWSON MALLARD	BENJAMIN COLLINS	JAMES McDANIEL
LEMUEL H. SIMMONS	MICIJAH PETAWAY	JOSEPH BROCK
JOHN STANLY SR	LEWIS WILLIAMS	WILLIAMS JONES
JOHN ANDREWS	WILLIAM H. MEADOWS	ENOCH FOY
WILLIAM M. GILES	JOHN ROUSE	JOHN GODWIN
JAMES W. HOWARD	WILLIAMS ISLER	JAMES TURNAGE
JOHN MALLARD	JAMES MARRET	THOMAS DUDLEY

JOHN J____ (This may have been JONES, but it was smudged.)

HARDY MUNDINE	WILLIAM RHEM	FREDERICK FOSCUE
JOHN M. FRANKS	FREDERICK I. BECTON	EDWIN BECTON
LEWIS KINSEY		

Bills of sale and deeds, mortgages, etc. registered by JAS REYNOLDS, registrar:
WILLIAM HUGGINS, sheriff, to JOHN STILL?

Jones Cty Court of Common Pleas Minutes 1829

CLARK? and MASTER? in equity to WILLIAM HUGGINS
JAMES McDANIEL to WILLIAM HUGGINS
JOHN STILL/STILE to WILLIAM HUGGINS
LEWIS KINSEY to EVAN WILLIAMS
LEWIS KINSEY to EVAN WILLIAMS
WM HUGGINS, sheriff, to DURANT RICHARDS
WM HUGGINS, sheriff, to RICHARD REYNOLDS
JOHN WOOD and wife to WM GILBERT
MELTIRE? ARNOLD to SOLOMAN COLLINS
JESSE CARMACK and wife to JOHN STANLY
RIGDON HEWIT to BARTHALAMEW MEADOWS
ALFRED HARGET to NANCY HARRISON
Admr of BENJN HARRISON to ALFRED HARGET
CHRISTOPHER BRYAN to TOBIAS KOONCE
WILLIAM HUGGINS to BENJAMIN HUGGINS
BENJM KOONCE to BENJAMIN HUGGINS
SIMMONS ISLER and B. KOONCE to ALFRED HARGET
JOHN H. HAMMOND and F.G. HERETAGE? to ALFRED HARGET
WILLIAM MEADOWS and BARTHELAMEW MEADOWS, agreement
ISAAC KORNEGAY, J. BROCK, M. PITTEWAY, J. W. BROCK, and B. BROCK, agreement
WILLIAM B. PENUEL to JOHN H. HAMMONS
BENJM COLLINS and others to SIMMONS COLLINS
MORRIS WARD_____ to ELIZABETH B. LAVENDER
JOHN D/B. DAVIS to HARDY BRYAN

JUNE TERM, 1829
TRENTON, Monday June 8th

Justices: OWEN B. COX, SIMMONS ISLER, and ROSCO BARRUS, esquires
Sheriff: WILLIAM HUGGINS, esq.
Clerk: HARDY BRYAN

Grand jurors for the term:
WILLIAM ISLER, foreman

JOHN ANDREWS	WILLIAM H. MEADOWS	WILLIAM RHIME
WILLIAM M. GILES	JOHN MALLARD	JOHN FRIZZE?
JAMES MARRET	WILLIAMS JONES	HARDY MUNDINE
JOSEPH BROCK	JOHN ROUSE	LEWIS WILLIAMS

Petit jurors:

MICAJAH PITEEWAY	JAMES W. HOWARD	JAMES McDANIEL
FREDERICK I. BECTON	ENOCK FOY	JOHN JONES
FREDERICK FOSCUE	BENJAMIN COLLINS	JOHN PARSONS
LEMUEL H. SIMMONS	LUKE SHELFER	ISAIAH WOOD

  THOMAS H. DAVIS, DURANT HATCH JR., and AMOS AMYET to audit accounts of FRANCIS AMYET, admr. of ENOCK AMYET, decd
  HARDY BRYAN, FRANCIS DUVAL, and RESDON McDANIEL to audit accounts of AMOS AMYET, guardian to heirs of ADONIJAH ANDREWS, decd
  Will of JOSEPH KEY proved in open court by oath of JAMES MADES one of

the witnesses; DANIEL SMITH qualified as one of the executors [Gwynn abstracted this will (pp. 427-428) which was written 9 Jan 1828. It names his wife, ANN; grandsons, JOSEPH, SAMUEL and BENJAMIN SMITH; daughter, PININ SCOTT; granddaughter, NANCY SMITH (who was to get nothing); granddaughters, MARY and ELIZA SMITH. Also mentioned, but not named, is a child of PININ's by her apparently late, second husband, SAMUEL SCOTT. Her late first husband was CALEB SMITH. He named his friends, JAMES ROBERTS, DANIEL SMITH and JOSIAH SMITH, exrs. ROBERT DICKSON and JAMES MADES were witnesses.]

Will of JAMES WESTBROOK, decd, proved in open court by oath of JOSEPH SMALL, a witness; BRYAN WESTBROOK qualified as the executor [Gwynn also abstracted this will (p. 451) which was written 27 Feb 1829. It mentions his son, BRYAN; grandson, CURTIS; and daughters, RILLY TURNER, ELIZABETH WESTBROOK, and MARY WESTBROOK. BRYAN WESTBROOK was named exr. and witnesses were JOSEPH SMALL and SARAH SMALL.]

WALTER HELLEN, JAMES N. SMITH, JAMES ROBERTS, THOMAS GILLET, and LEVI EUBANKS to audit accounts of _____, admr of SUSANNAH READ, decd

Same men to audit accounts of _____ executors of WILLIAM READ, decd (Note: These two underlines were blank spaces.)

Letters of admin. granted to IVEY ANDREWS on the estate of WILLIAM McDANIEL, decd; $500.00 bond with NATHAN B. BUSH and DANIEL MALLARD JR., sureties

Letters of admin. to JOHN H. HAMMON on estate of JOSEPH PARSONS, decd; $1000.00 with FREDERICK I. BECTON and JAMES B. SHINE, sureties

JAMES HARRISON, FREDERICK I. BECTON, and JOHN M. FRANK to audit accounts of OWEN B. COX, guardian to WILLIAM COX, minor

RICHARD REYNOLDS, JAMES REYNOLDS, and BENJM KOONCE to audit accounts of PETER HARGET, executor of DANIEL SIMMONS, decd

PETER HARGET appointed guardian to ABRAHAM and NANCY SIMMONS, heirs of DANIEL SIMMONS, decd; $3000.00 bond with SIMMONS ISLER and ISAAC KORNEGAY, sureties

ASA SMITH, JAMES ROBERT, and MICAJAH F. MATTOCK to audit accounts of ARCHIBALD B. OWENS, executor of SELBY H. WISE, decd

HARDY BRYAN, WILLIAM HUGGINS, and HARDY PARRY to audit accounts of BRADDOCK NOBLE, guardian to the several heirs of EMANUEL KOONCE, decd

JAMES HARRISON, FREDERICK I. BECTON, and JOHN M. FRANKS to audit accounts of OWEN B. COX, guardian to JESSE A. GREGARY

THOMAS J. FONVIELLE to oversee road from TRENT BRIDGE in place of WILLIAM DUNKEN, resigned

JOHN H. HAMMON, SAMUEL DILLAHUNT, and SIMMONS HARRISON to audit accounts of FURNIFOLD G. HERRITAGE, admr of THOMAS STELLY, decd

Division of lands of THOMAS MURPHY, decd, so as to allot to widow her dower agreeable to petition, was returned

Freeholders drawn as jurors for next county court:

THOMAS HARRISON	HARDY COLLINS	WILLIAM GOODING, SR.
ISAAC H. MEADOWS	DANIEL WILLIAMSON	JAMES WILLIAMS
ZEADOCK MEADOWS	JACOB HUGGINS JR.	JOHN TURNER
JOHN BALL	HARDY HILL	LEWIS FOSCUE, JR.
AMOS TAYLOR	SAMUEL DILLAHUNT	JOHN PARSONS
MARTIN F. BROCK	JAMES READ	OWEN ADAMS
JOHN H. HAMMONS	PETER HARGET	JAMES WALLACE
ELIJAH KOONCE	FRANCIS ANDREWS	WILLIAM ADAMS

BARTHALAMEW MEADOWS   WILLIAM HELLEN   THOMAS McDANIEL
JOSEPH RHEM   LEWIS O. BRYAN   LEWIS W. KORNEGAY

Freeholders drawn as jurors for the next Superior Court:

LUKE SHELFER	ISAIAH WOOD	WILLIAMS BROWN
NATHAN FOSCUE	RIGDON HEWIT	ROSCO BARRUS
JOSEPH HAY	JOHN STILL?	IVEY ANDREWS
SIMMONS ISLER	DURANT RICHARDS	ASA SMITH
BENJAMIN HUGGINS	DURANT HATCH JR.	JOHN POLLOCK
RISDEN McDANIEL, "son of R."		HARDY PARRY
DANIEL SMITH	THOMAS SMITH	THOMAS GILLET
JOHN WOOD	OWEN B. COX	WILLIAM GOODING
ISAAC KORNEGAY	ELIJAH MARKET	DANIEL YATES
SIMMONS HARRISON SR.	ALFRED HARGET	JAMES G. HERRITAGE
WALTER HELLEN	ELIJAH SIMMONS	LEVI EUBANKS
THOMAS POLLOCK	JOHN HEATH	BRADDOCK NOBLE

Inventory and account of sale of estate returned for each of the following: JAMES MILLER, ENOCK AMYET, WILLIAM McDANIEL, and THOMAS WILCOX, all decd

Settlement of estate returned for both BENJM KOONCE, decd, and JOHN ANDREWS, decd

WILLIAM T. DICKSON to oversee road from the crossroads on WHITE OAK to a black sorrel in the middle of the POCOSIN in place of DANIEL YATES, resigned

Debt case: MOSES JARVIS vs BENJM KOONCE and BENJM HUGGINS. The following jury found for the plantiff:

MICAJAH PETTEWAY	JAMES W. HOWARD	JAMES McDANIEL
FREDERICK I. BECTON	ENOCH FOY	JOHN JONES
FREDK FOSCUE	BENJAMIN COLLINS	LEMUEL H. SIMMONS
JOHN PARSONS	LUKE SHELFER	ISAIAH WOOD

Judgment: $106.59

DURANT HATCH JR to the use of SYLVESTER BROWN vs WILLIAM HELLEN and WALTER HELLEN: same jury as above found for plaintiff; judgment: $301.45 (Note: This was probably another debt case although the type of case was not specified.)

JAMES AYKSAY (Note: This name is probably ASKEY; see Potter.) vs GEO. OLDFIELD, ASA SMITH, JAMES ROBERTS, JAS N. SMITH, and ROBERT V. ORME. Same as above; judgment: $138.90

JAMES ASKEY vs ASA SMITH, JAMES ROBERTS, JAS N. SMITH, and ROB V. ORME. Same as above; judgment: $115.93

JOHN H. BRYAN to use of JOHN T. BOYD vs WILLIAM HELLEN. Same as above; judgment $309.00

WM P. FERONOL? to use of SILVESTER BROWN vs THOMAS J. FONVIELLE. Same as above; judgment: $111.82

DURANT HATCH vs JAMES W. HOWARD. Same as above; judgment: $143.74

HENERY W. JONES vs THOMAS H. HILL (debt). Same as above; judgment: $162.50

SALLY MILLER vs F.G. HERITAGE admr of JAS MILLER; petition for year's provision

MARY MURPHY vs THOS MURPHY: petition for partition

LEVIN B. LANE vs RESDEN M. McDANIEL, admr of MOSES McDANIEL (case): Plea of fully administered admitted to be true; judgment of $135.00 set. Interest from 1 Jan 1827 until paid; real estate in hands of heirs at law of MOSES McDANIEL, decd, who are: MITCHEL McDANIEL, JOHN, CALVIN, DRUSILLIA, SILVESTER, and MOSES McDANIELS, all infants; JACOB HUGGINS JR is their special guardian

Tuesday, 9 June 1829

Justices: OWEN B. COX, SIMMONS ISLER, and DURANT HATCH

Accounts of NATHAN B. BUSH, county trustee, filed
FREDERICK I. BECTON, JAMES R. CONNER, and DANIEL Y. SHINE to audit accounts of NATHAN B. BUSH, county trustee
EMANUEL JARMAN, FREDERICK I. BECTON, and ISAAC BROWN to audit accounts of MARY OLIVER, guardian to MARY OLIVER (minor)
Accounts of BRADDOCK NOBLE, guardian to heirs of EMANUEL KOONCE, decd, filed
The justices (a majority of those in the county) elected the county officers; the justices present for the election: ISAAC BROWN, DURANT HATCH JR., HARDY PARRY, RISDEN M. McDANIEL, JAMES HARRISON, OWEN B. COX, ROSCO BARRUS, SIMMONS HARRISON, JAMES N. SMITH, EMANUEL JARMAN, ABNER GREEN, DANIEL Y. SHINE, FRANCIS DUVAL. Officers elected:
WILLIAM HUGGINS, sheriff; RICHARD REYNOLDS and EMANUEL JARMAN, sureties for his bond
NATHAN B. BUSH, county trustee; WILLIAM HUGGINS and RISDEN M. McDANIEL, sureties for his bond
DANIEL DICKSON, constable for DISTRICT 1; LEMUEL H. SIMMONS and JAMES W. HOWARD, sureties
ALFRED HARGET, constable for DISTRICT 2; OWEN B. COX and R.M. McDANIEL, sureties
WM BROWN, constable for DISTRICT 3; OWEN B. COX and EML JARMAN, sureties
LEVI JONES, constable for DISTRICT 4; EML JARMAN and OWEN B. COX, sureties
JOSHUA B. OLIVER?, constable for DISTRICT 5; DANL Y. SHINE and JAMES G. OLIVER?, sureties
HARDY SHELFER, constable for DISTRICT 6; EML JARMAN and RESDEN M. McDANIEL, sureties

WILLIAM HUGGINS, sheriff, allowed $92.57 for extra services to the county last year
HARDY BRYAN, clerk, allowed $40.00 for same
BRADDOCK NOBLE, constable, allowed $23.20? for court attendance
LEVI JONES, constable, allowed $4.00 for court attendance
WILEY F. HIGGINS allowed $24.00? for court attendance as constable
RISDEN M. McDANIEL, HARDY PARRY and HARDY BRYAN, commissioners for building the court house, to put out bids for its construction
WILLIAM BROWN, constable, allowed $6.40 for court attendance

The following justices are to take the tax list:

Jones Cty Court of Common Pleas Minutes 1829

District 1: THOMAS GILLET   District 4: EMANUEL JARMAN
District 2: WALTER HELLEN   District 5: ABNER GREEN
District 3: FRANCIS DuVAL   District 6: ROSCO BARRUS

JAMES N. SMITH and ROSCO BARRUS appointed to assess repairs to TRENT BRIDGE and let bids for its repair

NATHAN B. BUSH, admr <u>debones non</u> of ELIZABETH HARRISON vs NANY HARRISON and A. BRYAN, admx and admr of BENJN HARRISON, decd: petition for partition. The pltff to receive the sum of $128.55 with interest from the 6th August 1820 being the distributive share of PENELOPE LEARY. This suit dismissed as to the other matters. Defendants to pay cash.

PERY ORTON, surviving partner of _____ vs CHRISTOPHER A. HATCH, admr of WM B. HATCH: case. Defendants plead fully administered but the following jury finds "other issues for pltff and assesses damages to $493.15 of which $428.92 is principal." Jury: MICIJAH PETTEWAY   JAS W. HOWARD   JAMES McDANIEL

ENOCH FOY	JOHN JONES	FREDERICK FOSCUE
FREDERICK I. BECTON	BENJN COLLINS	ISAIAH WOODS
LEMUEL H. SIMMONS	JAMES SIMMONS	JAMES B. SHINE

EMANUEL JARMAN, admr of HENCHEY KILLEBREW vs ABNER KILLEBREW, infant, by JACOB GILES, his guardian: Case. Same jury as above finds for pltff and assesses damages at $170.13 with interest from 8 Sept 1823.

DURANT HATCH JR. vs OWEN B. COX, admr of HALL HUMPHREY. Same jury as above finds for pltff. Judgment: $66.26.

ROBT V. ORME, admr of WM ORME to use of THOMAS McLIN vs WM HUGGINS, shff. Dismissed.

SIMMONS ISLER, guardian to WILLIAM BRYAN vs NANCY HATHAWAY: Case. Writ amended by making minor pltff. Application granted. FREDK I. BECTON and NATHAN B. BUSH, sureties.

LEML ISLER, guardian to JOS BRYAN, minor, vs NANCY HATHAWAY. Case. Writ amended by making minor pltff. Pltff called and failing to appear; a nonsuit declared. Appeal prayed and granted. FREDERICK I. BECTON and NATHAN B. BUSH, sureties.

Next of kin of MICHAEL KOONCE vs SIMMONS HARRISON, JAMES REYNOLDS, and RESDEN M. McDANIELS. Although difficult to read it appears that the case was decided for the pltff and the debt was $1515.38.

WILLIAM DUNKEN vs WINIFORD HEWITT/HERRITT. Case. Same jury as above. Damages assessed by justices, ISAAC BROWN, ROSCO BARRUS, and HARDY PARRY.

At the request of HARDY PARRY, admr of SAMUEL L. WIGGINS, any two of these men: WILLIAMS BROWN, RISDON M. McDANIEL and EMANUEL JARMAN should audit and settle the accounts of the said admr

State vs HARDY MOORE: Bastardy. Defendant pleads that he is not the father. Following jury found for defendant but he had to pay court costs:

NATHAN B. BUSH	SAMUEL DILLAHUNT
DANIEL MALLARD	DANIEL STANLY
JAS HUGGINS	HARDY HUGGINS
DANIEL WILLIAMSON	DAVID GREEN
RICHARD KOONCE	JOHN MESSAW/MESSAN
LEWIS SMALL	DURANT RICHARDS

State vs AMOS KOONCE. Defendant pleads that he is not the father. The following jury found for the defendant:

Jones Cty Court of Common Pleas Minutes 1829

WILLIAM McDANIEL	LUKE SHELFER	ELIAS FORDHAM
GEORGE WILCOX	BENJN KOONCE	TOBIAS KOONCE
SILAS McDANIEL	JOHN STANLY	JACOB HUGGINS
JOSEPH RHEM	BENJN HUGGINS	JOHN FORDHAM

HARDY BRYAN, clerk, allowed $12.00 to purchase record books
Sheriff directed to have a good wall or fence erected around the jail as soon as possible

Deeds proved this term with JAS REYNOLDS, registrar:
WM. HUGGINS, shff to SIMON FOSCUE
WM. HUGGINS, shff to SIMON FOSCUE
JAS N. SMITH to SIMON FOSCUE
THOMAS J. FONVILLE to SIMON FOSCUE
DURANT WESTBROOK to JOSEPH SMALL
THOMAS B. IVES to JAMES N. SMITH
RIGDEN HEWIT to BARTHOLOMEW MEADOWS
LEMUEL H. SIMMONS to JNO. OLIVER for MARY HATCH
JONATHAN KEY to THOMAS GELLET
RUBEN RICE to THOMAS GELLET
BENJAMIN KOONCE to RUBIN KNISE?
DURANT HATCH to JOHN MISSAW? (Note: The index to the 1820 census has a WILLIAM MESSER in JONES COUNTY.)
BENJN D. GRAY to JOHN E. FOSCUE
LEVIN B. LANE to DANIEL Y. SHINE
LEMUEL H. SIMMONS to WILLIAM HUGGINS
JOHN WOOD to JOSEPH SMALL
DURANT HATCH, JR. to WILLIAM HUGGINS
LETITIA KORNEGAY to WILLIAM HUGGINS
WM HUGGINS, shff to LEML H. SIMMONS
WM HUGGINS, shff to LEML H. SIMMONS
JOHN S. STANLY to SUSAN FOY (deed of trust)
Division of lands of THOS MURPHY, decd

WILLIAM S. BLACKLEDGE and EDMD HATCH, guardians to EDMOND and RICHARD HATCH (minors) vs THOMAS B. IVES, SAML C. FISHER and THOS D. BARBER. *fi fa*. (Note: This is short for *fieri facias* which is a writ commanding the sheriff to levy, make, or raise money.) BRICE FONVIELLE, sheriff of ONSLOW CO. fined $100.00 for deglect of duties under Act of Assembly for 1821, Chap. 1100. Guardians of the minors are to recover this fine.
GEORGE C. HATCH, arrested at the insistance of CATHERINE ANTHONY, for debt, was permitted to take the oath for the relief of debters. The following were notified: JAMES ROBERTS, R. DICKSON, DURANT HATCH, EDWARD S. JONES, DANIEL DICKSON, JOSEPH LOFTEN, president of the bank of NEWBERN, pres. & directors of branch of state bank of N.C., EDWD GRAHAM, JOHN T. BOYD, WM. S. BLACKLEDGE, SILVESTER BROWN, and WILLIAM GASTON of NEWBERN

SEPTEMBER TERM, 1829
TRENTON, 14 Sept 1829

Justices: RESDEN M. McDANIEL, SIMMONS ISLER, JAMES N. SMITH,

esquires
Shff: WILLIAM HUGGINS
Clerk: HARDY BRYAN

Grand jurors: JOHN H. HAMMON, foreman
JOSEPH RHEM   HARDY COLLINS
BARTHOLOMEW MEADOWS   LEWIS O. BRYAN
SAMUEL DILLAHUNT   WILLIAM ADAMS
JOHN BALL   OWEN ADAMS
MARTIN F. BROCK   THOMAS HARRISON
THOMAS McDANIEL   JACOB HUGGINS, JR

Petition of THOMAS GILLET vs EDWARD S. JONES for damages read and heard by court. Defendant to be notified and a jury summoned.

State vs JAS B. WATSON: (charge not stated). AMOS TAYLOR, ELI__ FORDHAM, WILLIAM HELLEN, DANIEL WILLIAMSON, JONAS WILLIAMS, ELIJAH KOONCE, JOHN SHELFER, JONAS JONES JR., WILLIAM McDANIEL, BRADDOCK NOBLE, JOSEPH KINSEY, and LEWIS (last name left blank). (This must have been the jury but no judgment was given.)

WILLIAM HUGGINS, shff, ordered to pay balance of sum to ADONIJAH PARRY from sale of said PARRY'S lands after satisfaction of sundry executions

SIMMONS HARRISON, JOHN H. HAMMON, and SAMUEL DILLAHUNT again ordered to audit accounts of FURNIFOLD G. HERITAGE, admr of THOMAS STELLEY

JAMES HARRISON, esq., FREDERICK I. BECTON, and JOHN M. FRANKS to audit accounts of MRS. MARY OLIVER, guardian to MARY OLIVER (now MARY LARAQUE)

JOHN KOONCE appointed guardian to heirs of MICHAEL KOONCE, decd, in room of THOMAS SPEIGHT, resigned; $10,000 bond with RICHARD REYNOLDS and ELIJAH KOONCE sureties

HARDY BRYAN, HARDY PARRY, and NATHAN B. BUSH to audit accounts of CHRISTOPHER A. HATCH, admr of WILLIAM B. HATCH, decd

EMANUEL JARMAN, WILLIAM L. LAROQUE, JOHN M. FRANKS, JACOB GILES, BENJAMIN BROCK, and LEWIS KORNEGAY to be patroles in DISTRICT 4 for 1 yr

Pay charge by JORDAN L. CARROW for his services in case of State vs JOHN D. DAVIS

Court to pay costs for superior court in case State vs Negro MOSES

ELIJAH SIMMONS, EDMOND HATCH, and ENOCH FOY to audit accounts of JOSEPH WALLACE, admr of STEPHEN WALLACE, decd

WILLIAMS ISLER, JAMES OLIVER, and AMOS HEATH to audit accounts of SIMMONS ISLER, guardian to JOSEPH and WILLIAM BRYAN (minors)

Court to pay costs in cases: State vs ELIJAH S. BELL and State vs BENJN COLLINS

ISAAC H. MEADOWS ordered to remit penalty for his non-attendance as witness in case: State vs BENJN WALLACE

JAMES ROBERTS, esq., MICAJAH F. MATTOCKS, and BARTHOLOMEW MEADOWS to be patroles in DISTRICT 1 for 1 yr

RESDEN M. McDANIEL, SIMMONS ISLER, and WALTER HELLEN, esqs, appointed to board of appeals to sit at courthouse in TRENTON on 3rd Monday in September 1829

HUBARD STANLY to oversee road in place of PETER HARGET resigned

ASA SMITH, EML JARMON, and CHRISTR GREEN to audit accounts of ABRAHAM MITCHEL, exec. of E.S. FRANKS, decd, and appointed guardian to W.W. FRANKS (minor)

Jones Cty Court of Common Pleas Minutes 1829 67

Tuesday, 15 Sept 1829

Justices: ISAAC BROWN, SIMMONS ISLER, and HARDY PARRY, esqs

JAMES HARRISON, SIMMONS HARRISON, and DANIEL Y. SHINE to "value and divide" the Negroes of the estate of JEREMIAH PARSONS, decd, among the heirs of said decd (Note: inbetween the lines was written "alott off WRIGHT PARSONS equal share")

JAMES N. SMITH, and ROSCO BARRUS to audit accounts of OWEN ADAMS, guardian to heirs of KADER KNIGHT, decd

EMANUEL JARMAN, HARDY PARRY, and SIMMONS ISLER to be a committee to draft rules and conditions for the government of patroles in JONES COUNTY

State vs BENJN COLLINS: Indictment for harboring runaway Negro. Pleads not guilty. Following jury found him guilty:

AMOS TAYLOR	ELIAS FORDHAM	WILLIAM HALLEN
DANL WILLIAMSON	JOHN SHELFER	PETER HARGET
BRADDOCK NOBLE	BENJN KOONCE	TOBIAS KOONCE
JOHN BENDER	ELIJAH PARRY	ELIJAH KOONCE

Fined $50 and 3 mos in jail. Defendant asked for an appeal in Superior Court. Appeal granted and he to appear in Sup Court March Term 1830

State vs JAMES B. WATSON: Indictment for an "affray" (Note: This is fighting in public.) Same jury as above finds defendant not guilty

State vs JOHN HARPER: Indictment for larceny. Pleads not guilty. Same jury found him guilty. Punishment: 15 lashes the next Thursday and to stay in prison until that time. Defendant appeals to Superior Court. He is surrendered to sheriff.

DANIEL DICKSON to use of JNO H. HILL vs ANTHONY HATCH, GEO HATCH, and DURANT HATCH, exec of (This name was smugged.) MURPHY: Debt. Judgment for pltff of $173.43. (A mention was made concerning the heirs of THOS MURPHY)

HARDY BRYAN, ALFRED HARGET, and WILLIAM BROWN to audit accounts of MORRIS McDANIEL, former guardian to WILLIAM POLLOCK, with RISDEN M. McDANIEL, present guardian to said WILLIAM

Same men to audit and settle accounts of RISDEN M. McDANIEL, guardian to heirs of JAMES McDANIEL, decd

Same men to settle accounts of EML JARMON, exec of DURANT McDANIEL, decd, as guardian to JAMES HENERY, with RISDEN M. McDANIEL, his present guardian

JOHN H. HAMMON to oversee road from JACK CABIN to RED OAK in room of WILLIAM HELLEN, resigned

JAMES FOY to oversee road from MILL CREEK BRIDGE to REEDY BRANCH in room of DANIEL WILLIAMSON, resigned

CALVIN KOONCE, WRIGHT STANLY, BENJM KOONCE, WILLIAM McDANIEL, WILLIAM COOMBS JR., BRADDOCK NOBLE, ELIJAH PARRY, HARDY PARRY, NEEDHAM SHELFER, SAMUEL HILL, and ABNER GREEN to be patrols for DISTRICT 5 for one year

JAMES ROBERT, ASA SMITH, and MICAJAH F. MATTOCKS to settle accounts of ARCHIBALD B. OWENS, exec. of SELBY H. WISE, decd

Letters of admin. on estate of LEMUEL ANDREWS, decd, granted to RISDEN McDANIEL "(son of RISDEN);" $200.00 bond; GEORGE WILCOX and JOHN G. RAMSEY, sureties

Jones Cty Court of Common Pleas Minutes 1829

next day? Although no date was given, when justices were named it meant that the court was in session the next day.

Justices: ISAAC BROWN, DURANT HATCH JR., NATHAN FOSCUE, THOMAS GILLET, SIMON FOSCUE, HARDY PARRY, and ABNER GREEN

NATHAN FOSCUE to repair bridge at TRENTON with county trustees to pay his bills
    ROSCO BARRUS to repair TRENT BRIDGE
    WILLIAM HUGGINS to allow 24 insolvent taxable poles for 1828

Freeholders drawn as jurors for next term:

EDMOND HATCH	EDWARD DEBRULE	JAMES GODIN
WILLIAM STANLY	JAMES MADES	DANIEL STANLY SR
SHADERACK MALLARD	JAMES REYNOLDS	FURNIFOLD G. HERITAGE
JOHN SHELFER	JOHN FORDHAM	REAVIS R. FOSCUE
SILAS McDANIEL	ELIJAH PARRY	JAMES SIMMONS
JACOB GILES	LEMUEL BUSICK	BENJAMIN KOONCE
JOSEPH SMALL	FRANCIS ANDREWS	JOHN McDANIEL
JOHN ROUSE	JOSEPH BROCK	FREDERICK I. BECTON
JOHN TURNER	JOHN STANLY SR	JACOB HUGGINS JR
HARDY COLLINS	WILLIAM WATERS	BRYAN LAVENDER

Deeds registered with JAS REYNOLDS, registrar:
ARCHIBALD B. OWENS to RIGDEN HEWIT
WILLIAMS JONES to MERRITT JONES
JAMES BARNET to WILLIAMS JONES
ELIJAH FRANKS to JONAS JONES
JASON MEADOWS to THOMAS GILLET
OWEN B. COX, adm. to JONAS JONES
LEWIS KINSEY to JONAS JONES
WILLIAMS JONES to JONAS JONES
WILLIAM HUGGINS to EDWD GILBERT
WM HUGGINS, shff to SHADRACK ERWIN
JAMES HATCH to JAMES McDANIEL
WM HUGGINS, shff to S. BROWN & S. ISLER
HENERY H. NICHOLSON to WM HUGGINS
JONATHAN LEE & others to JOHN BENDER
JAMES HUGGINS to SOLOMON CARY
JOHN YOUNG to GEO POLLOCK

DECEMBER TERM, 1829
TRENTON, 14 DEC 1829

Justices: EMANUEL JARMAN, ROSCOE BARRUS and THOMAS GELLET, esquires
Shff: WILLIAM HUGGINS
Clerk: HARDY BRYAN

Jurors: JACOB GILES, foreman   JACOB HUGGINS
            JOHN STANLY SR   JOHN SHELFER

Jones Cty Court of Common Pleas Minutes 1829

LEMUEL BUSICK	JAMES SIMMONS
JOSEPH BROCK	WILLIAM WATERS
ELIJAH PARRY	RICHD R. FOSCUE
DANIEL STANLY	JOHN ROUSE
SILAS McDANIEL	

The jurors were charged by JAMES W. BRYAN, solicitor.
(Note: I read the name REAVIS R. FOSCUE in the list of freeholders drawn as jurors during the SEPTEMBER TERM to serve this term. However, RICHD R. FOSCUE is the name in the list of jurors for this term.)

FREDERICK FOSCUE, NATHAN FOSCUE, JAMES MARRET, OWEN ADAMS, and ROSCO BARRUS to divide among the heirs of ISAAC KORNEGAY, decd, a piece of land lying beside the main road leading to NEWBERN

JOSEPH WALLACE appointed guardian to APLES/ASLES WALLACE (minor); $100.00 bond; JAMES N. SMITH and CHARLES WHITTY, sureties

ENOCK FOY, JAMES FOY, JOHN YOUNG, ELIJAH SIMMONS, and JAMES N. SMITH to divide lands of STEPHEN WALLACE, decd, among his heirs

JOHN H. HAMMON, admr of JOSEPH PARSONS, decd, has leave to sell a Negro boy named SIMON and a girl named ELIZA in order to make a division among the heirs of said decd

HARDY SHELFER appointed admr of estate of LUKE SHELFER, decd; $1500.00 bond; BENJM HUGGINS and JOHN H. HAMMON, sureties

EMANUEL JARMAN, HENERY RHODES SR and ISAAC BROWN "to divide the Negroes of estate of CHRISTOPHER KINSEY, decd, so as to alott off to LEVI JONES his distributive share..."

RISDEN M. McDANIEL, JAMES REYNOLDS, and WILLIAM RHEM "to alott off to LANY SHELFER, widow of LUKE SHELFER, decd" one yr's provisions for herself and family

JOHN HEATH "orphan son of ABEJAH HEATH, decd" aged about 17 yrs to be bound to SAMUEL DILLAHUNT who should provide the boy with 6 mos schooling

THOMAS GILLET, ASA SMITH, DANIEL YATES, and WALTER HELLEN "to divide Negroes of estate of RICHARD ROBERTS, decd, so as to alott off to GEORGE ROBERTS and EDWD S. JONES (in right of his wife, SARAH) their equal shares agreeable to the will of said RICHARD, decd"

HARDY BRYAN, WILLIAM HUGGINS, and CHRISTOPHER A. HATCH to settle accounts of JAMES HARRISON, guardian to heirs of BRYAN MUMFORD, decd

JOSEPH PEARCE vs HARDY SHELFER, RICHD REYNOLDS, and LUKE SHELFER: Debt. The following jury:

EDWD DEBRULE	JOHN McDANIEL	FRANCIS ANDREWS
JOHN FORDHAM	JOSEPH SMALL	HENERY RHODES
BRYAN LAVENDER	LEMUEL H. SIMMONS	ISAIAH WOOD
JOHN STANLY	JOHN WOOD	SIMMONS HARRISON JR

find for the plaintiff. Judgment: $185.30.

HARDY BRYAN, admr of JAS GREEN vs ASA SMITH, JAS N. SMITH, and URBAN OLDFIELD: Debt. Same jury finds for plantiff. Judgment: $680.29.

President & directors of State Bank vs THOMAS B. IVES, GEO. A. THOMPSON, THOS D. BARBER, URBAN OLDFIELD, AGRIPPA ROBERTS, JAMES W. HOWARD, and MOSES JARVIS: Case. Same jury finds for plantiff. Judgment: $602.80.

GEORGE A. HOWARD to use of JAS. W. HOWARD vs RICHARD B. HATCH: Debt. Same jury finds for plaintiff. Judgment: $169.05.

ISAAC KOONCE vs JOSEPH RHEM and WM RHEM: Debt. Same jury finds for plaintiff. Judgment: $621.25.

Jones Cty Court of Common Pleas Minutes 1829

PETER CURTIS vs RICHD B. HATCH: Debt. Same jury finds for plaintiff. Judgment: $177.32.

BANK OF NEWBERN assignee of JNO. M. BRYAN vs THOS H. HILL, WM S. HITE, and JACOB GOODING: Debt. Same jury find for plaintiff. Judgment: $128.93.

JOHN JUSTICE, guardian, vs LOVICK G. MOORE and MOSES JARVIS: Same jury finds for plaintiff. Judgment: $239.39.

JONAS JONES may sell liquor by small measure

JOHN JONES may also sell liquor by small measure

GRAHAM? ANTWINE to admr estate of JOSHUAY? SAWYER, decd; $300.00 bond; JOHN FORDHAM and LEMUEL BUSICK, sureties

F.G. HERITAGE to oversee rd in room of WILLIAM ANTWINE, resigned

JONAS JONES to be guardian to BENJM RHODES (minor); $2,000.00 bond; JOHN JONES and JOSEPH KINSEY, sureties

EMANUEL JARMAN to admin. estate of JAMES RHODES, decd; $4,000.00 bond; JOSEPH KINSEY and JOHN JONES, sureties

BRYAN BALL arrested for not paying debts

LITTLEBERRY HUTSON arrested for not paying debts. BRYAN LEVANDER, JOHN FRANKLIN, AMOS FOSCUE, THOS SPEIGHT, B. WALLACE, and JNO. D. DAVIS were notified. HUTSON allowed to take oath for the relief of debtors.

THOMAS H. DAVIS, WILLIAM HUGGINS, and HARDY BRYAN "to divide Negroes of F.G. SIMMONS, decd, among the minor heirs, also...to divide the share of MARY ELIZABETH, decd, between her brother, F.G. SIMMONS, and her mother"

SAML DILLAHUNT, JOHN H. HAMMON, and HARDY PARRY "to divide Negroes of THOMAS STILLEY, decd, between THOMAS STILLEY (minor), his child, and DAVID GREEN and wife"

EMANUEL JARMAN, ISAAC BROWN, and JONAS JONES "to divide Negroes belonging to the estate of CHRISTOPHER KINSEY, decd, between LEVI JONES and wife and CHARITY and JAMES KINSEY..."

FURNIFOLD G. HERRITAGE to be guardian to THOMAS STILLEY (minor); $1500.00 bond; JAMES HARRISON and SAML DILLAHUNT, securities

HARDY BRYAN was reelected clerk (He being elected Dec 1825) by the votes of the following justices: DURANT HATCH JR., SIMON FOSCUE, THOMAS GILLET, ROSCO BARRUS, JAS ROBERTS, ASA SMITH, JAMES HARRISON, ABNER GREEN, NATHAN FOSCUE, JAMES N. SMITH, and EML JARMAN.

Division of Negroes of estate of JEREMIAH PARSONS, decd, returned

Settlement of OWEN ADAMS, guardian to the heirs of KADER KINSEY?, decd, returned

Settlement of WENDAL DAVIS, guardian to CHARITY, JAMES D., and SARAH KINSEY (minors), returned

Settlement of FURNIFOLD G. HERRITAGE, admr of THOS STILLEY, decd, returned

Settlement of estate of SUSAN READ, decd, approved

Settlement of estate of STEPHEN WALLACE, decd, approved

15 Dec 1829

Justices: ASA SMITH, THOMAS GILLET, and ABNER GREEN, esqs

Settlement of estate of THOS STILLEY, decd, with F.G. HERRITAGE, his admr, returned

Settlement of accounts of JOSEPH WALLACE, guardian to APLES WALLACE

Jones Cty Court of Common Pleas Minutes 1829

(minor) filed

Settlement of LEMUEL H. SIMMONS, guardian to AMOS and SOPHIA SIMMONS (minors) filed

Account of sale of estate of LEMUEL ANDREWS, decd, filed

State vs WILLIAM McDANIELS: assult and battery: Defendant pleads not guilty. Following jury found for defendant:

EDWD DEBRULE	JOHN McDANIEL	FRANCIS ANDREWS
JOHN FORDHAM	JOSEPH SMALL	BRYAN LAVANDER
NATHAN B. BUSH	JOSEPH RHEM	RISDEN McDANIEL JR
JOHN STANLY	WILLIAM RHEM	NEEDHAM SHELFER

State vs AGRIPPA ROBERTS: Affray (Note: According to Black an affray is a public fight.): Defendant pleads not guilty but same jury found defendant guilty and imposed a $.50 fine plus costs

State vs LIM/SIM MOORE: Affray: Defendant pleads not guilty. Same jury, except B. HUGGINS in place of JOSEPH RHEM, gave a ruling but it was not written in the book.

State vs SOLOMAN CARY: Petit Larceny: Defendant pleads not guilty. Same jury finds defendant not guilty and orders JOHN FORDHAM, the prosecutor, to pay costs. JOHN FORDHAM's place on the jury was taken by WILLIAM HELLEN.

THOS H. LEGGET to use of JAMES WORSTES? vs BENJM KOONCE: Case: The jury was:

EDWD DEBRULE	JOHN McDANIEL	FRANCIS ANDREWS
JOHN STANLY	RISDON McDANIEL	NATHAN B. BUSH
BRYAN LAVENDER	DAVID GREEN	JOSIAH ASKEY
WILLIAM McDANIEL	JOSEPH KINSEY	GEORGE KING

Plaintiff did not appear.

WILLIAM McDANIEL and wife vs T. SPEIGHT, guardian to heir of M. KOONCE: Case: The following jury:

EDWD DEBRULE	FRANCIS ANDREWS	JOHN STANLY
BRYAN LAVENDER	JOSIAH ASKEY	GEORGE KING
JOSEPH KINSEY	JOB SMITH	JOHN G. RAMSEY
JOHN FORDHAM	ROBERT GILBERT	JOSEPH SMALL

finds "for defendant and say there is no course of action."

JAMES N. SMITH and CHARLES WHITTY to be securities for JOSEPH WALLACE in place of those named yesterday for guardianship to APLS WALLACE; $100.00 bond

JAMES N. SMITH, SIMON FOSCUE, and HARDY BRYAN to settle accounts of FRANCIS DuVAL, guardian to the minor heirs of THOMAS MURPHY, decd

DURANT HATCH JR., WILLIAM HUGGINS, and WILLIAMS BROWN to settle accounts of HARDY BRYAN, admr of the estate of BENJM HARRISON, decd, and of CHRISTOPHER BRYAN, decd, and of JOSEPH GREEN, decd, and of JOSHUAY DAVIS, decd

JAMES McDANIEL, WILLIAM HUGGINS, WMS BROWN, and LEMUEL H. SIMMONS or either three of them to divide Negroes of estates of BENJM HARRISON and CHRISTOPHER BRYAN, decd, among their lawful heirs

An order of last term to settle estate of WM B. HATCH, decd, with C.A. HATCH, admr, be renewed

ISAAC BROWN, HENERY RHODES SEN., and EMANUEL JARMON to settle accounts of JONAS JONES, guardian to JOHN and LEVINA COX (minors)

Wednesday, 16 Dec 1829

Justices: SIMON FOSCUE, JAMES ROBERTS, and ASA SMITH, esquires

EMANUEL JARMON to admin. estate of THOMAS MURPHY (minor), decd; $4000.00 bond; THOMAS J. FONVIELLE and WILLIAMS BROWN, sureties

EML JARMON to admin. estate of THOMAS SHELFER, decd; $500.00 bond; JOHN FORDHAM and JOSEPH SMALL, sureties

WALTER HELLEN, JAMES N. SMITH, JAMES SIMMONS, BRYAN LAVENDER, and ELIJAH SIMMONS to "divide lands left to DENSEE LOVET and DAVID LOVET by the will of JNO. LOVET their father..."

JAMES N. SMITH to admin. estate of THOMAS LITTLETON, decd; $300.00 bond with ASA SMITH and JAMES ROBERTS

HARDY BRYAN to be paid $5.00 from county funds for a book to be used by the court

FREDERICK I. BECTON, JACOB GILES, JAMES B. SHINE, and DANIEL Y. SHINE to see if a bridge over CYPRESS CREEK on rd from SHINE's to NEWBERN is necessary and to estimate cost (Note: CYPRESS CREEK arises, according to Powell, in ONSLOW COUNTY and flows north into the TRENT RIVER. It is on the COLLET MAP of 1770, and a study of that map indicates it is just west of WHITE OAK SWAMP.)

Deeds registered with JAS REYNOLDS, registrar:
WM HUGGINS, shff, to MOSES JARVIS (3 deeds)
WILLIAMS BROWN and wife to MOSES JARVIS
URBAN OLDFIELD to JOB SMITH
LITTLEBERRY HUTSON to GEORGE W. HUTSON
SIMMONS HARRISON and A. HARGET to MICAJAH PETTAWAY
JAMES FRAZER to ASA SMITH
JOHN L. PARSONS to JOHN H. HAMMON
SIMMONS HARRISON to JOHN JONES
RICHARD REYNOLDS to PETER ANDREWS
RICHARD REYNOLDS to WILLIAMS ISLER
PETER ANDREWS and wife to JOHN HARRISON
JAMES ANDREWS and wife to SINGLA? READ
RISDEN M. McDANIEL to JAMES McDANIEL
JAMES RHODES to HENERY RHODES JR
JAMES MORGEN to HENERY RHODES SEN
WILLIAM RHODES JR to HENERY RHODES JR
GEORGE KING to JOSEPH KINSEY
URBAN OLDFIELD to JOB SMITH
Marriage contract of WILLIAM L. HILL/HILE and ANN GREEN
"deed from the BRYANS to G. HARRISON left for to be handed to register"

WILLIAM DUNKEN vs SIMON FOSCUE: Case: The following jury:

LAWSON MALLARD	JOSEPH SMALL	SILAS McDANIEL
JOHN HARRISON	BRADDOCK NOBLE	JACOB HUGGINS
JOHN MESSAU	HARDY SHELFER	JOHN MALLARD
JAMES McDANIEL	FRANCIS ANDREWS	JOHN McDANIEL

finds for plaintiff and assesses damage at $30.00 with interest from 12 Mar 1828 and costs. Defendant dissatisfied and appeals to superior court. Bond granted by court and waived by plaintiff's attorney "considering defendant sufficiently good."

Governor to use of DAVID GREEN vs BRADDOCK NOBLE and others: Debt: The jurors were:

EDWARD DEBRULE	LAWSON MALLARD	JOHN G. RAMSEY
JOSEPH SMALL	JOHN HARRISON	JACOB HUGGINS
JOHN MESSAU	HARDY SHELFER	JAMES McDANIEL

FRANCIS ANDREWS   JOHN McDANIEL   JOHN FORDHAM
Plaintiff did not come. Appeal granted, and bond waived.

Freeholders drawn as jurors for next county court:

JAMES WALLACE	BARTHALOMEW MEADOWS	JOHN H. HAMMON
EDWARD DEBRULE	OWEN ADAMS	DANIEL YATES
ASA EUBANKS	HUBBARD STANLY	GEORGE WILCOX
MARTIN F. BROCK	PETER HARGET	MICAJAH PETTAWAY
DANIEL STANLY	ENOCK FOY	SHADRACK MALLARD
HARDY HILL	JAMES TURNAGE	DANIEL WILLIAMSON
JAMES MADES	LEVI EUBANKS	WILLIAM GOODING
JAMES WILLIAMS	JOHN ROUSE	JOHN BALL

Freeholders drawn as jurors for next superior court during Spring term:

WILLIAM HELLEN	JOHN POLLOCK	WILLIAMS JONES
JOHN H. BECTON	LEWIS WILLIAMS	WILLIAM GOODING JR
JAMES B. SHINE	HARDY MUNDINE	WILLIAM H. MEADOWS
JAMES HARRISON	DANIEL SMITH	JOHN STANLY (TRENTON)
LOT EUBANKS	JOHN M. FRANKS	WILLIAMS ISLER
WILLIAM M. GILES	JAMES W. HOWARD	MILLINGTON MEADOWS
RIGDON HEWIT	PETER ANDREWS	COUNCIL GOODING
WILLIAM GILBERT	ZADOCK MEADOWS	JAMES MARRET
ISAAC BROWN	JOHN FRIEZE	SAML DILLAHUNT
SIMMONS ISLER	ROBERT GILBERT	SIMMONS HARRISON JR
JOHN JONES	JOHN WOOD	RISDEN M. McDANIEL
JOHN ANDREWS	FREDERICK FOSCUE	THOMAS McDANIEL

Jones Cty Court of Common Pleas Minutes 1830

MARCH TERM, 1830
8 MARCH 1830

Justices: ISAAC BROWN, OWEN B. COX, ROSCO BARRUS, esqs.
Sheriff: WILLIAM HUGGINS
Clerk: HARDY BRYAN

Grand jury: ENOCK FOY, foreman

PETER HARGET	JAMES MADES	MICAJAH PETTAWAY
EDWD DEBRULE	DANIEL STANLY	JOHN BOLE/BALL
ASA EUBANKS	HUBARD STANLY	DANIEL WILLIAMSON
JOHN BENDER	LEVI EUBANKS	BARTHALOMEW MEADOWS

EMANUAL JARMON, exec. of RISDON McDANIEL, decd, may sell Negro slave, LUCY, of his intestate at a credit of six mos. to pay debts

Letters of Admin. to be issued to EMANUEL JARMON on goods and chattles of ADENIJAH PARRY, decd; $1200.00 bond; ISAAC BROWN? and HARDY BRYAN, sureties

State vs LEVI MOORE: Jury:

WILLIAM GOODING	SHADERACK MALLARD	JONAS WILLIAMS
JOHN H. HAMMON	OWEN ADAMS	MARTIN F. BROCK
DANIEL YATES	GEORGE WILSON	JAMES McDANIEL
JOHN MISSAU	JOSEPH KINSEY	JOHN KOONCE

found defendant not guilty (No indication of the charges were given.)

State vs TOM LEWIS: Same jury finds defendant guilty and finds him $.50 plus costs; again no indications of charges

State vs JNO. KILLINGSWORTH: assult & battery: Defendant pleaded guilty; no jury; fined 5 (shillings?) and costs

State vs THOS J. FONVIELLE: assult & battery: defendant "submitts to court" and was fined $.50 and costs

President and directors of the State Bank vs GEORGE? C. HATCH and JOS. N. SMITH: Same jury as above finds for plaintiff and assess damage at $829.32 of which $711.62 is principal.

ROSCO BARRUS, guardian of? J.S.H. FRESHWATER vs THOS SPIEGHT and JOS. N. SMITH: Same jury finds for plaintiff and assesses damages at $113.00 as principal with interest from 11 Dec 1828 until paid and costs

FRANCIS GAMATE? to use of T.B. GOODWIN vs ANN B. WATSON: Debt. Same jury finds for plaintiff and assesses damage at $308.14 of which $262.17 is principal; jury also finds there was a payment of $39.00 on 11 Sept 1828

HENERY RHODES SEN, EML JARMON, and OWIN B. COX to settle accounts of JONAS JONES, guardian to JOHN and LEVINA COX (minors), heirs of JOHN B. COX, decd

DURANT HATCH JR, AMOS AMYET, and JOHN McDANIEL to settle accounts of JOHN ANDREWS, admr of estate of LEWIS HARRISON, decd

HARDY BRYAN, CHRISTOPHER A. HATCH, and WILLIAM HUGGINS to settle accounts of SIMMONS ISLER, guardian to heirs of BENJAMIN KOONCE, decd

Same men to also settle accounts of SIMMONS ISLER, guardian to heirs of JOSEPH BRYAN, decd

Same men to settle accounts of SIMMONS ISLER, guardian to RICHD KOONCE, minor

JOSHUA B. OLIVER to be paid $4.00 for his services as constable in attending the grand jury in Sept and Dec 1829

ASA SMITH, THOMAS GELLET, and CHRISTOPHER R. GREEN to settle accounts of ABRAHAM MITCHEL, guardian to WILLIAM FRANKS, minor

Jones Cty Court of Common Pleas Minutes 1830

ASA SMITH, JAMES ROBERTS, and MICAJAH MATTACKS to audit and settle accounts of ARCHIBALD B. OWENS, executor of SELBY H. WISE, decd

JOHN HATCH, an orphan aged between 10 and 15 years, bound to ISAIAH WOOD until he is 21 yrs and said WOOD to have him taught reading and writng for 12 months

FREDERICK I. BECTON, JOHN M. FRANKS, and HENERY RHODES SENR to settle accounts of MARY OLIVER, guardian to MARY OLIVER, minor

JAMES HARRISON, FREDERICK I. BECTON, and HENERY RHODES SEN to settle accounts of JACOB GILES, guardian to ABNER KILLIBREW, minor

STARKY IPOCK, orphan aged about 12 years, to be bound to LEMMOS MOORE to be an apprentice until he is 21 and MOORE is to give him 12 months schooling

FREDERICK I. BECTON, HENERY RHODES SEN and JACOB GILES to settle acounts of EMANUAL JARMON, admr to estate of HINCHEY KILLEBREW, decd

CHRISTOPHER A. HATCH, THOMAS W.C. WENGET, and HARDY BRYAN to settle accounts of JOHN HARRISON, admr of LEVI HARRISON, decd

CHRISTOPHER A. HATCH, esq., is a justice of the peace for JONES CO.

WHITFIELD TURNER, M. JONES, and LEVI JONES own land in JONES CO.

Account of sale of estate of LUKE SHELFER, decd, filed

Same for JOSHUA SAWYER

Division of Negroes of estate of CHRISTOPHER KINSEY, decd, returned

Division of lands of ISAAC KORNEGAY, decd, returned

Settlement of E. JARMON, guardian to heirs of S. WESTBROOK, filed

Settlement of E. JARMON, guardian to J. KOONCE, minor, filed

Settlement of TOBIAS KOONCE, guardian to ELIZABETH WRIGHT, minor, filed

Settlement of HARDY PARRY, guardian to heirs of SILAS PARRY, decd, filed

Settlement of JOSEPH LOFTON, guardian to heirs of F.G. SIMMONS, filed

Will of RICHARD KOONCE, decd, proved in open court by oath of EDWD M. GILBERT, witness; CALVIN KOONCE, executor [Gwynn abstracted this will (p. 430) which was written 25 Feb 1826. It names the deceased's sons, CALVIN and MICHAEL KOONCE; daughters, PENELOPE and ELIZABETH KOONCE; and wife, ELIZABETH. The exr. named was the son, CALVIN, and the witness was EDWARD M. GILBERT.]

LOVECK G. MOORE to oversee rd in place of JOHN OLIVER, resigned, from BEVER DAM near JAS MARRET'S to fork of rd at the 10 mile house [Note: According to Powell, BEAVERDAM BRANCH rises in southern JONES COUNTY and flows north into MILL RUN. BEVERDAM CREEK rises in eastern JONES COUNTY and flows south into the TRENT RIVER. These are distinguished from BEAVER CREEK which rises in northwest LENOIR COUNTY and flows east into the TRENT RIVER in JONES COUNTY. These are the only relevant references in Powell to anything close to BEVER DAM. MILL RUN, according to Powell, rises in central JONES COUNTY and flows northeast into the TRENT RIVER.

Also, according to Kammerer (Vol. 1, p. 81), JOHN OLIVER and PENELOPE B. LOFTIN were married 9 Jan 1830.]

JOHN HOUSTON to oversee rd from bridge near R.B. HATCH'S in room of THOMAS HALE, resigned

JAMES SIMMONS to oversee rd from TRENT BRIDGE to TOM SWAMP in room of ELIJAH LOVET, resigned

Tuesday, 9 March 1830

Present: ELIJAH SIMMONS, NATHAN FOSCUE, and CHRISTOPHER A. HATCH, esquires

CHRISTOPHER A. HATCH, ALFRED HARGET, and HARDY BRYAN to settle accounts of RISDEN M. McDANIEL, admr of MORRIS McDANIEL, decd

EML JARMON appointed guardian to heirs of EMANUEL KOONCE, decd, in place of B. NOBLE, resigned; $10,000 bond; HARDY BRYAN and PETER HARGET, securities

RESDEN M. McDANIEL, HARDY BRYAN, and HARDY PARRY to settle accounts of B. NOBLE, former guardian to heirs of EML KOONCE, decd, with EML JARMON, their present guardian

ALFRED HARGET, THOS W.C. WINGET, and HARDY BRYAN to settle accounts of CHRISTOPHER BROCK, guardian to his children

JOHN S. PARSONS to be constable in room of J.B. OLIVER, resigned, until JUNE TERM; JOHN H. HAMMON and RESDEN M. McDANIEL, sureties

DANIEL Y. SHINE and MICAJAH PETTAWAY to turn the road begining near SHINE'S house and ending near PETTEWAY'S

Governor to use of THOS M. LIN vs HARDY PARRY, admr of S.S. WIGGINS: finds for defendant; JAS W. BRYAN and W.C. STANLY, securities

Freeholders drawn for jury JUNE TERM:

SHADERACK ERWIN	BENJAMIN HUGGINS	ELIJAH KOONCE
RISDON McDANIEL (Capt.)	JAMES McDANIEL	DURANT RICHARDS
JOHN STILE	AMOS TAYLER	WILLIAM RHEM
ISAAC KORNEGAY	WILLIAM STANLY	THOS SMITH
NATHAN B. BUSH	TOBIAS KOONCE	JOHN C. WOOD
JOHN S. PARSONS	LEWIS FOSCUE	EDWIN BECTON
BRADDOCK NOBLE	JOSEPH RHEM	JAMES REYNOLDS
SAMUEL HILL	JOHN HEATH, SENR	WILLIAM ADAMS
ISAIAH WOOD	JACOB HUGGINS	JOHN MALLARD
LEWIS O. BRYAN	WILLIAM McDANIEL JR	JOSIAH ASKEY

Deeds ordered to be recorded by JAS REYNOLDS, registrar:
BENETER ALPHEN to WM STANLY
DURANT HATCH JR to CALVIN I/S MORRIS
WM HELLEN and B. LAVENDER to ALFRED HARGET
AMOS FOSCUE to DANIEL SMITH
SEARS BRYAN to HARDY BRYAN
FRANCIS DuVAL to DURANT HATCH JR
THEOFELUS ADEM to THOMAS CANNON
TOBIAS KOONCE to MARY POLLOCK
ROSCO BARRUS to ALFRED M. FRESHWATER
H. BRYAN, admr of JOS. GREEN, to SARAH GREEN
H. BRYAN, admr of JOS. GREEN, to WILLIAM S. MORRIS
JOHN G. RAMSEY to JOHN POLLOCK
SARAH GREEN to WILLIAM S. MORRIS
JAMES B. SHINE to DANIEL Y. SHINE
JOB SMITH to THOMAS HALE
SIMONS HARRISON to JOHN WOOD
WILLIAM FOSCUE to EDMOND HATCH JR
SOLOMON COLLINS to LEVI ARNOLD
JOHN POLLOCK to JOHN G. RAMSEY
DURANT HATCH JR to HARDY O. CONNER
JOHN WOOD to AARON WOOD
JOHN WILLIAMS to DANIEL Y. SHINE

Mortgage from ALFRED M. FRESHWATER to ROSCO BARRUS submitted to the registrar by JAMES W. HOWARD

JUNE TERM, 1830
TRENTON, Monday the 14th

Justices: ISAAC BROWN, SIMMONS ISLER, and CHRISTOPHER A. HATCH, esquires
Sheriff: WILLIAM HUGGINS
Clerk: HARDY BRYAN

Jurors:
JOHN HEATH, foreman
JAMES McDANIEL	WILLIAM RHEM	JOHN STILE/STILL
DURANT RICHARDS	JOSEPH RHEM	SAMUEL HILL
WILLIAM McDANIEL	ELIJAH KOONCE	JOHN MALLARD
TOBIAS KOONCE	ISAIAH WOOD	SHADRACH ERWIN

CHRISTOPHER A. HATCH, SIMMONS ISLER, and THOMAS W.C. WINGET to settle accounts of NATHAN B. BUSH, trustee of county

Clerk to enter piece of land in county books for JOHN HEATH, JR

ASA SMITH, JAMES ROBERTS, and ABRAHAM _____ (Name in fold of book) to settle accounts of ELIZABETH WHARTON, guardian of ALICE, FANNY, EDWARD, and JEREMIAH WARTON, minors

JAMES G. HERRITAGE, Esq., and JOHN H. BECTON to examine ELANY ANDREWS, wife of JOHN ANDREWS, on her consent to sale of land to JOHN HARRISON

JAMES HARRISON, JACOB GILES, and BRYAN SHINE to settle accounts of F.I. BECTON, admr of BRYAN BECTON, decd

Justices of the Peace in JONES COUNTY who are to take the tax list:
District 1: JAMES ROBERTS, Esq.
District 2: JAMES N. SMITH, Esq.
District 3: CHRIST A. HATCH, Esq.
District 4: DANIEL Y. SHINE, Esq.
District 5: OWEN B. COX, Esq.
District 6: SIMMONS ISLER, Esq.
District 7: NATHAN FOSCUE, Esq.

The following persons to see that elections are held:
District 1: THOS GILLET, esq., DANIEL YATES, and LEVI EUBANKS
District 2: ROSCO BARRUS, esq., ENOCH FOY, and DANL WILLIAMSON
District 3: C.A. HATCH, esq., LEML BUSECK, and N.B. BUSH
District 4: D.Y. SHINE, esq., F.I. BECTON, and JACOB GILES
District 5: EML JARMON, esq., HENERY RHODES, and J.S. KINSEY
District 6: JAS G. HERITAGE, esq., WM ISLER, and _____ HEATH

Patrols for one year:
District 1: WILLIAM BINUM, CHRISTOPHER R. GREEN, DAVID BALL, and HARDY MUNDINE
District 2: JOHN HOUSTON, JAMES W. HOWARD, THOMAS HALL, and JOSEPH WHITTY
District 3: CHRISTOPHER A. HATCH, JACOB HUGGINS, JOHN G. RAMSEY, and HARDY WATSON
District 4: JACOB GILES, BRYAN SHINE, MICAJAH PETTAWAY, and LEWIS KORNEGAY
District 5: EML JARMON, JOHN M. FRANKS, and LEWIS WILLIAMS
District 6: SIMMONS ISLER, WILLIAM COBB, RICHARD STANLY, NEEDHAM SHELFER
District 7: RISDEN M. McDANIEL, NATHAN FOSCUE, NATHAN B. BUSH, LEMUEL H. SIMMONS, and JOHN OLIVER
[Note: NATHAN B. BUSH served in the North Carolina House of Commons in 1830 (Wheeler).]

Settlements filed:
JACOB GILES, guardian to ABNER KILLEBREW
JOHN ANDREWS, admr of LEWIS HARRISON
SAML B. HEATH, guardian to his children
EML JARMON, admr of HINCHEY KILLEBREW
JONAS JONES, guardian to LEVINA and J. COX, minors
JOHN HARRISON, admr of LEVI HARRISON
C.A. HATCH, admr of WM B. HATCH, decd
SIMMONS ISLER, guardian to WINIFRED KOONCE, MARTHA KOONCE, and WILLIAM and JOSEPH BRYAN (minors)

Inventory of property of RICHD KOONCE, decd, filed

JNO MARSHEL vs HOUSTON ROBERTS: ROBERTS was arrested for non payment of debt to MARSHAL. THOS GILLET, ASA SMITH, and J.S.N. SMITH heard his plea and court allowed him to take the oath of insolvency and he is discharged

Freeholders to serve as jurors at next superior court:

JOSEPH KINSEY	JAMES ROBERTS	ASA SMITH
LEML H. SIMMONS	ELIJAH LOVET	THOS HARRISON
JOHN GODWIN	EML JARMON	ALFRED HARGET
DAVID GREEN	JOSEPH KAY	D.Y. SHINE
WM D. COBB	HENERY RHODES SR.	THOMAS H. HILL
BENJN COLLINS	WILLIAMS BROWN	SIMMONS HARRISON SR
NATHAN FOSCUE	ADAM ANDREWS	THOMAS POLLOCK
AARON WOOD	THOS J. FONVIELLE	MOSES ADAMS
JAMES N. SMITH	JOHN WOOD	MICHAEL KOONCE
JAMES S. MILLER	LEWIS W. KORNEGAY	ALFRED M. FRESHWATER
ELIAS LANE	LEWIS SMALL	ELIJAH SIMMONS
GEORGE ROBERTS	MARRET JONES	HARDY O. CONNER

Jurors to serve at county court SEPT TERM:

WILLIAM HARRISON	NEEDHAM SHELFER	CALVIN J. MORRIS
JOB SMITH	JOHN OLIVER	JOHN G. RAMSEY
LEVI JONES	JOHN HOUSTON	CHRISTOPHER R. GREEN
JOHN FROST	JOHN ADAMS	HENERY RHODES JR
BRYAN MISSAU	ZACHUS BROWN	JAMES MISSAU
CALVIN KOONCE	WILLIAM DUNKEN	JOHN S. KOONCE
LOVACK G. MOORE	JOHN SIMMONS	THOS W.C. WINGET
VINCENT ANDREWS	JAMES FOY	HARDY SHELFER
EDWD GILBERT	DANIEL ANDREWS	ELIJAH SMALL
STEWARD SCOTT	JONAS JONES JR	

WILLIAM P. FEROND vs GEORGE C. HATCH: Debt. Jury:

JAMES REYNOLDS	WILLIAM ADAMS	NATHAN B. BUSH
JACOB HUGGINS	BENJN HUGGINS	THOS SMITH
JOHN MISSAU	J.S.B. SHINE	RISDEN McDANIEL (esq.)
JNO STANLY	BRYAN LAVENDER	BENJN WALLACE

find for pltff; $455.89 judgment plus costs

Governor to use of STEPHEN B. FORBES vs ALFRED HARGET, WM BROWN, and ELIJAH KOONCE: Debt. Find for pltff and assess damages at $96.64

Since a quorum of county justices were present, viz:

ISSAC BROWN	SIMMONS ISLER	DURANT HATCH
OWEN B. COX	RESDEN McDANIEL	ROSCO BARRUS

Jones Cty Court of Common Pleas Minutes 1830

JAMES N. SMITH	ASA SMITH	CHRISTOPHER A. HATCH
NATHAN FOSCUE	DANIEL Y. SHINE	ALFRED HARGET
ABNER GREEN	JAMES ROBERTS	JAMES HARRISON

they proceeded to the election of county officers.

Constables elected:

District 1: DANIEL DICKSON with JAMES W. HOWARD, and JOSEPH WHITTY, sureties
District 2: JAS LARAQUE
District 3: WILLIAMS BROWN with EML JARMON and JOSEPH KINSEY, sureties
District 4: JOHN S. PARSONS with RISDON M. McDANIEL and JOHN H. HAMMOND, sureties
District 5: BRYAN WESTBROOK
District 6: HARDY H. SHELFER with RESDON M. McDANIEL and GEORGE WILCOX, sureties
District 7: JAMES H. FRESHWATER

    WILLIAM HUGGINS, sheriff, renewed his bond

    NATHAN B. BUSH, county trustee, renewed his bond

    JAMES REYNOLDS, registrar, renewed his bond

    Clerk of County Court renewed his bond

    JAMES FOY appointed _____ for TRENT BRIDGE; ROSCO BARRUS and JAMES N. HOWARD, sureties

    OWEN B. COX, DURANT HATCH, and NATHAN FOSCUE to state the accounts of the commissioners of the court house

    DANIEL Y. SHINE, ISAAC BROWN, and SIMMONS ISLER to district TRENT RIVER from TRENTON to TUCKHOE CREEK

    JAMES FOY to inspect turpentine for lower part of county

    DANIEL Y. SHINE, EML JARMON, and JACOB GILES to see that a bridge is built across CYPRESS CREEK

    The order from a former court term to settle accounts of RESDON M. McDANIEL, admr of MORRIS McDANIEL, decd, be reported next court

    NATHAN B. BUSH to be reappointed trustee

    HARDY O. CONNOR to oversee road in TRENTON in room of JOHN STILE, resigned

    JAMES H. FRESHWATER, LOVICK G. MOORE, THOS J. FONVILLE, and JOHN OLIVER to be patrols for one year in DISTRICT 7

    HARDY BRYAN, WILLIAM HUGGINS, and FRANCIS DuVAL to settle accounts of JOHN MORRIS, late guardian to LEWIS MORRIS, decd

    EML JARMON to admin. estate of LEWIS MORRIS, decd; SIMMONS HARRISON and JAMES HARRISON, sureties

    ASA SMITH, JAMES ROBERTS, and MICAIJAH MATTOCKS to settle accounts of ARCHIBALD B. OWENS, executor of SELBY H. WISE, decd

    CHRISTOPHER A. HATCH, esq., HARDY BRYAN, and WILLIAM HUGGINS to settle accounts of JAMES HARRISON, guardian to heirs of BRYAN MUMFORD, decd

    JOSEPH SMALL to oversee road from BLACK SWAMP to the county line in place of ELIAS FORDHAM

    ALFRED HARGET, esq., is justice of the peace

    THOMAS McDANIEL to oversee road from head of the straight reach to the INDIAN GROVE in place of GEORGE WILCOX, resigned

    NATHAN B. BUSH, NATHAN FOSCUE, and OWEN B. COX to sell the old courthouse

    JAMES N. SMITH to be removed as guardian of DAVID LOVICK with BRYAN LEVANDER named guardian in his place; $2500 bond; ROSCO BARRUS and BENJN WILCOX, securities

Jones Cty Court of Common Pleas Minutes 1830

WILLIAMS BROWN to be paid $12.00 for his duties as constable

WILLIAM HUGGINS, sheriff, to be paid $73.30 for services and $37.50 for upkeep of state prisoners, JOHN HOSPER/HARPER and THOMAS NORRIS

HARDY BRYAN, clerk, to be paid $40.00 for extra services

Inventory and sale of property of ADONIJAH PARRY, decd, filed by E. JARMON, admr

JAS REYNOLDS, guardian to NANCY McQUETTIN and WINIFERD ISLER, filed accounts

Year's provisions allowed ELIZABETH PARRY, widow of ADONIJAH PARRY

DANIEL DICKSON to be paid $20.60 by trustees

Division of lands of CHRISTOPHER KINSEY, decd, returned

Deeds registered:
JOHN GILDERSLEEVE to SIMMONS ISLER
ROBERT V. ORME to MARY KINCEY
N.B. and BENJN WESTBROOK to JAS and PATIENCE WESTBROOK
AMOS TAYLOR to ENOCH FOY
LEMUEL H. SIMMONS to JAMES MARRET
LUKE? KOONCE to PETER HARGET, power of attorney
WILLIAM and PENELOPE McDANIEL to JEREMIAH NOBLE
CALVIN J. MORRIS to ELIAS LANE
JOHN M. FRANK to ISAAC BROWN
MARY A. McDANIEL to ELIJAH SMALL
THOS and MATILDA POLLOCK to ELIJAH SMALL
WILLIAM MISSAW to BRYAN MISSAW
DURANT HATCH to WILLIAM MISSAW
JOHN POLLOCK to THOMAS POLLOCK
EML JARMON to RACHEL McDANIEL
EML JARMON to RACHEL McDANIEL
JAS S. MILLER and ELIZABETH OLIVER: mortgage contract
ELIAS LANE to R. REYNOLDS and JNO. COBB
GEORGE C. HATCH to JAMES HATCH

JAMES ACKROYD vs ASA SMITH, JAS N. SMITH, JAMES ROBERTS and ROBT V. ORME: *fieri facias* Also: JAMES ACKROYD vs GEO. OLDFIELD, ASA SMITH, JAS ROBERTS, JAS N. SMITH and ROBERT V. ORME: *fieri facias*. In both cases JAMES ACKROYD to collect $100 penalty from WILLIAM HUGGINS, sheriff, because he failed "*nesi*" his duty

SEPTEMBER, 1830
TRENTON, Monday the 13th

Justices: OWEN B. COX, NATHAN FOSCUE, and DANIEL SMITH, esqs
"Shffs. D:" WM BROWN
Clerk: HARDY BRYAN
Assistant Clerk: ROSCO BARRUS
County Solicitor: JAS W. BRYAN

Jurors: HENERY RHODES, JR., foreman
    ELIJAH SMALL   JONAS JONES JR   DANIEL ANDREWS
    EDWD GILBERT   BRYAN MISSAW   JOHN SIMMONS
    JOHN ADAMS   JOHN G. RAMSEY   STEWART SCOTT
    JOHN OLIVER   CHRISTOPHER R. GREEN

Freeholders of the original <u>vinera</u> sworn and employed: (Note: <u>Vinera</u> is possibly <u>venire</u> which, according to Black, is a summons for jurors to come to court.)

JOHN FROST	JOHN S. KOONCE	WM HARRISON
JAMES FOY	WILLIAM DUNKIN	JOHN HOUSTON
ZACHEUS BROWN	WINSTON ANDREWS	HARDY H. SHELFER
JAMES MISSAW	CALVIN KOONCE	NEEDHAM SHELFER

JAMES H. FRESHWATER, a constable elected JUNE TERM had his bond with JAS N. SMITH and ROSCO BARRUS, sureties, approved by justices: OWEN B. COX, CHRIST A. HATCH, and THOS GILLET

EMANUEL JARMON, JOHN M. FRANKS, and HENERY RHODES SR. to settle accounts of JOHN FORDHAM, admr of will of PHYLPENEA KOONCE, decd

BENJAMIN CLARK, aged 10 years, to be bound to DANIEL YATES until 21 years old as an apprentice

LOT EUBANKS to oversee rd from crossroads on WHITE OAK to BLACK CORREL in middle of the POCOSIN in place of WILLIAM DICKSON, resigned (Note: Powell does not list BLACK CORREL. Perhaps this should be BLACK SORREL in reference to a tree used as a landmark.)

AMOS MOORE, an orphan, to be bound to JAMES H. FRESHWATER until 21 years of age

JAMES HARRISON, JAMES B. SHINE, and JACOB GILES to settle accounts of FREDERICK I. BECTON, admr of BRYAN BECTON, decd

JAMES ROBERTS, ASA SMITH, and ABRAHAM MITCHELL (Note: this last surname was written to fit on the edge of the page, so this is a best guess.) to settle accounts of ELIZABETH WHARTON, guardian to ALICE, FANNY, EDWARD, and JEREMIAH WHARTON, minors

HARDY BRYAN, WM HUGGINS, and CHRISTOPHER A. HATCH to settle accounts of JAMES HARRISON, guardian to JAMES and PENELOPE MUNFORD, minors

FREDERICK I. BECTON, DANIEL Y. SHINE, and RESDON M. McDANIEL to divide Negroes of JAMES GREEN, decd, among the heirs

JOHN STANLY to oversee rd from bridge at TRENTON to BEVER DAM BRANCH and from fork of road at R.M. McDANIEL's up to MUSSELSHELL BRANCH on road leading to KINSTON

HARDY BRYAN, CHRISTOPHER A. HATCH, and JAMES R. CONNER to settle accounts of SUSAN FOY, guardian to WM FOY, minor

Since a majority of justices were present, viz.:

DURANT HATCH JR.	ALFRED HARGET	CHRISTOPHER A. HATCH
ABNER GREEN	OWEN B. COX	NATHAN FOSCUE
DANIEL SMITH	DANIEL Y. SHINE	ELIJAH SIMMONS
THOMAS GILLET	RISDON M. McDANIEL	ISAAC BROWN and

ROSCO BARRUS, WILLIAM HUGGINS, esq., sheriff elect, was sworn in; his bond with ISAAC BROWN, EML JARMON, JAMES McDANIEL, and LEMUEL H. SIMMONS, sureties, was approved

An additional $400 approved to help finish the new courthouse

ELIAS LANE approved to retail liquor by the small measure

Rules of the court for better government by the patrols:
1) No slave may have any kind of stock (horses, cattle, etc.); such stock to be seized and sold with the profit to the poor
2) No slave shall have any unlawful weapon (15 lashes is penalty)

3) Slaves may not hold public worship except to bury their dead (15 lashes)
4) Slave owners must give patrols the names of their slaves above 12 years old
5) Slaves must travel with permit from masters
6) Slaves found off master's premises without a permit to receive 15 lashes
7) No slave from another county with a permit may be hired in this county
8) Patrols are not exempted from taxes or road work
9) Any patrol failing to carry out the enforcement of the above shall pay $10.00 to the informant and $10.00 to the use of the poor
10) The clerk of courts is to furnish the patrols with the above list

The following are patrols:
District 1 (WHITE OAK): GEORGE ROBERTS, DANIEL DICKSON, CHRISTOPHER R. GREEN, G.S. BENDER, DANIEL YATES, and EDMOND WHARTON
District 2 (TRENTON BRIDGE): JOSEPH WHITTY, JAMES W. HOWARD, THOMAS HALL, DANIEL WILLIAMSON, EDMD HATCH, and JOSEPH FOY
District 3 (TRENTON): JOHN G. RAMSEY, JAMES McDANIEL, CHRIST A. HATCH, HARDY WATSON, SAMUEL HILL, and ADAM ANDREWS
District 4 (CYPRESS CREEK): DANIEL Y. SHINE, MICAJAH PETTAWAY, DAVID GREEN, JACOB GILES, JAMES B. SHINE, and BENJAMIN BROCK
District 5 (TUCKEHOE): EML JARMON, OWEN B. COX, JOHN M. FRANKS, JOSEPH KINCEY, LEVI JONES, and JONAS WILLIAMS
District 6 (BEVER CREEK): SIMMONS ISLER, JOSEPH RHEM, NEEDHAM SHELFER, FREDERICK WISE, JOHN SIMMONS, and ABRAHAM SIMMONS
District 7 (McDANIEL's): ALFRED HARGET, JOHN OLIVER, LOVICK G. MOORE, RISDEN M. McDANIEL, NATHAN FOSCUE, and THOS J. FONVIELLE

Those men working the roads should also clean the river subject to the overseers of the roads
Districts of the river from TRENTON to mouth of TUCKEHOE:
Dist. 1: from TRENTON to mouth of JOSHWAYS RESOLUTION (Note: Although Powell does not list a Joshway's Resolution, he does list RESOLUTION BRANCH which rises in northern JONES COUNTY and flows southerly into TRENT RIVER.)
Dist. 2: from thence to mouth of BEVER CREEK
Dist. 3: from thence to mouth of BIG CHINQUAPIN
Dist. 4: from thence to mouth of LITTLE CHINQUAPIN
Dist. 5: from thence to mouth of CYPRESS CREEK
Dist. 6: from thence to mouth of RUDY BRANCH
Dist. 7: from thence to mouth of TUCKAHOE
(Note: Powell does not list a RUDY BRANCH. Powell does list CHINQUAPIN BRANCH which he describes as rising in western JONES COUNTY and flows 4 1/2 miles east to flow into the TRENT RIVER; it is also known as BIG CHINQUAPIN BRANCH. LITTLE CHINQUAPIN BRANCH rises in western JONES COUNTY and flows about 3 1/2 miles east into the TRENT RIVER. Also note that these districts do not seem to coorespond to the usual districts, and these districts seem to cover only the part of the county west of TRENTON. This may be explained by the next entry which indicates that these river districts were all within the usual DISTRICT 1.)

Hands set out to work the river should be divided as follows:
District 1 (River districts as above): ELIJAH SMALL's and LEMUEL BUSECK's
District 2: all hands

Jones Cty Court of Common Pleas Minutes 1830

District 3: all hands
District 4: all hands
District 5: all hand
District 6: from BLACK SWAMP to JOSEPH BROCK's place; all hands including those on BROCK's place
District 7: all hands

Overseers of the above divisions:
1: WMS BROWN   5: D.Y. SHINE
2: LEML ISLER   6: J.B. SHINE
3: WRIGHT STANLY   7: ISAAC BROWN
4: ELIJAH PARRY

Tax of ten cents on all black poles to be levied and collected to pay the patrols

BRYAN JONES to be guardian to ELIZA M. WRIGHT in room of TOBIAS KOONCE, resigned; $200.00 bond; JAMES MARRET and HARDY BRYAN, sureties

HARDY BRYAN, JACOB HUGGINS, and FRANCIS DuVAL to settle accounts between TOBIAS KOONCE, former guardian to ELIZA M. WRIGHT, and BRYAN JONES, present guardian

DURANT HATCH, admr of JOHN MORRIS, decd, shall sell Negroes of his intestate on credit of 6 mos to satisfy a debt from JOHN MORRIS to LEWIS MORRIS, decd

OWEN B. COX, ENOCH FOY, and NATHAN B. BUSH to be a board of appeals for JONES CO. to set Monday next to hear complaints of people on their land assessments

Entry made for JOSEPH KINSEY for 15 acres of land adjoining lands of EML JARMON and said JOSEPH KINSEY's lands on south side of TRENT RIVER

Entry made for ISAAC BROWN for 5 acres adjoining lands entered by JOSEPH KINSEY, EML JARMON and others on so. side TRENT RIVER

Will of JAMES HUGGINS, decd, proved by oath of HARDY WATSON, one of the witnesses; BENJN HUGGINS, executor [The will is abstracted in Gwynn, p. 420. It was written 27 Jun 1830; he left everything to his wife (unnamed) and, after her death, to his five children: JACOB, SUSANNAH, JAMES, NANCY and HARDY HUGGINS. The exr was BENJAMIN HUGGINS, and the witnesses were HARDY BRYAN and HARDY WATSON.]

Tuesday, 14 Sept 1830

Justices: OWEN B. COX, NATHAN FOSCUE, CHRISTOPHER A. HATCH, Esquires
Shff: WMS BROWN (pro term)
Clerk: HARDY BRYAN

CHRISTOPHER A. HATCH, HARDY PARRY, and HARDY BRYAN to settle accounts of EML JARMON, exec of both RISDEN McDANIEL, decd, and DURANT McDANIEL, decd

FREDERICK I. BECTON to be permitted to draw from the clerk's office the papers pertaining to a judgment which he had against JOHN B. HARGET with JAS HUGGINS, surety; said execution was levied on lands of said HARGET, returned to court and court not satisfied

HENERY RHODES JR. to oversee road in place of LEVI JONES from RATTLESNAKE BRANCH to DUPLIN CO. line at crossroads from ONSLOW to LENOIR CO.

Jones Cty Court of Common Pleas Minutes 1830

line
County attorney should purchase up to date law reports
Settlement of JAS MARRET, guardian to BENJN and JAS SIMMONS, minors, filed
Account of sales and inventory of estate of JNO B. HARGET and ZELPY HARGET filed by A. HARGET
MOSES JARVIS vs GEORGE C. HATCH: Case. Pltff failed to appear
JAMES E. BETNER vs JAMES B. SHINE: Debt. The following jury:

JOHN FROST	JOHN I. KOONCE	WILLIAM HARRISON
JAMES FOY	WILLIAM DUNKEN	JOHN HOUSTON
ZACHEUS BROWN	WINSON ANDREWS	HARDY H. SHELFER
JAMES MISSAW	CALVIN KOONCE	NEEDHAM SHELFER

find for pltff. Dept of $167.63 with interest of $15.40 for a judgment of $183.03 plus costs

Governor to use of JACOB GOODING vs A. HARGET, WMS BROWN, and E. KOONCE: Debt. Same jury as above, except JOB SMITH replaced JAMES FOY, found for pltff. $31.30 judgment. Pltff granted an appeal

Pres. and directors of State Bank vs JAMES N. SMITH: Case. Same jury as above except, HARDY PARRY in place of JOB SMITH, finds for defendant. Pltff appeals

HARDY BRYAN, WM HUGGINS, and RISDEN M. McDANIEL to settle accounts of WILLIAM S. BLACKLEDGE, admr of LEML HATCH, decd, and (as admr de bonas Nov) of MARY ANN HATCH, decd

FRANCIS DuVAL, WILLIAM HUGGINS, and HARDY BRYAN to settle accounts of DURANT HATCH JR., admr of JOHN MORRIS, decd

ELIZABETH WHARTEN must appear next term to reassess her guardian bond as guardian to her children

CHRISTOPHER A. HATCH, WILLIAM HOLLAND, and F. DuVAL to settle accounts of RISDEN M. McDANIEL, admr of McCULLEN POLLOCK, decd

CHRISTOPHER A. HATCH, WILLIAMS BROWN, and NATHAN B. BUSH to settle accounts of RESDEN M. McDANIEL, admr of MORRIS McDANIEL, decd

JOHN JONES to take over combined road companies adjoining CYPRESS CREEK

Freeholders drawn as jurors for next term:

WILLIAMS JONES	WILLIAM M. GILES	WILLIAM McDANIEL
ROBERT GILBERT	WILLIAM MESSOR	DANIEL STANLY, SR
STEWART SCOTT	THOMAS SMITH	HARDY COLLINS
JOHN STILL	FREDERICK I. BECTON	SHADK MALLARD
JACOB HUGGINS JR	LEML BUSICK	JOHN FRIEZE
BRYAN MESSOR	JOHN FORDHAM	EDWIN BECTON
HUBARD STANLY	MARTIN F. BROCK	ELIJAH KOONCE
PETER ANDREWS	JOSEPH SMALL	WILLIAM BROWN
BENJAMIN COLLINS	JOHN JONES	WILLIAM GOODING
THOMAS McDANIEL	MICAJAH PETERWAY	JAMES GODWIN

JAMES AYROYD vs GEORGE OLDFIELD, ASA SMITH, JAMES ROBERTS, JAS N. SMITH and ROBT V. ORME: fieri facias. WILLIAM HUGGINS, shff, fined $100.00 for failure of duty in this case. (Note: a fieri facias is also called fi fa and is a writ commanding the sheriff to levy, make, or raise money.)

Deeds and bills of sale registred with JAS REYNOLDS, registrar:
JOHN FROST to IVEY ANDREWS
WILLIAM HUGGINS, shff, to THOMAS GILLET

Jones Cty Court of Common Pleas Minutes 1830

WILLIAM HUGGINS, shff, to THOMAS McDANIEL
RICHARD REYNOLDS to PETER ANDREWS
JAMES N. SMITH to DANIEL SMITH
JAMES N. SMITH to AMOS HEATH
BRADDOCK NOBLE, const, to AMOS HEATH
JONAS WILLIAMS to LEWIS WILLIAMS
ALFRED HARGET to WM BROWN, R.M. McDANIEL and JAS REYNOLDS
ditto
WINSTON ANDREWS to JACKSON ASKEY, mortgage

Heirs of LEVI HARRISON to JOHN HARRISON, deed with (?) and private examination
Clerk's accounts sworn to before N. FOSCUE, justice
CHRISTOPHER A. HATCH, WILLIAM HUGGINS, and HARDY BRYAN to settle accounts of RICHARD REYNOLDS, guardian to heirs of JAMES GREEN, decd
More deeds delivered for registration:
Power of attorney and deed from STEPHEN MILLER to SARAH MILLER
WM HUGGINS, shff, to JAS McDANIEL
EML JARMON to JAMES McDANIEL
WM HUGGINS, shff, and R.B. HATCH to DAVID GREEN
Election returns for sheriff:
WM HUGGINS   349
JOHN H. HAMMOND   37
312 majority for HUGGINS

ELIZABETH KOONCE, widow of the late RICHARD KOONCE, filed petition for dower in the lands of her late husband. Court ordered same to be issued
CALVIN KOONCE, MICHAEL KOONCE, and FURNIFOLD G. HERRITAGE and PENELOPE, his wife, filed their petition for partition in the lands of RICHD KOONCE, decd, "they being heirs at law of said RICHD KOONCE." Court appoined HARDY PARRY, ELIJAH PARRY, SAMUEL DILLAHUNT, JOHN HARTY SEN., and EDWD GILBERT to handle the partition
HENERY RHODES filed his petition for partition of the land of JONES RHODES, decd, among the heirs. OWEN B. COX appointed special guardian to JACOB RHODES (minor) "to defend for him and accept the service of process" and the other heirs should be prepared to defend next term
The heirs at law of MICAJAH ADAMS, decd, viz., JOHN ADAMS, WILLIAM ADAMS, MOSES ADAMS, JAMES ADAMS, MICAJAH ADAMS, OWEN ADAMS, and BRADDOCK JARMON and wife, filed their petition for partition in the real estate of "their father" to be set off to them individually. Petition granted. ISAAC BROWN, EMANUEL JARMON, HENERY RHODES SEN., JOHN M. FRANKS, and JACOB GILES to effect said partition
Petition of JOHN MALLARD to alter names of two children of ANN McKINEY, viz., FRANCES ANN McKINEY to be changed to FRANCES ANN MALLARD and WILLIAM HARDY McKINEY to WILLIAM HARDY MALLARD, was approved. The said children of ANN McKINEY shall enjoy all of the privileges they would have had had they been born in lawful wedlock and shall be considered as legitimate and lawful children who may inherit and transmit property according to the act of assembly of 1829

Jones Cty Court of Common Pleas Minutes 1830

DECEMBER TERM, 1830
TRENTON, Monday the 18th

Note: On 11 Nov 1830 ABNER GREEN reported the results of his taking of the census of JONES COUNTY to the U.S. Department of Census. His total was 5,608 persons but the U.S. figured 5,628 with 3,095 of those being slaves. I have heavily annotated the December Term with census results in order to obtain a perspective on the men who served in public office, who were on the juries, and who came to court.

Justices: NATHAN FOSCUE, JAMES ROBERTS, and THOMAS GILLET, esquires
Sheriff: WILLIAM HUGGINS
Clerk: HARDY BRYAN

[Note: NATHAN FOSCUE was a young man between 30 and 40 years old. Although a slave owner (with eight), his holdings were not large. JAMES ROBERTS was about the same age as FOSCUE, but he owned 42 slaves. THOMAS GILLET was older. He was between 50 and 60 years old, and he owned 17 slaves. WILLIAM HUGGINS was 30 to 40 years old and owned 11 slaves. HARDY BRYAN was 40 to 50 years old and owned 19 slaves. These were rather young men of material substance.]

The following freeholders were drawn as jurors:
MARTIN F. BROCK, foreman

BRYAN MESSOR	FREDERICK I. BECTON	WILLIAM MESSOR
JOSEPH SMALL	LEMUEL BUSICK	MICAJAH PETEWAY
JOHN FORDHAM	JACOB HUGGINS	JOHN STILL
WILLIAM M. GILES	HUBBARD STANLY	JOHN JONES
WILLIAM GOODING		

[Note: MARTIN F. BROCK was 40 to 50 years old and owned 20 slaves. BRYAN MESSOR was not a head of household in 1830 in Jones County. JOSEPH SMALL was just 20 to 30 years old and owned three slaves. JOHN FORDHAM was 50 to 60 years old and owned nine slaves. WILLIAM M. GILES was 30 to 40 years old and owned seven slaves. WILLIAM GOODING was 30 to 40 years old and owned one slave. FREDERICK I. BECTON was 40 to 50 years old and owned 20 slaves. LEMUEL BUSICK was 30 to 40 years old and owned four slaves. JACOB HUGGINS was 30 to 40 years old and owned no slaves. HUBBARD STANLY was 30 to 40 years old and owned four slaves. WILLIAM MESSOR was 50 to 60 years old and owned one slave. MICAJAH PETEWAY was 20 to 30 years old and owned 12 slaves. JOHN STILL was 40 to 50 years old and owned four slaves. JOHN JONES was 30 to 40 years old and owned 15 slaves.]

HARDY BRYAN, CHRISTOPHER A. HATCH, and WILLIAMS BROWN to settle accounts of SIDNEY JARMAN, admr of HARDY JARMON, decd
DANIEL WILLIAMSON to oversee road from MILL CREEK BRIDGE in room of JAMES FOY, resigned
ASA SMITH, JAMES ROBERTS, and THOMAS GILLET to divide the Negroes of EDMD WHARTON, decd, among heirs of said decd agreeable to partition petition
JONAS JONES may sell liquor by small measure in his house for one year
JOHN JONES may do same
[Note: According to the census, CHRISTOPHER H. HATCH was 20 to 30 years old and owned 20 slaves. WILLIAMS BROWN was 30 to 40 years old and owned 11 slaves. SIDNEY JARMAN was not head of a household in Jones County. DANIEL

Jones Cty Court of Common Pleas Minutes 1830

WILLIAMSON was 30 to 40 years old and owned 21 slaves. JAMES FOY was not head of a household in Jones County. ASA SMITH was 50 to 60 years old and owned 19 slaves. JONAS JONES could have been either the father or the son. JONAS SR. was 50 to 60 years old and owned 13 slaves. JONAS JR was 20 to 30 years old and owned eight slaves.]

    ENOCK FOY, ROSCO BARRUS, DANIEL YATES, and LEVI EUBANKS to divide Negroes of JOSEPH KEY, decd, among heirs of CALIB SMITH, decd, agreeable to wife of said KEY
    JONAS JONES, guardian to JACOB RHODES, minor, entered bond of $500.00; JOHN JONES and EML JARMON, sureties
    JAMES HARRISON, guardian to heirs of B. MUMFORD, to renew his bond of $1200.00; FREDK I. BECTON, DANIEL Y. SHINE, and JAS B. SHINE, sureties
    DANIEL YATES, guardian to ELISHA STAFFORD, minor, to renew his bond of $500.00; JAMES ROBERTS and BRYAN LAVENDER, sureties
    JAMES B. SHINE, guardian to heirs of DANIEL MASHBURN, to renew his bond of $100.00 with DANIEL Y. SHINE and FREDERICK I. BECTON, sureties
    [Note: ENOCK FOY was 50 to 60 years old and owned 53 slaves. ROSCO BARRUS was 20 to 30 years old and owned seven slaves. DANIEL YATES was 40 to 50 years old and owned two slaves. LEVI EUBANKS was 40 to 50 years old and owned nine slaves. EMANUEL JARMON was 40 to 50 years old and owned 22 slaves. JAMES HARRISON (SR in the census) was 40 to 50 years old and owned 9 slaves. DANIEL Y. SHINE was 20 to 30 years old and owned 24 slaves. JAMES B. SHINE was also 20 to 30 years old and owned 30 slaves. BRYAN LAVENDER was 30 to 40 years old and owned 11 slaves.]

    OWEN ADAMS, guardian to heirs of KADER NIGHT, decd, to renew bond of $1,000.00; JAMES N. SMITH and BRYAN LAVENDER, sureties
    HARDY PARRY, guardian to heirs of SILAS PARRY, to renew his bond of $10,000 with ELIJAH PARRY and WM RHEM, sureties
    JOHN H. HAMMOND, guardian to heirs of JEREMIAH PARSONS, decd, to renew his bond of $5,000 with HARDY PARRY and EML JARMON, sureties
    JOHN H. HAMMOND, guardian to FREDK BRYAN, minor, to renew his bond of $1,000 with JOHN JONES and FREDERICK I. BECTON, sureties
    HEPSABETH BRAY, guardian to heirs of WILLIAM BRAY, decd, to renew her bond of $2,000 with DANIEL YATES and GEORGE ROBERTS, sureties
    SARAH OLDFIELD, guardian to heirs of RICHD OLDFIELD, decd, to renew her bond of $12,000 with GEORGE ROBERTS and JAMES N. SMITH, sureties
    [Note: OWEN ADAMS was 40 to 50 years old and owned four slaves. JAMES N. SMITH was 20 to 30 years old and owned nine slaves. HARDY PARRY was 50 to 60 years old and owned 32 slaves. ELIJAH PARRY was also 50 to 60 years old and owned 29 slaves. WILLIAM RHEM was 40 to 50 years old and owned 19 slaves. JOHN H. HAMMOND was 30 to 40 years old and owned 10 slaves. I found no BRAY or GEORGE ROBERTS in the 1830 census for JONES COUNTY. SARAH OLDFIELD was 40 to 50 years old and owned 18 slaves.]

    THOMAS GILLETT, guardian to CATHARINE HAY, minor, to renew his bond of $1,000 with JAMES ROBERTS, security
    WINDEL DAVIS, guardian to JAMES and CHARITY KINSEY, minors, to renew his bond of $10,000 with EMANUEL JARMON and JOHN M. FRANKS, sureties
    LEMUEL H. SIMMONS, guardian to AMOS and SOPHIA SIMMONS, minors, to renew his bond of $10,000 with JAMES McDANIEL and WILLIAM HUGGINS, sureties

Jones Cty Court of Common Pleas Minutes 1830

SIMMONS ISLER, guardian to MARTHY and WINIFRED KOONCE, minors, to renew his bond of $5,000 with RICHD REYNOLDS and WILLIAMS ISLER, sureties

SIMMONS ISLER, guardian to JOSEPH and WILLIAM BRYAN, minors, to renew his bond of $3,000 with WILLIAMS ISLER and RICHD REYNOLDS, sureties

[Note: I found no WINDEL DAVIS in the census. JOHN M. FRANKS was 20 to 30 years old and owned 14 slaves. LEMUEL H. SIMMONS was 30 to 40 years old and owned 52 slaves. JAMES McDANIEL was 40 to 50 years old and owned 21 slaves. SIMMONS ISLER was 30 to 40 years old and owned 19 slaves. RICHARD REYNOLDS was 70 to 80 years old and owned 19 slaves, but it is likely that the RICHD REYNOLDS attending court was a younger man not listed as head of household in the census. WILLIAMS ISLER was 50 to 60 years old and owned 39 slaves.]

RICHARD REYNOLDS, guardian to heirs of JAMES GREEN, decd, to renew his bond of $10,000 with SIMMONS ISLER and WILLIAMS ISLER, sureties

Inventory and sale of property of JAMES HUGGINS, decd, filed by executor

Division of lands of RICHD KOONCE, decd, filed

LEMUEL H. SIMMONS, guardian to AMOS and SOPHIA SIMMONS rendered his accounts and processed them

Settlement of estate of PHILPENEA KOONCE, decd, filed

State vs JOHN CONWAY and RE(CORON?) SANDERSON: Affray: defendants found guilty and fined $10 for CONWAY and $8? for SANDERSON

State vs SIMMONS COLLINS and LEWIS ALLAGOOD: Affray: defendant COLLINS found guilty but ALLAGOOD found not guilty. COLLINS fined $5.00 plus costs

[Note: JOHN CONWAY was 20 to 30 years old and owned no slaves. I found no SANDERSON in the census. SIMMONS COLLINS was 20 to 30 years old and owned five slaves. LEWIS ELLIGOOD was enumerated in the 1830 federal census for JONES COUNTY. He was 20-30 years old with three people in his household and no slaves.]

Tuesday, 19 Dec 1830

NATHAN FOSCUE, CHRISTOPHER A. HATCH, and DANIEL SMITH, esquires, justices

Settlement of JNO MORRIS as admr of LEWIS MORRIS, decd, returned and filed

Settlement of FREDK I. BECTON, admr of BRYAN BECTON, filed

Settlement of ROSCO BARRUS, guardian to W. FRANK, filed

JESSE ELLIT to be bound to JOHN G. RAMSEY and said RAMSEY to comply with the usual indentures

ISAAC BROWN, HENERY RHODES SENR and JOHN M. FRANKS to divide and allot off to WILLIAM COX his share of the Negroes of the estate of JOHN B. COX, decd

[Note: DANIEL SMITH Jr was 50 to 60 years old and owned no slaves. DANIEL SMITH SR, also 50 to 60 years old, owned 38 slaves. Which one was the J.P.? JNO MORRIS was not a head of household. JOHN RAMSEY was 30 to 40 years old and owned ten slaves. ISAAC BROWN was 50 to 60 years old and owned 18 slaves. HENRY RHODES SR was 30 to 40 years old and owned 9 slaves. WILLIAM COX was not listed as a head of household.]

CHRISTOPHER A. HATCH, LEMUEL H. SIMMONS, and HARDY BRYAN to divide and set off to WILLIAM DuVAL and ELIZA, his wife, their "equal portion" of Negroes of THOMAS MURPHY, decd

Account of WINDAL DAVIS, guardian to JAMES D. and CHARITY KINSEY, minors, filed

ALFRED M. FRESHWATER to oversee rd from TRENT BRIDGE to DEEP GULLY BRIDGE in room of THOS J. FONSVILLE, resigned

ANN REBECAH BRYAN to be guardian to "her son" WILLIAM HENERY BRYAN, minor; $2000 bond with WALTER P. ALLEN and HARDY O. CONNER, sureties

HARDY BRYAN appointed guardian to DARCUS FOSCUE; $3000 bond with NATHAN FOSCUE and CHRISTOPHER A. HATCH, sureties

WALTER P. ALLEN appointed guardian to WILLIAM FOY, minor; $3000 bond with HARDY O. CONNER and RACHEL CONNER, sureties

[Note: WILLIAM DuVAL was 20 to 30 years old and owned no slaves. ALFRED M. FRESHWATER was not listed as a head of household. THOMAS "FONVEAL" was 20 to 30 years old and owned eight slaves. ANN REBECAH BRYAN may have been the REBECCAH BRYAN who was listed as head of the household in the 1830 census. She was 30 to 40 years old and owned two slaves. Neither WALTER P. ALLEN nor HARDY O. CONNER was listed as a head of household. However, RACHEL CONNER was head of household. She was 50 to 60 years old and owned 11 slaves. This is a rare instance of a woman acting as security for a bond.]

JOHN O. SIMMONS to be admr of estate of PENELOPE SIMMONS, decd; $1000 bond with WALTER P. ALLEN and JACOB HUGGINS, JR., sureties

AMOS AMYET, guardian to SUSAN ANDREWS, minor, to renew bond of $200 with JOHN G. RAMSEY and ADAM ANDREWS, sureties

RISDEN M. McDANIEL, FRANCES DuVAL, and CHRISTOPHER A. HATCH to settle accounts of AMOS AMYET, guardian to SUSAN ANDREWS, minor

HARDY BRYAN, guardian to FRANKLIN BENJAMIN HARRISON, minor, to renew his bond of $3000 with EML JARMON and WM HUGGINS, sureties

ROSCO BARRUS, EMANUEL JARMON, and CHRISTOPHER A. HATCH, esquires, to settle accounts of SIMON FOSCUE, former guardian to DORCUS FOSCUE, with HARDY BRYAN, present guardian of said DARCUS

EMANUEL JARMON to admr estate of SOLM CARY, decd; $10,000 bond with HARDY PARRY and BENJM HUGGINS, sureties

[Note: Although JOHN O. SIMMONS was not listed as a head of household in the 1830 census returned by ABNER GREEN 11 Nov 1830, PENELOPE SIMMONS was. She was 50 to 60 years old and owned ten slaves. JACOB HUGGINS JR was 20 to 30 years old and owned seven slaves. AMOS "AMITT" was 50 to 60 years old and owned no slaves. ADAM ANDREWS was 20 to 30 years old and owned five slaves. RISDON M. McDANIEL was 40 to 50 years old and owned seven slaves. FRANCIS DuVAL was 40 to 50 and had four slaves. SIMON FOSCUE was 50 to 60 years old and owned 25 slaves. When ABNER GREEN took the 1830 federal census for JONES COUNTY, reported 11 Nov 1830, SOLOMON CARY was listed as head of the household. However, 23 of the 24 members of the household were slaves. The one remaining household member was a free white woman 60-70 years old. One would assume this was SOLOMON's widow. BENJAMIN HUGGINS was 30 to 40 years old and owned five slaves.]

JAMES N. SMITH and ROSCO BARRUS to take the private examination of ELIZA SMITH, wife of JOB SMITH, concerning her consent to the sale of a piece of land. (Note: JOBE SMITH, as enumerated in the 1830 federal census for JONES COUNTY, was the largest slave owner in the county. He owned 198 slaves.)

County trustee to pay $4.00 to GEORGE S. ALTMON as his fee due him as attorney for court in suit vs D. HATCH, executor of THOS MURPHY, decd, as former county trustee

Clerk to determine fees to be paid to JAMES W. BRYAN, county attorney in state cases where county is liable for costs

County trustee to pay GEO. S. ALTMAN and JOHN HAWKS $10 for their defence of the Negro, MOSES, in the Superior Court for his indictment for murder

EDMD HATCH to admr estate of BUCKNER HATCH, decd; $800 bond with JOHN G. RAMSEY and JOSEPH WHITTY, sureties

ISAAC BROWN, HENERY RHODES SENR and JOHN M. FRANKS to take private examination of ELIZABETH HINES, wife of CHARLES A. HINES, concerning her approval of the sale of a piece of land to ISAAC STROUD?

[Note: DURANT HATCH was 40 to 50 years old and owned 71 slaves. GEO. S. ALTMAN, JAMES W. BRYAN and JOHN HAWKS were not listed as heads of household. EDMOND HATCH SR was 40 to 50 years old and owned 46 slaves. EDMOND B. HATCH was 15 to 20 years old and owned 34 slaves or this may have been EDMOND HATCH who was 20 to 30 years old and owned 38 slaves. JOSEPH WHITTY was 30 to 40 years and owned 24 slaves. I found neither HINES nor STROUD in the census.]

EML JARMON, guardian to heirs of SAMUEL WESTBROOK, to renew bond of $3000 with HARDY BRYAN and WILLIAM HUGGINS, sureties

EML JARMON, guardian to BENJM and JOHN ASKEY, to renew bond of $1000 with HARDY BRYAN and WILLIAM HUGGINS, sureties

WML JARMON, guardian to JOHN KOONCE, minor, to renew bond of $1500 with same sureties

EML JARMON, guard to WILLIAM SHELFER, to renew bond of $1000 with same sureties

DANIEL DICKSON, guardian to MARY C. WEINTROUGH?, to renew bond of $1500 with GEORGE ROBERTS and JOSEPH WHITTY, sureties

[Note: I found neither GEORGE ROBERTS nor DANIEL DICKSON in the census.]

The following deeds were registered with JAS REYNOLDS, registrar:
JOSEPH WHITTY to JOHN YOUNG
JOHN MALLARD to DANIEL HARRISON
JOHN STANLY to WRIGHT, NATHAN, & BENJM F. STANLY
Shff of JONES COUNTY to JOSEPH PEARCE
MARY MURPHY to WILLIAM C. MURPHY
SOLN E. GRANT to JOHN BENDER JR
ASA SMITH to WILLIAM BINAM
WILLIAM WATERS to SIMMONS COLLINS
N.G. BLUNT to JOSEPH KINSEY
AGREPPA ROBERTS to JAMES ROBERTS
WILLIAM HUGGINS, shff, to JOHN JONES
DANIEL MALLARD to PETER ANDREWS
MOSES JARVIS to CHRISTOPHER A. HATCH
ALLEN JONES to JOHN TURNER
MICHAEL FISHER? & FRANCES WHARTON (mortgage contract)
CALVIN & MICHAEL KOONCE & F.G. HERITAGE to JNO M. FRANKS
ELIAS LANE to JAMES B. LARAQUE

Jones Cty Court of Common Pleas Minutes 1830

  JAMES B. LARAQUE to R. REYNOLDS & JNO COBB
  JOHN JONES & wife to JONAS JONES SENR
  DURANT HATCH to JNO M. ROBERTS

[Note: JAMES REYNOLDS, the registrar of deeds, was 40 to 50 years old and owned 26 slaves. JOHN YOUNG was 30 to 40 years old and owned 10 slaves. JOHN MALLARD was 50 to 60 years old and owned four slaves. DANIEL HARRISON was 20 to 30 years old and owned 4 slaves.

JOHN STANLY SR was 60 to 70 years old and owned 19 slaves. JOHN STANLY JR was 30 to 40 years old and owned three slaves. WRIGHT, NATHAN, and BENJAMIN STANLY were not listed as heads of households in 1830 JONES COUNTY. Neither was JOSEPH PEARCE. MARY was the only MURPHY listed as head of household. She was 50 to 60 and owned 9 slaves. SOL GRANT was not listed, but a JOHN BENDER was listed. He could have been JOHN BENDER SR since he was 50 to 60 years old. He owned 11 slaves. WILLIAM BINUM was 30 to 40 years old and owned two slaves. WILLIAM WATERS was 40 to 50 years old and owned one slave.

No BLUNT was listed but JOSEPH KINSEY was 50 to 60 years old and owned 32 slaves. No AGREPPA ROBERTS was listed as head of household. DANIEL MALLARD SR was either 50 to 60 or 90 to 100 years old (each was marked); he owned no slaves. DANIEL MALLARD JR was 30 to 40 years old and owned five slaves. Neither PETER ANDREWS nor MOSES JARVIS was listed as head of household. ALLEN JONES was 30 to 40 years old and owned no slaves. JOHN TURNER was 50 to 60 years old and owned no slaves.

The only FISHER listed was DOLLY, a free Black with two others in her household. Two WHARTONs were heads of households, both women; they were ELIZABETH and SARAH. Although several KOONCEs were heads of household, CALVIN and MICHAEL were not among them.

FURNIFOLD G. HERITAGE was 40 to 50 years old and owned 13 slaves. The only LANE was BARBARY who was 50 to 60 years old, had three people in her household and no slaves. JAMES B. LAROQUE was 15 to 20 years old and owned five slaves. Neither JNO COBB nor JNO M. ROBERTS were listed as heads of household in the 1830 federal census for JONES COUNTY.]

  DURANT HATCH, admr of JOHN MORRIS, decd, to sell Negroes of his intestate, and to distribute the proceeds among the "distributees of said JOHN MORRIS" subject to payment of debts
  ENOCK FOY, JOSEPH WHITTY, CHARLES WHITTY, JOHN HOUSTON, and JAMES MARRIT to divide real estate of BUCKNER HATCH, decd, and all other real estate which may belong to said BUCKNER'S two sons, EDMD B. HATCH and RICHD W. HATCH, and settle to each his distributive share agreeable to a petition filed this term
  ENOCK FOY, JOSEPH WHITTY, and JOHN HOUSTON to divide the Negroes belonging to EDMD B. HATCH and RICHD W. HATCH, heirs of BUCKNER HATCH, decd, between said EDMD and RICHARD agreeable to petition

[Note: CHARLES WHITTY was 40 to 50 years old and owned six slaves. JOHN HOUSTON was 20 to 30 years old and owned 27 slaves. JAMES MERRITT was 40 to 50 years old and owned 22 slaves. RICHARD W. HATCH was not listed as a household head.]

  ENOCK FOY, JAMES W. HOWARD, and ROSCO BARRUS to settle accounts of WILLIAM DUNKEN, admr of ISAAC KINSEY/KORNEGAY, decd
(Note: Neither an ISAAC KINSEY nor an ISAAC KORNEGAY was listed as a head of household in the 1830 federal census for JONES COUNTY.)

WILLIAMS ISLER, BLUNT COLEMAN, and JOHN HEATH to divide and allot to MARY BECTON, widow and one of the distributees of BRYAN BECTON, decd, her distrubutive share of said BRYAN BECTON'S personal estate in the hands of FREDK I. BECTON, admr of said BRYAN BECTON

Court orders the sale of the Negroes asked to be divided by the petition of THOMAS GILLET and others (filed this term). Since they are held in common by the petitioners, the division must be by their sale which will be handled by HARDY BRYAN at the house of THOMAS GILLET in JONES CO.

(Note: JAMES W. HOWARD was 20 to 30 years old and owned 34 slaves. WILLIAM DUNCAN was 40 to 50 years old and owned 13 slaves. BLUNT COLEMAN was not listed. Two JOHN HEATHS were heads of household. One was 60 to 70 years old and owned eight slaves. The other was 20 to 30 years old and owned no slaves. MARY ANN BECTON was 30 to 40 years old and owned three slaves.)

The following freeholders were drawn as jurors for next Superior Court:

CHRISTOPHER A. HATCH	GEORGE WILCOX	EMANUEL JARMON
JOSEPH RHEM	AMOS TAYLOR	BENJM HUGGINS
DANIEL WILLIAMSON	SIMMONS HARRISON	SIMMONS ISLER
HENERY RHODES SR	ELIJAH SIMMONS	JOHN ROUSE
WILLIAM GILBERT	LEML H. SIMMONS	RIGDEN HEWETT
SILAS McDANIEL	CHRISR R. GREEN	PETER HARGET
ASA SMITH	JAMES HERRITAGE	DANIEL YATES
JOHN MALLARD	ASA EUBANKS	JOSEAH ASKEY
JAMES SIMMONS	JAMES B. SHINE	JOHN M. FRANKS
THOMAS HARRISON	AARON WOOD	JAMES ROBERTS
RICHD R. FOSCUE	DANIEL ANDREWS	EDMOND HATCH
JONAS WILLIAMS	THOMAS GILLET	FRANCIS ANDREWS

[Note: JOSEPH RHEM was not listed in the 1830 federal census for JONES COUNTY. WILLIAM GILBERT was 50 to 60 years old and owned no slaves. SILAS McDANIEL was 50 to 60 years old and also owned no slaves. JAMES SIMMONS was 40 to 50 years old and owned 12 slaves. THOMAS HARRISON was 30 to 40 years old and owned six slaves. RICHARD FOSCUE was 60 to 70 years old and owned no slaves. JONAS WILLIAMS was 20 to 30 years old and owned six slaves.

GEORGE WILCOX was 30 to 40 years old and owned one slave. AMOS TAYLOR was 30 to 40 years old and owned no slaves. SIMMONS HARRISON SR was 60 to 70 years old and owned 28 slaves; SIMMONS HARRISON JR was 20 to 30 years old and owned three slaves. ELIJAH SIMMONS was 40 to 50 years old and owned 32 slaves. CHRISTOPHER R. GREEN was 20 to 30 years old and owned 23 slaves. JAMES HERITAGE was 40 to 50 years old and owned five slaves. ASA EUBANKS was 40 to 50 years old and owned no slaves.

Although several WOODs were heads of households, AARON was not one of them. DANIEL ANDREWS was 60 to 70 years old and owned two slaves. JOHN ROUSE was 30 to 40 years old and owned 13 slaves. RIGDON HEWIT was 50 to 60 years old and owned 14 slaves. PETER HARGET was 40 to 50 years old and owned 16 slaves. JOSIAH ASKEY was not listed. There were two FRANCIS ANDREWS. One was FRANCIS SR who was 60 to 70 years old and owned 7 slaves. The other was FRANCIS JR who was 20 to 30 years old and owned one slave.]

The following freeholders were drawn as jurors for the next county court:

LEWIS O. BRYAN	ELIAS LANE	HARDY MUNDINE

Jones Cty Court of Common Pleas Minutes 1830

JOHN ANDREWS	JACOB HUGGINS JR	LEWIS W. KORNEGAY
DAVID GREEN	IVEY ANDREWS	JOHN GODWIN
FREDERICK FOSCUE	WILLIAMS ISLER	LAWSON MALLARD
THOMAS H. HILL	WILLIAM ADAMS	COUNCIL GOODING
ENOCK FOY	JAMES W. HOWARD	JONAS JONES JR
SHADRACK ERWIN	JOHN WOOD	BRYAN LAVENDER
MILENTON MEADOWS	JOHN SHELFER	TOBIAS KOONCE
THOS J. FONVIELLE	JACOB GILES	LEWIS SMALL
BENJAMIN KOONCE	SAMUEL DILLAHUNT	

[Note: LEWIS O. BRYAN was 40 to 50 years old and owned four slaves. JOHN ANDREWS was 30 to 40 years old and owned no slaves. DAVID GREEN was 30 to 40 years old and owned ten slaves. FREDRICK FOSCUE was 60 to 70 years old and owned nine slaves. THOMAS H. HILL was not listed. SHADRACK IRVIN was 50 to 60 years old and owned no slaves. MILLINGTON MEADOWS was 50 to 60 years old and owned five slaves.

BENJAMIN KOONCE was 20 to 30 years old and owned 11 slaves. IVEY ANDREWS was not listed. WILLIAM ADAMS was 30 to 40 years old and owned one slave. JOHN WOOD was 40 to 50 years old and owned 11 slaves. JOHN SHELFER was 20 to 30 years old and owned one slave. JACOB GILES was 30 to 40 years old and owned 14 slaves. SAMUEL DILLAHUNT was 30 to 40 years old and owned 11 slaves. HARDY MUNDINE was 40 to 50 years old and owned four slaves.

LEWIS KORNEGAY was 60 to 70 years old and owned three slaves. JOHN GODWIN could have been listed as JOHN GODDIN. He was 30 to 40 years old and owned 16 slaves. LAWSON MALLARD was 50 to 60 years old and owned two slaves. COUNCIL GOODING was 30 to 40 years old and owned one slave. TOBIAS KOONCE was 50 to 60 years old and owned six slaves. LEWIS SMALL was 30 to 40 years old and owned five slaves.]

WILLIAM S. BLACKLEDGE and MARY, his wife, and WM S. BLACKLEDGE, admr of LEML HATCH, and EDMOND HATCH, admr de bonis non of BUCKNER HATCH, petition for division of four Negroes held in common: the woman, CLARY, and ther three children, SAM?, SILVIA, and JANE. Court agrees to the sale in order to effect division with each of the petitioners receiving 1/3 proceeds of the sale.

ROBERT V. ORME vs ROE and ISAAC H. MEADOWS: Ejectment.

Jury:

JOHN MESSER	DANIEL ANDREWS	JOHN STANLY
JOHN SIMMONS	DURANT RICHARDS	NATHAN S. WESTBROOK
LEWIS WILLIAMS	JONAS JONES JR	JONAS JONES SR
ELIJAH PARRY	BRYAN SHINE	JACOB GILES

find for defendant (no cause for action). Plantiff asks for appeal to superior court and appeal is granted; JOB SMITH and ROSCO BARRUS, securities

[Note: BLACKLEDGE was not listed in the census. ROE could be JOBE MEADOWS, who was 60-70 years old in 1830 according to the census and owned one slave; ISAAC MEADOWS was 20-30 years old and owned one slave. ROBERT ORME was not found in the 1830 census. JOHN MESSOR was 30 to 40 years old and owned one slave. JOHN SIMMONS was not listed as a head of household. LEWIS WILLIAMS was 30 to 40 years old and owned 10 slaves. BRYAN SHINE was not listed. NATHAN WESTEBROOK was 20 to 30 years old and owned one slave.]

Governor to use of MARTIN STEPHENSON JR vs ALFRED HARGET, BRADDOCK NOBLE, OWEN B. COX, and SAML DILLAHUNT: Debt. Same jury finds for plff and assesses damages at $44.62 plus costs.

CALVIN KOONCE, MICHAEL KOONCE, and FURNIFOLD G. HERRITAGE and wife to the court: Petition for partition. Report returned and recorded

JOHN S. KOONCE and others to the court: Petition for division of Negroes. Returned and filed

JOHN ADAMS, WILLIAM ADAMS, MARY? ADAMS, JAMES ADAMS, MICAJAH ADAMS, OWEN ADAMS, and B. JARMON and wife petition the court for partition. Returned and registered

ELIZABETH KOONCE vs heirs of RICHD KOONCE: Petition for dower. Report returned and recorded

[Note: No STEPHENSON appears as head of household in JONES COUNTY in the 1830 federal census. ALFRED HARGET was 40 to 50 years old and owned 14 slaves. BRADDOCK NOBLE was not listed. OWEN B. COX was 30 to 40 years old and owned 11 slaves. Neither CALVIN nor MICHAEL KOONCE was listed. JOHN KOONCE was 30 to 40 years old and owned seven slaves. WILLIAM and OWEN were the only ones of these ADAMSes who were listed. WILLIAM was 30 to 40 years old and owned one slave; OWEN was 40 to 50 years old and owned four slaves. No B. JARMON was listed. ELIZABETH KOONCE was 50 to 60 years old and owned 19 slaves, but ELIZABETH W. KOONCE was 40 to 50 years old and owned no slaves.]

Will (found among deceased's valuable papers) of SOLOMON CAREY, decd, proved by oath of JOSEPH KINSEY and by oaths of JOS. KINSEY, GEORGE KING, and ELIJAH KOONCE, witnesses to the will. At the same time, TABITHA SAWYER, one of the heirs at law of said SOLO. CARY came to court by Atto. J.H. BRYAN and entered protest against this will.

[Note: ABNER GREEN reported the results of the 1830 federal census for JONES COUNTY 11 Nov 1830. His enumeration of the CARY household has SOLOMON CARY as its head. However, out of the 24 members of the household only the one white woman aged 60-70 years old was not a slave. One might assume that SOLOMON had died so recently that his widow, no doubt the one white woman, had given his name instead of hers. Note the earlier reference to SOLOMON CARY.]

Some further notes: Wheeler (1851, 1964 reprint) listed members of the North Carolina General Assembly from Jones County. RISDEN McDANIEL was the senator from Jones County from 1824 through 1831. EMANUEL JARMAN, LEML. H. SIMMONS, JAMES N. SMITH, OWEN B. COX, ENOCH FOY, ALFRED STANLY, NATHAN B. BUSH, AND JAMES W. HOWARD served at times in the House of Commons during the period 1824 - 1831. Others familiar to the county court served in the General Assembly during the period 1800 - 1824. These included: DURANT HATCH, JAS. C. BRYAN, CHRISTOPHER BRYAN, and HARDY PERRY.

MARCH TERM, 1831
TRENTON, Monday the 14th

Justices: NATHAN FOSCUE, SIMMONS ISLER, and CHRISTOPHER A. HATCH
Sheriff: WILLIAM HUGGINS
Clerk: HARDY BRYAN

Jurors for the state:
ENOCK FOY, foreman

DAVID GREEN	TOBIAS KOONCE	WILLIAM ADAMS
MILLENTON MEADOWS	JOHN WOOD	IVEY ANDREWS
SHADERACH IRWIN	JOHN SHELFER	JOHN ANDREWS
BENJAMIN KOONCE	FREDERICK FOSCUE	HARDY MUNDINE

Petit jurors for this term:

JAMES W. HOWARD	SAMUEL DILLAHUNT	WILLIAMS ISLER
LEWIS W. KORNEGAY	LEWIS O. BRYAN	COUNCEL GOODING
JOHN G. RAMSAY	JOHN H. HAMMOND	LEWIS SMALL
LEMUEL H. SIMMONS	ROBERT GILBERT	JAMES HATCH

(Note: JAMES W. HOWARD served, according to Wheeler, in the North Carolina House 1831, 1835, and 1836 and in the Senate in 1842 and 1846.)

JOHN E. FOSCUE to oversee rd from TRENT BRIDGE down to DEEP GULLY BRIDGE in room of ALFRED M. FISH__ who resigned

$40.50 to be paid to ALFRED ROWLAND, jailor of ROBESON COUNTY, for keeping MOSES, a slave, committed to ROBESON COUNTY jail. MOSES was found guilty and "executed" in CRAVEN COUNTY

$30.00 to be paid to A.S. BROWN, Shff of ROBESON COUNTY, for apprehending Negro slave, MOSES, and bringing him to JONES; MOSES charged with murder in JONES COUNTY

$180.80 appropriated to pay costs in JONES and CRAVEN COUNTIES in suit, State vs. MOSES, slave, who was tried, convicted, and executed for murder and whose owner is not yet ascertained

$46.90 to pay costs in JONES and CRAVEN SUPERIOR COURTS in suit, State vs DONUM, a slave, who was tried for murder and acquitted

$77.71 to pay 1/2 costs in JONES and CRAVEN SUPERIOR COURTS in case, State vs DONUM, TOM and others for conspiracy in which all of the defendants were discharged by a *not pros.* and DONAM was acquitted. The other half of costs to remain as TOM has not been tried (Note: *non pros.*, according to Black, is an abbreviation of *non prosequitier* meaning he does not follow up or pursue; that is, if the plantiff neglects to take the proper steps as prescribed by the court, the defendant may enter this judgment against the pltff resulting, possibly, in dismissal of the original action or a default judgment for the defendant.)

HARDY BRYAN, NATHAN B. BUSH, and THOMAS W.C. WENGET to settle accounts of SIMMONS ISLER, guard to PATSEY KOONCE, minor

$35.80 to pay costs in SUPERIOR COURTS of JONES and CRAVEN COUNTIES in suit, State vs TOM, a slave, the property of SIMON FOSCUE, for grand larceny in which TOM was acquitted

AMOS MOON, a 9 yr old orphen, apprenticed to SIMMONS ISLER until he is 21 yrs

Jones Cty Court of Common Pleas Minutes 1831

HARDY BRYAN, LEML H. SIMMONS, and FREDERICK I. BECTON to settle accounts of JOSEPH LOFTEN, former guard to FURNIFOLD G. SIMMONS, with JOHN OLIVER, present guard

JOHN OLIVER to be guard to FURNIFOLD G. SIMMONS, minor, in place of JOSEPH LOFTEN, resigned; $4,000 bond; FREDK I. BECTON and DANIEL Y. SHINE, sureties

$10.29 to be paid to ABRAHAM MITCHEL for attending court as a witness in case, State vs BENJN COLLINS, "lately tried in LENOIR SUPERIOR COURT in which defendant was acquitted"

$5.30 to be paid to DAVID (Perhaps this was the name; it was smugged) SANDERS for being a witness in same case as above

$5.25 to be paid to RIGDON HEWIT for same case as above

$5.05 to ISAAC EUBANKS for same as above

"MARGERY, NANCY and ANGELENA (daughters) and GEORGE and EDMUND (sons), children of RHODA, a free woman of color," to be bound to DANIEL DICKSON

HARDY PARRY, ALFRED HARGET, and HARDY BRYAN to settle accounts of JOHN McDANIEL, executor of AMY POLLOCK, decd

JAMES HARRISON, FREDK I. BECTON, and JACOB GILES to settle accounts of OWEN B. COX, guard to WILLIAM A. COX

WILLIAM D. COBB to oversee rd from fork at JAS REYNOLDS' to fork at JNO WISE's in place of WILLIAMS ISLER, resigned

JAMES MILLER to oversee rd from the INDIAN GROVE/GRAVE? OLDFIELD to JACK CABBIN BRANCH and from HARRISON'S bridge to same rd as immediately above in place of F.G. HERRITAGE, resigned

FREDK I. BECTON to oversee rd from fork at SHINES' to RED HILL on work side of RUBY BRANCH in place of JAS B. SHINE, resigned (Note: RED HILL is a community in DUPLIN COUNTY, but Powell does not list RUBY BRANCH.)

DANIEL Y. SHINE, JOHN H. HAMMON, and HARDY BRYAN to settle accounts of FURNIFOLD G. HERRITAGE, admr of JAMES MILLER, decd

Clerk of Court to enter land for ISAAC STRAND, "agreeable to act of Assembly in that case made as provided"

Trustees of JONES COUNTY to pay DAVID LEWIS, jailer of CRAVEN COUNTY, $52.30 in jail fees for Negro MOSES

JAMES N. SMITH and ROSCO BARRIS to take the private examination of ELIZA SMITH, wife of JOB SMITH, concerning the sale of their land from WHITE OAK RIVER to MICAJAH F. MATTOCK's

Jurors for next term:

JOHN McDANIEL	WILLIAM STANLY	JAMES MADES
HARDY O. CONNER	SAMUEL HILL	WILLIAM RHEM
JOHN H. HAMMOND	JOSEPH HAY	MARRET JONES
WILLIAM GOODING SR	JOSEPH KENSEY	JAMES WALLACE
SIMMONS HARRISON JR	LEWIS WILLIAMS	VINCENT ANDREWS
JOHN POLLOCK	LOT EUBANKS	JAMES MESSER
EDWARD GILBERT	JOHN BENDER	ELIJAH PARRY
COUNCEL GOODING	ELIJAH SMALL	JOHN BALL
WILLIAM HARRISON	JOHN ADAMS	WILLIAM DUNKEN
EDWARD C. DEBRULE	JOB SMITH	JAMES FOY

Inventory and sale of property of PENELOPE SIMMONS, decd, filed

Same for SIMON FOSCUE, decd, filed by JNO E. FOSCUE, exr [Note: SIMON FOSCUE JR. left a will (Gwynn, p. 412) which was written 11 May 1826 and probated this March term 1831. He mentions his wife but does not name her. His six youngest children were named: ELIZA, POLLY, NANCY, HANNAH, JOHN

EDWARD and CHRISTIANA FOSCUE. He left a tract of land to JOSEPH RHEM, SR. of CRAVEN COUNTY, in trust for his daughter, JULIA, wife of LEWIS SANDERSON. His son, JOHN EDWARD FOSCUE, was named exr and the witnesses were J. STANLY and EDWD. STANLY.]

Will of BENJAMIN ASKEY, decd, proved in court by oath of LEWIS BRYAN, a witness; JOHN ASKEY qualified as an executor [Note: Gwynn abstracted this will (pp. 400-401). It was written 18 Jun 1811 and names wife, SUSANNAH; sons, JOHN, JOSIAH, NATHAN and ZADOCK ASKEY; daughters, SUSANNAH ASKEY, ELIZABETH HAWKINS, and PEGGY TILMAN. SUSANNAH ASKEY and JOHN ASKEY were named exrs, and the witnesses were LEWIS BRYAN and DANIEL SIMMONS.]

Will of DANIEL MALLARD, decd, proved in court by oath of FREDERICK FOSCUE, a witness; RISDEN M. McDANIEL appointed admr; $1,000 bond; LAURA MALLARD and SHADERACK MALLARD, sureties [Gwynn abstracted this will (p. 433). DANIEL MALLARD, SR. was 88 years old. He wrote his will 15 Dec 1819. (Was he 88 then or when the will was probated?) He named his granddaughter, POLLY HARRISON, and his daughter, KESIAH MALLARD, who was to take care of her "aged mother." Witnesses were FREDERICK FOSCUE and WM. H. CONNER.

Will of SIMON FOSCUE, decd, proved in court by oath of E. STANLY, a witness; JOHN E. FOSCUE qualified as executor

Division of estate of BRYAN BECTON, decd, returned
Division of Negroes of JOHN B. COX, decd, returned
Same for ISAAC KORNEGAY, decd, and SIMON FOSCUE, decd
Division of lands of JAMES RHODES, decd, returned
Account current of F.I. BECTON, guard to JAS. C. BRYAN, minor, filed
Same for AMOS AMYET, guard to SUSAN ANDREWS, minor, filed
Same for HARDY PARRY, guard to heirs of SILAS PARRY, decd
Same for JOHN S. KOONCE, guard to NANCY, MARY, SIMEON E., MICHAEL, and AMOS S. KOONCE, heirs of MICHAEL KOONCE, decd
Same for JNO H. HAMMOND, guard to heirs of J. PARSONS, decd
Same for ROSCO BARRUS, guard to WM FRANKS, minor

TRENTON, Tuesday 15 Mar 1831

Justices: ALFRED HARGET, NATHAN FOSCUE, and CHRISTOPHER A. HATCH, esquires

SPARTLEY M. DOYLE granted license to sell liquor at his residence in TRENTON for one yr

THOMAS W.C. WENGET granted letters of admin. on estate of MARY DAVIS, decd; $100 bond; CHRISR A. HATCH and BENJN HUGGINS, sureties

ENOCK FOY, ROSCO BARRUS, and ASA SMITH to settle accounts of DANIEL SMITH, executor of JOSEPH HAY, decd

FREDK I. BECTON appointed guard to heirs of BRYAN BECTON; $4,000 bond; JACOB GILES and DANIEL Y. SHINE, sureties

MARY W. BECTON, widow of BRYAN BECTON, allowed $90 for board and clothing for her children from the guardian

JAMES REYNOLDS vs WM COOMBS: WILLIAM COOMBS was arrested within 20 days of this term upon writs of capeas ad satisfaciendum at the instance of JAMES REYNOLDS, pltff. COOMBS gave bond conditioned upon his appearance at this term rather than at next term as required by act of 1822. Since COOMBS appeared this term, he is discharged. [Note: capias ad satisfaciendum or ca. sa. is a writ issued after final judgment in a case compelling the defendant to make satisfaction (according to Swaim.)]

Jones Cty Court of Common Pleas Minutes 1831

THOMAS GILLET and others: Petition for sale of Negroes of SETH GILLET, decd. The amount of the sale was $1830. The clerk directed by the court to deduct costs and divide remainder as follows: to THOMAS GILLET, 1/10; ISAAC GILLET, 1/10; JOHN G. RAMSEY, 1/10; JOHN THOMPSON and ESTHER, his wife, 1/10; JOHN AMYET and RACHEL, his wife, 1/10; CALVIN J. MORRIS, 1/10; ELIAS LANE and VASTY, his wife, 1/10; SETH MORRIS, 1/10; REDDING MORRIS, 1/10; LEMUEL GILLET's children, 1/10.

Clerk directed to make these entries in the entry book and to issue warrents:

for GEORGE POLLOCK, 20 acres of land joining his own land in POCOSIN on head of western branch of MILL CREEK; also 640 acres on CATFISH LAKE

for ISAAC STRAND/STROUD, 150 acres within GRAPE BRANCH on north side of TUCKAHOE and on south side of BUTERY BRANCH, then joining own land and that of CHARITY KINSEY (Note: GRAPE BRANCH rises in southern JONES COUNTY and flows south east into WHITE OAK RIVER; Powell does not have an entry for BUTERY BRANCH.)

Sale of Negroes of estate of JOHN MORRIS, decd, by DURANT HATCH, admr, to pay debts and effect division; report filed

Division of Negroes of EDMD WHARTEN, decd, returned and confirmed by court

Inventory and account of sale of SOLOMON CARY, decd, returned by E. JARMON, admr, recorded

Accounts of SIDNEY JARMON, admr of HARDY JARMON, decd, returned

GEORGE OLDFIELD vs AMOS FOSCUE: Case. Jury found for pltff and assessed damage at 6 pence and costs

President and directors of State Bank vs DURANT HATCH SR, D. HATCH, and EDWD HATCH: debt. case dismissed at defendants cost

Same vs JAMES R. CONNER, RACHEL CONNER and ANN R. BRYAN: debt. jury found for pltff; $551.04 judgment

HENERY RHODES, JAS J. RHODES, BENJN RHODES, DELIA RHODES, and JACOB RHODES petition for partition of lands; report returned

WILEY N. TINDAL vs CHRISTOPHER R. GREEN: appeal. "judgment of justice affirmed" for $1.75 and costs

President and directors of Bank of Newbern vs THOS H. HILL, WM S. HILL, and EDWD S. JONES: case. jury found for pltff; judgment of $1095.42 but stay of execution ordered

DURANT HATCH JR to use of JOHN SNEED vs THOMAS H. HILL and EDWD S. JONES: case. jury found for pltff; judgment of $512.40 and costs

JAS. N. SMITH to use of BRUSH & NELSON vs THOMAS H. HILL: debt. jury found for pltff; judgment of $245.52 and costs

DAVID COOPER vs WALTER HELLEN, exr of WILLIAM MITCHEL who was exr of BANISTER LESTER: case. jury found for pltff; judgment of $259.08

HARDY BRYAN to use of MOSES W. JARVIS vs ALFRED HARGET: (no description was given of the type of dispute) jury found for pltff; judgment of $150.61

Chairman of the court to use of THOS HALL vs heirs at law of J. PARSONS: debt. case dismissed

Governor to the use of JOHN STANLY vs ALFRED HARGET, WILLIAMS BROWN, JAMES REYNOLDS, and BRADDOCK NOBLE: debt. jury found for pltff; judgment for penalty of bonds of $4,000 to be discharged on payment of $85.00 to JOHN STANLY and $12.50 to Geo. S. ALTMAN?

ALICE, FANNY, EDWD, & JEREMIAH WHARTEN petition court for division of

Jones Cty Court of Common Pleas Minutes 1831

Negroes; division made

WM HOTESTER? to use of S. KINSEY vs GEO. P. KINSEY and J.S. CROOM: levy on land

EDMD B. HATCH & RICHD W. HATCH vs EDMD HATCH, their guardian: petition for division of Negroes. division made

DURANT HATCH, admr of JNO. MORRIS: petition for sale of Negroes. division made

WILLIAM S. BLACKLEDGE, admr of LEML HATCH and heirs of B. HATCH by their guardian: petition for division of Negroes. Report by H. BRYAN, commissioner made and confirmed by court

EML JARMON, exr of SOLO. CARY vs TABETHA SAWYER and others: "whether the paper writing offered as the last will and testament of SOLOMON CARY be so or not" jury found NOT; appeal granted

MOSES W. JARVIS vs THOMAS S. SMITH: execution levied on land; sum of $59.40 with interest from 10 June 1829 and costs; "ordered that Vend. Expor. issued to sell land lived on" (Note: According to Black, Vend. Expos. is Venditioni exponas which is a writ commanding the sheriff to sell property that has been seized by the court.)

Deeds and bills of sale proved and registered with JAS. REYNOLDS, registrar:

    LEMUEL & JAMES STEELE to DURANT HATCH
    C.B. WOOD & LANEY WOOD to EPHRIAM HARRISON
    WILLIAM HUGGINS & RICHARD REYNOLDS to WILLIAM S. LARAQUE
    JOHN A. AVERET to JOHN S. KOONCE
    WILLIAMS ISLER to SIMMONS ISLER
    AMOS S. KOONCE to JOHN S. KOONCE
    NATHAN F. PARSONS to JOHN H. HAMMOND
    DURANT HATCH to CHRISTOPHER A. HATCH
    DURANT HATCH to CHRISTOPHER A. HATCH
    JOHN P. DAVIS & others to DURANT HATCH SR
    EPHRIAM HARRISON to COUNCEL WOOD
    COUNCEL S. WOOD to OWEN HARRISON
    JOHN WILLIAMS to MARTIN F. BROCK
    CHRISTOPHER A. HATCH to WILLIAM D. COBB
    FRANCIS J.W. NELSON to DANIEL WILLIAMSON
    CHARLES WESTBROOK to MICHAEL KOONCE
    DURANT HATCH JR to CALVIN KOONCE
    WM H. MEADOWS to BARTHOLOMEW MEADOWS
    DANIEL SIMMONS to ISAAC HATHAWAY
    ISRAEL GRAY to LEMUEL H. SIMMONS
    LEMUEL H. SIMMONS to JOHN H. HUTSON
    HARDY BRYAN, commissioner? to LEML H. SIMMONS
    LEML H. SIMMONS to CHARLES WHITTY
    COLEMAN & GOTLEN to SIMMONS ISLER
    ELIAS LANE to WM HUGGINS, C.J. MORRIS, & R. REYNOLDS
    HARDY BRYAN to SARAH J.C. McDANIEL
    WM HUGGINS, shff, & R.B. HATCH to NATHAN FOSCUE
    WILLIAM HELLEN to SIMMONS ISLER
    CHRISTOPHER A. HATCH to JAS McDANIEL
    CHARLES WESTBROOK to JACOB GILES

DURANT HATCH, admr, to JAMES McDANIEL
PETER ANDREWS to JAMES McDANIEL
JOHN M. ROBERTS to JAS McDANIEL
JNO. VANN & LEWIS GREGORY to DURANT HATCH
DURANT HATCH to WILLIAMS BROWN
DURANT HATCH SR. to DURANT HATCH JR.
DURANT HATCH, admr., to WILLIAMS HATCH
DURANT HATCH JR. to R. REYNOLDS & WM HUGGINS
PETER CUSTIS to WILLIAM HOLLISTER
LEMUEL D. HATCH to PETER CUSTIS
DURANT HATCH to PETER CUSTIS
JAMES MARRET to GEO. M. HUTSEN

Received of HARDY BRYAN, clerk, the following division of lands for registration: MICAJAH ADAMS, decd; RICHARD KOONCE, decd; CHRISR KINSEY, decd; STEPHEN WALLACE, decd; ISAAC KORNEGAY, decd

JUNE TERM, 1831
TRENTON, Monday the 13th

Justices: RISDEN M. McDANIEL, OWEN B. COX, & CHRISTOPHER A. HATCH, esquires
Sheriff: WILLIAM HUGGINS
Clerk: HARDY BRYAN

Grand jurors for this term:
JOHN BINDER, foreman

ELIJAH SMALL	LEWIS WILLIAMS	JOHN BALL
EDWARD C. DEBRULE	LOT EUBANKS	JAMES MESSER
JOHN McDANIEL	ELIJAH PARRY	WILLIAM RHEM
HARDY O. CONNER	WILLIAM DUNKEN	WILLIAM HARRISON

Petit jurors:

JOHN H. HAMMON	JAMES MADES	SAMUEL HILL
SIMMONS HARRISON	EDWARD GILBERT	JOHN ADAMS
WILLIAM GOODING SR	JOSEPH KINSEY	COUNSEL GOODING
JAMES McDANIEL	WILLIAM GILBERT	LEMUEL H. SIMMONS

SAMUEL DILLAHUNT, ABNER GREEN and FURNIFOLD G. HERRITAGE to settle accounts of JOHN H. HAMMON, admr of JOSEPH M. PARSONS, decd

NATHAN B. BUSH to oversee rd in place of BENJN KOONCE, resigned, from bridge at TRENTON to "Words hite and from fork of B. HUGGINS' down to M_cehshill" (Mitchell?)

ENOCK FOY allowed #33.14 for his and Negro's attendance as witnesses in suit: State vs DONAN & TOM (Negro slaves) which was tried in CRAVEN COUNTY Superior Court

Clerk to note land transfer for ROBERT DICKSON

CHRISTOPHER A. HATCH, ROSCO BARRUS, and NATHAN FOSCUE to settle accounts of NATHAN B. BUSH, county trustee

WILLIAM DUNKEN allowed $11.68 for his appearance as witness in suit: State vs Negro TOM and others, tried in Superior Court of CRAVEN COUNTY

Sic fu to be issued to JOHN GILBERT of ONSLOW COUNTY to appear next term of this court and renew his bond as guardian to heirs of JAS REYNOLDS, decd

Jones Cty Court of Common Pleas Minutes 1831

RICHARD PARRY to be bound to JOHN M. FRANKS until he is 21 yrs old

LEWIS SMALL to oversee rd in place of WILLIAM ADAMS, resigned, from fork at MICHAEL KOONCE's to BLACK SWAMP

JOHN H. HAMMON and CALVIN KOONCE commissioned as justices

Settlement of FURNEFOLD G. HERRITAGE, admr of JAMES MILLER, decd, to be reported next court

DANIEL Y. SHINE to oversee rd in place of JOHN H. HAMMOND, resigned, from JACK CABBIN up to the RED OAK

CHRISTOPHER A. HATCH, NATHAN B. BUSH, and RESDON M. McDANIEL to settle acounts of IVEY ANDREWS, admr of WILLIAM McDANIEL, decd

SHADERACK LOFTON and MICHAEL KOONCE to patrol district no. 6 in place of NEEDHAM SHELFER and JOHN SIMMONS

EMANUEL JARMON to be guardian to CURTIS WESTBROOK; $50 bond with ISAAC BROWN and RISDON M. McDANIEL, sureties

Jurors for next term of Superior Court:

DANIEL Y. SHINE	ISAIAH WOOD	JAMES HARRISON
JAMES REYNOLDS	NATHAN FOSCUE	JOHN HEATH SR
RISDEN McDANIEL (Capt/Const.)	OWEN ADAMS	JOSEPH BROCK
JOHN L. PARSONS	JOHN SIMMONS	GEORGE ROBERTS
DANIEL STANLY SR	PETER HARGET	JAMES N. SMITH
JOHN G. RAMSAY	ISAAC BROWN	DANIEL SMITH
JOHN TURNER	JOHN STANLY SR	LEWIS FOSCUE
WILLIAM D. COBB	JOHN STANLY JR	JAMES TURNAGE
FURNIFOLD G. HERRITAGE	DURANT RICHARDS	WILLIAM WATERS
BARTHOLOMEW MEADOWS	ALFRED HARGET	JOHN OLIVER
RESDEN M. McDANIEL	DURANT HATCH	OWEN B. COX
NATHAN B. BUSH	JAMES MARRET	LEVI EUBANKS

ALFRED HARGET to admr estate of ZELPHA HARGET, decd; $1,000 bond; WILLIAM BROWN and RESDEN M. McDANIEL, sureties

Jurors for next term of county court:

HENERY RHODES JR	MOSES ADAMS	ELIJAH LOVECK
JOHN S. KOONCE	LOVECK G. MOON	JAMES S. MILLER
THOMAS W.C. WINGET	WILLIAM BROWN	ADAM ANDREWS
ALFRED M. FRESHWATER	MICHAEL KOONCE	CALVIN J. MORRIS
THOMAS POLLOCK	LEVI JONES	JOHN FROST
CHRISTOPHER R. GREEN	HARDY H. SHELFER	JOHN HOUSTON
JONAS WILLIAMS	JOHN WOOD	JOSEPH SMALL
SHADERACK MALLARD	FREDERICK FOSCUE	JOHN ANDREWS
HARDY MUNDINE	LEWIS SMALL	ROBERT GILBERT
SIMON S. BECTON	FREDERICK WOOD	JOHN SHELFER

Settlement of OWEN B. COX, guard to WM COX, minor, proved and filed

Settlement of SIMMONS ISLER, guard to JOSEPH and WILLIAM BRYAN, minors, proved and filed

Settlement of SAMUEL B. HEATH, guard to LEVIAH and WILLIAM HEATH, minors, proved and filed

Inventory and account of sale of estate of DANIEL MALLARD, decd, returned and filed by R.M. McDANIEL, exr

President & directors of Bank of Newbern vs ALFRED HARGET, JAS REYNOLDS, RESDEN M. McDANIEL, & WMS BROWN: Case. Plea withdrawn; judgment by default:

$259.39

C.J. MORRIS to use of MOSES W. JARVIS vs ALFRED HARGET: Debt. Jury found for pltff. $161.54 judgment

SPAROW & HOWARD vs JAMES SIMMONS, JAMES N. SMITH & ELIJAH SIMMONS: Case. The following jury found for pltff:

JOHN H. HAMMOND	JAMES MADES	SAMUEL HILL
SIMMONS HARRISON JR	EDWARD GILBERT	JOHN ADAMS
WILLIAM GOODING SR	JOSEPH KINSEY	COUNSEL GOODING
JAMES McDANIEL	WILLIAM GILBERT	LEMUEL H. SIMMONS

Judgment of $483; case appealed by JAMES SIMMONS to next Superior Court; JAMES MARRET and DANIEL DECKSON, sureties

ALONZO T. JERKINS vs ELIAS LANE, WM HUGGINS, and JAMES MARRET: Debt. Same jury as above found for pltff and awarded judgment of $125 plus interest from 25 Oct 1830

JOHN G. RAMSEY to oversee rd from TRENTON to ASA HATCH's gate in place of JAS McDANIEL, resigned

JOSEPH WHITTY to oversee rd from BUCKNER HATCH's mill down to bridge near RICHD B. HATCH's and to POCOSIN on rd by (HOWARD's?) in room of JAMES W. HOWARD, resigned

Since a majority of justices were present, patrols for the various disticts were appointed:
WHITE OAK, DIST 1: JOHN BINDER, RIGDON HEWIT, & DANIEL SMITH
TRENT BRIDGE, DIST 2: ROSCO BARRUS, ENOCH FOY, & EDMOND HATCH
TRENTON, DIST 3: HARDY BRYAN, WILLIAMS BROWN, & WILLIAM HUGGINS
CYPRESS CREEK, DIST 4: JAMES HARRISON, ISAAC BROWN, & SIMMONS HARRISON
TUCKAHOE, DIST 5: OWEN B. COX, HENRY RHODES, & JOSEPH KINSEY
BEVER CREEK, DIST 6: MARTIN F. BROCK, WILLIAMS ISLER, & JOHN STANLY
BEVERDAM, DIST 7: RISDON M. McDANIEL, FREDERICK FOSCUE, & NATHAN B. BUSH

A tax for JONES COUNTY for 1831 was levied and collected as follows: for every $100 value of land and town lots $.20 and for each taxable pole $.40

ADAM ANDREWS to be guardian to SETH MORRIS and READING MORRIS, minors; $1500 bond; JOHN G. RAMSEY and CALVIN J. MORRIS, securities

NATHAN B. BUSH, county trustee, to make diligent inquiry into trial of Negro man, MOSES, removed from JONES to CRAVEN COUNTY, so as to determine if ZEADOCK MUMFORD of ONSLOW COUNTY is liable for costs and if a suit should be filed in Superior Court of this or another county to recover costs

The district of river lying above mouth of BEVER CREEK on which WRIGHT STANLY is overseer, shall be extended from said BEVER CREEK up to PARRY's bridge instead of stopping at CHINQUAPIN CREEK thus making the districts more equal

County trustee ordered to pay JORDAN S. CARRAW/CONNER? $185.40 1/2 for sundry charges stemming from removing prisoners from JONES COUNTY to CRAVEN COUNTY for trial and for several witness tickets

County trustee to pay $88.36 in claims from Superior Court of CRAVEN in case State vs Negro man, TOM and others and State vs Negro man DECK, property of SIMON FOSCUE

JAMES W. HOWARD, JOSEPH WHITTY, and ROSCO BARRUS to settle accounts of exr of JOSEPH HAY

Sheriff to be paid $96.85 for this year's extra services

HARDY BRYAN paid $40 for extra services this yr as clerk
ALEXANDER MITCHEL granted license to sell liquor at TRENT BRIDGE
SOPHIA, a free woman of color, has leave to peddle
LEMUEL H. SIMMONS allowed $6.10 for his man attending as a witness in trial: State vs TOM and others

The following justices to take list of taxable property in JONES COUNTY:
District 1 (WHITE OAK): THOMAS GELLET, exq.
District 2 (TRENT BRIDGE): ROSCO BARRUS, esq.
District 3 (TRENTON): CHRISTOPHER A. HATCH, esq.
District 4 (CYPRESS CREEK): JOHN H. HAMMOND, esq.
District 5 (TUCKAHOE): EMANUEL JARMON, esq.
District 6 (BEVER CREEK): CALVIN KOONCE, esq.
District 7 (BEVERDAM): ALFRED HARGET, esq.
County Trustee to pay $588.72 to NATHAN FOSCUE, constable, to repair bridge at TRENTON

Court to be hereafter held by these justices:
March Term: ISAAC BROWN, NATHAN FOSCUE, ROSCO BARRUS, ALFRED HARGET & ELIJAH SIMMONS
June Term: DURANT HATCH, OWEN B. COX, CHRISTOPHER A. HATCH, ASA SMITH, JNO. H. HAMMOND, & CALVIN KOONCE
September Term: RISDEN McDANIEL, THOMAS GILLET, EMANUEL JARMON, JAMES G. HERRITAGE, & JAMES HARRISON
December Term: JAMES N. SMITH, SIMMONS ISLER, ABNER GREEN, DANIEL SMITH, DANIEL Y. SHINE, & JAMES ROBERTS

The following persons were to hold elections:
Dist. 1: THOS. GILLET, DANIEL YATES, & LEVI EUBANKS
Dist. 2: ROSCO BARRUS, JNO. OLIVER, & OWEN ADAMS
Dist. 3: WILLIAM HUGGINS, CHRIST. A. HATCH, & HARDY BRYAN
Dist. 4: DANL Y. SHINE, ROBT GILBERT, & FREDK I. BECTON
Dist. 5: ISAAC BROWN, JOSEPH KINSEY, & HENRY RHODES SENR
Dist. 6: ABNER GREEN, WMS ISLER, & PETER HARGET
Constables elected for JONES COUNTY:
Dist. 1: DANIEL DICKSON
Dist. 3: WILLIAMS BROWN
Dist. 6: HARDY H. SHELFER
Dist. 7: JOHN L. PARSONS
No appointments made for districts 2,4, and 5
N.B. BUSH was reelected county trustee and entered his bond
HARDY BRYAN, clerk, renewed his bond
WILLIAMS BROWN allowed $8.80 from county funds for his services as constable for one yr ending this term
DANIEL DICKSON allowed $10.40 for his yr as constable
JOHN L. PARSONS paid $11.20 for his yr as constable
Will of MARY MURPHY, decd, proved in open court by oath of HENRY SHEETS; EML JARMON, the therein named exr, qualified as such [Note: Gwynn abstracted this will (p. 438) which was written 5 Jan 1831. It mentioned her three children, WILLIAM E. MURPHY, MARINDA MURPHY, and DEBORAH MURPHY and a grandson, FREDERICK, son of THOMAS J. FONVILLE. EMANUEL JARMAN was named exr. and the witness was HENRY SHUTE.]

Jones Cty Court of Common Pleas Minutes 1831

EML JARMON, guard to WM SHELFER, (accounts?) proved and filed; also same for his guardianship to NANCY WESTBROOK, JOHN & BENJAMIN ASKEY, JOHN P. KOONCE, and the heirs of E. KOONCE

F.G. HERRITAGE, (guard?) to THOS STELLY (accounts?) proved and filed
JOSEPH LOFTEN, guard to F.G. SIMMONS, (accounts?) filed and approved
Inventory and sale of BENJM ASKEY, decd, filed by JNO. ASKEY, exr
Inventory and sale of MARY McDANIEL, decd, filed by THOS W.C. WINGET, admr

Deeds and bills of sale proved this term and registered by JAS REYNOLDS, registrar:
TOBIAS KOONCE to MATILDA HUGGINS
WILLIAM JARMON to HARDY PARRY
JOB SMITH and others to MICAJAH F. MATTOCKS
JOHN KOONCE to HARDY PARRY
BENJAMIN WESTBROOK to NATHAN B. WESTBROOK
DANIEL Y. SHINE to IGNATIOUS BROCK
SIMMONS HARRISON to WILLIAM HUGGINS
WILLIAM HUGGINS to LEMUEL H. SIMMONS
BRYAN LAVENDER to OWEN ADAMS & ROSCO BARRUS (mortgage)
E.S.F. GILES to JACOB GILES & JNO. M. FRANKS (mortgage)
MARY MURPHY & WM MURPHY (agreement)
Clerk of County Court issued this term
D. HATCH to the Director of State Bank proved before the judges and ____? the register, July 12th? 1831

H. BRYAN, clerk

SEPTEMBER TERM, 1831
TRENTON, Monday the 12th

Justices: RISDON M. McDANIEL, JAMES HARRISON, and EMANUEL JARMON, esquires
Sheriff: WILLIAM HUGGINS
Clerk: HARDY BRYAN

Grand Jurers this term:
FREDERICK FOSCUE, foreman

JONAS WILLIAMS	JOHN WOOD	JOHN S. KOONCE
JAMES I. MILLER	MOSES ADAMS	JOHN FROST
SHADERACK MALLARD	LEVI JONES	ADAM ANDREWS
ROBERT GILBERT	ELIJAH LOVECK	FREDERICK WOOD

Justices were called and the following appeared:

ISAAC BROWN	JAMES HARRISON	CHRISTOPHER A. HATCH
JAMES ROBERTS	THOMAS GILLET	DANIEL SMITH
JAMES G. HERRITAGE	NATHAN FOSCUE	ALFRED HARGET
JOHN H. HAMMOND	ABNER GREEN	CALVIN KOONCE

These twelve were sufficient to conduct business so WILLIAM HUGGINS renewed his bond as sheriff with JAMES McDANIEL, WILLIAMS BROWN, and JAMES B. SHINE, securities

HARDY MUNDINE to oversee rd from the cross roads on WHITE OAK to a black sorrel in the middle of the pocosin in place of LOT EUBANKS, resigned

RISDEN M. McDANIEL, Esq., to take private examination of FANNY FONVIELLE, wife of THOMAS J. FONVIELLE, for her approval of the sale of land in this county to EMANUEL JARMON

DANIEL STANLY to be guardian to "his grandchild, LEAH M. STANLY;" $2,000 bond; RISDEN M. McDANIEL and JOHN L. PARSONS, securities

County trustee to pay JOHN YOUNG $5.20 for witnessing in trial of State vs TOM and others

JACOB HUGGINS to oversee rd from bridge at TRENTON to head of street and one mile above TRENTON in room of HARDY O. CONNER, resigned

DANIEL Y. SHINE, JAMES B. SHINE, and FREDERICK I. BECTON to divide the Negroes of JEREMIAH PARSONS, decd, so as to allot to NATHAN F. PARSONS his distributive share

DANIEL HARRISON to oversee rd from the bridge at TRENTON down to (This word was partially smeared.)___DON BRANCH and from fork at RISDEN M. McDANIEL's to MUSSELSHELL BRANCH on road to KINSTON in place of JOHN STANLY, resigned

Patrols in Districts 1 and 5 to be paid their portion of tax levied by court

SAMUEL DILLAHUNT had a complaint lodged against him concerning damages incurred on the road; court ruled that no damages would be paid

ISAAC BROWN, EMANUEL JARMON, and JOHN H. HAMMOND to look into the DILLAHUNT matter

PETER HARGET authorized to sell on credit of six months the following slaves, property of DANIEL SIMMONS, decd, ROSE, JIM, JACK, SHARPER, LOT, and LITTLE ROSE, for distribution among the heirs

Lists of taxable property in districts 1,3,4,6, & 7 were returned by the justices appointed to take the lists & R. BARRUS, Esq., for DISTRICT 2

DANIEL SMITH, executor of JOSEPH KAY, decd, filed affidavit

FURNIFOLD G. HERRITAGE, admr of JAMES MILLER, decd, filed affidavit

JOHN H. HAMMOND, admr of JOSEPH M. PARSONS, decd, aft. filed

ROSCO BARRUS, guard to OLIVER E. STRONG, aft. filed

Account of sale of property of JOSEPH KEY, decd, filed

Account of JAS N. SMITH filed by ROSCO BARRUS, his trustee

HARDY BRYAN, HARDY PARRY, and CHRISTOPHER A. HATCH to settle accounts of EMANUEL JARMON, exec. of DURANT McDANIEL, decd

ISAAC BROWN, HENRY RHODES, and JOHN M. FRANKS to settle accounts of EMANUEL JARMON, admr of THOS SHELFER, decd

HARDY BRYAN, NATHAN B. BUSH, and THOMAS W.C. WINGET to settle accounts of RISDEN M. McDANIEL, admr of MORRIS McDANIEL, decd, and McCULLEN POLLOCK, decd

County trustee should pay WILLIAM COOMBS what he needs to go as an express (messenger) in DUPLIN with a Black insurrection

Patrols should follow same rules as before with this addition: slaves are "prohibited from holding public worship on any pretense whatever and that no slave shall be permitted to pass except to see his wife: and for that he must have written permission from his owner and the owner of his wife. These restrictions are only good for three months.

[Note: This seemingly curious entry and the previous entry about a Black insurrection in DUPLIN COUNTY stem directly from the famous NAT TURNER slave revolt which occurred in SOUTHAMPTON COUNTY, VIRGINIA just a couple of weeks previous to this term of the JONES COUNTY COURT. During the early morning hours and the day of 22 Aug 1831 NAT TURNER, a slave and a preacher, and several other slaves killed about 55 white men, women, and children. They accomplished their feat by pretending to be out hunting, it being common for slaves to leave their homes to come together for a late night or early morning hunt, and so were ignored by their victims until it was too late. By the next day TURNER's slave army, which had at one point swelled to 50 or 60 mounted men, had all been captured, killed, or dispersed. TURNER, alone, remained free (Tragle, 1971). Although slave revolts were an ever-present danger in the slave holding states, the NAT TURNER insurrection caught North Carolinians by surprise. The northeastern counties were the first to react due to their proximity to SOUTHAMPTON COUNTY, VIRGINIA, but within two weeks fear had swept across southeastern North Carolina also (Morris, 1985) as can be attested to by these court entries. Even though JONES COUNTY had a greater slave population than it did white, it was not one of the North Carolina counties where white reaction was to rumor of local slave revolts (Morris, 1985). DUPLIN was one of those counties as can be seen in these records. Other neighboring counties, LENOIR and CRAVEN also had rumors of slave revolts (Morris, 1985). Meanwhile, NAT TURNER remained at large until 30 Oct 1831 when he was captured near his home place in SOUTHAMPTON CO., VIRGINIA. He was tried 5 Nov, 1831 and sentenced to death. He was hung at noon 11 November (Tragle, 1971).]

GEORGE HAZZARD to oversee rd from BEVERDAM near JAS MARRET's to fork of road at S./I. GRANT's in place of LOVICK G. MOORE, resigned

F. WISE and ABRAHAM SIMMONS shall be paid for their work as patrols

RISDON M. McDANIEL, N.B. BUSH, and WM HUGGINS to settle accounts of HARDY BRYAN, admr of C. BRYAN, decd

Deeds and bills of sale recorded with Registrar, JAS REYONLDS:
JAMES SIMMONS to ELIJAH SIMMONS
THOS J. FONVIELLE & wife to EML JARMON
R. BARRUS, trustee of JAS N. SMITH to WM HUGGINS
Same to EDMD HATCH
JOSEPH WHITTY to JNO YOUNG
DANIEL WILLIAMSON to SAMUEL HILL
STEWARD SCOTT to READING SCOTT
ABIJAH DAVIS to JAS H. FRESHWATER, mortgage
SAMUEL HILL to DANIEL WILLIAMSON
FREDK PARKER/PACKER to JOHN H. HAMMOND
JAMES SIMMONS to DANIEL WILLIAMSON, bill of sale

List of taxable property in Dist. 2 returned by ROSCO BARRUS

Jurors for next term:

JACOB HUGGINS JR	LEWIS WILLIAMS	ENOCK FOY
THOMAS McDANIEL	JAMES MESSER	BRYAN MESSER
WM McDANIEL SR	DANIEL YATES	JOHN WOOD
FREDK I. BECTON	HENRY RHODES	RICHARD R. FOSCUE
SIMMONS HARRISON SR	MILENTON MEADOWS	WILLIAM ADAMS
SAMUEL HILL	MARTIN F. BROCK	JAMES WALLIS
ELIJAH SMALL	IVEY ANDREWS	JOHN STILE
ELIJAH KOONCE	WILLIAM GILBERT	ELIJAH PARRY
JOHN McDANIEL SR	JOSEPH KINSEY	JAMES GODWIN

Jones Cty Court of Common Pleas Minutes 1831

JOHN MALLARD   JOHN BENDER   LEMUEL BUSECK

DECEMBER TERM, 1831
TRENTON, Monday the 12th

Justices: DANIEL SMITH, DANIEL Y. SHINE, and ABNER GREEN, Esquires
Sheriff: WILLIAM HUGGINS, Esquire
Clerk: HARDY BRYAN

Jurors this term:
MARTIN F. BROCK, foreman

MILLENTON MEADOWS	SAMUEL HILL	ELIJAH KOONCE
WILLIAM GILBERT	ELIJAH SMALL	JOHN McDANIEL
IVEY ANDREWS	JOHN WOOD	JOHN MALLARD
THOMAS McDANIEL	JAMES MESSER	JOHN STILE/STILL

SIMEON MEADOWS to admin. estate of DELILA MEADOWS, decd; $1,000 bond; MILLENTON MEADOWS and EDMOND WHARTON, sureties

STEPHEN KINSEY and WILLIAM W. HYNEN may sell liquor by small measure for one yr at their store at TRENT BRIDGE

ENOCK FOY to oversee rd from MILL CREEK BRIDGE including 1/2 of said bridge to REEDY BRANCH in place of DANIEL WILLIAMSON, resigned

SHADERACK ERWIN to oversee rd from head of straight rd one mile above TRENTON up to INDIAN GROVE OLDFIELD in place of THOMAS McDANIEL, resigned

ROSCO BARRUS, DANIEL YATES, and LOTT EUBANKS to divide Negroes belonging to heirs of CALEB SMITH, decd

OWEN B. COX to admin. estate of HENRY RHODES JR, decd; $2,000 bond; WILLIAMS BROWN and JONAS WILLIAMS, sureties

JACOB GILES to admr estate of FREDERICK WOOD, decd; $1,000 bond; JAMES B. SHINE and MICAJAH PETIEWAY, sureties

JAMES REYNOLDS, PETER HARGET, and JOHN S. KOONCE to settle accounts of HARDY H. SHELFER, admr of LUKE SHELFER, decd

County trustee to pay HARDY BRYAN $3.00 for entertaining the guard placed at the TRENTON jail by the Col. Weds. night

Clerk to enter in "entrytakers" book land for ALLEN JONES JR; the land was 25 acres on the south side of TUCKAHOE and north side of NEW RIVER SWAMP joining lands of JOHN JONES JR, JAMES MILLS, BENJN RHODES, and heirs of JAMES RHODES SR (Note: According to Powell NEW RIVER rises in north western ONSLOW COUNTY near the JONES COUNTY line and flows in a south easterly direction until it empties into ONSLOW BAY. It appeared as the CORANI RIVER on the MOLL MAP of 1729 and as the NEW RIVER on the MOSELEY MAP of 1733.)

WILLIAM STANLY to oversee rd from bridge at TRENTON up to WARDS HILL and from fork at B. HUGGINS' down to MUSSELSHELL BRANCH on rd from NEWBERN to KINSTON in place of N.B. BUSH, resigned

RISDEN M. McDANIEL, FRANCIS DUVAL, and CALVIN J. MORRIS to settle accounts of AMOS AMYET, guard to (this was smeared) ANDREWS

JOHN H. HAMMOND, FURNIFOLD G. HERRITAGE, and JAMES S. MILLER to settle accounts of ABNER GREEN, admr of MARY GREEN, decd

SIMMONS ISLER to be paid $40 from county funds for bringing arms from RALEIGH for the use of the county [Note: This entry and the one about "entertaining the guard" at the jail (on previous page) probably have to do with the tension over the NAT TURNER revolt.]

JAMES H. FRESHWATER to oversee rd from TRENT BRIDGE to (this was torn) SWAMP in place of JAMES SIMMONS, resigned

WHITFIELD TURNER to oversee rd from RATTLESNAKE BRIDGE up to DUPLIN COUNTY line and the cross roads from ONSLOW to LENOIR COUNTY line in place of HENRY RHODES JR

JOHN OLIVER to oversee rd from ASA HATCH's gate down to BUCKNER HATCH's mill in place DURANT HATCH

HARDY BRYAN, WILLIAM HUGGINS, and NATHAN FOSCUE to divide Negroes of the estate of THOMAS and CAROLINA MURPHY, minor heirs of THOS MURPHY, decd, among the lawful heirs

HARDY BRYAN, WILLIAM HUGGINS, and HARDY PARRY to settle accounts of EMANUEL JARMON, executor of DURANT McDANIEL, decd

ISAAC BROWN, HENRY RHODES, and JOHN M. FRANK to divide Negroes of estate of SAML WESTBROOK, decd, so as to allot to EDMD WESTBROOK his distributive share

Petit jurors:

HENRY RHODES	BRYAN MESSER	RICHARD R. FOSCUE
DANIEL YATES	LEWIS WILLIAMS	WILLIAM McDANIEL
JOHN BENDER	WILLIAM ADAMS	FREDK I. BECTON
ELIJAH PARRY	JOSEPH KINSEY	SIMMONS HARRISON

State vs RILEY JONES and EDWD OVERTON: affray. Above jury found JONES guilty (judgment of $.50 fine and costs) and OVERTON not guilty

State vs RILEY JONES and WM MORGIN: affray. Above jury found both defendants guilty (judgment of $.05 fine and costs)

Will of RISDEN McDANIEL SR proved in court by oaths of THOMAS McDANIEL and JOHN POLLOCK, witnesses; RISDEN McDANIEL, the named executor, qualified as such [Note: Gwynn abstracted this will (p. 436) which was written 19 Jan 1822. It names his wife, MARY; sons, JAMES, RISDON and deceased son, JOHN; grandsons, JOHN McDANIEL, JOHN LEWIS McDANIEL, and LEMUEL (or SAMUEL) McDANIEL. Five daughters were not named but mentioned. RISDON McDANIEL was named exr, and the witnesses were THOMAS McDANIEL and JOHN POLLOCK.]

Division of Negroes of the estate of JEREMIAH PARSONS, decd, returned and filed

Settlement of E. JARMON, admr of THOS SHELFER, decd, filed

Settlement of D. STANLY, guard to LEAH M. STANLY, filed

Settlement of estate of AMY POLLOCK, decd, with JNO. McDANIEL, executor, filed

NATHAN B. BUSH, county trustee, filed his settlement made wilth the county

Commissioners report of road condition at foot of HARRISONS (on the pier) BRIDGE and (This had something about an agreement.) with SAML DILLIHUNT (The last surname is probable, but not certain, since it was deep in the binding.)

Tuesday, 13 Dec 1831

Justices: SIMMONS ISLER, ABNER GREEN, and NATHAN FOSCUE, esquires

HARDY BRYAN, WILLIAM HUGGINS, and HARDY PARRY to settle accounits of EMANUEL JARMON, admr of ADONIJAH PARRY, decd

Jones Cty Court of Common Pleas Minutes 1831

The same men to settle accounts of EML JARMON, admr of JAMES RHODES, decd

HARDY BRYAN, WILLIAMS BROWN, and THOMAS W.C. WINGET to settle affairs of GEORGE WILCOX, admr of THOMAS WILCOX, decd

COUNCEL MILLER, minor about 12 or 13, to be bound to JOHN SHELFER until 21 years old

Sie fa to be issued to WM RHODES JR to appear at next court and show why ABNER SANDERS should not be bound to some person approved by the court

EMANUEL JARMON to be guardian to heirs of CULLEN POLLOCK, decd; $1000 bond; ISAAC BROWN and SIMMONS ISLER, sureties

HARDY BRYAN, HARDY PARRY, and WILLIAMS BROWN to settle accounts of RISDEN M. McDANIEL, admr of CULLEN POLLOCK, decd

NATHAN FOSCUE, HARDY PARRY, JACOB HUGGINS, and HARDY O. CONNER to divide lands of ADONIJAH and LEM ANDREWS "between" the heirs at law

GEORGE WILCOX to be guardian to heirs of THOMAS WILCOX, decd; $5000 bond; EMANUEL JARMON and SAMUEL DILLAHUNT, sureties

EMANUEL JARMON, admr of JAMES RHODES, decd, may sell Negroes CATE and FRANK of the estate of "the intestate" in order to pay debts of the estate

WILLIAM P. FEROND vs LEML H. SIMMONS and JAS C. COLE: Sie fa - bail. GEORGE C. HATCH, whose bail the defendants in this case are cited, came into court. The court was satisfied that GEORGE C. HATCH "had been admitted to the benefit at the act of 1822 for the relief of insolvent debtors" at June term 1829 of this court. HATCH permitted to go without delay

ABNER GREEN, admr of MARY GREEN, decd, may sell Negro man, LONDON, in order to make a distribution among heirs of MARY GREEN

ISAAC BROWN, chairman, to use of EML JARMAN, admr of LEWIS MORRIS vs WILLIAM DUNKEN: debt. Jury found for plantiff and assessed damages at $57.63 plus costs

NATHAN I. HARGET vs BENJAMIN HUGGINS, executor of JAMES HUGGINS: appeal. Jury found for pltff and assessed damages at $15.00 plus costs

GEORGE WILSON, guardian to use of MICHAEL N. FISHER vs JAMES N. SMITH, JAMES W. HOWARD, ROSCO BARRUS, and EDWD S. JONES: debt. Jury found for pltff and judgment was to pay principal on note of $1175.58 with $115.38 interest for total judgment of $1290.96 and costs

JOHN CHADWICK to use of B.W. VEIL vs MICHAEL N. FISHER: case: Jury found for pltff and assessed damage at $93.30 of which $90 is balance of principal and costs

MOSES W. JARVIS vs RESDON M. McDANIEL, THOS McDANIEL, and JAS McDANIEL: debt. Jury found for pltff. Principal=$220; interest and costs= $6.60; total judgment=$226.60

President and directors of State Bank of North Carolina vs BRYAN LAVENDER, BENJM WALLACE, and MICIJAH F. MATTOCKS: case. Jury found for pltff. Principal=$330; interest and damage and costs=$8.60; total judgment=$338.60

JAMES N. SMITH to use of ROSCO BARRUS for LEGGIT FOX vs JAMES W. HOWARD: debt. Jury found for pltff and assessed damage at $426.27

DANIEL SMITH vs JAMES W. HOWARD: debt. Jury found for pltff. Balance of principal=$461.80; interest=$9.23; total judgment=$471.03 and costs

Gov. to use of MICHAEL H. LENT vs ALFRED HARGET, BRADDOCK NOBLE, OWEN B. COX, and SAML DILLAHUNT: debt. Jury found for pltff. "Judgment for penalty of bond to be discharged by payment of $95 plus costs" $39.38 due to M.H. LENT and $54 due to W.G. STANLY for total of $95.08

GEO S. ATTMORE to use of SPAFFORD and TALISTON vs JAMES W. HOWARD: case. Jury found for pltff. Principal=$433.65; interest=$56.15; total judgment=$489.80 plus costs

Jurors for next county court:

LEWIS O. BRYAN	JAMES MADES	PETER ANDREWS
HARDY O. CONNER	JOSEPH HAY	TOBIAS KOONCE
SIMMONS HARRISON JR	LOT EUBANKS	WILLIAM GOODING SR
STEWART SEATE/LEOTE	JOHN BALL	WM M. GILES
EDWIN BECTON	JOSIAH ASKEY	SILAS McDANIEL
BENJ HUGGINS	JAMES W. HOWARD	JONAS JONES JR
WILLIAMS ISLER	JOHN JONES	WM RHEM
WM HARRISON	JAS McDANIEL	RIGD HEWIT
JNO ROUN	JNO FREIZE	JNO GODWIN
DANL WILLIAMSON	JACOB GILES	MICAJAH PETEWAY

Jurors drawn for Superior Court:

SAML DILLAHUNT	JNO M. FRANKS	AARON WOOD
VINCENT ANDREWS	THOMAS HARRISON	EML JARMON
BENJ KOONCE	ABNER GREEN	AMOS TAYLOR
WM GOODING	WM STANLY	ASA EUBANKS
JNO H. BECTON	JNO POLLOCK	EDMD HATCH
JAS B. SHINE	THOS GILLET	GEO WILCOX
JOSEPH RHEM	EDWD C. DEBRULE	JNO FORDHAM
JNO H. HARRISON	WM DUNKEN	LEML ISLER
CALVIN KOONCE	HARDY COLLINS	ELIJAH SIMMONS
JAMES G. HERRITAGE	ASA SMITH	JAMES FOY
LEWIS W. KORNEGAY	WM MESSER	COUNCIL GOODING
LEMUEL H. SIMMONS	DAVID GREEN	JERD? HUGGINS JR

Deeds proved and registered with JAS REYNOLDS, registrar:
NATHAN G. BLUNT and others to JOHN WILLIAMS
JAS McDANIEL to WM HUGGINS
JNO POLLOCK to WM HUGGINS
JNO STANLY to WM HUGGINS
SINGLA READ to JNO THOMPSON
ROSCO BARRUS to OWEN ADAMS
PETER ANDREWS to N.B. BUSH
LEML ISLER to D.Y. SHINE
EDMD HATCH to JNO SMED
C.B. GREEN to EDWD I. JONES
M.F. MATTOCKS to F. MATTOCKS
M.F. MATTOCKS to F. MATTOCKS
N.B. BUSH to PETER ANDREWS
DURANT RICHARDS to IVEY ANDREWS
Shff HUGGINS to D. MALLARD
D. RICHARDS to PETER ANDREWS
PETER ANDREWS to JNO MALLARD
?.D. WILLIAMS and wife to PETER ANDREWS
F. TAYLOR to E. FOY
MICAJAH ADAMS to MOSES ADAMS
EZEKIEL JONES to WM JONES
JAS C. COLE to LILY MOORE
JNO P. DAVIS to D. WILLIAMSON

N.B. BUSH to SIMMONS HARRISON
President and directors of the Bank of Newbern to EDMOND HATCH
    JONAS JONES SR and JOHN JONES may sell liquor at their homes in JONES COUNTY for one year

Jones County Court of Common Pleas Minutes 1832

MARCH TERM, 1832
TRENTON, Monday the 12th

Justices: ISAAC BROWN, NATHAN FOSCUE, and ALFRED HARGET, esquires
Sheriff: WILLIAM HUGGINS
Clerk: HARDY BRYAN

Grand jury made up of the following freeholders:
WILLIAMS ISLER, foreman

JAMES McDANIEL	WILLIAM HARRISON	JOHN JONES
JONAS JONES JR	BENJAMIN HUGGINS	TOBIAS KOONCE
HARDY O. CONNER	RIGDON HEWIT	LOT EUBANK
JAMES W. HOWARD	JAMES MADES	JOHN ROUSE

The jurors were charged by JAMES W. BRYAN, solicitor for the county

HARDY BRYAN, WILLIAM HUGGINS, and JACOB HUGGINS to examine the accounts of ALFRED HARGET, admr of ZILPHA HARGET, decd. HARGET allowed some money from the estate to cover the "expense and trouble" of the infant children of the intestate; the accounts were settled and filed

JOHN SHELFER to oversee road in place of ABNER GREEN, resigned

HENRY RHODES (The surname was written over but it was probably RHODES.) to oversee road in place of JNO M. FRANKS, resigned

Clerk to make an entry of land for HENRY SHIELE bounded by JNO KORNEGAY, CHARLES THOMAS?, SIMMONS ?

FREDERICK TAYLOR to oversee road in place of ENOCH FOY, resigned

JAMES B. SHINE permitted to rebuild a mill on REEDY BRANCH at the old mill site lately owned by FREDERICK I. BECTON

RISDEN M. McDANIEL, CALVIN J. MORRIS, and FRANCIS DUVAL to settle accounts of AMOS AMYET, guardian to SUSAN ANDREWS

JAMES W. HOWARD to oversee road in place of JOSEPH WHITTY, resigned and moved

ELIZABETH WHARTON, guardian to JEREMIAH WHARTON, minor, should come before the court next term to renew her guardian's bond

$18 to be paid to .... (The original has dots to hold a space; no name was ever written.) in the case of "conspiracy, State vs DONAM, TOM, and others lately removed from this to CRAVEN COUNTY" in addition to $77.71 already allowed in same case

[Note: This case concerns the fear of slave insurrection in the wake of the NAT TURNER revolt. Taylor provides some background on slave and freedman laws in North Carolina: According to a law of 1741 no slave could be set free except for meritorious service which was to be judged by the county court. However this law was flagrantly violated by Quakers in PERQUIMANS and PASQUOTANK COUNTIES. Because of these violations the General Assembly reaffirmed the law in 1777. Nevertheless, from 1801-1828 there was considerable sentiment favoring freeing the slaves in North Carolina due to the work of the Colonization Society and the North Carolina Manumission Society which was organized by Quakers in GUILFORD, CHATHAM and RANDOLPH COUNTIES in 1816. The Quakers were responsible for sending many slaves to LIBERIA, HAITI, ILLINOIS, and INDIANA.

However, numerous slave insurrections in North Carolina in the early 19th century probably prompted the General Assembly in 1830 to pass legislation requiring slave owners to petition the Supreme Court in order to free a slave. The requirements were daunting: the petitioner had to give public notice of his or her intent six weeks prior in the *Star Gazette* and at the county courthouse. Plus, he or she had to post a bond of $1,000 per slave. These same terms were required for emancipation by a will.

While uprisings in SAMPSON and DUPLIN COUNTIES occurred in 1831 (the same year as the NAT TURNER uprising), the only law enacted as a direct consequence in North Carolina was the one forbidding Negroes to preach. NAT TURNER's rebellion silenced all black ministers.

The plight of the free Negro grew steadily worse during the first half of the 19th century. In 1830 a law was enacted in North Carolina which exiled from the state freed slaves under 50 years old. Further restrictions followed in the 1840s. Free blacks were not allowed to purchase liquor or own slaves of their own. In the state of VIRGINIA they could not even own a dog! After 1832 they were not allowed a trial by jury in VIRGINIA, but this right was never rescinded in North Carolina.]

JONAS JONES, JACOB GILES, and HENRY RHODES to allot off to WILLIAM A. COX and "his wife, CHARITY," their shares of the Negroes of the estate of CHRISTOPHER KINSEY (This name is probably correct, but it was partially hidden in the binding.), decd

Clerk to enter 40 acres of land for JOSEPH KINSEY adjoining heirs of DAVID FONVIELLE, decd, EML JARMON & J. KINSEY

JOHN JONES to oversee road in place of DANIEL Y. SHINE, resigned

OWEN B. COX to be guardian to MARY RHODES & JACKSON RHODES, minors; $1000 bond with ISAAC BROWN & WILLIAM HUGGINS, sureties

JACOB HUGGINS may "turn the road leading from TRENTON to MUSSELSHELL so as to lean his field to the left hand"

HARDY BRYAN may sell spiritous liquors by the small measure at his dwelling in TRENTON

State vs SIM MOORE} Affray. The jury:
SIMMONS HARRISON JR	WILLIAM M. GILES	PETER ANDREWS
MICAJAH PETEWAY	DANIEL WILLIAMSON	JOSEPH SMALL
WILLIAM GOODING SR	SILAS McDANIEL	JAMES MESSER
RISDEN McDANIEL	BENJN KOONCE	SAMUEL HILL

found the defendant innocent.

State vs BRICE MOON & BRYAN JONES} Affray. The same jury as above found MOON not guilty but JONES guilty. JONES fined $2.50 & costs

State vs WALTER P. ALLEN} F & L: Same jury as above found ALLEN guilty - fined $1.00 & costs

Account of sale & inventory of estate of FREDK WOOD, decd, filed by J. GILES

Division of Negroes of C. SMITH, decd, filed

EML JARMON, executor of D. McDANIEL, decd, filed affidavit

ROSCO BARRIS, guardian to W.W. FRANKS, minor, filed affidavit

Affidavit of W. DAVIS, guardian to JAMES D. & CHARITY KINSEY, minors, filed

HARDY H. SHELFER, admr of LUKE SHELFER, decd, filed affidavit

HARDY PARRY, guardian to heirs of SILAS PARRY, decd, filed affidavit

GEO WILCOX, admr of THOS WILCOX, decd, settlement

Jones County Court of Common Pleas Minutes 1832

JOHN S. KOONCE, guardian to heirs of MICHAEL KOONCE, decd, filed affidavit
JOHN OLIVER, guardian to F.G. SIMMONS, minor, filed affidavit
EML JARMON, admr of JAMES RHODES, decd, filed affidavit
Division of Negroes of estate of SAML WESTBROOK, decd, filed
JOHN H. HAMMOND, guardian to heirs of J. PARSONS, filed
[Note: JOHN H. HAMMOND served in the North Carolina House of Representatives 1832-1835 (Wheeler).]
EML JARMON, admr of A. PARRY, decd, filed affidavit
Inventory and sale of DELILA MEADOWS, decd, filed

Next day at 10 o'clock

Judges present: ISAAC BROWN, NATHAN FOSCUE, & ALFRED HARGET, esquires

Sci fa issued to WALTER P. ALLEN, guardian of WILLIAM FOY, minor, to renew his guardian's bond (Note: Sci fa is probably short for Scire facias which means cause it to be known. A writ thus issued is for the purpose of asking a defendant, in this case a guardian, to show cause.)
Same to ANN R. BRYAN, guardian to WILLIAM HENRY BRYAN, minor, to renew her bond
JOSEPH S. FOY to oversee road in place of JOHN YOUNG, resigned
HARDY BRYAN, WILLIAMS BROWN, & NATHAN FOSCUE to settle accounts of RISDEN M. McDANIEL, admr of MORRIS McDANIEL, decd
Inventory & sale of RISDEN McDANIEL SR, filed
NATHAN FOSCUE, WILLIAMS BROWN & HARDY BRYAN to settle accounts of MORRIS Mc(DANIEL?), former guardian to WILLIAM POLLOCK, minor, with RESDEN M. McDANIEL, present guardian to said minor
DANIEL DICKSON to oversee road in place of MICAJAH F. MATTOCKS, resigned
BENJAMIN BROCK to oversee road in place of LEWIS SMALL, resigned
OWEN B. COX to hire "some fit person" to convey fire arms belonging to JONES COUNTY from their "place of deposit" to the courthouse at TRENTON
SIMON I. BECTON to oversee road in place of WILLIAM D. COBB, resigned
ROSCO BARRIS to settle accounts of HARDY BRYAN, admr of BENJN HARRISON, decd
THOMAS POLLOCK to oversee road in place of JOHN G. RAMSEY, resigned
HARDY SHELFER, admr of LUKE SHELFER and others vs COUNCIL SHELFER and others} Petition for partition. Court determined that the land mentioned in the petition (unspecified in these minutes) should be sold and that out of the money received $95.20 plus interest from this day (13 Mar 1832) should be paid to HARDY SHELFER, "that being the amount...due him from the estate of LUKE SHELFER, decd" - the costs should be equally divided among petitioners and defendants.
Will of ESTHER HOLLAND, decd, proved in court by oath of ROSCO BARRUS who testified to the hand writing of HARRIET A. SMITH one of the witnesses; also DANIEL SMITH, the executor therein named qualifed as such
Division of lands of heirs of BUCKNER HATCH, decd, returned
OWEN ADAMS, guardian to heirs of KADER KNIGHT, decd, accounts settled
Settlement of accounts of ABNER GREEN, admr of MARY GREEN, decd, filed
Governor to the use of EML JARMON vs F. DUVAL - WM HUGGINS} debt. This case was carried forward ("Null" was written across it) but it mentioned that WILLIAM & CAROLINA MURPHEY, minors, owed money to their former guardian,

Jones County Court of Common Pleas Minutes 1832

FRANCIS DUVAL. Also mentioned were THOMAS, MARINDA and DEBORAH MURPHY to whom DUVAL owed money.

State vs SUSAN ALLEN} F.I. The jury:

SIMMONS HARRISON	WILLIAM M. GILES	PETER ANDREWS
MICAJAH PETEWAY	DANIEL WILLIAMSON	SILAS McDANIEL
WILLIAM GOODING	RISDON McDANIEL	WILLIAM RHEM
LEMUEL H. SIMMONS	JOSEPH WHITTY	ISAIAH WOOD

found defendant not guilty

State Bank vs JAS R. CONNER, RACHEL CONNER, & ANN R. BRYAN} dept. Same jury as above found for pltff in the amount of $500 & interest from 1 July 1829 & costs

Bank of New Bern vs BRYAN LAVENDER} judgment by default of $645 plus interest from 3 July 1831

MOSES JARVIS vs BRYAN LAVENDER} judgment by default of principal & interest which equals $130.59

WM HALLENTIN vs BRYAN LAVENDER} judgment by default of $161.71 with interest from 14 Mar 1832

Bank of New Bern vs BRYAN LAVENDER} judgment by default of $199 plus interest from 18 Aug 1831

State Bank vs BRYAN LAVENDER} judgment by default of $326 plus interest of $12.67

JOHN HAIRSTON vs BRYAN LAVENDER} judgment by default (no amount given)

ELIJAH SIMMONS vs JAMES N. SMITH} judgment by default of $299 plus interest and costs

"guarnishee having been called and failing to appear judgment - nici against the said guarnishee, DANIEL SMITH, for the sum of $299 with interest and costs issue Sci fa"

Deeds, bills of sale, and mortgages filed this term with registrar, JAS REYNOLDS

CALVIN J. MORRIS to WM HUGGINS & HARDY BRYAN
GEORGE HAZZARD to JAMES MARRIT
ELIAS FORDHAM to JOHN FORDHAM
ALFRED HARGET to WILLIAM BROWN
PETER HARGET, exec. of D. SIMMONS, to WILLIAM GOODING
ABNER GREEN to DAVID GREEN
FREDERICK I. BECTON to JAMES B. SHINE
JAMES MARRIT to LEML H. SIMMONS
JOHN D. & FREDK COLVITS to RESDON M. McDANIEL
CHARLES WHITTY to OWEN ADAMS
WINSTON ANDREWS to JOHN JACKSON
WM HUGGINS, shff, to OWEN ADAMS
WM HUGGINS, shff, to OWEN ADAMS
DURANT HATCH JR to HARDY WATSON
BENJAMIN KOONCE to SAML HILL
BENJAMIN KOONCE to SAML HILL
JNO HOUSTON/HAIRSTON, clerk of Superior Court bond

JAS McDANIEL to WILLIAMS BROWN, decd, delivered the rights, 24 Apr 1832
JAMES SIMMONS vs JAMES N. SMITH} attachment. default.
Governor to use of EML JARMON vs FRANCES DUVAL, WM HUGGINS & JAS MARRIT} debt. Judgment for pltff "for penalty of bond $10,000 to be discharged by the payment of $508.10 with credit of $143.37 which said amount is made as follows

Jones County Court of Common Pleas Minutes 1832

by amount due THOMAS MURPHY, minor, from DUVAL $152.88 & amount due MARINDA MURPHY, minor, from DUVAL $130.86" & same "due DEBORAH MURPHY...$224.32" JARMON is present guardian of the minors WILLIAM MURPHY & CAROLINA MURPHY are indebted to FRANCIS DUVAL, former guardian. JARMON to pay debts from the minors' accounts.

Freeholders drawn as jurors for next court, June term 1832:

1. WILLIAM JONES
2. EDWARD GILBERT
3. SHADERACK ERWIN
4. MERRIT JONES
5. DANIEL ANDREWS
6. FRANCIS ANDREWS
7. HUBBARD STANLY
8. JOHN ADAMS
9. FURNIFOLD G. HERRITAGE
10. JOHN STANLY SENR
11. JOHN FORDHAM
12. JOHN POLLOCK
13. COUNCIL GOODING
14. PETER HARGET
15. EDWARD C. DEBRULE
16. JOHN ANDREWS
17. JOSEPH RHEM
18. JOSEPH KINSEY SENR
19. JOSEPH WHITTY
20. JAMES GODWIN
21. JOHN FRIEZE
22. ISAIAH WOOD
23. EDWIN BECTON
24. JACOB HUGGINS (JR?)
25. (LEMUEL BUSICK?)
26. LEWIS WILLIAMS
27. HARDY COLLINS
28. JOHN H. BECTON
29. JOHN WOOD
30. OWEN ADAMS

GEORGE W. HOWARD to use of JAMES W. HOWARD vs JAMES N. SMITH} (*ca sa* and bond?) Judgment against defendant and his sureties, DANIEL DICKSON and EDWD I. JONES, for $94.30 and costs. (**Note**: This was very difficult to read.)

HARDY BRYAN to use of WM POLLOCK vs WILLIAM I. HILL and JOSEPH WHITTY} debt. Judgment for pltiff for $338.00 plus interest, but JOSEPH WHITTY asked for and received an appeal to Superior Court of Jones County. His securities: JAMES W. HOWARD and LEMUEL H. SIMMONS.

ELIJAH SMALL vs RISDEN M. McDANIEL, JAS REYNOLDS, and adm. of C. BRYAN} debt. Judgment by default for $800.00 and damages assesed at $210.19 and costs.

President and Directors of the State Bank vs BENJN WALLACE, BRYAN LAVENDER and JOSEPH WALLACE} debt. Favor of pltff for $150.00 and interest from 12 Sep 1831 and costs.

ROSCO BARRES vs DAVID W. DUDLEY and JOSEPH WHITTY} debt. Favor of pltff for $1245.69 with interest from 9 May 1831 until paid and costs.

PENNY WOOD vs JACOB GILES, adm. of F. WOOD} petition for yr's provisions. Recorded.

JAMES I/S. MILLER and others to the court} petition to sell Negroes for.... Court agreed to sale (but no listing given for owner of Negroes).

RACHEL CONNERS vs JAMES HAZZARD} *Cos Ta* and bond. The defendant appeared in court and took the oath of insolvency and was discharged. (**Note**: *Cos Ta* may refer to costs, interest, and bond.) HATCH (no given name was written) and CALVIN J. MORRIS were named (but no connection was made to the pltff or def).

JUNE TERM, 1832
TRENTON, 2nd Monday

Justices: OWEN B. COX, JOHN H. HAMMOND, and CALVIN KOONCE, esquires
Shff: WILLIAM HUGGINS
Clerk: HARDY BRYAN

Freeholders drawn as jurors for the state:
1. FURNIFOLD G. HERRITAGE, foreman
2. HARDY COLLINS
3. JOSEPH RHEM
4. FRANCIS ANDREWS
5. JOHN POLLOCK
6. EDWD C. DEBRULE
7. OWEN ADAMS
8. JAMES GODWIN
9. JOHN ADAMS
10. JOHN WOOD
11. SHADRACK ERWIN
12. JOHN ANDREWS
13. EDWARD GILBERT

JAMES TAYLOR, esq. atty....

Petit Jury:
1. ISAIAH WOOD
2. JOSEPH WHITTY
3. COUNCIL GOODING
4. DANIEL ANDREWS
5. PETER HARGET
6. MARRIT JONES
7. HUBBARD STANLY
8. JOSEPH KINSEY
9. OWEN HARRISON
10. FREDK I. BECTON
11. BRYAN WESTBROOK
12. MICHAEL KOONCE

JOSEPH BROCK to oversee rd from fork at SHINEs up to RED HILL on west side of REEDY BRANCH in place of FREDK I. BECTON (moved?)

County trustees to pay THOS W.C. WINGET $8.00 for ammunition he furnished the regiment during the alarm of insurrection of the Negroes Sep 1831.

Hands liable to work the public roads and living on the plantations of MRS. OLDFIELD, CLINTON? SIMMONS and DAVID BALL should be taken from DANIEL SMITH's district to work the road from the cross through the middle of the pocosin under overseer of that district.

Freeholders drawn for Superior Court Fall term:
1. JOSEPH SMALL
2. DANL STANLY SENR
3. GEO WILCOX
4. WM STANLY
5. JNO JONES
6. HENRY RHODES SENR
7. RISDEN M. McDANIEL
8. WMS ISLER
9. JAMES WALLACE
10. JONAS WILLIAMS
11. ISAAC BROWN
12. VINCENT ANDREWS
13. LEML HARRISON JR
14. LOT EUBANKS
15. THOS GILLET
19. JAMES B. SHINE
20. ELIJAH SMALL
21. JOHN H. HAMMOND
22. JOHN BALL
23. RICHD R. FOSCUE
24. FREDK FOSCUE
25. JNO M. FRANKS
26. ASA SMITH
27. DANL SMITH
28. JAMES MARRIT
29. ELIJAH SIMMONS
30. IVEY ANDREWS
31. THOMAS HARRISON?
32. OWEN B. COX
33. WM GILBERT

Jones County Court of Common Pleas Minutes 1832

16. NATHAN FOSCUE
17. JAMES ROBERTS
18. JAMES W. HOWARD
34. JNO BINDER
35. JAMES MADES
36. BENJN HUGGINS

[Note: Juror #16, NATHAN FOSCUE, served in the North Carolina House 1832-1834 (Wheeler). Kammerer (Vol. 2, pp. 21-22) transcribed a biography of FOSCUE which appeared in the *New Bern Daily Journal*, 2 Jan 1886. According to this article FOSCUE was born in 1791 and married SUSAN OLDFIELD in 1833. They had three sons, CYRUS, MACON and JOSEPHUS FOSCUE, and two daughters, JOSEPHINE, who married FRANKLIN FOY but died a few years later, and SUSAN CAROLINE, who married J.W. WOOTEN and died in 1884 or 1885. The three sons were living in 1886. NATHAN FOSCUE was described as a self-made man who had only nine months schooling. At his death he owned over 80 slaves and $40,000 worth of land. He died in 1858 and his wife survived him for only two months.]

Jurors for September Court:
1. JAS I. MILLER
2. ASA EUBANKS
3. JOHN L. PARSONS
4. MICAJAH PITWAY
5. LOVICK G. MOORE
6. HARDY HILL
7. JAMES KINSEY
8. WM A. COX
9. WRIGHT STANLY
10. JNO STANLY JR
11. BENJN F. STANLY
12. BRYAN MISSAU
13. SAML HILL
14. WM GOODING SENR
15. JOHN HEATH SENR
16. LEVI? JONES
17. CHRIST R. GREEN
18. ENOCK FOY
19. JNO OLIVER
20. F.I. BECTON
21. DANL YATES
22. LEWIS SMALL
23. LEVI EUBANKS
24. R. McDANIEL
25. MICHAEL KOONCE
26. L.H. SIMMONS
27. JAMES TURNAGE
28. ALFRED M. FRESHWATER?
29. ELIJAH KOONCE
30. JAS MISSAU

Account of sale of property of HENRY RHODES JR returned.

SIMMONS ISLER, guardian to JOSEPH and WILLIAM BRYAN, acc. filed
Same for SAML B. HEATH, guardian to LIVIA and WM HEATH, minors.
Same for AMOS AMYET, guardian to SUSAN ANDREWS, minor.

FREDERICK KESSAN vs JAMES SIMMONS} debt. Jury (ISAIAH WOOD, JOSEPH WHITTY, COUNCIL GOODING, JOHN FORDHAM, DANIEL ANDREWS, PETER HARGET, MARRIT JONES, HUBBARD STANLY, JOSEPH KENSEY, OWEN HARRISON, FREDK I. BECTON, and BRYAN WESTBROOK) found for pltff. Damages: $578.50 and costs.
TIMOTHY I. KESSAN vs JAMES SIMMONS} debt. Same jury as above found for pltff and assessed damages at $140.71.
Gov. to use of JOHN BIRQURN? vs HARDY H. SHELFER, RISDEN McDANIEL and GEORGE WILCOX} debt. Same jury as above found for pltff; judgment of $4000 penalty of bond to be discharged upon payment of $41.36 and costs.
State vs JNO FORDHAM and LEWIS SMALL} affray. SMALL submits to court and is fined fifty cents and costs. Same jury finds FORDHAM not guilty.

Jones County Court of Common Pleas Minutes 1832

Tuesday, 12 June 1832

Justices: ISAAC BROWN, RISDEN M. McDANIEL, and OWEN B. COX, esg.

HARDY BRYAN, WILLIAMS BROWN, and THOMAS W.C. WINGET to settle acc. of RISDEN M. McDANIEL, admr of CULLEN POLLOCK, dec'd.

Renew orders of last term for (1) settlement of accounts of MORRIS McDANIEL, former guardian of WILLIAM POLLOCK, minor, with RISDEN M. McDANIEL, present guardian to said WM and (2) settlement of RISDEN M. McDANIEL, admr of MORRIS McDANIEL, dec'd.

EMANUEL JARMON to be guardian to WILLIAM HENRY BRYAN, minor, in place of ANN R. BRYAN; $2000 bond; ISAAC BROWN and HARDY BRYAN, sureties.

ISAAC BROWN, HARDY PARRY, and RISDEN M. McDANIEL to settle acc of HARDY BRYAN, admr of CHRISTOPHER BRYAN, dec'd.

EML JARMON to be guardian of RICHARD, ELIZA, and JOSEPH PARRY, minors; $200 bond; ISAAC BROWN and HARDY BRYAN, sureties.

JAMES REYNOLDS allowed money to pay for his account books needed for county records.

OWEN B. COX to be allowed $40.00 for conveying all of the ? of arms belonging to Jones Co. from FAYETTEVILLE to court house in TRENTON including 32 swords yet deficient.

Since a majority of the County Justices were present (ISAAC BROWN, RISDEN McDANIEL, JAMES HARRISON, OWEN B. COX, EMANUEL JARMON, ABNER GREEN, ELIJAH SIMMONS, NATHAN FOSCUE, and ROSCO BARRUS), court elected county officers, levied the county tax, and made appointments.

The county tax levied was same as last year. Every black tithable pole was taxed ten cents to pay patrols in the county.

WILLIAM HUGGINS, shff, was to be paid $80.60 for extra services in the last yr.

HARDY BRYAN, clerk, allowed $40.00 for extra services.

WILLIAM BROWN, constable, allowed $7.20 for extra services.

DANIEL DICKSON/DURKSON, constable, allowed $8.00 for attending court last yr.

JOHN L. PARSONS allowed $9.60 for attending court.

RISDON M. McDANIEL, Esq., appointed to care for the public arms belonging to the county deposited at the courthouse in TRENTON. He was to furnish a lock to the office room wherein the arms were secured and to have them cleaned.

County Officers elected by the court:
County Trustee: EMANUAL JARMON, 1 yr., bond with ISAAC B..... and HARDY BRYAN
Constables:
District 1, White Oak - DANIEL DICKSON, bond with WILLIAM HINES and JOSEPH WHITTY
District 2, Trent Bridge - no candidate
District 3, Trenton - WMS BROWN with JACOB HUGGINS, and NATHAN FOSCUE, securities
District 4, Cypress Creek - no candidate
District 5, Tuckahoe - no candidate
District 6, Biver Creek - BENJAMIN HUGGINS with WM HUGGINS and EML JARMON, sureties
District 7, McDaniel's - JOHN L. PARSONS with EML JARMON and JAS W. HOWARD, sureties

Jones County Court of Common Pleas Minutes 1832

The following justices were ordered to take the list of taxable property in the county for the present year:
- District 1, White Oak - DANIEL SMITH
- District 2, Trent Bridge - ELIJAH SIMMONS
- District 3, Trenton - RISDON M. McDANIEL
- District 4, Cypress Creek - JAMES HARRISON
- District 5, Tuckahoe - OWEN B. COX
- District 6, Bever Creek - SIMMONS ISLER?
- District 7, McDaniels - NATHAN FOSCUE

The following persons were appointed to hold elections:
- District 1: THOS GILLET, DANL DICKSON, LEVI EUBANKS
- District 2: ROSCO BARRUS, ENOCK FOY, JOHN HOUSTON
- District 3: ABNER GREEN, WILLIAMS BROWN, HARDY BRYAN
- District 4: JNO H. HAMMOND, MICAJAH PETERWAY, JACOB GILES
- District 5: ISAAC BROWN, HENRY RHODES, JOSEPH KINSEY
- District 6: SIMS/LIML ISLER, WMS ISLER, PETER HARGET
- District 7: to go to the other elections

County Trustees were to pay L. SCOTT $.... (not filled in) as an indemnity against a bill of cost in superior court March term, 1832, he having been a militia man at the time

Damages sustained by patrols in suit filed by JOHN H. BUTON against the patrols for hogs taken as Negro property and then sold by the patrols. BUTON was to be paid such charges in his settlement as trustee.

ABNER GREEN, ELIJAH PARRY, HARDY PARRY, JAMES HUGGINS and WILLIAM RUSSEL petitioned court and court ordered that HARDY PARRY, ELIJAH PARRY, and ABNER GREEN were to direct hands residing on the plantation wherein GREEN lived and who were cleared from road work in their present district, were now liable to work for three years to open a good highway from said GREEN's across the run at or in the neighborhood of PARRY's bridge and into the Trenton rd below MRS. RACHEL McDANIEL's. Then they were to go back to work on roads in their district.

Monies collected as patrol tax were to be distributed to the persons who served as patrols the last two years.

RICHARD DISMAL/DIRMAL, an orphan boy aged about nine years, was to be bound to ABNER GREEN as an apprentice and servant

ABNER SANDERS, an orphan boy aged about .... (not filled in) years, was to be bound as an apprentice and servant of SHADERACK EVERET? until he reaches lawful age.

JACOB GILES, guardian to ABNER KILLIBREW, filed accounts.

EML JARMAN, guardian to JEROD KOONCE, filed accounts.

EML JARMAN also filed guardian accounts for these wards: JNO P. KOONCE, NANCY WESTBROOK, ISA WESTBROOK, C.B. KOONCE, E.F. KOONCE, CURTIS WESTBROOK, JOHN and BENJN ASKEY.

Account of sale of balance of property of MARY MURPHY, dec'd, filed by E. JARMAN, exr.

Inventory of estate of LEWIS MORRIS, dec'd, returned by EML JARMAN, admin.

Division of Negroes of estate of CHRISTOPHER KINSEY, dec'd, returned by commissioners.

JAMES HAZZARD vs RACHEL CONNER} appeal. The jurors (GEORGE WILCOX,

Jones County Court of Common Pleas Minutes 1832

BENJAMIN HUGGINS, CALVIN J. MORRIS, JOHN MISSAW, ISAIAH WOOD, JOSEPH WHITTY?, COUNCIL GOODING, JOHN FORDHAM, DANIEL ANDREWS, PETER HARGET, MERRIT JONES, and HUBBARD STANLY) found for pltff. Damages set at $44.00 and costs.

WILLIAM DUNKEN vs WINIFORD/WINFORD HERRICK/HERRIOT} debt. Same jury found for pltff. Judgement of $172.80 and costs.

CALVIN J. MORRIS was allowed a license to serve retail spirits for one yr in TRENTON.

Deeds proved and left for registration:
1. WILLIAM MUMFORD, trustee, to WILLIAM HUGGINS
2. ELIJAH LOVIT to DAVID LOVIT
3. WILLIAM HUGGINS, shff, to JAMES C. COLE
4. ALFRED HARGET to WILLIAM HUGGINS
5. SIMMONS HARRISON to JACOB GILES
6. DURANT HATCH to JOHN BINDER
7. THOS J. FONSVILLE to EML JARMON
8. WM HILLEN and wife to JACOB HUGGINS
9. LOVICK G. MOORE to Pres. and directors of .... Bank
     JAS REYNOLDS, registrar

SEPTEMBER TERM, 1832
TRENTON, 2nd Monday

Justices: RESDEN M. McDANIEL, DANIEL SMITH, CALVIN KOONCE, Esquires
Sheriff: WILLIAM HUGGINS
Clerk: HARDY BRYAN

Jurors for term:
JOHN HEATH	JAMES D. KINSEY	ELIJAH KOONCE
LIML H. SIMMONS	RISDEN McDANIEL	FREDK I. BECTON
JAMES S. MILLER	JOHN OLIVER	ASA EUBANKS
LEWIS SMALL	WILLIAM A. COX	BENJN F. STANLY
WRIGHT STANLY		

ENOCK FOY, EDMD HATCH SENR and LEMUEL H. SIMMONS to audit and settle accounts of STEPHEN B. FORBES, admr of THOMAS O. BRYAN, dec'd, and report this term.

JOHN MISSAW was to oversee rd from BEVER DAM near JAMES MARRIT's down to fork of rd at TEN MILE HOUSE in place of GEO HAZZARD. (**Note**: according to Powell, TEN MILE FORK is a community in eastern Jones County.)

GEORGE I. BENDER to oversee rd from his house towards TRENT BRIDGE to the main rd and to work all hands on said rd (except his Negro man, YORK, SARAH OLDFIELD's hands, B.C. LIMON/SIMMONS and DAVID BALL's hands, who were taken off last court and put on the other rd.

SIMMONS HARRISON, JAMES B. SHINE, and ABNER GREEN to divide Negroes of estate of JEREMIAH PARSONS, dec'd, so as to allot off to THOMAS PARSONS his equal and distributive share of said Negroes agreeable to law.

LEMUEL H. SIMMONS to oversee rd from bridge at TRENTON down to BEVER DAM BRANCH and from fork of rd at RISDEN M. McDANIEL's to MUSSELSHELL BRANCH on rd leading to KINSTON in room of DANIEL HARRISON.

WILLIAM L. LARAQUE to oversee rd from bridge at TRENTON to head of straight reach one mile above TRENTON including streets of said town in place of JACOB HUGGINS.

    RISDEN M. McDANIEL, ABNER GREEN, and WILLIAMS BROWN to audit and settle accounts of BENJAMIN HUGGINS, exr of JAMES HUGGINS, decd.

    JAMES G. OLIVER to oversee rd in place of DANIEL Y. SHINE (The rest was written over and made illegible.)

    CATY? COLLINS was to admin. estate of JOHN COLLINS, decd; $2500 bond with HARDY COLLINS and LOTT EUBANKS, sureties. Also CATY? COLLINS permitted to sell the personal estate of the intestate and Negroes: MARIA, LISHEY?), TOM & LINDA. ASA SMITH, Esq., LEVI EUBANKS, ASA EUBANKS, & RIGDON HEWIT appointed to set off to said CATY? COLLINS, widow, one yr's support for herself & family out of estate of her late husband, JOHN COLLINS.

    WILLIAM HUGGINS, Esq., shff, gave bond.

    Settlement of HARDY BRYAN, admr of CHRISTOPHER BRYAN, returned.
    Settlement of HARDY BRYAN, admr of BENJAMIN HARRISON, decd, approved.
    Settlement of RESDEN M. McDANIEL, admr of CULLEN POLLOCK, decd, returned.
    Settlement of STEPHEN B. FORBES, admr of THOMAS O. BRYAN, decd, returned & filed in office.
    Settlement of JAMES HARRISON, guard to JAMES & PENIT? MUMFORD, minors, filed.
    Tax list of Districts 1,5,6,& 7 returned & filed.

Tuesday, September 11, 1832

Justices: JAMES HARRISON, JAMES G. HERRITAGE, & ELIJAH SIMMONS, Esquires

Petit Jurors:

WILLIAM GOODING	MICHAEL KOONCE	WRIGHT STANLY
MICAJAH PETERWAY	SAMUEL HILL	JAMES MISSAW/MIPAW
DANIEL YATES	ENOCK FOY	JOHN STANLY
BRYAN MISSAW/MIPAW	COUNCIL GOODING	BENJAMIN BROCK

    NICHOLAS A. BRAY, orphan boy aged 11 yrs, to be bound to DANIEL YATES as an apprentice until he reaches lawful age.

    WILLIAM HUGGINS, WILLIAMS BROWN, & RISDEN M. McDANIEL to audit accounts of THOMAS W.C. WINGET, admr of MARY McDANIEL, decd.

    JOSEPH RHEIM to oversee rd in room of WRIGHT STANLY, resigned, from mouth of BEVER CREEK up to BIG CHINQUIPEN & to work all hands from said BEVER CREEK to ? the north side of river & on south from BUSECK's and C. SMITH's.

    OWEN ADAMS to oversee rd from TRENT BRIDGE down to ? GULLY BRIDGE in room of JOHN C. FOSCUE, resigned.

    AARON WOOD to oversee rd from the INDIAN (gran of field?) up to JACK CABBIN in place of JAMES S. MILLER, resigned.

    County Trustees to pay ELIJAH SIMMONS $9.97 for four witness tickets: attendance of Negro, ISAAC, the property of said SIMMONS in favor of the state against TOM and others lately tried in Craven Superior Court, three others for attendance of JOHN CONWAY in same suit.

    HARDY BRYAN, WILLIAMS BROWN, & WILLIAM HUGGINS to settle accounts of RISDEN M. McDANIEL, admr of MORRIS McDANIEL, decd.

Jones County Court of Common Pleas Minutes 1832

Same committee as immediately above to settle accounts of MORRIS McDANIEL, guard of WILLIAM POLLOCK, minor.

RISDEN M. McDANIEL, FREDERICK FOSCUE, & LEMUEL H. SIMMONS to be patrols for one yr in District #7.

Country Trustees to pay $7.00 to JAMES REYNOLDS, registrar, for books for his office.

Tax list for districts 2, 3, & 4 returned & filed.

District of River (**Note:** This must be BEVER as there did not seem to be a River District; District 6 was called BEVER CREEK.) from PARRY's BRIDGE to LITTLE CHINQUIPIN CREEK to be divided into two districts; the first to commence at PARRY's BRIDGE & end at mouth of BUCK BRANCH running through WILLIAM GILBERT's field; the second to commence at mouth of BUCK BRANCH and end at mouth of LITTLE CHINQUIPIN CREEK. SAMUEL DILLAHUNT to oversee district from BUCK BRANCH to mouth of LITTLE CHINQUIPIN.

Jurors drawn for December term, 1832:

HARDY M(?)	JOHN ROUN?	SILAS McDANIEL
TOBIAS KOONCE	SIMMONS HARRISON JR.	JOHN FROST
JOSEPH HAY	WHITFIELD TURNER	ADAM ANDREWS
WILLIAM McDANIEL	WILLIAM MISSOW/MIPOW	PETER ANDREWS
LEWIS O. BRYAN	WILLIAM M. GILES	JOHN SHELFER
AARON WOOD	MILLENTON MEADOWS	RIGDEN HEWIT
JAMES GODWIN	JOSEPH ASKEW	STUART SCOTT
ELIJAH PARRY	JONAS JONES JR.	THOMAS McDANIEL
JOHN MALLARD	WILLIAM D. COBB	

WILLIAM HUGGINS, shff, returned his audit of taxes on retailors, peddlers, exhibitors.

Governor to use of FREDERICK I. BECTON vs WILLIAM S. BLACKLEDGE & N.B. BUSH} debt. The following jury: WILLIAM GOODING, MICHAEL KOONCE, MICAJAH PETTAWAY, LOVICK G. MOORE, SAMUEL HILL, JAMES MIPAW, DANIEL YATES, ENOCK FOY, JOHN STANLY, BRYAN MIPAW, COUNCIL GOODING, & BENJAMIN BROCK find for pltff & assess damage at $3827.20.

EARLINA HARGET vs BENJN HUGGINS, exr of JOS HUGGINS} appeal. Motion to amend warrent allowed from which defendant prays an appeal to superior court; granted.

RUFUS W. DAVIS, admr of RACHEL GREEN vs THOMAS GELLET} covr?. Judgment admitted for $99.88 with interest & costs.

Heirs & ? of MARY GREEN, decd, vs ABNER GREEN, JAS N. SMITH, & NATHAN B. BUSH} debt. Same jury as above found for pltff with judgment of $70.67 with interest & costs.

JOHN GILBERT, admr, vs WM COOMBS, RICHD REYNOLDS, & EML JARMON, admr of A. PARRY} appeal. Same jury found for pltff with judgment of $26.75 & costs.

DAVID GEORGE to use of JOHN JONES vs SIMMONS ISLER & WILLIAMS ISLER} debt. Same jury found for pltff with judgment of $117.91 with interest since 1830 & costs.

DAVID GEORGE to use of JOHN JONES vs OWEN B. COX} debt. Same jury found for pltff with judgment of $171.65 plus interest & costs.

Bank of Newbern to use of JOHN GILDERSLEEVE vs ASA SMITH, WILLIAM JONES, & EDWD L. JONES} Writ amended by striking out WM JONES.

WILLIAM HUGGINS to use of NATHAN FOSCUE vs EDWARD S/L. JONES} Same jury found for pltff; judgment of $112.90 & costs. (Note: I could not decipher what kind of case this one was or the one just above.)

Governor to use of Z. SLADE vs DANL DICKEN, JAS W. HOWARD, & ELIJAH LOVIT} debt. Same jury, except WRIGHT STANLY in place of L.G. MOORE, found for pltff.

MARY BRYAN, widow of THOS O. BRYAN, to the court} petition for year's provision. Report returned & confirmed. Judgment against the admr for amount of report & costs. S.B. FORBES, admr.

FREDERICK BLUNT to use of DAVID LEWIS vs HENRY SHUTE. On motion ordered clerk issue $16.20 to defendant with interest from 15 September 1831.

Deeds proved at this term for registration:
JOHN H. DILLAHUNT to SAMUEL DILLAHUNT
DANIEL MALLARD to IVEY ANDREWS
SIMMONS HARRISON to JAMES HARRISON
HARDY BRYAN to BENJN HUGGINS
DANIEL ANDREWS to IVEY ANDREWS
JAMES J. RHODES to OWEN B. COX
WILLIAM HUGGINS, Shff, to JAMES FOY
JAMES CAHOON to ENOCK FOY
WILLIAM L. LARAQUE to CALVIN J. MORRIS
SAML C. FISHER, CLARK & MASTERS to RD B. HATCH
RICHD REYNOLDS to SARAH GREEN
RICHD REYNOLDS to SARAH GREEN
SARAH B. GREEN to RICHD REYNOLDS
WALTER HILLEN proved ? ? ENOCK FOY

DECEMBER TERM, 1832
TRENTON, Monday, December 10, 1832

Justices: ASA SMITH, ROSCO BARRUS & SIMMONS ISLER, esquires
Sheriff: WILLIAM HUGGINS
Clerk: HARDY BRYAN

Jurers:
    WILLIAM M. GILES, foreman

MILLENTON MEADOWS	JOHN MALLARD	PETER ANDREWS
JOHN SHELFER	JOHN FROST	JOHN GODWIN
WILLIAM McDANIEL	AARON WOOD	ADAM ANDREWS
LEWIS O. BRYAN	ELIJAH PARRY	RIGDON HEWIT

JAMES W. BRYAN, esq., gave the charge; JOHN PARSONS, constable, sworn to attend grand jury.

DAVID BALL to oversee rd from cross roads on WHITE OAK to a black sorrel in the middle of the POCOSIN in place of HARDY MUNDINE (removed).

GEORGE DEBRULE to oversee rd from TRENT BRIDGE to DEEP GULLY in place of OWEN ADAMS, due to age.

ENOCK FOY & JOSEPH S. FOY to take the private examination of CATHARINE CONWAY, wife of JOHN CONWAY, on the execution of a deed to GEORGE POLLOCK.

LEMUEL H. SIMMONS, JAMES McDANIEL & BENJAMIN HUGGINS to divide Negroes of estate of BENJN HARRISON, decd, among heirs.

RESIDEN M. McDANIEL, ABNER GREEN, & JOSEPH/JACOB HUGGINS JR. to divide Negroes of MRS. LAROQUE, late wife of Dr JAS. B. LARAQUE in order to give an

Jones County Court of Common Pleas Minutes 1832

equal share to JAMES E. LARAQUE.

HARDY O. NEWTON may sell spirits at the fork of the rd in Jones County for one yr.

JONAS JONES JR. & JOHN JONES may sell spirits in each of their houses in Jones County for one yr.

LEMUEL H. SIMMONS' hands who have worked rds from BEVERDAM down to fork were to work from TRENTON down to BEVERDAM.

Patrols for TRENTON for one yr: JACOB HUGGINS, WILLIAMS BROWN, THOS. W.C. WIG..., WM HUGGINS, JAMES E. LAROQUE, FRANCIS ANDREWS, HARDY O. CONNER, & FRANCES DUVAL.

Jury to be summoned to lay off dower to SUSAN ALLEN ... . of THOS. FOY, decd of ..... (**Note:** the dots indicate illegible words.)

JAMES REYNOLDS to oversee rd from WARDS HILL up to JACOB BRANCH including BEEN CREEK BRIDGE in place of HUBBARD STANLY, resigned.

JESSE LITTLE, a colored boy, to be bound to OWEN CONNER.

DAVID GREEN to oversee rd from bridge at TRENTON up to WARDS HILL and from fork of rd at B. HUGGINS down to MUSSELSHELL? on the rd to NEWBERN in place of WILLIAM STANLY, resigned.

County Trustees were to pay costs of judgment against JAS. B. SHINE as overseer of (Trent run?).

MARTIN MILLER was to be guard to heirs of JAMES? MILLER, decd, in place of JAMES MILLER, resigned; $2,000 bond; JAMES B. SHINE & CALVIN KOONCE, sureties.

WILLIAM HUGGINS, HARDY BRYAN & WILLIAMS BROWN were to divide and allot to JEROME? KOONCE his portion "of his father, EML KOONCE's, estate."

Same committee were to divide estate of CAROLINA MURPHY & THOS MURPHY, decd, among heirs.

HARDY BRYAN, FURNIFOLD G. HERITAGBE, & MICAJAH PETEWAY to audit & settle accounts between JAMES MILLER, former, & MARTIN MILLER, present guard, to heirs of JAMES MILLER, decd.

Sheriff was to draw $25 or $30 from county funds to purchase vacant lot adjoining courthouse from DURANT RICHARDS for county.

Jury to be summoned to ascertan lunacy of MARTHA COLLINS.

SAMUEL HILE/HILL to admin estate of ELIJAH SMALL, decd; $3,000 bond; BENJN HUGGINS & ADAM ANDREWS, sureties.

JAMES G. HERRITAGE, JOHN H. BECTON, & AMOS HEATH to audit & settle accounts of JOHN ASKEY, exr of BENJN ASKEY, decd.

Court concurred that JOHN R. FOY of DYER CO., TN, was to be appointed and qualified as guard to infants, BRYAN BECTON & MARY BECTON, in the aforesaid county and state.

Tuesday

Justices: ISAAC BROWN, RISDEN M. McDANIEL & ASA SMITH, esquires
Sheriff: WM HUGGINS
Clerk: H. BRYAN

Motion of RISDEN M. McDANIEL for suit to show cause why execution in case of Governor to use of ELIJAH SMALL vs RISDEN M. McDANIEL and others should not be set aside; refused.

Jones County Court of Common Pleas Minutes 1832

WILLIAM HUGGINS, LEMUEL H. SIMMONS & HARDY BRYAN were to settle accounts of FREDERICK BECTON, guard to BRYAN & MARY BECTON, minors.

THOS GILLET, ASA SMITH, & GEO. OLDFIELD were to settle ... of SARAH OLDFIELD, guard to PRUDENCE OLDFIELD.

WALTER P. ALLEN & wife vs WILLIAM FOY, heir of THOS FOY} petition for dower. Since the petitioners were guardians of the defendant, ENOCH FOY was appointesd to be special guard to defend the suit. Petition granted.

HARDY SHELFER vs COUNCEL SHELFER & others} petition for sale of land.

Note: The next section was very difficult to read. It appeared to be two cases. The first mentioned Governor to use of T.W. ? and the second was Governor to use of JNO BIRGIVEN.

Freeholders drawn as jurors for March Term of Superior Court for 1833:

WM M. GILES	ENOCH FOY	SIMS HARRISON JR
LEML H. SIMMONS	JAMES W. HOWARD	DANIEL YATES
WMS BROWN	EDWD C. DEBRULE	JNO ROUN
RISDEN McDANIEL	RIGDON HEWIT	TOBIAS KOONCE
JOHN STANLY (Trenton?)	PETER ANDREWS	JNO H. HAMMOND
BENJN HUGGINS	IVEY ANDREWS	JOSEPH HAY
WILLIAMS ISLER	ASA SMITH	JAMES ROBERTS
HENRY RHODES SR	GEO WILCOX	SHADK ERWIN
EDWD M. GILBERT	COUNCIL GOODING	JONAS WILLIAMS
HUBBARD STANLY	JOHN POLLACK	JOSEPH SMALL
JAMES HARRISON	LEVI JONES	JAMES G. HERRITAGE
ASA EUBANKS	JOHN H. BECTON	JOHN HEATH, SR

Jurors drawn for county court March Term, 1833:

DANIEL WILLIAMSON	JOHN SHLE?	WM WATERS
WM HARRISON	EDMD HATCH	WM ADAMS
WM GOODING	NATHAN STANLY	JNO McDANIEL SR
SIMON S. BECTON	DAVID GREEN	MARTIN F. BROCK
THOS POLLACK	SHADRACK MALLARD	F.H. JARMAN
BARTHOLMY MEADOWS	CALVIN J. MORRIS	JOHN WOOD
WM DUNKEN	MOSES ADAMS	JAMES FOY
ELIJAH LOVIT	HARDY O. CONNER	JOHN S. KOONCE
JOHN FORDHAM	WM RHEM	LOTT EUBANKS
JAMES MARRIT	HARDY COLLINS	

Settlement of T.W.C. WINGET, admr of MARY McDANIEL, decd, filed.
Division of Negroes of estate of J. PARSONS filed.
Settlement of R.M. McDANIEL, admr of MORRIS McDANIEL, filed.
Settlement of MORRIS McDANIEL, guard to WM POLLACK, minor, approved.
Inventory & sale of estate of JNO S. COLLINS filed.
Deeds proved & ordered to be recorded:
JOHN M. FRANKS to F. GOODING
JAS C. COLE to E.C. DEBRULE SR & others
JOHN COLLINS to MILENTIN MEADOWS
JOHN COLLINS & others to SIMEON COLLINS
JAMES SIMMONS to JOHN HOUSTON
WILLIAM MISSITFORD? to JOHN HOUSTON
WM HUGGINS, shff, to JOSEPH BELL

WM HUGGINS, shff, to JOHN HOUSTON
JNO HOUSTON to WILLIAM HUGGINS
JNO POLLACK to WILLIAM HUGGINS
WILLIAM HUGGINS, shff, to RIGDEN HEWIT
L.W. KORNEGAY to I.W. BROCK
ISAAC KORNEGAY to L.W. KORNEGAY
THOS POLLACK & wife to IVEY ANDREWS
JOHN FORDHAM to WILLIAM GOODING
JAMES S. MILLER to MARTIN MILLER
JOHN M. FRANK to MICHAEL KOONCE
MARY McDANIEL to IVEY ANDREWS
E.M. FRANKS to JNO M. FRANKS
        JAS REYNOLDS, registrar

The paper on the left side of the volume has one note: Tobacco to Negro LEMUEL/LEMONT MARTIN on the 20th or the 28th of September 1837.

The records begin:

MARCH TERM, 1833
TRENTON, 2nd Monday in March, 11 March 1833

Justices: OWEN B. COX, NATHAN FOSCUE, & CALVIN KOONCE, Esquires
Sheriff: WILLIAM HUGGINS
Clerk: HARDY BRYAN

Grand Jurors:
JOHN FORDHAM, foreman	MOSES ADAMS	WILLIAM GOODING
DANIEL WILLIAMSON	LOT EUBANKS	JAMES FOY
JOHN McDANIEL SR	JOHN WOOD	HARDY COLLINS
FURNIFOLD H. JARMON	WILLIAM WATERS	WILLIAM DUNKIN
SHADERACK MALLARD		

Jurors charged under direction of JAMES W. BRYAN, county solicitor, & JOHN L. PARSONS, constable sworn to attend the jury.

Power of attorney given to JOSEPH T. RHODES by JACOB RHODES to be registered.

HARDY BRYAN, WILLIAM HUGGINS & WILLIAM BROWN to settle accounts of EMANUEL JARMON, admr de bonis non of LEWIS MORRIS, decd.

THOMAS DUDLEY to oversee rd from crossroads on WHITE OAK to a black sorral in middle of POCOSIN in place of DAVID BALL.

EDMUND HATCH to oversee road from MILL CREEK BRIDGE including one half of said bridge to REEDY BRANCH in place of FREDERICK TAYLOR, resigned.

LEWIS WILLIAMS to oversee rd in place of HENRY RHODES, resigned.

The portion of road formerly extending from MILL CREEK BRIDGE including one half of said bridge to JOSEPH HATCH's run was to be altered so as to extend from said bridge to fork of the road near BUCKNER HATCH's mill and the hands of ELIJAH SIMMONS were to work said road in addition to those who were already employed on said rd and JOHN HOUSTON was to be the overseer.

The portion of road formerly leading from the POCOSIN to BUCKNER HATCH's mill to the bridge over HATCH's run was to be so altered as to extend from the middle of said Pocosin to BUCKNER HATCH'S mill only and that the overseer of said road was to use the hands of EDWD MUMFORD in addition to those already assigned.

JAMES FOY was to oversee rd from TEN/TOW SWAMP to TRENT BRIDGE including one half of said bridge in place of JAMES H. FRESHWATER, resigned.

GEORGE POLLOCK's hands were ordered to work road extending from MILL CREEK BRIDGE, including one half of said bridge, to the fork of rd below HATCH's mill and the same number of hands of JOHN BURGWIN and all the hands at TRENT BRIDGE were to work rd extending from TRENT BRIDGE to DEEP GULLY.

ADAM ANDREWS was to oversee rd in place of THOMAS POLLACK, resigned.

ROSCO BARRUS, AMOS AMYET, JOHN BENDER, JAMES FOY & DAVID LOVETT were to allot off to NANCY WHITTY, widow of CHARLES WHITTY, decd, one yr's support for herself & family out of her late husband's estate.

WILLIAM JONES was to be guard to heirs of FREDERICK WOOD, decd; $400 bond; JAMES RHODES & JOHN ADAMS, sureties.

$5.70 was to be paid on a witness ticket to JACOB I. DALEY/DOBY in case: State vs BENJAMIN COLLINS, which was removed to LENOIR COUNTY and defendant acquitted.

JAMES W. HOWARD, JOSEPH L. FOY, FREDERICK I. BECTON, & JOHN S./L. KOONCE qualified as justices.

$5.10 was allotted to ABNER GREEN, admr of MARY GREEN, decd, for voucher omitted in his settlement, plus 5% commission on sale of a Negro man who sold for $250; clerk assigned to pay remainder to heirs.

County trustee ordered to pay JAMES W. BRYAN, soliciter, $35 for his services in state cases when defendants were not able to pay.

JOHN H. HAMMON, SIMMONS HARRISON, & HARDY PARRY were to inspect the free bridge over TRENT RIVER & ascertain what repairs would be necessary and to employ persons to make repairs not to exceed $25, but if said bridge is determined to be not worth repairing and in a dangerous situation, they should report this to the next court.

State vs JAMES TIPPET} assult & battery. Defendant submitted and was fined by the court five cents plus costs.

ASA SMITH vs A. HARGET, B. NOBLE, B. COX, & SAML DILLEHUNT} **sie fa**. The jury: WILLIAM HARRISON, SIMON S. BURTON, DAVID GREEN, BARTHALOMAS MEADOWS, C.J. MORRIS, MARTIN F. BROCK, G.O. CONNER, THOS. POLLOCK, JAS. MARRET, WM. RHODES, NATHAN STRONG?, & LEML H. SIMMONS, found for pltff & fixed damages at $49.60 plus costs. Judgment for penalty of bond $400. (**Note:** The last lines of this page were very difficult to read, but at least two more names were mentioned in this case: B. HUGGINS & JOHN H. HAMMON who may have been appointed to see that the judgment was carried out.)

Tuesday, 12 March 1833

Justices: NATHAN FOSCUE, JOHN H. HAMMON, & JOHN S. KOONCE, Esquires

SAMUEL HILL to oversee rd in place of WILLIAMS BROWN, resigned.

DAVID McDANIEL to oversee rd extending from head of the straight reach above TRENTON to the INDIAN GROVE...OLDFIELD.

NATHAN F. PARSONS to oversee rd in place of JOHN JONES, resigned.

HARDY PARRY, WILLIAM HUGGINS & WILLIAMS BROWN were to settle accounts of ANN R. BRYAN, former guard to WILLIAM HENRY BRYAN, minor, with EMANUEL JARMON, present guard.

EMANUEL JARMON was appointed guard to SUSAN ANDREWS in place of AMOS AMYET; $500 bond; HARDY BRYAN & WILLIAM HUGGINS, sureties.

HARDY BRYAN, HARDY PARRY, & WILLIAM HUGGINS were to settle accounts of AMOS AMYET, former guard to SUSAN ANDREWS, minor, with EMANUEL JARMON, present guard.

Jurors drawn for June term:

THOMAS McDANIEL	JOSIAH ASKEY	ISAIAH WOODS
JEROD KOONCE	SAMUEL HILL	PETER ANDREWS
A.M. FRESHWATER	RICHD R. FOSCUE	ELIJAH PARRY
JOSEPH WHITTY	JAMES MADES	ELIJAH KOONCE
JAMES MAPAN/MASSAN	FREDERICK FOSCUE	JAMES McDANIEL

Jones Cty Court of Common Pleas Minutes 1833

BENJN F. STANLY	BENJN C. SIMMONS	LEWIS SMALL
LEVI EUBANKS	MICAJAH PETEWAY	JOHN BAER
FURNIFOLD G. HERRITAGE	JOHN HERRITAGE?	SIMMONS HARRISON SR
JAMES B. SHINE	JOHN SHELFER	THOMAS HARRISON
LEMUEL BUSICK	JAMES GODWIN	THOMAS ORMAN?

Deeds, etc., registered with JAS REYNOLDS, registrar:

JACOB GILES to F.H. JARMON
MARY FRANKS to ENOCK FOY
JOSEPH WHITTY to JNO YOUNG
HENRY RHODES to C.H. RHODES
MARY FRANKS to ENOCK FOY
JAS T. RHODES to O.B. COX
WM SHELFER to E. MATTS
RACHEL McDANIEL to HARDY PARRY
THOMAS SPEIGHT to WM HUGGINS
WM GILBERT to SAML DILLAHUNT
CHARLES WHITTY and wife to JAS WALLAN
LEWIS SMALL to EDWD WESTBROOK
D. RICHARDS to WM HUGGINS
SILAS McDANIEL to HARDY PARRY
WM ADAMS to JAS ADAMS
EDMD HATCH to LEWIS SMALL
LEML HARRISON to WM HUGGINS
JNO POLLOCK to BENJN HUGGINS
WM HUGGINS to JAS BALL?
JAS BALL? to WM HUGGINS
LANY SMALL to IVEY ANDREWS
JAS MALLARD to PETER ANDREWS
DURANT HATCH to FRANCIS DUVAL
JOHN M. FRANKS to JACOB GILES
JAMES G. OLIVER to JOSHUA B. OLIVER
WILLIAMS BROWN to SAMUEL HILL
LANTON? C. FULTON? ... to RICD R. HATCH (**Note:** This line was crossed out.)
JOSHUA B. OLIVER to CALVIN KOONCE
Mortgage between WM McDANIEL & JACOB? KOONCE
WILLIAM ADAMS to EDMD WESTBROOK
JAS G. OLIVER to BENJAMIN BROCK
THOMAS C. PARSONS to JOHN H. HAMMOND
R. BARRUS & O. ADAMS to JOSEPH MALLARD/WALLAND
HINDS & KINSEY to JOSEPH KINSEY & ELIJAH SIMMONS
JOSEPH RHEM to PETER HARGET
JAMES G. OLIVER to JACOB GILES
JACOB RHODES to JOSEPH T. RHODES
SAML HILL to DAVID GREEN

Estate settlements & divisions returned:

JOHN H. HAMMOND, guard to heirs of JEREMIAH PARSONS, decd, & of FREDK BRYAN, minor.

JAMES S. MILLER, guard to heirs of JAMES MILLER, decd.

JOHN S. KOONCE, guard to heirs of MICHAEL KOONCE, decd.

HARDY PARRY, guard to SUSANNAH PARRY, SILAS PARRY, minor, & GEORGE PARRY.

Jones Cty Court of Common Pleas Minutes 1833

JOHN ASKEY, exr of BENJ ASKEY, decd.
OWEN ADAMS, guard to heirs of KNIGHT.
JONAS JONES, guard to SUSAN COX, minor.
JOHN OLIVER, to F.G. SIMMONS
ROSCO BARRUS, guard to WM W. FRANKS
EML JARMON, admr of LEWIS MORRIS, decd.
Division of Negroes of CAROLINA & THOS. MURPHY, decd.
Division of Negroes of LOIS? LARAQUE, decd.
JONAS JONES, guard to JOHN A. COX
F.I. BECTON, guard to heirs of BRYAN BECTON
Division of Negroes of BENJAMIN HARRISON, decd.
Sale of estate of ELIJAH SMALL, decd, by S. HILL, admr.

JUNE TERM 1833
TRENTON, 2nd Monday, 10 June 1833

Justices: OWEN B. COX, FREDERICK I. BECTON, & CALVIN KOONCE
Sheriff: WILLIAM HUGGINS
Clerk: HARDY BRYAN

Grand Jurors:
FURNIFOLD G. HERRITAGE, foreman
PETER ANDREWS	JEROD KOONCE	JAMES B. SHINE
JOHN ANDREWS	ISAIAH WOOD	LEVI EUBANKS
BENJN F. STANLY	SAMUEL HILL	JOHN SHELFER
LEMUEL BUSICK	ELIJAH PARRY	THOMAS HARRISON

Petit Jurors:
JAMES GODWIN	RICHARD R. FOSCUE	JOSEPH WHITTY
ELIJAH KOONCE	LEWIS SMALL	SIMMONS HARRISON
JAMES McDANIEL	THOMAS McDANIEL	MARTIN F. BROCK
JOHN OLIVER	JOHN MASSAN	DAVID GREEN

JAMES B. SHINE was to oversee rd from fork at SHINE's to hill on west side of REEDY BRANCH in place of JOSEPH BROCK, resigned.
LEMUEL H. SIMMONS was to be guard to ELIZABETH ANN SIMMONS, minor; $1000 bond; NATHAN FOSCUE & WILLIAM HUGGINS, sureties.
Clerk ordered to enter in ... book for F.R. DICKSON for 100 acres of land.
CHARLES GARICK was licensed to retail spirituous liquors at his store in TRENTON for one yr.
JONATHON WOOD was licensed to retail spirituous liquors at his store at TRENT BRIDGE for one yr.
OWEN B. COX was licensed to retail spirituous liquors at (This was blank.) in said county for one yr.
RISDEN M. McDANIEL, JOHN STANLY, & SAMUEL DILLAHUNT were to examine the accounts of the office of EML JARMAN, county trustee, & report to court

DAVID M. CROSSLAND vs WILLIAM McDANIEL} Jury found for pltff. Damages assessed at 6 pence & costs.
ELINOR? HARGET vs BENJN HUGGINS, exr of JAS HUGGINS} Jury found for

pltff; damages $2.00 with interest from 5 Mar 1831 until paid plus costs.
LUKE HUGGINS vs MICAJAH F. MATTOCKS & DAVID W. SANDERS} debt. Jury found for pltff. Debt equaled $173 with $6.87 interest.
ISAIAH? GRINGE to use of JOHN JONES vs FRANCIS GOODING} debt. Plea was withdrawn. Debt was $119.14 with $2.61 interest. Judgment was for same plus costs.
EMANUEL JARMON, exr of DURANT McDANIEL vs devise of DURANT McDANIEL. Defendant, as heir of DURANT McDANIEL, indebted to pltff to sum of $278.21 plus interest from 8 Mar 1833. (**Note**: There may have been more than one defendant.)

CHARLES WILLIAMS was granted letters of admin for the estate of SARAH MORRIS, decd; $1000 bond; FREDERICK FOSCUE, surety.
ELIZABETH CARY appointed to admin estate "of her late husband SOLOMON CARY, decd," $10,000 bond; EMANUEL JARMON & JOHN STANLY sureties.

The following settlements & accounts were filed:
WMS BROWN, guard to heirs of B. SMALL (settlement).
EML JARMON, guard to JNO P., C.B., & E.F. KOONCE, & to NANCY & CURTIS WESTBROOK, & to heirs of A. PARRY, decd, & to HOLLON POLLOCK, minor, & to BENJN & JNO ASKEY (accounts).
L.B. HEATH, guard to his own children (accounts).
SIMMONS ISLER, guard to JOSEPH & WILLIAM BRYAN (settlement).
E. JARMON, county trustee (settlement).

Tuesday, 11 June 1833, 10 a.m.

Justices: ISAAC BROWN, OWEN B. COX, & NATHAN FOSCUE

These justices were ordered to take the list of taxable property in their districts for the present year:
    District 1: White Oak - JAMES ROBERTS
    District 2: Trent Bridge - JAMES W. HOWARD
    District 3: Trenton - RISDON M. McDANIEL
    District 4: Cypress Creek - ISAAC BROWN
    District 5: Tuckahoe - OWEN B. COX
    District 6: Bever Creek - JOHN S. KOONCE
    District 7: Bever Dam - NATHAN FOSCUE

The following persons were to hold elections:
District 1: THOS GILLET, DANIEL YATES & FRANCIS MATTOCKS
District 2: ROSCO BARRUS, JAMES FOY & DANIEL WILLIAMSON
District 3: sheriff, SAMUEL HILL & JAMES B. LARAQUE
District 4: CALVIN KOONCE, SIMMONS HARRISON & JOSEPH BROCK
District 5: ISAAC BROWN, HENRY RHODES, & JOSEPH KINSEY
District 6: FREDERICK I. BECTON, WILLIAMS ISLER & PETER HARGET
District 7: not given

Election of county officers took place since enough justices were present. The justices present were: ISAAC BROWN, NATHAN FOSCUE, OWEN B. COX, ABNER GREEN, JAMES HARRISON, RISDEN M. McDANIEL, & JOHN S. KOONCE. Constables

Jones Cty Court of Common Pleas Minutes 1833

they elected were: BENJAMIN HUGGINS, DANIEL DICKSON & JOHN L. PARSONS.

County trustee was ordered to pay JOHN L. PARSONS $10.40 for services to court during past yr.
Shff WM HUGGINS was allowed to draw $80.80 from county funds for services rendered.
Clerk HARDY BRYAN was allowed $40 for extra services.
BENJAMIN HUGGINS was allowed $4.80 for services.
DANIEL DICKSON was allowed $6.40 for services.
WILLIAMS BROWN was allowed $2.40 for services.
RESDEN M. McDANIEL was allowed $1.80 "for a lock furnished...buttons to the windows of courthouse."
The tax levied & collected this yr shall be the same as last yr.
The tax for pay for patrols should be levied & collected.
The same persons appointed as patrol committies in the county districts at June term 1831 were to be reappointed except NATHAN FOSCUE was to replace NATHAN B. BUSH who moved.

ROSCO BARRUS, JOHN BENDER & J. FOY were to allot off to NANCY WHITTY, widow of the late CHARLES WHITTY, one yr's provisions for herself & family.
HARDY BRYAN, WM HUGGINS & JACOB HUGGINS were to settle accounts between EML JARMON & ELIZABETH CARY, admr of SOLOMON CARY, decd.

President & directors of the State Bank vs RESDEN M. McDANIEL, WM HUGGINS & H. BRYAN} vendi... (Note: This was probably vendition). WM HUGGINS failed to execute a "process" from the bank. Court ordered sie fa to WM HUGGINS. No mention of other defendants.
President & directors of the State Bank of N.C. vs SIMMONS HARRISON (Note: These names were written in as defendants but were crossed through: JACOB GILES & NATHAN B. BUSH)} fi fa. Same finding and order as above.

The last will & testiment of DAVID LOVETT, decd, proved by oath of ROSCO BARRUS, one of the witnesses to the will; ELIJAH LOVETT named exr. [Gwynn abstracted this will (pp. 432-433) which was written 8 Apr 1833. Named in the will are the wife, MARY H. LOVETT and son, JAMES MONROE (It was not clear if the surname should be Lovett or Monroe.). The deceased's brother, ELIJAH LOVETT, was named exr, and the witnesses were HENRY ROWE, ROSCO BARRUS, and DAVID WEEKS.]
HARDY BRYAN, NATHAN FOSCUE, & C.J. MORRIS were to audit & settle accounts of RESDEN M. McDANIEL, admr of DANIEL MILLER, decd.

Freeholders drawn as jurors for next Superior Court:

JOHN MALLARD	JOHN JONES	JOHN WOOD
JAMES FOY	JAMES McDANIEL	FRANCIS ANDREWS
OWEN ADAMS	EDWD C. DEBRULE SR	JAMES W. HOWARD
DANIEL YATES	WILLIAM MURPHY	JOHN FORDHAM
JOSHUA BROWN	DAVID BALL	HENRY RHODES
SAML DILLAHUNT	BENJN HUGGINS	BENJN C. SIMMONS
DAVID McDANIEL	DANIEL WILLIAMSON	SIMMONS COLLINS
JAMES D. KINSEY	ISAIAH WOOD	BENJN F. STANLY
ELIJAH PARRY	ROSCO BARRUS	AMOS SIMMONS
WM RHEM SR	OWEN B. COX	THOMAS ORMAN

ABRAM SIMMONS	AMOS SHELFER	EDWIN BECTON
JAMES MESSAN	JAMES HARRISON	JOHN FRIEZE

Jurors for next county court:

SIMS HARRISON SR	MOSES ADAMS	JOHN HEATH SR
LEML H. SIMMONS	JOSEPH KINCEY	LEWIS O. BRYAN
WILLIAM D. COBB	ENOCK FOY	JNO McDANIEL SR
SHADRACK ERWIN	LEWIS WILLIAMS	FURNIFOLD H. JARMON
AARON WOOD	HOUSTON ROBERTS	SAMUEL HILL
DANIEL MALLARD	JAMES B. SHINE	RICHD R. FOSCUE
WM GOODING SR	HUBBARD STANLY	JOHN POLLOCK
NATHAN STANLY	LEWIS KINCEY	JAS H. FRESHWATER
THOMAS POLLOCK	HARDY MUNDINE	CHRISTOPHER ROBERTS
THOMAS MATTOCKS	THOMAS CANNON	THOMAS PARSONS

Deeds registered by JAS REYNOLDS, registrar:
JOHN WOOD to OWEN HARRISON
EPHRAM HARRISON to OWEN HARRISON
WILLIAMS BROWN to MATHEW OUTLAW?
BRYAN MESSAN to SIDNEY JARMAN
JOHN BARRUS to JULIA T. BERQUIN
OLIVER E. STRONG to JULIA T. BERGWIN
Marriage contract JAMES PIDCOCK & others

SEPTEMBER TERM 1833
TRENTON, 9 September 1833

Justices: RESDEN M. McDANIEL, JAMES HARRISON & JOSEPH FOY, esquires
Sheriff: WILLIAM HUGGINS
Clerk: HARDY BRYAN

Jurors:
ENOCK FOY, foreman

DANIEL MALLARD	HUBBARD STANLY	MOSES ADAMS
SHADERACK ERWIN	JOHN McDANIEL	NATHAN STANLY
HOUSTON ROBERTS	FURNIFOLD H. JARMON	HARDY MUNDINE
FRANCIS MATTOCKS	LEWIS WILLIAMS	JOHN HEATH SR

JAMES W. BRYAN, Esq., county solicitor, charged the grand jury & JOHN L. PARSONS, constable, was sworn to attend them during the term.

HARDY BRYAN, WILLIAM HUGGINS, & JACOB HUGGINS were to correct the settlement returned by EMANUAL JARMAN, admr de bonis non of LEWIS MORRIS, dec.
WILLIAM GOODING was exempted from jury duty.
JAMES B. LARAQUE, WILLIAM HUGGINS, & HARDY BRYAN were to divide Negroes of estate of JAMES GREEN, decd, among heirs & allot off to "ELIZABETH GREEN, one of the children & heir of said JAMES, decd, her distributive share in said Negroes."
An order was made at a former time, appointing a committee to settle accounts of RESDEN M. McDANIEL, exr of DANIEL MALLARD, decd, was mentioned in order to afford a settlement.

BENJAMIN GRIFFEN, an orphan boy, was bound to JOHN H. HAMMOND until he reached lawful age.

WILLIAM HUGGINS, CALVIN J. MORRIS, & HARDY BRYAN were to settle accounts of RESDEN M. McDANIEL, admr of GEORGE POLLOCK, decd.

JOHN ADAMS was to oversee rd in place of JOSEPH SMALL, resigned.

JAMES H. FRESHWATER was to admin estate of ALFRED M. FRESHWATER, decd; $1000 bond; JOSEPH WHITTY & BENJAMIN HUGGINS, sureties.

EMANUEL JARMON was appointed guard to heirs of FREDERICK WOOD, decd; $500 bond; JAMES KINCEY & HARDY BRYAN, sureties.

JAMES HARRISON, IGNATIOUS BROCK, & HENRY RHODES were to settle accounts of JACOB GILES, admr of FREDK WOOD, decd.

FRANCIS B. AMYET was to oversee rd in place of JAMES W. HOWARD, resigned.

JAMES MESSAN to oversee rd in place of JOHN MESSAN, resigned.

JOHN HEATH SR exempted from jury duty.

JOHN L. PARSONS appointed guard to LEAH STANLY, minor; $1500 bond; NATHAN F. PARSONS & BENJAMIN HUGGINS, sureties.

MARY H. LOVET, "widow of the late DAVID LOVIT" brought the will of her husband to court.

NATHAN FOSCUE, RESDEN M. McDANIEL, & WILLIAMS BROWN were to settle accounts of the (infants?) ADLINE & RACHEL MOORE with the exr of JOHN ANDREWS, decd, & with DANIEL MOORE of DUPLIN CO., their guard.

Since a majority of the county justices were in court, namely: RESDEN M. McDANIEL, JAMES HARRISON, JAMES FOY, OWEN B. COX, JOHN H. HAMMOND, ABNER GREEN, JOHN L. KOONCE, JAMES G. HERRITAGE, FREDERICK I. BECTON, & NATHAN FOSCUE, the renewed bonds of WILLIAM HUGGINS, sheriff, & HARDY BRYAN, clerk, were received & accepted.

WILLIAMS BROWN, constable, was allowed $10.20 for services in summoning a jury of inquiry on the body of JAMES HAZZARD, decd.

Court was adjourned until 10:00 the next morning:

Justices: RESDEN M. McDANIEL, JOHN H. HAMMOND & JAMES G. HERRITAGE

HARDY BRYAN, CALVIN J. MORRIS & JACOB HUGGINS were to settle accounts of DAVID STANLY, former guard to LEAH M. STANLY, minor, with JOHN L. PARSONS, present guard to said minor.

SARAH OLDFIELD, guard to RICHD HALFORT?, was permitted to renew her bond, as such, of $2500 with NATHAN FOSCUE & CHRISTOPHER ROBERTS, securities.

ENOCH NOBLE was to admin estate of BRADDOCK NOBLE, decd; $2800 bond; JAMES B. SHINE & JOSEPH KINSEY, securities.

BENJAMIN HUGGINS was to oversee river from mouth of RESOLUTION to mouth of BEVER CREEK

JOHN S. KOONCE was to oversee river from mouth of BEVER CREEK to PARRY'S BRIDGE.

JOHN JONES was to oversee river from mouth of LITTLE CHINQUIPEN to mouth of CYPRESS CREEK

JOSEPH BROCK to oversee river from mouth of CYPRESS CREEK to REEDY BRANCH

SAMUEL WHITE, an orphan boy, was to be bound to DAVID McDANIEL until he reached lawful age.

Jones Cty Court of Common Pleas Minutes 1833

"Doe on the Dimin" (**Note:** I could find nothing to clarify this.) of JAMES C. COLE vs RICHARD ROE & MORRIS WARD} ejectment. Jury charged & found defendant guilty; assessed damages at five pence and costs. An appeal was asked for and was granted.

JAMES HALL vs FRANCIS DUVAL & C.J. MORRIS} debt. Jury found for pltff on principal of $123.78 and interest of $3.77 = $127.55; judgment was for the same and costs.

JAMES HALL vs CALVIN J. MORRIS} case. Jury found for pltff. Judgment for principal of $295.32, interest of $10.32, for balance of $305.64 plus costs.

ELIZABETH CARY, admr, returned inventory & account of sale of property of estate of SOLOMON CARY, decd.

Settlement of SARAH OLDFIELD, guard to RICHARD OLDFIELD, minor, returned.

Settlement of BENJN HUGGINS, exr of JAMES HUGGINS, decd, filed.

Shff WILLIAM HUGGINS filed account of insolvents for year of 1832 and the peddlers' taxes.

Clerk HARDY BRYAN filed an account of monies remaining in his office from the years before his term.

Tax lists returned from:
District 1 by JAMES ROBERTS, Esq.
District 2 by JAMES W. HARRISON, Esq.
District 3 by RESDEN M. McDANIEL, Esq.
District 4 by ISAAC BROWN, Esq.
District 5 by OWEN B. COX, Esq.
District 6 by JOHN S. KOONCE, Esq.
District 7 by NATHAN FOSCUE, Esq.

Jury drawn for next term:

MICAJAH F. MATTOCKS	LOTT EUBANKS	LEWIS SMALL
WILLIAM L. LARAQUE	COUNCIL GOODING	JOSEPH WHITTY
JOHN MASSAN	DAVID GREEN	EDWARD M. GILBERT
EDWARD C. DEBRULE	JOHN ROUSE	JAMES ADAMS
IVEY ANDREWS	ELIJAH KOONCE	WILLIAM A. COX
JONAS WILLIAMS	WRIGHT STANLY	BARTHOLOMEW MEADOWS
SIMMONS HARRISON JR	DAVID HARTEN	PETER ANDREWS
IGNATIOUS W. BROCK	JOHN BENDER	MERIT JONES
WHIFFINTEN TURNER	JOSEPH HAY	JAMES J. RHODES
JOSEPH SMALL	THOMAS McDANIEL	GEORGE WILCOX

Shff WILLIAM HUGGINS presented his account for jailing Negro MOSES and others for sum of $32.20 which was allowed out of county funds.

Deeds, etc. filed with JAS REYNOLDS, registrar:
DANIEL ANDREWS to PETER ANDREWS
LEMUEL H. SIMMONS to OWEN ADAMS
WILLIAM M. GILES to JONAS JONES
JAMES HATCH to JOHN OLIVER
EDMUND WESTBROOK to JOSEPH SMALL
LEMUEL D. HATCH to JAMES HATCH
JOHN KILLEBREW to JONAS JONES
ELIZABETH & COUNCIL GOODING to WILLIAM GOODING
WINIFRED GOODING to WILLIAM GOODING

Jones Cty Court of Common Pleas Minutes 1833

MARY GOODING to ISOBEL SMALL
LEVI JONES to JAMES D. KINSEY
ELIAS FORDHAM to CALVIN KOONCE
ADONIJAH ANDREWS to DURANT HATCH
SIMEON MEADOWS to SIMMONS COLLINS
JAMES D. KINSEY to JOSEPH GILES
AMOS AMYET & ADON/ADAM ANDREWS to JAMES HATCH
Clerk of County Court bonds

President & directors of the State Bank vs SIMMONS HARRISON} (<u>fieri facias</u>?). Shff HUGGINS failed to execute a "process" delivered by the State Bank. Court ordered that the bank may recover of HUGGINS $100 which was "the penalty for such neglect."

DECEMBER TERM 1833
TRENTON, Monday 9th December 1833

Justices: ISAAC BROWN, ELIJAH SIMMONS & CALVIN KOONCE, Esqs.
Sheriff: WILLIAM HUGGINS
Clerk: HARDY BRYAN

Jurors:
JOHN BENDER, foreman

EDWARD C. DEBRULE	PETER ANDREWS	GEORGE WILCOX
BARTHOLOMEW MEADOWS	THOMAS McDANIEL	JAMES J. RHODES
WRIGHT STANLY	LEWIS SMALL	EDWARD M. GILBERT
JONAS WILLIAMS	IVEY ANDREWS	ELIJAH KOONCE

JOHN L. PARSONS, constable, sworn to attend jury.

"It being satisfactorly stated to the court that SAMUEL DAVIS of this county died on the 4th day of November 1833 intestate..." He had no personal property and "about $100 due on account of a pension as a soldier in the Revolution." Letters of admin granted to LEMUEL H. SIMMONS; $200 bond; JACOB HUGGINS & AMOS L. SIMMONS, securities.

JAMES ROBERTS, THOMAS GELLET & CHRISTOPHER ROBERTS to settle accounts of SIMEON MEADOWS, admr of DELILA MEADOWS, decd.

Petit jurors:
WILLIAM A. COX	JOSEPH SMALL	JAMES ADAMS
IGNATIOUS W. BROCK	LOTT EUBANKS	SIMMONS HARRISON JR
MICAJAH F. MATTOCKS	ELIJAH PARRY	ADAM ANDREWS
DANIEL MALLARD	BRYAN WESTBROOK	SAMUEL HILL

HARDY O. NEWTON was allowed to sell spiritous liquors at his house by small measure for one yr.

THOMAS HARRISON was to oversee rd in place of DAVID GREEN, resigned.

FRANCIS MUNDINE to have letters of admin on estate of HARDY MUNDINE, decd; $2000 bond; DAVID DICKSON & BARTHOLOMEW MEADOWS, securities.

ASA SMITH, JAMES MADES, RIGDON HEWIT & LEVI EUBANKS were to allot to "the widow of the late HARDY MUNDINE" one year's provisions for herself and her family.

JAMES McDANIEL, JACOB HUGGINS & HARDY BRYAN were to divide Negroes of estate of NEEDHAM SIMMONS, decd, between AMOS & SOPHIA SIMMONS

JAMES HARRISON, HENRY RHODES, & IGNATIOUS W. BROCK were to settle accounts of JACOB GILES, admr of FREDK WOOD, decd.

ROSCO BARRUS & JOHN HOUSTON were to look into the situation of TRENT BRIDGE & contract for masonary work.

CALVIN KOONCE & PETER HARGET were to report on condition of bridge across BEVER CREEK and to contract for masonary work.

CHARLES GERACK was to admin estate of "his father SAML GERACK, decd;" 200 pound bond; MATHEW S. BECTON, surety.

HENRY RHODES, LEWIS WILLIAMS, & JONAS JONES to divide Negroes of estate of SAMUEL WESTBROOK so as to allot to IRA WESTBROOK his share.

RACHEL McDANIEL was appointed guard of EDNEY L. McDANIEL, minor; $1000 bond; EMANUEL JARMON, HARDY PERRY, & RESDEN M. McDANIEL, sureties.

EMANUEL JARMON appointed guard to ABNER KILLEBREW in place of JACOB GILES, resigned; $1000 bond; SAMUEL HILL & HARDY BRYAN, sureties.

JAMES HARRISON, HENRY RHODES & IGNATIUS W. BROCK were to settle accounts between JACOB GILES, former guard & EML JARMON, present guard to ABNER KILLEBREW, minor.

State vs ARTHUR DOW? & JOHN POLLOCK} affray. ARTHUR DOW? submitted to court & was charged 50 cents & costs; jury found JOHN POLLOCK not guilty on his plea of not guilty.

State vs JOHN MASSAN} A & B (**Note**: This was probably assult & battery.) Defendant found guilty & fined $5.00 & costs.

State vs JOHN MASSAN} A & B. Again, he was found guilty and this time was fined $1.00 & costs.

JAMES S. MILLER to the use of JAMES HATCH vs JAMES G. HERRITAGE, F.G. HERRITAGE & JNO OLIVER. Jury found for pltff; $130 judgment.

Inventory & accounts of sale of property of DAVID LOVITT, decd, filed by ELIJAH LOVETT, exr.

EMANUEL JARMON, guard to heirs of THOMAS MURPHY, decd, filed accounts.

Last will & testament of MARY GOODING, decd, was exhibited in court & proved by oath of SHADERACK LOFTON who testified to the signature of SAMUEL LOFTON, the subscribing witness. IMILA N. MILLER seems to have been named exr - but this was difficult to decipher. [Note: Gwynn abstracted this will (pp. 415-416) which was written 25 Oct 1828 with a codicil attached 24 Jan 1829. Named in the will are sons, FRANCIS, WILLIAM and COUNCIL GOODING; and daughters, ELIZABETH GRIFFITH, WINIFORD LANE, and ISABELLA GOODING. DANIEL MILLER was named exr, and the witnesses were SAMUEL LOFTON and IMLA N. MILLER.]

Last will & testament of WILLIAM RHEM, decd, exhibited & proved by oath of JOHN S. KOONCE, a witness to the will; WILLIAM B. RHEM qualified as exr. [Note: Gwynn also abstracted this will (p. 441) which was written 1 May 1830. Named in the will were daughters, MARY I. PERRY, SUSAN KINSEY, ELIZABETH LOFTIN, and HANNAH PERRY; and sons, JOSEPH RHEM, WILLIAM B. RHEM, and MELCHOIR RHEM. Son, WILLIAM B. RHEM, and HARDY PARRY were named exrs, and JOHN S. KOONCE and AMOS I. KOONCE were witnesses.]

HARDY BRYAN, WILLIAM HUGGINS & JACOB HUGGINS to audit & settle accounts of ELIZABETH CARY, admr of SOLOMON CARY, decd.

Jones Cty Court of Common Pleas Minutes 1833

Deeds, etc. filed with JAS REYNOLDS, registrar:
SIMMONS HARRISON & wife to ISAAC BROWN
ELIJAH KOONCE to JACOB GILES
WILLIAM M. GILES to ISAAC BROWN
CALVIN KOONCE to JOHN STANLY SR
JOSEPH T. RHODES to LEWIS KINCEY
DANIEL SANDERS to LEMUEL H. SIMMONS
SIMMONS HARRISON to CALVIN KOONCE
ELIJAH KOONCE to JACOB GILES
MICAJAH PETTEWAY to DANIEL Y. SHINE
JAMES MUMFORD to LEMUEL H. SIMMONS
ELIJAH LOVETT to MARY LOVETT
ELIJAH KOONCE to JOHN STANLY
JONAS JONES to JACOB GILES
IMILA N. MILLER to SIMMONS MORE
JAMES HATCH to AMOS AMYETT & ADAM ANDREWS
LEWIS SMALL to ISRAEL HOWARD
WILLIAMS BROWN to LEMUEL H. SIMMONS
RACHEL McDANIEL to JAMES McDANIEL, guard to heirs of RISDEN
ISRAEL HOWARD to LEWIS SMALL

Marriage settlement: C. DAVIS, E. GREEN & L.B. GREEN
C.J. MORRIS, Clerk of Court Bond

The following justices: JAMES W. HOWARD, RISDEN M. McDANIEL & FREDERICK I. BECTON, drew the jury for the next Superior Court:

JAS G. HERRITAGE	THOMAS GILLET	HARDY PARRY
JOHN H. HAMMOND	NATHAN B. WESTBROOK	WILLIAMS JONES
MILLENTON MEADOWS	FREDK PARKER	NATHAN FOSCUE
WILLIAM BINAM	CALVIN KOONCE	OWEN HARRISON
FURNIFOLD G. HERRITAGE	JAS MARRIT	JOHN OLIVER
DANIEL HARRISON	ASA SMITH	GEORGE L. DEBRULE
SIMMONS ISLER	HARDY COLLINS	WILLIAM GOODING
MARTIN F. BROCK	JONAS JONES SR	JOHN GODWIN
EDMD HATCH SR	JAMES ROBERTS	EDMD B. HATCH
JOHN STANLY JR	GEORGE KING	JOHN S. KOONCE
RISDEN McDANIEL (Cof?)	FREDK I. BECTON	JOHN YOUNG
SIMON S. BECTON	ADAM ANDREWS	BENJN BROCK

County court jurors:

JOHN STANLY (Trenton)	ASA EUBANKS	EMERY METTS
WILLIAM WATERS	WALTER P. ALTON?	JOHN HARRISON
GEORGE HAZZARD	RIGDON HEWIT	BENJN ASKEY
JOHN H. BECTON	JOHN BALL	JONAS JONES JR
THOMAS HARRISON	JOHN E. FOSCUE	JEROD KOONCE
JOHN SHELFER	JOHN ADAMS	EDMOND WESTBROOK
HARDY A. CONNER	LEMUEL BUSACK	PETER HARGET
MICHAEL KOONCE	IVEY ANDREWS	JAMES MADES
EDWIN BECTON	JOHN FORDHAM	ISAIAH WOOD
WILLIAM MURPHY	JAMES B. SHINE	JAMES J. RHODES

MARCH TERM, 1834
TRENTON, Monday 10 March 1834

Justices: ROSCO BARRUS, JOSEPH FOY, & JOHN S. KOONCE, Esquires
Sheriff: WILLIAM HUGGINS
Clerk: HARDY BRYAN

Freeholders who served as jurers:
RIGDON HEWIT, foreman

IVEY ANDREWS	ISAIAH WOOD	JOHN HARRISON
JOHN ADAMS	ASA EUBANKS	PETER HARGET
JEROD KOONCE	EDMD WESTBROOK	HARDY O. CONNER
THOMAS HARRISON	BENJAMIN ASKEY	MICHAEL KOONCE

JOHN L. PARSONS, constable, attended jury

Petit jury summoned:

JOHN SHELFER	GEORGE HAZZARD	WILLIAM WARTISS?
JONAS JONES JR	WALTER P. ALLEN	JOHN E. FOSCUE
LEMUEL BUSICK	JOHN STANLY	WILLIAM MURPHY
HARDY O. NEWTON	SAMUEL HILL	JOHN H. DILLAHUNT

JOHN E. FOSCUE to oversee rd from TRENT BRIDGE to DEEP GULLY in place of GEORGE C. DEBRULE, resigned.

Last will and testament of WILLIAMS ISLER, decd on 3 Dec 1833, offered to court for probate by exr, COUNCIL WOOTEN. Proved by oaths of FREDK I. BECTON, EMANUEL JARMAN & WILLIAM HUGGINS who testified it was handwriting of WILLIAMS ISLER. Oath of EULINOR? HARGET proved it "was found among the valuable papers of said decd after his death carefully locked up in a desk." Letters of admin granted COUNCIL WOOTEN. [Note: Gwynn abstracted this will (pp. 420-421) which was written 3 Dec 1833. Named in the will are wife, ANN, sons, SIMMONS and EDWIN B. ISLER, and daughters, ELIZA WOOTEN, REBECCA HERRING, and E.B. ISLER. His heirs were to support OLD MOLL and ALEX, his slaves. His son-in-law, COUNCIL WOOTEN, was named exr, and the witnesses were FREDERICK I. BECTON, EMANUEL JARMAN, and WILLIAM HUGGINS. EXELINA HARGET swore to the will being found in the desk.]

The following justices being in court: ABNER GREEN, ROSCO BARRUS, JOSEPH FOY, JOHN S. KOONCE, OWIN B. COX, & JAMES HARRISON, the election returns from District 5 were shown to court. ERASMUS KINSEY elected constable.

FREDERICK PARKER was to oversee rd from JACK CABIN to the RED OAK in place of N.F. PARSONS, resigned.

EDMUND B. HATCH was to oversee rd from MILL CREEK BRIDGE to fork of rd near BUCKNER HATCH's mill & hands of EDMUND B. HATCH & ELIJAH SIMMONS were to be subject to work said rd in addition to those liable to work same rd under overseer JOHN HOUSTON, resigned.

MICHAEL KOONCE was to oversee rd from HARRISON's bridge to RHEMS' rd in place of JOHN SHELFER, resigned.

HARDY BRYAN, WILLIAM HUGGINS, & JACOB HUGGINS were to settle accounts of EML JARMAN, guard to JOHN P. KOONCE, minor.

JOHN E. FOSCUE, GEORGE HAZZARD, & HARDY O. NEWTON were to be a patrol committee according to Act of Assembly in District 7.

HARDY BRYAN, FRANCIS DUVAL & WILLIAM HUGGINS were to settle accounts of

RICHARD REYNOLDS, guard to heirs of JAMES GREEN & report next court.

THOMAS HUGGINS was to oversee rd from straight reach one mile above TRENTON to the INDIAN GROVE in place of DAVID McDANIEL, resigned.

JOSEPH BROCK was to oversee rd from REEDY BRANCH to the fork at SHINE's in place of JAS B. SHINE, resigned.

All hands of JOHN BERGWIN who were subject to work rd from MILL CREEK to fork near HATCH's Mill should, rather, work rd from TRENT BRIDGE down to DEEP GULLY & five of GEORGE POLLOCK's hands who were subject to work rd from TRENT BRIDGE to town were to help from MILL CREEK to fork near HATCH's Mill.

FURNIFOLD JARMON was to oversee rd from the RED HILL on the north side of REEDY BRANCH up to RATTLESNAKE BRIDGE in place of LEWIS WILLIAMS, resigned.

JOHN HOUSTON & FURNIFOLD JARMON, Esquires, qualified as justices of the peace for Jones County.

HARDY BRYAN was to admin estate of TABITHA SAWYER?, decd; $3000 bond; EML JARMON & JOHN HOUSTON, sureties.

HARDY BRYAN, WILLIAM HUGGINS, & JACOB HUGGINS were to settle accounts of RISDEN McDANIEL, admr of GEORGE POLLOCK, decd.

Same men were to settle accounts of RISDEN McDANIEL, admr of LEMUEL ANDREWS, decd.

Same men to settle accounts of RISDEN McDANIEL, exr of RISDEN McDANIEL SR, decd.

THOMAS McLIN vs SAML C. FORBES} judgment according to *sie fie*; see Trial Docket No. 7.

FRANCIS ANDREWS was to oversee rd from fork at the bridge at TRENTON up to head of straight reach one mile from TRENTON in place of WILLIAM L. LARAQUE, resigned.

County trustee was to pay RISDEN M. McDANIEL $2.40 for holding inquest on body of JAMES HAZZARD, decd.

County trustee was to pay costs as county is by law bound in suit: State vs JAMES R. CONNER, tried in Superior Court of Jones County, "for the killing of JAS HAZZARD" March Term, 1833.

Freeholders drawn as jurors for June term:

MICAJAH F. MATTOCKS	JOHN FREIZE	JOHN ROUN
THOMAS McDANIEL	ENOCK FOY	SAMUEL DILLAHUNT
JOHN MALLARD	JOHN HEATH SR	JOSEPH WHITTY
LEWIS WILLIAMS	JOHN McDANIEL SR	SIMMONS COLLINS
JOHN MESSAN	DANIEL WILLIAMSON	JOSEPH SMALL
AARON WOOD	MARRIT JARVIS	WILLIAM L. LAROQUE
JAMES MESSAN	EDWD M. GILBERT	LOT EUBANKS
WILLIAM GOODING JR	ISAAC BROWN	AMOS L. SIMMONS
CHRISTOPHER ROBERTS	ELIJAH KOONCE	COUNCIL GOODING
PETER ANDREWS	JOHN WOOD	JOSEPH HAY

Letters of admin issued to JOSEPH WALLIS on estate of CELIA WALLAN (**Note**: Could the clerk have meant Wallis?), decd; $100 bond; ELIJAH SIMMONS & JOSEPH KINSEY, securities. JOSEPH WALLAN qualified as admr (**Note**: Perhaps the name should, instead, be Wallan.)

Last will and testament of TOBIAS KOONCE, decd, exhibited in court by BENJAMIN HUGGINS, exr, & admitted to probate. Proved by oaths of WILLIAM HUGGINS & HARDY BRYAN, the witnesses. [Gwynn abstracted this will (p. 431) which was written 23 Dec 1833. Named in the will are the wife, BENETER; daughters, MARY POLLOCK and MATILDA HUGGINS. His son-in-law, BENJAMIN HUGGINS, was named exr, and the witnesses were WILLIAM HUGGINS, MARY ANN HUGGINS, and HARDY BRYAN.]

The following settlements were filed:
- JNO H. HAMMOND, guard to heirs of PARSONS and of F. BRYAN, minor.
- EML JARMAN, guard to ABNER KILLEBREW, minor.
- F.I. BECTON, guard to J.C. BRYAN, minor.
- F.G. HERRITAGE, guard to THOS STELLEY, minor.
- JNO S. KOONCE, guard to heirs of M. KOONCE, decd.
- L.H. SIMMONS, guard to ELIZABETH A. SIMMONS
- S. MEADOWS, admr of DELILA MEADOWS, decd.
- OWIN ADAMS, guard to heirs of KADER KNIGHT, decd.
- PETER ANDREWS with RACHEL MORRIS, minor.
- JACOB GILES, guard to ABNER KILLEBREW.
- JACOB GILES, admr of FREDK WOOD.

The following inventories & accounts of sales of property were filed: MARY GOODING, decd, WILLIAM ISLER, decd, HARDY MUNDINE, decd, & SAMUEL DAVIS, decd.

Division of Negroes of SAML WESTBROOK, decd, filed.

Settlement of HARDY PARRY, guard to heirs of S. PARRY, filed.

An order of last term appointing a committee to settle accounts of ELIZABETH CARY, admx of SOLOMON CARY, decd, was reissued.

Inventory & account of sale of property of WILLIAM RHEM, decd, returned by WM A. RHEM, exr.

Deeds, etc. registered with JAS REYNOLDS, registrar:
JOHN M. FRANKS to ISAAC BROWN
Shff to HARDY COLLINS
Agreement between AMOS AMYET & ADAM ANDREWS
JOHN STANLY to JOHN WESTBROOK
HANNAH WOOD to SALLY KOONCE
RICHARD REYNOLDS to JAMES REYNOLDS
JAMES (S?) MILLER to JOHN OLIVER, power of att
WM L. LAROQUE to WILLIAM HUGGINS
WILLIAM POLLOCK to JOHN POLLOCK
WINIFORD HARRIET to HENRY? SHUTE
JAROD KOONCE to ISRAEL WOOD
RISDEN McDANIEL to SAMUEL HILL
JAMES REYNOLDS & others to RICHARD REYNOLDS
MICAJAH F. MATTOCKS to TOBIAS KOONCE
MARY H. LOVET to ELIJAH SIMMONS
JONAS JONES to DANIEL Y. SHINE
JOSEPH SMALL to WILLIAM GOODING
SIMMONS HARRISON JR to ISAAC BROWN
JAMES REYNOLDS to DANIEL WILLIAMSON
WILLIAM POLLOCK to JOHN POLLOCK
C.J. MORRIS to ADAM ANDREWS
HARDY BRYAN to WILLIAM HUGGINS
WILLIAM HUGGINS to JACOB HUGGINS
JACOB HUGGINS to JAMES McDANIEL
D.W. DUDLEY to D.B. WHORTON, "power before the judge"

Jones Cty Court of Common Pleas Minutes 1834

JUNE TERM, 1834
TRENTON, 9 JUNE 1834

Justices: OWEN B. COX, SIMMONS ISLER, & JOSEPH FOY, Esqs.
Shff: WILLIAM HUGGINS
Clerk: HARDY BRYAN

Jurors:
ISAAC BROWN, foreman

MICAJAH F. MATTOCKS	ENOCK FOY	JOHN McDANIEL
LEWIS WILLIAMS	JOHN MISSAW	AARON WOOD?
EDWD M. GILBERT	LOT EUBANKS	ELIJAH KOONCE
THOMAS McDANIEL	PETER ANDREWS	JOHN WOOD

Jurors were charged by JAMES W. BRYAN, Esq., att. for this county & JOHN L. PARSONS was sworn as officer to attend jury.

State vs JAROD KOONCE} affray. The following jury: MERRIT JONES, JOSEPH SMALL, JOSEPH WHITTY, DANIEL WILLIAMSON, JAMES MISSAW, AMOS L. SIMMONS, JAMES H. FRESHWATER, JOHN OLIVER, LEMUEL H. SIMMONS, LEWIS SMALL, SAMUEL HILL, & JOSEPH KINSEY found for defendant; not guilty.

HARDY HUGGINS, charged with an affray, submitted to court & was fined (no amount was given) plus costs.

HARDY BRYAN, WILLIAM HUGGINS, & JACOB HUGGINS were to settle accounts of EMANUEL JARMAN, guard to JOHN (B.?) KOONCE, minor.

Same committee was to settle accounts of EML JARMAN, present guard of WM HENRY BRYAN, minor, with ANN R. BRYAN, former guard.

JOSEPH WHITTY was to oversee rd from FURNIFOLD McDANIEL's gate down to B. HATCH's mill in place of JOHN OLIVER, resigned & that this district road be altered so as to (return?) only from POLLY BRANCH instead of F. McDANIEL's gate.

NATHAN FOSCUE, JAMES W. HOWARD, & JOHN H. HAMMOND, Esq., were to settle accounts of EMANUEL JARMAN, county trustee.

County trustee was to pay ROSCO BARRUS $29.61 for repairs to TRENT BRIDGE.

IGNATIOUS BROCK was to oversee the part of TRENT RIVER under care of JOSEPH BROCK, resigned.

JAMES HARRISON, Esq., was to oversee rd from the fork at SHINE's up to the RED HILL on the west side of REEDY BRANCH in place of JOSEPH BROCK, resigned.

STANLY WOOD was to be bound to MARRET JONES until he reached 21 years of age.

JAMES FOY was appointed surveyor for Jones County.

WILLIAM BRAY was bound to NATHAN FOSCUE, Esq., until he reached 21 years of age.

OWEN B. COX allowed to sell liquors by small measure at his store in Jones County for one year.

CHARLES GEROCK allowed to sell liquor by small measure at his store in TRENTON for one year.

JONATHAN WOOD allowed to sell liquor at the store at TRENT BRIDGE for one year.

ZACHARIAH WESTBROOK was bound to JAMES McDANIEL until he reached 21 years of age.

Jones Cty Court of Common Pleas Minutes 1834

RILEY DAVIS, a boy of color, was bound to JOSEPH SMALL until he would reach 21 years of age.

The following were to be patrols for Jones County:
District 1, White Oak: JAMES ROBERTS, LEVI EUBANKS, & DANIEL YATES
District 2, Trent Bridge: JOSEPH FOY, WALTER P. ALLEN, & DANIEL WILLIAMSON
District 3, Trenton: JAMES McDANIEL, HARDY BRYAN, & JOHN HOUSTON
District 4, Cyrpress Creek: CALVIN KOONCE, JAMES B. SHINE, & JOHN H. HAMMOND
District 5, Tuckahoe: EMANUEL JARMON, HENRY RHODES, & OWEN B. COX
District 6, Bever Creek: SIMMONS ISLER, MARTIN BROCK, & FREDK I. BECTON
District 7, (Clerk left rest blank.)

HARDY BRYAN was to purchase a (jury caller?) "a 6 or 8th" and have it mounted and placed at the courthouse in Trenton.

Justices of the county were called and a majority appeared & proceeded to elect county officers & made allowances to the officers as follows:
WILLIAM HUGGINS, shff, $73.70.

County trustee ordered to pay HARDY BRYAN, clerk, $40 for extra services.

BENJAMIN HUGGINS, constable, was to be paid $8.80 for services.

JOHN L. PARSONS, constable, was to be paid $9.60 for services.

MARY ANN MILLER, DANIEL W. MILLER, ELIZABETH JANE MILLER, & MARTIN F. MILLER had removed to TWIGS CO., GEORGIA. JAMES S. MILLER had been appointed guard to these children by the TWIGGS COUNTY court & had given bond. Therefore, the Jones County court ordered that MARTIN MILLER, heretofore appointed guard to these children by the Jones County court, should be removed from his guardianship & he was ordered to pay to JAMES S. MILLER all such monies & other property belonging to these children that he may or ought to have in his hands.

WILLIAM HUGGINS was paid $3.60 for plank & nails for repairs of the bridge at TRENTON.

SAMUEL HILL, admr of ELIJAH SMALL, decd, refunded $1500.36 in payment of debts of his intestate which was a larger amount than the assets which he had on hand from the estate. Therefore, he may sell a Negro from the estate, TIMOTHY, in order to discharge claims on the estate.

JOHN H. HAMMOND was appointed guard to the infant heirs of DAVID FONVIELLE, decd, to wit: DAVID, JOHN, MARY, & NARCISSA, & to defend their estate from the claims against them by FREDERICK PARKER.

Inventory of the property of TABITHA IVEY, decd, filed by HARDY BRYAN, admr.

It was ordered that tax would be collected the same as last year, and the following would take the list of taxable property for 1834:
District 1, White Oak: THOMAS GILLET
District 2, Trent Bridge: JOSEPH S. FOY
District 3, Trenton: JOHN HOUSTON
District 4, Cypress Creek: CALVIN KOONCE
District 5, Tuckahoe: FURNIFOLD H. JARMON
District 6, Bever Creek: FREDERICK I. BECTON
District 7, Bever Dam: NATHAN FOSCUE

The following will "hold the poles for elections:"

Jones Cty Court of Common Pleas Minutes 1834

Dist. 1: JAMES ROBERTS, LEVI EUBANK & DANIEL YATES
Dist. 2: ROSCO BARRUS, DANIEL WILLIAMSON, & JOHN YOUNG
Dist. 3: Shff WM HUGGINS, HARDY BRYAN & JOHN HOUSTON
Dist. 4: CALVIN KOONCE, JAS B. SHINE, & FURNIFOLD G. HERRITAGE
Dist. 5: FURNIFOLD H. JARMON, HENRY RHODES, & JOSEPH KINSEY
Dist. 6: SIMMONS ISLER, JOHN S. KOONCE, & FREDK I. BECTON
(no dist. 7 was given)

    Constables elected for this year by the court:
    (no dist. 1 given)
Dist. 2: JOHN YOUNG, neglected to appear & give bond
    (no dist. 3 given)
Dist. 4: JOHN L. PARSONS, entered into bond with JNO H. HAMMOND & OWEN B. COX, sureties.
    (no dist. 5 given)
Dist. 6: BENJAMIN HUGGINS, bond with WILLIAM HUGGINS & EMANUEL JARMON, sureties.
    (no dist. 7 given)

EMANUEL JARMON, county trustee, renewed his bond.

Freeholders drawn as jurors for Superior Court, Fall Term, 1834:

RESDON M. McDANIEL	SHADERACK ERWIN	DANIEL SMITH
JOSEPH S. FOY	JAS H. FRESHWATER	WM B. RHEM
IGNATIOUS W. BROCK	OWEN B. COX	JOHN MISSAW
BENJN C. SIMMONS	JOSEPH KINSEY SR	JOHN E. FOSCUE
RICHD R. FOSCUE	ABNER GREEN	JNO H. HAMMOND
JOHN BENDER	WM A. COX	AARON WOOD
OWEN ADAMS	ELIJAH PARRY	JOHN YOUNG
LEMUEL H. SIMMONS	MOSES ADAMS	JOSEPH SMALL
WILLIAM D. COBB	JAMES HARRISON	MICAJAH F. MATTOCKS
DAVID GREEN	ROSCO BARRUS	JOHN WOOD
BENJN HUGGINS	JAMES W. HOWARD	FREDK I. BECTON
FURNIFOLD H. JARMON	JAMES D. KINSEY	NATHAN B. WESTBROOK

Jurors for the next county court, Sept Term, 1834:

HOUSTON ROBERTS	JAMES ADAMS	JOHN JONES
THOMAS POLLOCK	ABRAM SIMMONS	JAS McDANIEL
BARTHALMEW MEADOWS	LEWIS SMALL	THOMAS BALEY
EDWD C. DEBRULE SR	LEWIS KINSEY	JAMES FOY
GEORGE WILCOX	DAVID WHARTEN	WRIGHT STANLY
ZACHEAUS BROWN	DAVID BALL	DANIEL MALLARD
EDWD C. DEBRULE JR	AMOS SHELFER	NATHAN STANLY
DAVID McDANIEL	BENJN F. STANLY	FRANCIS ANDREWS
WHITFIELD TURNER	JOHN POLLOCK	HENRY RHODES
JONAS WILLIAMS	LEWIS O. BRYAN	DANIEL YATES

    Inventory & sale of property of CELIA WALLAN, decd, filed by JOSEPH WALLAN, admr.
    Settlement of SAMUEL B. HEATH, guard to WM HEATH, filed.
    Settlement of EML JARMON, guard to JOHN P. KOONCE, SALYAR? RICHARD, JAMES PARRY, J.C. KOONCE, E.F. KOONCE, CAROLINA & HOLLON POLLOCK, ANN D.

Jones Cty Court of Common Pleas Minutes 1834

POLLOCK, MARINDA & DEBRULE? MURPHY, heirs of FREDK WOOD, and NANCY & CURTIS WESTBROOK.

Deeds recorded by JAS REYNOLDS, registrar:
RESDON M. McDANIEL to JAMES McDANIEL
RIGDON WHITE to WILLIAM ISLER
JOHN STANLY to JAMES McDANIEL
IRA WESTBROOK to JOSEPH SMALL
JOHN WOOD to JOHN DILLAHUNT
SIMMONS HARRISON to JAMES B. SHINE
JULIA R. HOWARD to JAMES W. HOWARD
JEROD KOONCE to EML JARMAN for J.C.B. & E.F. KOONCE
EDMD B. HATCH to JOHN HOUSTON
EDMD B. HATCH to JOHN HOUSTON
EDMD B. HATCH to JOHN HOUSTON
JOHN ADAMS to JAMES ADAMS
LANY SMALL to JAMES McDANIEL
MICHAEL KOONCE to JOHN S. KOONCE
CALVIN J. MORSE/MOSES to ADAM ANDREWS
JOSEPH WHITTY to JOHN P. DAVIS
JOHN P. DAVIS to JOSEPH WHITTY

Letters of admin were granted to MICAJAH PETTEWAY on estate of CATHARINE KORNEGAY, decd; $2000 bond; IGNATIOUS BROCK & JOSEPH BROCK, sureties.

SEPTEMBER TERM 1834
TRENTON, Monday the 8th of September

Justices: ABNER GREEN, ROSCO BARRUS, & CALVIN KOONCE, Esqs.
Shff: WILLIAM HUGGINS
Clerk: HARDY BRYAN

The shff had to give bond agreeable to the acts of assembly. The Justices were called and the following came & took their seats:
JAMES HARRISON   NATHAN FOSCUE   JOHN HOUSTON
JOHN S. KOONCE   FURNIFOLD JARMAN   DANIEL SMITH
ROSCO BARRUS   ABNER GREEN   FREDERICK I. BECTON
CALVIN KOONCE   JOHN H. HAMMOND
Whereupon RISDEN M. McDANIEL presented the bond which was received by the court. (**Note**: As will be seen next term, he became the new sheriff.)

HARDY BRYAN, WILLIAM HUGGINS & JACOB HUGGINS were to settle the accounts of MARTIN MILLER, guard to heirs of JAMES MILLER, decd.
DANIEL SMITH, ASA SMITH, & RIGDEN HEWIT were to settle the accounts of CASSANDRA COLLINS, admx of JOHN S. COLLINS, decd.
OWEN B. COX, FREDERICK I. BECTON, & NATHAN FOSCUE were to settle the accounts of "the superintendants...?...building the court house" & report all facts which they can relative to this business.
THOMAS HALE was to oversee rd from TRENT BRIDGE to TOM SWAMP in place of JAMES FOY, resigned.
NATHAN STANLY was to oversee rd from JACOB's BRANCH to the County Line

Jones Cty Court of Common Pleas Minutes 1834

(near?) RIGDON WHITE in place of MARTIN F. BROCK, resigned.

H..?.TON ROBERTS was to oversee rd from house of GEORGE S. BENDER to TRENT BRIDGE through the POCOSIN in place of GEORGE S. BENDER, resigned.

JAMES ADAMS was to oversee rd from BLACK SWAMP to LENOIR COUNTY line in place of JOHN ADAMS, resigned.

CALVIN KOONCE was to oversee rd from INDIAN GROVE OLDFIELD to JACK CABBIN & from HARRISON's Bridge to the above named rd in place of JOHN H. DILLAHUNT, resigned & hands of DILLAHUNT to be subject to work sd rd.

NATHANIEL P. MASSLES/MAPLES was to oversee rd from BEVERDAM BRANCH near JAMES MARRET's to fork of rd at HARDY A. NEWTON's in place of JAMES MISSAU, resigned.

FRANCIS D. SMITH, a child of THOMAS SMITH, decd, aged about eight years, was to be bound to DANIEL HARRISON until 21 years.

The following was to be a "jury to lay off a ...?... near MRS BANETER KOONCE:"

JAMES McDANIEL	HARDY BRYAN	DAVID GREEN
JAMES REYNOLDS	WILLIAM RHEM	HARDY O. CONNER
PETER HARGET	SAMUEL HILL	DANIEL MALLARD
PETER ANDREWS	THOS HARRISON	JOHN WOOD

JOHN HOUSTON, WILLIAM HUGGINS, & NATHAN FOSCUE were to be a court of appeals to sit agreeable to act of assembly.

Letters of admin granted EML JARMON on estate of HUBBISON STANLY, decd; $8000 bond; HARDY BRYAN & WILLIAM HUGGINS, sureties.

JOHN H. HAMMOND, ABNER GREEN, & CALVIN KOONCE were to contract for building a bridge across TRENT RIVER at the place called the (FREE?) BRIDGE.

JAMES FOY, who was appointed county surveyor at the June Term of this court, entered his bond.

HARDY BRYAN, clerk, filed his affidavit.

Inventory of property of CATHERINE KORNEGAY, decd, filed by MICAJAH PETERWAY, admr.

Settlement of OWEN B. COX, guard to MARY & JACKSON RHODES, minors, filed.

Settlement of ANN R. BRYAN, former guard to WILLIAM & HENRY BRYAN, minors, filed.

Settlement of ELIZABETH CAREY, admx of SOLOMAN CARY, decd, filed.

Settlement of JAMES HARRISON, guard to PENELOPE MUMFORD, minor, filed.

WILLIAM HUGGINS, shff, filed his account of taxes from "Rotactus Padless Exhibitors" (?!) for year 1833.

Freeholders drawn as jurors for next term:

DANIEL HARRISON	OWEN HARRISON	GEORGE KING
FREDK PARKER	WHITFIELD TURNER	WILLIAM BYNUM
BENJN C. SIMMONS	HARDY COLLINS	BENJN F. STANLY
DANIEL WILLIAMSON	ENOCK FOY	SIMMONS COLLINS
FURNIFOLD G. HARRITAGE	EMERY METTS	JAMES FOY
JNO STANLY (Trenton)	EDWD M. GILBERT	HARDY PARRY
JONAS JONES SR	JOHN STANLY SR	JAMES MISSAW
MARTIN F. BROCK	ASA EUBANKS	WRIGHT STANLY
GEORGE S. DEBRULE	JEROD KOONCE	CHRISTOPHER ROBERTS
JONAS JONES JR	JOHN H. BECTON	SAMUEL DILLAHUNT

Jones Cty Court of Common Pleas Minutes 1834

Deeds registered by JAS REYNOLDS, registrar:
EDWARD DEBRULE to GEORGE DEBRULE
SAMUEL MIDDLETON to JONAS JONES SR
RICHARD REYNOLDS to CALVIN DAVIS
JAMES J. RHODES to BENJAMIN RHODES
HARDY BRYAN to BANETER SIMMONS (? smudged)
THOMAS WHITLEDGE to HENRY RHODES
BARNET HEATH to HENRY RHODES

DECEMBER TERM, 1834
TRENTON, Monday the 8th of December

Justices: ABNER GREEN, THOMAS GILLET, & JOSEPH FOY, Esqs.
Shff: RISDEN M. McDANIEL
Clerk: HARDY BRYAN

Jurers, charged by JAMES W. BRYAN, Esq., County Solicitor:
HARDY PARRY, foreman

JAMES MESSAW	CHRISTOPHER ROBERTS	JAMES FOY
FREDERICK PARKER	FURNIFOLD G. HERRITAGE	SIMMONS COLLINS
GEORGE KING	WILLIAM BYNAM	DANIEL HARRISON
EMERY METTS	JONAS JONES JR	OWEN HARRISON

FRANCIS ANDREWS was to admr estate of "his son IVEY ANDREWS, decd;" $1000 bond; JAMES MARRETT, security.

FRANCIS ANDREWS SR, appointed guard to MARY McDANIEL, minor; $2000 bond; JACOB HUGGINS, security.

Letters of admin on the estate of JAMES REYNOLDS, decd, granted to FREDERICK I. BECTON; $20,000 bond; JOSEPH KINSEY & JAMES McDANIEL, sureties.

FREDK I. BECTON, admr of JAMES REYNOLDS, decd, to sell the perishable property of his intestate agreeable to law.

HARDY BRYAN was to have charge of the public arms which were in the county for purpose of keeping them in order & he was to be paid $10.00 out of the county funds.

CALVIN DAVIS appointed guard to WINIFRED GREEN, SARAH GREEN, & RICHARD GREEN, minors, in place of RICHARD REYNOLDS, former guard, resigned; $12,000 bond; CALVIN KOONCE & OWEN B. COX, sureties.

HARDY BRYAN, JOHN HOUSTON, BLUNT COLEMAN & OWEN B. COX were to settle accounts of RICHD REYNOLDS, former guard to WINIFRED, SARAH, & RICHD GREEN.

WILLIAM BYNUM was granted letters of admin on the estate of DAVID BALL, decd; $2000 bond; JOHN BALL & GEO BENDER, sureties.

DANIEL SMITH, LEVI EUBANKS, DANIEL YATES, & LOTT EUBANKS were to alott off to HULDAH BALL, "widow of DAVID BALL, decd, one yrs provisions for herself & 5 children out of estate of her late husband."

THOMAS GILLET, ASA SMITH, & JAMES MADES were to divide Negroes of estate of RICHD OLDFIELD, decd, "among the heirs."

ROSCO BARRUS, JOSEPH S. FOY, & JAMES FOY were to settle accounts of ELIJAH LOVETT, exr of DAVID LOVETT, decd.

County trustees were to pay JOHN I. PASTEUR? $8.00 for advertising orders of Superior Court of Jones Co. in case of HANNAH WOOD vs HARDY WOOD for divorce & alimony (**Note:** Wood could be Ward.)

Jones Cty Court of Common Pleas Minutes 1834

ALFRED REYNOLDS was to oversee rd from bridge at TRENTON to (ROMA?) BRANCH; also from fork near BENJN HUGGINS down to MUSSELSHELL BRANCH on the road leading to NEW BERN in place of THOS HARRISON, (decd?).

CALVIN KOONCE, ABNER GREEN, & HARDY PARRY were to divide Negroes of estate of MICHAEL KOONCE, decd, so as to alott off to MICHAEL KOONCE his distributive share.

CALVIN KOONCE, JAMES McDANIEL, & BENJN KOONCE were to divide Negroes of estate of JEREMIAH PARSONS, decd, so as to alott to JOHN S. KOONCE in right of his wife their distributed share.

HARDY O. NEWTON given permission to sell liquor at his place of residence for one year.

Clerk of this court was authorized to make two entries of land in the entrytakers book for ROBERT DICKSON.

Clerk of court authorized to make an entry for land in entry book for ALLEN? JONES.

SIMMONS ISLER was appointed guard to EDWIN BECTON ISLER, minor; $2000 bond; JOSEPH KINSEY & COUNCIL WOOTON, sureties.

A tax of 12 cents on the $100 value of real estate and 40 cents on the pole was to be levied & collected for the purpose of purchasing a proper site & erecting a bldg suitable for the accommodation of the poor of the county & for other purposes relative to the case of the sd poor.

EMANUAL JARMON appointed guard to the minor heirs of DAVID FONVIELLE, decd; $500 bond; JOHN H. HAMMOND & BENJAMIN HUGGINS, sureties.

Letters of admin issued on the estate of JOHN PHELYAN?, decd, to EMANUEL JARMON; $? bond; JOHN H. HAMMOND & HARDY BRYAN, sureties.

JOHN H. HAMMOND, WILLIAM HUGGINS & HARDY BRYAN were to settle accounts of the admr of DAVID FONVIELLE, decd.

Freeholders sworn as petit jurors to this term:
JOHN STANLY	WRIGHT STANLY	BENJN F. STANLY
GEORGE I. DEBRULE	ASA EUBANKS	JOHN SHELFER
ENOCK FOY	JEROD KOONCE	NATHAN F. PARSONS
JOHN MISSAW	BENJN KOONCE	JAMES H. FRESHWATER

JONAS JONES SR vs OWEN B. COX, admr of HENRY RHODES} Jury found for pltff & assessed damages at $109.09 with interest from 28 Jan 1834.

President & directors of the state bank vs JAMES B. LARAQUE & RICHARD REYNOLDS} Case. Same jury found for pltff. Debt of $150 plus $3.50 interest.

Settlement of estate of J.L. COLLINS was filed.

Settlement of LEML ISLER, guard to JOSEPH & WILLIAM BRYAN, minors, was filed.

Inventory of property of estate of CATHARINE KORNEGAY, decd, was filed.

Account of sale & inventory of HUBBAN STANLY, decd, filed by E. JARMON, admr.

Last will & testament of MOSES WARD, decd, exhibited & proved in open court; DAVID W. DUDLY, exr therein named, qualified as same. [Note: Gwynn abstracted this will (p. 451) which was written 27 Oct 1834. It named only the deceased's friend, DAVID W. DUDLEY, of CRAVEN CO., who was willed all of WARD's land in CRAVEN and JONES COUNTIES and who was named exr. Witnesses were JAMES MARRETT and RICHARD RICHARDSON.]

Jones Cty Court of Common Pleas Minutes 1834

Tuesday, the 9th of December

Justices: JOSEPH FOY, JOHN HOUSTON & FURNIFOLD JARMON, Esqs.

WILLIAM HUGGINS was to see that the bridge at TRENTON was repaired & the county trustees were to pay him for same.

WILLIAM HUGGINS, HARDY BRYAN & BENJN HUGGINS were to settle accounts of SAMUEL HILL, admr of ELIJAH SMALL, decd.

Magistrates held an election to elect a registrar for the county in place of JAMES REYNOLDS (died) & JOHN S. KOONCE was duly elected; he entered into bond with EMANUEL JARMON, FURNIFOLD JARMAN & JOHN H. HAMMOND, sureties.

Clerk to issue sie fa to Shff directing him to have before the court next term EGBERT GRIFFEN & RUFUS FARRIER, orphan children that the court may have them bound to someone to take care of them or otherwise as court shall direct.

SAMUEL WHITE, son of CLANCY? WHITE, aged about ten yrs, to be bound to JAMES McDANIEL to learn the art of farming until he attains lawful age.

WILLIAM HUGGINS, HARDY BRYAN, & JACOB HUGGINS were to settle accounts of ? JARMON, guard to JOHN ASKEY.

Jurors for next Superior Court:

SIMMONS ISLER	IGNATIUS BROCK	JAMES ADAMS
RIGDON HEWET	DANIEL SMITH	SIMON I. BECTON
WILLIAM GOODING JR	LEWIS SMITH	ADAM ANDREWS
NATHAN FOSCUE	AMOS SIMMONS	HARDY O. CONNOR
SHADERACH ERWIN	JOHN ROSEN	DAVID GREEN
THOMAS GILLET	DAVID WHARTON	OWEN ADAMS
ASA SMITH	JAMES W. HOWARD	RICHARD R. FOSCUE
JAMES ROBERTS	LEMUEL H. SIMMONS	BENJAMIN HUGGINS
JAMES MAIDS	BENJAMIN BROCK	ABNER GREEN
JOHN POLLOCK	EDWARD C. DEBRULE	CALVIN KOONCE
DANIEL MALLARD	JOSEPH WHITTY	BENJN ASKEY
GEORGE WILCOX	LOT EUBANKS	LEWIS O. BRYAN

Jurors for next county court:

JOHN BENDER SR	PETER HARGET	MOSES ADAMS
JOHN MALLARD	EDMUND WESTBROOK	ISAAC BROWN
JOHN FORDHAM	LEMUEL BUSICK	COUNCIL GOODING
JOSEPH HAY	JOSEPH KINSEY	ELIJAH PARRY
WILLIAMS JONES	EDWIN BECTON	THOMAS BALEY
ISAIAH WOOD	THOMAS McDANIEL	THOMAS CANNON
WILLIAM A. COX	JONAS WILLIAMS	MERRITT JONES
JOHN SHELFER	JOHN HARRISON	JOHN GODWIN
JOHN ADAMS	BARTHOLOMEW MEADOWS	
WALTER P. ALLEN	JOHN OLIVER	JOHN BALL

Deeds, etc., registered with JNO S. KOONCE, regestrar:
JOHN ANDREWS to ADAM ANDREWS
WINIFRED MERRIOT to WILLIAM GOODING
JOHN OLIVER to ADAM ANDREWS
ADAM ANDREWS to JOHN ANDREWS
JAMES WALLIS to JOSEPH WALLIS

APLIS WALLIS TO JOSEPH WALLIS
EDMUND B. HATCH to AMOS L. SIMMONS
JAMES HATCH to JACOB HUGGINS
JAMES HATCH to JOHN HOUSTON
ADAM ANDREWS to JOHN McDANIEL
LEVIAH HEATH to JONAS JONES SR
SAM KEY to JEREMIAH CANNON & THOMAS CANNON/CONNOR
JOHN H. & SIMON I. BECTON to JOHN HEATH
ANDREW WALLIS to JOSEPH WALLIS
DANIEL Y. SHINE to JOSEPH BROCK
JOSEPH K. STOKES to JOSEPH KINSEY/KINCEY
DANIEL SMITH to NATHAN F. PARSONS
JOHN THOMPSON to JOHN G. RAMSAY
WM HUGGINS, shff, to JOHN HOUSTON
HARDY BRYAN to JAMES MISSAW
SIDNEY JARMON & BRYAN MISSAW to JAMES MISSAW
EDMUND WESTBROOK to IRA WESTBROOK
NATHAN F. PARSONS to JOHN S. KOONCE

Jones Cty Court of Common Pleas Minutes 1835

MARCH, 1835
TRENTON, 9 March 1835

Justices: JOHN H. HAMMOND, FURNIFOLD H. JARMON, JAMES W. HOWARD & JOSEPH L. FOY, esqs.
Shff: RESDON M. McDANIEL
Clerk: HARDY BRYAN

Freeholders sworn as jurors for the state by JAS W. BRYAN, solicitor for county:
WALTER P. ALLEN, foreman

JONAS WILLIAMS	JOHN HARRISON	PETER HARGET
JOHN MALLARD	JOHN ADAMS	JOHN OLIVER
MARRITT JONES	JOHN SHELFER	THOMAS BALEY
ISAIAH WOOD	LEMUEL BUSICK	BARTHALOMEW MEADOWS

Letters of admin. on estate of RICHARD FOSCUE, decd, granted to WILLIAM FOSCUE; $1000 bond; JONATHAN WOOD & WALTER P. ALLEN, sureties.

JAMES FOY was authorized by court as county surveyor.

LEMUEL BUSICK was to oversee rd in place of THOMAS HUGGINS resigned.

EGBERT GRIFFIN, an orphan boy, was bound to JONAS/JAMES GRIFFIN until he would be of age.

Letters of admin. granted to EMANUAL JARMON on estate of MARY A. McDANIEL, decd; $500 bond; HARDY BRYAN & JOSEPH L. FOY, sureties.

JAMES W. HOWARD, ROSCO BARRUS, & JOSEPH L. FOY were to audit & settle accounts of JOSEPH WHITTY, admr of CHARLES WHITTY, decd, & at same time to make division & set off to ALFRED WHITTY, one of the heirs of said CHARLES, "his share of the estate of his father."

LEMUEL BUSICK was appointed to oversee rd in place of ?

LEWIS O. BRYAN was to oversee rd in place of JOHN H. BECTON, resigned.

Court ordered that the order made last term for the division of Negroes of RICHARD OLDFIELD, decd, be rescinded as the division was made under a previous order.

CAROLINA POLLOCK, minor, was to be bound to JOHN HARRISON.

CALVIN DAVIS appointed guard to RICHARD HATCH, minor; $5000 bond; EMANUEL JARMON & WILLIAM HUGGINS, sureties.

NATHAN FOSCUE, JOHN HOUSTON, & WILLIAM HUGGINS were to settle accounts of ADAM ANDREWS, guard to the heirs of JOHN MORRIS, decd, & at same time to divide & set off to SETH MORRIS, one of the heirs, his distributive share.

JOSEPH WHITTY appointed guard to "the children of CHARLES WHITTY, decd;" $3000 bond; JAMES W. HOWARD, surety.

EMANUEL JARMON appointed guard to CHRISTOPHER McDANIEL, "son of DURANT McDANIEL;" $500 bond; HARDY BRYAN & ADAM ANDREWS, sureties.

Clerk was to audit accounts of JORDAN S. CARSON.

Tuesday, 10 March 1835

Justices: JOHN HOUSTON, ABNER GREEN & NATHAN FOSCUE

Freeholders sworn as petit jurors:
MOSES ADAMS	CHARLES GEROCK	EDMD WESTBROOK

Jones Cty Court of Common Pleas Minutes 1835   153

BENJN KOONCE	THOMAS HARRISON	HARDY O. CONNOR
JOSEPH KINSEY	LEML H. SIMMONS	JOSEPH WHITTY
ADAM ANDREWS	JAMES RHODES	JAMES McDANIEL

    HARDY BRYAN appointed guard to NANCY R. LARAQUE, "infant dau of JAS B. LARAQUE;" $5000 bond; EML JARMON & WM HUGGINS, sureties.
    County trustees were to pay persons appointed to board of appeals last yr $2.00 per day each.
    Persons to hold elections in April:
District 1, White Oak: JOHN YOUNG & LEVI EUBANKS
District 2, Trent Bridge: ROSCO BARRUS & JAMES FOY
District 3, Trenton: ABNER GREEN & JOHN HOUSTON
District 4, Cypress Creek: JOHN H. HAMMOND & CALVIN KOONCE
District 5, Tuckehoe: FURNIFOLD JARMON & OWEN B. COX
District 6, Bever Creek: JAS S. KOONCE & FREDK I. BECTON

    JOHN HARRISON was to oversee rd from TRENTON to FRENCH BRANCH.
    WILLIAM HUGGINS, HARDY BRYAN, & JACOB HUGGINS were to settle accounts of EML JARMON, exr of MARY MURPHY, decd.
    WILLIAM HUGGINS, JACOB HUGGINS, & HARDY BRYAN were to settle accounts of ANN R. BRYAN, former guard to WILLIAM HENRY BRYAN & EML JARMON, present guard to said WM H.

    JAMES H. FRESHWATER, admr of ALFRED M. FRESHWATER vs EDWARD C. DEBRULE} writ case. The following jury:

MOSES ADAMS	CHARLY GEROCK	EDMUND WESTBROOK
BENJAMIN KOONCE	THOMAS HARRISON	HARDY O. CONNOR
JOSEPH KINSEY	LEMUEL H. SIMMONS	JOSEPH KINSEY
ADAM ANDREWS	JAMES RHODES	JAMES McDANIEL

found for the defendant.

    Report of committee to allot off to HULDAH BALL, widow of DAVID BALL, decd, year's provisions for self & children, returned to court & recorded.
    Report of committee to divide Negroes of heirs of JEREMIAH PARSONS, decd, returned & filed.
    Report of division of Negroes of MICHAEL KOONCE, decd, returned & filed.
    Account of sale & inventory of estate of JAMES REYNOLDS, decd, filed by F.I. BECTON, admr.
    Account of sale of property of HUBBARD STANLY filed by EML JARMON, admr.
    Account of sale & inventory of estate of MARY A. McDANIEL, decd, filed by EML JARMON, admr.
    Setlements of JOHN S. KOONCE, guard to heirs of MICHAEL KOONCE, filed.
    Settlements of HARDY PARRY, guard to heirs of SILAS PARRY, decd, filed.
    Settlement of JOHN OLIVER, guard to F.G. SIMMONS, minor, filed.
    Settlements of JOHN H. HAMMOND, guard to FREDK BRYAN, minor, & heirs of JEREMIAH PARSONS, decd, filed.
    Settlement of EML JARMON, guard to JNO ASKEY, filed.

    Last will & testament of FREDERICK FOSCUE, decd, produced in open court & admitted to probate by oath of LEMUEL H. SIMMONS, a witness; NATHAN FOSCUE, exr. [Note: Gwynn abstracted this will (p. 411) which was written 4 Oct 1834. Named are sons, AUGUSTUS, NATHAN; wife, DOVE; grandson, FREDERICK

FOSCUE. Son, NATHAN FOSCUE, was named exr, and the witnesses were LEMUEL H. SIMMONS and DANIEL MALLARD.]

Jurors for next term:

ZACKEUS BROWN	PETER ANDREWS	LEWIS WILLIAMS
EDMUND HATCH SR	ELIJAH KOONCE	LEWIS KINSEY
EDMUND B. HATCH	JAMES H. FRESHWATER	ABRAM SIMMONS
NATHAN STANLY	MELATON MEADOWS	JOHN McDANIEL SR
THOMAS POLLOCK	JOHN JONES	EDWARD C. DEBRULE SR
JAMES McDANIEL	WILLIAM D. COBB	FRANCIS ANDREW
THOMAS HARRISON	MICHAEL KOONCE	WILLIAM GOODING SR
SAMUEL HILL	JAMES K. RHODES	WILLIAM L. LAROQUE
HENRY RHODES	GEORGE HAZZARD	DANIEL YATES
AMOS SHELFER	JAMES MARRETT	JAMES D. KINSEY

Deeds, etc. registred with JNO S. KOONCE, registrar:
ASA SMITH to RICHARD REYNOLDS
ASA SMITH to RICHARD REYNOLDS
SETH G. MORRIS to JOHN McDANIEL
JAMES B. LARAQUE to CHARLES GEROCK
JOHN P. KOONCE to EDWARD GILBERT
JOSIAH SMITH to DAVID SMITH bond
EMANUEL HARGET to SIMON E. KOONCE
WILLIAM H. MEADOWS to his (sureties?)
NATHAN FOSCUE & wife to SARAH OLDFIELD
SARAH OLDFIELD to NATHAN FOSCUE
Pres. & directors of State Bank to JOSEPH WHITTY

JUNE TERM 1835
TRENTON, 8 June 1835

Justices: ABNER GREEN, JOSEPH I. FOY, & CALVIN KOONCE, esqs.
Shff: RESDON M. McDANIEL
Clerk: HARDY BRYAN

Letters of admin. on estate of WILLIAM GEORGE, decd, granted to EMANUEL JARMON on motion of GEORGE I. ALTMAN?, esq; $1200 bond; HARDY BRYAN & JOHN H. HAMMOND, sureties.
JOHN ADAMS was to oversee rd in place of JOHN E. FOSCUE, resigned.
JOHN B. REYNOLDS was to oversee rd in place of JAMES REYNOLDS, decd.
The hands of HARDY PARRY, ELIJAH PARRY, & those employed on the plantation where ABNER GREEN lives were to be exempted from working on the public rd for three years provided they make & keep in good repair a rd leading from ABNER GREEN's across PARRY's bridge & to the public rd leading to TRENTON.
JOHN YOUNG was permitted to turn the public rd leading from BLACK SWAMP to TRENTON so as to afford him (opportunity to enter?) his yard around his dwelling house.
County trustees to pay GEORGE WILCOX $2.40 for services to the court last term.

Jones Cty Court of Common Pleas Minutes 1835

ROSCO BARRUS, JONATHAN WOOD & GEORGE P. KINSEY were to settle accounts of ELIJAH LOVITT, exr of DAVID LOVITT, decd.

JAMES FOY, esq., qualified as a justice of the peace for Jones Co.

Justices were called & a majority appeared so the court levied a tax for the county. These persons were appointed to take the list of taxables in these districts:
District 1, White Oak: THOMAS GILLET
District 2, Trent Bridge: ROSCO BARRUS
District 3, Trenton: JOHN HOUSTON
District 4, Cypress Creek: JOHN H. HAMMOND
District 5, Tuckahoe: OWEN B. COX
District 6, Bever Creek: ABNER GREEN
District 7, (smudged); NATHAN FOSCUE

These persons should hold the poles of elections in the several districts:
District 1: LEVI EUBANKS, DANIEL YATES & THOS GILBERT
District 2: W.P. ALLEN?, DANIEL WILLIAMSON & J..? FOY
District 3: H. BRYAN, LEML BUSACK & JNO HOUSTON
District 4: JNO JONES, JOSEPH BROCK & CALVIN KOONCE
District 5: HENRY RHODES, ROSCO BROWN & FURNIFOLD JARMON
District 6: SIMON I. BECTON, AMOS HEATH & SIMMONS ISLER
District 7: AMOS SIMMONS, HARDY O. NEWTON & NATHAN FOSCUE

The following tax was to be levied & collected for 1835: for every $100 value of land, $.10 for improvements, & $.20 for taxable poles.

ABNER GREEN, esq, to take private examination of HARRIET KOONCE, wife of JOHN S. KOONCE, concerning her voluntary consent in executing a deed conveying lands to JOHN H. HAMMOND.

IGNATIOUS BROCK to oversee rd in place of JAS HARRISON, resigned.

COUNCIL CONNER, a boy aged about (blank) was bound to JOHN STANLY.

FREDERICK I. BECTON, SIMMONS ISLER, & JOHN HEATH were to settle accounts of DANIEL MILLER, exr of MARY GOODING, decd.

On motion of CALVIN DAVIS it was ordered that all hands of CALVIN DAVIS who were liable to work the public rd were to be taken from the district leading from the free bridge to WILLIAM RHEM's & placed to work under the overseer of that part of rd extending from the fork of rd to BLACK SWAMP.

OWEN B. COX licensed to sell spirituous liquors by small measure for one year at his store house on TUCKAHOE.

FREDERICK I. BECTON, JOHN HOUSTON & NATHAN FOSCUE were to make settlements with the several officers in Jones County.

JOHN H. HAMMOND, NATHAN FOSCUE & CALVIN KOONCE were to settle accounts of EML JARMON, county trustee.

HARDY BRYAN, WILLIAM HUGGINS, & JAMES McDANIEL were to select a suitable place to erect a poor house situated within one mile of TRENTON. They were authorized to purchase 100 acres of land for sd purpose drawing on county funds from trustee for payment.

R.G. REYNOLDS & wife vs PENELOPE, REBECAH, & NANCY HARGET} petition for sale & division of slaves. JACOB HUGGINS, appointed special guard of defendants, stated satisfactorily to the court that the slaves mentioned in the petition cannot be divided without a sale. It was ordered that they be sold by the Clerk of Court.

Jurors for next Superior Court:

THOMAS POLLOCK	THOMAS HARRISON	RIGDON HEWET
SIMON S. BECTON	EDWIN BECTON	AMOS SHELFER
JAMES MISSAW	WILLIAM L. LARAQUE	JAMES HARRISON
HARDY COLLINS	JOHN HEATH SR	FREDERICK PARKER
LEMUEL BUSICK	ROSCO BARRUS	WRIGHT STANLY
JOSEPH KINSEY	MARRETT JONES	JAMES ADAMS
ABNER GREEN	SAMUEL HILL	JOHN OLIVER
LEWIS KINSEY	OWEN HARRISON	FURNIFOLD H. JARMON
JAMES J. RHODES	DAVID WHARTON	JASON JONES JR
JOHN H. BECTON	THOMAS CONNOR/CANNON	JOHN YOUNG
JOHN E. FOSCUE	BENJAMIN C. SIMMONS	JAMES ROBERTS
NATHAN FOSCUE	JOHN STANLY (Trenton)	DANIEL WILLIAMSON

Jurors for next county court:

JOHN WOODS	DANIEL MALLARD	JAMES McDANIEL
AMOS SIMMONS	JOHN GODWIN	IGNATIOUS W. BROCK
WILLIAM B. RHEM	WILLIAM D. COBB	JACHIUS BROWN
ISAAC BROWN	HARDY PARRY	LOTT EUBANKS
EMORY METTS	THOMAS McDANIEL	HARDY O. CONNOR
SAMUEL DILLAHUNT	SHADRACK ERWIN	BENJAMIN HUGGINS
COUNCIL GOODING	ASA EUBANKS	SIMMONS COLLINS
JOHN POLLOCK	JOHN BROWN	FRANCIS ANDREWS
(OWEN?) ADAMS	WILLIAM JONES	BARTHALOMEW MEADOWS
(JAMES?) ADAMS	GEORGE WILCOX	GEORGE KING

Division of Negroes of NANCY LARAQUE filed.
Account of sale of estate of HUBBARD STANLY, decd, filed by E. JARMON, admr.
Settlement of OWEN ADAMS, guard to heirs of KADER KNIGHT, filed.
Settlement of SAMUEL B. HEATH, guard to WILLIAM HEATH, filed.
Settlement of EMANUEL JARMON, exr of MARY MURPHY, decd, filed.
Settlement of E. JARMON, guard to WM H. BRYAN, minor, filed.
Settlement of E. JARMON, guard to SUSAN ANDREWS, minor, filed.
Settlements of E. JARMON, guard to heirs of FREDK WOOD; to JNO C.B. KOONCE, minor, to E.F.B. KOONCE, minor; to heirs of A. PARRY; to heirs of C. POLLOCK; to CURTIS & NANCY WESTBROOK; to DEBORAH & MARINDA MURPHY, all filed.
Will of ASA SMITH, decd, produced in court; STEPHEN B. FORBES qualified as exr. [Note: Gwynn abstracted this will (p. 447) which was written 18 Jan 1835. Named is his minor daughter, SALLY SMITH and his "kinsman" STEPHEN B. FORBES who was also named exr. Witnesses were JAMES GOODING and SAMUEL G. BATTLE.]
Will of DANIEL STANLY, decd, proved in court. [Note: This will was also abstracted by Gwynn (p. 449). It was written 11 Dec 1834. It names the deceased's son, DANIEL C. STANLY, who was also named exr. Witnesses were ROSCO BARRUS and GEORGE HAZZARD.]
Deeds, etc., recorded by J.S. KOONCE, registrar:
FREDERICK FOSCUE to W. HUMPHREY & others

Jones Cty Court of Common Pleas Minutes 1835

STEPHEN B. FORBES, exr of ASA SMITH, to JOHN YOUNG
HARDY COLLINS to JOHN HUGGINS
JOHN STANLY to EMANUEL JARMON
WILLIAM MUMFORD, trustee of R.B. HATCH, to ELIJAH SIMMONS
BENJAMIN RHODES to OWEN B. COX
JOHN PARKER to OWEN B. COX
WILLIAM HUGGINS, shff, to OWEN B. COX
ISAAC BROWN & H. RHODES, agreement
JACOB HUGGINS "Clerk & (Master?)" to OWEN ADAMS
RICHARD REYNOLDS to ALFRED H. REYNOLDS
RICHARD REYNOLDS to JOHN B. REYNOLDS
RICHARD REYNOLDS to RICHARD G. REYNOLDS
OWEN B. COX to THOMAS ALPHEN
JOHN POLLOCK to BENJAMIN HUGGINS
EDWD MEADOWS to SIMEON MEADOWS
ARCHIBALD R. OWENS & FRANCIS OWENS to SIMEON MEADOWS
MILLENTON MEADOWS to SIMEON MEADOWS

SEPTEMBER TERM, 1835
TRENTON, 14 September 1835

Justices: JOSEPH I. FOY, FURNIFOLD H. JARMON, & JAMES W. HOWARD
Shff: RESDEN M. McDANIEL
Clerk: HARDY BRYAN

Jurors charged by JAMES W. BRYAN, County Solicitor, & sworn in by JOHN L. PARSONS, Constable:
ISAAC BROWN, foreman

SHADRACK ERWIN	GEORGE KING	FRANCIS ANDREWS
ZACHEUS BROWN	JOHN POLLOCK	SIMMONS COLLINS
DANIEL MALLARD	ASA EUBANKS	HARDY O. CONNER
AMOS SIMMONS	JOHN WOOD	THOMAS McDANIEL

ROSCO BARRUS, JONATHAN WOOD, & ENOCH FOY were to settle accounts of ELIJAH LOVETT, exr of DAVID LOVETT, decd.
JAMES STANLY was to oversee rd in place of CALVIN KOONCE, resigned.
JOHN H. DILLAHUNT was to oversee river in place of JOHN S. KOONCE, resigned.
FERDIAN DICKSON was to oversee rd in place of DANIEL DICKSON, resigned.
OWEN B. COX & FURNIFOLD H. JARMON, esq., were to take the private exam of CHARITY COX, wife of WILLIAM COX, touching her voluntary consent to a deed.
JAMES W. HOWARD & CALVIN MORRIS were to settle accounts of LEMUEL H. SIMMONS, admr of SAMUEL DAVIS, decd.
JONATHAN WOOD licensed to sell spirituous liquors at his store at TRENT BRIDGE for one yr by small measure.
$6.83 1/2 was paid to LOFTEN QUIN for four witness tickets in State vs SHADERACK ERWIN; three of sd tickets an ..?.. of WRIGHT QUIN, to be paid by county trustee.
EMANUEL JARMON was to admr estate of JOHN CONNER; $1000 bond; HARDY BRYAN & FREDERICK I. BECTON, sureties.

ROSCO BARRUS to admr de bonis non with will of ROSCO LEPSEY, decd; $500 bond; ELIJAH SIMMONS & ELIJAH LOVETT, securities.

WALTER P. ALLEN was to oversee rd in place of EDMUND HATCH, resigned.

County trustee was to pay to the shff of ROBESON COUNTY $62.50.

The hands on the south side of the main rd leading from TRENTON (who belong to District 3 including JOHN R. OLIVER, THOMAS McDANIEL, STEPHEN LEE, & DEMPSEY HARPER) up to the branch this side of JOHN DILLAHUNT's house were to be transfered to District 1.

FURNIFOLD H. JARMON, ZACHIUS BROWN, WILLIAM HARRISON, JAMES B. SHINE, CALVIN KOONCE, THOS PARSONS & CALVIN DAVIS were to be patrols in District 4.

$75.10 was allowed RESDON M. McDANIEL, shff, for services.

$4.60 paid to R.M. McDANIEL, shff, in settlement of tax for 1834 for insolvant taxables.

OWEN B. COX, LEWIS WILLIAMS, JONAS WILLIAMS, NEEDHAM PENUEL, JOHN KINSEY, & IVEY KING were named patrols for District 5.

NATHAN FOSCUE, JAMES MARRIETT, & HARDY O. NEWTON named as patrols for District 7.

ELIJAH SIMMONS was to oversee rd in place of EDMD B. HATCH, resigned.

$4.80 paid to BENJAMIN HUGGINS, Constable, for services.

RESDEN McDANIEL, Shff, filed his affidavit for 7 white poles and 16 black poles listed for 1834.

$6.43 paid to CALVIN J. MORRIS for witness ticket in Superior Court of CRAVEN COUNTY in case: State vs PETER GODETT.

JAMES MUMFORD, MICHAEL KOONCE & JOHN S. KOONCE were to settle accounts of COUNCIL WOOTEN, exr of WILLIAMS ISLER, decd.

Since the residue bequeathed by will of WILLIAMS ISLER, decd, was insufficient to satisfy debts of the estate, JAMES MUMFORD, MICHAEL KOONCE & JOHN S. KOONCE, were to value the specific legacies bequeathed & ascertain the appropriate proportions of contributions to debts.

Will of SARAH LIPSEY, decd, proved in court by oath of AMOS AMYET, a witness; ROSCO BARRUS named exr & he qualified as such. [Note: Gwynn abstracted this will (p. 432) written 5 Dec 1831. It names her granddaughter, ELIZA HARGET, and grandsons, ABNER and WILLIAM HARGET and JOHN and ROSCO BARRUS, who was also named exr. The witnesses were AMOS AMYETT and JAMES HATCH.]

Inventory & sale of estate of WM GEORGE, decd, filed by EML JARMON, admr.

Current accounts of exr of DAVID LOVETT filed.

Current accounts of LEML H. SIMMONS, admr of SAMUEL DAVIS, decd, filed.

Governor to the use of JOHN WASHINGTON vs HARDY H. SHELFER, R.M. McDANIEL & EML JARMON} (debt on Constable BROWN?).

The jurors:

MOSES ADAMS	ALFRED REYNOLDS	GEORGE WILCOX
JAMES MARRET	LOT EUBANKS	GEORGE HAZZARD
HARDY PARRY	LEMUEL H. SIMMONS	IGNATIUS W. BROCK
JAMES MISSAW	JOHN MISSAW	JOHN E. FOSCUE

found for the defendant from which verdict pltff craved an appeal to Superior Court which was granted; JOHN C. WASHINGTON & BENJAMIN HUGGINS signing appeal bond.

BENJN HARRISON, chairman, to the use of CHRISTOPHER R. GREEN, SARAH B. GREEN, & others vs F.K. BECTON, admr of JAS REYNOLDS & JNO E. FOSCUE, exr of SIMON FOSCUE & JAS B. SHINE} debt. Same jury as above found for pltff;

penalty of bond to be remitted on payment of $1179.60 & costs. Clerk allowed $10.00.

JOHN M. ROBERTS, agent, vs OWEN B. COX, LEWIS KINSEY & JOSEPH KINSEY} case. Plea withdrawn; judgment: $105.04.

RICHARD G. REYNOLDS & wife, BETSY, vs PENELOPE HARGET, REBECAH HARGET & NANCY HARGET} petition to sell slaves. Report of sale returned.

LEML H. SIMMONS qualified as a justice.

THOMAS McDANIEL vs EML JARMON, admr of MARY McDANIEL} appeal; pltff paid costs.

Tuesday, 15 September 1835

Justices: JOSEPH S. FOY, LEMUEL H. SIMMONS, & ABNER GREEN.

BENJN KOONCE was to be admr of JAMES HILL, son of JAS HILL, formerly of this county; $100 bond; SAMUEL HILL, surety.

JOHN HEATH, SIMMONS ISLER, & FREDERICK I. BECTON were to settle accounts of DANIEL MILLER, exr of MARY GOODING, decd.

SAML HILL appointed guard to ANN E. SMALL, minor; $500 bond; BENJN HUGGINS & BENJN KOONCE, sureties.

BENJN KONCE, JOHN H. DILLAHUNT, THOMAS HUGGINS, THOMAS LEE & HARDY O. CONNER appointed patrols in District 3.

ADAM ANDREWS, FURNIFOLD McDANIEL, & STARKEY McDANIEL appointed patrols in District 3. (**Note**: Perhaps one of these entries should be a different district. If so, the second entry is probably the one in error since Hardy O. Conner had been in District 3 in 1831.)

BENJN ASKEY was to oversee rd in place of FRANCIS ANDREWS, resigned.

WILLIAM STANLY, FREEMAN SMITH, AUTUS GILBERT, JOHN B. REYNOLDS, MICHAEL SHELFER & BENJN F. STANLY appointed patrols for District 6.

JOHN L. PARSONS was paid $8.80 for services.

$40.00 allowed HARDY BRYAN, clerk, for extra services.

STEPHEN SMITH, ISRAEL HOWARD, ALFRED WHITTY, JAMES MORTON, JOSEPH S. FOY & GEORGE S. BENDER appointed patrols for District 2.

GEORGE KING exempted from jury duty on "account of affliction."

JOHN L. PARSONS & BENJN HUGGINS, constables, entered bonds.

JAMES McDANIEL, WILLIAM HUGGINS, & HARDY BRYAN were to ascertain on what terms a suitable site for a poor house could be purchased & to "draft buildings for that purpose."

Tax list for District 1 returned by THOS GILLET, esq.
Tax list for District 2 returned by ROSCO BARRUS, esq.
Tax list for District 3 returned by JOHN HOUSTON, esq.
Tax list for District 4 returned by F.H. JARMON, esq.
Tax list for District 5 returned by O.B. COX, esq.
Tax list for District 6 returned by ABNER GREEN, esq.
Tax list for District 7 returned by N. FOSCUE, esq.

HARDY BRYAN, clerk, filed his affidavit as to monies in his office for 3 yrs previous to this term.

Jurors drawn for December term:
PETER ANDREWS	MICHAEL KOONCE	ABRAM SIMMONS
JOHN MALLARD	WILLIAM GOODING SR	EDMUND HATCH SR

Jones Cty Court of Common Pleas Minutes 1835

HENRY RHODES	MARTIN F. BROCK	FURNIFOLD G. HERRITAGE
JOSEPH WHITTY	WALTER P. ALLEN	JOHN McDANIEL SR
JOHN MISSAW	JAMES B. KINSEY	MICAJAH F. MATTOCKS
JOHN HARRISON	BENJAMIN ASKEY	DANIEL HARRISON
LEWIS SMALL	JOHN BENDER SR	EDWARD C. DEBRULE
ADAM ANDREWS	EDWD M. GILBERT	NATHAN B. WESTBROOK
JAMES B. SHINE	JOHN ADAMS	THOMAS BALEY
PETER HARGET	JOHN BALL	JAMES MARRET

Deeds, etc., recorded by JNO S. KOONCE, registrar:
JAMES MUMFORD to FREDERICK I. BECTON & M.F. BROCK
LEWIS BRYAN to ELIJAH KOONCE
JOHN S. KOONCE & wife to JOHN H. HAMMOND
JNO YOUNG & J. WHITTY to JOHN BENDER SR
HANNAH H. KINSEY & NANCY M. FOSCUE to LEML H. SIMMONS
A.H. REYNOLDS to JOHN B. REYNOLDS
RICHD G. REYNOLDS to A.H. REYNOLDS
BENJAMIN HUGGINS to WILLIAM B. RHEM
EML K. HARGET to WILLIAM B. RHEM
LEWIS KINSEY to WILLIAM GEORGE
R. GREEN to JAS TAYLOR proved before the judge, I.R. DONNER

DECEMBER TERM, 1835
TRENTON, December 14, 1835

Justices: ROSCO BARRUS, JOHN HOUSTON & JOSEPH S. FOY, esqs.
Shff: RESDEN M. McDANIEL
Clerk: HARDY BRYAN

Jurors who were sworn to attend by JOHN L. PARSONS, Constable, and charged by the county attorney:
JOHN BENDER, foreman

JOHN MALLARD	ADAM ANDREWS	DANIEL HARRISON
JOHN HARRISON	LEWIS SMALL	MICAJAH F. MATTOCKS
EDWARD C. DEBRULE	JOHN McDANIEL	NATHAN B. WESTBROOK
JOHN MISSAW	HENRY RHODES	ABRAM SIMMONS

HARDY A. NEWTON licensed to retail spirituous liquors at his home for one year.

ROSCO BARRUS licensed to retail same at his store at TRENT BRIDGE for one year.

JOSEPH B. LOFTON appointed admr of the estate of MARY LOFTEN; $1000 bond; FREDERICK I. BECTON & SIMMONS ISLER, sureties.

JAMES PADRICK appointed guard to JOSEPH H. WATSON, minor; $2500 bond; DANIEL YATES & MICAJAH F. MATTOCKS, sureties.

JOHN YOUNG was to oversee rd from cross roads on WHITE OAK to a black sorrel in the middle of the POCOSIN in place of THOS DUDLY, resigned.

JOSEPH SMALL was to oversee rd from BLACK SWAMP to the LENIOR COUNTY line in place of JAMES ADAMS, resigned.

SAMUEL HAZZARD, infant son of JAMES HAZZARD, decd, was bound to THOMAS McDANIEL.

Jones Cty Court of Common Pleas Minutes 1835

CHARLES GEROCH licensed to retail spirituous liquors at his store in TRENTON for one year.

SAMUEL HILL qualified as a justice of the peace.

JAMES FOY appointed guard to JOSEPH HATCH, minor; $1000 bond; EDMUND HATCH & JOSEPH S. FOY, sureties.

EML JARMON appointed guard to JESSE TAYLOR, minor, $500 bond; HARDY BRYAN & BENJN HUGGINS, sureties.

BENJN HUGGINS reappointed Constable for three months.

WILLIAM B. RHEM appointed guard to METAHU? RHEM, minor; $20,000 bond; RESDEN McDANIEL & SAMUEL HILL, sureties.

SAMUEL HILL, BENJAMIN KOONCE, & LEML BUSICK were to settle accounts of BENJN HUGGINS, exr of TOBIAS KOONCE, decd.

HARDY BRYAN, WILLIAM HUGGINS, & EML JARMON were to settle accounts of HARDY PARRY, guard to SALLY PARRY, minor.

ELIZABETH HARRISON, surviving extx of the will of JOHN HARRISON, decd, qualified as same.

JASON G. TAYLOR, an orphan boy, was bound to JOHN JARMON SR until he would come of age.

Inventory & account of sale of property of JOHN CONNOR, decd, returned by EML JARMON, admr.

DANIEL MILLER, exr of MARY GOODING, decd, returned settlement which was filed.

Last will of FRANCIS MUNDINE, decd, proved in court by oath of B. MEADOWS, a witness to will; DANIEL DICKSON, named exr by will, qualified as same. [Gwynn abstracted this will (p. 438) which was written 26 Mar 1835. It names the deceased's mother, ANN MUNDINE, brother, WILLIAM MUNDINE, and sister, HESSY/HEPSEY MUNDINE. DANIEL DICKSON was named exr, and THOMAS GILLET and BARTHOLOMEW MEADOWS were witnesses.]

Jurors drawn for Superior Court March term 1836:

JAMES WILLIAMS	JOHN MISSAW	JAMES W. HOWARD
THOMAS GILLET	JAMES G. HERRITAGE	JOHN BALL
COUNCIL GOODING	MOSES ADAMS	BARTHALOMEW MEADOWS
FREDK I. BECTON	BENJN ASKEW	WILLIAM B. RHEM
JAMES McDANIEL	JOSEPH S. FOY	DAVID WHARTON
CALVIN KOONCE	NATHAN B. WESTBROOK	EDMD HATCH SR
WILLIAM JONES	LEML H. SIMMONS	JOHN H. HAMMOND
OWEN B. COX	GEORGE WILCOX	ABNER GREEN
JAMES FOY	DANIEL HARRISON	THOMAS POLLOCK
JOSEPH WHITTY	ROSCO BARRUS	EDWD C. DEBRULE SR
JOSEPH KINSEY SR	IGNATIUS BROCK	WALTER P. ALLEN
DANIEL WILLIAMSON	JOHN YOUNG	
FURNIFOLD G. HERRITAGE		

Freeholders drawn for jury duty in the county court March term 1836:

JOSEPH SMALL	EDMUND WESTBROOK	LEWIS WILLIAMS
EDMUND B. HATCH	WHITFIELD TURNER	JOHN STANLY SR
MILLINTON MEADOWS	WILLIAM BYMAN	EDWD C. DEBRULE JR
WILLIAM GOODING	JAMES MADES	BENJAMIN BROCK
LEWIS O. BRYAN	ELIJAH KOONCE	BENJAMIN F. STANLY
ELIJAH PARRY	ENOCK FOY	JOHN SHELFER
ISAIAH WOOD	RICHARD P. FOSCUE	GEORGE HAZZARD

Jones Cty Court of Common Pleas Minutes 1835

DANIEL YATES	JOHN FORDHAM	JOSEPH HAY
JONAS JONES SR	DAVID GREEN	GEORGE S. DEBRULE
NATHAN STANLY	JOHN JONES	AARON WOOD

Deeds, etc., recorded with JNO S. KOONCE, registrar:

EMANUEL JARMON to NEEDAM B. BEASLEY
EDMUND WESTBROOK to JOHN STRICKLIN
JAMES D. KINCEY to GEORGE D. JONES
JOB SMITH to JOSEPH WHITTY
SIMMONS MOORE to BRICE MOORE/MOSES
JOHN L. PARSONS to JOHN E. HUSEY/HUPEY
EML JARMON, agent for WM ADAMS, to EZEKIEL JONES
EML JARMON to ELIZABETH REYNOLDS
EML JARMON to ALFRED REYNOLDS
JACOB HUGGINS to WILLIAM HUGGINS
JOHN B. REYNOLDS to ELIZABETH REYNOLDS
JOSEPH K. SMITH to SIMMONS COLLINS
JOHN TURNER to J.E. HUPEY/HUSSEY
LEMUEL HATCH to JOSEPH WHITTY

Jones Cty Court of Common Pleas Minutes 1836

MARCH TERM 1836
TRENTON, Monday 14 March 1836

Justices: JAMES FOY, ROSCO BARRUS, & JOSEPH S. FOY, Esq.
Shff: RESDEN M. McDANIEL
Clerk: HARDY BRYAN

Jurors:
ENOCK FOY, foreman	JOHN SHELFER	JAMES MADES
GEORGE HAZZARD	DAVID GREEN	BENJAMIN BROCK
BENJAMIN F. STANLY	LEWIS O. BRYAN	ELIJAH PARRY
EDWD C. DEBRULE	WILLIAM GOODING	JOHN JONES

Grand jury charged by JAMES W. BRYAN, solicitor; BENJA HUGGINS, constable, sworn to attend jurors.

JAMES FOY, JOSEPH S. FOY & ROSCO BARRUS were to settle accounts of JOSEPH WALLACE, admr of CELIA WALLACE, decd.

COUNCIL FIELDS to oversee rd from middle of pocosin to BUCKNER HATCH's mill in place of FRANCIS B. AMYETT, removed.

ABNER GREEN & OWEN B. COX were to take the private exam of CHARITY COX, wife of WILLIAM COX.

FERDINAN DICKSON was appointed constable in WHITE OAK district; he entered into bond with DANIEL YATES, JAMES W. HOWARD & DANIEL DICKSON, sureties.

County trustee was to pay ROSCO BARRUS $19.99 for timber furnished by him for repair of TRENT BRIDGE.

Order of last term to appoint a committee to settle accounts of BENJN HUGGINS, exr of TOBIAS KOONCE, decd, was renewed with report due next term.

ANN MUNDINE was appointed admx of estate of HARDY MUNDINE, decd; $6,000 bond; BARTHALAMEW MEADOWS & DANIEL DICKSON, sureties.

JAMES FOY was to see that TRENT BRIDGE was repaired.

RICHARD G. REYNOLDS was appointed guard to the "infant heirs of ZILPHA HARGET, decd;" $2,000 bond; JAMES B. SHINE & CALVIN KOONCE, sureties.

WILLIAM HUGGINS appointed guard to ELIZABETH REYNOLDS, "dau of JAMES REYNOLDS, decd;" $3,000 bond; EML JARMAN & BENJN HUGGINS, sureties.

EMANUEL JARMAN, guard to JAMES STANLY, minor, "son of HUBBARD STANLY, decd;" $5,000 bond; WILLIAM HUGGINS & HARDY BRYAN, sureties.

JAMES G. HERRITAGE was to oversee rd from GUM SWAMP on the DOVER RD to the county line near JOHN COBB's & from JOHN WISE's to the southwest in place of LEWIS O. BRYAN, resigned.

EML F. JONES appointed constable in District 5.

JOHN PARSONS was to oversee rd from the SAND RIDGE to fork at JAMES FRAZER's place & from fork below FRAZER's to state rd leading towards TRENT BRIDGE in place of HOUSTON ROBERTS, moved.

County trustees were to pay FREDK I. BECTON, admr of JAMES REYNOLDS, decd, $7.00 for a bank record furnished the office of registrar.

THOMAS POLLOCK was to oversee rd from ...?... to "French house" in place of JOHN HARRISON, resigned.

THOMAS GILLET, LEVI EUBANKS, & DANIEL DICKSON were appointed patrols for District 1.

HARDY PARRY, WILLIAM HUGGINS, & HARDY BRYAN were to settle accounts of EML JARMON, guard to NANCY WESTBROOK.

Jones Cty Court of Common Pleas Minutes 1836

WILLIAM HUGGINS was to see that repairs were made to the county jail.
County trustees were to pay WILLIAM HUGGINS $31.50 for extra services while shff.
DANIEL DICKSON, esq., qualified as justice of the peace "& took his seat in court."

These settlements were filed:
- JOHN S. KOONCE, guard to heirs of MICHAEL KOONCE, decd
- HARDY PARRY, guard to heirs of SILAS PARRY
- CALVIN DAVIS, guard to R. HATCH, WINIFRED GREEN, SARAH GREEN, & RICHD GREEN, minors
- JOHN OLIVER, guard to F.G. SIMMONS, minor
- ROSCO BARRIS, guard to W.W. FRANKS
- E. JARMON, guard to WM E. MURPHY
- OWEN ADAMS, guard to heirs of K. KNIGHT
- RACHEL McDANIEL, guard to EDNEY McDANIEL
- COUNCEL WOOTEN, exr of WM JOHN, decd
- SAMUEL HILL, admr of ELIJAH SMALL
- Division of the Negroes of EMANUEL KOONCE filed
- Division of the Negroes of SILAS PARRY filed
- Inventory of estate of MARY LOFTEN, decd, filed by F.B. LOFTEN

Tuesday, 15 Mar 1836

Justices: JOSEPH S. FOY, SAMUEL HILL & JOHN HOUSTON, esqs.

THOMAS GILLET, JAMES ROBERTS, & JAMES MADES were to settle accounts of ANN MUNDINE, admx of HARDY MUNDINE with DANIEL DICKSON, who was admr.
BENJAMIN HUGGINS was appointed constable in District 6; bond with LEMUEL BUSACK & JOHN H. DILLAHUNT, sureties.
WILLIAM HUGGINS was to contract to purchase about 90 acres near TRENTON owned by JOHN MALLARD for $600.00 for the erection of a poorhouse.
JOHN A. SANDERS vs NATHAN SMITH, et al} Pltff to pay.

Freeholders drawn for June term:

MICHAEL KOONCE	JOSEPH WOLLON	RICHARD G. REYNOLDS
JOHN HAGINS	WHITFIELD TURNER	EDMD D. WHARTON
ENOCK FOY	ELIJAH McDANIEL	RICHARD R. FOSCUE
JNO HANDCOCK	NATHAN F. PARSONS	CHARLES GAROCK
JONATHAN WOOD	JAMES ADAMS	EDWD C. DEBRULE (JR?)
AMOS AMYETT	JAMES MUMFORD	MICHAEL SHELFER
JAMES D. KINSEY	JOHN B. REYNOLDS	LEWIS WILLIAMS
RIGDON HEWET	NATHAN P. SMITH	GEORGE S. DEBRULE
EMANUEL KOONCE	ELIJAH KOONCE	HARDY POLLOCK
JNO STRICKLINE	CALVIN DAVIS	ISRAEL HOWARD

Deeds & bills of sale recorded by JNO S. KOONCE, registrar:
- THOMAS BALEY to E. KOONCE
- CATHARINE CROFT to JAMES SHINE
- ELANOR IPOCK to ELARY IPOCK
- HARDY BRYAN, (const?), to WILLIAM HUGGINS

JONATHAN WOOD to JAMES FOY
WM A. COX & wife to ISAAC STROUD?
WILLIAM HUGGINS, shff, to JONATHAN WOOD
WILLIAM HUGGINS, shff, to JONATHAN WOOD
JOHN G. RAMSAY to THOMAS POLLOCK
JAMES H. FRESHWATER to BENJN LEATH?
LANEY SMALL to THOMAS POLLOCK
JOHN E. HUSSEY to JOHN HEATH
MARY GEROCK to CHARLES GEROCK
EDWIN BECTON to EMANUEL JARMON
JOHN H. BECTON to EMANUEL JARMON
JONAS JONES to FELIA KING
SIMON I. BECTON to ELIZABETH CASEY & D. HALE/HILL
Marriage contract signed by N.P. SMITH, MARY N. LOVET & B. MARKET
WM HUGGINS, clerk of superior court, bond
CHARLES GEROCK, clerk & master in equity, bond
H. BRYAN, (cons?) to JAS ROBERTS proven before the judge

JUNE TERM 1836
TRENTON, Monday 13 June 1836

Justices: OWEN B. COX, ABNER GREEN, JOSEPH S. FOY, & JAMES FOY
Shff: RESDEN M. McDANIEL
Clerk: HARDY BRYAN

Jurors:
CALVIN DAVIS, foreman	JAMES ADAMS	JOHN B. REYNOLDS
JOHN STRICKLIN	MICHAEL SHELFER	RICHARD G. REYNOLDS
EMANUEL KOONCE	MICHAEL KOONCE	HARDY POLLOCK
EDWD C. DEBRULE, JR	JNOTHAN WOOD	ELIJAH McDANIEL
JAMES MUMFORD		

Jurors charged by JAMES W. BRYAN, county solicitor. BENJAMIN HUGGINS, constable, sworn to attend jurors.

ABNER GREEN was appointed to take the private exam of Mrs. HARRIET KOONCE
ENOCK NOBLE was to be guard to heirs of BRADDOCK NOBLE, decd; $10,000 bond; JAMES B. SHINE & JOHN JONES, sureties.
DANIEL O'SHAUGHNESSY? was bound to JAMES FOY.
OWEN B. COX & JNOTHAN WOOD were granted the right to sell liquor at their respective homes.
Order of last court for JAMES FOY to make repairs to TRENT BRIDGE was renewed.
GABULON H. SIMPSON was granted license to peddle goods, wares & merchandise.
Trustees were to pay DANIEL DICKSON $9.60 for services up to 14 June 1833.
HARDY BRYAN, WILLIAM HUGGINS & CHARLES GERACK to audit & settle accounts of EMANUEL JARMON, county trustee.
JAMES CRAFT, DAVID CRAFT, & FREDERICK CRAFT, orphans, were bound to FREDERICK PARKER

Jones Cty Court of Common Pleas Minutes 1836

The road allotted to JOHN S. PARSONS as overseer during March Term 1836 shall be up WHITE OAK as far as BENDER's hands instead of to the SAND RIDGE as mentioned in that earlier order & the hands of JOHN BALL & BENJ C. SIMMONS were subject to work the rd under PARSONS

The following are to hold the election poles for Jones County the first Thursday in August next for the election of members to the next General Assembly, County Sheriff, & Governor of the State:

District 1: DANIEL DICKSON, justice; LEVI EUBANKS & NATHAN F. PARSONS, inspectors
District 2: ROSCO BARRUS, justice; JOSEPH S. FOY & JONATHAN WOOD, inspectors
District 3: NATHAN FOSCUE, justice; WM HUGGINS & HARDY BRYAN, inspectors
District 4: CALVIN KOONCE, justice; JOHN JONES & JAMES B. SHINE, inspectors
District 5: OWEN B. COX, justice; JOSEPH KINCEY & LEWIS WILLIAMS, inspectors
District 6: SIMMONS ISLER, justice; ALFRED H. REYNOLDS & MICHAEL KOONCE, inspectors
District 7: (nothing written)

The following persons were to take the list of taxable property in the county:
District 1: DANIEL DICKSON
District 2: JAMES FOY
District 3: SAMUEL HILL
District 4: JOHN H. HAMMOND
District 5: OWEN B. COX
District 6: FREDERICK I. BECTON
District 7: LEMUEL H. SIMMONS

BENJAMIN HUGGINS was to remain constable until next court.

Commissioners of the poorhouse were to draw funds from the trustees as needed.
JAMES W. HOWARD, JAMES FOY & JOSEPH I. FOY were named patrols in District 2.

Freeholders drawn as jurors for next county court:

FELIA/FELIX KING	JOHN BENDER SR	ADAM ANDREWS
AMOS KOONCE	ABRAHAM SIMMONS	HENRY RHODES
JOHN MALLARD	JAMES HARRISON JR	FRANCIS ANDREWS
HARDY PARRY	MICAJAH F. MATTOCKS	BENJN C. SIMMONS
JOHN JONES	AMOS SIMMONS	AARON WOOD
JOHN POLLOCK	DANIEL MALLARD	LEWIS SMALL
JOHN JONES JR	SIMON I. BECTON	FREDK PARKER
LOTT EUBANKS	BENJAMIN HUGGINS	ISAAC BROWN
ZACHEUS BROWN	JOHN GOULDING	JAMES J. RHODES
SIMMONS COLLINS	JOHN SHELFER	JAMES WHALEY

Freeholders drawn for next superior court, September term 1835 (sic):

SHADERACH ERVIN	EDMUND M. GILBERT	JOSHUA MILLER
BENJN SCOTT	NATHAN P. MAPLES?	EDWARD SCOTT
ABNER KILLIGREW	JOHN E. FOSCUE	MERRIT JONES
JOHN OLIVER	OWEN ADAMS	DANIEL YATES
GEORGE HAZZARD	MARTIN F. BROCK	GEORGE KING
JOSEPH SMALL	JOHN HOUSTON	WRIGHT C. STANLY
JAMES MISSAW	JOHN HARRISON	EMORY METTS
LEWIS O. BRYAN	JOHN McDANIEL SR	SAMUEL HILL
JAMES MADES	SAMUEL DILLAHUNT	JOHN ROUSE
HARDY O. CONNER	THOMAS McDANIEL	THOMAS HARRISON
NATHAN STANLY	JOHN H. DILLAHUNT	AMOS SHELFER
LEMUEL BUSACK	DAVID GREEN	THOMAS BALEY

EMANUEL JARMON, guard, filed the following settlements of his wards: SUSAN ANDREWS; heirs of A. PARRY; E.F.B. & J.C.B. KOONCE; MARIA & DEBORAH MURPHY; HOLLON, CAROLINA, & ANN D. POLLOCK; heirs of F. WOOD; CHRISTOPHER McDANIEL; IVEY HARRISON in right of his wife; & CURTIS WESTBROOK.
    Settlement of D. DICKSON, exr of HARDY MUNDINE, decd, filed.
    Settlement of JOSEPH WALLACE, admr of C. WALLIS, filed.
    Settlement of LEML B. HATCH, guard to WM HEATH, filed.
    Inventory of estate of MORRIS WARD, decd, filed by (first name smudged) W. DUDLEY, his exr.
    Account of sale of property of JOHN HARRISON, decd, filed.

JAS J. RHODES to use of JOHN JONES vs OWEN B. COX} debt. Plea withdrawn & judgment by default. Debt of $300; interest from 25 Jan 1833. Appeal prayed & granted.

Deeds registered with JNO S. KOONCE, registrar:
MICAJAH PETERWAY to subscribers for meeting & school house
ELIJAH SIMMONS to JONATHAN WOOD
JAMES MARRIT to GEORGE HAZZARD
ELIZABETH CAREY & D. HALE to SIMON I. BECTON
RICHARD REYNOLDS to LEML H. SIMMONS
EML JARMON to WILLIAM C. MURPHY
HARDY PARRY to BENJN HUGGINS
BENJN RHODES to JONAS JONES SR
ELIJAH KOONCE to ELIJAH B. KOONCE
ELIJAH KOONCE to EML KOONCE
OWEN ADAMS to ROSCO BARRUS

SEPTEMBER TERM, 1836
TRENTON   12 September 1836

Justices: ROSCO BARRUS, NATHAN FOSCUE & LEMUEL H. SIMMONS, esquires
Shff: RESDEN McDANIEL
Clerk: HARDY BRYAN
    JAMES TAYLOR attended as solicitor for JAMES W. BRYAN, county solicitor.

Shff returned his _vinera_ of jurors summoned to attend this term & the jury was discharged by the court.

HARDY BRYAN appointed admr of estate of PETER ANDREWS, decd; $4,000 bond; WILLIAM HUGGINS & BENJAMIN HUGGINS, sureties. In addition BRYAN is to sell the perishable property of the estate at 6 mos credit.

JOHN WOOD was to oversee public rd in place of JAMES STANLY, resigned.

ZACHEUS BROWN was to oversee rd in place of FURNIFOLD H. JARMON, resigned.

JOHN C. FOSCUE was to oversee rd in place of JOHN ADAMS, resigned.

Power of attorney, executed by FURNIFOLD GREEN of Georgia, to DAVID GREEN of Jones County, authorizing said DAVID to receive certain monies from HARDY BRYAN, clerk of court, due from his office of this county.

Clerk to receive from EML JARMON his list of taxable property from District 5.

An order of March Term 1836 appointing a committee to settle accounts of BENJAMIN HUGGINS, exr of TOBIAS KOONCE, decd, be readied for report this term.

JAMES W. HOWARD, JONATHAN WOOD, & ROSCO BARRUS to settle accounts of WILLIAM BENUM, admr of DAVID BALLARD.

RICHARD G. REYNOLDS was to oversee rd in place of IGNATIOUS BROCK, resigned.

FURNIFOLD H. JARMON, ZACHEUS BROWN & JOHN HANCOCK were appointed patrols for District 4 for one yr.

HARDY O. NEWTON, JAMES MARRET, & NATHAN FOSCUE named patrols in District 7.

HARDY BRYAN, WILLIAM HUGGINS, & CALVIN J. MORRIS named in District 3.

SAMUEL DILLAHUNT excused from jury & attendance to public roads during "his inability & afflictions."

HARDY BRYAN was to be paid $40 for services to the county in his office as clerk for one yr ending June Term 1836.

JOSEPH S. FOY was appointed surveyor for the county; he entered bond with LEMUEL H. SIMMONS, surety.

GEORGE WILCOX was allowed $1.60 from county funds for two days attendance at court March Term 1836.

BENJAMIN HUGGINS was appointed constable for one yr; he entered bond with ADAM ANDREWS & WILLIAM HUGGINS, sureties.

RISDEN McDANIEL, shff, was allowed 9 absent taxable poles listed for year 1835, viz:

EMANUEL ALPHIN	EDWARD CRAFT/CROFT	WILLIAM CONNER
GRAYLIN MORRIS	CHRISTOPHER R. GREEN	BENTLY WESTUN
ELIAS LANE	FRANCIS ANDREWS	WILLIAM M. KINCEY

Jurors for next term:

JAMES B. SHINE	JOHN MALLARD	JOHN FORDHAM
IVA WESTBROOK	BENJN F. STANLY	OWEN HARRISON
JOSEPH KINCEY SR	PETER HARGET	WM D. COBB
ASA EUBANKS	HARDY O. NEWTON	EDMD B. HATCH
BENJN BROCK	WILLIAM MURPHY	WHITFIELD TURNER
ALFRED H. REYNOLDS	ELIJAH PARRY	EDMD HATCH SR
WILLIAM BINUM	NATHAN F. PARSONS	ISAIAH WOOD
HARDY COLLINS	FURNIFOLD H. JARMON	JOHN HAGANS
WM GOODING	JAMES MARRET	ELIJAH McDANIEL
JOHN ADAMS	MILLENTON MEADOWS	EDWD D. WHARTON

HARDY BRYAN, WILLIAM HUGGINS, & CHARLES GEROCK were to settle accounts of ELIZABETH HARRISON, extx of JOHN HARRISON, decd.
    Settlement of B. HUGGINS, exr of TOBIAS KOONCE, decd, filed.
    Account of sale of property of DAVID BALL filed.
    Inventory of estate of DAVID BALL filed.
    Tax list for District 1 filed by D. DICKSON, J.P.; for District 3 filed by SAML HILL, J.P.; for District 4 filed by JNO H. HAMMOND, J.P.; for District 5 filed by JAMES FOY, Esq.; for District 6 filed by F.I. BECTON, J.P.; and for District 7 filed by LEML H. SIMMONS, J.P. (**Note**: District 2 was not in the list.)

    RESDEN M. McDANIEL, Shff, presented his bonds and they were filed; LEMUEL H. SIMMONS & JAMES McDANIEL, sureties.
    Papers, deeds, etc. recorded by JNO S. KOONCE, registrar:
FURNIFOLD GREEN to DAVID GREEN, power of attorney
EDWD S. FERROND, WINIFRED GREEN, & ABNER GREEN: Morgt. contract
R. McDANIEL, shff, to GEORGE KING: deed
STEPHEN KINCEY & IVA/IRA PRESCOT to ISREAL HOWARD: deed
Sheriff WM HUGGINS to EDWD L. JONES: deed

    Settlement of BENJN HUGGINS, exr of TOBIAS KOONCE, decd, filed.
    Settlement of EML JARMON, county trustee, filed.
    Settlement of SIMMONS ISLER, guard to EDWIN B. ISLER, minor, filed.

DECEMBER TERM, 1836
TRENTON, Monday 12 December 1836

Justices: ABNER GREEN, JOHN H. HAMMOND & SAMUEL HILL, esquires
Shff: RESDEN M. McDANIEL
Clerk: HARDY BRYAN

    County trustee was to pay HARDY O. CONNER $5.50 for articles furnished for the jail. (**Note**: Although it seems EMANUEL JARMON was the only trustee, often the word appeared to be plural.)
    JAMES HARRISON, JAMES B. SHINE, & CALVIN KOONCE were to divide the Negroes of heirs of JEREMIAH PARSONS, decd, among the heirs.
    Last will & testament of SHADERACK ERWIN, decd, produced & admitted to probate. Proved by oath of LEMUEL BUSECK, one of the witnesses thereto. HARDY BRYAN, the exr therein named, qualified as such. [Note: Gwynn abstracted this will (p. 410) which was undated. It names the deceased's nephews, JOHN, CALVIN, WILLIAM and RICHARD ERWIN (sons of his brother, WILLIAM ERWIN), LIKERGUS ERWIN (son of his brother, RICHARD ERWIN) and ABNER ERWIN (son of his brother, EDWARD ERWIN); neices, ALICE (daughter of his brother, ROBERT ERWIN), CAROLINE, WINIFRED and ELIZABETH (daughters of his brother WILLIAM ERWIN); and brothers, WILLIAM, EDWARD, ABSALOM, and EVAN ERWIN. HARDY BRYAN "of TRENTON" was named exr, and the witnesses were: LEMUEL BUSICK and GEORGE WILCOX.]
    ELIJAH LOVETT appointed guard to JAMES MONROW LOVETT, minor; $10,000 bond; ELIJAH SIMMONS & DANIEL DICKSON, securities.
    JOHN H. HAMMOND, ABNER GREEN & CALVIN KOONCE were to divide Negroes of

estate of MICHAEL KOONCE, decd, in order to allot off to SIMON KOONCE his distributive share of same.

THOMAS ALCOT allowed to peddle goods in the county for one yr.

JONATHAN WOOD and ROSCO BARRUS were allowed to sell spirituous liquors at POLLOCKSVILLE for one yr.

GEORGE I. BENDER was to oversee rd from fork to upper MILL CREEK BRIDGE in place of JOSEPH I. FOY, resigned.

HENRY RHODES, JOSEPH KINCEY, & EMANUEL JARMON were to divide Negroes of JOHN B. COX, decd, so as to allot off to LEVINA COX, "one of the heirs," her distributive share.

JAMES D. KINCEY appointed guard to GEORGE D. JONES & MARY JONES, minors; $1500 bond; JOHN H. HAMMOND & EML JARMON, sureties.

JAMES MUMFORD was to oversee rd from WOODS/WARDS HILL to JACOB'S BRANCH including BEVER CREEK BRIDGE in place of I./S. B. REYNOLDS, resigned.

WILLIAM ERWIN appointed guard to "his children:" WILLIAM, RICHARD, CAROLINE, & JOHN ERWIN, minors; $1000 bond; JAMES D. KINCEY & JOSEPH KINCEY, sureties.

The jail fee ordered to be increased to $.40 per day for the maintenance of prisoners.

JOHN S. KOONCE, registrar, gave his resignation as such.

CHRISTOPHER C. RHODES was elected by court as new registrar of county to fill vacancy occasioned by resignation of JNO S. KOONCE, RHODES entered into bond with HARDY BRYAN & BENJN HUGGINS, sureties.

FREDERICK I. BECTON, admr of JAMES REYNOLDS, decd, allowed to sell on 6 mos credit so many of the slaves of the intestate as will raise the sum of $1100 in order to settle the estate.

JOSEPH S. FOY, county surveyor, gave his resignation.

JAROD KOONCE was to oversee rd from HARRISON's BRIDGE including one half of said bridge to WM RHEM's rd in place of MICHAEL KOONCE, resigned.

Overseer of rd from TRENT BRIDGE to TOM SWAMP was to work & keep up rd as far as the crossroads on WHITE OAK.

Overseer of rd (BLACK SWAMP) was to work up to WHITE OAK.

ELBERT I. CLARK allowed to "peddle & hawk" goods in the county for one yr.

HARDY BRYAN, WILLIAM HUGGINS, & CHARLES GEROCK were to settle accounts of EMANUEL JARMON, admr of HUBBARD STANLY, decd.

WILLIAM HUGGINS to oversee rd from bridge at TRENTON to head of the straight reach in place of BENJAMIN ASKEY, resigned.

EMANUEL JARMON was to admin. estate of SUSAN ANDREWS, decd; $200 bond; H. BRYAN & JNO HOUSTON, sureties.

LEWIS HARGET was to oversee rd from JACK CABBIN to the "RIAL OAKE" in place of FREDK PARKER, resigned.

HARDY BRYAN, WILLIAM HUGGINS & CHARLES GEROCK were to settle accounts of WILLIAM B. RHEM, exr of WM RHEM, decd.

HARDY BRYAN, WILLIAM HUGGINS & FRANCIS DUVAL were to settle accounts of EMANUEL JARMON, guard to MARINDA MURPHY, minor.

BRYAN JONES was to admr estate of HOLLAN/HOLBAN KOONCE, decd; $2000 bond; JAMES MARRET & EMANUEL JARMON, sureties.

JOSEPH WHITTY was to admr estate of EDWARD S. FERROND, decd; $6000 bond; HARDY O. NEWTON & WALTER P. ALLEN, sureties.

CALVIN DAVIS & wife & others vs RICHARD REYNOLDS} debt. Jury found for pltff; judgment of $1318.12 & interest from 1 Sep 1836 to be paid according to report of commission/council I./J.G. STANLY; judgment for penalty of bond $20,000. It appeared to court that CALVIN DAVIS was out of the state; clerk ordered to issue notice of CALVIN DAVIS as guard of WINIFRED FERRAND, SARAH GREEN & RICHARD GREEN & RICHARD HATCH to appear at next term & show why he has not removed his guardianship. Clerk to issue copies to ABNER GREEN as agent of said DAVIS & to send a copy to DAVIS by mail.

Tuesday 13 Dec 1836

Justices: JOHN H. HAMMOND, ABNER GREEN & SAMUEL HILL
Solicitor: JOHN H. BRYAN

JOHN B. MAURHAUN? allowed to "hawk & peddle goods" in the county for one yr.
HARDY BRYAN, CHARLES GEROCK & BENJAMIN ASKEY were to settle accounts of RISDON M. McDANIEL1, exr of DANIEL MALLARD, decd.
CALVIN J. MORRIS allowed to retail spirituous liquors by small measure at his store in TRENTON for one yr.
ALMREN PRATT allowed to peddle goods in the county for one yr.

Freeholders drawn as jurors to next county court:

MARTIN F. BROCK	JAMES I./S. RHODES	EDMD B. HATCH
MOSES ADAMS	JOHN SHELFER	GEORGE HAZZARD
HARDY O. CONNER	DANIEL MALLARD	PETER HARGET
JOHN H. DILLAHUNT	ENOCH FOY	JOHN ROUSE
AMOS KOONCE	LEWIS SMALL	JOSHUAY MILLER
OWEN ADAMS	JOHN POLLOCK	JOHN GODDING
ISRAEL HOWARD	IGNATIOUS W. BROCK	EMERY METTS
JAMES MARRET	BENJAMIN SCOTT	ABNER KILLEBREW
ZACHAUS BROWN	EDWARD M. GILBERT	JOHN ADAMS
EDWD C. DEBRULE JR	FRANCIS ANDREWS	GEORGE WILCOX
SIMMONS COLLINS	JAMES ADAMS	

Freeholders drawn as jurors for next Superior Court (Spring term 1837):

NATHAN FOSCUE	WILLIAM GOODING JR	HARDY PARRY
GEORGE S. DEBRULE	BENJAMIN BROCK	MERRIT JONES
FURNIFOLD H. JARMON	LEWIS O. BRYAN	ISAIAH WOOD
FELIX KING	THOMAS McDANIEL	JAMES ROBERTS
SIMON S. BECTON	FURNIFOLD G. HERRITAGE	CALVIN KOONCE
JOHN WOOD	ISAAC BROWN	SAMUEL HILL
FRANCIS GOODING	JAMES G. HERRITAGE	LOT EUBANKS
ROSCO BARRUS	JONAS JONES JR	AMOS AMYET
NATHANIEL P. WAPLES	RICHARD G. REYNOLDS	LEWIS WILLIAMS
BENJAMIN C. SIMMONS	IVY WESTBROOK	JOHN E. FOSCUE
ALFRED H. REYNOLDS	JAMES FOY	HENRY RHODES
EMANUEL K. HARGET	DANIEL WILLIAMSON	JOSEPH WALLACE

Deeds, etc., recorded with CHRISR C. RHODES, registrar:
SAMUEL HILL to EMANUEL K. HARGET

JOHN S. KOONCE to FREEMAN SMITH
SAMUEL SMITH to SIMMONS COLLINS
FREDERICK PARKER to JOHN SHELFER
RICHD PARSONS to JOHN H. HAMMOND
JOHN HAGINS to HARDY COLLINS
DAVID GEORGE to JOHN JONES
JOHN S. KOONCE to JOHN H. HAMMOND
RICHARD REYNOLDS to WILLIAM B. RHEM
WILLIAM HUGGINS, shff, to LEWIS SMALL
JAMES STEEL to LEWIS SMALL
JOHN M. FRANKS to JAMES D. KINCEY
THOMAS ALPHEN to JAMES D. KINCEY
CALVIN DAVIS to ABNER GREEN
CALVIN DAVIS to FRANCIS GOODING, agreement
JOHN B. REYNOLDS to RICHARD G. REYNOLDS

Jones Cty Court of Common Pleas Minutes 1837

SPECIAL COURT FOR JONES COUNTY
COURTHOUSE, TRENTON, 20 Jan 1837

Justices: LEMUEL H. SIMMONS, NATHAN FOSCUE, & SAMUEL HILL
Clerk: HARDY BRYAN

ADAM ANDREWS appointed special admr of estate of CALVIN J. MORRIS, decd; $5000 bond; RESDEN M. McDANIEL & BENJAMIN HUGGINS, sureties. ADAM ANDREWS was to have power in securing goods & chattles of said intestate and to sell such part "as should be in a wastfule condition." Signed: NATHAN FOSCUE, J.P., L.H. SIMMONS, J.P., S. HILL, J.P.

SPECIAL COURT FOR JONES COUNTY
TRENTON, Tuesday 24 Jan 1837

Justices: JAMES FOY, SAMUEL HILL, & ROSCO BARRUS, esquires

ROSCO BARRUS was appointed special admr of estate of COUNCIL FIELDS, decd; $200 bond; JAMES FOY & HARDY BRYAN, sureties. Admr allowed to sell portions of estate as needed. Signed: JAS FOY, J.P., S. HILL, J.P., & R. BARRUS, J.P.

Jones Cty Court of Common Pleas Minutes 1837

MARCH TERM 1837
TRENTON, Monday 13 Mar 1837

Justices: ABNER GREEN, JOHN H. HAMMOND & JAMES W. HOWARD
Shff: RESDON M. McDANIEL
Clerk: HARDY BRYAN

NEEDHAM BEASLEY was to oversee rd from GUM SWAMP to county line & down road near JOHN COBB & from fork at JNO WISE's to SOUTH WEST BRIDGE in place of JAMES G. HERRITAGE, resigned.

An order from last term which appointed a committee to settle accounts of RISDON M. McDANIEL, admr of DANIEL MALLARD SR, decd, was renewed with report due next term.

AMOS L. SIMMONS was to oversee rd from fork at HARDY O. NEWTON's to BEVERDAM in place of N.P. WAPLES, resigned.

JAMES MORTON was to oversee rd from a branch, the dividing line between WILLIAM W. FRANKS and JOHN BURQWIN, to MILL CREEK BRIDGE; also rd from TRENT BRIDGE to corner of JOHN E. FOSCUE's fence near his house & that MORTON have the hands of JOHN BERQWIN alone to keep up said rd & that he receive the piece of new rd lately made by JOHN BERQWIN heading from the WHITE OAK ROAD towards TRENTON agreeable to act of assembly of 1834.

JOHN E. FOSCUE was to oversee rd from corner of his fence near his house to fork at HARDY O. NEWTON's & that he keep up same with labor of his own hands.

AMOS L. SIMMONS was to oversee rd from BEVERDAM to ...?... GULLY BRIDGE & to work all hands subject to road work from TRENT BRIDGE to DEEP GULLY in addition to those he now has except JOHN E. FOSCUE's & JOHN BERQWIN's.

ROSCO BARRUS appointed admr of estate of COUNCIL FIELDS, decd, $200 bond; HARDY BRYAN & ELIJAH SIMMONS, sureties.

JAMES W. HOWARD was to oversee rd from HATCH's MILL to middle of the POCOSIN in place of COUNCIL FIELDS, decd.

CALVIN DAVIS, guard to "WINIFRED FERRAND (formally WINIFRED GREEN), SARAH GREEN, RICHARD GREEN & RICHARD HATCH, minor," has left the state to reside elsewhere & has left the property of his wards in Jones County. He was to have been removed from his guardianship of said wards.

OWEN B. COX appointed guard of WINIFRED FERRAND, SARAH GREEN & RICHARD GREEN "heirs of JAMES GREEN, decd; $12,000 bond; JOHN H. HAMMOND & HARDY BRYAN, sureties.

HARDY BRYAN appointed guard to RICHARD HATCH, minor; $5,000 bond; EMANUEL JARMON & WILLIAM HUGGINS, sureties.

FERDINAN DICKSON named constable for District 1; bond with BENJAMIN HUGGINS & DANIEL DICKSON, sureties.

HARDY BRYAN, WILLIAM HUGGINS & CHARLES GERACK were to settle accounts of EMANUEL JARMON, admr of MARY A. McDANIEL, decd.

Freeholders summoned by shff to serve as petit jurors for this term:
MOSES ADAMS	JAMES MARRET	HARDY O. CONNER
ZACHUES BROWN	PETER HARGET	FRANCIS ANDREWS
AMOS KOONCE	DANIEL MALLARD	OWEN ADAMS
JOHN POLLOCK	ISRAEL HOWARD	BENJAMIN SCOTT

JOHN ADAMS & wife & others to the court} petition for partition.

Report returned, confirmed, recorded.
 FREDERICK PARKER vs ALFRED H. REYNOLDS & J.B. SHINE} debt. Jury found for pltff; principal of $100 and interest of $72.
 EMANUEL JARMON vs ALFRED H. REYNOLDS & WM B. RHEM} debt. Jury found for pltff. $650 principal & $56.55 in interest.
 EMANUEL K. HARGET to the use of BENJN KOONCE vs AMOS KOONCE & ALFRED H. REYNOLDS} debt. Jury found for pltff. $160 principal and $4.56 interest. (**Note**: AMOS KOONCE was on the jury - unless there was more than one man by that name.)
 President & directors of the Merchants Bank of Newbern vs ALFRED H. REYNOLDS, RICHD G. REYNOLDS & BRYAN HUGGINS} debt. Jury found for pltff. $375 principal & $12.18 interest.
 President & directors of Merchants Bank of Newbern vs RICHD REYNOLDS, ALFRED H. REYNOLDS, BENJN HUGGINS, & JAS B. SHINE} debt. Jury found for pltff. $400 principal & $12 interest.
 WILLIAM B. RHEM to use of Z. SLADE vs ALFRED H. REYNOLDS} debt. Jury found for pltff. $125 principal & $9 interest.

 HARDY BRYAN licensed to sell spirituous liquors at his house in TRENTON for one yr.
 FRANCIS GOODING was to oversee the part of TRENT RIVER from mouth of LITTLE CHINQUIPEN CREEK up to mouth of CYPRESS CREEK in place of JOHN JONES, resigned.
 An order was made by the court: when blankets were required by any person in the Jones County jail, the jailor was to furnish them from those provided by the county & charge two and one half cents each for every day used. The jailor was required to render an account of the monies collected for blanket use to the court each December term.
 County trustee was to pay BENJAMIN ASKEY $6.50 for (jail fees?).
 WILEY W. HIGGINS was to oversee rd from dividing line between FRANKS & BERQWIN to fork at JAMES W. HOWARD's field in place of ELIJAH SIMMONS, resigned.
 GEORGE P. KINCEY allowed to peddle & hawk goods in the county for one yr.
 CHARLES GEROCK licensed to retail spirituous liquors in TRENTON for one yr.
 JOSEPH WHITTY was to oversee rd from TRENTON to BUCKNER HATCH's mill "both districts being put into one."
 WILLIAM HUGGINS was to oversee rd from TRENTON to JOSHWAYS RESOLUTION in place of SAML HILL.
 WILLIAM HUGGINS, CHARLES GEROCK & JOHN H. HAMMOND were to settle accounts of CALVIN DAVIS as guard to "the minor heirs of JAMES GREEN, decd."
 Same men were to settle accounts of said DAVIS as guard to RICHD HATCH, minor.
 IGNATIOUS BROCK was to oversee rd from SHINE's up to the RED HILL on the west side of REEDY BRANCH in place of RICHARD G. REYNOLDS, resigned.

Tuesday 14 Mar 1837
Justices: OWEN B. COX, ABNER GREEN, & LEMUEL H. SIMMONS

 WILLIAM STANLY, ALFRED H. REYNOLDS, FREEMAN SMITH, ARETUS GILBERT, &

Jones Cty Court of Common Pleas Minutes 1837

BENJAMIN F. STANLY were appointed patrols for one yr in District 6.

WILLIAM HUGGINS & CHARLES GEROCK, esquires, came into court & qualified as justices of the peace for Jones County

JOHN WILLIAM, BRYAN THOMAS SR., FARNIFOLD McDANIEL, BAZEL McDANIEL, & JOHN HARRISON were appointed patrols in District 3 for one year.

JAMES KINCEY, LEWIS WILLIAMS, JOHN KINCEY, JOHN JARMON & HENRY RHODES were appointed patrols in District 5 for one yr.

WILLIAM HARRISON, CALVIN KOONCE, FARNY H. JARMON, JAMES B. SHINE, RICHARD PARSONS & JNO HANCOCK were appointed patrols for one yr in District 4.

ADAM ANDREWS was to admin. estate of CALVIN J. MORRIS, decd; $2000 bond; RESDEN M. McDANIEL & JOHN S. PARSONS, sureties.

The overseer of rd from RED HILL on west side of REEDY BRANCH up to RATTLESNAKE on which F.H. JARMON lived came to court &, not objecting, the court ordered that said overseer receive the new rd made by said Furnifold H. Jarman & sd JARMON would be permitted to shut up the old rd so altered as the court was satisfied that the new rd was in good & lawful order.

The following settlements were filed:
JOHN S. KOONCE, guard to NANCY E. & SUSAN E. KOONCE
RACHAEL McDANIEL, guard to EDNEY I./S. McDANIEL
SAMUEL HILL, guard to ANN E. SMALL
JOHN OLIVER, guard to FURNIFOLD G. SIMMONS
EMANUEL JARMON, trustee to ELIZA DUVAL
HARDY PARRY, guard to GEORGE & SILAS PARRY
WILLIAM B. RHEM, exr of WILLIAM RHEM
EMANUEL JARMON, admr of HUBBARD STANLY
EMANUEL JARMON, guard to MARINDA MURPHY

Divisions filed this term:
Negroes of the infant heirs of MICHAEL KOONCE
Lands of ABRAM KORNEGAY
Negroes of estate of JOHN B. COX

Inventories & accounts of sales filed:
Estate of EDWD S. FERRAND by JOSEPH WHITTY, admr
Estate of SUSAN ANDREWS by EML JARMON, admr
Estate of SHADERACK ERWIN by HARDY BRYAN, exr

Freeholders drawn as jurors at June term 1837:

JAMES WHALEY	ASA EUBANKS	WALTER P. ALLEN
MILLENTON MEADOWS	NATHAN P. SMITH	BENJAMIN ASKEY
JOSEPH WHITTY	BENJAMIN STANLY	WILLIAMS JONES
JAMES D. KINCEY	THOMAS POLLOCK	JOHN BALL
DANIEL HARRISON	BARTHOLOMEW MEADOWS	AARON WOOD
EMANUEL KOONCE	JOHN BENDER SR	EDWARD C. DEBRULE SR
HARDY COLLINS	JAMES McDANIEL	COUNCIL GOODING
WILLIAM BROWN	JOHN YOUNG	ELIJAH PARRY
JOHN JONES	MICHAEL KOONCE	JOHN STRECKLIN
JOHN FORDHAM	GEORGE KING	ELIJAH KOONCE

Deeds & bills of sale recorded by C.C. RHODES, registrar:
GEORGE HAZZARD to JOHN MARRET
WILLIAM HUGGINS, shff, to JONAS JONES

RICHARD REYNOLDS to HARDY POLLOCK
EDMUND HATCH to ROSCO BARRUS
RICHARD REYNOLDS to MICHAEL KOONCE
SAMUEL SIMPSON to SIMMONS ISLER
VOLNY VINTERS & wife to EMANUEL JARMON
JAMES J. RHODES to OWEN B. COX
WILLIAM STANLY to RICHARD REYNOLDS
WINIFRED HERRIOT to GEORGE HERRIOT
WILLIAM HUGGINS, shff, to JOSEPH BELL
SOPHIA E. SIMMONS to LEMUEL H. SIMMONS
WILLIAM B. RHEM to MITCHEL RHEM
JAMES HARRISON to EMANUEL JARMON
IRA WESTBROOK to LIM MOORE
JOHN POLLOCK to BENJAMIN HUGGINS
JAMES B. SHINE to ALFRED REYNOLDS
BENJAMIN C. SIMMONS to ISRAEL HOWARD
JOSEPH W. BRYAN to WILLIAM HUGGINS
HARDY POLLOCK to WILLIAM HUGGINS
HANNAH WOOD to JAMES TAYLOR
SOPHIA E. SIMMONS to OWEN ADAMS
EDMUND B. HATCH to JAMES McDANIEL
HARRIS HUTCHING to JAMES McDANIEL
HARRIS HUTCHING to JAMES McDANIEL
WILLIAM HUGGINS, shff, to HARDY BRYAN (**Note**: Generally the fee to register deeds, etc. was 40 cents. Sometimes the fee was 50 or 60 cents, but this transaction cost 70 cents to register.)
WILLIAM HUGGINS, shff, to HARDY BRYAN
WILLIAM HUGGINS, shff, to HARDY BRYAN
WILLIAM HUGGINS, shff, & RICHD HATCH to HARDY BRYAN
FRANCIS DUVAL to HARDY BRYAN
WILLIAM HUGGINS, shff, to SARAH GREEN
SARAH GREEN to HARDY BRYAN
SARAH GREEN to HARDY BRYAN
DURANT HATCH to HARDY BRYAN
WM HUGGINS, shff, to CHRISTOPHER BRYAN
CHRISTOPHER R. GREEN to RICHARD REYNOLDS
RICHARD REYNOLDS to SARAH OLDFIELD
DANIEL ANDREWS to NATHAN FOSCUE
DANIEL R. YATES to DANIEL ANDREWS
NEEDHAM SIMMONS to FREDERICK FOSCUE

SPECIAL COURT
TRENTON, Thursday 25 Mar 1837

Justices: FREDRICK I. BECTON, SIMMONS ISLER, & CHARLES GEROCK

COUNCIL WATERS? was appointed special admr of estate of NANCY ISLER, decd; $10,000 bond; SIMMONS ISLER & FREDERICK I. BECTON, sureties. Signed: SIM. ISLER, J.P.; CHAS GEROCK, J.P., F. ISLER BECTON, J.P. (**Note**: These looked like actual signatures.)

Jones Cty Court of Common Pleas Minutes 1837

SPECIAL COURT
TRENTON, 17 April 1837

Justices: WILLIAM HUGGINS, CHARLES GEROCK & CALVIN KOONCE, esq.

Special letters of admin. granted to JOHN H. DILLAHUNT on the goods & chattles of SAMUEL DILLAHUNT, decd; $5000 bond; JOHN WOOD & CALVIN KOONCE, sureties. JOHN DILLAHUNT allowed to sell perishable goods as needed at public auction. Test.: (signed) H. BRYAN; signed: WM HUGGINS, J.P.; CHARLES GEROCK, J.P.; CALVIN KOONCE, J.P.

JUNE TERM, 1837
TRENTON, Monday, 12 June 1837

Justices: OWEN B. COX, ABNER GREEN & CALVIN KOONCE, esqs.
Shff: RISDON M. McDANIEL
Clerk: HARDY BRYAN

County trustee was to pay $4.80 to FURDINAN DICKSON.
WILLIAM WASHINGTON was to be county solicitor in place of JAS W. BRYAN, resigned at former term.
County trustee was to pay HARDY BRYAN, clerk, $7.00 for blank record book for his office.
County trustee was to pay CHRISTOPHER C. RHODES $7.50 for purchase of a blank record book for the registrar's office.
CHARLES GEROCK, WILLIAM HUGGINS & HARDY BRYAN were to settle accounts of EMANUEL JARMON, admr of WILLIAM GEORGE, decd.
CHARLES GEROCK, WM HUGGINS & HARDY BRYAN were to settle accounts of EML JARMON, admr of JOHN CONNER.
Same men were to settle accounts of EML JARMON, county trustee.
EML JARMON was reappointed county trustee.
WYAT ROBINS, a boy, was bound to JOHN MARRET, agreeable to law; indentures filed.
OFFA? ROBINS was bound to WM C. MURPHY agreeable to law; indentures filed.
GEORGE WILCOX was appointed overseer of rd in place of LEMUEL BUSACK, resigned.
County trustee was to pay HARDY BRYAN $40 for extra services to the county for one yr concluding at end of this term.
LEWIS B. HUMPHREY was appointed guard to ANN ELIJAH SMALL, minor; $200 bond; SAMUEL HILL & BENJAMIN HUGGINS, sureties.
WILLIAM HUGGINS, CHARLES GEROCK & HARDY BRYAN were to settle accounts of SAMUEL HILL, former guard to ANN E. SMALL, minor, & furnish same to present guard, LEWIS B. HUMPHREY.
COUNCIL WOOTEN was to admin. estate of ANN ISLER, decd; $10,000 bond; WILLIAM D. MOSLEY & SIMMONS ISLER, sureties.

"Whereas by the last will & testament of WILLIAMS ISLER, decd; certain Negro slaves were bequeathed to his widow, ANN ISLER, for and during her life and afterwards to be divided among ELIZA, wife of COUNCIL WOOTEN; REBECCA, wife of WILLIAM HERRING; CAROLINE, wife of WM FORBS, and EDWIN B. ISLER, children of said WILLIAMS ISLER, and whereas the said widow died intestate and at the present term (June) 1837, COUNCIL WOOTEN was appointed her admr and the Negros belonging absolutely to said ANN are distributable among all her children viz-those above named-Now to effect a division of all the said Negroes both those held for life by said widow and those held absolutely among the persons respectively written as aforesaid-FREDERICK I. BECTON, MARTIN F. BROCK & JAMES MUMFORD are appointed a committee to divide said Negroes according to the rights as aforesaid."

JAMES D. KINCEY was appointed guard to JOHN H. COX, minor; $5,000 bond; OWEN B. COX & JAMES B. SHINE, sureties.

HENRY RHODES, EMANUEL JARMON, & FURNIFOLD H. JARMON were to settle accounts of JONAS JONES, former guard to JOHN H. COX, minor.

JAMES D. KINCEY was appointed admr of estate of LEVINA COX, decd; "with the will annexed ...?..," $2500 bond; EML JARMON & JOSEPH WHITTY, sureties. [Note: Gwynn abstracted this will (p. 408) which was written 13 May 1831. It names daughter, LEVINA, and son, JOHN H. COX. Other children were mentioned but not named. JONAS JONES, SR was named exr, and EML JARMAN was the witness.]

JOHN H. DILLAHUNT was appointed admr of estate of SAMUAL DILLAHUNT, decd; $10,000 bond; CALVIN KOONCE & JOHN WOOD, sureties.

BENJAMIN HUGGINS was reappointed constable.

COUNCIL WOOTEN, admr of ANN ISLER, decd, filed inventory & account of sale of property of the intestate.

Inventory of COUNCIL FIELDS, decd, filed by R. BARRUS, admr.

Inventory of SARAH LEPSAY?, decd, filed by R. BARRUS, exr.

The last will & testament of LEVINA COX, decd, proved by oath of EML JARMON, a witness.

EML JARMON, guard to "sundry minors" filed his accounts.

OWEN ADAMS, guard to heirs of KADER KNIGHT, filed his accounts.

Inventory and account of sale of property of C.J. MORRIS, decd, filed by A. ANDREWS, admr.

court adjourned until next day

Justices: WM HUGGINS, JAMES W. HOWARD, JOHN H. HAMMOND, NATHAN FOSCUE, LEML H. SIMMONS, SAMUEL HILL, & CHARLES GEROCK

The following justices were appointed to take the tax list for 1837:
District 1, White Oak: DANIEL DICKSON, JNO BINAM SR & JOHN YOUNG
District 2, Trent Bridge: JAMES W. HOWARD, E. FOY & J. WHITTY
District 3, Trenton: CHARLES GEROCK, WM HUGGINS & JAS McDANIEL
District 4, Cypress Creek: CALVIN KOONCE, JAS B. SHINE & F.H.   JARMON
District 5, Tuckahoe: OWEN B. COX, J.S. KINCEY, & EML JARMON
District 6, Bever Creek: ABNER GREEN, H. PARRY & F.I. BECTON
District 7, Beverdam: NATHAN FOSCUE, A. SIMMONS, & J.S. MARROTT

The following persons appointed to hold elections in August:
District 1: THOMAS GILLET, MICAJAH F. MATTOCKS & LEVI EUBANKS
District 2: ROSCO BARRUS, JOSEPH WHITTY & ENOCH FOY

Jones Cty Court of Common Pleas Minutes 1837

District 3:   R.M. McDANIEL, shff; LEML BUSICK & SAMUEL HILL
District 4:   JOHN H. HAMMOND, JAMES B. SHINE & JAMES HARRISON
District 5:   OWEN B. COX, LEWIS WILLIAMS, & HENRY RHODES
District 6:   FREDK I. BECTON, PETER HARGET & DAVID GREEN

It was ordered that the following tax be levied & collected for 1837 to defray county expences: 15 cents on every $100 value of lands, town lots, & improvements and 30 cents on every taxable pole.

JOHN ADAMS was to oversee rd from fork at HARDY O. NEWTON's to DEEP GULLY BRIDGE & the district now under AMOS L. SIMMONS, overseer, was to be stopped at said NEWTON's as formerly & all hands formerly belonging to that district leading from TRENT BRIDGE to said Gully was to be subject to the orders of said ADAMS, except those of JOHN F. BERQUIN & JOHN E. FOSCUE.

Freeholders drawn as jurors to next Superior Court, Fall Term 1837:

JOHN McDANIEL SR	AMOS SHELFER	FELIX KING
THOMAS GILLET	DAVID GREEN	GEORGE S. DEBRULE
CHARLES GEROCK	JOHN H. HAMMOND	JOHN H. DILLAHUNT
RIGDON WHALEY	JAMES HARRISON	BENJN C. SIMMONS
JAMES W. HOWARD	RIGHT STANLY	THOMAS McDANIEL
OWEN B. COX	MILCHER RHEM	RICHD G. REYNOLDS
JONATHAN WOOD	ELIJAH PARRY	ALFRED H. REYNOLDS
FURNIFOLD G. HERRITAGE	SIMMONS ISLER	JAMES J. RHODES
JOSEPH SMALL	ELIJAH McDANIEL	CALVIN KOONCE
FREDERICK I. BECTON	EML K. HARGET	SIMON S. BECTON
ABNER GREEN	ENOCK FOY	LEWIS O. BRYAN
LEMUEL H. SIMMONS	JOHN SHELFER	EDWD M. GILBERT

Freeholders drawn for jurors to next term of Court of Pleas & Quarter Sessions:

HARDY O. NEWTON	ELIJAH KOONCE	OWEN HARRISON
JOHN OLIVER	LEML BUSACK	RICHD R. FOSCUE
JAS MUMFORD	JOHN HARRISON	ABRAM SIMMONS
JAS KINCEY SR	JNO HANCOCK SR	JAMES MISSAW
NATHAN B. WESTBROOK	THOS BALEY	ADAM ANDREWS
BENJN SCOTT	RIGDON HEWET	DANIEL YATES
JNO STANLY (Trenton)	JOHN B. REYNOLDS	MICAJAH F. MATTOCKS
WM C. MURPHY	NATHAN STANLY	THOMAS HARRISON
FREDK PARKER	JOHN MISSAW	AMOS L. SIMMONS
JONAS WILLIAMS	MICHAEL SHELFER	JAMES MADES

The following "instruments of writing" were proved & recorded by registrar, C.C. RHODES:
   LEWIS D. KINCEY to OWEN B. COX
   F. PARKER & JAS B. SHINE to J. ROBINSON & wife
   ENOCK FOY to MILES FOY "not pd."
   NATHAN G. BLUNT to MARTHA B. FOY
   OWEN B. COX to SUSAN JARMON
   GEORGE DEBRULE to EDWARD DEBRULE
   MELCHIR RHEM to SAMUEL HILL
   D.W. MILLER to M. MILLER
   E. GILBERT to W.B. RHEM

MELCHIR RHEM to WM B. RHEM
LEML H. SIMMONS to WM B. RHEM

SEPTEMBER TERM, 1837
TRENTON, Monday 11 September 1837

Justices: OWEN B. COX, NATHAN FOSCUE, JAMES ROBERTS & ABNER GREEN, Esquires
Shff: RISDON M. McDANIEL
Clerk: HARDY BRYAN
Solicitor: WILLIAM WASHINGTON

The following freeholders were sworn in as jurors for the state:
HARDY O. NEWTON, foreman

AMOS L. SIMMONS	NATHAN B. WESTBROOK	JAMES MADES
JOHN HARRISON	MICHAEL SHELFER	JOHN MISSAW
JAMES MUMFORD	JOHN B. REYNOLDS	THOMAS BALEY
OWEN HARRISON	JAMES MISSAW	DANIEL YATES

HARDY BRYAN, being elected clerk of court, presented his bond.
RISDEN M. McDANIEL renewed his bond as sheriff.
AMOS HEATH was to oversee rd in place of SIMON S. BECTON, resigned.
JAMES ROBERTS, overseer of rd from BLACK SWAMP to JARVIS MILL dam, was exempted from working that part of said rd which had heretofore been kept up by SIMMONS COLLINS
JAMES B. SHINE & JOHN JONES were to examine the CYPRESS CREEK BRIDGE & have repairs made.
WILLIAM HUGGINS was to have the bridge at TRENTON repaired.
CALVIN KOONCE & JOHN H. HAMMOND were to have necessary repairs made to the free bridge across TRENT RIVER.
The clerk of court was to issue certificates to THOMAS JARMON & DANIEL/DAVID HARPER exempting them from working the rds & paying pole tax.
WILLIAM HUGGINS, JOHN H. HAMMOND & CHARLES GEROCK were to settle accounts of CALVIN DAVIS, former guard to WINIFRED FERREN (GREEN) and RICHARD & SARAH GREEN with ABNER GREEN, trustee of said CALVIN DAVIS & OWEN B. COX, present guard.
LEMUEL H. SIMMONS was to administer estate of MARGARET FOY, "late the wife of FREDERICK FOY;" $5000 bond; AMOS L. SIMMONS & JAMES McDANIEL, sureties.
JOHN OLIVER asked to resign as guard of FURINIFOLD G. SIMMONS (minor); court approved & appointed LEMUEL H. SIMMONS in his stead; $7000 bond; AMOS L. SIMMONS & JAMES McDANIEL, sureties.
WILLIAM HUGGINS, CHARLES GEROCK, & HARDY BRYAN were to settle accounts between JOHN OLIVER, former guard to FURNIFOLD G. SIMMONS (minor) & LEMUEL H. SIMMONS, present guard.
FREDK I. BECTON, SIMON S. BECTON & AMOS HEATH were to settle accounts of FREDERICK A. LOFTON, admr of MARY LOFTON, decd.
ELIJAH SIMMONS, JONATHAN WOOD & JAMES FOY were to settle accounts of ROSCO BARRUS, exr of SARAH LEFERY/LEPECY. (**Note**: Potter has an Issac LIPSEY (p. 20) and a Timothy LIPSEY (p. 19) in Onslow County in the 1820 census and a John LISSEY? (p. 38) in Anson County for the same census.)

Same men were to settle accounts of ROSCO LESSERY/LAFSEY, decd, with the (wil? am?....).

JONATHAN WOOD, ROSCO BARRUS, & JAMES FOY were to settle accounts of OWEN ADAMS, guard to heirs of KADER KNIGHT, decd.

County trustee was to pay HENRY LOCKEY $6.00 for his care & attention to the TRENT BRIDGE during last term.

SAMUEL SMITH & others to the court} petition to divide slaves. Report returned & confirmed & registered.

SARAH BERT to the court} petition for dower. Report made & confirmed & registered.

NANCY MORRIS to the court} petition for yr´s provisions. "Report made & confirmed. Judgment accordingly for the sum & costs."

LEWIS SMALL to the use of JOSEPH SMALL vs FREDERICK PARKER & WILLIAM STANLY} debt. The following jury:

JOSEPH KINCEY	NATHAN STANLY	BENJN SCOTT
JOHN STANLY	RIGDON HEWET	MICAJAH F. MATTOCKS
ELIJAH KOONCE	JNO OLIVER	JONAS WILLIAMS
JOSEPH SMALL	WM C. MURPHY	IGNATIOUS W. BROCK

found for plft; $128.45 principal & $4.50 interest.

JACOB GOODING vs RICHD G. REYNOLDS & JNO B. REYNOLDS} debt. Same jury found for pltff; $399.54 principal; $17.97 interest & costs.

SARAH DILLAHUNT vs the heirs at law of SAML DILLAHUNT} petition for dower. Report returned & confirmed.

Tuesday 12 September 1837

Justices: DANIEL DICKSON, LEMUEL H. SIMMONS & JAMES ROBERTS

County trustee was to pay expenses of the different boards of valuation appointed by the court agreeable to direction of act of assembly passed in 1836.

HARDY O. NEWTON, JAMES MARRIT & NATH FOSCUE were to be patrols for District 7.

NATHAN I. PARSONS, THOMAS GILLET & DANIEL DICKSON appointed patrols in District 1.

Freeholders drawn as jurors to next court:

JOHN WOOD	JOHN E. FOSCUE	NATHANIEL WASSLES/WAPLES
ISRAEL HOWARD	MILLENTON MEADOWS	BARTHLOMEW MEADOWS
ZACHEUS BROWN	OWEN ADAMS	FRANCIS ANDREWS
LEWIS SMALL	WALTER P. ALLEN	PETER HARGET
JOHN STRICKLIN	JAMES McDANIEL	JOHN HAGINS
F.H. JARMON	JAMES MARRET	JOHN JONES
DANIEL HARRISON	JOSHUA MILLER	JOHN HARRISON
FRANCIS GOODING	WILLIAM BYNUM	IGNATIOUS BROCK

LEMUEL H. SIMMONS, AMOS S. SIMMONS & SOPHIA SIMMONS & FURNIFOLD G. SIMMONS by his guard, LEML H. SIMMONS to the court} petition to sell slaves. Court ordered HARDY BRYAN to sell the Negroes named in the petition at the courthouse in Trenton after giving 30 days notice upon a credit of six months taking bonds with two good & sufficient securities for the purchase money. Also BRYAN should take the said bonds in such amounts as to correspond with the interests of the petitioners.

WINIFRED FERRAND & others to the court} petition for division of Negroes. Prayer of petitioners granted. WILLIAM HUGGINS, JOHN H. HAMMOND & CHARLES GEROCK were to divide the Negroes.

Settlement of EML JARMON, county trustee, filed.
Settlement of admr of WM GEORGE, decd, filed.
Settlement of admr of JNO CONNER, decd, filed.
Inventory & account of sale of property of LEVINIA COX, decd, returned & filed by JAS D. KINCEY, admr.
Settlement of JONAS JONES, late guard to JOHN H. COX, minor, filed.
Inventory & account of sale of property of SAMUEL DILLAHUNT, decd, filed by JOHN H. DILLAHUNT, admr.
JOHN H. DILLAHUNT was to oversee road in place of JOHN WOOD, resigned.
Tax list for 1837 for the different districts was returned by the separate boards of valuation.

Deeds proved & recorded by C.C. RHODES, registrar:
WILLIAM B. RHEM to LEMUEL H. SIMMONS
JONAS JONES JR to JAMES JONES SR
JAMES B. SHINE to JOHN S. KOONCE
N.P. SMITH to R. BARRUS & by him to ELIJAH SIMMONS, (endowed?)
JONAS JONES to OWEN B. COX
MARY BRONSON to NATHAN FOSCUE
GEORGE W. HOWARD to JAMES W. HOWARD
ALFRED H. REYNOLDS to JOHN HEATH
GEORGE POLLOCK to NATHAN FOSCUE
JAMES TIPPET to WM B. RHEM
JOHN E. FOSCUE to NANCY M. FOSCUE
JOHN E. FOSCUE to CHRISTIANNA FOSCUE
HARDY BRYAN, clerk bonds 1837
WM HUGGINS, clerk superior court bonds

DECEMBER TERM, 1837
TRENTON, Monday 11 December 1837

Justices: JOHN H. HAMMOND, CALVIN KOONCE, ABNER GREEN, Esqs.
Shff: RISDON M. McDANIEL
Clerk: HARDY BRYAN

Freeholders summoned as jurors for the state & charged by JAMES W. BRYAN, county solicitor:
JOHN JONES, foreman

PETER HARGET	ZACHEUS BROWN	MILLENTON MEADOWS
JOHN HUGGINS	WILLIAM BYNAM	BARTHALOMEW MEADOWS
JOSHUA MILLER	LEWIS SMALL	IGNATIOUS W. BROCK
ISRAEL HOWARD	JOHN HARRISON	WALTER P. ALLEN

Freeholders summoned as petit jurors:

DANIEL HARRISON	JOHN WOOD	JAMES MARRETT
JOHN STRICKLIN	JAMES McDANIEL	FURNIFOLD H. JARMON
FRANCIS GOODING	ELIJAH McDANIEL	JOHN E. FOSCUE
FRANCIS ANDREWS	DANIEL WILLIAMS	EDWARD M. GILBERT

WILLIAM WASHINGTON resigned as county solicitor & JAMES W. BRYAN was appointed to the post.

CALVIN KOONCE was to be paid $44 for repairs made to the free bridge.

EMANUEL JARMON was appointed guard to ALFRED, JAMES, REBECAH, JOHN, SUSANNA, RILA & AMANDA CONNER, minors & "children of JOHN CONNER, decd;" $500 bond; H. BRYAN & R.M. McDANIEL, sureties.

WILLIAM HUGGINS, CHARLES GEROCK, & HARDY BRYAN appointed to set off to I.C.B. KOONCE his distributive share in estate of "his father EMANUEL KOONCE, decd."

Same men were to settle accounts of EMANUEL JARMON as guard of I.C.B. KOONCE.

ROSCO BARRUS allowed to retail spirituous liquors by small measure for one year at his store or residence at TRENT BRIDGE.

HARDY O. NEWTON allowed to retail liquor at his residence for one year.

WATSON DEWEY allowed to peddle in the county for one year.

JOHN JONES was to oversee rd from JACK CABBIN up to the RED OAK at the county line in place of LEWIS HARGET, resigned.

GEORGE W. SIMMONS, FREDERICK MARKET, JAMES MORTON, HENRY FOY & JAMES PRIGET? appointed patrols in District 2 for one yr.

BURTON HAWLEY & JOHN B. MOORHOUSE allowed to peddle & hawk goods in the county for one year.

FREDERICK I. BECTON appointed to administer estate of WILLIAM RHODES, decd; (amount of bond left blank); HARDY BRYAN & JOHN H. HARRISON, sureties.

SIMMONS COLLINS appointed guard to MARTHA COLLINS (lunatic); $1000 bond; JONATHAN WOOD & JOHN HUGGINS, sureties.

WILLIAM RHODES was appointed surveyor for the county.

NATHAN STANLY appointed guard to PENELOPE STANLY, minor; $4000 bond; BENJN F. STANLY & WRIGHT STANLY, sureties.

JAMES D. KINCEY, admr of LAVINIA COX, allowed to sell Negro, NELSON, belonging to the estate for payment of debts according to the will.

WILLIAMS ISLER, late of Jones County, by his last will & testament directed that an old Negro woman named MOLLY should be supported out of his estate. The widow kept her until the widow's death. After which, COUNCIL WOOTEN, as admr, exposed her at public auction to "the lowest bidder for her support for life" and she was bid off by SIMMONS ISLER at the sum of $190. Therefore COUNCIL WOOTEN, as exr of WILLIAMS ISLER, was allowed to add the sum of $190 as a credit to his account already returned & filed in court.

The last will & testament of JOHN STANLY SR, decd, admitted to probate. [Note: Gwynn abstracted this will (pp. 448-449). It named sons, JAMES STANLEY (now of state of GEORGIA), JOHN STANLEY (now of state of GEORGIA), WRIGHT, NATHAN, BENJAMIN and EDWARD STANLEY; daughters, LEAH CANNON and WINIFRED WEST (both now of state of GEORGIA) and PENELOPE; grandson, JAMES STANLEY (son of deced's son, HUBBARD); and housekeeper, SALLY SANDERS. Sons, NATHAN and BENJAMIN STANLEY, were named exrs, and the witnesses were B. COLDMAN, N. KOONCE, and NATHAN B. GILBERT.]

The last will & testament of WILLIAM HARRISON, decd, admitted to probate

Jones Cty Court of Common Pleas Minutes 1837

& THOS HARRISON qualified as exr. [Note: Gwynn also abstracted this will (p. 417) which was written 30 Mar 1814. It names sons, JAMES, THOMAS, and DANIEL HARRISON; daughter, MARY HARRISON; and wife, SARRY. SARRY HARRISON, wife, and sons, JAMES and THOMAS HARRISON were named exrs, and the witnesses were IVY ANDREWS, FRANCIS ANDREWS, and GEORGE HARRISON.]

Settlement of R. BARRUS, admr of ROSCO LIPSEY, decd, filed.
Settlement of R. BARRUS, exr of SARAH LIPSEY, decd, filed.
Settlement of F.B. LOFTEN, admr of MARY LOFTEN, decd, filed.

Tuesday, 12 December 1837

Justices: OWEN B. COX, SIMMONS ISLER, & SAMUEL HILL, esquires.

State vs JAMES DAVIS: A & B. Defendant pleaded not guilty. Jury found DAVIS guilty of the assult & battery & not guilty on the first count. Fined by court $50 & costs.

County trustee was to pay BENJAMIN ASKEW $31 out of county funds.

JOHN OLIVER appointed guard to FURNIFOLD G. SIMMONS, minor, in place of LEML H. SIMMONS, resigned; $10,000 bond; JAMES W. HOWARD & SAMUEL HILL, sureties.

BENJAMIN ALRY? was to pay county trustee $5.02 for use of blankets while in jail.

Shff ordered to collect no more than a "single tax out of SAMUEL HILL ...(this was smudged)... his labour in giving his tax to the justice appointed to take the same."

HARDY BRYAN, WILLIAM HUGGINS, & CHARLES GEROCK were to settle accounts of SAML HILL, former guard to ANN ELIJAH SMALL, minor, with present guard.

WRIGHT STANLY was to oversee TRENT RIVER extending from mouth of BUSH/BUCK BRANCH to mouth of LITTLE CHINQUIPEN in place of SAML DILLAHUNT (dead). (**Note**: Powell does not list a Bush Branch, but he does list several Buck Branches none of which, however, appear to run through Jones County.)

JONATHAN WOOD allowed to retail liquor at his "place at TRENT BRIDGE (or POLLOCKSVILLE)" for one year.

An order from last term to divide Negroes of JAMES GREEN, decd, was to be renewed.

Agreeable to the recommendation of the field officers of the 25th Regiment of Militia of Jones County, since GIDIAN WHITEHEAD has been appointed regiment musician, court orders that he be exempt from public service while remaining in the county.

"Doe an dimera of" SAMUEL SIMPSON vs ROE & WALTER P. ALLEN} ejectment. Since a defence witness was absent, the case was sent to Superior Court for trial. (**Note**: I was unable to find the meaning of the quoted phrase.)

Freeholders drawn as jurors for March term of this court 1838:

BENJN SCOTT	WILLIAM GOODING	JOHN STANLY (Trenton)
THOMAS POLLOCK	ABRAM SIMMONS	WRIGHT STANLY
JOHN BALL	JAMES MISSAW	THOMAS HARRISON
EDMD WHARTON	THOS BALEY	BENJAMIN ASKEW
DAVID GREEN	SIMMONS COLLINS	OWEN HARRISON
MICHAEL SHELFER	HENRY RHODES	WILLIAM PRITCHARD
ADAM ANDREWS	JOSEPH SMALL	MOSES ADAMS

Jones Cty Court of Common Pleas Minutes 1837

COUNCIL GOODING	JOSEPH WALLACE	WILLIAM ERWIN
JOHN POLLOCK	ABNER W. KILLEBREW	JONAS WILLIAMS
DANIEL YATES	JOSEPH WHITTY	DANIEL WILLIAMSON

Freeholders drawn as jurors for next Superior Court, Spring Term 1838:

JAMES MADES	JAMES WHALEY	RIGDON HEWET
JONAS JONES JR	DANIEL MALLARD	JAMES G. HERRITAGE
JOHN OLIVER	JAMES HARRISON	OWEN B. COX
NATHAN STANLY	JOHN B. REYNOLDS	FREDERICK I. BECTON
LEMUEL BUSICK	ROSCO BARRUS	JOSEPH KINCEY
ISAAC BROWN	ABNER GREEN	WILLIAM C. MURPHY
CHARLES GEROCK	THOMAS GILLET	JOHN McDANIEL SR
MARTIN F. BROCK	NATHAN FOSCUE	LEMUEL H. SIMMONS
HARDY PARRY	JAMES ROBERTS	BENJAMIN F. STANLY
SAMUEL HILL	MARRITT JONES	JOHN BENDER SR
AMOS SHELFER	WILLIAM JONES	JAMES W. HOWARD
BENJAMIN BROCK	SIMMONS ISLER	HARDY O. CONNER

Deeds, etc. recorded by C.C. RHODES, registrar:

JONAS JONES JR to JONAS JONES SR
JONAS JONES JR to JONAS JONES SR
WILLIAM TAYLOR to DANL KORNEGAY
MELCHER RHEM to PETER HARGET
NATHAN FOSCUE to GEORGE POLLOCK
PETER HARGET to MELCHER RHEM
RICHARD W. HATCH to LEML H. SIMMONS
JOHN OLIVER to SAMUEL HILL
HARDY HILL to SAMUEL HILL
AMOS L. SIMMONS to EDMD B. HATCH
EDMD B. HATCH to RICHARD W. HATCH
RICHARD W. HATCH to JOHN OLIVER
JONAS JONES to FREDERICK JONES
EDMUND WESTBROOK to JOSHUA MILLER
DANIEL KNIGHT to JOHN E. FOSCUE
PETER HARGET to I.C.B. KOONCE
ISAAC TAYLOR to HARDY COLLINS
RICHARD W. HATCH to JOHN OLIVER

MARCH TERM 1838
TRENTON, Monday 12 March 1838

Justices: JAMES W. HOWARD, NATHAN FOSCUE & ROSCO BARRUS, esqs.
Shff: RISDEN M. McDANIEL
Clerk: HARDY BRYAN

Jurors for the state charged by JAMES W. BRYAN, county solicitor:
JOSEPH WHITTY, foreman

WILLIAM PRICHARD	WILLIAM ERWIN	ABNER W. KILLEBREW
MICHAEL SHELFER	DANIEL YATES	THOMAS POLLOCK
THOS HARRISON	JOHN POLLOCK	ADAM ANDREWS
THOMAS BALEY	JAMES MISSAW	JOSEPH SMALL
BENJAMIN SCOTT	HENRY RHODES	JONAS JONES
MOSES ADAMS	JOHN BALL	

GEORGE WILCOX was sworn as officer to attend the jury.

JAMES ROBERTS appointed guard to JOSEPH HATCH WATSON, minor; $3000 bond; LEMUEL H. SIMMONS & NATHAN FOSCUE, sureties.

WILLIAM HUGGINS, CHARLES GEROCK & HARDY BRYAN were to settle accounts of FREDERICK I. BECTON, admr of JAS REYNOLDS, decd.

[Note: WILLIAM HUGGINS, who had served as sheriff for a number of years, was now serving in the North Carolina House of Representatives. According to Wheeler, he served both in 1838 and 1840. JAMES B. STANLY of TRENTON wrote a biography of WILLIAM HUGGINS in the New Bern *Weekly Journal* for 21 Jul 1899 (Kammerer, Vol. 2, pp. 34-37). According to the article, HUGGINS was born near TRENTON 25 Jun 1795 to JACOB and PATSEY HUGGINS. He married ELIZABETH BRYAN. They resided in a "small red house on the hill on Webber Street" until about 1834 when they purchased the house on the corner of Cherry and Trent Streets. They raised an "interesting family of children:" SARAH A. HUGGINS, who married WILLIAM FRANKS, Esq.; ELIZA HUGGINS, who married R.F. GREEN and resided at the time of writing in KINSTON; CAROLINA HUGGINS, who married E.F. COX and who also lived in KINSTON; MARIANNA HUGGINS, who married JOHN N. HYMAN of NEW BERN; LEWIS SEARS HUGGINS; and W.F. HUGGINS, who married and died in RALEIGH. HUGGINS was a "farmer, turpentine raiser, ginner and miller" and was nearly always in some office from magistrate to sheriff. He was elected to the "lower House" in 1838 and 1840. "The HUGGINS, the DUVALS, and the BRYANS, and a few others were the leaders of TRENTON society at that day." HUGGINS, DR. DUVAL and Mr. HARDY BRYAN hunted foxes on the BEAVERDAM savannas. "When I heard them blow their horns I would crawl on top of fences to see their beautiful many colored hounds trotting along and hear them yelping as an encouragement to the hunters, showing that they too enjoyed the sport." HUGGINS died 10 Jan 1852 "a friend to all." His monument in the TRENTON Cemetery was the largest at the time.]

JOHN BINDER was to oversee rd in place of JOHN L. PARSONS, resigned.

NICHOLAS BARRY/BEERY/BOSEY, orphan, formerly bound to DANL YATES, was to be bound to MICHAEL N. FOSCUE, "the said YATES being willing to (give?) him up."

BENJAMIN HUGGINS allowed to retail liquor at his residence in TRENTON for one year.

FERDINAN DICKSON appointed constable for District 1, WHITE OAK; bond with DANIEL DICKSON & DANIEL YATES, sureties.

JAMES W. HOWARD, WILLIAM HUGGINS, NATHAN FOSCUE, JOHN H. HAMMOND & DANIEL DICKSON were elected special justices to hold Court of Common Pleas & Quarter Sessions for Jones County for one year & they were to be paid out of county funds $3.00 each day served in court.

County trustee was to pay $4.80 to FERDINAN DICKSON out of county funds for his attendance as an officer of the present term of Superior & County Court.

JOHN B. REYNOLDS was to oversee rd from FREE BRIDGE to RHEM's road in place of JAROD? KOONCE, removed.

JAMES G. STANLY was to oversee rd from bridge at TRENTON up to WARD's Hill & from fork near BENJN HUGGINS' down the NEWBERN ROAD to MUSSELSHELL BRANCH in place of J.M. BRYAN, resigned "(mistake in name?)" (**Note**: The quote is what it looked like to me; I do not know what it could mean. Perhaps, assuming I read it correctly, the name of one of the people named in the entry was a mistake, the clerk wrote this as a note to himself, and forgot to go back to it to make a change.)

JOHN S. KOONCE was to oversee rd from fork at SHINE's up to the RED HILL on west side of REEDY BRANCH in place of IGNATIOUS W. BROCK, resigned.

FREEMAN SMITH was to oversee TRENT RIVER from BEVER CREEK up to PARRY's bridge in place of JOHN H. DILLAHUNT, resigned.

SAMUEL HILL, esq., was to oversee rd heretofore worked by JAMES W. HOWARD, resigned, and, in addition, the rd belonging heretofore to that district from the sign post to the bottom at which HILL's fence terminates & that the said HILL's hands be attached to said road.

WILLIAM HUGGINS, CHARLES GEROCK & EML JARMON were to settle accounts of ENOCH NOBLE, admr of BRADDOCK NOBLE, decd.

ANDREW GOODING was to oversee rd in place of BENJN BROCK, resigned.

JOHN ANDREWS was exempted from public duties.

HARDY BRYAN asked if he could give up his guardianship of DORCUS FOSCUE and that another guard be appointed; court ordered that that should be entered into the minutes & published in the Newbern *Spectator*, & that relatives & friends of DORCUS should make appropriate arrangements, & that amount be returned to proper officers for adjustment.

Sie fa was to be issued to shff commanding him to bring to court at June Term, 1838 the following children: WRIGHT WESTBROOK, FURNEY WESTBROOK, CURTIS SIMPSON & JOHN BALL to be disposed of for some person to keep & raise.

WINIFRED FERRAND & others to the court} petition to divide slaves. Report returned & confirmed.

JOSEPH KINCEY vs WM B. RHEM} debt. The following jury:

DAVID GREEN	COUNCEL GOODING	JOSEPH WALLACE
DANIEL WILLIAMSON	WILLIAM GOODING	JNO B. REYNOLDS
ABRAHAM SIMMONS	JOHN HARRISON	JOHN OLIVER
ZACHEUS BROWN	THOS HUGGINS	JOHN H. DILLAHUNT

found for pltff. Principal #389.02 & interest $11.65; judgment of $400.67 plus costs.

HARDY PARRY vs WILLIAM B. RHEM} case. Same jury as above found for pltff & assessed damages at $400.67 plus costs.

EML JARMON vs FREDK PARKER & ABRAM W. KILLEBREW} debt. Same jury found for pltff. Principal of $339.12 with $7.00 interest. Judgment of $346.12

Jones Cty Court of Common Pleas Minutes 1838

plus costs.

NATHAN STANLY & others to the court} petition to divide Negroes. Report returned & confirmed.

MELCHER RHEM & others to the court} petition for partition. Leave to amend petition. Report returned & confirmed.

Inventory & sale of property of WILL W. RHODES, decd.

HARDY BRYAN vs ADAM ANDREWS, admr of C.J. MORRIS} justices' judgment. Def. pleads no assets which is admitted & judgment signed for $22 & costs. Pltff prays process to subject & estate desended to heirs at law. CHARLES GEROCK appointed special guard "for infant heir."

HARDY BRYAN vs same as above} justices' judgment. Admr pleads no assets which is admitted & judgment signed for $40 & costs. Rest is same as above.

Inventory & accounts of sale of property of JOHN STANLY, decd, filed.

Account of sale of property of SAMUEL DILLAHUNT, decd, filed by JNO H. DILLAHUNT, admr.

Account of sale of Negro, NELSON, property of LEVINA COX, decd, filed by J.D. KINSEY, admr.

Inventory of property of WM HARRISON, decd, filed by THOS HARRISON, exr.

Accounts of JNO S. KOONCE, guard to NANCY & MARY KOONCE, minors, filed.

Account of sale & inventory of property of WILLIAM W. RHODES, decd, filed by F.I. BECTON.

Settlement of F.I. BECTON, admr of JAS REYNOLDS, decd, returned.

Settlement of HARDY PARRY, guard to SILAS & GEORGE PARRY, minors, returned.

ROSCO BARRUS, guard to WM W. FRANKS, settlement returned.

Settlement of JOS FOY, guard to JOSEPH HATCH, minor, returned.

Freeholders drawn as jurors for June Term:

EDWARD C. DEBRULE SR	LEWIS O. BRYAN	JOHN MISSAW
JAMES WHALEY	JOHN YOUNG	EDWARD D. WHARTON
ASA EUBANKS	JOHN OLIVER	JOHN FORDHAM
ISAAC BROWN	LOT EUBANKS	EDWARD M. GILBERT
RICHARD R. FOSCUE	JAMES McDANIEL	JOSEPH KINCEY SR
PETER HARGET	MARTIN F. BROCK	JOHN McDANIEL SR
JOHN E. FOSCUE	EMERY METTS	GEORGE S. DEBRULE
JAMES MISSAW	JAMES MADES	NATHAN B. WESTBROOK
JOHN B. REYNOLDS	JAMES HARRISON	JOHN STRICKLIN
WALTER P. ALLEN	AMOS SHALFER	JOHN WOOD

Deeds, etc., filed with C.C. RHODES, registrar:
FRANCIS DUVAL to WILEY MERRITTS/MERRELLS
LEVI JONES to JAMES D. KINCEY
DANIEL KNIGHT to ROSCO BARRUS
SAMUEL HILL to THOMAS McDANIEL
ALFRED H. REYNOLDS to EDWD M. GILBERT
DAVID McDANIEL & others to FRANCIS DUVAL
FRANCIS DUVAL to WILLIAM HUGGINS
FRANCIS DUVAL to WILLIAM HUGGINS
FREDERICK COLVITT to NATHAN FOSCUE
ISAAC BROWN to JOHN JARMON SR

MELCHER RHEM to WILLIAM B. RHEM
WILLIAM B. RHEM to RICHARD REYNOLDS
JOHN E. HUSEY to JAMES D. KINCEY
MELCHER RHEM to THOMAS HUGGINS
SIMON E. KOONCE to AMOS S. KOONCE
EDWD C. DEBRULE SR & GEO I. DEBRULE to EDWD C. DEBRULE JR
JAMES HARRISON to IGNATIOUS BROCK
FRANCIS DUVAL to JAMES C. BRYAN
LEMUEL HUDLER to EDWD C. DEBRULE
ISAAC H. MEADOWS & wife CASSA? to MICAJAH F. MATTOCKS

JUNE TERM, 1838
TRENTON, Monday 11 June 1838

Justices: JAMES W. HOWARD, NATHAN FOSCUE, DANIEL DICKSON, JOHN H. HAMMOND & WILLIAM HUGGINS
Shff: RISDEN M. McDANIEL
Clerk: HARDY BRYAN

Jurors charged by JAS W. BRYAN, Esq., solicitor:
WALTER P. ALLEN, foreman

JOHN OLIVER	JOHN YOUNG	JAMES McDANIEL
JOHN STRICKLEN	EDWARD D. WHARTON	JAMES MISSAW
LOT EUBANKS	JAMES MADES	EDWARD M. GILBERT
AMOS SHELFER	JOHN McDANIEL	NATHAN B. WESTBROOK
JNO E. FOSCUE	JNO B. REYNOLDS	RICHARD R. FOSCUE
MARTIN F. BROCK	JOSEPH KINCEY	

and GEORGE WILCOX was officer of the court.

EML JARMON renewed his bond as guard to WILLIAM HENRY BRYAN for $5,000 with HARDY BRYAN & WM HUGGINS, sureties.

EML JARMON renewed his bond as guard to heirs of ADONIJAH PARRY, decd; $200 bond; HARDY BRYAN & WILLIAM HUGGINS, sureties.

EML JARMON renewed his bond as guard to heirs of CULLEN POLLOCK, decd; $500 bond; HARDY BRYAN & WM HUGGINS, sureties.

EML JARMON renewed his bond as guard to infant heirs of DAVID FONVIELLE, decd; $200 bond; HARDY BRYAN & WILLIAM HUGGINS, sureties.

EML JARMON renewed his bond as guard to DEBORAH MURPHY, minor; $10,000 bond; HARDY BRYAN & WILLIAM HUGGINS, sureties.

EML JARMON renewed his bond as guard to E.F.B. KOONCE, minor; $10,000 bond; HARDY BRYAN & WILLIAM HUGGINS, sureties.

EML JARMON renewed his bond as guard to CURTIS WESTBROOK, minor; $50 bond with H. BRYAN & WM HUGGINS, sureties.

RACHEL McDANIEL renewed her bond as guard to EDNEY I. MCDANIEL, minor; $2,000 bond; HARDY PARRY, RISDEN M. McDANIEL & EML JARMON, sureties.

HARDY BRYAN renewed his bond as guard to FRANKLIN B. HARRISON, minor; $15,000 bond; EML JARMON & WM HUGGINS, sureties.

HARDY PARRY renewed his bond as guard to GEORGE & SILAS PARRY, minors; $20,000 bond; EML JARMON & R.M. McDANIEL, sureties.

SIMMONS ISLER renewed his bond as guard to EDWIN B. ISLER, minor; $10,000 bond; R.M. McDANIEL & SAMUEL HILL, sureties.

Jones Cty Court of Common Pleas Minutes 1838

ISAAC BROWN excused from jury duty "from & after this term."

THOMAS COLLINS appointed admr of HARDY COLLINS, decd; $10,000 bond; SIMMONS COLLINS, DANIEL YATES & JONATHAN WOOD, sureties.

JOHN H. HAMMOND renewed his bond as guard to JEREMIAH PARSONS, minor; $2,000 bond; WM HUGGINS & NATHAN FOSCUE, sureties; he also renewed his bond as guard to F. BRYAN, minor; $5,000 bond; WM HUGGINS & NATHAN FOSCUE, sureties.

JOHN L. PARSONS renewed his bond as guard to LEAH M.? STANLY, minor; $2,000 bond; GEORGE BENDER & DANIEL YATES, sureties.

DANIEL DICKSON, F. DICKSON, & JAMES MADES were to settle accounts of DANIEL YATES, guard to heirs of ELISHA STAFFORD, decd.

FURNIFOLD G. HERRITAGE renewed his bond as guard to THOMAS STILLY, minor; $3,000 bond; JAMES B. SHINE & CALVIN KOONCE, sureties.

GEORGE WILCOX renewed his bond as guard to THOMAS & STEPHEN WILCOX, minors, $3,000 bond; SAML HILL & EML JARMON, sureties.

FURNIFOLD G. HERRITAGE exempted from jury duty until able to serve.

WALTER P. ALLEN renewed his bond as guard to WILLIAM FOY, minor; $2,000 bond; ZACHEUS BROWN & HARDY O. CONNER, sureties.

JAMES B. SHINE appointed guard to "infant heirs of JOHN B. HARGET, decd;" $2,000 bond; JOHN S. KOONCE & CALVIN KOONCE, sureties.

JOHN S. KOONCE renewed his bond as guard to NANCY & MARY KOONCE, minors; $4,000 bond with CALVIN KOONCE & JNO H. HAMMOND, sureties.

FRANCIS ANDREWS renewed his bond as guard to MARY McDANIEL, minor; $100 bond; WM HUGGINS & J.W. HOWARD, sureties.

DANIEL DICKSON, Esq., RIGDEN HEWIT, JOHN YOUNG & JAMES MADES were to allot & set off to the widow of HARDY COLLINS, decd, one year's provisions out of the estate of said HARDY.

CHARLES GEROCK, WM HUGGINS, & HARDY BRYAN were to settle accounts of RISDEN M. McDANIEL, exr of DANIEL MALLARD, decd.

JOHN S. KOONCE, JOHN JONES & JOHN H. HAMMOND were to settle accounts between RICHARD G. REYNOLDS, former, & JAMES B. SHINE, present guard of heirs of JOHN B. HARGET, decd.

NATHAN FOSCUE, CHARLES GEROCK & HARDY BRYAN were to settle accounts of LEMUEL H. SIMMONS, guard to ELIZABETH ANN SIMMONS, minor.

EMANUEL JARMON renewed his bond as county trustee; $5,000 bond; HARDY BRYAN & WM HUGGINS, sureties.

County trustee was to pay costs that would be incurred by Clerk of Superior Court of Jones County in suit: State vs HENRY ADAMS, sent from Jones to CARTERET COUNTY.

JOHN H. HAMMOND, NATHAN FOSCUE, & CHARLES GEROCK were to settle accounts of EMANUEL JARMON, county trustee.

MARY LOVETT to the court} petitioners declined to return a report.

Governor to use of JNO WASHINGTON vs HARDY H. SHELFER} debt on (Constable?) bond. Each party was to pay his own costs.

JONATHAN WOOD to the use of Pursons & Co. vs JOHN B. POLLOCK & ELIJAH SIMMONS} case. The following jurors:

PETER HARGET	IGNATIOUS W. BROCK	JNO WOOD
ASA EUBANKS	HARDY B. NEWTON	JAMES C. BRYAN
JOHN MISSAW	FREEMAN SMITH	LEWIS WILLIAMS
ADAM ANDREWS	HARDY O. CONNER	JOHN S. KOONCE

found for pltff & assessed damages at $137.43 of which $125 was principal, and costs.

LEWIS WILLIAMS vs BENJN HUGGINS & ISAAC BROWN} debt. Same jury found for pltff. Debt of $330 plus $71 interest. Judgment of $401 plus costs.

CALVIN KOONCE vs RICHARD REYNOLDS} debt. Same jury found for pltff. Principal of $900 and interest of $37.50. Judgment of $937.50 and costs.

JAS HARRISON, guard, to the use of JAMES MUMFORD vs FRANCIS DUVAL & WM HUGGINS. Same jury found for pltff. Principal of $230; interest of $6.13; judgment of $236.13 plus costs.

JAMES C. BRYAN & WM H. BRYAN to the court} petition for partition; report confirmed & returned.

Tuesday, 12 June 1838

County trustee was to pay RISDEN M. McDANIEL, shff, $62.60 & HARDY BRYAN, clerk, $40, both for extra services.

BENJAMIN HUGGINS was reappointed constable for District 3; bond with EML JARMON & ZACHEUS BROWN, sureties.

WILLIAM POLLOCK appointed constable in District 6; bond with BENJAMIN HUGGINS & RISDEN M. McDANIEL, sureties.

NATHAN FOSCUE was to be guard to DARCY FOSCUE in place of HARDY BRYAN, resigned; $10,000 bond; WM HUGGINS & JAS W. HOWARD, sureties.

County trustee was to pay JAMES W. HOWARD, NATHAN FOSCUE, WM HUGGINS, JOHN H. HAMMOND & DANIEL DICKSON, special justices, for holding court at this term $8 each for two days attendance.

County trustee was to pay HARDY BRYAN $40 for services in recording tax list for 1837.

The following justices in addition to the special court are present in making above allowances & appointments of officers: THOS GILLET & CHARLES GEROCK, esquires.

JAMES KINCEY, JOSEPH KINCEY JR. & JOHN JARMON were to be patrols in District 5 for one year.

JACOB GOODING licensed to sell liquor by small measure.

JAMES C. BRYAN, ADONIJAH McDANIEL & FURNIFOLD McDANIEL appointed patrols in District 3 for one year.

GEORGE SIMMONS, ALFRED WHITTY & JOHN HANCOCK were to be patrols in District 2 for one year.

ZACHEUS BROWN, BENJN BROCK & FURNIFOLD JARMON were to be patrols in District 4 for one year.

GEORGE WILCOX was allowed $3.20 for services rendered in waiting on the court up to this term inclusive.

Court ordered that patrols who would provide an account of their expenses at the end of their year's duty should be paid out of county funds the amount requested.

GEORGE WILCOX appointed constable; bond with EMANUEL JARMON & RISDEN M. McDANIEL, sureties.

Following justices were to take tax list for 1838:
District 1: DANIEL DICKSON
District 2: ROSCO BARRUS
District 3: WM HUGGINS
District 4: CALVIN KOONCE
District 5: OWEN B. COX
District 6: FREDERICK I. BECTON
District 7: LEML H. SIMMONS

Jones Cty Court of Common Pleas Minutes 1838

Following persons were to hold elections for 1838:
Dist. 1: THOS GILLET, esq., N.F. PARSONS & M.F. MATTOCKS
Dist. 2: JAS FOY, esq., W.P. ALLEN & JNO OLIVER
Dist. 3: CHARLES GEROCK, esq., JNO McDANIEL & LEMUEL BUSICK
Dist. 4: JNO H. HAMMOND, esq., JAS B. SHINE & JNO JONES
Dist. 5: CALVIN KOONCE, esq., HENRY RHODES & EML JARMON
Dist. 6: SIMS ISLER, esq., BENJN KOONCE & JNO B. REYNOLDS
(**Note**: District 7 was not listed.)

Jurors drawn for next Superior Court:

WM BYNAM	IGNATIOUS BROCK	JOHN BALL
SIMS ISLER	FURNIFOLD H. JARMON	RIGDON HEWET
JOSHUA MILLER	JOHN MERRITT	GEORGE HERRIOT
BENJN ASKEY	DANIEL DICKSON	BENJN HUGGINS
JOSEPH SMALL	THOMAS HARRISON	DANIEL HARRISON
MOSES ADAMS	FREDK I. BECTON	DAVID GREEN
WM ERWIN	ABRAHAM SIMMONS	WRIGHT STANLY
NATHAN STANLY	LEML H. SIMMONS	WILLIAMS JONES
WM GOODING	BENJN BROCK	COUNCIL GOODING
SAMUEL HILL	WM PRICHARD	JAMES JONES JR
HARDY PARRY	BENJN SCOTT	JAS W. HOWARD
WM MURPHY	SIMMONS COLLINS	FRANCIS GOODING

Jurors for next county court:

ISRAEL HOWARD	JAMES HANCOCK	DANIEL MALLARD
ADAM ANDREWS	JONAS WILLIAMS	JOHN HAGINS
EML KOONCE	MARRIT JONES	WILY N. MERRIT
ELIJAH KOONCE	JAMES C. BRYAN	NATHAN P. WAPLES
JONATHAN WOOD	OWEN HARRISON	AMOS SIMMONS
OWEN ADAMS	THOMAS HUGGINS	JNO H. DILLAHUNT
THOMAS BALEY	ELIJAH McDANIEL	BARTHALOMEW MEADOWS
JOHN JONES	FRANCIS ANDREWS	NATHAN F. PARSONS
LEML BUSICK	DANIEL WILLIAMSON	MILLENTON MEADOWS
FELIX KING	JAMES MERRIT	BENJN C. SIMMONS

Affidavits of EML JARMON, guard, filed this term for DEBORAH MURPHY, CURTIS WESTBROOK, CHRISTOPHER McDANIEL, WM H. BRYAN, J.C.B. KOONCE, E.F.B. KOONCE, JAMES A. STANLY; JAMES and RICHARD PARRY; MARY & JOHN FONVIELLE; HOLLON, CAROLINE & ANN D. POLLOCK; JOHN, ALFRED, JAMES, REBECCA, SUSAN, AMANDA & (?) CONNER

Settlement of SIMMONS ISLER, guard to EDWIN BECTON ISLER, minor, filed.
Settlement of OWEN ADAMS, guard to FANNY KNIGHT & others, filed.
Deeds, stc., recorded by C.C. RHODES, registrar:
PENELOPE MUMFORD & WILLIAM K. LEWIS?, marriage contract
LEWIS KINCEY to JAMES HARRISON, bill of sale
THOMAS LIN? to BENJN HUGGINS & JAS C. BRYAN, bill of sale
ALFRED H. REYNOLDS to ELIZABETH REYNOLDS, bill of sale
ROBERT KORNEGAY to JAMES MERRIT, deed
WILLIAM HUGGINS to JAMES C. BRYAN, deed
WINIFRED HERROT (?) to JAS FRESHWATER & by him to H.O. NEWTON

Jones Cty Court of Common Pleas Minutes 1838

SPECIAL COURT
Clerk's Office, TRENTON
16 Aug 1837 (**Note:** Although it would seem that 1838 would have been the correct date, this is what the clerk wrote.)

Justices: JOHN H. HAMMON, WILLIAM HUGGINS, & CHARLES GEROCK, esquires
Clerk: HARDY BRYAN

JESSE HEATH was appointed special admr on the estate of McLENDAL TURNER, decd; $500 bond; JONAS JONES JR, surety. HEATH was allowed to sell perishable property of the estate at public venue on credit of six months. Signed: W.H. HAMMOND, WM HUGGINS, CHARLES GEROCK.

SEPTEMBER TERM, 1838
TRENTON, Monday 10 September 1838

Justices: NATHAN FOSCUE, JOHN H. HAMMOND, DANIEL DICKSON, & WILLIAM HUGGINS, Esqs.
Shff: RESDEN M. McDANIEL
Clerk: HARDY BRYAN

The grand jury was dispensed with since the solicitor, JAS W. BRYAN, was sick & not in attendance.
Jurors sworn in for both civil & state cases:

ISRAEL HOWARD	JAMES HANCOCK	ADAM ANDREWS
JOHN HAGINS	ELIJAH KOONCE	JAMES C. BRYAN
OWEN HARRISON	JONATHAN WOOD	OWEN ANDREWS
JOHN H. DILLAHUNT	MILENTON MEADOWS	BARTHLOMEW MEADOWS

The justices of the county were called, in addition to those already in attendance, until a majority of the J.P.s in the county were in court. The following came in:

ROSCO BARRUS	SIMMONS ISLER	LEMUEL H. SIMMONS
CALVIN KOONCE	OWEN B. COX	JAMES FOY
SAMUEL HILL		

whereupon (1) RESDEN M. McDANIEL presented his bond as shff elect with LEMUEL H. SIMMONS, JAMES McDANIEL & HARDY PERRY, sureties. (2) HARDY BRYAN presented his bonds renewed as clerk. (3) CHRISTOPHER C. RHODES renewed his bond as registrar.

JOHN COART? was licensed to sell liquor by small measure at his store in POLLOCKSVILLE for one year.
County trustee was to pay JAMES B. SHINE $69.16 for services rendered.
EDWARD C. DEBRULE was to oversee road in place of JOHN ADAMS.
A former order clearing the hands of HARDY & ELIJAH PERRY & ABNER GREEN from public road work for purpose of keeping up the PERRY ROAD was renewed for three years.
PETER HARGET was appointed guard to his daughter, OLIVE; $2,000 bond; JOHN S. KOONCE & FREEMAN SMITH, sureties.
NATHAN FOSCUE was to act with WILLIAM HUGGINS, formerly appointed to superintend the building of a poorhouse in Jones County, and they were to

proceed to have said poorhouse completed. They were impowered to use such monies as the shff had collected for such use as they saw fit to get the job done.

OWEN B. COX, JAMES D. KINCEY & JONAS WILLIAMS were to lay off to the widow of McLENDAL TURNER, decd, one year's provisions for herself & family.

CHARLES ANDREWS was exempted from county duties and from pole taxes as long as he continued to be a (minister?) in Jones County.

CHARLES GEROCK, NATHAN FOSCUE & WILLIAM HUGGINS, Esq., with the Clerk of the Jones County Court were to revise and arrange names placed in the jury box as per the last tax list & when completed to draw the jurors to attend next court.

The order was renewed for the settlement of DANIEL YATES, guard of heirs of STAFFORD; report next term.

ZACHEUS BROWN appointed constable in District 4; bond with EMANUEL JARMON & JAMES B. SHINE, sureties.

JOHN HAGGINS/HUGGINS, JOHN L. PARSONS & BARTHLOMEW MEADOWS were to be patrols for District 1 for one year.

WILLIAM C. MURPHY, DANIEL HARRISON & FRANCIS MERRETT appointed patrols in District 7 for one year.

Affidavit of HARDY BRYAN, clerk, as to monies remaining in office for three years prior to the current term, was filed.

Settlement of RESDEN M. McDANIEL, admr, with the will annexed, of DANIEL MALLARD, decd, returned.

Accounts of ELIJAH LOVITT, guard to JAMES M. LOVITT, minor, filed.

Account of sale, inventory & widow's provisions of HARDY COLLINS, decd, filed by the admr.

Tax list filed.

MARY McKINLEY vs OWEN B. COX, WILLIAM HUGGINS, & HARDY BRYAN} debt. Jury found for pltff: principal of $500; interest of $7.50 and costs. Appeal prayed & granted. ADAM ANDREWS & BENJAMIN HUGGINS, sureties.

RACHEL CONNER to use of HARDY O. CONNER vs JAMES FOY & WILLIAM HUGGINS} debt. Jury found for pltff. Principal of $250 plus $10.25 interest plus costs.

FRANCIS DUVAL vs ADAM ANDREWS, admr of CALVIN J. MORRIS} judgment of justice. Judgment by default & judgment of justice affirmed for $54.85 and costs.

The same pltff and defendant as above} same kind of case; same finding for $40 and costs.

The State of N.C. to the use of RICHARD HATCH, minor, vs WILLIAM HUGGINS & EML JARMON} debt on guard bond of C. DAVIS. Report made by C. GEROCK. Jury assessed damage at $1165.18. Judgment was for this amount. Bond was to be remitted by payment of above sum and costs. C. GEROCK was allowed $5.00 for making report.

ROSCO BARRUS vs JOHN STANLY} levy on lands. Judgment of justice affirmed for $10 and costs.

ROSCO BARRUS vs WILLIAM FOSCUE} levy on land. Judgment of justice affirmed for $8.70 and costs.

CHARLES GEROCK vs JOHN STANLY} levy on land. Judgment of justice affirmed for $35.54 & costs.

MATHEW A. AUSTIN vs JOHN STANLY} constable levy on land. Judgment of justice affirmed for $2.30 with interest from 12 Sep 1833 and costs.

Jones Cty Court of Common Pleas Minutes 1838

Deeds, etc. recorded by C.C.RHODES, registrar:
DAVID KINCEY to JAMES D. KINCEY
EMANUEL JARMON to E. KOONCE
MARY OLIVER to EML JARMON, power of attorney
ELIJAH LOVETT to MARY H. LOVETT
ELIZABETH CAREY to ELIJAH KOONCE
EDMD B. HATCH to SAML HILL
SAML HILL to EDMD B. HATCH
THOS McDANIEL to EDMD B. HATCH
SAML HILL to EDMD B. HATCH
ZEDOC M. MASEY to EDMD D. WHORTER
ISAAC COLLINS to HARDY COLLINS
ABNER W. KILLEBREW to JAMES B. SHINE
JAMES D. KINCEY to JOHN H. COX
READING MORRIS to WM HUGGINS, power of attorney
JOHN R. FOY to LEML H. SIMMONS, power of attorney

Jurors for December term:

JOHN POLLOCK	AMOS AMYETT	MICAJAH F. MATTOCKS
BENJAMIN KOONCE	JAMES MISSAW	JAMES HARRISON
JOHN BENDER SR	HARDY O. CONNER	JOHN STRICKLIN
ELIJAH S. KOONCE	DANIEL YATES	JAMES McDANIEL
JOHN HEATH	ZACHEUS BROWN	BENJAMIN F. STANLY
JAMES MUMFORD	MARTIN F. BROCK	JOSEPH WALLACE
FREDERICK PARKER	AMOS SHELFER	NATHAN B. WESTBROOK
WILLIAM MUNDINE	LEWIS O. BRYAN	GEORGE I. BENDER
SIMON I. BECTON	NEEDHAM BEASLEY	FREDERICK MARKET
JOHN ROUSE	JOHN HARRISON	

SPECIAL COURT
Clerk's Office, Trenton, 23 Nov 1838

Justices: CHARLES GEROCK, SAMUEL HILL & LEML H. SIMMONS, esquires

Court was certified that EDMUND B. HATCH of Jones County was dead and left a last will & testament appointing EDMUND HATCH of ALABAMA, executor. Since the perishable property of estate could not wait on the exr, the court appointed a special admr to handle the situation. HARDY BRYAN of TRENTON was appointed the special admr; $5,000 bond; JAMES C. BRYAN & BENJAMIN HUGGINS, sureties. Signed: CHS. GEROCK, S. HILL, LEML H. SIMMONS.

DECEMBER TERM, 1838
TRENTON, Monday 10 Dec 1838

Justices: NATHAN FOSCUE, JAMES W. HOWARD, DANIEL DICKSON & J.H. HAMMOND, Esqs.
Shff: RISDON M. McDANIEL
Clerk pro tem: C.C. RHODES

Jurors for the state, charged by G.S. ATMORE, Esq., solicitor pro tem

Jones Cty Court of Common Pleas Minutes 1838

for the county with GEORGE WILCOX attending the jury:
JOHN BENDER, foreman

LEWIS O. BRYAN	AMOS AMYET	JOHN STRICKLIN
JOHN HARRISON	JAMES MESSOR	NEEDHAM BEASLEY
JOHN ROUSE	ZACHEUS BROWN	MICAJAH F. MATTOCKS
JOHN HEATH	SIMON S. BECTON	NATHAN B. WESTBROOK
DANIEL YATES	JOHN POLLOCK	GEORGE S. BENDER
JAMES MONTFORD	BENJAMIN F. STANLY	

HARDY PARRY, CALVIN KOONCE & ABNER GREEN were to "value" the Negroes of MICHAEL KOONCE, decd, & allot to MARY & NANCY KOONCE, heirs of said decd, their portions.

SIMMONS ISLER was exempted from the tax of "seven pole" that he gave in the Jones County list but would "have to give & pay for in BRUNSWICK COUNTY."

F.I. BECTON, SIMON BECTON & SIMMONS ISLER were to settle accounts of COUNCIL WOOTON, admr of NANCY ISLER, decd.

JOHN (T?) PARSONS was appointed constable for District 1; JAMES W. HOWARD & DANIEL DICKSON?, sureties.

NATHAN FOSCUE, DANIEL DICKSON & JAMES ROBERTS were to allot off to the "widow of WILLIAM BRAY & two of her children to wit, HARDY & ELIZA BRAY, their proportionable part of said BRAY's Negroes."

ELIJAH SIMMONS JR was to oversee road from dividing line between FRANK's & BURGWIN's to the fork at JAMES W. HOWARD's fence in place of WILEY F. HUGGINS, resigned.

JONATHAN WOOD, HARDY O. NEWTON & ROSCO BARRUS were licensed to retail spirituous liquors for one year.

MICAJAH F. MATTOCKS appointed to oversee road from foot of BLACK SWAMP BRIDGE to the BAPTIST CHAPEL and from the crossroads to the foot of SMITH's MILL BRIDGE leaving out the hands from the crossroads to the BAPTIST CHAPEL.

JOHN B. MOOREHOUSE? allowed to peddle goods in Jones County for one year.

The jailor, BENJAMIN ASKEW, was ordered to pay the county trustee the rest of the money now in his hands: $5.92 1/2.

EMANUEL JARMON appointed guard to heirs of ISAIAH WOOD, decd, to wit: GEORGE, JOHN, AMOS, FURNIFOLD & ISAIAH WOOD; $2,000 bond; J.H. HAMMOND & RISDON M. McDANIEL, securities.

County trustee was to pay the special court for their services for two days December term, 1838.

EMANUEL JARMON was to be admr of the estate of McLENDAL TURNER, decd; $1,000 bond; J.H. HAMMOND & RISDON M. McDANIEL, sureties.

J.H. HAMMOND, JAMES D. KINCEY & F.H. JARMON were to lay off to the widow & family of McLENDAL TURNER, decd, one year's provisions.

HARDY BRYAN, CHARLES GEROCK & BENJAMIN ASKEW were to audit accounts of EMANUEL JARMAN, admr of the estate of ISAIAH WOOD, decd.

Shff was to proceed immediately to summon the justices of the peace of Jones County, who were then absent from TRENTON, to attend at the courthouse in TRENTON Tuesday 13 December at 12 o'clock; the majority, to wit:

JAMES FOY	JAMES HERRITAGE	CALVIN KOONCE
ROSCO BARRIS	DANIEL DICKSON	JAMES ROBERTS
ABNER GREEN	JAMES W. HOWARD	LEMUEL H. SIMMONS

SAMUEL HILL   OWEN B. COX   NATHAN FOSCUE

The following persons came forward as candidates for the office of county clerk, viz: J.H. HAMMOND, FRANCIS DUVAL, CHARLES GEROCK. Court voted and elected J.H. HAMMOND clerk. HAMMOND offered as securities for his bond JAMES McDANIEL, JAMES ROBERTS, & JAMES B. SHINE.

  Deeds, etc., recorded by C.C. RHODES, registrar:
JOSIAH ASKEW to LEWIS O. BRYAN
JOHN POLLOCK to BENJAMIN HUGGINS
WILLIAM MEADOWS/MUNDINE to BARTHOLOMEW MEADOWS
HOSEA BANDIN to JAMES WHALEY's children
HEPSEY MUNDINE to BARTHOLOMEW MEADOWS
RISDON M. McDANIEL to GEORGE W. HARRIOTT
WILLIAM H. ROGERS to BENJAMIN S. BRYAN
RILEY JACKSON to LEWIS O. BRYAN
JONAS JONES to JOHN JONES
JOHN H. HAMMOND, clerk's bond, 1838
EDMUND & RICHARD HATCH to JOHN MESSOR

  Last will & testament of SHADERACK MALLARD was proved by oath of BENJAMIN ASKEW, one of the witnesses, and was recorded. [Note: Gwynn abstracted this will (p. 434) which was written 13 Nov 1837. It names DANIEL, son of WILLIAM HARRISON; JOHN, son of WELTHY HARRISON; and MARY, daughter of STEPHEN HARRISON, decd. MARY HARRISON was named exr, and BENJAMIN ASKEW and C.W. BRYAN were witnesses. A biography of SHADRICK MALLARD appeared in the New Bern *Daily Journal* for 27 Feb 1886 (Kammerer, Vol. 2, pp. 19-20). According to the article, SHADRICK MALLARD was the son of DANIEL MALLARD SR, who reportedly died at about 100 years in 1831. Of his several children only five could be named: LAWSON, BETSY SUSAN, SARAH, KEZZIAH, and SHADRICK MALLARD. LAWSON married NANCY COLVETT and their children included: LANEY, who married RISDEN McDANIEL, DANIEL, and BETSY, who married ROBERT HANCOCK of NEW BERN in 1839. SARAH, daughter of DANIEL, SR. married WILLIAM HARRISON and had children: THOMAS, JAMES, DANIEL and MARY HARRISON. SHADRICK and KEZZIAH took charge of the "old homestead" a few years before their father's death. Youpon trees provided tea, bees provided honey, and they raised swine, sheep, cattle, and cotton. WEALTHY and MARY HARRISON were neices according to the article but how their were neices was not clear. Neither SHADRICK nor KEZZIAH married and both are buried on the east side of JUMPING RUN in unmarked graves. (Although Powell lists several Jumping Runs, none were in Jones County.)]
  Last will & testament of BENETEN? KOONCE was proved by oath of JAMES C. BRYAN, one of the witnesses, & was recorded. [Gwynn abstracted this will (p. 429-430) which was written 9 Jan 1836. In the will BENETER KOONCE named MARY, wife of JOHN POLLOCK; BENETER's sister, MARY SIMMONS; and MATILDA, wife of BENJAMIN HUGGINS. BENJAMIN HUGGINS was named exr, and the witnesses were H. BRYAN and JAMES C. BRYAN.]

  Jurors drawn for March term 1839 of this court:
EDWARD C. DEBRULE SR	EDWARD M. GILBERT	JOSEPH WHITTY
JONAS WILLIAMS	COUNCIL GOODING	WILLIAM BYNUN
RICHARD R. FOSCUE	THOMAS HARRISON	AMOS L. SIMMONS

DAVID GREEN	HENRY RHODES	EDMUND D. WHARTON
ASA EUBANKS	GEORGE W. HARRIETT	JAMES GODWIN
JOHN S. KOONCE	JOHN McDANIEL	DANIEL WILLIAMSON
JAMES MERRITT	ABNER HARGET	EDWARD C. DEBRULE JR
OWEN ADAMS	MICHAEL SHELFER	JOSEPH KINCEY
LEVI JONES	MERITT JONES	BENJAMIN SCOTT
JEREMIAH CANNON	THOMAS McDANIEL	JOHN E. FOSCUE

Jurors drawn for spring term of Superior Court:

JOHN MALLARD	J.H. HAMMOND	JOHN MERRITT
WRIGHT STANLY	JOHN HAGINS	HARDY PARRY
JOHN BALE/BALL	SIMMONS ISLER	BARTHOLOMEW MEADOWS
DANIEL MALLARD	THOMAS BAILEY	JOHN K. BENDER
ABRAM SIMMONS	SAMUEL HILE/HILL	WILLIAM C. MURPHY
WILLIAM HUGGINS	EMERY METTS	BRYAN BENDER
THOMAS HUGGINS	THOMAS POLLOCK	FREEMAN SMITH
ISRAEL HOWARD	JOHN C.B. KOONCE	ELIJAH PARRY
THOMAS GILLET	JOHN WESTBROOK	JOHN YOUNG
JOHN H. DILLAHUNT	LOTT EUBANKS	WILLIAM PRITCHETT
REUBIN WILLIAMS	JOHN JONES	NATHANIEL WAPLES
JOHN TURNER	JOHN KINCEY	MILLINGTON MEADOWS

RICHARD H. WATSON of MISSISSIPPI brought into court documents from probate court of HOLMES COUNTY, MISS. certifying his appointment as guard of JOSEPH H. WATSON in that county & now the residence of the minor, & made an affidavit that the bond given under his appointment is for $2,000; this court was satisfied with this bond & arrangement.

One mortgage deed filed from JAMES G. STANLY to JOHN MARRITT dated 16 Feb 1837.

SPECIAL COURT
Clerk's Office, Trenton, 2 Jan 1838 (**Note:** This should have been 1839.)

Justices: NATHAN FOSCUE, SAMUEL HILL & ABNER GREEN

It was certified to court that FRANCIS B. AMYET of Jones County was dead; no last will; LEMUEL H. SIMMONS appointed special admr to estate of FRANCIS B. AMYET, decd; $1,000 bond; JAMES W. HOWARD & RISDON M. McDANIEL, securities: said admr could sell perishable property of said decedant. Signed: S. HILL, ABNER GREEN, NATHAN FOSCUE.

Jones Cty Court of Common Pleas Minutes 1839

SPECIAL COURT
Clerk's Office, Trenton 12 Jan 1839

Justices: NATHAN FOSCUE, LEMUEL H. SIMMONS & CHARLES GEROCK

WILLIAM HUGGINS appointed special admr of the estate of HARDY BRYAN, decd; $4,000 bond; JAMES C. BRYAN & EMANUEL JERMAN, securities: said admr allowed to sell perishable items of the estate. Signed: CHS. GEROCK, NATHAN FOSCUE, LEML H. SIMMONS.

Note: According to Kammerer (Vol. 2, p. 25) a biography of HARDY BRYAN was published in the New Bern *Daily Journal* 24 Nov 1886. The biography states that he was born 30 Apr 1781 and died near Trenton 11 Dec 1838. He and his wife, WEALTHY, ran a hotel. They had two daughters, MARY, who married CHISTOPHER RHODES and JULIA, who married DR. JESSE D. HINES. He was remembered as a "great hunter of foxes and deer." WILLIAM HUGGINS was also a "great hunter" and friend of BRYAN. JAMES B. STANLY recalled in a New Bern Weekly Journal of 21 Jul 1899 that HUGGINS, BRYAN and DR. DUVAL would leave TRENTON in the early morning to hunt in the BEAVERDAM savannas (Kammerer, Vol. 2, pp. 35-37).

MARCH TERM, 1839
TRENTON, Monday 11 Mar 1839

Justices: JAMES W. HOWARD, WILLIAM HUGGINS, DANIEL DICKSON, NATHAN FOSCUE
Shff: RISDEN M. McDANIEL
Clerk: J.H. HAMMOND
Solicitor: JAMES W. BRYAN

Jurors:
JAMES MERRIT, foreman

JOHN McDANIEL	ABNER HARGET	JOHN E. FOSCUE
HENRY RHODES	ASA EUBANKS	EDWARD C. DEBRULE
BENJAMIN SCOTT	MICHAEL SHELFER	AMOS SHELFER
THOMAS McDANIEL	EDWARD M. GILBERT	MERRIT JONES
OWEN ADAMS	DANIEL WILLIAMSON	JEREMIAH CANNON
WILLIAM BINUM	JONAS WILLIAMS	

GEORGE WILCOX, as constable, attended the jury.

WILLIAM HUGGINS, NATHAN FOSCUE & HARDY PARRY were to settle accounts of JOSEPH WHITTY, admr of EDWARD S. FERRAND.
LEMUEL H. SIMMONS was to admin. estate of FRANCIS B. AMYET, decd; $1600 bond; JOSEPH WHITTY & AMOS L. SIMMONS, sureties.
CALVIN KOONCE, Esq., FURNIFOLD JERMAN, JAMES D. KINCY & JONAS WILLIAMS were to allot off to the widow of McLENDAL TURNER her year's provisions.
JAMES GODWIN was released from serving as juror for one year.
BENJAMIN HUGGINS was licensed to retail liquors for one year.
MICHAEL SHELFER was to oversee road in place of JAMES G. STANLY, resigned.
BENJAMIN (?) was to oversee rd in place of EDWARD C. DEBRULE, resigned.
HARDY PARRY, MICHAEL SHELFER & HARRISON HEATH were appointed patrols for

Jones Cty Court of Common Pleas Minutes 1839

one year in District 6.

JONAS WILLIAMS was to oversee rd in room of WHITFIELD TURNER, resigned.

JOHN AMYET, minor, was bound to ADAM ANDREWS.

JAMES W. HOWARD, JAMES FOY & WILEY F. HIGGINS were to settle accounts of ROSCO BARRUS, admr of COUNCIL FIELDS.

JAMES ADAMS was to oversee TRENT RIVER in room of ISAAC BROWN.

ISAAC BROWN removed from his appointment as overseer of TRENT RIVER.

WILLIAM HUGGINS, CHARLES GEROCK & J.H. HAMMOND were to settle estate of SUSAN ANDREWS with the admr, EMANUEL JERMAN.

WILLIAM HUGGINS allowed $64.18 for repairs to the bridge at TRENTON from county trustee.

The rd which is overseen by ELIJAH SIMMONS was to be extended to BUCKNER HATCH's mill & J.W. HOWARD was appointed overseer of rd from fork as far as the district of rd heretofore extended towards WHITE OAK.

A former order of this court which bound CAROLINE POLLOCK to JOHN HARRISON was rescinded & said HARRISON was relieved of any responsibility.

LEWIS WILLIAMS was to oversee rd in room of ZACHEUS BROWN, resigned.

JOHN L. PARSONS, RICHARD OLDFIELD, JOHN HAGGINS, & BARTHOLOMEW MEADOWS were to be patrols for District 1.

JAMES C. BRYAN, JOHN MERRITT, & JOHN H. DILLAHUNT qualified as justices of the peace for Jones County.

County trustee was to pay JOHN JONES $7.80.

CHARLES GEROCK, NATHAN FOSCUE, LEMUEL H. SIMMONS, JAMES W. HOWARD & WILLIAM HUGGINS were appointed special justices for one year.

County trustee was to pay O.B. COX for taking tax list and valuing land for 1837.

ABNER GREEN was appointed guard to FRANKLIN B. HARRISON; $20,000 bond; JOSEPH WHITTY & JOSEPH KINCEY, securities.

OWEN B. COX appointed admr de bonus non with the will annexed of SHADRACK ERWIN, decd; $4,000 bond; WILLIAM ERWIN & FRANCIS GOODING, sureties.

J.H. HAMMOND, CHARLES GEROCK & HARDY PERRY were to settle accounts between HARDY BRYAN, decd, late exr of SHADRACK ERWIN, decd, & OWEN B. COX, admr de bonus non.

Letters of admin. were issued to WILLIAM I. MORRIS on the estate of DURANT GREEN; $200 bond; JAMES HARRISON, security.

RICHARD W. HATCH granted letters of admin. with the will annexed on estate of EDMUND B. HATCH, decd; $50,000 bond; W.S. BLACK & JOSEPH WHITTY, securities.

EMANUEL JERMAN, admr of MARY McDANIEL, allowed to amend his settlement by charging vouchers paid counsel since his settlement.

EMANUEL JERMAN, CHARLES GEROCK & J.H. HAMMOND were to settle accounts of DORCUS FOSCUE, lunatic, with WILLIAM HUGGINS, admr of HARDY BRYAN, former guard.

Note: A Jones County Superior Court case, Dec. term (Vol. 37, p. 232), ELIZABETH FOSCUE vs JOHN E. FOSCUE explained that HARDY BRYAN had been guardian to DORCUS FOSCUE since 1830. He hired out the slaves left her by her father SIMON FOSCUE SR for her support (Kammerer, Vol. 1, p. 6).

(**Note:** A special court record was inserted at this point in the record.

I have elected to place it at the end of the proceedings for the regular March Term. Search here for it, howerer, in the original record.)

    CHARLES GEROCK, EMANUEL JERMAN and J.H. HAMMOND were to settle estate of F.B. HARRISON, minor, with WILLIAM HUGGINS, admr of HARDY BRYAN, former guard.
    Same men were to settle accounts of RICHARD HATCH, minor, with WILLIAM HUGGINS, admr of HARDY BRYAN, former guard.
    Same men were to settle accounts of NANCY LAROQUE, minor, with WILLIAM HUGGINS, admr of HARDY BRYAN, former guard.
    WILLIAM HUGGINS appointed guard to RICHARD HATCH, minor; $2,500 bond; J. BRYAN & SAMUEL HILL, sureties.
    WILLIAM HUGGINS appointed guard to NANCY LAROQUE, minor; $2,500 bond; J. BRYAN & SAMUEL HILL, sureties.
    WILLIAM HUGGINS issued letters of admin. on estate of HARDY BRYAN, decd; $20,000 bond; J. BRYAN & EMANUEL JERMAN, securities.

    Petit jurors called & sworn in:

JOSEPH WHITTY	THOMAS HARRISON	DAVID GREEN
JOSEPH KINCEY	JOHN S. KOONCE	COUNCIL GOODING
JOHN HARRISON	NATHAN F. PARSONS	ADAM ANDREWS
HARDY O. CONNER	AMOS AMYET	JOHN MESSOR

    State of MISSISSIPPI, (NONUBA?) County (**Note:** A check of Mississippi county names revealed three possibilities which I have ranked in order of my best guess: Neshoba, Noxubee, Itawamba.) 28 Jan 1839: "Be it known that I, EDMUND HATCH of the county & state aforesaid do by these presents fully & certainly quit claim & release to RICHARD W. HATCH & all others all the right that may be vested in me by law or otherwise to the executorship of the last will & testament of the late EDMUND B. HATCH, decd, of the State of North Carolina, Jones County.... I do further relinquish & quit claim to R.W. HATCH all the right that I may have to the administration on the estate of E.B. HATCH, decd, in witness whereof I have heretofore set my seal the day & date above, written EDMUND HATCH."
    [Note: Gwynn abstracted this will (p. 417) which was written 24 Jan 1837. It names sister, HENRIETTA B. HATCH, and brother, RICHARD B. HATCH, who were minors and were to be wards of the exr, EDMUND HATCH, who was given permission to move them to ALABAMA or any other place that would be in their interest. The exr named was the step-father of the deceased. The witnesses were F. DUVAL and WM. HUGGINS.]
    Inventory & account of sale of property of BRADOCK NOBLE returned.
    Inventory of property of McLENDALE TURNER returned.
    Committee appointed to lay off to widow of McLENDALE TURNER her year's provisions returned their report.
    Settlement of JOHN S. KOONCE, guard of heirs of MICHAEL KOONCE, decd, returned.
    Settlement of NATHAN STANLY, guard to PENELOPE STANLY, returned.
    Guard accounts of JAMES G. KINCEY with GEORGE H. IVERS? returned.
    Guard accounts of HARDY PERRY, guard to SILAS & GEORGE PERRY, recorded.
    Settlement of EMANUEL JARMAN, admr of estate of ISAIAH WOOD, returned.
    Settlement of COUNCIL WOOTEN, admr of NANCY ISLER?, decd, returned.
    The following guardian settlements were proved and recorded:
JOHN OLIVER, guard to FURNIFOLD G. SIMMONS

Jones Cty Court of Common Pleas Minutes 1839

RACHEL JARMON, guard to EDNEY S. McDANIEL
JAMES D. KINCEY, guard to JOHN H. COX
ROSCO BARRUS, guard to WILLIAM W. FRANK

Report of division of Negroes, who belonged to estate of MICHAEL KOONCE, decd, returned.
Settlement of JOSEPH WHITTY, admr to E./O.S. FERROND, returned.

State vs ZACHEUS BROWN} bastardy. The petit jury as listed above found for defendant; not guilty.
State vs GRAY NORRIS} affray. Same jury found defendant guilty; fine of $50 and costs.
WELTHY BRYAN to the court} petition for year's provisions.
Note: WELTHY/WEALTHY BRYAN's will, recorded Oct. term, 1855, named her two daughters, MARY E. RHODES and JULIA W. HINES, and a granddaughter, ELIZABETH H. RHODES. her sons-in-law, CHRISTOPHER C. RHODES and JESSE D. HINES were named exrs (Gwynn, 405).

Bills of sale, etc., recorded by C.C. RHODES, registrar:
SIMMONS ISLER to EDWARD M. GILBERT
EDMUND H. HATCH to RICHARD REYNOLDS
JOHN BURGUYN to JOHN C. BURGUYN
EDWARD R. STANLY to NATHAN & B.F. STANLY
LEWIS KINCEY to HENRY RHODES
JOHN HOUSTON to AMOS AMYET
NANCY M. FOSCUE to JAMES HANCOCK
MICHAEL & ELIZABETH KOONCE to RICHARD REYNOLDS
JESSE HEATH to JONAS JONES
R.M. McDANIEL to JAMES STANLY
WILLIAM HUGGINS to JOHN BURGUYN
PETER ANDREWS to RICHARD REYNOLDS
F.I. BECTON to SWITHERINGTON?
EDWARD M. GILBERT to AMOS JONES
LEVY JONES to JAMES D. KINCEY
JONAS JONES JR to ZACHEUS HOWARD
JOHN OLIVER to LEMUEL H. SIMMONS
MARTIN & BRYAN JONES to BAND? JONES
HANNAH WOOD to O.B. COX

Jurors drawn to next County Court:

IGNATIUS BROCK	JAMES G. STANLY	LEVY EUBANKS
WHITFIELD TURNER	NATHAN F. PARSONS	JOHN HEATH
WALTER P. ALLEN	LEMUEL BUSICK	JOHN ADAMS
JOHN CANNON	BENJAMIN COLLINS	MOSES ADAMS
JONAS JONES JR	WILLIAM GOODING	ENOCK FOY
JOSEPH SMALL	JOHN C. BURGWYN	JOHN MESSOR
RICHARD OLDFIELD	JOHN JARMAN	LEWIS KOONCE
HARDY O. NEWTON	JOSEPH HAY	LEWIS WILLIAMS
WILLIAM ERWIN	NATHAN STANLY	EMANUEL KOONCE
AMOS HEATH	JOHN B. REYNOLDS	JOHN WOOD

Jones Cty Court of Common Pleas Minutes 1839

SPECIAL COURT
25 March 1839

Justices: WILLIAM HUGGINS, CHARLES GEROCK & CHRISTOPHER BRYAN

    RICHARD M. McDANIEL was to admin. estate of HUSTON SIMMONS, decd; $5,000 bond; WILLIAM HUGGINS & JAMES McDANIEL, securities. Admr allowed to sell perishable property of the estate. Signed: CHS GEROCH, J.P.; WM HUGGINS, J.P.; JAS C. BRYAN, J.P.

JUNE TERM
TRENTON, 10 June 1839

Special Justices: WILLIAM HUGGINS, JAMES W. HOWARD, NATHAN FOSCUE, CHARLES GEROCK, LEMUEL H. SIMMONS
Shff: RISDEN M. McDANIEL
Clerk: J.H. HAMMOND
County Solicitor: JAMES W. BRYAN

    Jurors for the state:
WALTER P. ALLEN, foreman

HARDY O. NEWTON	LEWIS WILLIAMS	LEVI EUBANKS
JOHN B. REYNOLDS	IGNATIUS BROCK	JOHN JERMAN, JR
MOSES ADAMS	WILLIAM ERWIN	WHITFIELD TURNER
LEWIS KOONCE	NATHAN STANLY	LEMUEL BUSICK
JOHN C. BURGWYN	JOHN WOOD	BENJAMIN COLLINS
JONAS JONES JR	EMANUEL KOONCE	

    Petit jury dispensed with for this term.

    JOHN H. DILLAHUNT appointed guard to heirs of SAMUEL DILLAHUNT, decd; $15,000 bond; JOHN OLIVER & JOHN WOOD, securities.
    WILLIAM HUGGINS, EMANUEL JERMAN & CHARLES GEROCK were to settle accounts of JOHN H. DILLAHUNT, admr to estate of SAMUEL DILLAHUNT, decd.
    ARTHUR GILBERT to oversee rd in room of JAMES MUNTFORD, extending from WARD'S HILL to JACOB BRANCH including BEAVER CREEK.
    WILLIAM HUGGINS, CHARLES GEROCK & BENJAMIN HUGGINS were to settle accounts of ADAM ANDREWS, admr to estate of C.J. MORRIS, decd.
    ELIZABETH ANDREWS appointed admx de bonis non to the estate of PETER ANDREWS, decd; $4,000 bond; NATHAN FOSCUE & JAMES C. BRYAN, sureties. She was also appointed guard to heirs of PETER ANDREWS, decd; $5,000 bond; same sureties.
    Six cents tax was levied on every $100 value of land & town lots and a 20 cent tax was levied on every taxable pole in order to defray county expenses.
    County trustee was to pay BENJAMIN HUGGINS $9.60 for his services attending court.
    DREWEY HARPER & CANA CANNON exempted from public duties agreeable to act of assembly.
    Patrols appointed June term 1838 were to be paid $2.00 per month agreeable to order of that term.

Jones Cty Court of Common Pleas Minutes 1839

J.H. HAMMOND, CHARLES GEROCK & NATHAN FOSCUE were to settle accounts of HARDY BRYAN, admr to the estate of PETER ANDREWS, decd & ELIZABETH ANDREWS, admx de bonis non to same estate.

WILLIAM HUGGINS, J.H. HAMMOND & CHARLES GEROCK were to settle accounts of EMANUEL JERMAN, county trustee.

EMANUEL JERMAN was to continue as county trustee for one year from this time; $10,000 bond; WILLIAM HUGGINS & J.H. HAMMOND, securities.

County trustee was to pay admr of HARDY BRYAN, decd, $25 for extra services of said BRYAN for June & September 1838 terms of court.

County trustee was to pay JOHN H. HAMMOND, clerk, $15 for extra services up to this term.

These J.P.s were to take the list of taxables for 1839:
District 1: DANIEL DICKSON
District 2: JAMES FOY
District 3: JOHN H. DILLAHUNT
District 4: CALVIN KOONCE
District 5: OWEN B. COX
District 6: ABNER GREEN
District 7: JOHN MERRETT

The following were to hold the polls for an election for a member to Congress and for the school agreeable to act of Assembly for 1839:
District 1: THOMAS GILLET, M.F. MATTUCKS, & LEVI EUBANKS
District 2: R. BARRUS, E. FOY, & DANIEL WILLIAMSON
District 3: Shff SAMUEL HILL & WILLIAM HUGGINS
District 4: CALVIN KOONCE, JAMES B. SHINE & JOHN JONES
District 5: OWEN B. COX, HENRY RHODES, & ISAAC BROWN
District 6: FREDERICK I. BECTON, PETER HARGET, BENJAMIN KOONCE
(**Note:** District 7 was not listed.)

WILLIAM HINDS allowed to retail spirituous liquors at his "own house" in TRENTON.

County trustee was to pay GEORGE WILCOX $8 for his attendance at court up to June term inclusive.

County trustee was to pay BENJAMIN ASKEW as per "act" rendered $15.20.

County trustee was to pay GEORGE WILCOX 80 cents as costs on two warrents in favor of overseer of river.

County trustee was to pay WILLIAM POLLOCK 45 cents for costs in State vs LEVICY CONNER.

WILLIAM I. GIBSON & STARKEY McDANIEL were to admir estate of HESTER SIMMONS, decd; $10,000 bond; JAMES McDANIEL, JOHN H. DILLAHUNT, JAMES FOY, & RICHARD OLDFIELD, sureties.

JAMES C. BRYAN, CHARLES GEROCK & WILLIAM HUGGINS were to settle accounts of R.M. McDANIEL, special admr to the estate of HESTER SIMMONS, decd, & WILLIAM I. GIBSON & STARKEY McDANIEL, general admrs.

JAMES B. SHINE, IGNATIOUS BROCK & JOHN S. KOONCE were to settle accounts of JAMES D. KINCY, admr to estate of LAVINIA COX, decd.

Court ordered that the double tax incurred by the representative? of JOHN P. DAVIS, decd, by reason of his failing to give in a list of taxables last year, be remitted to the single or usual tax payable by persons who gave in their lists.

JAMES W. HOWARD, NATHAN FOSCUE & OWEN B. COX were to examine the books of the Registrar, and if they decide that they are in a "ruinous" and "dilapidated" condition, a new set of books shall be purchased & a contract let for one or more persons to transcribe the records of deeds in the old books into the new books.

The last will & testament of JONAS JONES was admitted for probate. Executor therein named qualified agreeable to law & letters testamentary issued to him. (**Note**: The man's name was not given.) [Note: Gwynn abstracted this will (p. 426) which was written 11 July 1838. Named are wife, MARY and nephew, JONAS, son of JOHN JONES. Nephew, JOHN JONES, was named exr, and the witnesses were HEN. RHODES and BENJAMIN RHODES.]

EMANUEL JERMAN renewed his bond as county trustee.
WILLIAM POLLOCK renewed his bond as constable.
GEORGE WILCOX renewed his bond as constable.

ALFRED HATCH vs BUCKNER HILL & JAMES ROBERTS} debt. Jury found for pltff. Judgment for $1600 principle & $52 interest plus costs. Appeal prayed & granted. THOMAS GILLET & DANIEL/DAVID DICKSON, securities. (**Note**: Jury members were not named.)

Deeds, etc. filed with Registrar, C.C. RHODES:
JAMES McDANIEL (deed) to LEWIS KOONCE
LEWIS KOONCE to JAMES McDANIEL (deed)
ELIJAH KOONCE (deed) to AMOS KOONCE
E. JARMAN to ELIJAH KOONCE (deed)
AMOS KOONCE to ELIJAH KOONCE (deed)
(J?)H. STANLY to E. JARMON (deed)
MARY OLIVER to JACOB GOODING (deed)
GEORGE POLLOCK to JONATHAN WARD/WOOD (deed)
RICHARD M. HATCH to JOHN OLIVER (deed)
I.C.B. KOONCE to RICHARD RUSSEL (deed)
JOHN B. BECTON to WRIGHT STANLY (bill of sale)

IMLA N. MILLER vs OWEN B. COX} debt. Plea withdrawn. Judgment final by default: bad debt of $673.38, interest of $30.30, total: $703.68 plus costs.

WEALTHY BRYAN to the court} petition for year's provisions report. Report returned & confirmed.

Jurors drawn for September term for County Court:

ENOCH FOY	COUNCIL GOODING	JOHN C. BUYQWIN
MILITON MEADOWS	THOMAS McDANIEL	ASA EUBANKS
JOHN S. KOONCE	MICAJAH F. MATTOCKS	HENRY RHODES
JOHN WOOD	EDWARD C. DEBRULE SR	LEVI EUBANKS
JOHN STRICKLIN	JEREMIAH CANNON	JOHN BALE/BALL
AMOS L. SIMMONS	JOHN BENDER SR	JOSEPH WHITTY
JOSEPH KINCY	BENJAMIN HUGGINS	I.C.B. KOONCE
JOHN JARMAN JR	JOHN CONNOR/CANNON	THOMAS POLLOCK
RICHARD OLDFIELD	MICHAEL SHELFER	LEMUEL BUSICK
ELIJAH PARRY	WILLIAM GOODING	AMOS SHELFER
ABNER HARGET	BENJAMIN ASKEW	JOHN HEATH SR
JOHN ADAMS	JOHN POLLOCK	ISRAEL HOWARD

Jones Cty Court of Common Pleas Minutes 1839

Jurors drawn for Superior Court September Term:

JAMES FOY	F.I. BECTON	JOSEPH HAY
NATHAN FOSCUE	ELIJAH McDANIEL	SILAS M. TURNER
DANIEL HARRISON	ADAM ANDREWS	JOHN FOREST
JOHN FORDAM	JAMES G. HERRITAGE	ELIJAH SIMMONS
ABNER GREEN	CALVIN KOONCE	SIMMONS COLLINS
RIGDON HEWIT	DANIEL DICKSON	F.H. JARMAN
FRANCIS GOODING	PETER HARGET	MARTIN MIL(ERS?)
AARON WOOD	JAMES D. KINCY	NATHAN F. PARSONS
OWEN B. COX	JAMES W. HOWARD	NATHAN STANLY
ELIJAH KOONCE	BENJAMIN BROCK	LEVI JONES
FELIX KING	AMOS S. KOONCE	GEORGE WILCOX
JOHN OLIVER	LEMUEL H. SIMMONS	JAMES G. STANLY
LEWIS KOONCE	ABRAM SIMMONS	BENJAMIN KOONCE
LEWIS O. BRYAN	JOHN MALLARD	BENJAMIN COLLINS

SEPTEMBER TERM, 1839
Monday, 9 September 1839

Justices: WILLIAM HUGGINS, NATHAN FOSCUE, JAMES W. HOWARD, & LEMUEL H. SIMMONS
Shff: R.M. McDANIEL
Clerk: J.H. HAMMOND

Both juries were dispensed with this term.
Court ordered that JAMES ROBERTS should add BARTHOLOMEW MEADOWS' piece of road to the portion said ROBERTS oversees.
Mr. JOHN BENDER was exempted from jury duties due to his infirmities.
AMOS I. KOONCE was appointed constable in BEAVER CREEK District with R.M. McDANIEL, BENJAMIN HUGGINS, & JOHN B. REYNOLDS, securities.
JOHN H. HAMMOND was appointed admr of estate of LEWIS HARGET, decd; $2,000 bond; EMANUEL JARMON & NATHAN STANLY, securities.
JAMES B. SHINE, CALVIN KOONCE, JAMES HARRISON & JOHN JONES were to allot to MARY HARGET, "widow of LEWIS HARGET," her year's provisions for herself & family.
County trustee was to pay WILLIAM C. MURPHY, FRANCIS MERRITT, & DANIEL HARRISON their wages as patrols in District 7.
SAMUEL HILL was appointed guard to heirs of SILAS PARRY, decd, "by the name of GEORGE PARRY & SILAS PARRY;" $20,000 bond; ELIJAH PARRY & EMANUEL JARMON, sureties.
OWEN B. COX, WILLIAM HUGGINS & NATHAN FOSCUE were to settle accounts of HARDY PARRY, former guard of heirs of SILAS PARRY, decd, & SAMUEL HILL, present guard.
ZACHEUS BROWN was appointed constable for three months; EMANUEL JARMAN & JAMES B. SHINE, sureties.
County trustee was to pay shff $94.10 as per accounts received by clerk.
LEMUEL H. SIMMONS ordered to "sell & dispose of a certain old Negro woman (formerly belonging to F.B. AMGET, decd) to the best advantage."
BENJAMIN BROCK was to oversee rd in room of ANDREW GOODING, resigned.
WILLIAM HUGGINS, EMANUEL JARMAN & CHARLES GEROCK were to settle accounts of JOHN H. DILLAHUNT, admr of estate of SAMUEL DILLAHUNT, decd.

Jones Cty Court of Common Pleas Minutes 1839

A former order was renewed appointing JAMES W. HOWARD, OWEN B. COX & NATHAN FOSCUE to examine the Registrar's Books.

JOSEPH KINSEY, JOHN JARMAN JR. & EMORY METTS were appointed patrols in District 5.

DANIEL HARRISON, WILLIAM C. MURPHY & FRANCIS MARRITT were appointed patrols in District 7.

County trustee was to pay JOSEPH KINSEY for his services as patrol in district 5.

FURNIFOLD McDANIEL was to oversee rd from FRENCH BRANCH to TRENTON. (**Note**: According to Powell, French Branch arises in central Jones County and flows north into the Trent River.)

County trustee was to pay JOHN L. PARSONS for services as patrol in District 1.

Justices present at the appointment of superintendents of common schools:

JAMES FOY	DANIEL DICKSON	LEMUEL H. SIMMONS
SAMUEL HILL	NATHAN FOSCUE	ROSCO BARRUS
OWEN B. COX	CALVIN KOONCE	ABNER GREEN
JOHN MARRITT	JOHN H. DILLAHUNT	WILLIAM HUGGINS
JAMES W. HOWARD	F.I. BECTON	

The following were elected as superintendents of common schools:
District 1: DANIEL DICKSON
District 2: ROSCO BARRUS
District 3: SAMUEL HILL
District 4: ABNER GREEN
District 5: OWEN B. COX
District 6: F.I. BECTON
District 7: LEMUEL H. SIMMONS & JAMES MARRETT

The above named superintendents allowed $1.00 per day for their services as prescribed by law.

LEMUEL H. SIMMONS, NATHAN FOSCUE & CHARLES GEROCK were to settle accounts of ELIZABETH ANDREWS, admx <u>de bonis non</u> of PETER ANDREWS, decd, with said ELIZABETH guard to heirs of said ANDREWS.

OWEN B. COX, LEWIS WILLIAMS & HENRY RHODES were to examine the state of TUCKAHOE CREEK from its mouth to the bridge on the road & ascertain if the road hands would be able to clear it out.   (**Note**: Their report was returned immediately and from the following entry, it appears the hands could manage.)

OWEN B. COX, LEWIS WILLIAMS & HENRY RHODES were to lay off above named portion of TUCKAHOE CREEK into districts for the hands to work thereon & that OWEN B. COX & HENRY RHODES were to oversee said districts of said creek; COX above & RHODES below.

JOHN H. DILLAHUNT was to administer <u>de bonis non</u> the estate of SUSAN DILLAHUNT, decd; $500 bond; CALVIN KOONCE & OWEN B. COX, sureties.

ABNER GREEN was to admin. estate of SERENA GREEN; $500 bond; CALVIN KOONCE & OWEN B. COX, securities.

EMANUEL JARMON was to admin. estate of HARDY PARRY, decd; $20,000 bond; SAMUEL HILL & J.H. HAMMOND, securities.

EMANUEL JARMON was to admin. estate of FURNIFOLD H. JARMON; $7,500 bond; HENRY RHODES & ZACHEUS BROWN, securities.

Jones Cty Court of Common Pleas Minutes 1839

The last will & testament of MELISSA T. ROBERTSON was admitted to probate. [Note: Gwynn abstracted this will (p. 443) which was written 2 Nov 1837. Named are grandson, RIGHT ROBERTSON; daughter, HESTER ROBERTSON; daughter, REBECCAH COX; granddaughter, DOROTHY ROBERTSON, and ELISHA ROBERTSON (no relationship given). No exr was named; witnesses were PETER HARGET and I.H. HAMMOND. (This should be J.H. Hammond since he was identified as the Clerk of Courts or C.C.)]

R.M. McDANIEL renewed his bond as sheriff.

Deeds, etc. recorded by C.C. RHODES, registrar:
Mortgage from JONAS JONES to O.B. COX
FRANCIS MATTOCKS to M.F. MATTOCKS
FRANCIS MATTOCKS to M.F. MATTOCKS
ELISHA STAFFORD to M.F. MATTOCKS
JAMES MUMFORD to IVY HARRISON
RICHARD REYNOLDS to DAVID GREEN
ALLEN JONES to SILAS TURNER, deed
JOSHUAY MILTON? to DANIEL WILLIAMSON, deed
READING EUBANKS to LOTT EUBANKS, bill of sale
JAMES G. STANLY to JOHN MARRETT, deed
E. JARMON to L.E. METTS?, deed
IVY HARRISON to JOHN HARRISON, deed
AMOS KOONCE to E. JARMAN, deed
IVY HARRISON to E. JARMAN, deed
ISAAC EUBANKS & AMOS HARRISON to JOHN HARRISON, ded
JAMES MUMFORD to WILLIAM HARRISON, deed
WILEY S. MERRILS to SARAH ANN HAYWOOD, deed

S. & I. BATTLE to the use of JOSEPH W. ALLEN vs O.B. COX} debt. Plea withdrawn. Judgment final by default. Principal of $239.82. Judgment for same & costs.

WILLIAM HINES? vs I.B. REYNOLDS, A.S. KOONCE & DAVID GREEN} debt. Plea withdrawn. Judgment for $139.55 principal plus $11.45 interest and costs. Final by default.

J.E. FOSCUE vs JAMES HANCOCK & WILLIAM HANCOCK} debt. Plea withdrawn. Judgment for $436.65 principal, $13.93 interest, and costs. Final by default.

Jurors drawn for December 1839 term:

WILLIAM PRITCHET	THOMAS HARRISON	JOHN HARRISON
JOSEPH SMALL	WRIGHT STANLY	WILLIAM C. MURPHY
DANIEL YATES	JAMES G. STANLY	WILLIAM BINUM
JAMES MAIDS	RUBIN WILLIAMS	DANIEL WILLIAMSON
EDWARD M. GILBERT	ZACHEUS BROWN	EMANUEL KOONCE
AMOS HEATH	JOHN McDANIEL	JAMES MARRETT
LEWIS WILLIAMS	EMERY METTS	BARTHALOMEW MEADOWS
OWEN ADAMS	EDWARD WHARTON	DANIEL MALLARD
WILLIAM MUNDINE	FREEMAN SMITH	NATHAN B. WESTBROOK
JOHN HEATH	NEEDHAM BEASLEY	JOHN JONES

Jones Cty Court of Common Pleas Minutes 1839

DECEMBER, 1839
TRENTON, Monday, December 9th

Justices: WILLIAM HUGGINS, NATHAN FOSCUE, JAMES W. HOWARD & LEMUEL H. SIMMONS
Shff: RESDON M. McDANIEL
Clerk: JOHN H. HAMMOND
Solicitor: JAMES W. BRYAN

Jury: JAMES MARRETT, foreman
EDWARD M. GILBERT	EMERY METTS	JOHN JONES
EMANUEL KOONCE	THOMAS HARRISON	FREEMAN SMITH
WILLIAM BINUM	LEWIS WILLIAMS	NEEDHAM BEASLY
BARTHALOMEW MEADOWS	JOHN HEATH	JOHN McDANIEL
NATHAN B. WESTBROOK	WRIGHT STANLY	OWEN ADAMS
DANIEL MALLARD	JAMES MADES	

GEORGE WILCOX sworn to attend the jury; petit jury dispensed with this term.

Order renewed for OWEN B. COX, WILLIAM HUGGINS, & NATHAN FOSCUE to settle accounts of HARDY PARRY, decd, former guard to heirs of SILAS PARRY, decd, & now in the hands of EMANUEL JARMAN, admr, with SAMUEL HILL, present guard to sd heirs.

With a majority of the justices present, to wit:
CALVIN KOONCE	NATHAN FOSCUE	R. BARRUS
WILLIAM HUGGINS	L.H. SIMMONS	THOMAS GILLET
O.B. COX	JOHN H. DILLAHUNT	DANIEL DICKSON
J.W. HOWARD	SAMUEL HILL	

it was decided that jurors for March & September terms shall be dispensed with agreeable to act of assembly.

County trustee was to pay FURNIFOLD McDANIEL, patrol, agreeable to former regulation.

GEORGE WILCOX was to admr estate of NEEDHAM SHELFER, decd; $2,000 bond; JOHN S. KOONCE & SAMUEL HILL, securities.

SAMUEL HILL, PETER HARGET, DAVID GREEN, THOMAS HUGGINS & FREEMAN SMITH were to divide lands of JESSE SHELFER, decd, "between the heirs of said SHELFER."

ALFRED HATCH, agent for WM FOY, released from a double tax incurred from failure to give in the land of sd WM FOY & the same be allowed the sheriff in his settlement.

BENJAMIN ASKEW, jailor, was allowed $8.60 & the trustees allowed same in his settlement.

The report of the committee appointed to apportion the TUCKAHOE into districts and apportion hands accordingly entered into minutes.

Hands of ELIJAH KOONCE, JOSEPH SMALL, BRYAN WESTBROOK & all those hands on north side of the road & above the BLACK SWAMP shall be placed on the upper district of TRENT RIVER instead of the district below.

County trustee was to pay Clerk $40.00 for services copying lists.

RILEY JONES was relieved agreeable to 18th Sec. militia law (revised statues).

WILLIAM HUGGINS, L.H. SIMMONS & NATHAN FOSCUE were to settle estate of WILLIAM HARRISON, decd, with executor, THOMAS HARRISON.

WILLIAM W. FRANKS was to oversee rd from TRENT BRIDGE to TRENTON beginning at the dividing line of lands of said FRANKS & BURGWIN & extending to the BUCKNER HATCH mill run.

J. GOODING & R. BARRUS were licensed to retail spirituous liquors by the small measure at their store in Jones County for one year.

JOHN L. PARSONS was appointed constable for Jones County; $4,000 bond; DANIEL DICKSON & DANIEL YATES, sureties.

FRANCIS MARRETT was to be removed from patrol duty & THOMAS HARRISON was appointed in his room.

HARDY O. NEWTON was licensed to retail liquor by the small measure.

JOHN B. MOOREHOUSE was licensed to peddle goods in Jones Co. for one year.

The committee assigned to lay off TUCKAHOE CREEK into districts from its mouth to TUCKAHOE BRIDGE at the road made their report: They suggested two districts with the dividing spot at a place called the KINCY OLD BRIDGE. Dist. 1 (or lower dist.) would comprise that part of the creek from its mouth to KINCY OLD BRIDGE and it would have the following boundary lying below RATTLESNAKE BRANCH and above TUCKAHOE BRANCH on the south side of TUCKAHOE CREEK except ABNER KILLEBREW's hands and all that portion of inhabited territory lying on the west side of TRENT & JOSHUA CREEK & on the lower eastern side of JOSHUAY BRANCH and north side of TUCKAHOE CREEK. The boundaries of the lower district extend a distance of 5 miles from the said TUCKAHOE CREEK on both sides.

The upper or second district would take in all portions of the said creek above the old KINCY BRIDGE up to the road at the Bridge within the following boundaries: all the portion of territory above RATTLESNAKE BRANCH on the south and all above JOSHUA BRANCH on the north side of TUCKAHOE CREEK with the various county lines of LENOIR, DUPLIN and ONSLOW as the boundaries of the upper or 2ed district within the distance of 5 miles to the nearest point of said creek. Signed: OW. B. COX, HEN. RHODES. (Note: According to Powell, Joshua Creek rises in south east Lenoir County and flows south east into Jones County where it enters the Trent River.)

The court ordered that all hands above TUCKAHOE BRANCH & above the "prong of TRENT" and on the west side of JOSHUA CREEK be taken off their portion of the TRENT in order to be put on TUCKAHOE CREEK.

JOHN H. HAMMOND, CALVIN KOONCE, & EMANUEL JARMAN were to settle accounts of NATHAN STANLY & BENJAMIN F. STANLY, executors of JOHN STANLY, decd.

COUNCIL WOOTEN, exr of SIMMONS ISLER, allowed to sell ten of the slaves of his testator in order to pay debts.

F.I. BECTON, N.B. BEASLY & BENJAMIN KOONCE were to settle accounts of SIMMONS ISLER as guard to EDWIN B. ISLER with the present guard.

SIMON S. BECTON appointed guard to EDWIN B. ISLER; $25,000 bond; N.B. BEASLY & COUNCIL WOOTIN, sureties.

SIMON S. BECTON was appointed guard to SUSAN H. ISLER, REBECCA H. ISLER, JOHN W. ISLER; $20,000 bond; N.B. BEASLY & COUNCIL WOOTIN, sureties.

EMANUEL JARMAN was appointed guard to HANNAH PARRY, JOSEPH A. PARRY, FARNIFOLD PERRY, CALVIN PARRY, ELI H.G.F. PARRY, WILLIAM F. PARRY & ERASMUS PARRY; $75,000 bond; SAMUEL HILL, J.H. HAMMOND & JOHN H. DILLAHUNT, sureties.

WILLIAM HUGGINS, CHARLES GEROCK & J.C. BRYAN were to settle accounts of WILLIAM J. GEBRON & STARKEY McDANIEL, admrs of HUSTIN SIMMONS.

WILLIAM HUGGINS, admr of HARDY BRYAN, allowed to sell three of the slaves of his intestate for payment of debts.

JOHN H. HAMMOND, CHARLES GEROCK & NATHAN FOSCUE were to settle accounts of HARDY BRYAN, late exr of SHADRACH ERWIN, decd.

The last will & testament of SIMMONS ISLER was admitted to probate & proved by oath of N.B. BEASLEY, one of the witnesses; COUNCIL WOOTIN qualified as exr. [Note: Gwynn abstracted this will (p. 420) which was written 24 Sep 1839. Named are the three eldest children: SUSAN HERRING ISLER, REBECCA HARRISON ISLER, and JOHN WILLIAMS ISLER (all minors); wife, BARBARA ISLER; and three youngest children: GEORGE MILLER ISLER, STEPHEN WILLIAMS ISLER, and SIMMONS HARRISON ISLER. Wife, BARBARA, friend, COUNCIL WOOTEN, and JAMES W. HICKS were named exrs and JAMES G. HERRITAGE was the witness. (The three older children were by another wife since it mentions land left them by their mother.)]

The last will & testament of LAWSON M. MOORE? was admitted to probate & proved by oath of NATHAN FOSCUE, one of the witnesses; DANIEL MALLARD, qualified as exr. [This will of LAWSON MALLARD was abstracted by Gwynn (pp. 433-434) and was written 29 July 1839. Named are son, DANIEL; wife, NANCY; granddaughter, ELIZABETH L. HANCOCK; grandson, JOHN A. McDANIEL; granddaughter, ELENDER MALLARD; daughter, LANY McDANIEL. DANIEL MALLARD was named exr, and NATHAN FOSCUE and GEORGE W. HARRELL were witnesses.]

JOHN L. PARSONS gave his bond as constable with DANIEL DICKSON & DANIEL YATES, securities.

Jurors drawn for Superior Court, March Term 1840:

LOTT EUBANKS	HARDY O. CONNER	BENJAMIN F. STANLY
NATHAN FOSCUE	NATHANIEL WAPLES	JOHN YOUNG
JOHN ROUSE	WILLIAM ERWIN	JAMES MESSER
RICHARD R. FOSCUE	GEORGE S. BENDER	JOSEPH WALLIN
THOMAS BALEY	JOHN H. DILLAHUNT	THOMAS COLLINS
BENJAMIN SCOTT	JOHN B. REYNOLDS	WALTER P. ALLEN
MARTIN F. BROCK	DAVID WHARTON	JOHN TURNER
MARRETT JONES	HARDY O. NEWTON	MOSES ADAMS
BRYAN BENDER	AMOS AMYETT	JOHN MARRETT
WHITFIELD TURNER	ABNER W. KILLEBREW	JAMES ADAMS
SAMUEL HILL	JAMES McDANIEL	JOHN MESSER
JOHN HAGINS	JOHN E. FOSCUE	SIMON S. BECTON

Deeds & bills of sale, etc., recorded by C.C. RHODES, registrar:
JEREMIAH HEATH & H.O. NEWTON to SCOTT (deed)
(Note: Scott was the only name given.)
EMANUEL JARMON, agent of J.H. BECTON to N.B. BEASLEY
JOHN BENDER to BRYAN BENDER (deed)
DANIEL MALLARD to NATHAN FOSCUE (deed)
JOHN BENDER to JOHN K. BENDER (deed)
JAMES B. SHINE to JOHN S. KOONCE (deed)
JONAS JONES to JONAS JONES SR (bill of sale)
LINNIE B. HUMPHREY to JOHN H. DILLAHUNT (bill of sale)
JOHN BENDER to GEORGE S. BENDER (deed)
ELIJAH SIMMONS to THOMAS HALE (deed)
WILLIAM B.F. FORT to N.B. BEASLEY (deed)

SPECIAL COURT
Clerk's Office
Trenton, 2 Jan 1840

Justices: NATHAN FOSCUE, JAMES C. BRYAN, & CHARLES GEROCK

SIMON S. BECTON was appointed special admr of the estate of JOHN L. STANLY, decd; $20,000 (or $10,000?) bond; WILLIAM HUGGINS & CALVIN KOONCE, securities. BECTON was given leave to sell perishable property of estate.
Signed: JAS C. BRYAN, J.P.; NATHAN FOSCUE, J.P.; CHS. GEROCK, J.P.

MARCH TERM, 1840
TRENTON, Monday 9 Mar 1840

Justices: WILLIAM HUGGINS, NATHAN FOSCUE, JAMES W. HOWARD, & LEMUEL H. SIMMONS
Shff: RISDON M. McDANIEL
Clerk: JOHN H. HAMMON
Solicitor: JAMES W. BRYAN

The jury was dispensed with this term.

BIGTON (probably RIGDEN) HEWIT was released from the double tax penalty for not handing in his taxables as required by law for 1839 on condition that he make oath before the clerk of his amount of taxables for said year.
County Trustee was to pay JOHN JARMON $12.00 for patrol service.
A.S. KOONCE was appointed overseer of the River in place of RIGHT STANLY from BUCK BRANCH to the mouth of LITTLE CHINQUIPEN.
JOHN FORDHAM was to be refunded one half the tax paid by him in 1838 since it was a double tax.
FURNIFOLD McDANIEL, BAUDE (probably BAZEL) McDANIEL & HARDY O. CONNER were to be patrols for District 3 for one year.
A tax of ten cents on each taxable pole of the county and of four cents on the $100 worth of lands including town property is to be levied for support of the common schools.
A Negro man named VIRGIL, the property of FREDERICK I. BECTON, is disabled according to oath of said BECTON, and was, therefore, cleared from working on the roads.
A Negro man named JOHN, the property of JAMES W. HOWARD, is disabled according to oath of said HOWARD, and was, therefore, released from taxes.
O.B. COX was to be paid $5.00 for his services in making the report for the School Committee.
DAVID GREEN was to oversee rd from fork near TRENTON up the KINSTON ROAD to WARD's HILL then down the NEWBERN ROAD crossing the run of MUSSELLSHELL BRANCH to the Division between that and the next District.
COUNCIL GOODING was to oversee rd from JACOB's BRANCH up to the county line near BLOUNT COLEMAN's in place of NATHAN STANLY, resigned.
F.I. BECTON was to oversee rd from JAMES REYNOLDS, decd, up to the fork formerly JOHN WEIER's? in place of AMOS HEATH, resigned.
The order of last court to divide lands of JESSE SHELFER, decd, was renewed with report due next term.

NEEDHAM SAMPSON, a "coloured" boy four years old, was bound to DANIEL YATES.

STEPHEN WILCOX was to oversee a portion of TRENT RIVER in place of FREEMAN SMITH.

J.H. HAMMOND, clerk, was allowed $3.25 for postage & paper.

JAMES MESSER was cleared from certain duties "as per edict? of the legislature."

F.I. BECTON, N.B. BEASLEY, & BENJAMIN KOONCE were to allot off to the widow of JOHN STANLY, decd, her year's provisions.

LEMUEL H. SIMMONS, admr of MARGARET FOY, decd, allowed to sell one of the slaves belonging to the intestate to pay debts of the estate.

COUNCIL WOOTIN, exr of SIMMONS ISLER, decd, allowed to sell 10 other Negros in addition to those already sold in order to settle the estate.

All hands above BLACK SWAMP & on the north side of the main road leading from the QUAKER MEETING HOUSE to CHINQUIPEN CHAPEL were taken off that portion of TRENT RIVER in District 6 and placed in District 7.

Jurors drawn for June Term, 1840:

DAVID GREEN	NATHANIEL WAPLES	JOHN K. BENDER
THOMAS COLLINS	IGNATIOUS W. BROCK	RICHARD OLDFIELD
JONAS WILLIAMS	JOHN JARMAN, JR	WILLIAM W. FRANK
JOHN ADAMS	LEWIS O. BRYAN	MILLINTON MEADOWS
J.C.B. KOONCE	SIMON S. BECTON	RIGDON HEWIT
NATHAN F. PARSONS	WRIGHT STANLY	BARTHOLOMEW MEADOWS
WILLIAM ERWIN	JAMES G. STANLY	WALTER P. ALLEN
BRYAN BENDER	PETER HARGET	ELIJAH McDANIEL
JOHN BALL	ADAMS ANDREWS	COUNCIL GOODING
EDWARD M. GILBERT	THOMAS BAILEY	JOHN S. KOONCE
SILAS M. TURNER	AARON WOOD	BENJAMIN BROCK
ELIJAH KOONCE	JOHN HAGAINE	JOHN TURNER

Deeds, etc., recordeds by C.C. RHODES, registrar:
WILLIAM GOODING to GEORGE S. DEBRULE (deed)
DAVID W.G. DUDLY to GEORGE DEBRULE (deed)
H.B. MITCHELL to S.H. SIMMONS (bill of sale)
NATHANIEL WAPLES to ROSCOE BARRUS (bill of sale)
"A release from his heirs to JOHN BENDER"
JOHN MALLARD to WILLIAM HUGGINS (deed)
HENRY RHODES to LEWIS KINCY (bill of sale)
RICHARD W. HATCH to WILLIAM HUGGINS (deed)
ADAM ANDREWS to JOSEPH WHITTY (deed)
E.R. STANLY to RICHRD REYNOLDS (bill of sale)
JOSEPH WHITTY to ADAM ANDREWS (deed)
J.J. JARMAN to JOHN JARMON (bill of slae)
JOHN WESTBROOK to JOHN WESTBROOK (?) (deed)
JAMES NUNCE? to WILLIAM GOODING (bill of sale)
JOHN WESTBROOK to HARMON WESTBROOK (deed)
EDMOND WHARTON to M.F. MATTUCKS (deed)
JAMES HANCOCK to JACOB FIELDS (deed)
ENOCK FOY to JOSEPH FOY (deed)
WILLIAM HUGGINS, attor for MORRIS, to JOHN McDANIEL
MICAJAH PETTWAY to J.H. HAMMOND (deed)

JOHN FONVIELLE to EMORY METTS (deed)
GEORGE S. DEBRULE to WILLIAM GOODING Ideed)
JAMES/JONAS JONES to OW B. COX & others (mortgage)

SPECIAL COURT
TRENTON, 4 April 1840

Justices: NATHAN FOSCUE, JAMES C. BRYAN, & SAMUEL HILL

ELIZABETH SHEPHARD appointed special admr of the estate of HENRY SHEPHERD, decd; $500 bond; LEWIS KOONCE, security. She was allowed to sell the perishable property of the estate.
Signed: NATHAN FOSCUE, J.P.; S. HILL, J.P.; JAS C. BRYAN, J.P.

Note: The extensive school committee report, which follows, appeared to be part of the March Term.

Report of the committee appointed by the Jones County Court of Common Pleas & Quarter Sessions, in compliance with the Act of Assembly called the Common School Law, to apportion Jones County into school districts, taking into consideration the local situation of roads "covered as it is with pocosin up each side of the RIVER TRENT running immediately through the county and the various tributary streams which let into said River & so obstructed in many places that this situation renders it impossible for children to pass in safety owing to the peculiar situation of the county your superintendents have had a grate deal of difficulty in laying of the districts...and wile much be to the inconvenience of some of the citizens of said county yet your superintendents have been compelled to make more districts than would be to the lay of the inhabited part of the county into districts six miles square you committee have been compelled to extend the length much greater than the width owing to the situation having therefore taken these matters into consideration" your committee has done its best beginning at WHITE OAK & extending from Number one to 16 bounded in the manner & form herein given:

District 1: Begins at the mouth of TONEYS? BRANCH where it empties into WHITE OAK RIVER and running up said branch to the POCOSIN then to CARTERET COUNTY line at HUNTERS CREEK and with the same to WHITE OAK RIVER. Then up the River to the first station. The center of District 1 is to be between EDWARD JONES'mill and PITCH HOLE BRANCH.

District 2: Begins at the mouth of TANEY BRANCH where it empties into WHITE OAK RIVER at the upper line of District 1. Runs with said Branch and line of District 1 to the POCOSIN. Up the POCOSIN and opposite L. EUBANKS' then southwesterly to WHITE OAK RIVER at LEVI EUBANKS' landing, then down said river to the mouth of TANSY'S BRANCH. (**Note:** Powell offers no help as to the name of the branch. He has no Toney's, Taney, or Tansy's Branch.)

District 3: Commences at LEVI EUBANKS' landing on WHITE OAK RIVER at the upper line of District 2 and runs with the said line northeasterly to the POCOSIN. Up the POCOSIN & with its various meanderings to the head of WHITE OAK RIVER. The center of the district is on the branch near JOHN L. PARSONS.

Jones Cty Court of Common Pleas Minutes 1840

District 4: Lies below RACCOON BRANCH on the south side of the TRENT RIVER....to the CRAVEN CO. line commencing at the mouth of RACCOON BRANCH at TRENT RIVER and running with the river to the CRAVEN COUNTY line. Then with said line to the POCOSIN; then with the POCOSIN to the head of RACCOON BRANCH. Then with said branch to TRENT RIVER. The center of the district is near ISLAND CREEK. (**Note**: According to Powell, Island Creek arises in eastern Jones County and flows north into Trent River. It appeared on the Moseley map of 1733 which also showed Murfy's Ferry across the Trent River near the mouth of Island Creek.)

District 5: Lies above District 4 and commences at the mouth of RACCOON BRANCH at the TRENT RIVER at the corner of District 4. It extends up TRENT RIVER opposite the mile post below WILLIAM FRANKS. Then in a line with said mile post in a south-westerly direction to HOWARD's POCOSIN. Then with said pocosin to the head of MILL CREEK and with the MILL CREEK pocosin to the head of RACCOON BRANCH. Then down said Branch to TRENT RIVER. The center was supposed to be at the fork of the road at MILL CREEK "where the school house now stands."

District 6: Lies between the mile post near FURNIFOLD McDANIEL's down to the mile post below WILLIAM FRANKS. Commences at the River opposite the mile post below FRANKS at upper part of District 5 and extends up TRENT RIVER opposite mile post near F. McDANIEL's. Then with and in a direction of said mile post near south west corner to the POCOSIN. Then with the POCOSIN so as to include JAMES HOWARD's opposite the mile post below FRANKS to the intersection with line of District 5. The center was supposed to be at the fork of the road leading to JOSEPH WHITTY's.

District 7: To extend from TRENTON (which is the center) up the FAYETTEVILLE ROAD to the Branch below JOHN DILLAHUNT's and down the WHITE OAK ROAD to the mile post at FURNIFOLD McDANIEL's gate and down the NEWBERN RD to the mile post below JOHN FROST and up the BEAVER CREEK ROAD to the RESOLUTION BRANCH. District 7 commences at the mouth of RESOLUTION BRANCH, runs up the branch to the POCOSIN, then with the POCOSIN opposite the mile post below JOHN FROST. Then in a south westerly direction to TRENT RIVER at or near WILLIAM HUGGINS' landing. Then down river to District 6's upper line southwesterly to the WHITE OAK POCOSIN. Then with the same to the head of PALACO? BRANCH below JOHN DILLAHUNT's. Then with the said branch to TRENT RIVER and down said river to the mouth RESOLUTION.

District 8: Lies below TRENTON on the north side of TRENT RIVER. It begins at the mile post below NATHANIEL WAPLES' and runs south westerly to the TRENT RIVER. Then down river to the mouth of the DEEP GULLY. Then with the DEEP GULLY and the county lines of CRAVEN & JONES up said gully so as to include all the inhabitants about the head of BACHELOR CREEK that belong to Jones County opposite the beginning and then in a southwest course to the beginning. The school house will be placed in the center on TRENT ROAD at the corner of the old field near HARDY O. NEWTON's. (**Note**: Bachelor Creek rises in GREAT DOVER SWAMP in north east Jones County and flows north east into central Craven County according to Powell. It was named for EDWARD BATCHELOR and appears as Batchellors Creek on the 1733 Moseley map.)

Jones Cty Court of Common Pleas Minutes 1840

District 9: Lies on the north side of TRENT RIVER. It begins at a mile post just below JOHN FROST and extends in a southwesterly direction to the TRENT RIVER and in a northeasterly direction from the said mile post to the POCOSIN and extends down the main road to the mile post below N. WAPLES to the upper line of District 8 to run with said line in a southwesterly direction to the TRENT RIVER and in a northeasterly direction to the POCOSIN. The river on the south and the pocosin on the north form the two sides of said district. The school house will remain where it is now.

District 10: Lies above TRENTON on both sides of TRENT RIVER between the PALACE? BRANCH and CYPRESS CREEK. It begins at the mouth of the PALACE BRANCH and runs up TRENT RIVER to the mouth of the CHAPEL BRANCH in the north side of TRENT. Then with the said CHAPEL BRANCH to the main road. Then with the main road to LITTLE CHINQUIPIN BRIDGE and including the residence of AARON WOOD. Then in a southerly direction to TRENT RIVER opposite the mouth of CYPRESS CREEK. Then with CYPRESS CREEK to the POCOSIN and then with the POCOSIN to the head of the PALAIC? BRANCH and down said Branch to the River. The center of the district is just below CALVIN KOONCE's. (**Note:** Powell has no Chapel Branch in Jones County and was not helpful in determining the name of the Branch which I read variously as Palace, Palaic, Palaco.)

District 11: Extends from CYPRESS CREEK up to TUCKAHOE BRANCH. Commences at the mouth of CYPRESS CREEK and extends up the same to the POCOSIN so as to include the inhabited territory up to the head of the TUCKAHOE BRANCH. Then down same to TRENT RIVER. Then a direct line to the mouth of CYPRESS CREEK to include the inhabitants on the south side of TRENT. The center of district is near IGNATIUS W. BROCK's.

District 12: Extends from TUCKAHOE BRANCH up to PATRICK BRANCH above MERRITT JONES. Commences at mouth of TUCKAHOE BRANCH at TRENT RIVER and runs up to the mouth of TUCKAHOE CREEK. Then up said Creek to the mouth of JOSHUA BRANCH. Then with said branch to LENOIR COUNTY line. Then with said line to where it strikes the GREAT BRANCH. Then southerly to the head of the long branch that "lites into OWEN B. COX's mill pond." Then with said branch to the mill pond and up said mill pond to the mouth of PATRICK BRANCH on the south side of the pond and with said branch and in a SE course to the ONSLOW COUNTY line. Then with said county line and the POCOSIN to the head of TUCKAHOE BRANCH. Then down the same to the start. Center nearly opposite "OWEN B. COX's plantation" on the road. (**Note:** Powell does not list a Patrick Branch or a Great Branch in Jones County.)

District 13: Extends from District 12 to the upper end of the county. Commences at the mouth of PATRICK BRANCH and runs up the same with District 12 line to ONSLOW COUNTY line and then with various county lines of ONSLOW, DUPLIN, and LENOIR round to the GREAT BRANCH where it intersects with the line of District 12. Then with said district line to the start. The school house would be located between the BEAVER DAM BRANCH and where HILERY BISHOP now lives.

District 14: Starts at the mouth of JOSHUA BRANCH and extends up same running with the line of District 13 to LENOIR COUNTY line. Then with said county line to where it intersects with District 15. Then with said district

line to the head of the LITTLE CHINQUIPEN. Then with same to road at the
bridge to District 10. Then with said District 10 line in a southerly course
to opposite the mouth of the CYPRESS CREEK to District 11. Then with said
District 11 line up TRENT RIVER opposite the mouth of TUCKAHOE BRANCH. Then
up TRENT RIVER and TUCKAHOE CREEK to the mouth of JOSHUA BRANCH. The school
house would be located as near the county line as possible "suppose at QUAKER
MEETING HOUSE."

District 15: Begins at District 16 and runs with said line so as to
include the WILLIAM ISLER and JOHN STANLY plantations to the head of the
LITTLE CHINQUIPEN. Then with the same down to the bridge at the main road.
Then with the line of District 10 to CHAPEL BRANCH. Then with the said branch
to the TRENT RIVER. Then down the river to the mouth of the
RESOLUTION at District 7 TRENTON. Then up river to the POCOSIN. Then with
the POCOSIN to the start. The school house would be located in the center.

District 16: Begins at the POCOSIN opposite the WILLIAM ISLER
plantation and runs in said POCOSIN to the CRAVEN and LENOIR COUNTY line.
Then with said county line round opposite COLEMAN's to the main road. Then
with the LENOIR COUNTY line to the west of WILLIAM GOODING. Then a direct
course to the head of LITTLE CHINQUIPEN. Then a direct line to start. The
school house would be located in the center.

The superintendents in accordance with the said act of assembly have
appointed school committees in each district; viz:
- District 1:   THOMAS GELLIT, JAMES ROBERTS, & BARTHOLOMEW MEADOWS
- District 2:   RIGDON HEWIT, MICAJAH F. MATTOCKS, & JOHN YOUNG
- District 3:   NATHAN F. PARSONS, WILLIAM BINUM, & THOMAS PERSON/PARSON?
- District 4:   WALTER P. ALLEN, DANIEL WILLIAMSON, & WILLIAM PRITCH(ERD?)
- District 5:   ENOCK FOY, GEORGE S. BENDER, & JAMES FOY
- District 6:   JOSEPH WHITTY, WM W. FRANK, & JOHN OLIVER
- District 7:   WILLIAM HUGGINS, DR. FRANCIS DUVAL, & CHARLES GEROCK
- District 8:   BENJAMIN SCOTT, OWEN ADAMS, & GEORGE DEBRULE
- District 9:   NATHAN FOSCUE, RISDEN M. McDANIEL, & NATHANIEL WAPLES
- District 10: JOHN H. HAMMOND, CALVIN KOONCE, & JOHN JONES
- District 11: JAMES B. SHINE, IGNATIOUS W. BROCK, & JOHN S. KOONCE
- District 12: HENRY RHODES, ISAAC BROWN, & JONAS WILLIAMS
- District 13: JOHN HEATH, WHITFIELD TURNER & JONAS JONES
- District 14: JOSEPH KINSEY, JOSEPH SMALL & WILLIAM BON(D?)
- District 15: SIMON BECTON, AMOS RHEIM & NEEDHAM (B...?) (**Note:** This could be BRYAN.)
- District 16: DAVID GREEN, BENJAMIN KOONCE & PETER HARGET

The above report was submitted to the court 9 March 1840 and signed: OWEN B.
COX, chairman, LEMUEL H. SIMMONS, F. ISLER BECTON, JAMES MARRITS, R. BARRUS,
S. HILL.

SPECIAL COURT
Clerk's Office in Trenton
13 June 1840
Justices: (**Note:** This was left blank.)
JOHN H. HAMMOND was appointed special admr on the estate (blank); $1,000

bond with (blank) securities. HAMMOND may sell perishable property of decd. (**Note**: It appears that HAMMOND might have come to the clerk who made out a "standard form.")

JUNE TERM, 1840
TRENTON

Justices: WILLIAM HUGGINS, NATHAN FOSCUE, JAMES W. HOWARD & LEMUEL H. SIMMONS
Shff: R.M. McDANIEL
Clerk: J.H. HAMMOND
Solicitor: J.W. BRYAN

Jurors for the state:

THOMAS BALEY	JOHN JARMAN JR	JOHN ADAMS
BENJAMIN BROCK	WILLIAM ERWIN	RICHARD OLDFIELD
WILLIAM W. FRANKS	JOHN HAGAINS	ELIJAH McDANIEL
ELIJAH KOONCE	SIMON S. BECTON	ADAM ANDREWS
JONAS WILLIAMS	SILAS M. TURNER	DAVID GREEN
MILETON MEADOWS	AARON WOOD	BARTHALOMEW MEADOWS

Petit Jurors:

EDWARD M. GILBERT	BRYAN BENDER	RIGHT STANLY
WALTER P. ALLEN	RIGDON HEWIT	COUNCIL GOODING
IGNATIOUS W. BROCK	NATHAN F. PARSONS	THOMAS COLLINS
JOHN K. BENDER	PETER HARGET	JOHN S. KOONCE

MICAJAH F. MATTICKS, SIMEON MEADOWS & DANIEL DICKSON were to settle the accounts of THOMAS COLLINS, admr of HARDY COLLINS, decd.

The same men were to divide the Negroes of the estate of HARDY COLLINS, decd, among the heirs of the decd.

ELIZABETH SHEPARD was to admin. estate of HENRY SHEPARD, decd; $500 bond; LEWIS KOONCE, security.

JAMES McDANIEL, JOHN OLIVER, & THOMAS POLLOCK were to allot to ELIZABETH SHEPARD one yr's provisions.

ABNER GREEN & CALVIN KOONCE were to take the private examination of NARCISSA NORRIS, wife of GRAY NORRIS, & SARAH VENTERS, wife of VOLNEY VENTERS. (**Note**: This was probably for property the husbands were selling.)

The following taxes were levied in order to defray county expences for the present year: six cents per $100 land evaluation and twenty cents per taxable poll.

WILLIAM STANLY, JOHN B. REYNOLDS & FREEMAN SMITH were appointed patrols in District 6 for one year.

SAMUEL HILL, CHARLES GEROCK, & LEMUEL H. SIMMONS were to settle the accounts of NATHAN FOSCUE & WILLIAM HUGGINS, commissioners for building the poor house.

ELIJAH SIMMONS, JR, JOHN HALL, & GEORGE S. BENDER were appointed patrols for District 2 for one year.

The following J.P.s were to take the list of taxable property for the present year:
District 1: THOMAS GILLET, Esq.

Jones Cty Court of Common Pleas Minutes 1840

District 2: JAMES W. HOWARD
District 3: JAMES C. BRYAN
District 4: CALVIN KOONCE
District 5: SAMUEL HILL
District 6: FREDERICK I. BECTON
District 7: NATHAN FOSCUE

The following persons were appointed to hold the polls for an election for members to the legislature and sheriff for the next two years:
District 1: DANIEL DICKSON, Esq. & MICAJAH F. MATTICKS
District 2: ROSCO BARRUS, Esq., DANIEL WILLIAMS & JOSEPH WHITTY
District 3: LEMUEL H. SIMMONS, SAMUEL HILL, & J.C. BRYAN
District 4: CALVIN KOONCE, JAMES B. SHINE & JOHN JONES
District 5: JOHN H. DILLAHUNT, HENRY RHODES & LEWIS WILLIAMS
District 6: ABNER GREEN, Esq., PETER HARGET & AMOS (HINSH? but probably HEATH)
(**Note**: No District 7 was given.)

WILLIAM HINDS was given license to retail spirituous liquors by small measure.

EMANUEL JARMAN was continued as County Trustee for one year.

N. FOSCUE, W. HUGGINS, & J.H. HAMMOND were to settle accounts of the County Trustee and report next court.

County Trustee to pay GEORGE WILCOX $6.10 for attending court and cost of state warrent.

JOHN H. HAMMOND was appointed admr of estate of SARAH C. BRYAN, decd; $10,000 bond; SAMUEL HILL & EMANUEL JARMAN, securities.

JONAS WILLIAMS, LEWIS JONES, & JOHN A. COX were appointed patrols in District 5.

NATHAN FOSCUE was appointed to have necessary repairs made to this court house and draw on the county trustee for the money.

JOHN MESSER was to oversee the public road from BEAVER DAM to HARDY O. NEWTON's - the fork of said road in place of AMOS S. SIMMONS, resigned.

JOHN HEATH was to admin. estate of MATILDA RANDEL/RENDALE; $1,000 bond; R.M. McDANIEL & JOHN S. KOONCE, securities.

JOHN LOFTIN vs FRANCIS GOODING & COUNCIL GOODING (**Note**: There was no further information.)

NATHAN FOSCUE vs BENJAMIN HUGGINS & ALFRED WHITTY} Jury found in favor of pltff: $168.00 & $4.38 interest. Judgment for same & costs.

WILLIAM I. GIBSON vs JAMES FOY & JAMES W. HOWARD} Jury found for pltff. Debt was $900.00 with $124.50 interest. Judgment for same & costs.

GEORGE S. BENDER vs JAMES FOY & ROSCO BARRUS} Jury found for pltff. Debt of $221.36 & $18.82 interest. Judgment for same and costs.

SIMON S. KOONCE to use of JOHN S. KOONCE vs BENJAMIN HUGGINS & WILLIAM HUGGINS} Jury found for pltff. Debt of $256.00 & $24.16 interest. Judgment for same and costs.

NATHAN STANLY & BENJ F. STANLY vs BENJ HUGGINS & OWEN B. COX & ADAM ANDREWS} Jury found for pltff. Debt of $110.00 with $13.00 interest. Judgment for same & costs.

BENJAMIN McDANIEL to use of ELIJAH McDANIEL vs FRANCIS DUVAL & WILLIAM HUGGINS} Jury found for pltff. Debt of $230.00 with $17.86 interest.

Judgment for same & costs.

EZEKIEL JONES vs FRANCIS DUVAL} Jury found for pltff. Debt of $150.00 and interest of $12.75. Judgment for same and costs.

G.W. HOWARD to the use of EW(G?) W. MONTFORD vs FRANCIS DUVAL} Jury found for pltff. Debt of $17.31. Judgment for same & costs.

JACOB GOODING vs JOHN B. REYNOLDS & AMOS KOONCE} Jury found for pltff. Debt of $200.79 with $3.81 interest. Judgment for same & costs.

JACOB GOODING vs JOHN B. REYNOLDS} Jury found for pltff. Debt of $262.36 with $20.98 interest. Judgment for same & costs.

ELIJAH PARRY & others to the court} Petition for partition of land. Report returned & confirmed & ordered to be registered. "Costs to be paid equally by E. PARRY & the heirs of HARDY PARRY."

LEVIN B. LANE vs WILLIAM HUGGINS, admr of HARDY BRYAN} Jury found for pltff & assessed damages at $691.10 "of which $670.98 & they further find that there is a payment by the amt of $205.83 on the ____ day of June 1839 & that the balance is the amt of this judgment." Judgment for same & costs. (**Note:** The underline indicates a blank where, apparently, the clerk meant to fill it in later.)

Freeholders drawn as jurors for Superior Court September Term, 1840:

BENJAMIN F. STANLY	DAVID WHARTON	ASA EUBANKS
JOHN HARRISON	ISRAEL HOWARD	EMANUEL KOONCE
JOHN MALLARD	JOHN MESSER	JAMES HARRISON
JOSEPH WHITTY	HARDY O. NEWTON	LEVY EUBANKS
JOHN ROUSE	ABRAM SIMMONS	ZACHEUS BROWN
DANIEL YATES	THOMAS HUGGINS	JAMES ADAMS
JAMES G. HERRITAGE	MERRITT JONES	RICHARD R. FOSCUE
JOHN CANNON	LEWIS WILLIAMS	JOHN FROST
SIMMONS COLLINS	NATHAN B. WESTBROOK	RABIN WILLIAMS
THOMAS McDANIEL	MICAJAH F. MATTOCKS	NATHAN STANLY
ENOCH FOY	AMOS HEATH	WILLIAM GOODING
AMOS L. SIMMONS	JOHN MARRITT	WILLIAM C. MURPHY

Deeds & bills of sale registered by C.C. RHODES, Registrar:
WILLIAM POLLOCK to JONAS WILLIAMS (bill of sale)
LEMUEL H. SIMMONS to FREDERICK FOSCUE (deed)
JAMES SMITH to FREDERICK FOSCUE (deed)
WILLIAM C. MURPHY to JOHN MERRITT (deed)
EDWARD C. DEBRULE to GEORGE S. DEBRULE (deed)
IGNATIOUS W. BROCK & wife to ISAAC BROWN
JONAS WILLIAMS to POLINA ANN JONES (bill of sale)
WILLIAM D. COBB to FREDRICK I. BECTON (deed)
F.I. BECTON to AMOS HEATH (deed)
JOHN MARRETT to JAMES MARRETT (deed)
ABNER W. KILLEBREW & J.B. SHINE to EMANUEL JARMON (deed)

JOHN HEATH & wife & others to the court} Petition to sell slaves. Court determined that the sale was necessary to effect a division; therefore, sale was to occur the 4th Saturday of July, next, at public auction at JAMES STANLY's in Jones County.

AMOS AMYET & others} Petition for partition of lands. Since the defendant in this case, FANNY POLLOCK, was not an inhabitant of the state, the court ordered the publication of the plea for the defendant to appear and plead answer or demur on this petition for six wks in the Newbern *Spectator*.

SPECIAL COURT
Clerk's Office, Trenton
11 August 1840

Justices: CHARLES GEROCK, JAMES C. BRYAN & JOHN MARRITT, esquires

EMANUEL JARMAN was appointed special admr of the estate of SAMUEL B. HEATH; $300 bond; J.H. HAMMOND & CHARLES GEROCK, securities. JARMAN allowed to sell the perishable property of the decd & the slaves of same at public auction.
Signed: CHS GEROCK, J.P., JAS C. BRYAN, J.P., JOHN MARRETT, J.P.

SEPTEMBER TERM
Monday, 14 September 1840
Trenton

Justices: WILLIAM HUGGINS, NATHAN FOSCUE, JAMES W. HOWARD, & LEMUEL H. SIMMONS
Sheriff: R.M. McDANIEL
Clerk: J.H. HAMMOND
Solicitor: W.H. WASHINGTON

Both juries were dispensed with for this term.

THOMAS HARRISON, DANIEL HARRISON, & JAMES HARRIET were appointed patrols in District 7 for one year.
NEEDHAM SMALL was appointed overseer of road extending from HARRISON BRIDGE to "what is called" WILLIAM RHEM's Road in place of JOHN B. REYNOLDS, resigned.
JAMES W. HOWARD was granted letters of admin. on the estate of JULIA N. HOWARD. Will attached. $5,000 bond; WILLIAM HUGGINS & SAMUEL HILL, securities. [Note: Her will is abstracted in Gwynn, p. 420. It was written 17 Jun 1834. Named are her son, GEORGE W. HOWARD; granddaughter, FRANCES HOWARD, "child of my son, GEORGE;" son, JAMES W. HOWARD; daughter, LOUISA MONTFORD; and grandson, WILLIAM HENRY MONTFORD. JAMES W. HOWARD was named admr, and the witnesses were JAMES G. STANLY and H. STANLY.]
ROSCO BARRUS was appointed commissioner to have TRENT BRIDGE put into proper order with county funds.
FARNIFOLD GOODING was to oversee road in place of BENJAMIN BROCK, resigned.
The hands of ELIJAH SIMMONS were subject to work on the road from HATCH's Mill to the Branch on the line between the lands of W.W. FRANK & JOHN DEVEREUIX, formerly POLLOCK's lands.
The hands of JOHN DEVERIUX, under the charge of THOMAS HALL on MILL CREEK, were subject to work the road leading from the Cross Roads on WHITE OAK

Jones Cty Court of Common Pleas Minutes 1840

to POLLACKSVILLE

An order of last court appointing SAMUEL HILL, CHARLES GEROCK, & LEMUEL H. SIMMONS to audit the accounts of NATHAN FOSCUE & WILLIAM HUGGINS as commissioners to build the Poor House was renewed and was to be returned at the next court.

CALVIN KOONCE was to oversee the road from the INDIAN GRAVE OLDFIELD up to JACKS CABBIN BRANCH & from the fork to the FREE BRIDGE in place of JOHN H. DILLAHUNT, resigned.

CHARLES GEROCK, ABNER GREEN, NATHAN STANLEY, JOHN H. DILLAHUNT & LEMUEL BUSICK were to divide and allot off to HANNAH PARRY her portion of the Negroes belonging to the estate of HARDY PARRY, decd.

EMANUEL JARMAN was to admr estate of SAMUEL B. HEATH, decd; $1,000 bond; JOHN H. HAMMOND & THOMAS C. PARSONS, securities. [Note: EMANUEL JARMAN served in the North Carolina House of Commons 1820-1824 (Wheeler). His will is abstracted in Gwynn, p. 421-422. It was written 5 Feb 1841 and probated March term, 1843. He named his wife, SARAH; daughter, SALOME; his brother, AMOS JARMAN; son, JOHN JARMAN; three sons of his deceased son, F.H. JARMAN; daughter, ELIZABETH JARMAN; son-in-law, JOB L. JARMAN. JOHN JARMAN was exr. and the witnesses were WILLIAM HUGGINS and NATHAN FOSCUE.]

CALVIN KOONCE, JOHN S. KOONCE, HENRY RHODES, & IGNATIOUS W. BROCK were to allot off to LOVEY HEATH, "widow of SAMUEL B. HEATH," decd, her year's provisions.

CHARLES GEROCK, JAMES C. BRYAN & NATHAN FOSCUE were to settle the accounts of LEMUEL H. SIMMONS, admr of the estate of FRANCIS B. AMYET, decd.

JOHN JONES, CALVIN KOONCE & EMANUEL JARMAN were to allot off and divide the Negroes belonging to the estate of SARAH C. BRYAN, decd, "among the heirs."

GEORGE W. HOWARD was appointed guardian to "his daughter, FRANCES;" $1,000 bond; JACOB GOODING & JOSEPH WHITTY, securities.

JOHN YOUNG, JAMES FOY & JOHN E. FOSCUE were to settle accounts of OWEN ADAMS, guardian of the heirs of KADER KNIGHT, JR., decd.

WILLIAM HUGGINS, admr of HARDY BRYAN, was authorized to sell six Negroes of the estate of said BRYAN to enable him to settle debts of the estate.

NATHANIEL WAPLES, L.H. SIMMONS, & NATHAN FOSCUE were to run the line between CRAVEN COUNTY & Jones County from the head of DEEP GULLY westwardly and to appoint a surveyor for same.

Persons appointed to hold the polls for election of President & Vice President of the United States:
District 1: DANIEL DICKSON, J.P., MICAJAH F. MATTOCKS, N.F. B... (The rest of the name was lost in the binding.)
District 2: R. BARRUS, J.P., WILLIAM W. FRANK, & JOHN BENDER, JR.
District 3: Shff JAMES C. BRYAN & JOHN H. DILLAHUNT
District 4: CALVIN KOONCE, J.P., JOHN JONES, & JAMES B. SHINE
District 5: OWEN B. COX, J.P., HENRY RHODES & JOSEPH KINCEY
District 6: FRED. I. BECTON, SIMON S. BECTON, & DAVID GREEN

GEORGE SIMMONS, STEWART SCOTT & READING SCOTT were appointed patrols in District 1 for one year.

GEORGE SIMMONS was allowed $6.00 for expenses & labor involved in bringing to jail JOHN M. SUGGS & he was to pay each of his guards $1.25.

JOHN H. HAMMOND, clerk, was allowed $40.00 for extra services up to June 1840 plus $1.00 postage for county business.

ELISHA ROBERTSON, musician, was cleared from public duties.

The jailor of Jones County was to receive $.30 per day for the board of prisoners until further ordered.

I.W. BROCK & WILLIAM BROWN, executors of ISAAC BROWN, decd, allowed to sell perishable property of said decd.

The last will & testament of JULIA N. HOWARD was proved in open court by oath of JAMES G. STANLY & ordered recorded; JAMES W. HOWARD was granted letters of admin. with the will annexed. [Gwynn abstracted this will (p. 420), which was written 17 Jun 1834. She named her son, GEORGE W. HOWARD and his daughter, FRANCES HOWARD; son, JAMES W. HOWARD, and daughter, LOUISA MONTFORD and grandson, WILLIAM HENRY MONTFORD. JAMES W. HOWARD was named administrator, and the witnesses were JAMES G. STANLY and H. STANLY.]

The last will and testament of ISAAC BROWN was proved in open court by the oath of HENRY RHODES, one of the subscribing witnesses, & ordered to be recorded; I.W. BROCK & WILLIAM BROWN, qualified as executors. [Gwynn abstracted this will (pp. 404-405). It was written 31 Jul 1840. Although his wife is mentioned but not named, he names his daughters, LEAH, ORPAH, POLLY and NANCY BROWN and LEVICY ISAAC, and sons ZACHEUS, WILLIAM, ISAAC and CYRUS. Exrs were son, WILLIAM BROWN, and friend, IGNATIOUS BROCK. The witnesses were HENRY RHODES, NANCY PACKER, and MARY PACKER.]

The last will and testament of JOHN JARMAN was proved in open court by the oaths of JARMAN KOONCE, JESSE ISLER?, & NANCY BROWN & ordered recorded; ZACHIUS BROWN, one of the executors, qualified as such. [This will was abstracted by Gwynn (p. 422). It was written 7 May 1840 and names his wife, ELIZABETH. He also names his "apprentice lad," JESSE TAYLOR; friend, ISAAC BROWN; friend, ZACCHUS (no surname given, but this was a woman); and BARNABAS GILES and JOHN GILES, "sons of WILLIAM GILES, and grandsons, one to my first wife and the other to my said present wife, ELIZABETH." He listed his siblings: WILLIAM JARMAN (deceased), ANN MASHBURN (deceased), BARBARA JARMAN (deceased), RISDON JARMAN, McLENDAL JARMAN, CASSANDRA McDANIEL, MARY HAZZARD and THOMAS JARMAN. Exrs were ISAAC and ZACCHEUS BROWN, his "trusty friends." The witnesses were JARMON KOONCE, JESSE TAYLOR, NANCY BROWN, and ISAAC BROWN.]

The petition of JAMES ROBERTS, EDWARD S. JONES & wife, SARAH, HOUSTON ROBERTS, RICHARD ROBERTS, GEORGE ROBERTS, & CHRISTOPHER ROBERTS, as tenants in common of the following slaves viz: HARDY, LILLY, CORNELIUS, & DAIVD, which they have devised lately from the estate "of their father, RICHARD ROBERTS," was presented to court. As each is entitled to 1/6 part of said slaves (that is, JAMES is entitled to 1/6, EDWARD in the right of his wife, to 1/6, HOUSTON to 1/6, RICHARD to 1/6, GEORGE to 1/6, & CHRISTOPHER to 1/6) and since the said slaves cannot be divided, they pray the appointment of a commissioner to sell said slaves & to make such a division. Court granted petition & appointed JAMES ROBERTS to be the commissioner to make the sale at the Court House door in TRENTON after advertising for the space of 30 days upon a credit of 6 months. In addition the cash received from the sale should include enough to defray court costs of this petition.

R.M. McDANIEL presented his bond as sheriff where upon the BEAVER CREEK return was contested on the ground that it was not returned agreeable to law & it was decided by ballot. Those who voted in the affirmation: LEMUEL H.

SIMMONS, ABNER GREEN, CALVIN KOONCE, ROSCO BARRUS, JAMES FOY, OWEN B. COX, JAMES C. BRYAN, JOHN H. DILLAHUNT, JOHN MARRETT, F.I. BECTON, NATHAN FOSCUE. Those who voted against: JAMES W. HOWARD & WILLIAM HUGGINS. Then the WHITE OAK return was objected to for not being handed to the clerk by one of the inspectors. Those who voted for receiving were: WILLIAM HUGGINS, LEMUEL H. SIMMONS, ABNER GREEN, CALVIN KOONCE, JAMES FOY, OWEN B. COX, JAMES C. BRYAN, JOHN H. DILLAHUNT, JOHN MARRETT, F.I. BECTON, & NATHAN FOSCUE. Those in the negative: JAMES W. HOWARD & ROSCO BARRUS. In the end R.M. McDANIEL was confirmed as sheriff and his bond was received.

Jurors drawn for December 1840 term:

BENJAMIN COLLINS	JOHN McDANIEL	LOTT EUBANKS
FREEMAN SMITH	GEORGE S. BENDER	BENJAMIN SCOTT
WILLIAM W. FRANK	AMOS SHELFER	FELIX KING
JOSEPH WALLACE	HENRY RHODES	EMERY METTS
JAMES MARRETT	JOSEPH KINCEY	LEMUEL BUSICK
WHITFIELD TURNER	AMOS S. KOONCE	DANIEL MALLARD
JOHN B. REYNOLDS	BENJAMIN HUGGINS	OWEN ADAMS
GEORGE WILCOX	HARDY O. CONNER	JOSEPH HAY
MARTIN MILLER	DANIEL WILLIAMSON	JOHN HEATH JR
NEEDHAM BEASLEY	MOSES ADAMS	FRANCIS GOODING
WILLIAM BINUM	JOHN HEATH SR	JOHN K. BENDER
JAMES MAIDS	JOHN POLLOCK	JOHN E. FOSCUE

Deed & Bills of Sale recorded by C.C. RHODES, registrar:
"Clerk & Master of Equity" to JOHN McDANIEL (deed)
Power of attorney: ELIZABETH FOSCUE to ROSCO BARRUS
JOHN B. REYNOLDS to AMOS S. KOONCE (deed)
EDWARD C. DEBRULE JR to GEORGE S. DEBRULE (deed)
EDWARD C. DEBRULE & GEORGE S. DEBRULE to E.C. DEBRULE (deed)
GEORGE S. DEBRULE to EDWARD C. DEBRULE (deed)
SAMUEL B. HEATH to EMANUEL JARMAN (deed)
E. JARMAN agreement with S.B. HEATH
MICAJAH MORGAN to E. JARMAN (deed)
WILLIAM PRITCHELL to WILLIAM A. HOWARD (deed)
NANCY THOMPSON to JAMES McDANIEL (bill of sale)
GEORGE Q. ROBERTS to EDWARD D. WHARTON (deed)
EDWARD D. WHARTON to JAMES ROBERTS (deed)

County Trustee was to pay R.M. McDANIEL, shff, $56.70 for extra services up to this term.
ZACHIUS BROWN allowed to sell perishable property of JOHN JARMAN, decd.
The undersigned, who examined the public rd from LITTLE CYPRESS CREEK to the fork & west, thought it would be advantageous to JAMES B. SHINE & to the public for the rd to run from LITTLE CYPRESS CREEK directly by the dwelling house of sd SHINE, it being on the west side of sd house. The proposed rd was in good condition and was little farther than the old way. 3 Dec 1840. Signed: JNO S. KOONCE, JAS D. KINSY, CALVIN KOONCE. (**Note**: The date of this entry would seem to indicate that the clerk wrote these last entries some time after the events occurred.)
WILLIAM BROWN (**Note**: This name was at the top of the next page in the original but it appears to have nothing to do with either the preceding or

succeeding entries.)

JOHN H. HAMMOND sold three Negroes, MARY, PENNY, & MONDAY, the property of MATILDA RANDAL, decd. The said Negroes were "bid off by JAMES B. SHINE at $863.00" and HAMMOND took the "note of THOMAS McDANIEL for the amount sold" 25 July 1840.

AMOS I. KOONCE was appointed constable; $4,000 bond; R.M. McDANIEL & JOHN B. REYNOLDS, his sureties.

DECEMBER TERM, 1840
TRENTON, Monday December 12th

Justices: JAMES W. HOWARD, LEMUEL H. SIMMONS, NATHAN FOSCUE, Esquires
Shff: RESDON M. McDANIEL
Clerk: J.H. HAMMOND
Solicitor: J.W. BRYAN

JAMES HARRISON, EML JARMAN & ABNER GREEN were to divide and allot off to heirs of SARAH BRYAN, decd, the Negroes of sd decd.

JOHN JARMAN was to oversee rd in room of LEWIS WILLIAMS, resigned.

Clerk of Court should take the list of taxables of NATHANEL WAPLES, delinquent.

JOHN HEATH, SR was cleared from jury duty for either court.

GEORGE S. DEBRULE was to oversee rd in place of BENJAMIN SCOTT.

Shff ordered to refund JAMES ROBERTS "so far as a double tax is concerned in a failure to list his taxables in the year 1839."

JAMES B. SHINE, BENJAMIN BROCK, & SIMON KOONCE were appointed patrols in District 4.

"Ordered that the road laid off by JOHN S. KOONCE, JAMES D. KINCY, and CALVIN KOONCE be received by the court & they take the same as per report dated 3 Dec 1840."

WILLIAM HUGGINS allowed to sell Negroes of HARDY BRYAN, decd, as per order of last court.

AMOS SHELFER was appointed guardian to IVY, SARAH, & CAROLINE ALPHEN and to JESSE & JAMES SHELFER; $200 bond; FARNIFOLD McDANIEL & FREEMAN SMITH, securities.

JAMES B. SHINE was required to send two of his hands to work the public rd in the upper district where JOHN S. KOONCE was overseer.

County Trustee was to settle accounts of B. ASKEW, jailor, he receiving $12.52 1/2 and paying his account $18.60.

County Trustee was to pay JOHN H. HAMMOND $40.00 for his services concerning the tax list.

THOMAS D. FOY was granted license to retail spirituous liquors by small measure at POLLOCKSVILLE.

ROSCO BARRUS was also granted license to retail spirituous liquors by small measure at POLLOCKSVILLE.

HARDY O. NEWTON was granted license to retail spirituous liquors at his residence.

RICHARD H. PARSONS was appointed constable "particularly" for the TRENT BRIDGE District; NATHAN F. PARSONS & JOHN KOONCE were securities for his bond.

JAMES H. PRICHELL was appointed admr of estate of WILLIAM PRITCHELL,

Jones Cty Court of Common Pleas Minutes 1840

decd; $25,000 bond; P.M. BRYAN & J.W. HOWARD, securities.

Jurors this term:

HARDY O. CONNER	LOTE EUBANKS	AMOS S. KOONCE
J.B. REYNOLDS	JOHN McDANIEL	AMOS SHELFER
JOSEPH KINCY	JAMES MARRETT	BENJAMIN COLLINS
MARTIN MILLER	NEEDHAM BEASLEY	FREEMAN SMITH
GEORGE S. BENDER	MOSES ADAMS	DANIEL WILLIAMSON
W.W. FRANK	JOHN HEATH	HENRY RHODES

Petit Jurors this term:

FELIX KING	GEORGE WILCOX	OWEN ADAMS
BENJAMIN SCOTT	JOHN K. BENDER	WILLIAM BINUM
JOHN E. FOSCUE	NATHAN STANLY	BENJAMIN HUGGINS
JOHN POLLOCK	EMERY METTS	THOMAS POLLOCK

WILLIAM BROWN vs FRANCIS DUVAL} debt. The petit jury (composed of the men listed above) found for pltff. Balance of debt = $175.10. Interest $10.50. Judgment for $185.60 & costs.

NATHAN FOSCUE, guard of DORCUS FOSCUE, vs CHARLES STEVESON, WILLIAM C. MURPHY, & LEMUEL HUDLER} debt. Same jury found for pltff. Debt = $203.00 with $11.66 interest. Judgment for $214.66 & costs.

D.Y. SHINE vs FRANCIS DUVAL & WILLIAM HUGGINS} debt. Same jury found for pltff. Debt = $200.00 with $11.40 interest. Judgment for $211.40 & costs.

ALEXANDER MITCHEL vs FRANCIS DUVAL} debt. Same jury found for pltff. $178.16 debt with $12.04 interest. Judgment for $190.20 & costs. Defendant appealed & gave N.F. PARSONS & JOHN OLIVER as sureties.

JOHN HEATH & wife & JOHN HEATH, admr of MATILDA RANDAL, petitioned court to sell slaves. Court ordered clerk to make sales, collect monies, pay court costs out of the purchase money & pay to "JOHN HEATH & wife 1/3 of the remainder as 'distributee' of N. RANDILE and the remaining 2/3 he is directed to pay to the admr of MATILDA RANDOLL to be by him distributed according to law."

BAZEL JONES vs FRANCIS GOODING} appeal. Each party was to pay his own costs. Tax attorney's fee for each counsel.

State of N.C. vs COUNCIL WOOTEN, exec of SIMMONS ISLER} Same jury as above found for pltff & assessed damages of $328.73 of which $287.48 was principle. Judgment for same & costs.

WILLIAM C. MURPHY vs WILEY S. MERRITTS & R.M. McDANIEL} Same jury found for pltff. $150 debt with $26.62 1/2 interest = $176.62 1/2. Judgment for same & costs.

JOHN OLIVER vs JOHN MESSER, WILLIAM HUGGINS & R.M. McDANIEL} Same jury found for pltff. $112.00 debt with $6.44 interest = $118.44. Judgment for same & costs.

WILLIAM H. MORRIS vs FRANCIS DUVAL} debt. Same jury found for pltff. $182.50 debt with $10.48 interest + $192.98. Judgment for same & costs.

AMOS AMYETT & others vs FANNY POLLOCK} "Report set aside & issue a new writ of partition."

Jurors drawn for March Term of Superior Court:

DANIEL DICKSON	DAVID GREEN	SAMUEL HILL
THOMAS HARRISON	JOHN YOUNG	JAMES FOY

Jones Cty Court of Common Pleas Minutes 1840

ROSCO BARRUS	E.C. DEBRULE SR	AMOS AMYETT
F.I. BECTON	ELIJAH SIMMONS	THOMAS POLLOCK
J.H. DILLAHUNT	DANIEL HARRISON	JAMES WILLIAMS
NATHAN FOSCUE	ABNER HARGET	JAMES G. STANLY
JOHN STRICKLIN	JAMES McDANIEL	WILEY M. MERRITS
CALVIN KOONCE	ABNER GREEN	LEVY JONES
JOSEPH SMALL	DANIEL WILLIAMSON	JAMES D. KINSY
JAMES MESSER	THOMAS GILLETT	LEWIS KOONCE
JOHN OLIVER	JOHN WOOD	ELIJAH PARRY
WILLIAM HUGGINS	J.W. HOWARD	J.W. BROCK

Deeds & Bills of Sale recorded by C.C. RHODES, Registrar:
JOHN HARRISON to ELIJAH McDANIEL (deed)
WILLIAM HUGGINS to WILLIAM POLLOCK (deed)
NATHAN EASON to AMOS AMYET (deed)
WILLIAM MESSER to SUSAN MESSER (deed)
BENJAMIN C. SMITH to SIMMONS COLLINS (deed)
JOSEPH KINSEY to JOSEPH B. KINSY (deed of gift)
Clerk & Master in Equity to L.H. SIMMONS (deed)
WILLIAM POLLOCK to AMOS AMYET (deed)
THOMAS D. FOY to ENOCH FOY & W.W. FRANK (mortgage)
JOSEPH KINSY to JULIA E. COX (deed of gift)
SUSAN SCOTT to GEORGE HARRIOTT (deed)
JAMES MESSER to FREDERICK ISLOR/TALOR (bill of sale)
WM C. MURPHY to JOHN MARRETT (bill of sale)
FRANCIS GOODING to JOSEPH KINSY, JAMES D. KINSY & O.B. COX (mortgage)
JAMES MESSER to ELIZABETH ANDREWS (mortgage)
WILLIAM C. MURPHY to JOHN MARRITT (bill of sale)
COUNCIL WOOTEN to FARNIFOLD McDANIEL (bill of sale)
JAMES MESSER to FREDERICK TALOR (deed)
ARETICES JONES to DAVID GREEN (deed of gift)
ARETICES JONES to LEWIS WILLIAMS (deed of gift)
JONATHAN WOOD to THOMAS D. FOY (deed)

EDMOND H. HATCH and wife and others petitioned the court for partition; JAMES C. BRYAN, SAMUEL HILL & CHARLES GEROCK appointed to issue the order.

CHARLOTTE PRITCHELL petitioned court for year's provisions. "Prayer granted & JAMES HOWARD is appointed Justice of the Peace and freeholder to lay off and allot the same."

SPECIAL COURT
Clerk's Office in Trenton
23 Jan 1840
(Note: The clerk probably meant to write the year as 1841.)

WILLIAM HUGGINS, JAMES C. BRYAN & CALVIN KOONCE, esquires, held the court.
EMANUEL JARMAN & EMANUEL KOONCE were appointed special admrs to the estate of ELIJAH KOONCE, decd; $15,000 bond; JOHN H. HAMMOND & WILLIAM HUGGINS, securities. Admrs allowed to sell perishable property of the estate.
Signed: JAS C. BRYAN, WM HUGGINS, CALVIN KOONCE

MARCH TERM, 1841
TRENTON
Monday, 8 Mar 1841

Justices: WILLIAM HUGGINS, NATHAN FOSCUE, LEMUEL H. SIMMONS, & JAMES W. HOWARD
Shff: R.M. McDANIEL
Clerk: JOHN H. HAMMOND
Solicitor: JAMES W. BRYAN

SAMUEL HILL, JOHN OLIVER, & CHARLES GEROCK were to settle accounts of BRADDOCK NOBLE, guard to "heirs of ENOCK NOBLE."

BENJAMIN F. STANLY was to oversee rd in room of COUNCIL GOODING, resigned.

ADONIJAH McDANIEL was to oversee rd from FRENCH BRANCH to TRENTON in room of FURNIFOLD McDANIEL.

HARDY O. CONNER was to be paid for his services as patrol in District 3 for 1840.

EMANUEL HARGET, DANIEL PERRY, & RICHARD HERRITAGE appointed patrols in Districts 3,4, & 7.

WM PADRICK, STEPHEN WILCOX & _____ MORTON (**Note:** Only a space was left for the first name.) were appointed patrols for District 4, Cypress Creek.

JACOB GOODING granted license to retail spirituous liquors for 1841.

C.C. RHODES was granted a peddlers license to retail dry goods in Jones Co.

Special Court elected (March, 1841) JAMES C. BRYAN, LEMUEL H. SIMMONS, J.E. FOSCUE, NATHAN FOSCUE, WM HUGGINS. (**Note:** No indication was given as to what office or offices they were elected.)

CALVIN KOONCE & WILLIAM A. COX were to see that the center arch in the FREE BRIDGE was widened to 20 feet & they were to make their report at the next court.

JAMES FOY resigned as guardian of JOSEPH HATCH; resignation accepted by court and appointed WILLIAM HUGGINS in his stead upon his entering $10,000 bond with EMANUEL JARMAN & WILLIAM W. FRANKS, sureties.

GEORGE BINDER, NATHANIEL WAPLES, WM W. FRANK, RICHARD OLDFIELD, JOHN JARMAN, NATHAN STANLY, & JOHN E. FOSCUE qualified this term as justices of the peace.

DANIEL DICKSON, JAMES W. HOWARD, SAMUEL HILL, JAMES B. SHINE, OWEN B. COX, FREDERICK I. BECTON, & NATHAN FOSCUE were elected this term to serve as school committee for one year.

JOHN SHELFER and wife and others petitioned the court for partition; court commissioners (to effect the partition) were HENRY RHODES, WILLIAM BROWN, BENJAMIN F. STANLY, NATHAN STANLY & JOSEPH SMALL.

"MARY KOONCE, widow vs the heirs at law of ELIJAH KOONCE}" Petition for dower.

"MARY KOONCE, widow vs E. KOONCE & E. JARMAN, admrs of ELIJAH KOONCE}" Petition for partition; court commissioners to effect the partition were JOHN JARMON, HENRY RHODES, WILLIAM BROWN, BENJAMIN F. STANLY.

"MARY KOONCE & others" petition court to divide slaves} court appointed HENRY RHODES, WILLIAM BROWN, & BENJAMIN F. STANLY to do same.

Jones Cty Court of Common Pleas Minutes 1841

Jurors for June Term, 1841:

WHITFIELD TURNER	REUBEN WILLIAMS	JAMES McDANIEL
LOTT EUBANKS	NEEDHAM BEASLEY	GEORGE (HERRIETTS?)
RIGHT STANLY	BRYAN BINDER	WILLIAM ERWIN
JOHN C.B. KOONCE	SIMON S. BECTON	JONAS WILLIAMS
JOSEPH SMALL	PETER HARGET	THOMAS POLLACK
WILLIAM GOODING	JOHN McDANIEL	JAMES ADAMS
AMOS HEATH	OWEN ADAMS	THOMAS COLLINS
COUNCIL GOODING	HARDY O. CONNER	NATHAN PARSONS
MERRITT JONES	AMOS L. SIMMONS	JOHN ADAMS
EMANUEL KOONCE	THOMAS BALEY	JOHN MESSER
ABRAM SIMMONS	DANIEL MALLARD	THOMAS HUGGINS
JAMES G. STANLY	JOHN JONES	JOSEPH WHITTY

Deeds & Bills of Sale, etc., recorded by registrar, C.C. RHODES:
RICHARD REYNOLDS to JOHN CONNER (deed)
AARON WOOD to J.H. DILLAHUNT (deed)
JAMES JONES to JOHN S. KOONCE (deed)
DANIEL KNIGHT to MILES FOY (deed)
MILES FOY to ENOCH FOY (deed)
JAMES FOY to CHARLES FOY (deed)
J.H. HAMMOND to THOMAS McDANIEL (bill of sale)
JOSEPH KENNY/KENSY to J. KENSY (deed)
GEORGE W. HAMETE? to JOHN E. FOSCUE (deed)
ENOCK FOY to CHARLES K. FOY (deed)
SARAH OLDFIELD to RICHARD OLDFIELD (deed)
FREDERICK F. FOSCUE to NATHAN FOSCUE (deed)
JOHN E. FOSCUE to GEORGE W. HARRIETS? (deed)
FOLNEY VENTERS & wife, GREY NORRIS & wife, & JOHN FONVIELLE to JOS. KINSY
JOSEPH KINSEY to JOSEPH B. KINSY (deed)
J.B. REYNOLDS to JAMES B. SHINE (bill of sale)
J.B. REYNOLDS to JAMES B. SHINE (bill of sale)
JOSEPH KINSY to J. KINSY (bill of sale)

SPECIAL COURT
Clerk's Office, Trenton

Justices: NATHAN FOSCUE, JAMES C. BRYAN, & ABNER GREEN

Purpose: Appointments of inspectors to hold election for a member to the 24th Congress.
The following were appointed:
District 1: DANIEL DICKSON, Esq., JOHN YOUNG & F. PARSONS
District 2: WM W. FRANK, Esq., JOHN R. BENDER & HENRY FOY
District 3: Shff CHARLES GEROCK & BENJAMIN ASKEW
District 4: CALVIN KOONCE, Esq., JOHN JONES & JAMES B. SHINE
District 5: OWEN B. COX, Esq., JOHN JARMAN & LEWIS WILLIAMS
District 6: F.I. BECTON, Esq., SIMON S. BECTON & NEEDHAM BEASLY

Jones Cty Court of Common Pleas Minutes 1841

JUNE TERM, 1841
TRENTON
Monday, 14 June 1841

Justices: WILLIAM HUGGINS, LEMUEL H. SIMMONS, JAMES C. BRYAN & NATHAN FOSCUE, special justices
Shff: R.M. McDANIEL
Clerk: J.H. HAMMOND
Solicitor: J.W. BRYAN

Jurors for the State:

PETER HARGET, foreman	JAMES ADAMS	AMOS L. SIMMONS
JOHN ADAMS	THOMAS BALEY	EMANUEL KOONCE
JOHN MESSER	RIGHT STANLY	JOSEPH SMALL
ABRAM SIMMONS	BRYAN BENDER	MERRITT JONES
THOMAS COLLINS	LOTT EUBANKS	THOMAS HUGGINS
WHITFIELD TURNER	OWEN ADAMS	THOMAS POLLOCK

Petit Jurors:

NATHAN F. PARSONS	WILLIAM ERWIN	NEEDHAM B. BEASLY
HARDY O. CONNER	SIMON S. BECTON	WILLIAM GOODING
IGNATIOUS W. BROCK	JOHN JONES	DANIEL MALLARD
WILLIAM A. COX	FREEMAN SMITH	FELIX KING

County Trustee was to pay OWEN B. COX $12.50 for services & "account paid JOHN J. PASTURO, printer, in relation to the Common Schools."

RICHARD OLDFIELD was appointed to take the tax list in District 1 for 1841; WILLIAM W. FRANK had District 2; CHARLES GEROCK had District 3; CALVIN KOONCE, District 4; JOHN JARMAN, District 5; NATHAN STANLY, District 6; and NATHANIEL WAPLES, District 7.

THOMAS GILLETT, J.P., ELIJAH LOVETTE & THOMAS PARSONS were to hold poles in District 1 for an election to elect Clerks of County & Superior Courts. Those holding poles in the other districts were:
District 2: GEORGE BENDER, J.P., BRYAN BENDER & THOMAS HALL
District 3: R.M. McDANIEL, Shff, ADONIJAH McDANIEL & LEMUEL BUSECK
District 4: CALVIN KOONCE, J.P., JOHN JONES, & JAMES B. SHINE
District 5: OWEN B. COX, J.P., JOSEPH B. KINSY & JONAS JONES JR
District 6: JAMES G. HERRITAGE, J.P., AMOS RHEM & BENJAMIN KOONCE
(**Note:** Apparently, people in District 7 paid taxes but did not vote! No explanation has been given as to why District 7 often was left off the lists.)

NATHAN FOSCUE, JOHN H. HAMMOND & JAMES C. BRYAN were to settle accounts of EMANUEL JARMAN as county trustee and report next court.

County trustee was to pay WILLIAM POLLOCK $4.80 for attending the grand jury.

JAMES FOY, GEORGE BENDER, RICHARD OLDFIELD & ROSCO BARRUS were to lay off a year's provisions for MRS. NANCY NEWBOLE.

WILLIAM HINDS was licensed to retail spirituous liquors by the small measure for one year.

CHARLES GEROCK, JOHN H. DILLAHUNT, JOHN H. HAMMOND, SAMUEL HILL, & NATHAN FOSCUE were to divide Negroes of HARDY BRYAN, decd.

A tax of 6 cents on every $100 value of land and town lots and improvements and 20 cents on every taxable pole shall be levied and collected for the present year in order to defray county expenses.

County trustee was to pay JOHN H. HAMMOND, clerk, $40 for extra services.

County trustee was to pay JOHN H. HAMMOND $2.75 for postage and paper.

Colonel Commandant of Jones County is empowered to call in the public arms of said county and then loan them to such persons as have not arms to perform public duty and such persons shall give the Colonel a receipt for same and shall keep arms in good order and return them when called for.

RACHEL McDANIEL, guard to EDNEY S. McDANIEL shall renew her guardian's bond with EMANUEL JARMAN & RISDEN M. McDANIEL, securities.

MRS. NANCY NEWBOLES was appointed admix of the estate of "her husband BAZEL NEWBOLE;" $1,000 bond; RICHARD OLDFIELD & JAMES FOY, securities.

LEMUEL H. SIMMONS, NATHAN FOSCUE, & ROSCO BARRUS were to audit & settle accounts of JAMES FOY, former guard to RICHARD A. HATCH (minor) with WILLIAM HUGGINS, present guard to said minor.

DAVID GREEN was appointed to admr estate of LEAH? GREEN; $500 bond; FREDERICK I. BECTON & PETER HARGET, securities.

CHARLES GEROCK, SAMUEL HILL, JOHN H. DILLAHUT, JOHN H. HAMMOND & LEMUEL H. SIMMONS were to audit and settle accounts of WILLIAM HUGGINS, admr of estate of HARDY BRYAN.

ARNOLD, a slave and the property of RICHARD REYNOLDS, shall be exempted from working roads during lifetime of sd RICHARD REYNOLDS provided REYNOLDS furnishes another hand in place of sd ARNOLD.

NATHAN FOSCUE, CHARLES GEROCK & JOHN H. HAMMOND were to audit and settle accounts of CALVIN DAVIS, former guard, & ABNER GREEN, agent of said DAVIS, to the minor heirs of JAMES GREEN, decd.

WILLIAM HUGGINS, CHARLES GEROCK, & JAMES C. BRYAN were to audit and settle accounts of JOHN H. HAMMOND, admr of estate of LEWIS HARGET.

County trustee was to pay WILLIAM STANLY, FREEMAN SMITH, & AMOS I. KOONCE $24 each for serving as patrols last year.

OWEN B. COX, superintendent of Common Schools, shall give bond in the final sum of $1,500; FREDERICK I. BECTON & SAMUEL D. KINSEY, securities, for the faithful application of the funds which may come to his hands as superintendent.

County trustee to pay WILLIAM A. COX $40 for work done on the FREE BRIDGE.

WILLIAM STANLY allowed to draw from court a judgment of $68 plus interest which was returned to court and levied on lands of the defendant in case EMANUEL JARMAN vs JAMES G. STANLY 28 Nov 1839 by WILLIAM POLLOCK, constable 3 July 1841. Signed: WM STANLEY.

Jurors for Superior Court September Term 1841:

JOHN S. KOONCE	RICHARD OLDFIELD	FRANCIS GOODING
JOHN E. FOSCUE	EMERY METTS	DANIEL DICKSON
EDWARD M. GILBERT	JAMES MADES	JAMES W. HOWARD
JOHN WOOD	LEMUEL BUSECK	JOHN CANNON
NATHAN FOSCUE	WM W. FRANK	SAMUEL HILL
JOHN ROUSE	JOHN K. BENDER	JOSEPH KINSY
JOHN HEATH	MOSES ADAMS	THOMAS McDANIEL
ELIJAH PARRY	ABNER HARGET	LEWIS O. BRYAN

Jones Cty Court of Common Pleas Minutes 1841

JAMES G. HERRITAGE	ENOCH FOY	NATHAN B. WESTBROOK
JOHN HAGAINS	JEREMIAH CONNER	LEVY JONES
OWEN B. COX	AMOS AMYETT	WILLIAM HUGGINS
JOHN STRICKLIN	IGNATIOUS W. BROCK	JOHN OLIVER
LEVY EUBANKS	RICHARD R. FOSCUE	AMOS SHELFER
JOHN TURNER	ISRAEL HOWARD	HENRY RHODES

Deeds, etc., recorded this term by C.C. RHODES, registrar:
AMOS KOONCE to WILEY KOONCE (bill of sale)
GEORGE KING to FELIX KING (deed)
C. WOOTEN to AMOS RHEM (bill of sale)
MICHAEL SHELFER to AMOS SHELFER (deed)
JAMES FOY to JOHN K. BENDER (bill of sale)
E. JARMAN to JOSEPH KINSY (deed)
WILEY KOONCE to EMANUEL KOONCE (deed)
IVY HARRISON to ELIJAH McDANIEL (deed)
LEWIS BRYAN to BENJAMIN I./S. BRYAN (deed)
JOHN B. REYNOLDS to ELIZABETH REYNOLDS (bill of sale)
PIETY KILLBREW? to JAMES B. SHINE (bill of sale)
MARTIN F. BROCK to NATHAN F. PARSONS & J.H. HAMMOND

AMOS AMYETT and others vs FANY POLLOCK} Petition to divide. Report returned and confirmed.

HUGGINS & WOOD vs JAMES FOY} Debt. Jury:

NATHAN F. PARSONS	HARDY O. CONNER	NEEDHAM B. BEASLEY
WILLIAM GOODING	SIMON S. BECTON	IGNATIOUS W. BROCK
JOHN JONES	WILLIAM A. COX	DANIEL MALLARD
FREEMAN SMITH	WILLIAM ERWIN	FELIX KING

found for pltff; $138.72 debt with interest of $6.98. Judgment for same and costs.

SAMUEL HILL, guardian to PARRY heirs vs BENJAMIN HUGGINS, WILLIAM HUGGINS & HARDY O. CONNER} Debt. Same jury found for pltff. $500 debt with $63.25 interest. Judgment for same & costs.

"Doe on demise" of JOSEPH KINCEY vs ROE and GEORGE KING} (**Note**: No case type was given.) Same jury found "all issues in favor of pltff and assigned his damage to ? and costs. Judgment accordingly." (**Note**: According to Swaim, "demise" means a lease of lands.)

DANIEL Y. SHINE vs FRANCIS DUVAL & WILLIAM HUGGINS} Debt. Same jury. Dismissed at defendants' cost.

E.K. HARGET vs FRANCIS DUVAL, LEMUEL H. SIMMONS & WILLIAM HARGET} Debt. Same jury found for pltff. $470 debt with $11.75 interest. Judgment for same & costs.

JAMES McDANIEL to the use of IVY HARRISON vs FRANCIS DUVAL & JAMES C. BRYAN. Same jury found for pltff. $200 debt with $17.50 interest. Judgment for same & costs.

ELIZABETH DOWDY vs FRANCIS GOODING, JOSEPH KINSY & EML JARMON} Debt. Same jury found for pltff. $300 debt with $13.50 interest. Judgment for same and costs.

IGNATIOUS W. BROCK, exr of ISAAC BROWN vs FRANCIS GOODING} Debt. Same jury found for pltff. $102.88 debt with $31.16 interest. Judgment for same and costs.

F.I. BECTON vs NATHAN F. PARSONS & JOSEPH WHITTY} Debt. Same jury found for pltff. $464.85 debt with $58.79 interest. Judgment for same & costs. Defendants appealed and gave EML JARMAN & R.H. PARSONS as securities.

ELIZABETH ANDREWS, guard to heirs of PETER ANDREWS vs FRANCIS GOODING & OWEN B. COX} Debt. Dismissed at defts' costs.

ELIZABETH ANDREWS vs ADAMS ANDREWS & BENJAMIN HUGGINS} Debt. Same jury found for pltff. $500 debt with $13.75 interest. Judgment for same & costs.

EZEKIEL JONES vs FRANCIS DUVAL} Debt. Same jury found for pltff. $150 debt with $21.75 interest. Judgment for same & costs.

F.I. BECTON vs JOHN B. REYNOLDS, AMOS I. KOONCE & ELIZABETH REYNOLDS} Debt. Same jury found for pltff. $367.88 debt with $27.59 interest. Judgment for same & costs.

MARY KOONCE, widow of E. KOONCE vs EML JARMAN and EML KOONCE, admr of E. KOONCE} Petition for year's provisions. Report returned and confirmed. Judgment for same and costs.

MARY KOONCE, widow of E. KOONCE vs heirs at law of E. KOONCE} Petition for dower. Report returned & confirmed & ordered to be registered. Judgment for costs against the petitioner.

MARY KOONCE and others to the court} Petition to divide slaves. Report returned & confirmed & ordered to be registered. Judgment against petitioner for costs.

Merchants Bank vs JOSEPH WHITTY, EDWARD S. JONES & GEORGE W. FERRAND} Debt. Dismissed at defendants' costs.

end of records

REFERENCES

Black, H.C. *Black's Law Dictionary*, 5th edition. St. Paul, Minn: West Publishing Co., 1979.

Corbitt, David Leroy. *The Formation of the North Carolina Counties 1663-1943*. Raleigh: State Dept. of Archives and History, 1950.

Cumming, William P. *North Carolina in Maps*. Raleigh: Division of Archives & History, 1966.

Gwynn, Z. Hargett. *Abstracts of the Records of Jones County, N.C. 1779-1868, Vol. 1*, 1963.

Johnson, Guion Griffis. *Ante-Bellum North Carolina: A Social History*. Chapel Hill: University of N.C. Press, 1937.

Kammerer, Roger E. & David E. Carpenter. *Onslow Register: Records of Onslow and Jones County Citizens and Related Families, Vol. 1*, 1984.

Kammerer, Roger E. *Onslow Register: Records of Onslow and Jones County Citizens and Related Families, Vol. 2*, 1988.

Morris, Charles Edward. "Panic and Reprisal: Reaction in North Carolina to the Nat Turner Insurrection, 1831." *The North Carolina Historical Review*, Vol. LXII, No. 1 (Jan 1985) 29-52.

Potter, Dorothy. *Index to the 1820 North Carolina Census*. Baltimore: Genealogical Publishing Co., 1978/1974.

Powell, William S. *The North Carolina Gazetteer: A Dictionary of Tar Heel Places*. Chapel Hill: University of N.C. Press, 1968.

Swaim, Benjamin. "The North Carolina Justice," *North Carolina Genealogical Society Journal*, Vol. 13, No. 1 (Feb 1987) 45-48.

Taylor, R.H. "The Free Negro in North Carolina." *The James Sprunt Historical Publications*, Vol. 17, No. 1 (1920) 5-26.

Tragle, Henry Irving. *The Southampton Slave Revolt of 1831*. Amherst: University of Mass. Press, 1971.

Wadsworth, Mary Jane. *Wadsworth Family in America, 1663-1985: Maryland, Pennsylvania and Southern States, Bk. 2*. Utica, Ky: McDowell Publications, 1985.

Wheeler, John Hill. *Historical Sketches of North Carolina from 1584 to 1851*. Baltimore: Regional Publishing Co., 1964. (Originally published 1851)

Two other references which I did not cite in the text but have valuable information on anti-bellum North Carolina are:

Olmsted, Frederick Law. *A Journey in the Seaboard Slave States.* New York: Dix & Edwards, 1856.

Raper, Charles Lee. *The Church and Private Schools of North Carolina: A Historical Study.* Greensboro, N.C.: Jos. J. Stone, Book and Job Printer, 1898.

Census materials used:

The 1820, 1830 and 1840 Federal Censuses for Jones County, North Carolina (microfilm copies) and these government documents:

Census for 1820. Washington: Gales & Seaton, 1821.

Fifth Census or Enumeration of the Inhabitants of the United States 1830. Washington: Duff Green, 1832.

Sixth Census or Enumeration of the Inhabitants of the United States, as Corrected at the Department of State, In 1840. Washington: Blair & Rives, 1841.

Statistics of the U.S.A., 6th Census. Washington: Blair & Rives, 1841.

INDEX

Names may appear more than once on a page. Check alternative spellings.

ABOLITIONIST GROUPS
    Colonization
        Society
        112
    North Carolina
        Manumissio
        n Society
        112

BLACK INSURRECTION 105

BUSINESS
    Pursons & Co.
    191

DUTIES OF PATROLS 82

MILITARY UNIT
    25th Regiment of
        Militia
        185

NEGROES
    ALEX 140
    ANGELENA 96
    ARNOLD 232
    BYER 51
    CATE 109
    CLARY 93
    CORNELIUS 224
    DAVID 224
    DARBY 53, 57
    DECK 102
    DELIAH 13
    DENNIS 21
    DONAM 112
    DONAN 100
    DONUM 95
    EDMUND 96
    ELIZA 69
    EPOCKS 21
    FRANK 109
    GEORGE 96
    HARDY 224
    ISAAC 122
    JACK 105
    JANE 93
    JERRY 56
    JIM 105
    JOHN 213
    LEDIA 24
    LEMON 37
    LILLY 224
    LIMONE 56
    LINDA 122
    LISHEY? 122
    LITTLE ROSE 105
    LONDON 109
    LOT 105
    LOTT 53
    LUCY 74
    MARGERY 96
    MARIA 122
    MARY 226
    MARY ELIZA 51
    MOLLY 184
    MONDAY 226
    MOSES 66, 90,
        95, 96,
        102, 136
    NANCY 96
    NATHAN 53
    NELSON 184, 189
    OLD MOLL 140
    PATSY 48
    PENNY 226
    PETER 31
    RHODA 96
    ROSE 105
    SAM? 93
    SHARPER 105
    SILVEY 53
    SILVIA 93
    SIMON 69
    SOPHIA 103
    TAMIRS 24
    TEEL 43
    TIMOTHY 144
    TOM 95, 100,
        102, 103,
        105, 112,
        122
    VIOLET 25
    VIRGIL 213
    YORK 121

NEWSPAPERS
    New Bern Daily
        Journal
        11, 16,
        118, 198
    New Bern
        Sentinel
        29

    New Bern Weekly
        Journal
        187
    Newbern
        Spectator
        188, 222
    North Carolina
        Star 11,
        27
    Star Gazette 113

PLACES
    ? Gully Bridge
        122
    (Free?) Bridge
        147
    (Roma?) Branch
        149
    ___don Branch
        105
    Alabama 196, 202
    Anson County 182
    Bachelor Creek
        216
    Baptist Chapel
        197
    Beaufort County
        46
    Beaver 8, 30,
        54, 75,
        204, 207,
        216, 217,
        220, 225
    Beaver Creek 30,
        54, 75,

204, 207, 216, 225
Beaver Creek Road 216
Beaverdam 58, 200
Beaverdam Branck 29, 58, 75
Beaverdam Creek 5
Been Creek Bridge 125
Bever Creek 7, 37, 82, 102, 103, 120, 122, 123, 132, 135, 138, 144, 153, 155, 170, 179, 188
Bever Creek Bridge 170
Bever Dam 8, 43, 75, 81, 121, 132, 144
Bever Dam Branch 81, 121
Beverdam 106, 125, 174
Beverdam Creek 75
Big Chinquapin 82
Big Chinquipen 122
Black Correl 81
Black Creek 5
Black Sorrel 81
Black Swamp 5, 8, 11, 29, 34, 39, 59, 79, 83, 101, 147, 154, 155, 160, 170, 181, 197, 210, 214
Black Swamp Bridge 29, 197
Black Swan 34
Bogue Inlet 11
Brown's Mill 5
Buck Branch 123, 213
Buckner Hatch's Mill 140, 201
Bush/Buck Branch 185
Butery Branch 98
Carteret County 1, 45, 191, 215
Catfish Lake 98
Chapel Branch 217, 218
Chatham County 112
Chinquapin Creek 102
Chinquipen Chapel 214
Colvett's Ford 54
Comfort 5, 34, 42
Corani River 107
Craven County 1, 8, 12, 29, 39, 42, 45, 59, 95-97, 100, 102, 106, 112, 150, 158, 216, 223
Cypress Creek 5, 6, 8, 37, 53, 54, 72, 79, 82, 84, 102, 103, 119, 120, 132, 135, 144, 153, 155, 175, 179, 181, 217, 218, 225, 229
Deep Gully 8, 12, 35, 50, 89, 95, 124, 128, 140, 141, 174, 180, 216, 223
Deep Gully Bridge 35, 50
Dover 39
Dover Rd 5, 39, 163
Duplin County 1, 42, 84, 96, 105, 108, 113, 135, 211, 217
Dyer Co., TN 125
Fayetteville 119
Fayetteville Road 216
Fork at Shine's 96
Frank's Ferry 12
Free Bridge 129, 155, 181, 184, 188, 223, 229, 232
French Branch 153, 208, 229
French House 163
Georgia 21, 184
Ginger Branch 8, 11
Grape Branch 98
Great Branch 217
Great Dover Swamp 216
Guilford County 112
Gully Bridge 174
Gum Swamp 39, 163, 174
Haiti 112
Halifax 1
Harrison's Bridge 34, 58, 96,

108, 140,
147, 170,
222
Hatch's Mill 30,
128, 141,
174, 222
Hill's Fence 188
Holland 11
Holmes County,
Miss. 199
Howard's Pocosin
216
Hunters Creek
215
Illinois 112
Indian ? 122
Indian Grave
Oldfield
223
Indian Grove 8,
34, 42,
56, 57,
79, 96,
107, 129,
141, 147
Indian Grove
Oldfield
42, 107,
129, 147
Indiana 112
Island Creek 216
Jack Cabbin 34,
57, 96,
101, 122,
147, 170,
184
Jack Cabbin
Branch 96
Jack Cabin 8,
34, 52,
67, 140
Jack Cabin
Branch 34
Jacks Cabbin
Branch 223
Jacob Branch
125, 204
Jacob's Branch
147, 170,
213
Jarvis Mill 181
Joshua Branch
217
Joshua Creek 211
Joshuay Branch
211
Joshways
Resolution
82, 175
Jumping Run 198
Kincy Bridge 211
Kincy Old Bridge
211
Kinston 5, 58,
81, 105,
107, 121,
187, 213
Kinston Road 58,
213
Lenoir County 1,
5, 39, 59,
75, 84,
96, 106,
108, 129,
147, 160,
211, 217,
218
Liberia 112
Little
Chinquapin
8, 82
Little
Chinquapin
Bridge 217
Little
Chinquapin
Creek 123
Little Cypress
Creek 225
M_cehshill 100
Messelshell 29
Mill Creek 8,
12, 67,
86, 98,
107, 128,
140, 141,
170, 174,
216, 223
Mill Creek
Bridge 12,
67, 128,
174
Mill Run 29, 75
Millcreek 39
Mississippi 199
Musselshell 5,
8, 11, 53,
58, 81,
105, 107,
113, 121,
125, 149,
188
Musselshell
Branch 58,
105
New Bern 11, 16,
29, 115,
118, 149,
187, 198,
200
New River 107
New River Swamp
107
Newbern 29, 35,
65, 69,
70, 72,
98, 102,
107, 111,
123, 125,
175, 188,
213, 216,
222
Newbern Rd 216
Newbern Road
188, 213
Onslow Bay 107
Onslow County 1,
11, 16,
21, 44,
65, 72,
84, 100,
101, 102,
107, 182,
211, 217
Palace? Branch
217
Palaco? Branch
216
Palaic? Branch
217
Parry's Bridge
102, 123,
135, 188
Pasquotank
County 112
Patrick Branch

217
Perquimans County 112
Perry Road 194
Pitch Hole Branch 215
Pocosin 8, 30, 30, 62, 81, 98, 102, 105, 117, 124, 128, 147, 160, 163, 174, 215-218
Pocosin Branch 30
Pollacksville 223
Pollock Plantation 35
Pollocksville 170, 185, 194, 226
Polly Branch 143
Quaker Meeting House 214, 218
Raccoon Branch 216
Raleigh 108, 187
Randolph County 112
Rattlesnake 5, 8, 30, 42, 59, 84, 108, 141, 176, 211
Rattlesnake Branch 30, 84, 211
Rattlesnake Bridge 5, 59, 108, 141
Read Hill 30
Ready Branch 30
Red Hill 8, 96, 117, 141, 143, 175, 176, 188

Red Oak 8, 34, 52, 67, 101, 140, 184
Reedy Branch 5, 39, 59, 67, 107, 112, 117, 128, 131, 136, 141, 143, 175, 176, 188
Reedy Creek 5
Resolution 135
Resolution Branch 82, 216, 218
Rhem's Road 140, 188
Rial Oake 170
Richlands 34
Ridy Branch 39
River Trent 54, 215
Robeson County 95, 158
Royal Oak 34
Ruby Branch 96
Rudy Branch 82
Sampson County 113
Sand Ridge 39, 50, 163
Sandy Bottom 39
Sandy Ridge 39
Shine's 188
Smith's Mill Bridge 197
Smiths Mill 29
South West Bridge 174
Southampton County, VA 106
T. Bridge 30
Tandy Branch 215
Tansy'S Branch 215
Ten Mile Fork 121
Ten Mile House 121

Ten/Tow Swamp 128
Texas 16
Tom Swamp 75, 147, 170
Tom'S Swamp 29
Toneys? Branch 215
Tracey Swamp 39
Trent 1, 5, 8, 11, 12, 17, 20, 29, 30, 34, 35, 37, 39, 40, 46, 50, 54, 61, 64, 68, 72, 75, 79, 82, 83, 89, 95, 102, 103, 107, 108, 119-122, 124, 125, 128, 129, 131, 132, 138, 140, 141, 143, 144, 147, 147, 153, 155, 157, 160, 163, 165, 170, 174, 175, 179-182, 184, 185, 187, 188, 201, 208, 210, 211, 214-218, 222, 227
Trent & Joshua Creek 211
Trent Bridge 1, 5, 8, 17, 20, 30, 35, 37, 39, 40, 46, 50, 54, 61,

64, 68,
75, 79,
89, 95,
102, 103,
107, 108,
119-122,
124, 128,
131, 132,
138, 140,
141, 143,
144, 147,
147, 153,
155, 157,
160, 163,
165, 170,
174, 179,
180, 182,
184, 185,
211, 222,
227
Trent River 5,
8, 11, 12,
29, 30,
34, 72,
75, 79,
82, 83,
129, 143,
147, 175,
181, 185,
188, 201,
208, 210,
211, 214,
216-218
Trent Road 216
Trenton 1, 5, 6,
10-12, 14,
16, 17,
19, 22,
29, 30,
34, 36-39,
41, 42,
44, 45,
48, 49,
51-56,
58-60, 65,
66, 68,
73, 77,
79-82, 86,
95, 97,
100,
102-105,
107,
112-114,
117,
119-122,
124-126,
128, 129,
131, 132,
134, 137,
139-141,
143, 144,
146-150,
152-158,
160, 161,
163-165,
167,
169-171,
173-175,
177-181,
183, 185,
187, 188,
190, 194,
196, 197,
199-201,
204, 205,
208, 210,
211, 213,
215-219,
222, 224,
226,
228-231
Trenton Bridge
82
Tuckahoe 7, 37,
54, 82,
98, 102,
103, 107,
119, 120,
132, 144,
155, 179,
208, 210,
211, 217,
218
Tuckahoe Branch
211, 217,
218
Tuckahoe Bridge
211
Tuckahoe Creek
208, 211,
217, 218
Tuckehoe 8, 37,
54, 82,
153
Tuckhoe Creek 79
Twigs Co.,
Georgia
144
Union Parish,
Louisiana
42
Virginia 113
Wake County 45
Ward's Hill 107,
125, 188,
204, 213
White Oak 5, 9,
11, 29,
30, 37,
50, 54,
62, 72,
81, 82,
96, 98,
102, 103,
105, 119,
120, 124,
128, 132,
144, 153,
155, 160,
163, 166,
170, 174,
179, 188,
201, 215,
216, 223,
225
White Oak
Pocosin
216
White Oak River
9, 11, 29,
96, 98,
215
White Oak Road
174, 216
White Oak Swamp
72
William Rhem'S
Road 58,
222
Woods/Ward's
Hill 170
Words/Wards Hill
58

NO SURNAME GIVEN

Abraham 77
Amos 20
Benjamin 200
Bevin 37
Catharine 27
Lewis 66
Simmons 112
Sophia 20
T.W. 126
Winifred Herrot 193

ACKROYD
   James 80
ADAMS
   Hardy 54
   Henry 191
   James 85, 94, 136, 137, 145-147, 150, 156, 160, 164, 165, 171, 201, 212, 221, 230, 231
   James? 156
   Jas. 130
   John 19, 32, 53, 78, 80, 85, 94, 96, 100, 102, 116, 117, 129, 135, 139, 140, 146, 147, 150, 152, 154, 160, 168, 171, 174, 180, 194, 203, 206, 214, 219, 230, 231
   M. 35
   Mary? 94
   Micajah 29, 85, 94, 100, 111
   Moses 78, 85, 101, 104, 111, 126, 128, 134, 145, 150, 152, 153, 158, 161, 171, 174, 186, 187, 193, 203, 204, 212, 225, 227, 232
   O. 130
   Owen 5, 18, 22, 40, 43, 52, 59, 61, 66, 67, 69, 70, 73, 74, 85, 87, 94, 101, 103, 104, 110, 114-117, 122, 124, 131, 133, 136, 145, 150, 156, 157, 164, 167, 171, 174, 177, 179, 182, 193, 199, 200, 209, 210, 218, 223, 225, 227, 230, 231
   Owen? 156
   Owens 49
   Owin 142
   William 19, 27, 34, 35, 43, 49, 54, 55, 61, 66, 76, 78, 85, 93-95, 106, 108, 130
   Wm. 126, 130, 162
ADDAMS
   William 48
ADEM
   Theofelus 76
ALCOT
   Thomas 170
ALLAGOOD
   Lewis 88
ALLEN
   Joseph W. 209
   Roe 185
   Susan 115, 125
   W.P. 193
   Walter P. 5, 89, 113, 114, 126, 140, 144, 150, 152, 158, 160, 161, 170, 176, 182, 183, 185, 189-191, 203, 204, 212, 214, 218, 219
ALLEN?
   W.P. 155
ALPHEN
   Beneter 76
   Caroline 226
   Daniel 19
   Ivy 226
   Sarah 226
   Thomas 157, 172
ALPHIN
   Emanuel 168
ALRY?
   Benjamin 185
ALTMAN
   Geo. S. 90
ALTMAN?
   Geo. S. 98
   George I. 154
ALTMON
   George S. 90
ALTON?
   Walter P. 139
AMGET
   Amos 24
   F.B. 207
AMITT
   Amos 89
AMYET

.... 56
Amos 12, 20, 26,
    39, 41,
    57, 60,
    74, 89,
    97, 107,
    112, 118,
    128, 129,
    137, 142,
    158, 171,
    197, 202,
    203, 221,
    228
Enoch 58
Enock 60, 62
Francis 60, 223
Francis B. 58,
    135, 199,
    200
I. 52
John 98, 201
Rachel 98

AMYETT
    Amos 139, 158,
        164, 196,
        212, 228,
        233
    Francis B. 163

ANDREW
    Francis 154

ANDREWS
    107
    A. 179
    Ad 26
    Adam 30, 32, 78,
        82, 89,
        101, 102,
        104,
        123-125,
        128, 137,
        139, 142,
        146,
        150-153,
        159, 160,
        166, 168,
        173, 176,
        180, 186,
        187, 189,
        191,
        193-195,
        201, 202,
        204, 207,
        214, 219,
        220
    Adams 234
    Adon/Adam 137
    Adonijah 20, 41,
        52, 56,
        60, 109,
        137
    Charles 195
    Daniel 32, 55,
        78, 80,
        92,
        116-118,
        121, 124,
        136, 177
    Elany 77
    Elizabeth 204,
        205, 208,
        228, 234
    Francis 18, 27,
        29, 33,
        39, 44,
        45, 55,
        61, 68,
        69, 71-73,
        92, 116,
        117, 125,
        133, 141,
        145, 148,
        156, 157,
        159, 166,
        168, 171,
        174, 182,
        184, 185,
        191, 193
    Francis, Sen. 53
    Francis, Sr. 148
    Ivey 12, 29, 47,
        48, 61,
        62, 85,
        93, 95,
        101, 107,
        110, 117,
        124, 126,
        127, 130,
        136, 137,
        139, 140,
        148
    Ivy 18, 27, 39,
        41
    James 35, 72
    Jas. 42
    Jno. 34, 58
    John 30, 32, 35,
        39, 40,
        59, 60,
        62, 73,
        74, 77,
        78, 93,
        95, 101,
        116, 117,
        131, 135,
        151, 188
    John Jnr 32
    John Jr. 18, 20
    John Sr. 40
    Lem 109
    Leml 57
    Lemuel 68, 71,
        141
    Maryann 30
    Melito 30
    Nancy 40
    Owen 194
    P. 40
    Penelope 30, 35
    Peter 27, 30,
        32-34, 38,
        40, 46,
        50, 51,
        55, 57,
        58, 72,
        73, 84,
        85, 90,
        91, 100,
        110, 111,
        113, 115,
        123, 124,
        126,
        129-131,
        136, 137,
        141-143,
        147, 154,
        159, 168,
        203-205,
        208, 234
    Susan 30, 89,
        97, 112,
        118, 129,
        156, 167,
        170, 176,
        201
    Vincent 78, 96,
        110, 117

Winson 84
Winston 81, 85, 115
ANTHONY
    Catherine 65
ANTWINE
    Garsham 59
    Graham 59
    Graham? 70
    William 57, 70
ARNOLD
    Levi 76
    Meltire? 60
    Milton 14
    Sarah 42
ASKAY
    Josiah 42
ASKEW
    B. 226
    Benjamin 7, 185, 186, 197, 198, 205, 206, 210, 230
    Benjn 161
    Joseph 123
    Josiah 49, 52, 198
ASKEY
    62
    Benj. 131
    Benjamin 97, 104, 140, 160, 170, 171, 175, 176
    Benjn 90, 104, 120, 125, 132, 139, 150, 159, 193
    Jackson 85
    James 62
    Jno. 104, 132, 153
    John 90, 97, 104, 125, 131, 150
    Joseah 92
    Josiah 41, 71, 76, 92, 97, 110, 129
    Nathan 97
    Susannah 97
    Z. 33
    Zadock 97
    Zea 31
    Zeadock 23, 36
    Zeaduk 31
ATMORE
    G.S. 197
ATTMORE
    Geo. S. 35, 110
AUSTIN
    Mathew A. 196
AVERET
    John A. 99
AYKSAY
    James 62
AYROYD
    James 84

B...
    N.F. 223
    Needham 218
    Isaac 119
BAER
    John 130
BAILEY
    Thomas 199, 214
BALE/BALL
    John 199, 206
BALEY
    Thomas 51, 145, 150, 152, 160, 164, 167, 181, 187, 193, 212, 219, 230, 231
    Thos 180, 186
BALL
    Bryan 70
    David 39, 77, 117, 121, 124, 128, 133, 145, 148, 153, 169
    Huldah 148, 153
    John 27, 36, 50, 54, 55, 61, 66, 73, 96, 100, 110, 117, 139, 148, 150, 160, 161, 166, 176, 185, 187, 188, 193, 214
BALL?
    Jas. 130
BALLARD
    David 168
BANDIN
    Hosea 198
BARBER
    Thos D. 65, 70
BARNET
    James 68
BARRES
    Rosco 24, 31, 34, 46
BARRIER
    Rosea 46
BARRIS
    Rosco 21-23, 26, 34-36, 40
BARRUS
    John 134, 158
    R. 57, 105, 106, 130, 173, 179, 183, 185, 205, 210, 211, 218, 223
    Rosco 5, 41-43, 47, 48, 50, 53-56, 60, 62-64, 67-70, 74, 76, 77, 79-81, 87-89, 92, 93, 97, 100, 102-107, 109, 110, 114, 119, 120, 124, 128, 131-134, 138, 140,

143, 145,
146, 149,
152, 153,
155-161,
163,
166-168,
170, 171,
173, 174,
177, 180,
182, 184,
186, 187,
189, 192,
194, 195,
197, 201,
203, 208,
220, 222,
225, 226,
228, 231,
232
 Roscoe 68
BARRY/BEERY/BOSEY
 Nicholas 187
BATCHELOR
 Edward 216
BATTLE
 I. 209
 S. 209
 Samuel G. 156
 Thomas 43
BEASLEY
 James 38, 40
 N.B. 212, 214
 Needham 7, 174,
  196, 197,
  209, 225,
  227, 230
 Needham B. 162,
  233
BEASLY
 N.B. 211
 Needham 210, 230
 Needham B. 231
BECTON
 B. 18
 Bryan 15, 17,
  19-21,
  29-31, 36,
  39, 43,
  47, 48,
  54, 77,
  81, 88,
  92, 97,

  125, 126,
  131
 Edwd. 37
 Edwin 18, 20,
  23, 27,
  29, 30,
  37, 40,
  41, 49,
  53, 59,
  76, 84,
  110, 116,
  134, 140,
  150, 156,
  165
 F. Isler 178,
  218
 F.I. 18, 31, 53,
  77, 97,
  118, 131,
  142, 153,
  169, 179,
  189, 197,
  203, 207,
  208, 211,
  213, 214,
  221, 225,
  228, 230,
  234, 234
 Fred I. 5, 6,
  12, 13,
  223
 Frederick 2, 126
 Frederick I. 22,
  23, 36,
  42, 48,
  52, 54,
  59-64, 66,
  68, 72
 Fredk 35
 Fredk I. 12, 17,
  21, 22,
  24, 32,
  37, 42,
  43, 46-48,
  50, 51,
  56, 64,
  92, 153
 J.H. 212
 Jno. H. 110
 John B. 206
 John H. 14, 27,
  37, 39,

  47-49, 73,
  77, 116,
  125, 126,
  139, 148,
  151, 152,
  156, 165
 Mary 92, 125,
  126
 Mary Ann 92
 Mary W. 97
 Mathew S. 138
 Simon 197, 218
 Simon I. 114,
  150, 151,
  155,
  165-167,
  196
 Simon S. 101,
  126, 139,
  156, 171,
  180, 181,
  197,
  211-214,
  219, 230,
  231, 233
BELL
 Elijah 30
 Elijah S. 66
 Joseph 127, 177
BENDER 166
 Bryan 6, 199,
  212, 214,
  219, 231
 G.S. 82
 Geo. 148
 George 191, 219,
  231
 George I. 121,
  170, 196
 George S. 6,
  147, 159,
  197, 212,
  218, 220,
  225, 227
 Jno. 32
 John 20, 22, 27,
  39, 44,
  45, 49,
  52, 57,
  58, 67,
  68, 74,
  90, 91,

96, 107,
108, 128,
133, 136,
137, 145,
150, 160,
166, 176,
186, 196,
197, 206,
207, 212,
214, 223
John K. 199,
212, 214,
219, 225,
227, 232,
233
John R. 6, 230
John, Jr. 90,
223
John, Sr. 150,
166, 176,
186, 196,
206
BENUM
William 168
BERGWIN
John 141
BERQUIN
John F. 180
Julia T. 134
BERT
Sarah 182
BETNER
James E. 44, 84
BEVINS
James 44
BINAM
Jno., Sr. 179
John 6
William 90, 139
BINAM?
William 50
BINDER
Bryan 230
George 229
Jno 18, 118
John 5, 18, 100,
102, 121,
187
BINUM
William 77, 168,
200, 209,
210, 218,

225, 227
BIRGIVEN
Jno. 126
BIRQURN?
John 118
BISHOP
Hilery 217
BLACK
W.S. 201
BLACKLEDGE
Mary 93
Mary F. 56
W.S. 33
William I. 21
William S. 36,
47, 56,
65, 84,
93, 99,
123
Wm S. 29, 65, 93
BLUNT
Frederick 124
N.G. 90
Nathan G. 110,
180
BOLE/BALL
John 74
BON(D?)
William 218
BOYD
John T. 62, 65
BRAWER
Mr. 35
BRAY
Eliza 22, 31,
197
Hardy 22, 197
Hephzibah 22
Hepsabeth 87
Hepsey 31
Margaret 22, 31
Nichol.. 31
Nicholas 22
Nicholas A. 122
Thomas 31
William 22, 31,
87, 143,
197
Wm. 12
Wm. W. 17, 20
BROCK
B. 60

Benj 59
Benjamin 6, 59,
66, 82,
114, 122,
123, 130,
150, 161,
163, 171,
186, 207,
214, 219,
222, 226
Benjn 139, 168,
188, 192,
193
Catharine 59
Christopher 47,
49, 76
Elizabeth 49
I.W. 127, 224
Ignatious 59,
104, 135,
143, 146,
155, 168,
175, 182,
190, 193,
205, 224
Ignatious W.
136, 137,
182, 214,
218, 221,
233
Ignatius 50,
150, 161,
203, 204
Ignatius W. 217
J. 60
J.W. 60, 228
John 49
Joseph 6, 18,
20, 27,
41, 42,
48, 49,
59, 60,
68, 69,
83, 101,
117, 131,
132, 136,
141, 143,
146, 151,
155
M.F. 37
Martin 49, 49,
144

Martin F. 2, 7,
    16, 19,
    27, 29,
    37, 41,
    44, 45,
    50, 53,
    61, 66,
    73, 74,
    84, 86,
    99, 102,
    107, 126,
    129, 131,
    139, 147,
    148, 160,
    167, 171,
    179, 186,
    189, 190,
    196, 212,
    233
Miss 12
Susanna 47

BRONSON
Mary 183

BROWDER
M. 40

BROWN
A.S. 95
Cyrus 224
Dempsey 55
Hardy 14
Isaac 6, 7,
    18-21, 24,
    27, 29,
    31, 33-38,
    40, 42,
    43, 45-57,
    63, 64,
    67-70,
    72-74, 77,
    79-81, 83,
    85, 88,
    90,
    101-105,
    108, 109,
    112-114,
    117, 119,
    120, 125,
    132, 133,
    136, 137,
    139,
    141-143,
    150, 156,
    157, 166,
    171, 186,
    189-191,
    201, 205,
    218, 221,
    224, 233
Jachius 156
John 156
Joshua 133
Leah 224
Leroy 14, 15, 40
Nancy 17, 31,
    36, 224
Orpah 224
Polly 224
Rosco 155
S. 68
Silvester 38,
    62, 65
Stephen 30
Susan 59
Sylvester 62
T. 10
Thos 13, 19, 36
William 33, 35,
    43, 50,
    57, 63,
    67, 84,
    101, 115,
    119, 128,
    176, 224,
    226, 227,
    229
Williams 6, 19,
    21, 23-25,
    31, 33,
    35-37, 41,
    43, 51,
    54, 62,
    64, 71,
    72, 78-80,
    84, 86,
    87, 98,
    100,
    102-105,
    107, 109,
    114, 115,
    119, 120,
    122, 123,
    125, 129,
    130,
    133-135,
    139
Wm 51, 63, 78,
    80, 85
Wms 17, 36, 71,
    83, 84,
    102, 119,
    126, 132
Zaccheus 224
Zacchus 224
Zachaus 171
Zacheaus 145
Zacheus 6, 81,
    84, 157,
    166, 168,
    182, 183,
    188, 191,
    192,
    195-197,
    201, 203,
    207-209,
    221, 224
Zachius 158,
    224, 225
Zachues 174
Zachus 78
Zackeus 154

BROWN?
Constable 158

BRUSH & NELSON 98

BRYAN
A. 64
Ann R. 98, 114,
    115, 119,
    129, 143,
    147, 153
Ann Rebecah 89
Benjamin I./S.
    233
Benjamin S. 198
C. 10, 25, 27,
    30, 39,
    42, 106,
    116
C.W. 198
Chris 47
Chrisr 31, 35,
    37
Christ 12, 14,
    25, 27
Christopher 17,
    20, 21,
    23-26, 29,

34-38, 41,
46, 60,
71, 94,
119, 122,
177, 204
Elizabeth 187
F. 142, 191
Fredk 49, 56,
58, 87,
130, 153
H. 12, 13, 17,
18, 20,
27, 30,
33, 44,
62, 76,
94, 99,
104, 125,
133, 155,
156, 165,
170, 171,
178, 184,
190, 192,
193, 198
Hardy 2, 6, 10,
11, 14,
15, 17-20,
22-25,
29-31, 34,
35, 37-52,
55-58, 60,
61, 63,
65-67,
69-72,
74-77,
79-81,
83-86, 89,
90, 92,
95, 96,
98-100,
102-109,
112-117,
119-126,
128, 129,
131,
133-155,
157,
159-161,
163-171,
173-178,
181,
183-185,
187-192,

194-197,
200-202,
205, 212,
212, 221,
223, 226,
231, 232
Henry 147
J. 202
J.C. 142, 211,
220
J.H. 94
J.M. 188
J.W. 219, 226,
231
James C. 6,
190-194,
196, 198,
200, 201,
204, 205,
213, 215,
220, 222,
223, 225,
228-233
James Christophe
r 43
James W. 17, 69,
90, 112,
124, 128,
129, 134,
143, 148,
157, 163,
165, 167,
183, 184,
187, 200,
204, 210,
213, 229
Jas C. 94, 97,
193, 204,
213, 215,
222
Jas. W. 76, 80,
152, 178,
190, 194
Jno C. 19
Jno. M. 70
John C. 27
John H. 12, 17,
18, 20,
27, 44, 62
Jos. 64
Jos. W. 45
Joseph 11, 20,

23, 24,
32, 34,
66, 74,
78, 88,
101, 118,
132, 149
Joseph W. 177
Julia 200
Lewis 97, 160,
233
Lewis O. 21, 27,
37-39, 53,
62, 66,
76, 93,
95, 110,
123, 124,
134, 145,
150, 152,
161, 163,
167, 171,
180, 189,
196-198,
207, 214,
232
Mary 23, 27,
124, 200
P.M. 227
Rebeccah 89
Rebeckah 42
Rebekah 47
Rosco 7
Sarah 33, 226
Sarah C. 220,
223
Sears 76
Thomas O. 29,
121, 122
Thos. O. 30, 124
Wealthy 200, 206
Welthy 203
William 24, 33,
34, 64,
66, 78,
88, 101,
118, 132,
147, 149
William Henery
89
William Henry
114, 119,
129, 153,
190

Wm Henry 143
Wm. H. 156, 192, 193
BRYAN family 72
BURGUYN
    John 203
    John C. 203
BURGWIN 197, 211
    John 128
BURGWYN
    John C. 203, 204
BURQWIN
    John 174
BURTON
    Simon S. 129
BUSACK
    Leml 155, 180
    Lemuel 139, 164, 167, 178
BUSECK 122
    Leml 53, 59, 77
    Lemuel 83, 107, 169
BUSH
    N.B. 18, 29, 32, 35, 36, 39, 47, 50, 77, 103, 106, 107, 110, 111, 123
    Nathan B. 2, 7, 11, 17, 23-26, 36, 37, 42-45, 47-50, 61, 63, 64, 66, 71, 76-79, 83, 84, 94, 95, 100-102, 105, 108, 123, 133
BUSICK
    Leml 27, 30, 42, 48, 54, 84, 161, 193
    Lemuel 30, 44, 45, 48, 68-70, 86, 116, 130, 131, 140, 150, 152, 156, 169, 186, 193, 203, 204, 206, 223, 225
    Sally 30
    Sarah 51
    Thomas 51
BUSICK?
    Lemuel 116
BUTON
    John H. 120
BUYQWIN
    John C. 206
BYMAN
    William 161
BYNAM
    William 148, 184
    Wm. 193
BYNUM
    William 147, 148, 182
BYNUN
    William 199
CAHOON
    James 124
CANNON
    Cana 204
    Jeremiah 27, 151, 199, 200, 206
    John 203, 221, 232
    Leah 184
    Thomas 76, 134, 150
CANNON/CONNOR
    Thomas 151
CAREY
    Elizabeth 147, 167, 196
    Solomon 94
CARMACK
    Jesse 60
CARRAW/CONNER?
    Jordan S. 102
CARROW
    Jordan L. 66
CARSON
    Jordan S. 152
CARTER
    H. 38
CARY
    Elizabeth 132, 133, 136, 139, 142
    Solm 89
    Solo. 94, 99
    Soloman 71, 147
    Solomon 68, 89, 98, 99, 132, 133, 136, 139, 142
CASEY
    Elizabeth 165
CASY
    Solomon 43
CHADWICK
    John 109
CLARK
    Benjamin 81
    Elbert I. 170
CLARK & MASTERS 124
CLARK?
    60
COART?
    John 194
COBB
    Jno. 80, 91
    John 5, 163, 174
    William 77
    William D. 96, 99, 101, 114, 123, 134, 145, 154, 156, 221
    Wm. D. 78, 168
COBBS
    John 39
COLDMAN
    B. 185
COLE
    James C. 121, 136
    Jas. C. 109, 111, 126
COLEMAN 218
    Blount 213

Blunt 92, 148
COLEMAN & GOTLEN 99
COLLING
    Hardy 41
COLLINS
    Benj. 12
    Benjamin 8, 37,
        51, 59,
        60, 62,
        84, 129,
        203, 204,
        207, 225,
        227
    Benjn 26, 60,
        64, 66,
        67, 78, 96
    Cassandra 146
    Caty? 122
    Hardy 23, 41,
        48-50, 54,
        57, 61,
        66, 68,
        84, 110,
        116, 117,
        122, 126,
        128, 139,
        142, 147,
        156, 157,
        168, 172,
        176, 186,
        191, 195,
        196, 219
    Isaac 196
    J.L. 149
    Jno. S. 126
    John 18, 40,
        122, 126
    John S. 22, 146
    Marth 25
    Marth.. 26
    Martha 23, 125,
        184
    Marthey 57
    Marthy 33, 46,
        54
    Simeon 126
    Simmons 29, 60,
        88, 90,
        133, 137,
        141, 147,
        148, 156,
        157, 162,
        166, 171,
        172, 181,
        184, 186,
        191, 193,
        207, 221,
        228
    Soloman 60, 76
    Thomas 191, 212,
        214, 219,
        230, 231
COLVERT
    John D. 15
COLVET
    Frederick 32
    John D. 14, 27,
        31, 32
COLVETT
    Nancy 198
COLVITS
    Fredk 115
    John D. 115
COLVITT
    Frederick 190
COMBS
    Will 13
    William 12, 19
    Wm. 43
CONAWAY
    Ivy 12
    James 12
CONNER
    ? 193
    Alfred 184, 193
    Amanda 184, 193
    Council 155
    G.O. 129
    Hardy 6, 48
    Hardy A. 139
    Hardy O. 52, 76,
        78, 89,
        96, 100,
        105, 109,
        110, 112,
        125, 126,
        140, 147,
        157, 159,
        167, 169,
        171, 174,
        186, 191,
        195, 196,
        202, 212,
        213, 225,
        227,
        229-231,
        233
    James 184, 193
    James R. 63, 81,
        98, 141
    Jas. R. 115
    Jeremiah 27, 233
    Jno. 183
    John 157, 178,
        184, 193,
        230
    Levicy 205
    Molsey 40
    Owen 125
    R. 44
    Rachel 14, 89,
        98, 115,
        121, 195
    Rebecah 184
    Rebecca 11, 193
    Rila 184
    Susan 193
    Susanna 184
    William 168
    William H. 11,
        13
    Wm. H. 12, 16,
        97
CONNERS
    Rachel 116
CONNON
    Rubin G. 32
CONNOR
    Hardy O. 79,
        150, 153,
        156
    Jeremiah 18
    John 161
CONNOR/CANNON
    John 206
    Thomas 156
CONWAY
    Catharine 124
    Ivey 16, 45, 51
    James 16
    Jas 45
    John 46, 88,
        122, 124
    Jos 51
COOMBS
    58

  William 27, 36,
   43, 97,
   105
  William, Jr. 67
  Wm 97, 123
COOPER
  David 98
CORMAN
  Hannah 23
  Reubin G. 31
  Rubin G. 15
CORMON
  Reuben G. 38
  Rubin G. 14
COX
  .... B. 34
  ...C.B. 54
  A. 56
  Andrew 20, 26,
   54
  Archibald B. 18
  B. 129
  Charity 113,
   157, 163
  E. 54
  E.F. 187
  Elany 20, 26, 54
  Elena 56
  Felin 15
  Felix? 56
  Felon 20
  Filia? 54
  J. 78
  Jno B. 22, 33
  John 47, 72, 74
  John A. 7, 131,
   220
  John B. 74, 88,
   97, 170,
   176
  John H. 179,
   183, 196,
   203
  Julia E. 228
  Lavinia 22, 183,
   184, 205
  Levina 47, 72,
   74, 78,
   170, 179,
   189
  O.B. 17, 56,
   130, 159,
   201, 203,
   209, 210,
   213, 228
  O.W.B. 16
  Ow B. 211, 215
  Owen 31
  Owen B. 2, 7,
   10, 15,
   20-25,
   29-31, 35,
   36, 38,
   43, 45,
   46, 49-51,
   54, 60-64,
   68, 74,
   77, 79-83,
   85, 94,
   96,
   100-103,
   107, 110,
   113, 114,
   117, 119,
   120, 123,
   124, 128,
   131-136,
   143-149,
   153, 155,
   157-159,
   161, 163,
   165-167,
   174, 175,
   177-181,
   183, 185,
   186,
   193-195,
   198, 201,
   205-208,
   210, 217,
   218, 220,
   223, 225,
   229-234
  Owin B. 15, 20,
   74, 140
  Rebeccah 209
  Susan 131
  William 36, 61,
   88, 157,
   163
  William A. 31,
   54, 96,
   113, 121,
   136, 137,
   150, 229,
   231-233
  Wm A. 24, 118,
   145, 165
  Wm. 101
CRAFT
  David 165
  Frederick 165
  James 165
CRAFT/CROFT
  Edward 168
CROFT
  Catharine 164
CROOM
  J.S. 99
CROSSLAND
  David M. 132
CURTIS
  Peter 70
CUSTIS
  Peter 100

DALEY/DOBY
  Jacob I. 129
DAVIS
  Abijah 106
  Allen 38
  C. 139, 195
  Calvin 148, 152,
   155, 158,
   164, 165,
   171, 172,
   174, 175,
   181, 232
  J. 42
  James 185
  Jno. 34
  Jno. D. 70
  Jno. P. 111
  John 41
  John D. 59, 66
  John D./B. 60
  John P. 41, 99,
   146, 205
  Joshua 21, 40
  Joshuay 71
  Mary 97
  Riley 144
  Rufus W. 123
  Samuel 137, 142,
   157, 158
  Thomas 31

Thomas H. 56,
    56, 60, 70
Thos H. 56
Thos. 39
W. 113
Wendal 70
Windal 23, 89
Windel 88
DEBRUELE
    Edwd 18
DEBRULE
    E. 31
    E.C., Sr. 126,
        228
    Edwd C. 48, 49,
        163
    Edward 20, 38,
        68, 73,
        148, 180
    Edward C. 96
    Edward C., Jr.
        225
    Edwd 14, 27, 31,
        34, 37,
        69, 71, 74
    Edwd C., (Jr.?)
        164
    Edwd C., Sr. 133
    Geo. I. 190
    George 124, 148,
        180, 218
    George C. 140
    George I. 149
    George L. 139
    George S. 148,
        162, 164,
        171, 180,
        189, 214,
        221, 225,
        226
DECKSON (See Dickson)
    Daniel 36, 102
DEEKSON
    Daniel 24
    Fredk 36
DELAHUNT
    Saml 19
DELLAHUNT (See
        Dillahunt)
    Samuel 54
DEVAL (See DuVal)
    Francis 51

DEVEREUIX
    John 222
DEWEY
    Watson 184
DICKEN
    Danl 124
DICKESON
    Daniel 18
DICKSON
    D. 167, 169
    Daniel 5, 43,
        50, 51,
        63, 65,
        67, 79,
        80, 82,
        90, 96,
        103, 114,
        116, 119,
        133, 157,
        161,
        163-166,
        170, 174,
        179, 182,
        188,
        190-194,
        196-198,
        200, 205,
        207, 208,
        210-212,
        219, 220,
        223,
        228-230,
        232
    Daniel 63
    Daniel/David 206
    Danl 120
    F. 191
    F.R. 131
    Ferdian 157
    Ferdinan 6, 163,
        174, 188
    Furdinan 178
    R. 65
    Robert 61, 100,
        149
    Robt. 12
    William 81
    William T. 62
DICKSON/DURKSON
    Daniel 119
DILLAHUNT
    J.H. 228, 230

Jno. H. 189, 193
John 146, 158,
    178, 216
John H. 124,
    147, 157,
    159, 164,
    167, 171,
    178-180,
    183, 188,
    194, 199,
    201, 204,
    205, 207,
    208,
    210-212,
    223, 231
Saml 22, 48, 50,
    70, 73,
    94, 110,
    130, 133,
    182, 185
Saml. 13
Samuel 23, 32,
    42, 43,
    53, 61,
    64, 66,
    69, 123
Sarah 182
Susan 208
Susannah 48, 53
DILLAHUNTY
    Saml 18
DILLAHUT
    John H. 232
DISMAL/DIRMAL
    Richard 120
DONNER
    I.R. 160
DOW?
    Arthur 138
DOWDY
    Elizabeth 233
DOYLE
    Spartley M. 97
DUDLEY
    ? W. 167
    D.W. 143
    David W. 116,
        150
    Jacob 39
    Narcisa 42
    Thomas 23, 36,
        42, 53,

    59, 128
  Thos 52
  Ths. 44
DUDLY
  David W. 149
  David W.G. 214
  N. 52
  Thos. 160
DUNKEN
  William 13, 47,
    50, 61,
    64, 72,
    84, 92,
    96, 100,
    109, 121
  Wm. 110, 128
DUNKEN/DUNKER
  Wm 51
DUNKIN
  William 81, 128
  Wm 18
DuVAL
  Danl Francis 34
  Dr. 187, 200
  Eliza 89, 176
  F. 84, 114, 202
  Francis 14, 22,
    34, 41,
    43, 47,
    50, 52,
    55, 56,
    58, 60,
    63, 64,
    71, 76,
    79, 83,
    84, 89,
    107, 112,
    115, 116,
    130, 136,
    141, 170,
    177, 189,
    190, 192,
    195, 198,
    218, 221,
    221, 227,
    233, 234
  William 89
EASON
  Nathan 228
EASTON
  Nathan 54
ELLIGOOD
  Lewis 88
ELLIT
  Jesse 88
ERVIN
  Shaderach 167
ERWIN
  Abner 169
  Absalom 169
  Alice 169
  Calvin 169
  Caroline 169,
    170
  Edward 169
  Elizabeth 169
  Evan 169
  John 169, 170
  Likergus 169
  Richard 169
  Robert 169
  Shaderack 76,
    107, 116,
    134, 145,
    150, 157,
    169, 176
  Shadk 126
  Shadrack 68, 77,
    93, 117,
    134, 156,
    157, 201,
    212
  William 169,
    170, 186,
    187, 201,
    203, 204,
    212, 214,
    219, 230,
    231, 233
  Winifred 169
  Wm. 193
EUBANK
  Levi 55
  Lot 49
EUBANKS
  Aaron 18
  Asa 14, 17, 27,
    32, 34,
    51, 57,
    58, 73,
    74, 92,
    110, 118,
    121, 122,
    126, 139,
    140, 148,
    149, 156,
    157, 168,
    176, 189,
    191, 199,
    200, 206,
    221
  Isaac 96, 209
  L. 215
  Levi 5, 13, 14,
    17, 21,
    22, 24,
    43, 53,
    61, 62,
    73, 74,
    77, 87,
    101, 103,
    118, 120,
    122, 130,
    131, 138,
    144, 148,
    153, 155,
    163, 166,
    180,
    204-206,
    215
  Levy 203, 221,
    233
  Lot 5, 14, 27,
    73, 81,
    96, 100,
    105, 110,
    117, 128,
    141, 143,
    150, 158,
    171, 189,
    190
  Lote 227
  Lott 2, 15, 37,
    57, 107,
    122, 126,
    136, 137,
    148, 156,
    166, 199,
    209, 212,
    225, 230,
    231
  Reading 209
EVERET?
  Shaderack 120
FARRIER
  Rufus 150

FAY (See Foy)
    Enoch 34
    Enock 11, 39,
        40, 45
    Susan 44, 45
    Thos. 45
FEROND
    William P. 78,
        109
FERONOL?
    Wm. P. 62
FERRAND
    Edward S. 200
    Edwd S. 176
    George W. 234
    Winifred 171,
        174, 183,
        188
FERREN (Green)
    Winifred 181
FERROND
    E./O.S. 203
    Edward S. 171
    Edwd S. 169
FIELDS
    C. 16
    Councel 22
    Council 18, 29,
        53, 55,
        163, 173,
        174, 179,
        201
    E. 16
    Frederick M. 55
    Jacob 214
    Nancy 57
FISH....?
    Alfred M. 95
FISHER
    Dolly 91
    Michael N. 109
    S.C. 31
    Saml C. 25, 31,
        38, 43,
        65, 124
FISHER?
    Michael 91
FIZLOW
    John 44
FONSVILLE
    Thos J. 89
    Thos. J. 121

FONVEAL
    Thomas 89
FONVIELLE
    Brice 65
    David 53, 113,
        144, 149,
        190
    Fanny 105
    John 144, 193,
        230
    Mary 144, 193
    Narcissa 144
    Thomas I. 50
    Thomas J. 41,
        61, 62,
        72, 105
    Thos I. 50
    Thos J. 49
FONVILLE
    Brice 44
    David 16, 59
    Frederick 104
    Thomas J. 65,
        104
FORBES
    S.B. 30, 124
    Saml C. 23, 141
    Stephen B. 29,
        78, 121,
        122, 156,
        157
FORBIS
    Stephen B. 16
FORBS
    Caroline 179
    Wm. 179
FORDHAM
    Eli... 66
    Elias 40, 59,
        65, 67,
        79, 115,
        137
    Jno 110, 118
    Jno. 44, 45
    John 2, 14, 15,
        27, 36,
        40, 41,
        49, 50,
        52, 57,
        58, 65,
        68-73, 81,
        84, 86,
        115, 116,
        118, 121,
        126-128,
        133, 140,
        150, 162,
        168, 176,
        189, 213
    Mary 36
FOREST
    John 207
FORT
    William B.F. 212
FOSCUE
    Amos 17, 20, 42,
        54, 70,
        76, 98
    Augustus 154
    Christiana 97
    Christianna 183
    Cyrus 118
    D. 10
    Darcus 14, 23,
        42, 47, 89
    Darcy 192
    Darius 26
    Dorcus 89, 188,
        201, 227
    Dove 154
    Eliza 97
    Elizabeth 201,
        225
    Frederick 2, 7,
        36, 48,
        49, 59,
        60, 64,
        69, 73,
        93, 95,
        97, 101,
        102, 104,
        123, 130,
        132, 153,
        156, 177,
        221
    Frederick F. 230
    Fredk 15, 19,
        27, 50,
        62, 117
    Hannah 97
    J.E. 209, 229
    Jno. E. 96, 158,
        190
    John C. 122, 168

John E. 65, 95,
    97, 139,
    140, 145,
    154, 156,
    158, 167,
    171, 174,
    180,
    182-184,
    186, 189,
    199-201,
    212, 223,
    225, 227,
    229, 230,
    232
John Edward 97
Josephine 118
Josephus 118
L. 29
Lewis 12, 44,
    76, 101
Lewis Jr. 48, 61
Macon 118
Michael N. 187
N. 85, 159, 187,
    220
Nancy 97
Nancy M. 160,
    183, 203
Nath 182
Nathan 2, 6, 7,
    13, 15-18,
    20, 22,
    25, 31,
    32, 36,
    38, 40,
    42, 43,
    46, 50,
    53, 54,
    58, 62,
    68-70, 75,
    77-83, 86,
    88, 89,
    95, 97,
    99-101,
    103, 104,
    108, 109,
    112, 114,
    118-120,
    124, 128,
    129,
    131-133,
    135, 136,
    139, 143,
    144, 146,
    147, 150,
    152-156,
    158,
    166-168,
    171, 173,
    177, 179,
    181, 183,
    186-188,
    190-192,
    194-201,
    204-208,
    210, 212,
    213, 215,
    218-220,
    222, 223,
    225-232
Polly 96
Reaves R. 45
Reavis R. 68, 69
Reeves R. 44
Richard 32, 152
Richard P. 161
Richard R. 59,
    106, 108,
    131, 150,
    164, 189,
    190, 199,
    212, 221,
    233
Richd R. 57, 69,
    92, 117,
    129, 134,
    145, 180
Rieves R. 48
Rivers R. 49
S. 21
Simon 10, 14,
    20, 21,
    23, 26,
    31, 36,
    41, 42,
    45-47, 49,
    51, 53,
    54, 56,
    65, 68,
    70-72, 89,
    95-97,
    102, 158,
    201
Simon, Jr. 96
Simon, Sr. 201
Susan Caroline
    118
William 53, 55,
    57, 76,
    152, 195
FOSTER 23
FOX
    Leggit 109
FOY (See Fay)
    Caroline 45
    Charles 230
    Charles Henry 45
    Charles K. 230
    E. 111, 179
    Elizabeth 45
    Enoch 2, 5,
        23-24, 32,
        45, 47,
        48, 56,
        59, 62,
        64, 66,
        77, 80,
        83, 94,
        102, 112,
        126, 157,
        171, 180,
        206, 221,
        228, 230,
        233
    Enock 21, 27,
        45, 46,
        51-53, 60,
        69, 73,
        74, 87,
        91-93, 95,
        97, 100,
        106, 107,
        118,
        120-124,
        130, 134,
        141, 143,
        147, 149,
        161, 163,
        164, 180,
        203, 214,
        218, 230
    F. 10
    Francis 45
    Franklin 45, 118
    Frederick 181
    Fredk 27

Harriet 45
Henry 6, 184, 230
J. 133
J..? 155
James 5, 45, 59, 67, 69, 78, 79, 81, 84, 86, 87, 96, 110, 124, 126, 128, 132, 133, 135, 143, 145, 147, 148, 152, 153, 155, 161, 163, 165, 166, 169, 171, 173, 182, 182, 194, 195, 198, 201, 205, 207, 208, 218, 220, 223, 225, 228-233
Jas. 193
John R. 125, 196
Jos. 189
Joseph 45, 82, 129, 134, 140, 143, 144, 148, 150, 170, 214
Joseph I. 6, 154, 157, 166, 170
Joseph L. 129, 152
Joseph S. 5, 45, 114, 124, 144, 145, 149, 159-161, 163-166, 168, 170
Margaret 181, 214
Maria 16
Mariah 45
Martha B. 180
Miles 45, 180, 230
Rachel 45
Rebecca 45
Sally 45
Susan 65, 81
T. 10
T.D. 45
Thomas 46
Thomas D. 45, 226, 228
Thos 15, 20, 23, 125, 126
William 89, 114, 126, 191
Wm 81, 210

FRANER
Geo. 14
Jas. 14

FRANK 197
Edward S. 15
Edwd. S. 12, 14
Jno M. 22
John M. 31, 34, 61, 80, 108, 127
W. 88
W.W. 222, 227, 228
William W. 203, 214, 223, 225, 231
Wm. W. 6, 218, 229, 230, 232

FRANKLIN
John 70

FRANKS
E.M. 127
E.S. 24, 33, 67
Edward S. 56
Edwd S. 19, 25, 26, 57
Elijah 68
Jno M. 49, 54, 55, 91, 110, 112, 117, 127
John 73

John M. 17, 22, 43, 44, 47, 53, 56, 59, 61, 66, 73, 75, 77, 81, 82, 85, 88, 90, 92, 101, 105, 126, 130, 142, 172
Mary 25, 130
W.W. 67, 113, 164
William 74, 187, 216
William W. 25, 57, 174, 211, 219, 229
Wm W. 56, 131, 189
Wm. 97

FRANKS & BERQWIN 175

FRAZAR
James 39

FRAZER
James 72, 163
James Senr 25

FREIZE
Jno. 110
John 141

FRESHWATER
A.M. 129
Alfred M. 76, 78, 89, 101, 135, 153
J.S.H. 74
James H. 79, 81, 108, 128, 135, 143, 149, 153, 154, 165
Jas H. 106, 134, 145
Jas. 193

FRESHWATER?
Alfred M. 118

FRIEZD

John 44
FRIEZE
    John 73, 84,
        116, 134
FRIZE
    John 51
FRIZE/FIETZ/FRISZD/FIZLOW
    John 59
FRIZZE?
    John 60
FROST
    John 45, 78, 81,
        84, 85,
        101, 104,
        123, 124,
        216, 217,
        221
FULTON?
    Lanton? C. 130
GAMATE?
    Francis 74
GARICK (See Gerack,
        Gerock)
    Charles 131
GAROCK
    Charles 164
GASTON
    William 65
GEBRON
    William J. 211
GELLET
    Thomas 65, 68
GELLIT
    Thomas 17
    Thos 24
GEORGE
    Brice 21
    Christian 21
    Clarrisa 21
    David 21, 123,
        172
    F.G. 17, 51
    Furnifold 15,
        21, 47
    Furnifold G. 21
    Lewis 21
    R.G. 30
    William 154,
        160, 178
    Wm. 158, 183
GERACK

Charles 138,
    165, 174
Saml 138
GEROCH
    Charles 161
    Chs 204
GEROCK
    C. 195
    Charles 6, 143,
        152, 154,
        165,
        169-171,
        175-181,
        183-189,
        191-198,
        200-202,
        204, 205,
        207, 208,
        211-213,
        218, 219,
        222, 223,
        228-232
    Charly 153
    Chas 178
    Chs 200
    Chs. 213
    Mary 165
GIBSON
    William I. 205,
        220
GILBERT
    Aretus 176
    Arthur 204
    Autus 7, 159
    Daniel 59
    E. 181
    Edmund M. 167
    Edward 44, 57,
        58, 96,
        100, 102,
        116, 117,
        154
    Edward M. 75,
        136, 137,
        171, 184,
        189, 190,
        199, 200,
        203, 209,
        210, 214,
        219, 232
    Edwd 19, 27, 38,
        45, 68,

78, 81, 85
Edwd M. 51, 75,
    126, 141,
    143, 147,
    160, 180,
    189
I. 43
Jno. 59
John 43, 53,
    101, 123
Joseph 37
Nathan B. 185
Robert 6, 22,
    24, 25,
    41, 43,
    71, 73,
    84, 95,
    101, 104
Robt 43, 103
Thos. 6, 155
William 14, 27,
    43, 44,
    49, 57,
    58, 73,
    92, 100,
    102, 107,
    123
Wm 60, 117, 130
Wm. P. 14
Wm/W. 52
GILDERSLEEVE
    John 80, 123
GILES
    Barnabus 224
    E.S.F. 104
    J. 113
    Jacob 17, 18,
        22, 31,
        35, 40,
        42, 44-46,
        48-50,
        52-54,
        57-59, 64,
        66, 68,
        69, 72,
        75, 77-79,
        81, 82,
        85, 93,
        96, 97,
        100, 104,
        107, 110,
        113, 116,

120, 121,
130, 133,
135, 138,
139, 142
John 224
Joseph 137
P. 33
William 2, 19,
224
William M. 34,
44, 59,
60, 73,
84, 86,
113, 115,
123, 124,
136, 139
Wm. M. 32, 33,
36, 110,
126

GILLET
Isaac 98
Lemuel 98
Seth 98
Thomas 5, 11,
12, 20,
23, 31,
37, 41-43,
53, 61,
62, 64,
66, 68-71,
81, 85,
86, 92,
98, 103,
104, 139,
144, 148,
150, 155,
161, 163,
164, 180,
182, 186,
199, 205,
206, 210,
220
Thos 11, 12, 26,
37, 40,
45, 52,
77, 78,
81, 110,
117, 120,
126, 132,
159, 192,
193

GILLETT

Thaoma 87, 228,
231
GODDIN
John 93
GODDING
John 171
GODETT
Peter 158
GODIN
James 68
GODWIN
James 44, 51,
84, 107,
116, 117,
123, 130,
131, 199,
200
Jno. 110
John 43, 54, 59,
78, 93,
124, 139,
150, 156
GOODIN
Council 19
GOODING
Andrew 188, 207
Councel 27, 95,
96, 188
Council 2, 11,
49, 53,
55, 57,
73, 93,
110,
116-118,
121-123,
126,
136-138,
141, 150,
156, 161,
176, 186,
193, 199,
202, 206,
213, 214,
219, 220,
229, 230
Counsel 37, 100,
102
Elizabeth 137
F. 126
Farnifold 222
Francis 132,
138, 171,

172, 175,
182, 184,
193, 201,
207, 220,
225, 227,
228,
232-234
Isabella 138
J. 211
Jacob 16, 29,
70, 84,
182, 192,
206, 221,
223, 229
James 156
Mary 137, 138,
142, 155,
159, 161
William 27, 32,
34, 54,
61, 62,
73, 74,
84, 86,
96, 100,
102, 110,
113, 115,
122, 123,
127, 128,
134,
137-139,
141, 142,
150, 151,
154, 159,
161, 163,
171, 185,
188, 203,
206, 214,
215, 218,
221, 230,
231, 233
William, Jr. 73,
150, 171
William, Sr. 61,
96, 100,
102, 110,
113, 159
Winifred 137
Wm. 110, 126,
168
Wm., Senr. 118
Wm., Sr. 134
GOODWIN

T.B. 74
GOULDING
    John 166
GRAHAM
    Edwd 18, 44, 65
GRANT
    Isaac 44
    S./I. 106
    Sol E. 19
    Sole E. 26, 29
    Solm. E. 13, 90
    Soloman E. 39
    Solomon E. 11, 58
    Stephen 44
GRAY
    Benjn D. 65
    Israel 99
Green
    Abner 2, 6, 7, 13, 35-37, 40, 42, 44, 57, 58, 63, 64, 67, 68, 70, 71, 79, 81, 86, 89, 94, 100, 103, 104, 107-110, 112, 114, 115, 119-123, 125, 129, 133, 135, 140, 145-150, 152-156, 159, 161, 163, 165, 169-172, 174, 175, 178-181, 183, 186, 194, 197-199, 201, 205, 207, 208, 219, 220, 223, 225, 226, 228, 230, 232
    Ann 72
    C.B. 110
    Chrisr R. 92
    Christ. R. 118
    Christopher 2
    Christopher R. 74, 77, 78, 81, 82, 92, 98, 158, 168, 177
    Christr 67
    Cornelia 42
    Cornelius 57
    David 7, 42, 48, 52, 64, 70, 71, 73, 78, 82, 85, 93, 95, 110, 115, 125, 126, 129-131, 136, 137, 145, 147, 150, 162, 163, 167-169, 180, 186, 188, 193, 199, 202, 209, 210, 213, 214, 218, 219, 223, 228, 232
    Durant 201
    E. 139
    Elizabeth 134
    F. 18
    Furnifold 168, 169
    Hambleton 57
    Hamelton 42
    James 11, 16, 81, 85, 88, 134, 141, 174, 175, 185, 232
    Jas 10, 69
    John 42, 57
    Jos 47, 76
    Joseph 23, 27, 36, 42, 46, 50, 57, 71
    L.B. 139
    Leah? 232
    Mary 35, 37, 40, 58, 108, 109, 114, 123, 129
    R. 160
    R.F. 187
    Rachel 123
    Richard 148, 171, 174, 181
    Richd 148, 164
    S./L. 47
    Sarah 42, 76, 124, 148, 164, 171, 174, 177, 181
    Sarah Ann 57
    Sarah B. 124, 158
    Serena 208
    Winifred 148, 164, 169, 174
GREEN?
    G. 59
GREGARY
    Jesse A. 61
GREGORY
    Jesse B. 16
    Lewis 37, 100
GRIFFEN
    Benjamin 16, 135
    Benjm 20
    Egbert 150
    William 39
GRIFFIN
    Dicy 36
    Egbert 152
    Jonas/James 152
GRIFFITH
    Elizabeth 138
GRINGE

Isaiah? 132
GUNTER
    N. 19, 40
    Rezon 16

HAGAINE
    John 214
HAGAINS
    John 219, 233
HAGANS
    John 168
HAGGINS (See Huggins)
    John 201
HAGGINS/HUGGINS
    John 195
HAGINS
    John 164, 172,
        182, 193,
        194, 199,
        212
HAIRSTON
    John 115
HALE
    D. 167
    Lewis 46
    Thomas 75, 76,
        147, 212
HALE/HILL
    D. 165
HALFORT?
    Richd 135
HALL
    George A. 32
    James 136
    John 6, 219
    Thomas 6, 24,
        59, 77,
        82, 223,
        231
    Thomas H. 15
    Thos 18, 98
HALLEN (See Hellen)
    William 67
HALLENTIN
    Wm. 115
HAMETE?
    George W. 230
HAMMON
    Jno 54
    Jno. H. 49, 58
    John 56
    John H. 32, 48,
        58, 59,
        61, 66,
        67, 69,
        70, 72-74,
        76, 96,
        100, 101,
        129, 194,
        213
HAMMOND
    I.H. 209
    J.H. 196
    John H. 60, 153
    W.H. 194
HAMMONS
    Jno H. 15
    John 56
    John H. 17, 18,
        24, 30,
        36, 48,
        54, 60, 61
HANCOCK
    Elizabeth L. 212
    James 193, 194,
        203, 209,
        214
    Jno. 176
    Jno., Sr. 180
    John 6, 168, 192
    Robert 198
    William 209
HANDCOCK
    Jno. 164
HARDY
    Nercison? 55
HARGET
    A. 38, 40, 72,
        84, 129
    Abner 158, 199,
        200, 206,
        228, 232
    Alford 13
    Alfred 2, 7, 12,
        18, 22,
        25, 25,
        29, 31,
        32, 35-40,
        44, 49-54,
        56, 58,
        60, 62,
        63, 67,
        76, 76,
        78, 79,
        81, 82,
        85, 94,
        96-98,
        101-104,
        110, 112,
        114, 115,
        121
    Benj. W. 15
    Benjm 21, 22
    Benjn W. 38
    E.K. 233
    Earlina 123
    Elinor? 132
    Eliza 158
    Emanuel 56, 154,
        229
    Emanuel K. 171,
        172, 175
    Emanuel Koonce
        30
    Eml K. 160, 180
    Eulinor? 140
    Exelina 140
    J.B. 33
    Jno. 24
    Jno. B. 23, 84
    John B. 12, 14,
        19, 23,
        27, 38,
        39, 52,
        53, 83,
        191
    Lewis 56, 170,
        184, 207,
        232
    Mary 207
    Nancy 155, 159
    Nathan I. 109
    Olive 194
    Penelope 155,
        159
    Peter 7, 11, 19,
        24, 24,
        27, 29,
        30, 32,
        34, 38,
        41, 53,
        57, 61,
        66, 67,
        73, 74,
        76, 80,
        92, 101,

103, 105,
107,
115-118,
120, 121,
130, 132,
138-140,
147, 150,
152, 160,
168, 171,
174, 180,
182, 183,
186, 189,
191, 194,
205, 207,
209, 210,
214,
218-220,
230-232
    Rebecah 155, 159
    William 12, 158,
233
    Zelpha 101
    Zelpy 84
    Zetphey 39
    Zilpha 44, 112,
163
HARISON
    James 32
HARPER
    Daniel/David 181
    Dempsey 158
    Drewey 204
    John 67
HARRELL
    George W. 212
HARRIET
    James 222
    Winiford 142
HARRIETS?
    George W. 230
HARRIETT
    George 53
    George W. 199
HARRIOTT
    George 228
    George W. 198
HARRISON
    Amos 26, 209
    B. 33, 36, 40,
51
    Benj 14, 17, 18
    Benjamin 10, 20,

35, 122
    Benjn 19-21, 23,
25-27, 42,
45, 60,
64, 71,
114, 124
    Daniel 7, 19,
90, 105,
121, 139,
147, 148,
160, 161,
176, 182,
184, 185,
193, 195,
198, 207,
208, 222,
228
    Elizabeth 26,
64, 161,
169
    Ephram 134
    Ephriam 99
    F.B. 16, 202
    Franklin B. 35,
190, 201
    Franklin
Benjamin
89
    G. 72
    George 185
    Ivey 167
    Ivy 209, 233
    James 6, 17, 18,
20-24, 31,
36, 39,
42, 43,
47, 49-56,
61, 63,
66, 67,
69, 70,
73, 75,
77, 79,
81, 87,
96,
101-104,
119, 120,
122, 124,
126,
133-135,
138, 140,
143,
145-147,

156, 166,
169, 177,
180, 186,
189, 190,
193, 196,
201, 207,
221, 226
    James W. 136
    James, Jr. 166
    Jas 18, 35, 36,
53, 155,
192
    Jno 54
    Jno. H. 110
    John 6, 26, 30,
46, 72,
73, 75,
77, 78,
85, 139,
140, 150,
152, 153,
160, 161,
163, 167,
169, 176,
180-182,
184, 188,
196, 197,
201, 202,
209, 221,
228
    John H. 184
    Leml 17, 19, 38,
130
    Leml H. 19
    Leml, Jr. 117
    Levi 21, 26, 30,
41, 46,
51, 75,
78, 85
    Levy 26
    Lewis 39, 74, 78
    Mary 185, 198
    Nancy 35, 44, 60
    Nany 64
    Owen 99, 117,
118, 134,
139, 147,
148, 156,
168, 180,
181, 186,
193, 194
    Polly 97

Sarry 185
Simmons 13, 14,
    19, 32,
    34, 36,
    37, 43,
    46, 50-52,
    55, 57,
    58, 61,
    63, 64,
    66, 67, 72
Simmons, Senr 39
Simmons, Jr. 30,
    69, 73,
    142
Simmons, Sr. 62
Sims, Jr. 40,
    126
Sims, Sr. 134
Stephen 198
Thomas 7, 29,
    36, 45,
    49, 61,
    66, 92,
    110, 117,
    130, 131,
    137, 139,
    140, 153,
    154, 156,
    167, 180,
    185, 193,
    199, 202,
    209-211,
    222, 228
Thomas B. 22, 36
Thos 12, 21, 27,
    32, 45,
    52, 53,
    78, 147,
    149, 185,
    187, 189
Thos B. 11, 22
Wealthy 198
Welthy 47, 198
William 6, 78,
    84, 96,
    100, 112,
    129, 158,
    176, 185,
    198, 209,
    210
Wm. 81, 110,
    126, 189

HARRISON?
    Thomas 117
HARRITAGE
    Furnifold G. 147
HARRITT
    Winifred 53
HARTEN
    David 136
HARTY
    John, Sen. 85
HATCH 116
    Alfred 206, 210
    Alice 21, 24
    Anthony 45, 67
    Asa 102, 108
    B. 99, 143
    Buckner 21, 30,
        32, 33,
        36, 40,
        90, 91,
        93, 102,
        108, 114,
        128, 140,
        163, 175,
        211
    C.A. 54, 71, 77,
        78
    Chrisr A. 97
    Christ A. 50,
        77, 81, 82
    Christopher A.
        43, 49,
        64, 66,
        69, 74,
        75, 77, 79
    Christopher H.
        87
    D. 10, 44, 52,
        90, 98,
        100, 104,
        137
    D., Jr. 10, 52
    David 49
    Du 10
    Durant 2, 10,
        12, 16-18,
        22, 24,
        25, 32,
        35, 39,
        41, 43,
        47, 49,
        50, 54,
        55, 60,
        62-65, 67,
        68, 70,
        71, 74,
        76, 79-81,
        83, 84,
        90, 91,
        94,
        98-101,
        103, 108,
        115, 121,
        130, 137,
        177
    Durant, Jr. 12,
        16, 22,
        25, 32,
        39, 41,
        43, 47,
        49, 54,
        55, 60,
        62-65, 68,
        70, 71
    E.B. 202
    Edmd 18, 19, 21,
        24, 27,
        36, 37,
        39, 43,
        45, 48,
        55, 65,
        82, 90,
        99, 106,
        110, 126,
        130
    Edmd B. 91, 99,
        139, 146,
        158, 168,
        171, 186,
        196
    Edmd, Senr. 121
    Edmd, Sr. 139,
        161, 168
    Edmond 20, 21,
        65, 66,
        68, 90,
        92, 93,
        102, 111
    Edmond B. 2, 90
    Edmond H. 228
    Edmond, Jr. 76
    Edmund 54, 128,
        158, 161,
        177, 196,

198, 202
Edmund B. 140,
    151, 154,
    161, 177,
    196, 201,
    202
Edmund H. 203
Edmund, Sr. 154,
    159
Edwd 98
Geo. 67
Geo. B. 52
Geo. C. 23, 37
George C. 12,
    16, 31,
    33, 41,
    44, 48,
    57, 65,
    78, 80,
    84, 109
George? C. 74
Haskel F. 12,
    39, 42
Henrietta B. 202
James 68, 80,
    95,
    136-139,
    151, 158
John 75
Joseph 128, 161,
    189, 229
L. 40
Leml 14, 15,
    17-19, 21,
    25, 27,
    33, 42,
    44, 46,
    84, 93, 99
Leml B. 167
Leml Jr. 32
Lemuel 21, 24,
    36, 56,
    162
Lemuel D. 137
Lemuel L. 16
Mary 16, 65
Mary A. 25, 29,
    44, 47
Mary Ann 21, 84
Mrs. M.A. 35
Nancy 39
R. 164

R.B. 75, 85, 99,
    157
R.W. 202
Rd B. 124
Ricd R. 130
Rich. B. 13, 14
Richard 65, 152,
    171, 174,
    195, 198,
    202
Richard A. 232
Richard B. 12,
    70, 202
Richard M. 206
Richard W. 91,
    186, 201,
    202, 214
Richd 175, 177
Richd B. 30, 70,
    102
Richd W. 21, 91,
    99
Shff 14, 48
William 32
William B. 13,
    20, 23,
    25, 31,
    36, 38,
    39, 66
Williams 100
Wm B. 24, 38,
    43, 47,
    64, 71, 78
HATHAWAY 10
    Isaac 11, 13,
        14, 19,
        23-27,
        30-33, 36,
        38, 49, 99
    Nancy 25, 38, 64
    Susan 26
HAUGHTON
    Thomas B. 55
HAWKINS
    Elizabeth 97
HAWKS
    John 90
    T.L. 46, 47
HAWLEY
    Burton 184
HAY
    Catharine 87

Joseph 37, 49,
    62, 96,
    97, 103,
    110, 123,
    126, 136,
    141, 150,
    162, 203,
    207, 225
HAYWOOD
    L.G. 30
    Sarah Ann 209
HAZARD
    George 50
    Thomas 31
HAZZARD
    Geo. 121
    George 50, 106,
        115, 139,
        140, 154,
        156, 158,
        161, 163,
        167, 171,
        176
    James 116, 121,
        135, 141,
        160
    Jas. 141
    Mary 224
    Samuel 160
HEATH
    77
    Abejah 69
    Abijah 17, 33
    Amos 7, 31, 66,
        85, 125,
        155, 181,
        203, 209,
        213, 221,
        230
    Barnet 148
    Harrison 7, 201
    Henry 49
    Jeremiah 212
    Jesse 194, 203
    John 2, 11, 27,
        47, 54,
        59, 62,
        69, 77,
        92, 121,
        151, 155,
        159, 165,
        183, 196,

197, 203,
209, 210,
218, 220,
221, 227,
232
John, Jr. 225
John, Senr 76,
118
John, Sr. 43,
101, 126,
134, 135,
141, 156,
206, 225,
226
L.B. 132
Leviah 101, 151
Livia 118
Lovey 223
S.B. 225
Saml B. 78, 118
Samuel B. 49,
101, 145,
156, 222,
223, 225
Soleah? 49
William 49, 101,
156
Wm. 118, 145,
167
HEATH/HINSH?
Amos 220
HEGGINS
Wiley 50
HELLEN (See Hillen)
Mary 23
Walter 14, 18,
19, 21-25,
31, 36,
37, 39,
41, 43,
46, 48,
50, 52-54,
56, 61,
62, 64,
66, 69,
72, 98
William 23-24,
27, 33,
37, 38,
49, 52,
62, 66,
67, 71,
73, 99
Wm 23, 32, 58,
76
HELLIN
Walter 17, 21
HENERY
James 59, 67
HERETAGE
F.G. 18
Furnifold 29
HERETAGE?
F.G. 60
HERITAGE
F.G. 52, 62, 70,
91
Furney G. 27, 49
Furnifold 41,
57, 58
Furnifold G. 58,
66, 68
James 39, 43,
53, 92
James G. 38, 49,
51
Jas G. 77
HERRICK/HERRIOT
Winiford/Winford
121
HERRIETTS?
George 230
HERRING
Rebecca 140, 179
William 179
HERRIOT
George 177, 193
Winifred 177
HERRITAGE
F.G. 71, 96,
104, 138,
142
Farnifold G. 14
Furnifold G. 6,
61, 70,
94, 148,
180, 191
James 92
James G. 62, 77,
103, 104,
110, 122,
125, 126,
135, 161,
174, 186,
207
Jas G. 139
Penelope 85
Richard 229
HERRITAGE?
John 130
HEWET
Rigden 48
Rigdon 29, 48,
150, 164,
180
HEWETT
Rigden 92
HEWIT
Bigton/Rigden
213
Rigd 110
Rigden 50, 65,
68, 123,
127, 146
Rigdon 5, 19,
27, 37,
38, 60,
62, 73,
92, 96,
102, 112,
122, 124,
126,
138-140,
207, 214,
218, 219
HEWITT/HERRITT
Winiford 64
HICKS
Alexander 19, 32
James W. 212
HIGGINS
Wiley F. 63, 201
Wiley W. 175
HILE/HILL
Saml 58
Samuel 125, 199
HILES/HILL
Thos H. 49
HILL
Buckner 206
Erasmus 13
Hardy 18, 20,
25, 27,
36, 48,
61, 73,
118, 186

James 159
Jas. 159
Jno. H. 67
Leml 19
S. 131, 199,
    215, 218
Saml 18, 22, 48,
    115, 118,
    159, 169,
    175
Samuel 6, 7, 22,
    37, 42,
    48, 56,
    67, 76,
    77, 82,
    96, 100,
    102, 106,
    107, 113,
    122, 123,
    129-132,
    134, 137,
    138, 140,
    142-144,
    147, 150,
    154, 156,
    159, 161,
    164, 166,
    167, 169,
    171-173,
    176,
    178-181,
    185, 186,
    188, 189,
    191, 193,
    194, 196,
    198, 199,
    202, 205,
    207, 208,
    210-212,
    215, 219,
    220, 222,
    223, 228,
    229,
    231-233
Thomas 12
Thomas H. 14,
    15, 41,
    48, 57,
    62, 78,
    93, 98
Thos 17
Thos H. 21, 37,
    70, 98
William I. 116
Wm. S. 98
HILL/HILE
    William L. 72
HILLEN
    Walter 37, 53,
        55, 124
    Wm 121
HINDS
    William 205,
        220, 231
HINDS & KINSEY 130
HINES
    Betsy 42
    Charles A. 42,
        90
    Dr. Jesse D. 200
    Elizabeth 90
    Jesse D. 203
    Julia W. 203
    William 119
HINES?
    William 209
HITE
    Wm. S. 70
HOLDEN
    Elizabeth 38
    John 38
HOLLAND
    Esther 114
    William 84
HOLLISTER
    William 100
HOSPER/HARPER
    John 80
HOTESTER?
    Wm. 99
HOUSTON
    Jno 56, 115,
        127, 155,
        170
    John 6, 31, 41,
        56, 75,
        77, 78,
        81, 84,
        91, 101,
        120, 127,
        128, 138,
        140, 141,
        144-148,
        150-153,
        155, 159,
        160, 164,
        167, 203
HOUSTON?
    Jno. 56
HOUSTON/HAIRSTON,
    Jno. 115
HOWARD
    Frances 222, 224
    G.W. 18, 221
    Geo H. 15
    Geo. 30
    Geo. W. 18
    George A. 70
    George W. 116,
        183,
        222-224
    Israel 6, 139,
        159, 164,
        169, 171,
        174, 177,
        182, 184,
        193, 194,
        199, 206,
        221, 233
    J.W. 191, 201,
        210, 227,
        228
    James 228
    James N. 79
    James W. 2, 5,
        30, 41,
        42, 54,
        58-60, 62,
        63, 70,
        73, 77,
        79, 82,
        92-95,
        102, 109,
        110, 112,
        116, 118,
        126, 129,
        132, 133,
        135, 139,
        143, 145,
        146, 150,
        152, 157,
        161, 163,
        166, 168,
        174, 179,
        180, 183,
        185-188,

190, 192,
196-201,
204,
206-208,
210, 213,
219, 220,
222,
224-226,
229, 232
 Jas W. 53, 55,
64, 70,
119, 124,
192, 193
 Josiah 11
 Julia N. 222,
224
 Julia R. 146
 William A. 225
 Zacheus 203
HUDLER
 Lemuel 190, 227
HUGGENS
 William 10
HUGGIN
 Jacob Jr. 51
 William 19
HUGGINS 233
 Ann 57
 B. 5, 71, 100,
107, 125,
129, 169
 Benjamin 2, 6,
7, 43, 47,
49, 54,
56, 60,
62, 76,
83, 89,
109, 112,
119, 121,
122, 124,
133, 135,
141, 142,
144, 145,
149, 150,
156-158,
160,
164-166,
168, 173,
174,
177-179,
187, 192,
195, 196,
198, 200,
204, 206,
207, 220,
225, 227,
233, 234
 Benjn 22, 27,
36, 39,
52, 54,
58, 62,
65, 69,
78, 83,
97, 118,
123-126,
130, 132,
133, 136,
145, 149,
150, 159,
161, 163,
167, 169,
170, 175,
192, 193
 Bryan 175
 Carolina 187
 Eliza 187
 Hardy 64, 83,
143
 Isaac C. 14
 Jacob 6, 14, 44,
57, 61,
63, 65,
66, 68,
69, 72,
73, 76-78,
83, 84,
86, 89,
93, 105,
106, 109,
112, 113,
116, 119,
121, 122,
125,
133-135,
137-143,
146, 148,
150, 151,
153, 155,
157, 162,
187
 Jacob, (Jr.?)
116
 Jacob, Jr. 44,
57, 61,
63, 66,
68, 84,
89, 93,
106
 James 18, 68,
83, 88,
109, 120,
122, 136
 James Sen. 20
 James Snr 32
 James, Sr 11, 43
 Jas 64, 84, 132
 Jerd?, Jr. 110
 John 6, 157, 184
 Jos. 123
 Joseph/Jacob,
Jr. 125
 Josiah? 49
 Lewis Sears 187
 Luke 132
 Marianna 187
 Mary Ann 142
 Matilda 104, 142
 Nancy 83
 Patsey 187
 Sarah A. 187
 Sheriff 55
 Shff 14, 110
 Susannah 83
 Thomas 141, 152,
159, 190,
193, 221,
230, 231
 Thos. 188
 W. 220
 W.F. 187
 Wiley 57
 Wiley F. 197
 William 2, 6,
14, 17,
19, 20,
22, 24,
25, 29-32,
35-38, 41,
43-46,
48-50, 52,
55-61, 63,
65, 66,
68-71, 74,
77, 79-81,
84-86, 88,
90, 95,

99, 100,
102-104,
107-109,
112, 113,
117, 119,
121-129,
131,
134-137,
139-147,
149, 150,
152, 153,
155, 157,
159,
161-165,
168-170,
172,
174-178,
181,
183-185,
187-190,
193-195,
199-205,
207, 208,
210, 211,
213, 214,
216,
218-223,
225-229,
231-233
Wm 13, 14, 25,
27, 34,
37, 38,
48, 50,
52, 60,
64, 65,
68, 72,
81, 84,
85, 89,
99, 100,
102, 106,
110, 114,
115, 119,
125, 127,
130, 133,
145, 151,
153, 165,
166, 169,
177-179,
183,
190-192,
194, 196,
202, 204,

229
HUMPHREY
    H. 19
    Hall 64
    Lewis B. 178
    Linnie B. 212
    Sarah M. 20
    W. 156
HUNTINGTON
    Mary 43, 50
    Mary C. 24
HUPEY/HUSSEY
    J.E. 162
HUSEY
    John E. 190
HUSEY/HUPEY
    John E. 162
HUSSEY
    John E. 165
HUTCHING
    Harris 177
HUTSEN
    Geo. M. 100
HUTSON
    George W. 72
    John H. 99
    Littleberry 70,
        72
HYMAN
    John N. 187
HYNEN
    William W. 107

IHS?
    Jnos. 34
IPOCK
    Elanor 164
    Elary 164
    Starky 75
IRVIN
    Shadrack 93
IRWIN
    Shaderack 95
ISAAC
    Levicy 224
ISLER
    Ann 140, 178,
        179
    Barbara 212
    E.B. 140
    Edwin B. 140,
        169, 179,

191, 211
Edwin Becton
    149, 193
George Miller
    212
James 18
John 20, 23, 30
John W. 211
John Williams
    212
Leml 17, 64, 83,
    110, 149
Nancy 177, 197
Rebecca H. 211
Rebecca Harrison
    212
S. 68
Sim. 178
Simmons 7, 14,
    15, 18,
    24, 29-31,
    34, 37,
    41-43, 50,
    51, 53,
    55-64, 66,
    67, 73,
    74, 77-80,
    82, 88,
    92, 95,
    99, 101,
    103, 108,
    109, 118,
    120, 123,
    124, 132,
    139,
    143-145,
    149, 150,
    155, 159,
    160, 166,
    169, 177,
    178, 180,
    184-186,
    191, 193,
    194, 197,
    199, 203,
    211, 212,
    214, 227
Simmons Harrison
    212
Simms 54
Sims 193
Sims/Liml 120

Stephen Williams
212
Susan H. 211
Susan Herring
212
William 2, 15,
60, 142,
146, 218
Williams 18, 20,
27, 29-31,
37, 39,
51, 52,
59, 66,
72, 73,
88, 92,
93, 95,
96, 99,
102, 110,
112, 123,
126, 132,
140, 158,
179, 184,
212
Winiford 15
Winifred 39, 80
Wm 30, 77
Wms 23, 103, 117
ISLER?
Jesse 224
Nancy 202
Simmons 120
ISLOR/TALOR
Frederick 228
IVERS?
George H. 202
IVES
Penelope
Elizabeth
47
Thomas B. 65, 70
Thomas P. 47
IVEY
Tabitha 144
JACKSON
John 32, 115
Riley 198
JARMAN
Amos 223
Barbara 224
E. 120, 206,
209, 225,
229, 233

Elizabeth 223,
224
Emanuel 2, 7,
51, 52,
55, 58,
63, 64,
66-70, 94,
104, 134,
140, 143,
163, 197,
202, 207,
210, 211,
220, 222,
223, 225,
229, 231,
232
Eml 31, 42, 43,
49, 51,
57, 58,
63, 70,
109, 120,
131, 140,
142, 143,
146, 163,
179, 226,
234
F.H. 126, 207,
223
Furnifold 146
Furnifold H. 6,
176
J.J. 214
Job L. 223
John 203,
223-226,
229-231
John, Jr. 206,
208, 214,
219
McLendal 224
Risdon 224
Salome 223
Sarah 223
Sidney 86, 87,
134
Thomas 224
William 224
JARMEN
Emanuel 48
Eml 13, 35, 37,
51
Sidney 35

Wm. 34
JARMON (See Jerman)
? 150
B. 94
Braddock 85
E. 33, 75, 80,
98, 108,
132, 149,
156, 164,
206, 209
Emanuel 23, 25,
38, 46,
49, 57,
59, 72,
74, 75,
81, 85,
87-89, 92,
101, 103,
105, 108,
109, 119,
128, 129,
132, 135,
138, 144,
145, 149,
150, 152,
154, 156,
157, 162,
165, 167,
169, 170,
174-179,
184, 191,
192,
195-197,
207, 208,
212, 221
Eml 17, 18,
20-23, 29,
31-33,
35-38, 40,
42, 45-48,
50, 67,
67, 72,
74, 76-83,
85, 87,
89, 90,
99, 103,
104, 106,
109, 110,
113-115,
119, 121,
123,
131-133,

138, 141,
146, 147,
153, 155,
158, 159,
161-163,
167-170,
176, 178,
179, 183,
188,
190-193,
195, 196,
233
F.H. 130, 159,
176, 179,
182, 197
Farny H. 176
Furnifold 141,
150, 155,
192
Furnifold H. 7,
128, 134,
145, 156,
168, 171,
184, 193,
208
Hardy 14, 21,
35, 40,
86, 98
John 19, 32,
176, 192,
213, 214,
229
John, Jr. 7
John, Sr. 161,
190
Rachel 17, 203
Risdon 19
Sidney 98, 151
Susan 180
Thomas 181
William 14, 37,
41, 104
JARVIS
Marrit 141
Moses 44, 47,
59, 62,
70, 70,
72, 84,
90, 115
Moses W. 58, 98,
99, 102,
109

JENTRIES
    Vincent M. 34
JERKINS
    Alonzo T. 102
JERMAN
    Emanuel 200-202,
        204-206
    Furnifold 200
    John, Jr. 204
JOHN
    Wm. 164
JONES
    Allen 33, 90,
        107, 209
    Allen? 149
    Amos 203
    Aretices 228
    Arial 38, 40
    Band? 203
    Bazel 38, 227
    Bryan 83, 113,
        170, 203
    Calvin 19
    Edward 215
    Edward S. 65,
        66, 224,
        234
    Edward S./L. 124
    Edwd 42
    Edwd I. 110, 116
    Edwd L. 123, 169
    Edwd S. 44, 45,
        52, 69,
        98, 109
    Elijah 38
    Eml F. 7, 163
    Ezekiel 111,
        162, 221,
        234
    Frederick 186
    George D. 162,
        170
    Hardy 15, 20
    Henery W. 62
    James 56, 59,
        230
    James, Sr. 183
    Jason, Jr. 156
    Jno. 40, 155
    John 23, 24, 32,
        35, 40,
        47, 49,

60, 62,
64, 70,
72, 73,
84, 86,
87, 90,
91, 107,
110-113,
123, 125,
129, 132,
133, 135,
145, 154,
162, 163,
165-167,
172, 175,
176,
181-184,
191, 193,
198, 199,
201,
205-207,
209, 210,
218, 220,
223, 230,
231, 233
Jonas 2, 7, 26,
41, 43,
47, 52,
66, 68,
70, 72,
74, 78,
80, 86,
87, 91,
93,
110-113,
123, 125,
131,
136-140,
142,
147-149,
151, 162,
165, 167,
171, 177,
179, 183,
186, 187,
194, 198,
203, 204,
206, 209,
212, 215,
218, 231
Jonas, Jr. 66,
78
King G. 55

Levi 42, 63, 69,
    70, 75,
    78, 82,
    84, 101,
    104, 126,
    137, 189,
    199, 207
Levi? 118
Levy 203, 228,
    233
Lewis 7, 50, 220
M. 75
Marret 78, 96,
    143
Marrett 156, 212
Marriett 152
Marrit 117, 118,
    193
Marritt 186
Martin 203
Mary 170, 206
Merit 136
Meritt 199
Merrit 116, 121,
    143, 167,
    171, 200
Merritt 68, 150,
    217, 221,
    230, 231
Polina Ann 221
Reading 21
Riley 108, 210
Sarah 69, 224
T.B. 36
William 14, 52,
    116, 123,
    129, 156,
    161, 186
Williams 32, 34,
    44, 59,
    60, 68,
    73, 84,
    139, 150,
    176, 193
Willie 1
Wm 38, 111
Wm R. 19

JONES?
    John 59
JUSTICE
    John 70
KAY
    Joseph 38, 78,
        105
KELLEBREW
    Henery 45
KENNY/KENSY
    Joseph 230
KENSEY
    Joseph 96, 118
KENSY
    J. 230
KESSAN
    Frederick 118
    Timothy I. 118
KEY
    Ann 61
    Jonathan 65
    Joseph 61, 87,
        105
    Sam 151
KILLBREW?
    Piety 233
KILLEBREW
    Abner 31, 35,
        64, 78,
        138, 142,
        171, 211
    Abner W. 186,
        187, 196,
        212, 221
    Abram W. 189
    Henchey 51, 57,
        64
    Henchy 51
    Hinchey 78
    Hinchy 75
    John 137
    William 35, 40,
        51
KILLIBREW
    Abner 46, 75,
        120
    Hinchey 40, 46
    Hinchy 47
    William 46
KILLIGREW
    Abner 167
KILLINGSWORTH
    Jno. 74
KINCEY
    David 196
    George P. 175
    J.S. 179
    James 7, 135,
        176, 192
    James D. 162,
        170, 172,
        176, 179,
        184, 189,
        190,
        195-197,
        203
    James G. 202
    Jas D. 183
    Jas., Sr. 180
    John 7, 176, 199
    Joseph 82, 134,
        166, 170,
        182, 186,
        188, 190,
        199, 201,
        202, 223,
        225, 233
    Joseph, Jr. 7,
        192
    Joseph, Sr. 168,
        189
    Lewis 134, 139,
        193, 203
    Lewis D. 180
    Mary 80
    Stephen 169
    William M. 168
KINCY
    James D. 200,
        205, 207,
        226
    Joseph 206, 227
    Lewis 214
KING
    Felia 165
    Felia/Felix 166
    Felix 171, 180,
        193, 207,
        225, 227,
        231, 233
    Geo. 39
    George 12, 31,
        32, 34,
        46, 49,
        71, 72,
        94, 139,
        147, 148,
        156, 157,
        159, 167,

169, 176,
233
Ivey 158
Vartier 38
William 55
Wm 11
KINSEY
C. 42
Charity 70, 88,
89, 98,
113
Chrisr 33, 100
Christ. 42
Christopher 23,
47, 69,
70, 75,
80, 113,
120
Erasmus 140
Geo. P. 99
George P. 155
Hannah H. 160
J. 113
J.D. 189
J.G. 10
J.S. 77
James 70, 88,
118
James B. 160
James D. 70, 89,
113, 121,
134, 137,
145, 154,
164
Jay Robert 12
Jno J. 10
John 35, 158
John G. 19, 47
Jos. 94
Joseph 2, 7, 11,
12, 19,
21, 37,
49, 50,
52-54, 66,
70-72, 74,
78, 79,
83, 90,
94, 100,
102, 103,
107, 108,
113, 117,
130, 132,
135, 141,
143, 145,
148-150,
153, 156,
159, 208,
218, 228,
230
Joseph, Senr 116
Joseph, Sr. 11,
145, 161
Lewis 2, 20, 23,
27, 29,
33, 41,
48, 49,
59, 60,
68, 145,
154, 156,
159, 160
Mary 52
Maurice/Morris
11
S. 99
Samuel D. 232
Sarah 70
Stephen 27, 29,
107
Susan 138
KINSEY/KINCEY
Joseph 151
KINSEY/KORNEGAY
Isaac 92
KINSY
J. 230
James D. 228
Jas. D. 225
Jos. 230
Joseph 232, 233
Joseph B. 228,
230, 231
KNIGHT 34, 131
Asa 14, 40
Daniel 14, 40,
186, 189,
230
Fanney 40
Fanny 54, 193
K. 164
Kader 67, 114,
142, 156,
179, 182
Kader Jr. 31,
223
Matilda 40
KNIGHTS
Fanny 12
Kader 12
KNISE?
Rubin 65
KOONCE
A.S. 209, 213
Amos 65, 166,
171, 174,
175, 206,
209, 221,
233
Amos I. 7, 138,
207, 226,
232, 234
Amos S. 97, 99,
190, 207,
225, 227
B. 33, 44, 60
Beneten? 198
Beneter 142, 198
Benj. 14, 110
Benjamin 7, 19,
30, 44,
47, 52,
57, 65,
68, 74,
93, 95,
115, 153,
161, 196,
205, 207,
211, 214,
218, 231
Benjn 19, 27,
30, 33,
37, 47,
49, 58-62,
65, 67,
71, 100,
113, 149,
153, 159,
175, 193
Benjn Jr 27
Benjn M., Jr 13
C.B. 120, 132
Calvin 6, 7, 37,
54, 67,
75, 78,
81, 84,
85, 94,
99, 101,

271

103, 104,
110, 117,
121, 125,
128,
130-132,
137-139,
144-150,
153-155,
157, 158,
161, 163,
166,
169-171,
176,
178-181,
183, 184,
191-194,
197, 198,
200, 205,
207, 208,
210, 211,
213,
217-220,
223, 225,
226,
228-231
E. 84, 104, 164,
234
E.F. 120, 132,
146
E.F.B. 156, 167,
190, 193
Elijah 14,
17-19, 24,
27, 39,
44, 51,
62, 66,
67, 76-78,
84, 94,
107, 118,
121, 129,
131, 136,
137, 139,
141, 143,
154, 160,
161, 164,
167, 176,
180, 182,
193, 194,
196, 206,
207, 210,
214, 219,
229

Elijah B. 167
Elijah S. 196
Elizabeth 75,
85, 94,
203
Emanuel 61, 63,
76, 164,
165, 176,
184, 203,
204, 209,
210, 221,
229-231,
233
Eml 17, 20, 23,
31, 36,
76, 125,
167, 234
Harriet 155, 165
Hollan/Holban
170
Hollon 40
I.C.B. 184, 186,
206
Isaac 33, 70
J. 75
J.C. 146
J.C.B. 146, 167,
193, 214
J.S. 156
Jacob 29
Jacob? 130
Jarman 224
Jarod? 188
Jas. S. 153
Jerod 120, 129,
131, 139,
140, 142,
143, 146,
148, 149,
170
Jerome? 125
Jno. 33
Jno. C.B. 156
Jno. P. 120, 132
Jno. S. 142,
150, 154,
160, 162,
164, 167,
169, 170,
189, 225
John 14, 21, 33,
66, 74,

90, 94,
104, 227
John (B?) 143
John C.B. 199,
230
John I. 84
John L. 135
John P. 104,
140, 146,
154
John S. 7, 78,
81, 94,
97, 99,
101, 104,
107, 114,
126, 129,
130, 132,
133, 135,
136,
138-140,
145, 146,
149-151,
153, 155,
157, 158,
160, 164,
170, 172,
176, 183,
188, 191,
194, 199,
202, 205,
206, 210,
212, 214,
218-220,
223, 226,
230, 232
John S./L. 129
Lewis 203, 204,
206, 207,
215, 219,
228
Lidia 29, 40
Luke? 80
M. 71, 142
Martha 30, 78
Marthy 88
Mary 97, 189,
191, 197,
229, 234
Michael 7, 13,
16, 18,
23, 32,
46, 64,

66, 75,
78, 85,
91, 94,
97, 99,
101, 114,
117, 118,
122, 123,
127, 130,
139, 140,
146, 149,
153, 154,
158, 159,
164-166,
170, 176,
177, 197,
202, 203
Mrs. Baneter 147
N. 185
Nancy 97, 189,
191, 197
Nancy E. 176
Patsey 95
Penelope 15, 32,
36, 42,
45, 75
Penny 13
Philpenea 88
Philpenia 36
Philpiny 36
Phylpenea 81
Rich. 14
Richard 18, 20,
24, 64,
75, 85,
100
Richd 31, 34,
74, 78,
85, 88, 94
Sally 142
Simeon E. 97
Simon 6, 170,
226
Simon E. 154,
190
Simon S. 220
Susan E. 176
Tobias 13, 18,
20, 27,
30, 33,
41-43, 47,
49, 58,
60, 65,

67, 75-77,
83, 93,
95, 104,
110, 112,
123, 126,
141, 142,
161, 163,
168, 169
Wiley 233
Winifred 30, 78,
88
Zenos 24
Zilpah 30
KOONES
Benj. 12
KORNEGAY
Abram 176
Catharine 146,
147, 149
Danl 186
Hamilton 52
Isaac 13, 14,
18, 21,
22, 37,
46-48, 51,
53, 59-62,
69, 75,
76, 97,
100, 127
Jno. 112
L.W. 127
Letitia 52, 65
Lewis 59, 66, 77
Lewis W. 53, 55,
62, 78,
93, 95,
110
Margaret 52
Mary 52
R. 10, 44, 52
Rob. 49
Robert 13, 17,
18, 25,
52, 193
Robt 10, 27, 54
Susan 13
Thomas 52
KRUONCE (KOONCE?)
Felpinca 51
LANE
Barbary 91
Elias 78, 80,

81, 91,
93, 98,
99, 102,
168
Levin B. 14, 19,
63, 65,
221
Vasty 98
Winifred 138
LARAQUE
Dr. Jas. B. 125
James 26
James B. 6, 91,
132, 134,
149, 154
James E. 125
Jas 79
Lois? 131
Mary 66
Nancy 156
Nancy R. 153
William L. 53,
122, 124,
136, 141,
156
William S. 99
LAROQUE
Doct. 10
James B. 91
Mrs. 125
Nancy 202
William 2
William L. 66,
141, 154
Wm L. 142
LAVANDER
Bryan 71
LAVENDER
B. 76
Bryan 20, 21,
36, 39-41,
46, 46,
51, 53,
55, 68,
69, 71,
72, 78,
87, 93,
104, 109,
115, 116
Charlotte 51
Elizabeth 60
Lewis 51

LAVINDER
    B. 40
    Bryan 33, 39
LEARY
    Penelope 64
LEATH?
    Benjn 165
LEE
    J.W. 10, 21
    Jesse 19
    Jesse W. 19,
        23-24, 27,
        29, 31,
        33, 37,
        45, 52
    Jonathan 12, 13,
        22, 68
    Stephen 158
    Thomas 159
LEFERY/LEPECY
    Sarah 182
LEGGET
    Thos H. 71
LENT
    M.H. 110
    Michael H. 110
LEPSAY?
    Sarah 179
LEPSEY
    Rosco 158
LESSERY/LAFSEY
    Rosco 182
LESTER
    Banister 98
LEVANDER
    Betsy 21
    Bryan 70
    John 21
LEWIS
    David 96, 124
    Tom 74
LEWIS?
    William K. 193
LIETZ
    Nancy 48
LIMON/SIMMONS
    B.C. 121
LIN
    Thos M. 76
LIN?
    Thomas 193
LIPSEY
    Isaac 182
    Rosco 185
    Sarah 158, 185
    Timothy 182
LISSEY?
    John 182
LITTLE
    Jesse 125
LITTLETON
    Thomas 72
LOCKEY
    Henry 182
LOFTEN
    F.B. 164, 185
    J. 41
    Joseph 51, 65,
        96, 104
    Mary 160, 164,
        185
LOFTIN
    Elizabeth 138
    John 220
    Joseph 13, 45
LOFTON
    Frederick A. 181
    Joseph 16, 75
    Joseph B. 160
    Mary 181
    Samuel 138
    Shaderack 101,
        138
LOVECK
    Elijah 101, 104
LOVET
    David 72
    Densee 72
    Elijah 75, 78
    Jno. 72
    Mary H. 135, 142
    Mary N. 165
LOVETT
    David 56, 128,
        133, 149,
        157, 158
    Elijah 46, 133,
        138, 139,
        149, 157,
        158, 170,
        196
    James Monrow 170
    Mary 139, 191
    Mary H. 133, 196

LOVETTE
    Elijah 6, 231
LOVICK
    David 80
    John 44
LOVIT
    David 121, 135
    Elijah 121, 124,
        126
LOVITT
    David 55, 138,
        155
    Dempsey 55
    Elijah 155, 195
    James M. 195

M(?)
    Hardy 123
MADES
    James 18, 23,
        27, 30,
        37, 38,
        61, 68,
        73, 74,
        96, 100,
        102, 110,
        112, 118,
        129, 138,
        139, 148,
        161, 163,
        164, 167,
        180, 181,
        186,
        189-191,
        210, 232
    Jno. 30
MADES?
    James 61
MADIS
    James 27, 29
MAIDS
    James 49, 150,
        209, 225
MALLARD
    Betsy 198
    Betsy Susan 198
    D. 110
    Daniel 2, 16,
        40, 64,
        90, 97,
        101, 124,
        134, 135,

137, 145,
147, 150,
154, 156,
157, 166,
171, 174,
186, 191,
193, 195,
199, 209,
210, 212,
225, 230,
231, 233
Daniel, Jr. 61
Daniel, Sr. 97,
174, 198
Elender 212
Frances Ann 85
Jas. 130
Jno. 14, 27, 110
John 14, 15, 22,
24, 25,
27, 44,
45, 51,
59, 60,
72, 76,
77, 85,
90, 92,
107, 123,
124, 133,
141, 150,
152, 159,
160, 164,
166, 168,
199, 207,
214, 221
Kesiah 97
Kezziah 198
Laney 198
Laura 97
Lawson 40, 44,
49, 52,
59, 72,
73, 93,
198, 212
Nancy 212
Sarah 198
Shaderack 37,
38, 44,
45, 68,
74, 97,
101, 104,
128, 198
Shadk 84

Shadrack 49, 51,
52, 57,
73, 126
Shadrick 198
William Hardy 85
MALLARD/WALLAND
Joseph 130
MAPAN/MASSAN
James 130
MAPLES?
Nathan P. 167
MARKET
B. 165
Elijah 14, 15,
22, 41,
42, 49,
52, 62
Frederick 6,
184, 196
MARKET/MASKET
Elijah 41
MARRET
I.L. 13
James 7, 16, 22,
24, 25,
27, 46,
49, 50,
52, 58-60,
69, 73,
80, 83,
100-102,
147, 158,
160, 168,
170, 171,
174, 182
Jas 12, 75, 84,
106, 129
John 176, 178
MARRETT
Francis 211
James 148, 150,
154, 184,
209, 210,
221, 225,
227
James Marrett
227
John 209, 212,
225, 228
MARRIETT
James 158
MARRIT

James 15, 18,
29, 31,
32, 35,
36, 53,
91, 115,
117, 121,
126, 167,
182
Jas. 115, 139
MARRITS
James 218
MARRITT
Francis 208
James 20
John 199, 208,
221, 222,
228
MARROTT
J.S. 179
MARSHEL
Jno. 78
MARTIN
Clerk 48
Lemuel/Lemont
128
MASEY
Zedoc M. 196
MASHBERN
Daniel 52
MASHBIRN
Daniel 48
MASHBURN
Ann 224
Daniel 42, 59,
87
MASSAN
John 131, 136,
138
MASSLES/MAPLES
Nathaniel P. 147
MATTACKS
Micajah 75
MATTECKS
Micajah 29
Micajah F. 53
MATTICKS
Micajah F. 219
MATTOCK
Micajah F. 61,
96
MATTOCKS
F. 110

275

Francis 5, 132,
        134, 209
M.F. 110, 193,
        209
Micaijah 79
Micajah F. 6,
        22, 54,
        55, 61,
        66, 67,
        96, 104,
        114, 132,
        136, 137,
        141-143,
        145, 160,
        166, 180,
        182, 190,
        196, 197,
        206, 218,
        221, 223
Micijah F. 109
Thomas 134

MATTS
    E. 130
MATTUCKS
    M.F. 205, 214
MATTUKS
    M.F. 23
MAURHAUN?
    John B. 171
Mc(DANIEL?)
    Morris 114
McBINE
    Thos. 32
McDANIEL
    Adonijah 6, 192,
            229, 231
    Baude/Bazel 213
    Bazel 6, 176
    Benjamin 51, 221
    Buckner 51
    Cassandra 224
    Christopher 51,
            152, 167,
            193
    D. 113
    David 51, 129,
            133, 136,
            141, 145,
            189
    Durant 18, 25,
            32, 37,
            42, 51,
            67, 83,
            105, 108,
            132, 152
    Edney 51, 164
    Edney I. 190
    Edney I./S. 176
    Edney L. 138
    Edney S. 49,
            203, 232
    Elijah 51, 164,
            165, 168,
            180, 184,
            193, 207,
            214, 219,
            221, 228,
            233
    F. 143, 216
    Farnifold 6,
            176, 226,
            228
    Furnifold 143,
            159, 192,
            208, 210,
            213, 216,
            229
    James 6, 22, 27,
            40-42, 45,
            46, 49,
            51, 52,
            59, 60,
            62, 64,
            67, 68,
            71-74, 76,
            77, 81,
            82, 85,
            88, 100,
            102, 105,
            108, 112,
            124, 130,
            131, 133,
            138, 139,
            142, 144,
            146-150,
            153-156,
            159, 161,
            169, 176,
            177, 181,
            182, 184,
            189, 190,
            194, 196,
            198,
            204-206,
            212, 219,
            225, 228,
            230, 233
    Jas 45, 46, 85,
            99, 100,
            102, 109,
            110, 115,
            145, 179
    Jno. 39, 108
    Jno., Sr. 126,
            134
    John 7, 11, 27,
            30, 37,
            39, 43,
            43, 51,
            68, 69,
            71-74, 96,
            100, 107,
            108, 128,
            134, 141,
            143, 151,
            154, 160,
            167, 180,
            186, 189,
            190, 199,
            200, 209,
            210, 214,
            225, 227,
            230
    John A. 212
    John F. 45
    John Lewis 108
    John T. 37, 46
    John, Sr. 107,
            160
    Laney 45
    Lany 212
    Lemuel/Samuel
            108
    M. 10
    Mahala 24
    Mary 104, 108,
            122, 126,
            127, 148,
            159, 191,
            201
    Mary A. 80, 152,
            153, 174
    Mary Ann 51
    Mitchel 63
    Mitchel Busick
            30

Morris 14, 15,
    24, 25,
    30, 31,
    37, 67,
    76, 79,
    84, 105,
    114, 119,
    123, 126
Moses 63
Mrs. Rachel 120
Penelope 80
R. 169
R.M. 10, 25, 29,
    58, 63,
    85, 101,
    126, 158,
    180, 184,
    190, 191,
    203, 205,
    207, 209,
    219, 220,
    222,
    225-227,
    229, 231
Rachael 51, 176
Rachel 49, 55,
    80, 130,
    138, 139,
    164, 190,
    232
Resden 25, 51,
    51, 55,
    79, 158,
    161, 167
Resden M. 10,
    11, 26,
    30, 32,
    49, 52,
    58, 63, 66
Resdon 42, 58,
    60
Resdon M. 18,
    31, 38,
    42, 45,
    47, 54,
    56, 59
Richard M. 204
Risden 12, 21,
    22, 24,
    41, 139
Risden M. 17,
    19-22, 25,
    36, 37,
    43, 63,
    67, 69,
    72, 73
Risden, Jr. 71
Risden, son of
    Jas. 24,
    37
Risden, son of
    R. 62
Risden, son of
    Risden 68
Risdon 2, 13,
    16, 17,
    25, 36,
    44, 51,
    55, 71,
    74, 76,
    108, 115
Risdon M. 13-15,
    19, 25,
    29, 31,
    35, 37,
    39, 41,
    43, 50-52,
    64
Risdon, Capt. 76
Risdon, Jr. 17
Risdon, son of
    Jas. 36
Risdon, son of
    Ris. 36
Risen M. 35
Sarah J.C. 99
Silas 14, 15,
    27, 35,
    37, 38,
    51, 57,
    65, 68,
    69, 72,
    92, 110,
    113, 115,
    123, 130
Starkey 159,
    205, 211
Thomas 11, 44,
    45, 49,
    51, 52,
    62, 66,
    73, 79,
    84, 85,
    106-108,
    123, 129,
    131, 136,
    137, 141,
    143, 150,
    156-160,
    167, 171,
    180, 189,
    199, 200,
    206, 221,
    226, 230,
    232
Thos 27, 35, 52,
    109, 196
William 32, 34,
    37, 51,
    58, 61,
    62, 65-67,
    71, 77,
    80, 84,
    101, 108,
    123, 124,
    132
William Senr 36,
    48
William, Jr. 76
William, Sr. 57,
    59
Wm 46, 130
Wm. Senr 48
Wm., Sr. 106
McDANIELS
    Calvin 63
    Drusillia 63
    James 56
    John 63
    Moses 63
    Resden M. 54, 64
    Risdon 13
    Silvester 63
    William 71
McKINEY
    Ann 85
    Frances Ann 85
    William Hardy 85
McKINLEY
    Mary 195
McLIN
    Thomas 64, 141
    Thos. 44
McQUETTIN
    Nancy 80
MCQUILIN

Nancy 34
McQUILLIN
    Thomas 43
MEADOW
    William H. 51
MEADOWS
    B. 161
    Bartey 52
    Barthalomas 129
    Barthalomew 6,
        11, 60,
        62, 73,
        74, 145,
        152, 156,
        161, 163,
        184, 193,
        209, 210,
        219
    Barthlomew 182,
        194, 195
    Bartholmy 126
    Bartholomew 32,
        43, 65,
        66, 99,
        101, 136,
        137, 150,
        161, 176,
        198, 199,
        201, 207,
        214, 218
    Cassa? 190
    Charity 52
    Delila 107, 114,
        137, 142
    Edwd 157
    Isaac 22, 33, 93
    Isaac H. 22, 26,
        29, 32,
        34, 44,
        49, 52,
        53, 61,
        66, 93,
        190
    Isaac N. 37
    Jason 68
    Job 26
    Jobe 93
    Marcum 56
    Melaton 154
    Meriem? 48
    Milentin 126
    Milenton 57, 93,
        107, 194
    Mileton 219
    Militon 206
    Millenton 51,
        95, 107,
        123, 124,
        139, 157,
        169, 176,
        182, 183,
        193
    Milleton 27
    Millington 2,
        73, 93,
        199
    Millinton 161,
        214
    Roe 93
    S. 142
    Simeon 40, 54,
        57, 107,
        137, 157,
        219
    Thomas L. 11
    Thos 11, 16
    William 44, 60
    William H. 20,
        27, 44,
        59, 60,
        73, 154
    Wm. H. 18, 40,
        99
    Zadock 73
    Zeadock 44, 53,
        61
MEADOWS/MUNDINE
    William 198
MERRET
    James 43, 45
MERRETT
    Francis 195
    John 205
MERRILS
    Wiley S. 209
MERRIOT
    Winifred 151
MERRIT
    James 43, 193,
        200
    Wily N. 193
MERRITS
    Wiley M. 228
MERRITT
    Francis 7, 207
    James 199
    John 7, 193,
        199, 201
MERRITTS
    Wiley S. 227
MERRITTS/MERRELLS
    Wiley 189
MESSAN
    Bryan 134
    James 134, 135,
        141
    John 135, 141
MESSAU
    John 72, 73
MESSAW
    James 148
MESSAW/MESSAN
    John 64
MESSER
    Bryan 106, 108
    Caroline 45
    James 45, 96,
        100, 106,
        107, 113,
        212, 214,
        228
    John 93, 212,
        220, 221,
        227, 230,
        231
    Susan 228
    William 65, 228
    Wm. 110
MESSOR
    Bryan 84, 86
    James 197
    John 93, 198,
        202, 203
    William 84, 86
METTS
    Emory 7, 139,
        147, 148,
        156, 167,
        171, 189,
        199, 208-
        210, 225,
        227, 232
METTS?
    L.E. 209
MIDDLETON
    Delila 20

Samuel 148
MIL(ERS?)
    Martin 207
MILE?
    Elijah S. 47
MILLER
    Councel 109
    D.W. 181
    Daniel 133, 138, 155, 159, 161
    Daniel W. 144
    Danl. 14
    Eley 36
    Elizabeth Jane 144
    Imila N. 138, 139
    Imla N. 138, 206
    James 58, 62, 96, 101, 105, 130, 146
    James (S?) 142
    James I. 104
    James I./S. 116
    James S. 78, 101, 108, 121, 122, 127, 130, 138, 144
    James? 125
    Jas 39, 58, 62
    Jas I. 118
    Jas S. 80
    Jno 21
    Joshua 167, 182, 184, 186, 193
    Joshuay 171
    M. 181
    Martin 125, 127, 144, 146, 225, 227
    Martin F. 144
    Mary Ann 144
    N. 14
    Sally 62
    Sarah 58, 85
    Stephen 85
MILLS
    James 107

MILTON?
    Joshuay 209
MIPAW
    Bryan 123
    James 123
MISSAU
    Bryan 78, 118
    James 78, 147
    Jas 118
    John 74, 78
MISSAW
    Bryan 80, 81, 151
    James 81, 84, 143, 147, 151, 156, 158, 167, 180, 181, 185, 187, 189, 190, 196
    John 121, 143, 145, 149, 158, 160, 161, 180, 181, 189, 191
    William 80
MISSAW?
    John 65
MISSAW/MIPAW
    Bryan 122
    James 122
MISSITFORD?
    William 127
MISSOW/MIPOW
    William 123
MITCHEL
    Abraham 26, 67, 74, 96
    Alexander 103, 227
    William 98
MITCHELL
    Abraham 81
    H.B. 214
MONROE
    James 133
MONTFORD
    Ewg.? W. 221
    James 197
    Louisa 222, 224

    William Henry 222, 224
MOON
    Amos 95
    Brice 113
    Loveck G. 101
MOORE
    Adline 135
    Amos 81
    Daniel 135
    Hardy 64
    L.G. 124
    Lemmos 75
    Levi 74
    Lily 111
    Lim 177
    Lim/Sim 71
    Lovick C. 82
    Lovick G. 70, 75, 78, 79, 82, 106, 118, 121, 123
    Rachel 135
    Sim 113
    Simmons 162
MOORE?
    Lawson M. 212
MOORE/MOSES
    Brice 162
MOOREHOUSE
    John B. 211
MOOREHOUSE?
    John B. 197
MOORHOUSE
    John B. 184
MORE
    Simmons 139
MORGAN
    Micajah 225
MORGEN
    James 72
MORGIN
    Wm. 108
MORRIS 214
    Alexander 47
    Beneter 47
    C.J. 99, 102, 129, 133, 136, 139, 142, 179, 189, 204

Calvin I./S. 76
Calvin J. 6, 78,
    80, 98,
    101, 102,
    107, 112,
    115, 116,
    121, 124,
    126, 135,
    136, 158,
    168, 171,
    173, 176,
    195
Graylin 168
Jno 18, 34, 39,
    88, 99
John 12, 19, 21,
    22, 24,
    27, 29,
    34, 39,
    40, 47,
    51, 79,
    83, 84,
    91, 98,
    152
L. 34
Leml 47
Lewis 12, 18,
    22, 34,
    79, 83,
    88, 109,
    120, 128,
    131, 134
Nancy 182
Rachel 142
Reading 102, 196
Redding 98
Richard 26
Sarah 132
Seth 43, 98,
    102, 152
Seth G. 154
William H. 227
William I. 201
William S. 76
Wilson 26
Wm. 24
MORSE
    Uriah 51
MORSE/MOSES
    Calvin J. 146
MORTON 229
    James 6, 159,
        174, 184
MOSLEY
    William D. 178
MUMFORD
    B. 35, 87
    Bryan 17, 51,
        69, 79
    Edwd 128
    James 47, 122,
        139, 158,
        160, 164,
        165, 170,
        179, 181,
        192, 196,
        209
    Jas. 180
    Penelope 47,
        147, 193
    Penit? 122
    William 121, 157
    Zeadock 102
MUNDINE
    Ann 161, 163,
        164
    Francis 137, 161
    Hardy 5, 11, 17,
        22, 44,
        45, 49,
        52, 59,
        60, 73,
        77, 93,
        95, 101,
        105, 124,
        134, 137,
        138, 142,
        163, 164,
        167
    Hepsey 198
    Hessy/Hepsey 161
    William 161,
        196, 209
MUNFORD
    James 81
    Penelope 81
MUNTFORD
    James 204
MURPHEY
    Carolina 114
    Fanney 41
    T. 33
    Thomas 43
    Thos 10, 11
    Ths. 41
    William 114
MURPHY
    67
    Carolina 108,
        116, 125,
        131
    Caroline 16
    Deborah 104,
        115, 116,
        156, 167,
        190, 193
    Debrule? 146
    Eliza 16
    Frances (Fanny)
        16
    Maria 167
    Marinda 104,
        115, 116,
        146, 156,
        170, 176
    Mary 16, 63, 90,
        103, 104,
        120, 153,
        156
    Miranda 16
    Thomas 16, 61,
        71, 72,
        89, 108,
        115, 116,
        138
    Thos 46, 49, 54,
        63, 65,
        67, 90,
        108, 125,
        131
    William 116,
        133, 140,
        168, 227
    William C. 7,
        90, 167,
        186, 199,
        207-209,
        221, 227,
        228
    William Clark 16
    William E. 104
    Wm. 104, 193
    Wm. C. 178, 180,
        182, 195,
        228
    Wm. E. 164

NELSON
    Francis J.W. 99
NEWBOLE
    Bazel 232
    Nancy 231
NEWBOLES
    Nancy 232
NEWTON
    H.O. 193, 212
    Hardy A. 147,
        160
    Hardy B. 191
    Hardy O. 7, 55,
        125, 137,
        140, 149,
        155, 158,
        168, 171,
        174,
        180-182,
        184, 197,
        203, 204,
        211, 212,
        216, 220,
        221, 227
NICHOLSON
    Henery H. 68
NICKBIREN
    H. 44
NICKLESON
    Henery H. 51
NIGHT (See Knight)
    Kader 87
NOBLE
    B. 31, 36, 54,
        76, 129
    Braddock 36, 52,
        61-63, 66,
        67, 72,
        73, 76,
        85, 94,
        98, 110,
        135, 165,
        188, 202,
        229
    Bradeck 36
    Braderik 17
    Bradick 36, 37,
        39
    Brodrick 22, 43,
        50
    D. 47
    Daniel 42
    Enoch 135, 188
    Enock 165, 229
    Jeremiah 42, 80
    Richd 47
NOBLES
    Daniel 36
    Jerry 36
NORRIS
    Gray 203, 219,
        230
    Narcissa 219
    Thomas 80
NUNCE?
    James 214

O´SHAUGHNESSY?
    Daniel 165
OLDFIELD
    ... 36
    Geo. 19, 24, 32,
        62, 80,
        126
    George 11, 14,
        17, 22,
        84, 98
    Mrs. 117
    Prudence 126
    Prudy 45
    R. 54
    Rich. 41
    Richard 6, 16,
        45, 136,
        152, 201,
        203, 205,
        206, 214,
        219,
        229-232
    Richd 23, 35,
        53, 87,
        148
    Sarah 35, 41,
        45, 53-55,
        87, 121,
        126, 135,
        136, 154,
        177, 230
    Susan 45, 118
    Urban 2, 40, 48,
        50, 55,
        69, 72
OLDFIELD´s?
    57
OLIVE
    John 52
OLIVER
    Elizabeth 80
    J.B. 76
    James 37, 66
    James G. 31-33,
        122, 130
    Jas G. 15, 130
    Jno. 54, 65,
        103, 118,
        182
    John 50, 58, 75,
        77-79, 81,
        82, 96,
        101, 108,
        114, 121,
        131, 136,
        139, 142,
        143,
        150-153,
        156, 164,
        167, 176,
        180, 181,
        185, 186,
        188-190,
        203, 204,
        206, 207,
        218, 219,
        227-229,
        233
    John R. 158
    Joshua B. 52,
        74, 130
    Lewis 15
    Mary 63, 66, 75,
        196, 206
OLIVER?
    James G. 63
    Joshua B. 63
ONE/ORME
    Peter 40
ORMAN
    Thomas 134
ORMAN?
    Thomas 130
ORME
    Rob. V. 44, 62
    Robert 93
    Robert V. 24,
        62, 80, 93

281

Robt V. 36, 44,
    64, 80, 84
William 14, 15,
    20, 24
Wm 19, 21, 32,
    33, 44, 64
ORTON
    Pery 64
OUTLAW?
    Mathew 134
OVERTON
    Edwd 108
OWENS
    A.B. 57
    Archibald 61, 75
    Archibald B. 44,
        48, 49,
        67, 68
    Archibald R. 157
    Francis 157
OWINS
    Archibald B. 20,
        27, 29, 45

PACKER
    Mary 224
    Nancy 224
PADRICK
    James 160
    Wm. 229
PARKER
    F. 180
    Frederick 140,
        144, 148,
        156, 165,
        172, 175,
        182, 196
    Fredk 139, 147,
        166, 170,
        180, 189
    Jno. 14, 27
    John 157
PARKER/PACKER
    Fredk 106
PARRY (See Perry) 233
    A. 114, 123,
        132, 156,
        167
    Adenijah 74
    Adonijah 15, 18,
        19, 21,
        27, 35,
        66, 80,
        109, 190
    Calvin 211
    E. 221
    Eli H.G.F. 211
    Elijah 13, 18,
        22, 31,
        32, 34,
        37, 38,
        49, 50,
        52, 67-69,
        83, 85,
        87, 93,
        96, 100,
        107, 108,
        120, 123,
        124, 129,
        131, 134,
        137, 145,
        150, 154,
        161, 163,
        168, 176,
        180, 199,
        206, 207,
        221, 228,
        232
    Eliza 119
    Elizabeth 80
    Erasmus 211
    George 131, 176,
        189, 190,
        207
    H. 7, 33, 179
    Hannah 211, 223
    Hardy 14, 17,
        19-22, 31,
        32, 34,
        36, 40,
        42-50, 54,
        55, 57-59,
        61-64,
        66-68, 70,
        75, 76,
        83-85, 87,
        89, 96,
        97, 104,
        105, 108,
        109, 113,
        119, 120,
        129, 130,
        138, 139,
        142,
        147-149,
        153, 154,
        156, 158,
        161, 163,
        164, 166,
        167, 171,
        176, 186,
        188-190,
        193, 197,
        199, 200,
        207, 208,
        210, 221,
        223
    Isler 58
    James 146, 193
    Joseph 119
    Joseph A. 211
    Richard 101,
        119, 193
    S. 142
    Sally 161
    Silas 43, 47,
        75, 87,
        97, 113,
        131, 153,
        164, 176,
        189, 190,
        207, 210
    Susannah 131
    William F. 211
PARSONS 142
    F. 6, 230
    Harriet 58
    I. 30
    J. 97, 98, 114,
        126
    Jeremiah 23, 56,
        58, 67,
        70, 87,
        105, 108,
        121, 130,
        149, 153,
        169, 191
    Jno. 30, 58
    John 23, 32, 34,
        60-62, 124
    John L. 6, 7,
        51, 72,
        101, 103,
        105, 118,
        119, 128,
        133-135,

    137, 140,
    143-145,
    157, 159,
    160, 162,
    187, 191,
    195, 201,
    208, 211,
    212, 215
John S. 76, 79,
    166, 176
John T.? 197
Joseph 61, 69
Joseph M. 100,
    105
N. 30
N.F. 140, 193,
    227
Nathan 58, 230
Nathan F. 99,
    105, 129,
    135, 164,
    166, 168,
    193, 202,
    203, 207
Nathan I. 182
R.H. 234
Richard 6, 176
Richard H. 227
Richd 58, 172
Thomas 6, 121,
    134, 231
Thomas C. 130,
    223
Thos 59, 158
Wright 67

PASTEUR?
    John I. 149
PASTURO
    John J. 231
PEARCE
    Joseph 69, 90
PEARSON
    Joseph M. 51
PEIRCE
    Joseph 13
PENEUL
    Penelope 34
PENEWILL
    Anny 36
PENUEL
    George 57
    Needham 158

    Penelope 15
    Susanna 15
    William B. 60
    Wm. B. 19
PERRY (See Parry)
    Daniel 229
    Elijah 194
    Farnifold 211
    George 202
    Hannah 138
    Hardy 2, 51, 94,
        138, 194,
        201, 202
    Mary I. 138
    Silas 202
PERSON/PARSON?
    Thomas 218
PETAWAY
    Micijah 59
PETERWAY
    Micajah 84, 120,
        122, 147,
        167
PETEWAY
    Micajah 86, 110,
        113, 115,
        125, 130
PETHAWAY
    Mecajah 48
PETIEWAY
    Micajah 107
PETTAWAY
    Micajah 72-74,
        76, 77,
        82, 123
PETTEAWAY
    Micajah 48
PETTEWAY
    Micajah 59, 62,
        139, 146
    Micajiah 37
    Micijah 64
PETTWAY
    Micajah 214
PHELYAN?
    John 149
PICKERIND
    Elizabeth 17
PICKERING
    Elizabeth 21
PIDCOCK
    James 134

PITAWAY
    Micajah 22
PITEEWAY
    Micajah 60
PITTEWAY
    M. 60
PITTS
    Hardy 44
    Richd 44
PITWAY
    Micajah 118
POLLACK
    C. 39
    Cullen 14, 17,
        22, 24,
        36, 39
    Fanny 37
    Geo. 27, 40
    Jno. 127
    John 11, 32, 34,
        126
    Thomas 128, 230
    Thos 126, 127
    William 22
    Wm. 126
POLLOCK 222
    Amy 96, 108
    Ann D. 146, 167,
        193
    C. 156
    Carolina 146,
        152, 167
    Caroline 193,
        201
    Cullen 22, 109,
        119, 122,
        190
    Fanny 222, 228
    Fany 233
    Geo. 48, 68
    George 48, 98,
        124, 128,
        135, 141,
        183, 186,
        206
    Hardy 164, 165,
        177
    Hollon 132, 146,
        167, 193
    Jno. 110, 130
    John 19, 43, 50,
        62, 73,

76, 80,
96, 108,
116, 117,
134, 138,
142, 145,
150, 156,
157, 166,
171, 174,
177, 186,
187,
196-198,
206, 225,
227
John B. 191
Mary 76, 142,
198
Matilda 80
McCullen 52, 84,
105
Thomas 44, 53,
62, 78,
80, 101,
114, 134,
145, 154,
156, 161,
163, 165,
176, 185,
187, 199,
206, 219,
227, 228,
231
Thos 19, 55, 80,
129
William 7, 67,
114, 119,
123, 142,
192, 205,
206, 221,
228, 231,
232
Wm. 10, 116
PRATT
Almren 171
PRESCOT
Iva/Ira 169
PRICHARD
William 187
Wm. 193
PRICHELL
James H. 227
PRIGET?
James 6, 184

PRITCH(ERD?)
William 218
PRITCHARD
William 186
PRITCHELL
Charlotte 228
William 225, 227
PRITCHET
William 209
PRITCHETT
William 199

QUIN
Loften 157
Wright 157

RAMSAY
John G. 95, 101,
151, 165
RAMSEY
John 18, 54
John G. 68, 71,
73, 76-78,
81, 82,
88-90, 98,
102, 114
RANDAL
Matilda 226, 227
RANDEL/RENDALE
Matilda 220
RANDILE
N. 227
RANDOLL
Matilda 227
READ
Abigail 53
Hollon 53
James 14, 22,
31, 37,
38, 40,
53, 56, 61
Jas 17
Sarah 53
Singla 110
Singla? 72
Susan 57, 70
Susannah 57, 61
William 15, 56,
57, 61
Wm 53
REED
James 47

REN
James 47
RENOLDS
Richard 12
REYNOLDS
A.H. 160
Alfred 149, 158,
162, 177,
189
Alfred H. 7,
157, 166,
168, 171,
175, 176,
180, 183,
193
Betsy 159
Elizabeth 162,
163, 193,
233, 234
I./S. B. 170
I.B. 209
J.B. 227, 230
J.S. 15
James 10, 11,
13, 15-19,
23, 27,
29, 30,
34, 38,
39, 41,
43, 45,
53, 56,
57, 59,
61, 64,
68, 69,
76, 78,
79, 91,
97, 98,
101, 107,
119, 123,
125, 142,
147, 148,
150, 153,
154, 163,
170, 213
Jas 14, 18, 21,
26, 33,
34, 36,
38, 40,
44, 47,
52, 55,
59, 65,
68, 72,

76, 80,
85, 90,
101, 102,
104, 110,
115, 116,
121, 127,
130, 134,
136, 139,
142, 146,
148, 158,
187, 189
Jno B. 182, 188,
190, 193
John B. 7, 154,
157, 159,
160, 162,
164, 165,
172, 180,
181, 186,
188, 189,
203, 204,
207, 212,
219, 221,
222, 225,
226, 233,
234
R. 80, 91, 99,
100
R.G. 155
Rich. 13, 14, 47
Richard 13, 21,
60, 61,
63, 66,
72, 85,
88, 99,
141, 142,
148, 149,
154, 157,
167, 171,
172, 177,
190, 192,
203, 209,
230, 232
Richard G. 157,
159
Richd 15, 17,
21, 30,
51, 69,
88, 123,
124
Richd G. 160
Richrd 214

REYNOLDS?
    Richd 50
RHEIM
    Amos 218
    Joseph 122
RHEM
    Amos 7, 231, 233
    Joseph 21, 44,
        45, 53,
        55, 62,
        65, 66,
        70, 71,
        76, 77,
        82, 92,
        110, 116,
        117, 130,
        138
    Joseph, Sr. 97
    Melcher 186,
        189, 190
    Melchir 181
    Melchoir 138
    Metahu? 161
    Milcher 180
    Mitchel 177
    Susan 12
    W.B. 181
    William 14, 32,
        53, 55,
        59, 69,
        71, 76,
        77, 87,
        96, 100,
        115, 138,
        142, 147,
        155, 176
    William B. 138,
        156, 160,
        161, 170,
        172,
        175-177,
        183, 188,
        190
    Wm 15, 70, 87,
        110, 126,
        134, 170
    Wm A. 142
    Wm B. 145, 175,
        181, 183,
        188
    Wm., Sr. 134
RHIM

    William 49
RHIME
    William 60
RHODES
    Benjamin 148,
        157, 206
    Benjn 70, 98,
        107, 167
    C.C. 176, 180,
        183, 186,
        189, 193,
        197, 198,
        203, 206,
        209, 212,
        214, 221,
        225,
        228-230,
        233
    C.H. 130
    Chrisr. C. 172
    Christopher 200
    Christopher C.
        203
    Delia 98
    Elizabeth H. 203
    H. 157
    Hen. 206, 211
    Henery 23, 24,
        27, 31,
        35-37,
        41-43,
        46-49, 51,
        53, 54,
        56, 57,
        69, 72,
        74, 75,
        77, 78,
        80, 81,
        84, 85,
        88, 90,
        92, 98,
        101
    Henery Jr. 27,
        41, 42,
        51, 72
    Henery Senr 24,
        35, 37,
        46-48, 49,
        56, 57,
        72, 75
    Henery Sr. 36,
        23, 54, 69

Henry 2, 7, 42,
    50, 88,
    102, 103,
    105-108,
    112, 113,
    117, 118,
    120, 126,
    128, 130,
    132, 133,
    135, 138,
    144, 145,
    148, 149,
    154, 155,
    160, 166,
    170, 171,
    176, 179,
    180, 186,
    187, 193,
    199, 200,
    203, 205,
    206, 208,
    214, 218,
    220,
    223-225,
    227, 229,
    233
Henry Sr. 42, 50
Jackson 113, 147
Jacob 85, 87,
    98, 128,
    130
James 70, 72,
    97, 109,
    114, 129,
    153
James I./S. 171
James J. 124,
    136, 137,
    140, 148,
    156, 166,
    177, 180
James K. 154
James, Sr. 107
Jas. J. 98, 167
Jas. T. 130
Jones 85
Joseph T. 128,
    130, 139
Mary 113, 147
Mary E. 203
Will W. 189
William 184

William W. 189
William, Jr. 72
Wm. 129
Wm., Jr. 109
RICE
    Ruben 65
RICHARD
    Erwin 170
    Salyar? 146
RICHARDS
    D. 110, 130
    Durant 24, 25,
        27, 33,
        36, 38,
        44, 47,
        54, 60,
        62, 76,
        77, 93,
        101, 110,
        125
    Jno. 54
    John 54, 56
    Richards 64
    William 19, 29
    Wm 27
RICHARDSON
    Richard 150
RICHERSON
    Susan 23
RIMS
    William 34
ROADS
    Henry 18
ROBERT
    George 44
    James 61, 67
ROBERTS
    Agrippa 41, 70,
        71, 90
    Christopher 134,
        135, 137,
        141, 148,
        224
    George 49, 69,
        78, 82,
        87, 90,
        101, 224
    George Q. 225
    H..?.ton 147
    Houston 55, 78,
        134, 145,
        163, 224

I.S. 34
James 2, 5,
    10-13, 15,
    17-19, 23,
    24, 31,
    37, 41-43,
    49, 52,
    54, 57,
    61, 62,
    65, 66,
    72, 75,
    77-81, 84,
    86, 87,
    90, 92,
    103, 104,
    118, 126,
    132, 136,
    137, 139,
    144, 145,
    150, 156,
    164, 171,
    181, 182,
    186, 187,
    197, 198,
    206, 207,
    218,
    224-226
Jas 11, 17, 70,
    165
Jno. M. 91
John M. 100, 159
Richard 69, 224
ROBERTSON
    Dorothy 209
    Elisha 209, 224
    Hester 209
    Melissa T. 209
    Right 209
ROBINS
    Offa? 178
    Wyat 178
ROBINSON
    J. 180
ROE 185, 233
    Richard 136
ROGERS
    William H. 198
ROSEN
    John 150
ROUN
    Jno. 110, 126
    John 141

ROUN?
    John 123
ROUSE
    John 27, 29, 39,
        44, 45,
        53, 59,
        60, 68,
        69, 73,
        92, 112,
        136, 167,
        171, 196,
        197, 212,
        221, 232
ROWE
    Henry 133
ROWLAND
    Alfred 95
RUSSEL
    James 58
    Richard 206
    William 120

SAMPSON
    Needham 214
SANDERS
    Abner 109, 120
    Daniel 139
    David W. 132
    David? 96
    John A. 164
    Maps? M. 34
    Moses 44
    Rachel 44
    Sally 185
SANDERSON
    Julia 97
    L. 38
    Lewis 97
    Re(coron?) 88
SAWYER
    Joshua 75
    Joshuay? 70
    Tabetha 99
    Tabitha 94
SAWYER?
    Tabitha 141
SCOTT 212
    Benjamin 171,
        174, 187,
        199, 200,
        212, 218,
        225-227

    Benjn 167, 180,
        182, 185,
        193
    Edward 167
    James 15
    L. 120
    Pinin 61
    Reading 6, 106,
        223
    Samuel 61
    Steward 78, 106
    Stewart 6, 81,
        84, 223
    Stuart 123
    Susan 228
SEAT
    Jehu 26
SEATE/LEOTE
    Stewart 110
SHALFER
    Amos 189
SHEETS
    Henry 103
SHELFER
    Amos 134, 145,
        154, 156,
        167, 180,
        186, 190,
        196, 200,
        206,
        225-227,
        233
    Councel 126
    Council 114
    Hardy 7, 63, 69,
        72, 73,
        78, 114,
        126
    Hardy H. 79, 81,
        84, 101,
        103, 107,
        113, 118,
        158, 191
    James 226
    Jesse 15, 20,
        31, 57,
        210, 213,
        226
    Jno. 58
    John 15, 24, 33,
        43, 51,
        57, 66-69,
        93, 95,
        101, 109,
        112, 123,
        124, 130,
        131, 139,
        140, 149,
        150, 152,
        161, 163,
        166, 171,
        172, 180,
        229
    Lany 69
    Luke 11, 15, 17,
        22, 41,
        42, 60,
        62, 65,
        69, 75,
        107, 113,
        114
    Michael 7, 159,
        164, 165,
        180, 181,
        186, 187,
        199, 200,
        206, 233
    Needham 67, 71,
        77, 78,
        81, 82,
        84, 101,
        210
    Sally 15
    Sarah 31, 41
    Thomas 44, 72
    Thos 105, 108
    William 90
    Wm. 104, 130
SHEPARD
    Elizabeth 219
    Henry 219
SHEPHARD
    Elizabeth 215
SHEPHERD
    Henry 215
    Jane 16
SHIELE
    Henry 112
SHINE 117, 143
    59
    Bryan 77, 93
    D.Y. 52, 77, 78,
        227
    Daniel Y. 2, 6,

34, 36-39,
43, 45,
47, 49,
51, 53,
56-58, 63,
65, 67,
72, 76,
77, 79,
81, 82,
87, 96,
97, 101,
103-105,
107, 113,
122, 139,
142, 151,
233
Danl Y. 63, 103
J.B. 83, 175,
221
J.S.B. 78
James 47, 164
James B. 2, 5,
6, 11, 13,
22, 23,
32, 36,
38, 39,
42, 43,
45-51, 53,
56-59, 61,
64, 72,
73, 76,
81, 82,
84, 87,
92, 105,
105, 107,
112, 115,
117, 121,
125, 130,
131, 134,
135, 140,
144, 146,
158, 160,
163, 165,
166, 168,
169, 176,
177,
179-181,
183, 191,
194-196,
198, 205,
207, 212,
218, 220,
223, 225,
226,
229-231,
233
Jas B. 13, 34,
36, 52,
54, 125
Js. B. 48
SHLE?
John 126
SHUTE
Henry 104, 124
Henry? 142
SIMMONS
A. 179
A.W. 26
Abraham 61, 82,
106, 166,
188, 193
Abram 134, 145,
154, 159,
160, 180,
185, 199,
207, 221,
230, 231
Amos 7, 15, 47,
56, 71,
88, 134,
138, 150,
155-157,
166, 193
Amos D. 16
Amos L. 137,
141, 143,
151, 174,
180, 181,
186, 199,
200, 206,
221, 230,
231
Amos S. 183, 220
Amos W. 13, 15,
23
Baneter 148
Beneter 16
Benjamin C. 156,
171, 177
Benjamin
Franklin
16
Benjn 51, 84
Benjn C. 130,
133, 145,
147, 166,
180, 193
Clinton? 117
D. 115
Daniel 19, 27,
35, 61,
97, 99,
105
Danl 32
E. 27
Elijah 2, 6, 10,
12, 17-21,
23, 24,
35, 41,
43, 45-47,
52, 53,
55, 62,
66, 69,
72, 75,
78, 81,
92, 102,
106, 110,
115, 117,
119, 120,
122, 128,
130, 137,
140-142,
157, 158,
167, 170,
174, 175,
182, 183,
191, 197,
201, 207,
212, 219,
222, 228
Elijah, Jr. 6,
197
Eliza 26
Elizabeth 13,
15, 23, 56
Elizabeth A. 142
Elizabeth Ann
131, 191
Elizabeth Lane
16
Elizah 10
Emily 16
F.G. 12, 16, 33,
45, 51,
70, 75,
104, 114,

131, 153,
164
Frank 16
Furnifold 13,
20, 56
Furnifold G. 13,
41, 56,
96, 176,
181, 183,
185, 203
George 6, 192,
223
George W. 6, 184
Hester 205
Hustin 211
Huston 204
James 12, 19,
20, 22,
24, 31,
33, 41,
42, 44,
46, 49,
52, 55,
57, 59,
64, 68,
69, 72,
75, 92,
102, 106,
108, 115,
118, 127
Jas 24, 48, 51,
59, 84
Jno. 31, 46
John 22, 46, 78,
81, 82,
93, 101
John O. 89
L.H. 54, 118,
142, 210,
228
Lem H. 50
Leml 10, 13, 15,
43
Leml H. 7, 15,
19, 20,
22, 23,
26, 27,
31, 45,
47, 56,
58, 65,
78, 92,
96, 99,

109, 115,
126, 129,
134, 153,
158-161,
167, 169,
179, 181,
183, 185,
186, 193,
196, 200
Lemuel 2, 41
Lemuel H. 16,
32, 33,
46, 48,
50, 59,
60, 62-65,
69, 71,
214
M.A.F. 33
Maria 16
Mary 198
Mary A. 14
Mary Ann 16
Mary Elizabeth
70
Nancy 61
Needham 16, 138,
177
Penelope 20, 56,
89, 96
Penny 12
Polly 16
S.H. 214
Sophia 15, 47,
56, 71,
88, 138,
183
Sophia E. 177
W.A. 33
Wight 19
Wright 12, 13,
20, 24,
26, 33,
48, 54,
55, 59
Write 32
SIMPSON
    Curtis 188
    Gabulon H. 165
    Samuel 177, 185
SLADE
    Z. 124, 175
SMALL 33

Ann E. 159, 176,
178
Ann Elijah 178,
185
B. 132
Benj. 13
Benjamin 46
Benjn Jr. 27
Elijah 78, 80,
83, 96,
100, 107,
116, 117,
125, 126,
131, 144,
150, 164
Elizabeth 46
I. 33
Isobel 137
J. 34
John 46
Joseph 15, 61,
65, 68,
69, 71-73,
79, 84,
86, 101,
113, 117,
126,
135-137,
141-146,
160, 161,
167, 180,
182, 186,
187, 193,
203, 209,
210, 218,
228-231
Laney 165
Lany 130, 146
Leah 20, 57
Lewis 2, 11, 24,
31, 50,
64, 78,
93, 95,
101, 114,
118, 121,
130, 131,
136, 137,
139, 143,
145, 160,
166, 171,
172, 182,
184

Maria 57
Mariah 20
Needham 222
S. 33
Sarah 61
SMALL/SMAW
   John D. 50
SMART
   Thos 18
SMAW
   John D. 46
SMED
   Jno. 110
SMITH
   Asa 11-13, 17,
      19-25, 27,
      31, 36,
      41-43, 48,
      50, 54,
      56, 57,
      61, 62,
      67, 67,
      69-72, 74,
      75, 77-81,
      84, 86,
      87, 90,
      92, 97,
      103, 110,
      117,
      122-126,
      129, 138,
      139, 146,
      148, 150,
      154, 156,
      157
   Bazel Jr. 25
   Benjamin 61
   Benjamin C. 228
   C. 113, 122
   Caleb 61, 107
   Calib 87
   Christeen 25
   Daniel 5, 12,
      17, 18,
      23, 27,
      37, 45,
      47, 48,
      51-54, 61,
      62, 73,
      76, 80,
      81, 85,
      88, 97,
      101-105,
      107, 110,
      114, 115,
      117, 120,
      121, 145,
      146, 148,
      150, 151
   Daniel, Jr. 88
   Danl 117
   David 154
   Edwd Ward 25
   Eliza 61, 89, 96
   Francis D. 147
   Freeman 7, 159,
      172, 176,
      188, 191,
      194, 199,
      209, 210,
      214, 219,
      225-227,
      231-233
   Harriet A. 114
   J.S.N. 78
   James 52, 221
   James Cr. 41
   James N. 11, 14,
      20, 23-25,
      30, 32,
      34, 41-46,
      48-50,
      53-57, 61,
      63-67,
      69-72,
      77-80, 84,
      85, 87,
      89, 94,
      96,
      101-103,
      109, 115,
      116
   Jas N. 14, 21,
      35, 36,
      39, 53,
      62, 65,
      69, 98
   Job 47, 53, 57,
      71, 72,
      76, 78,
      84, 89,
      93, 96,
      104, 162
   Jobe 2, 90
   John 55
   Jos. N. 74
   Joseph 61
   Joseph K. 162
   Josiah 61, 154
   Lewis 150
   Mary 52, 61
   N.P. 165, 183
   Nancy 61
   Nathan 164
   Nathan P. 164,
      176
   Sally 156
   Sally Ann 25
   Samuel 61, 172,
      182
   Sarah 54, 56
   Stephen 6, 159
   Thomas 41, 53,
      62, 84,
      147
   Thomas S. 99
   Thos 55, 76, 78
SNEED
   John 98
SPAFFORD and TALISTON
   110
SPAIGHT
   Thos 39
SPAROW & HOWARD 102
SPEIGHT
   T. 71
   Thomas 66, 130
   Thos 32, 43, 70
SPIEGHT
   Thos 74
SPIGHT
   Ivy 14
   Miles 21
   Thos 13, 24, 50
STAFFERD
   Elisha 16
STAFFORD 195
   Elisha 13, 87,
      191, 209
   Elizabeth 13
   James 13
   Susan 13
STANLEY
   Benjamin 184
   Daniel 11
   Edward 184

Hubbard 185
John 184
John H. 11
Nathan 7, 223
Penelope 185
Wm. 232

STANLY
Alfred 59, 94
B.F. 203
Benj. F. 220
Benjamin 176
Benjamin F. 161,
 163, 176,
 186, 196,
 197, 211,
 212, 221,
 229
Benjn F. 7, 90,
 118, 121,
 130, 131,
 134, 145,
 147, 149,
 159, 168,
 184
D. 108
Daniel 15, 16,
 38, 40,
 45, 50,
 58, 64,
 69, 73,
 74, 105,
 156
Daniel C. 156
Daniel Sen. 53
Daniel, Sr. 68,
 84, 101
Danl, Senr. 117
David 135
E. 97
E.R. 214
Edward R. 203
Edwd. 97
H. 222, 224
Huband 33
Hubard 37, 38,
 49, 57,
 66, 74, 84
Hubban 149
Hubbard 52, 73,
 86,
 116-118,
 121, 125,
 126, 134,
 153, 156,
 163, 170,
 176
Hubbison 147
I./J. G. 171
J. 97
J? H. 206
James 157, 163,
 168, 203,
 221
James A. 193
James B. 187,
 200
James G. 188,
 199, 200,
 203, 207,
 209, 214,
 222, 224,
 228, 230,
 232
Jno. 14, 19, 78,
 110, 118,
 147, 180
Jno. (Trenton)
 147, 180,
 185
Jno. Sr. 40
Jno., Jr. 118
John 7, 16-18,
 27, 29,
 36, 41-44,
 49, 59,
 60, 65,
 68, 69,
 71, 73,
 81, 90,
 91, 93,
 98, 101,
 102, 105,
 116, 122,
 123, 126,
 131, 132,
 139, 140,
 142, 146,
 147, 149,
 155-157,
 161, 182,
 184, 185,
 189, 195,
 196, 211,
 214, 218
John H. 11, 16,
 34, 40
John Jr. 18
John L. 213
John of Trenton
 36, 42,
 44, 73
John S. 65
John Senr 27,
 29, 116
John Sr. 41-43,
 59, 68, 69
John V.? 40
Leah 135
Leah M. 105,
 108, 135
Leah M.? 191
Nathan 90, 126,
 134, 145,
 147, 154,
 162, 167,
 180, 182,
 184, 186,
 189, 193,
 202-204,
 207, 211,
 213, 220,
 221, 227,
 229, 231
Penelope 184,
 202
R. 54
Richard 77
Right 34, 180,
 213, 219,
 230, 231
W.C. 76
W.G. 110
William 7, 25,
 34, 37,
 48, 68,
 76, 96,
 107, 125,
 159, 176,
 177, 182,
 219, 232
Wini... 53
Wm. 76, 110, 117
Wm Jr. 14
Wright 18, 37,
 67, 83,
 90, 102,

118, 121,
122, 124,
136, 137,
145, 148,
149, 156,
184, 185,
193, 199,
206, 209,
210, 214
    Wright C. 167
STANLY (Trenton?)
    John 126
STANTON
    Nancy 45
STEEL
    James 172
STEELE
    James 99
    James P. 44
    Lemuel 99
STELE
    John 45
STELL/STELE/HILL/HILE
    John 59
STELLEY
    Thomas 66
    Thos 142
STELLY
    Thomas 61
    Thos 104
STEPHENS
    Rachel 21, 22, 32
STEPHENSON
    M. 38
    Martin, Jr. 94
STEVESON
    Charles 227
STILE
    John 76, 79, 107
STILE/STILL
    John 77, 107
STILL
    John 44, 45, 84, 86
STILL?
    John 59, 62
STILL/STILE
    John 60
STILLEY
    Leah 32
    T. 35
    Thomas 29, 70
    Thos 32, 34, 70, 71
STILLY
    Thomas 191
    Thos 18, 22
STOKES
    Joseph K. 151
STRAND
    Isaac 96
STRAND/STROUD
    Isaac 98
STRECKLIN
    John 11, 176
STRICKLEN
    John 190
STRICKLIN
    John 162, 165, 182, 184, 189, 196, 197, 206, 228, 233
STRICKLINE
    Jno. 164
STRONG
    O.E. 47
    Oliver E. 46, 105, 134
STRONG?
    Nathan 129
STROUD?
    Isaac 90, 165
SUGGS
    John M. 224
SWITHERINGTON? 203

TALOR
    Frederick 228
TAYLER
    Amos 76
TAYLOR
    Amos 41, 51, 61, 66, 67, 80, 92, 110
    F. 111
    Frederick 112, 128
    Isaac 186
    James 117, 167, 177
    Jas 160
    Jason G. 161
    Jesse 161, 224
    William 45, 186
    William G. 39
TENDALE
    Wiley N. 53
THOMAS
    Bryan, Sr. 6, 176
THOMAS?
    Charles 112
THOMPSON
    Esther 98
    Geo. A. 70
    Jno. 110
    John 98, 151
    Nancy 225
TILMAN
    Peggy 97
TINDAL
    Wiley N. 98
TIPPET
    James 129, 183
TURNAGE
    James 37, 53, 59, 73, 101, 118
TURNER
    Ann 31
    John 31, 33, 37, 46, 48, 49, 61, 68, 90, 101, 162, 199, 212, 214, 233
    Levi Jackson 55
    McLendal 194, 195, 197, 200
    McLendale 202
    Nat 106, 108, 112, 113
    Rilly 61
    Silas 38, 40, 55, 209
    Silas M. 55, 207, 214, 219
    Whiffinten 136
    Whitfield 75, 108, 123,

145, 147,
161, 164,
168, 201,
203, 204,
212, 218,
225, 230,
231

TWILLEY
    H. 47

VANN
    Jno. 100
    John 38

VEIL
    B.W. 109

VENTERS
    Folney 230
    Sarah 219
    Volney 219

VINTERS
    Volny 177

WADSWORTH
    Ignatious 59

WAINWRIGHT
    Elizabeth 57

WALLACE
    Aples/Asles 69, 71
    B. 70
    Benjn 52, 55,
        66, 78,
        109, 116
    Celia 163
    James 41, 53,
        61, 73,
        96, 117
    Joseph 39, 40,
        66, 69,
        71, 116,
        163, 167,
        171, 186,
        188, 196,
        225
    Robert 17
    Robt 17, 20
    Stephen 14, 21,
        22, 39-42,
        47, 66,
        69, 70,
        100

WALLAN
    Celia 145
    Jas. 130
    Joseph 141, 145

WALLAN/WALLIS?
    Celia 141

WALLIN
    Joseph 212

WALLIS
    Andrew 151
    Aplis 151
    C. 167
    James 107, 151
    Joseph 141, 151

WALTON
    Daniel 47
    Thomas 47

WAPLES
    N. 217
    N.P. 174
    Nathan P. 193
    Nathaniel 7,
        199, 212,
        214, 216,
        218, 223,
        229, 231
    Nathaniel P. 171

WARD
    Morris 12, 136, 167
    Moses 149
    W.E. 16
    William P. 16

WARD...
    Morris 60

WARD/WOOD
    Jonathan 206

WARTISS?
    William 140

WARTON
    Alice 77
    Edward 77
    Fanny 77
    Jeremiah 77

WASHINGTON
    Jno. 191
    John 158
    John C. 158
    W.H. 222
    William 45, 178, 181, 184

WASSLES/WAPLES
    Nathaniel 182

WATERS
    William 25, 29,
        37, 38,
        43, 68,
        69, 90,
        101, 128,
        139
    Wm. 126

WATERS?
    Council 177

WATSON
    Ann 12
    Ann B. 74
    Charles 17
    Hardy 77, 82, 83, 115
    I. 30
    Ivey 12
    Ivy 16
    James B. 67
    Jas B. 66
    Jeremiah 22
    Joseph 187
    Joseph H. 160, 199
    Nancy 12, 54
    Richard H. 199
    William 22
    Wm 14, 30

WEBBER
    Thomas 1

WEEKS
    David 133
    Rhodes 12

WEIER?
    John 213

WEINTROUGH?
    Mary C. 90

WENGET
    Thomas W.C. 75, 95, 97

WENNEY
    Patsey 31

WEST
    Winifred 184

WESTBROOK
    Benjamin 104
    Benjn 80
    Bryan 61, 79,
        117, 118,
        137, 210
    Charles 99, 100

Curtis 61, 101, 120, 132, 146, 156, 167, 190, 193
Durant 20, 22, 33, 39, 41, 42, 47, 48, 59, 65
Edmd 108, 130, 140, 152
Edmond 139
Edmund 136, 150, 151, 153, 161, 162, 186
Edwd 130
Elizabeth 61
Furney 188
Harmon 214
Ira 138, 146, 151, 177
Isa 120
Iva 168
Ivy 171
James 61
Jas 80
John 142, 199, 214
Mary 61
N.B. 80
Nancy 104, 120, 132, 146, 156, 163
Nathan 43, 57
Nathan B. 104, 139, 145, 160, 180, 189, 196, 197, 233
Nathan I./S. 47
Nathan S. 93
Patience 80
S. 33, 75
Saml 18, 20, 24, 43, 47, 108, 114, 142
Samuel 90, 138
Wright 188
Zachariah 144

WESTBROOKE
    Saml 47
WESTEBROOK
    Nathan 93
WESTUN
    Bently 168
WHALEY
    James 166, 176, 186, 189, 198
    Rigdon 31, 180
WHARTEN
    Alice 99
    David 145
    Edmd 98
    Edwd 99
    Elizabeth 84
    Fanny 99
    Jeremiah 99
WHARTON
    Alice 81
    David 150, 156, 161, 212, 221
    Edmd 86, 186
    Edmd D. 164
    Edmond 82, 107, 214
    Edmund D. 199
    Edward 81, 209
    Edward D. 189, 190, 225
    Edwd D. 169
    Elizabeth 77, 81, 91, 112
    Fanny 81
    Frances 91
    Jeremiah 81, 112
    Sarah 91
WHETTY
    Joseph 15
WHILLY
    Charles 58
    Joseph 40, 55
WHITE
    Clancy? 150
    Durant 37, 39
    Durant H. 16, 31, 32
    Modica 15
    Mordica 34, 39
    Mordicai 40
    Mordics? 53
    Rigdon 26, 55, 146, 147
    Samuel 136, 150
WHITEHEAD
    Gidian 185
WHITLEDGE
    Thomas 148
WHITTY
    Alfred 6, 152, 159, 192, 220
    Charles 12, 18, 20, 27, 37, 46, 48, 52, 69, 71, 91, 99, 115, 128, 130, 133, 152
    J. 160, 179
    Joseph 2, 6, 11, 24, 54, 77, 79, 82, 90, 91, 102, 106, 112, 115-119, 121, 129-131, 135, 136, 141, 143, 146, 150, 152-154, 160-162, 171, 175, 176, 179, 180, 186, 187, 199-203, 206, 214, 216, 218, 220, 221, 223, 230, 234, 234
    Nancy 128, 133
WHITTY?
    Joseph 121
WHORTER
    Edmd D. 196

WHORTON
    D.B. 143
WIG...
    Thos. W.C. 125
WIGGENS
    Samuel S. 31
WIGGINS
    S.S. 31, 76
    Saml 18
    Saml S. 34
    Samuel L. 64
    Samuel S. 32
WILCOX
    Benjn 26, 80
    Geo. 110, 113, 117, 126
    George 37, 38, 48, 56, 58, 65, 68, 73, 79, 92, 109, 118, 121, 136, 137, 145, 150, 154, 156, 158, 161, 168, 169, 171, 178, 187, 190-192, 197, 200, 205-207, 210, 220, 225, 227
    Stephen 191, 214, 229
    Thomas 15, 26, 31, 41, 58, 62, 109, 191
    Thos 52, 113
WILLCOX
    George 37
WILLIAM
    John 6, 176
WILLIAMS
    ?.D. 111
    Bartholomew 18
    Charles 132
    Daniel 184
    Evan 60
    Fauntin 56

    Founten 26
    Fountin 23, 43
    James 59, 61, 73, 161, 228
    John 76, 99, 110
    Jonas 7, 66, 74, 82, 85, 92, 101, 104, 107, 117, 126, 136, 137, 145, 150, 152, 158, 180, 182, 186, 193, 195, 199-201, 214, 218-221, 230
    Lewis 7, 11, 21, 31, 43, 59, 60, 73, 77, 85, 93, 96, 100, 106, 108, 116, 128, 134, 138, 141, 143, 154, 158, 161, 164, 166, 171, 176, 180, 191, 192, 201, 203, 204, 208-210, 220, 221, 226, 228, 230
    Rabin 221
    Reuben 230
    Reubin 199
    Rubin 209
    T. 47
WILLIAMSON
    D. 111
    Daniel 18-20, 27, 38, 39, 41, 53, 55, 61, 64, 66, 67, 73, 74, 82, 86, 87, 92, 99, 106, 107, 113, 115, 126, 128, 132, 133, 161, 171, 193
    Danl 54, 67, 77, 110
    Lewis 22
WILLS
    Esereal 36
WILSON
    Benjn 26
    George 74, 109
    Thomas 26, 49
    Thos 19, 57
WINGET
    T.W.C. 126
    Thomas W.C. 77, 101, 105, 109
    Thos W.C. 76, 78, 104, 117
WISE
    F. 106
    Frederick 82
    James 18, 21, 27, 39, 44, 51, 55
    Jno. 96, 174
    John 5, 14, 32, 39, 163
    Nancy 55
    Olive 55
    Selby H. 61, 67, 75, 79
WOLLON
    Joseph 164
WOOD 233
    Aaron 76, 78, 92, 110, 122-124, 134, 141, 145, 162, 166, 176,

207, 214,
217, 219,
230
Amos 197
C.B. 99
Councel 99
Councel S. 99
F. 116, 167
Frederick 101,
104, 107,
129, 135
Fredk 113, 135,
138, 142,
146, 156
Furnifold 197
George 197
Hannah 18, 142,
149, 177,
203
Hardy 149
Isaiah 41, 52,
53, 55,
60, 62,
69, 75-77,
101,
115-118,
121, 131,
134, 140,
150, 152,
161, 168,
171, 197,
202
Israel 142
J.L.C. 12
Jno. C. 22
Jnothan 165
John 13, 41, 48,
60, 62,
65, 69,
73, 76,
78, 93,
95, 101,
104, 106,
107, 116,
117, 126,
128, 133,
134, 141,
143,
145-147,
157, 168,
171, 178,
179,
182-184,
189, 197,
203, 204,
206, 228,
232
John C. 12, 22,
37, 49,
52, 57, 76
Jonathan 5, 131,
143, 152,
155, 157,
164-168,
170,
180-182,
184, 185,
191, 193,
194, 197,
228
Joseph 37, 53
Laney 99
Penny 116
Stanly 143
WOOD?
Aaron 143
WOODS
Isaiah 64, 129
John 156
WOOTEN
C. 233
Council 140,
158, 164,
178, 179,
184, 202,
211, 212,
227, 228
Eliza 140, 179
J.W. 118
WOOTIN
Council 211,
212, 214
WOOTON
Council 149, 197
WORSTES?
James 71
WRIGHT
E. 19, 40
E.M. 33
Elisa M. 47
Eliza M. 58, 83
Elizabeth 75
Mary 13, 16
Stanley 118

YATES
Councel S. 38
Council 14
Daniel 5, 11,
13, 17,
18, 21,
22, 27,
29, 43,
46, 53-55,
62, 69,
73, 74,
77, 81,
82, 87,
92, 103,
106-108,
122, 123,
126, 132,
133, 144,
145, 148,
154, 155,
160, 162,
163, 167,
180, 181,
186-188,
191,
195-197,
209, 211,
212, 214,
221
Danl 118, 187
Young
Jno 106, 130,
160
John 5, 6, 12,
22, 45,
68, 69,
90, 91,
105, 114,
139, 145,
153, 154,
156, 157,
160, 161,
176, 179,
189-191,
199, 212,
218, 223,
228, 230

www.ingramcontent.com/pod-product-compliance
Lightning Source LLC
Chambersburg PA
CBHW081416230426
43668CB00016B/2259